FAMILY LAW

IN THE

REPUBLIC OF IRELAND

SECOND EDITION

To Carol & Dylan

FAMILY LAW

IN THE

REPUBLIC OF IRELAND

(Second Edition)

ALAN JOSEPH SHATTER

B.A. Mod., Dip. E.I. Solr.

WOLFHOUND PRESS

British Library Cataloguing in Publication Data
Shatter, Alan Joseph
Family Law in the Republic of Ireland. — 2nd ed.
1. Domestic relations — Ireland
1. Title
346'. 417'015   KDK200

ISBN 0 905473 43 4

ISBN 0 905473 44 2 Pbk

© 1981 Alan Joseph Shatter
Published 1981 by Wolfhound Press. This second edition is
fully revised and updated. (1st Edition © 1977)

Published by:
WOLFHOUND PRESS
98 Ardilaun, Portmarnock, County Dublin

Distributed outside of Ireland by Sweet & Maxwell Ltd., UK.
Typeset by Lagamage Co. Ltd.
Printed and bound in the Republic of Ireland

PREFACE TO SECOND EDITION

Since publication of the first edition of this work in 1977 there have been very few new statutory provisions of importance enacted by the Oireachtas in the area of Family Law. There has been, however, a sharp increase in the number of written judgements delivered by the courts in dealing with family matters and over one hundred and fifty additional cases are referred to and discussed in this edition. Consequently, whilst some of the new material derives from new legislative provisions, the major portion of it is concerned with case law developments. Virtually every chapter contains some changes from the last edition but the major changes are to be found in the chapters dealing with the Constitution, Separation Agreements, Adoption, Guardianship and Custody of Children, Maintenance and Matrimonial Property. New sections have also been inserted to deal with the law relating to Family Planning, Passports and Child Kidnapping.

At the time of writing the Courts Bill, 1980, is still being discussed by the Oireachtas. This Bill, if enacted as initiated before Dáil Éireann, will introduce a number of important changes in the family law jurisdiction exercised by the lower courts. Thus, the contents of the Bill, as initiated, are referred to in those chapters to which they are relevant. The Family Law Bill, 1981, is also presently before the Oireachtas, and is also referred to where relevant. The Bill as initiated can be found in Appendix D.

A major disappointment in the last four years has been the minimal impact of the Law Reform Commission on this area of the law. Working Papers produced by the Commission have, in the main, concentrated on those areas of family law of least practical importance. Not a single Working Paper has yet dealt with areas of major concern such as the law as to nullity, judicial separation, domicile and recognition of foreign divorces, maintenance and matrimonial property. A further disappointment has been the failure of the Task Force on Children's Services, established in 1974, to produce the necessary recommendations for reforming children's law and children's services. Both of these bodies, rather than providing a stimulant to legislative action have, by their very existence, provided an excuse for legislative paralysis. The proposals to date made by the Law Reform Commission for reforming family law are examined and discussed in the chapters to which they are relevant.

A continual difficulty in the area of family law is the number of unreported judgements. A majority of the new cases discussed in this edition are unreported and most of the unreported cases discussed in the first edition remain unreported. There is an urgent need to change the present law reporting system so as to ensure that a proper public record is maintained of all written family law judgements. The absence of such a record renders it almost impossible for legal practitioners to keep up to date with case law developments. Unreported cases in both the footnotes and the table of cases are dealt with and cited exactly as in the first edition.

I must again thank my partner, Brian Gallagher for reading this edition at the proof stage and for his helpful comments. My thanks also go to all of those working in the High Court and Supreme Court offices for their help in tracing unreported judgements and to the Incorporated Law Society of Ireland for assistance towards some of the costs of publication.

My greatest thanks go to my wife, Carol, for her support, encouragement and assistance and for never once complaining when I worked late into the night and at weekends to complete this new edition. I must also thank our son, Dylan, who is just one year old, for not tearing up the proofs despite ambushing me on at least three occasions with a clear intent to do so.

The original manuscript for this edition went to my publishers in September of 1980 but it has been possible to update the manuscript at the proof stage to include legislative and case law developments up to the 1st April, 1981.

A. J. SHATTER   *3rd April, 1981*

PREFACE TO THE FIRST EDITION (1977)

This book is written not only with the legal practitioner and law student in mind, but also having regard to all those without legal training who in their professional or voluntary work may look to this area of the law for assistance. The absence of any other book on Irish Family Law has, of course, influenced the manner in which this book is written. I have tried to deal with the areas of family law that are of particular importance, and that arise most often in practice. It was also my intention when I started my research, to produce a work at a price which would not put it out of the reach of many of those who may wish to acquire it. Thus, in certain areas I have had to be deliberately selective and omit some material, that if not for cost factors, would have been otherwise included. For example, many problems of private international law that are of direct relevance to family law have been excluded or only briefly referred to. I have confined detailed discussion in this area to those matters that in practice arise most frequently, such as recognition of foreign divorces, enforcement of maintenance orders, etc. I have also taken into account the existence of other books in areas of Irish Law. Thus, the chapter on matrimonial property contains many references to topics dealt with in J. C. W. Wylie's recently published and excellent work on Irish Land Law. Certain matters have also been deleted that were in the original draft. Thus the chapter on the courts has been considerably shortened and much material of an historical nature, and some relating to matters of practice and procedure has either been omitted or reduced to footnote form. The chapter on the Constitution is also reduced. It may be possible to include some of this material in a future edition.

The book attempts not only to describe what the law is, but also to examine its deficiencies and stimulate discussion as to what it ought to be. However, so that the practitioner will easily discover what the law is when he needs to do so, without finding himself lost in a morass of critical comment, I have generally confined comment on the need for law reform to the end of the chapter to which it is relevant. The statement in January, 1977 by the recently established Law Reform Commission that it regards family law as a priority area for its deliberations[1] will, I hope, give at least some of the reforms suggested a real chance of implementation.

[1] See The Law Reform Commission, *First Programme for Examination of Certain Branches of the Law with a View to their Reform* (Dublin, January 1977) p. 4. See further pp. 6, 7 and 9 of the programme.

A particular difficulty in the area of family law is the number of unreported judgments. It is my hope that I have managed to trace all those of importance or of interest. Where a case is referred to in a footnote as unreported and the date of delivery of the judgment is stated, unless otherwise indicated, a written judgment is obtainable. The record number of each such judgment can be found in the table of cases. There are no written judgments available, however, in certain cases of interest, and where this is the position, I have had to rely on newspaper reports. Generally speaking where a named case is accompanied by a newspaper citation it means that no written judgement is obtainable.

The emphasis in the book is on Irish authorities. There is of course, considerable reference to pre-1922 English authorities and also to cases determined after that date, where relevant. Indeed, as shall be seen, in certain areas due to the absence of Irish authority, it has been necessary to examine English case law in some detail. Where this is done, however, reference is also made to the relevant English books or articles in which a more extensive discussion of the particular topic can be found. Reference is also made to many Northern Ireland authorities.

Whilst I am of course solely responsible for the law as set out in the book, I wish to thank all those who have given me assistance. I owe a particular debt to Mr. Brian Gallagher, Solicitor, and to Mr. Ercus Stewart, B.L., who have read drafts of the book at various stages and whose critical comments and helpful suggestions have been of great assistance. I am also indebted to Judge Conroy who read the final draft and the proofs, for the many helpful comments he made. Similarly, my thanks go to Mr. Donal O'Hagan and Mr. Gay McGann, whose assistance on the indexation and checking of case citations was invaluable. Others who call for mention are Mr. George Gill who read the section on the Children's Act, 1908, and made comments thereon, and those working in the High Court and Supreme Court Offices, for their tremendous assistance in helping me find unreported judgments. My thanks are also due to the Incorporated Law Society of Ireland for their generous financial assistance, which has helped to make the publication of this book possible.

My greatest debt is however owed to my wife Carol, who has spent most of the last year typing various drafts of this manuscript and without whose continuous support, inspiration and encouragement this book would never have been completed. Her enthusiasm for this project was infectious and often helped to allay doubts as to whether this book would ever be completed. I should also mention my late father whose respect for scholarship and whose critical mind has been an indelible influence.

I have tried to state the law as accurately as possible on the sources available to me on February 1st 1977. The final draft of the manuscript went to the printers in September 1976, but it has been possible to update the text to the latter date, at the proof stage.

A. J. SHATTER   *February 10th, Dublin, 1977.*

CONTENTS

Chapter 7

SEPARATION AGREEMENTS

Chapter 8

DIVORCE *A MENSA ET THORO* (JUDICIAL SEPARATION)

Chapter 9

DIVORCE *A VINCULO MATRIMONII*

Chapter 10

RECOGNITION OF FOREIGN DECREES OF DIVORCE A VINCULO

TABLE OF STATUTES

TABLE OF CASES

A

B

H

M

INTRODUCTION

Family Law in the Republic of Ireland attempts not only to describe the main legal rules applicable to various aspects of family life but also to examine the social impact of their application and to indicate the legislative provisions required to cure their deficiencies.

In Irish law, as shall be seen, marriage is an essential pre-requisite for the creation of a legally recognised family unit. Thus, although the pages that follow deal with the family both inside and outside wedlock, it is the "marital family" with which the majority of legal rules that come within the subject matter of family law are concerned.

The Marital Family: Despite much publicity being given in the last decade to the problem of marital breakdown in Irish society, marriage has not lost any of its popularity. In the period, 1970 to 1979 inclusive there were 213,844 marriages in the Republic of Ireland. In the previous 10 year period, 1960 to 1969 inclusive, there were 168,985 marriages. There was thus an additional 44,859 marriages celebrated in Ireland in the last decade as compared to the number of marriages celebrated in the previous decade.

Marriage can be said to have two dimensions. On the one hand, it is viewed by the law as a life long contract between a man and a woman which creates a status giving rise to mutual rights and obligations. On the other hand, it is a personal relationship between two people subject to all the stresses and strains that fluctuations of physical and mental health, as well as a variety of social pressures, bring to it. The fundamental presumption behind many of the criticisms made, and law reforms suggested, in this book, is that it is the relationship concept and not the contractual concept of marriage with which family law should be principally concerned. However, the great majority of legal rules at present applicable to spouses are based on the contractual concept of marriage.

It is submitted that a society which regards the family based on marriage as of prime importance has two fundamental obligations. Policies and programmes should be created which reflect its value in practical terms. Those entering marriage should, through education, be fully prepared for and aware of the relationship into which they are entering. Family counsellors should be made available to assist spouses overcome marital difficulties and the social conditions which put the family at greatest risk should be prevented from arising. However, recognition must also be given to the fact that irrespective of the state of the law or the conditions prevalent in society, marriages will always break down. When breakdown occurs, the object of the law should be to mitigate the harmful consequences of the breakdown, to ensure that the welfare of any children of the parties to the marriage is properly protected and to help the parties themselves reorganise their lives with the minimum of distress, bitterness and recrimination. Many of the suggestions for reforming family law to be found in the chapters that follow have this object in view.

1

CHAPTER 1

THE FAMILY, MARRIAGE AND THE CONSTITUTION

INTRODUCTION

Under Articles 41 and 42 of Bunreacht na hÉireann (The Constitution of Ireland) the family is recognised as the most important social unit within the State. As such, the State guarantees its protection and pledges itself to defend the institution of marriage on which it states the family to be founded. Whereas the State can require that children receive a certain minimum education, its role is secondary to that of the family which is said to be the primary and natural educator of the child. Only if parents fail in their duty to their children may the State intervene.

Since 1937 the family has been placed on a constitutional pedestal. The earlier Constitution of the Irish Free State (in force from 1922-1937) contained no corresponding provisions concerning the family. As the provisions of Articles 41 and 42 are the principal subject matter of this chapter and are referred to in a number of subsequent chapters it is necessary to quote them in full. They read as follows:

Article 41—The Family:

1.1. The State recognises the Family as the natural primary and fundamental unit group of Society, and as a moral institution possessing inalienable and imprescriptible rights, antecedent and superior to all positive law.

1.2. The State, therefore guarantees to protect the Family in its constitution and authority, as the necessary basis of social order and as indispensable to the welfare of the Nation and the State.

2.1. In particular, the State recognises that by her life within the home, woman gives to the State a support without which the common good cannot be achieved.

2.2. The State shall, therefore, endeavour to ensure that mothers shall not be obliged by economic necessity to engage in labour to the neglect of their duties in the home.

3.1. The State pledges itself to guard with special care the institution of Marriage, on which the Family is founded, and to protect it against attack.

3.2. No law shall be enacted providing for the grant of a dissolution of marriage.

3.3. No person whose marriage has been dissolved under the civil law of any other State but is a subsisting valid marriage under the law for the time being in force within the jurisdiction of the Government and Parliament established by this Constitution shall be capable of contracting a valid marriage within that jurisdiction during the lifetime of the other party to the marriage so dissolved.

Article 42—Education:

1. The State acknowledges that the primary and natural educator of the child is the Family and guarantees to respect the inalienable right and duty of parents to provide, according to their means, for the religious and moral, intellectual, physical and social education of their children.

2. Parents shall be free to provide this education in their homes or in private schools or in schools recognised or established by the State.

3.1. The State shall not oblige parents in violation of their conscience and lawful preference to send their children to schools established by the State, or to any particular type of schools designated by the State.

3.2. The State shall, however, as guardian of the common good, require in view of actual conditions that the children receive a certain minimum education, moral, intellectual and social.

4. The State shall provide for free primary education and shall endeavour to supplement and give reasonable aid to private and corporate educational initiative, and, when the public good requires it, provide other educational facilities or institutions with due regard, however, for the rights of parents, especially in the matter of religious and moral formation.

5. In exceptional cases, where the parents for physical or moral reasons fail in their duty towards their children, the State as guardian of the common good, by appropriate means shall endeavour to supply the place of the parents, but always with due regard for the natural and imprescriptible rights of the child.

THE FAMILY AND THE CONSTITUTION

The Family

The "family" and "parents" referred to in these Articles, although their definition is not to be found in the Constitution, have been held by the courts to be confined to the family and parenthood that is based on marriage.[1] The absence of one spouse does not impair or diminish the authority of the family or parental rights. Thus a deserted[2] or widowed[3] spouse and the children of his or her marriage are a family within the meaning of the Constitution. Moreover, orphaned children who were members of a family in the constitutional sense remain a family for the purposes of the Constitution even though their parents have died.[4]

The rights and duties recognised[5] by the State as being vested in the family and parents, and the State's guarantees in relation to them do not extend to the natural family or the family existing outside wedlock.

Walsh J., in *The State (Nicolaou)* v. *An Bord Ucthála* stated:

"While it is quite true that unmarried persons cohabiting together and the children of their union may often be referred to as a family and have many, if not all, of the outward appearances of a family, and may indeed for the purposes of a particular law be regarded as such, nevertheless so far as Article 41 is concerned the guarantees therein contained are confined to families based upon marriage."[6]

However, a child born out of wedlock has been said to have the same "natural and imprescriptible rights" (under Article 42) as a child born in wedlock.

These rights include the right to religious and moral, intellectual, physical and social education and the right to free primary education.[7]

---

1. *The State (Nicolaou)* v. *An Bord Uchtala and the A-.G.* [1966] I.R. 567. (S.C.) *G.* v. *An Bórd Uchtála* (1978) 113 I.L.T.R. 25 (S.C.); *The State (K.M. & R.D.)* v. *The Minister for Foreign Affairs & Ors.* [1979] I.R. 73 (H.C.). *McNally* v. *Lee* (Jan. 1970), unreported, (H.C.). See also *In re J.* [1966] I.R. 295 (H.C.); in this case it was stated that there is no difference between the constitutional position of a legitimate and legitimated child—See p. 169 below; "Family Law" by D. Barrington, The Society of Young Solicitors, Lecture No. 33.

2. *In re Doyle, an Infant* [1956] I.R. 217 (H.C.), and (Dec. 1955), unreported (S.C.).

3. See *In re O'Brien, an Infant*, [1954] I.R. 1; (1953) 87 I.L.T.R. 156 (S.C.).

4. See *G.* v. *An Bórd Uchtála, supra*, judgement of Walsh J. at p. 43.

5. The rights and duties are "recognised" by the Constitution rather than "created" or "conferred" by it. They are said to exist as part of the natural law and the Constitution merely "confirms their existence and gives them protection", Walsh J., *McGee* v. *A.-G. and the Revenue Commissioners*, (1973) 109 I.L.T.R. 29; [1974] I.R. 284 (S.C.). See further J.M. Kelly, *The Irish Constitution* (Jurist Publishing Co. Ltd., Dublin, 1980) pp. 328–336.

6. *Supra*, at p. 643–4.

7. *In re M., an infant* [1946] I.R. 334 (H.C.) at p. 344 "Under Irish law, while I do not think that the constitutional guarantee for the family . . . avails the mother of an illegitimate child, I regard the innocent little girl as having the same 'natural and imprescriptible rights' (under Article 42) as a child born in wedlock" per Gavan Duffy P. Confirmed by the Supreme Court in *The State (Nicolaou)* v. *An Bórd Uchtála and the Attorney General, supra*, at p. 642 where Walsh J. stated: Article 42.5 "speaks of 'the natural and imprescriptible rights of the child'. Those 'natural and imprescriptible rights' cannot be said to be acknowledged by the Constitution as residing only in legitimate children any more than it can be said that the guarantee . . . as to the provision of free primary education excludes illegitimate children. While it is not necessary to explore the full extent of 'the natural and imprescriptible rights of the child' they include the right to "religious and moral, intellectual, physical and social education. An illegitimate child has the same natural rights as a legitimate child." See also judgement of Walsh J. in *G.* v. *An Bórd Uchtála, supra*, at p. 41. In the later case Henchy J. whilst acknowledging that "All children have an equal claim to what the Constitution expressly or impliedly postulates as the fundamental rights of children" stated that the natural and imprescriptible rights referred to in Art. 42.5 "are those of a child whose parents have married (thereby creating a family in the Constitutional sense) . ." He held that an illegitimate child's right to the provision of religious and moral, intellectual, physical and social education was a personal right implicitly arising under Art. 40.3. See further 113 I.L.T.R. at p. 51, 52. See also the judgement of O'Higgins C.J. at p. 35.

As for the constitutional right to free primary education and the State's duty to make provision for such education see *Crowley & Ors.* v. *Ireland, The Minister for Education & Ors.* (July 1978) unreported (H.C.); (October 1979) unreported (S.C.). The Supreme Court

The constitutional family is the nuclear family, i.e. a husband, wife and their children, if any.[8] It is expressly recognised in the Constitution as the most important social group in the State and as possessing inalienable and imprescriptible rights antecedent and superior to all positive law.[9] These rights attach to each member of the family unit and are vested in both parents and children.[10] The Constitution does not however specify or define all the rights possessed by the family and each of its members.[11] It has been left to the courts, Walsh J. has stated, [12]

"to examine and to search for the rights which may be discoverable in the particular case before the court in which these rights are invoked . . . According to the preamble, the people gave themselves the Constitution to promote the common good with due observance of prudence, justice and charity so that the dignity and freedom of the individual might be assured. The judges must, therefore, as best they can from their training and their experience interpret these rights in accordance with their ideas"

of these virtues. Thus, the rights possessed by the family may vary from time to time, dictated by the ideas, concepts, and prevailing notions of these virtues possessed by the judges called upon to determine or discover their existence and ambit.

The influence of the Constitution

Articles 41 and 42 have been said to be wholly inspired or dictated by Roman Catholic moral and social teaching.[13] Their emphasis on the importance of the

held by a 3—2 majority that the State had not failed in its duty under Art. 42.4 where a strike by teachers who were members of the Irish National Teachers' Organisation (I.N.T.O.) prevented children in Drimoleague, West Cork, from attending at three schools in their parish. It was however held that a circular sent by the I.N.T.O. to all its members teaching in schools in the areas adjoining Drimoleague directing them not to enrol pupils from Drimoleague was an unlawful interference with the constitutional rights of the infant plaintiffs to free primary education.

8. In *McCombe and Another* v. *Sheehan and Another*, [1954] I.R. 183 (H.C.) a case on the Rent Restrictions Act, 1946, Murnaghan J. in the High Court referring to Article 41 said at p. 190 ". . . there can be no doubt, in my opinion, about the meaning to be attributed to the word, 'family', namely, parents and children". In the later case of *Jordan and Another* v. *O'Brien* [1960] I.R. 363; (1959) 95 I.L.T.R. 115 (S.C.) the Supreme Court gave the word "family" a broader meaning for the purposes of the Rent Restrictions Acts but Lavery J. said, "I will accept, without deciding that the word, [family] as used in the constitution does mean parents and children and does not include other relationships"–[1960] I.R. at p. 370; In *McGee* v. *A.-G.* [1974] I.R. 284 at p. 334 Griffen J. stated, "The word Family is not defined in the Constitution but, without attempting a definition it seems to me that in this case it must necessarily include the plaintiff, her husband and their children".

9. In *Ryan* v. *A.-G* [1965] I.R. 294, Kenny J. stated at 308, "'Inalienable' means that which cannot be transferred or given away while 'imprescriptible' means that which cannot be lost by the passage of time or abandoned by non-exercise". See, however, *G.* v. *An Bórd Uchtála, supra*, where Walsh J. stated at p. 48 "some inalienable rights are absolutely inalienable while others are relatively inalienable."

10. See *P.W.* v. *A.W. & Ors.* (April 1980) unreported (H.C.). At the time of writing a Supreme Court appeal is pending in this case.

11. See p. 7 *et seq.*

12. *McGee* v. *A.-G supra.* at pp. 318 and 319. This view was reiterated by O'Higgins C.J. in the *State (Healy)* v. *Donoghue* [1976] I.R. 325 (S.C.) at p. 347.

13. See J.M. Kelly, *Fundamental Rights*, p. 58, where the author states the articles to be inspired particularly by two Encyclicals of Pope Pius XI, *Divini Illius Magistri* (1929) and *Casti Connubi*; see also pages 194—196. See Jack White, *Minority Report* (Gill & MacMillan, Dublin 1975) p. 14; J.H. Whyte, *Church and State in Modern Ireland, 1923—1970* (Gill & MacMillan, Dublin, 1971) p. 51—56; Dr. A. O'Rahilly, *Thoughts on the Constitution*, (Dublin 1937) p. 60—63; L. Beth, *Development of Judicial Review in Ireland 1937—1966* (Institute of Public Administration, Dublin 1967) p. 34. I.D. Duchacek, *Rights and Liberties in the World Today* (Clio Press, California and Oxford 1973) p. 116.

family has not, in the 44 years since their enactment, produced a corresponding recognition of its importance by the legislature. Irish family law has, in the main, stagnated. The majority of reforms introduced have been piecemeal responses to particular problems highlighted by pressure groups and the news media, or reaction forced by judicial constitutional pronouncements rather than based on coherent social policy and organised research.[14] Whilst legislative indolence is no fault of the Constitution, the effect of these articles apart from conferring on the courts one of the greatest opportunities to act creatively, has been also to substantially limit the powers of the legislature in a number of areas.

The clearest limitation imposed on legislative action arises under Article 41.3.2. which prohibits the enactment of any law providing for dissolution of marriage.[15] Moreover Article 41.3.3. was at one time interpreted as prohibiting in any circumstances the recognition in this country of a decree of dissolution granted in any other State. However, it is now established that it has no such effect.[16]

Articles 41 and 42 have also been held to restrict the legislative power over children. Two legislative provisions have been held by the Supreme Court to be repugnant to the Constitution because they impinged upon parental rights. In one case part of section 10 of the Children Act, 1941, was held to be invalid because it empowered the authorities to retain custody of a child placed in an industrial school with parental consent even after a parent had regained his ability and expressed a desire to support his child.[17] In the other, the Supreme Court held invalid a section in a Bill aimed at giving the Minister for Education ultimate control over the manner in which a child between the ages of 6 and 14 should be educated.[18] Further, there is a suggestion arising from a number of judgements that upon a dispute occurring between a parent and an outsider, over the guardianship or custody of a legitimate child, a law that regards the child's welfare as the paramount consideration may be unconstitutional.[19] However the Supreme Court has recognised that in order to afford protection to the rights of the child it may curb parental rights,[20] and in *P.W.* v. *A.W. & Ors.*[21] the High Court held that to regard the welfare of the child as the paramount consideration in custody matters is not contrary to, but in accord with the Constitution. As between married parents, the courts have interpreted the Constitution so as to put an end to the paternal supremacy of the common law and replace it with joint parental authority.[22]

---

14. Reforming legislation within this category includes the Marriages Act, 1972, Adoption Acts, 1974—1976, Family Law (Maintenance of Spouses and Children) Act, 1976.
15. See chapter 9.
16. See chapter 10.
17. *In re Doyle, an Infant, supra.*
18. *In re Art. 26 and the School Attendance Bill 1942*, [1943] I.R. 334 (S.C.). See also *Report of the Committee on the Constitution*, (Dublin Stationery Office, December 1967) p. 46 and the comments on this case; see also Kelly, *Fundamental Rights*, p. 234—238.
19. See chapter 13.
20. *In re Frost, infants*; [1947] I.R. 3; (1945), 82 I.L.T.R. 24, (S.C.). *J.* v. *D. & Ors.* (June 1977) unreported (S.C.) in particular see judgement of Kenny J.; *G.* v. *An Bórd Uchtála, supra*, in particular see judgement of Walsh J. See also *Landers* v. *A.-G.* (1975) 109 I.L.T.R. 1, (H.C.). In this recent case Finlay J. recognised however that there are qualifications to the rights possessed by the family. He accepted counsels' contention that "the family had not got authority, for example, to decide and act in a fashion clearly to the moral or physical disadvantage of one of its members". He further distinguished between the right of a family to protection for its "internal or domestic family decisions" and the right of the state to intervene where such a decision "goes outside the internal or familial atmosphere of the family structure" and has a public impact.
21. (April 1980) unreported (H.C.). At the time of writing an appeal is pending.
22 See *In re Tilson, Infants* [1951] I.R. 1, (S.C.). See further p. 207 *et seq.*

Personal Rights

In the important case of *Ryan* v. *The Attorney General*[23] both the High Court and, on appeal, the Supreme Court rejected the plaintiff's contention that provisions of the Health (Fluoridation of Water Supplies) Act, 1960, were unconstitutional. It was held that the Act which provided for the addition of fluoride to public water supplies was neither a violation of the rights nor an attack on the authority of the family, and that it did not violate the State's guarantee in Article 41 to protect the family in its constitution and authority. O'Dalaigh C.J. pronouncing the judgement of the Supreme Court stated[24] that:

> "The aspect of that authority which is in question is the authority of the family or the parents to provide for the health of its members in the way it thinks best. It is sought to establish, as a corollary, that parents are entitled to omit to provide for the health of their children if they so think fit. One of the duties of parents is certainly to ward off dangers to the health of their children, and in the court's view there is nothing in the Constitution which recognises the right of a parent to refuse to allow the provision of measures designed to secure the health of his child when the method of avoiding injury is one which is not fraught with danger to the child and is within the procurement of the parent . . .".[25]

The court also rejected the plaintiff's submission that the Act infringed her personal rights guaranteed by Art. 40.3 of the Constitution[26] which rights, she alleged, included a right to bodily integrity. In doing so, however, in the High Court Kenny J. (with whom the Supreme Court on appeal agreed) stated that:

> "the personal rights which may be invoked to invalidate legislation are not confined to those specified in Art. 40 but include all those rights which result from the Christian and democratic nature of the State."[27]

Included in these unspecified personal rights were the right to bodily integrity, the right to marry and the right to free movement within the State.[28] The

23. [1965] I.R. 294 (S.C.).
24. *Supra* at p. 350.
25. As for the contention that the legislation violated the "inalienable right of parents to provide for the physical education of their children" O'Dalaigh C.J. continued at p. 350: "Mr. Mac Bride [counsel for the plaintiff] contends that the provision of suitable food and drink for children is physical education. In the Court's view this is nurture, not education. Education essentially is the teaching and training of a child to make the best possible use of his inherent and potential capacities, physical, mental and moral. To teach a child to minimise the dangers of dental caries by adequate brushing of his teeth is physical education for it induces him to use his own resources. To give him water of a nature calculated to minimise the danger of dental caries is in no way to educate him physically or otherwise, for it does not develop his resources"
For a further discussion of the meaning of education in the Constitution see comments of Kenny, J. at p. 309. See also Finlay J. in *Landers* v. *A.-G. supra*, p. 5.
26. Article 40.3 of the Constitution states:
   1. "The State guarantees in its laws to respect, and as far as practicable, by its laws to defend and vindicate the personal rights of the citizen."
   2. "The State shall, in particular, by its laws protect as best it may from unjust attack and, in the case of injustice done, vindicate the life, person, good name, and property rights of every citizen."
27. *Supra* at p. 312.
28. *Ryan* v. *Attorney General* [1965] I.R. at p. 313. Building on the right to freedom of movement, Finlay P. in *The State (K.M. & R.D.)* v. *The Minister for Foreign Affairs & Ors., supra,* enunciated the right to travel and the right of a citizen to a passport. In the context of a child the right, he stated, is one to be exercised "by the choice of its parent, parents or legally recognised guardian subject always to the right of the Courts by appropriate proceedings to deny that choice in the dominant interest of the welfare of the child." (See [1979] I.R. at p. 81). See further p. 114 *infra*.

concept of the existence of unspecified personal rights arising out of the Constitution, first fully articulated by the courts in Ryan's case, laid the foundations for the judicial development and protection of family and parental rights.[29]·

In *The State (Nicolaou)* v. *An Bord Uchtála*,[30] the Supreme Court held that a mother's right to the care and custody of her illegitimate child was a personal right which fell to be protected by Art. 40.3 and this was re-affirmed in *G.* v. *An Bord Uchtála*.[31] In the latter case, the Supreme Court for the first time, in detail, enumerated some of the personal rights of the child.

O'Higgins C.J. stated:

> "The child also has natural rights . . . . Having been born the child has the right to be fed and to live, to be reared and educated, to have the opportunity of working and of realizing his or her full personality and dignity as a human being. These rights of the child and others which I have not enumerated must equally be protected and vindicated by the State."[32]

The duty of the State to afford protection to the rights of the child, he asserted, arises under Art. 42.5, in the case of a legitimate child, and under Art. 40.3, in the case of an illegitimate child.[33]

Parke J. also stated that:

> "The child . . . has personal rights, which are recognised by Art. 40 of the Constitution to life, to be fed, to be protected, reared and educated in a proper way."[34]

The child in question in this case was in fact illegitimate, but it is clear that these rights also vest in legitimate children. In the same case, Henchy J. stated:

> "All children, whether legitimate or illegitimate, share the common characteristic that they enter life without any responsibility for their status and

The right to marry was expanded upon in *McGee* v. *Attorney General, supra*, at p. 333, by Griffin J. who stated that "the right of married persons to establish a home and bring up children is inherent in the right to marry." See also *Somjee and Anor.* v. *The Minister for Justice and Anor.* (December 1979) unreported (H.C.) in which it was held that legislation which precluded a wife who was an Irish citizen, from conferring an automatic entitlement to such citizenship on her husband, who was an alien, did not violate the right to marry.

29. In *The State (Nicolaou)* v. *An Bórd Uchtála, supra*, Walsh J. at p. 642 stated: "The Constitution does not set out in whole what are the rights of the citizen which are encompassed in this guarantee and while some of them are indicated in sub-section 2 of section 3 . . . the personal rights guaranteed are not exhausted by those enumerated in sub-section 2." In *G.* v. *An Bórd Uchtála, supra*, at p. 41 Walsh J. noted that: "It is now well accepted that the view, first enunciated by Kenny J. (in *Ryan* v. *The Attorney General*) that there are rights guaranteed by the Constitution other than those which are enumerated in the Constitution itself is the correct view."
In *McGee* v. *Attorney General, supra*, Henchy J. stated at p. 325 "The infinite variety in the relationships between the citizen and his fellows and between the citizen and the State makes an exhaustive enumeration of the guaranteed rights difficult if not impossible." For a detailed consideration of the unspecified personal rights found by the courts to emerge out of Article 40.3 see J.M. Kelly, *The Irish Constitution, supra*, p. 360 *et seq.*
30. *Supra.*
31. (1978) 113 I.L.T.R. 25. (S.C.) See judgements of O'Higgins C.J., Walsh J. and Parke J. Henchy J. and Kenny J. dissented on this issue. See also *S.* v. *E.H.B. & Ors.* (February 1979) unreported (H.C.). In Nicolaou, the Supreme Court expressed doubts as to whether a natural father has any natural or constitutional rights in relation to his illegitimate child. See further, *The State (K.M. and R.D.)* v. *The Minister for Foreign Affairs & Ors., supra*, where Finlay P. stated [1979] I.R. at p. 83 that he was "not satisfied that the Constitutional right to travel of an illegitimate child below the age of reason extends to a right to travel at the choice of its natural father." See further p.
32. (1978) 113 I.L.T.R. at p. 35.
33. See also judgement of Henchy J., (1978) 113, I.L.T.R. at pp. 51–52.
34. (1978) I.L.T.R. at p. 59.

with an equal claim to what the Constitution expressly or impliedly postulates as the fundamental rights of children."[35]

Moreover, Walsh J. stated that in his view there is

"no difference between the obligations of the unmarried parent to the child and those of the married parent. These obligations of the parent or parents amount to natural rights of the child and they exist for the benefit of the child[36] ... Not only has the child born out of lawful wedlock the natural right to have its welfare and health guarded no less well than that of a child born in lawful wedlock, but a fortiori it has the right to life itself and the right to be guarded against all threats directed to its existence whether before or after birth ... It lies not in the power of the parent who has the primary natural rights and duties in respect of the child to exercise them in such a way as intentionally or by neglect to endanger the health or life of the child or to terminate its existence ... In these respects the child born out of wedlock is in precisely the same position as the child born in lawful wedlock."[37]

It is thus clear that both legitimate and illegitimate children possess rights guaranteed by the Constitution other than those enumerated in the Constitution itself.[38]

This equality of rights as between children, it has been held, does not require identical legislative treatment of all children in all circumstances. Thus, the State can by legislation redress the inequalities imposed by circumstances on illegitimate children. For example, it may by the enactment of adoption legislation provide an opportunity for such children to secure the advantages of family life.[39] It may also by legislation treat an illegitimate child differently to the treatment afforded to a legitimate child if such differences in treatment are to afford protection to the welfare of an illegitimate child.[40]. Finally, in the context of children's rights, in *P.W.* v. *A.W. & Ors.*[41] the High Court held that one of the personal rights of the child that arises under Art. 40.3 is "the right to have his welfare regarded as the paramount consideration" in any dispute as to custody. Moreover, in holding that a legitimate child's constitutional rights were protected by both Articles 41 and 42 the court stated that "the only way the 'inalienable and imprescriptible' and 'natural and imprescriptible' rights of the child can be protected is by the courts treating the welfare of the child as the paramount consideration in all disputes as to its custody, including disputes between a parent and a stranger."[42]

In *McGee* v. *The Attorney General*[43] the Supreme Court by a 4-1 majority recognised the existence of a "right to marital privacy". The plaintiff, a married woman decided with her husband's agreement that she would have no more

35. *Ibid* at p. 51.
36. *Ibid* at p. 41.
37. *Ibid* at p. 42.
38. See also the High Court judgement of Finlay P. in *G.* v. *An Bórd Uchtála, supra,* at p. 30 where the learned judge referring to the rights of the child stated she has "an unenumerated right to an opportunity to be reared with due regard to her welfare, religious, moral, intellectual, physical and social."
39. See *The State (Nicolaou)* v. *An Bórd Uchtála* [1966] I.R. at p. 642.
40. See *The State (K.M. & R.D.)* v. *The Minister for Foreign Affairs & Ors., supra.*
41. *Supra.*
42. See further p. 240 *infra.*
43. *Supra.* See also N. Osborough, 'The Constitution, Contraception and the Supreme Court', *Irish Times* 20th and 21st March, 1974; M. Dooley, 'Contraception and the Constitution' (1974) 3 *Social Studies* 286; J. O'Reilly, 'Marital Privacy and Family Law' (Spring 1977) 65 *Studies* 8.

children as she had been medically advised that another pregnancy would have serious physical repercussions and could put her life at risk. She sought to import by post a contraceptive jelly which was unavailable in Ireland but the package was seized by the Customs Authorities. In subsequent proceedings, the Supreme Court held section 17(3) of the Criminal Law Amendment Act, 1935, the effect of which[44] was to prohibit the importation of contraceptives for any purpose to be inconsistent with the Constitution and no longer in force.[45]

Three members of the court relied on Article 40.3 in their judgement.

Henchy J. stated:

"In my opinion, s. 17 of the Act of 1935 violates the guarantee in subs-s.1 of s.3 of Article 40 by the State to protect the plaintiff's personal rights by its laws; it does so not only by violating her personal right to privacy in regard to her marital relations but, in a wider way, by frustrating and making criminal any efforts by her to effectuate the decision of her husband and herself, made responsibly, conscientiously and on medical advice to avail themselves of a particular contraceptive method so as to ensure her life and health as well as the integrity, security and wellbeing of her marriage and her family."[46]

Griffin J. stating the right of marital privacy to be one of the personal rights guaranteed by Article 40.3.1 continued:

"In my opinion, a statute which makes it a criminal offence for the plaintiff or her husband to import or to acquire possession of contraceptives for use within their marriage is an unjustifiable invasion of privacy in the conduct of the most intimate of all their personal relationships."[47]

Budd J. said:

"Whilst the 'personal rights' are not described specifically, it is scarcely to be doubted in our society that the right to privacy is universally recognised and accepted with possibly the rarest of exceptions and that the matter of marital relationship must rank as one of the most important of matters in the realm of privacy ... This Act does not defend or vindicate the personal rights of the citizen or his or her privacy relative to matters of the procreation of children and the privacy of married life and marital relations."[48]

Walsh J. relying primarily on Article 41 stated that:

"The sexual life of a husband and wife is of necessity and by its nature an area of particular privacy[49] ... the rights of a married couple to decide how many children, if any, they will have are matters outside the reach of positive law where the means employed to implement such decisions do not impinge upon the common good or destroy or endanger human life ... it is outside the authority of the State to endeavour to intrude into the privacy of the

---

44. Together with sections 42 and 186 of the Customs Consolidation Act, 1876.
45. The prohibition on the importation of contraceptives together with the prohibition on their sale, had the effect of making them unavailable within the law. There was no prohibition either on their manufacture or use within the State. In practise "the pill" was imported and sold in chemist's shops throughout the country and taken by many thousands of women for purely contraceptive purposes. The law was evaded by the legal fiction that it was used for health reasons only.
46. [1974] I.R. at p. 328.
47. *Ibid* at p. 335.
48. *Ibid* at p. 322.
49. *Ibid* at p. 312.

husband and wife relationship for the sake of imposing a code of private morality upon that husband and wife which they do not desire.

In my view, Article 41 of the Constitution guarantees the husband and wife against any such invasion of their privacy by the State. It follows that the use of contraceptives by them within that marital privacy is equally guaranteed against such invasion and, as such, assumes the status of a right so guaranteed by the Constitution. If this right cannot be directly invaded by the State, it follows that it cannot be frustrated by the State taking measures to ensure that the exercise of that right is rendered impossible."[50]

As a consequence of this judgement it was no longer contrary to the law to import contraceptives. However, the other provisions contained in section 17 of the Criminal Law Amendment Act, 1935, remained in force prohibiting the importation for sale, or the sale of contraceptives in the State. The Health (Family Planning) Act, 1979, which came into operation on the 1st of November, 1980 repeals the whole of section 17 of the 1935 Act and makes statutory provision for the operation of family planning services and the supply of contraceptives.[51]

In *Murphy* v. *The Attorney General*,[52] Article 41 was again relied upon by the Supreme Court in holding sections 192-198 of the Income Tax Act, 1967, to be repugnant to the Constitution in so far as they provided for the aggregation of the earned income of married couples. Upon marriage, in the vast majority of cases, the effect of these provisions if both a husband and wife had an independent income was to impose on the husband an income tax liability greater than the total sum of income tax which a husband and wife would have had to pay if they were assessed separately as single people on what each earned. The State argued that this extra income tax liability had to be viewed in the context of the other legislative advantages given by the State to married couples and their children. Delivering the judgement of the Court, Kenny J. stated:

"The Court accepts the proposition that the State has conferred many revenue, social and other advantages and privileges on married couples and their children. Nevertheless, the nature and potentially progressive extent of the burden created by s. 192 of the Act of 1967 is such that, in the opinion of the Court, it is a breach of the pledge by the State to guard with special care the institution of marriage and to protect it against attack. Such a breach is, in the view of the Court, not compensated for or justified by such advantages and privileges."[53]

Although the case itself related solely to earned income, it is submitted that as a result of this decision it is no longer within the competence of the State to require a married person to pay additional tax of any nature simply because of the fact of marriage.

In the same case, in the High Court, Hamilton J. rejected the argument that

---

50. *Ibid* at p. 313.

51. See further p. 103 *infra*. Section 17.1 of the 1935 Act rendered it unlawful "for any person to sell or expose, offer, advertise or keep for sale or to import or attempt to import . . . for sale any contraceptive". The section was not here challenged. However, Walsh J. stated in *McGee* v. *The Attorney General, supra*. at p. 315 "if, in the result, notwithstanding the deletion of sub-s. 3, the prohibition on sale had the effect of leaving a position where contraceptives were not reasonably available for use within marriage, then that particular prohibition must also fall. However, at the moment I do not think it is necessary to make any declaration in respect of that."

52. (October 1979) unreported (H.C.); (January 1980) unreported (S.C.). For the sequel to these proceedings see the unreported judgements delivered by the Supreme Court in April 1980.

53. p. 20 of judgement.

each spouse has a right to privacy in respect of his or her income and that legislation obliging a spouse to disclose his or her income to the other spouse violated that right.

> "In my opinion the Constitution does not guarantee any such privacy to either the husband or the wife . . . it is clear that the right of privacy (referred to in *McGee* v. *The Attorney General*) was the right to the privacy of their relationships which did not impinge upon the common good or destroy or endanger human life . . . The common good of . . . society requires that revenue be raised for the purposes of that society by taxation and that information be made available for the purposes of determining the amount payable by any individual. The Court does not guarantee the right to either spouse not to disclose to his or her spouse the source or amount of his or her income for the purpose of making (income tax) returns which are required by the common good."[54]

The Supreme Court in its judgement did not refer to this issue.

In *DeBurca and Anderson* v. *The Attorney General*[55] the majority of the Supreme Court granted a declaration that the Juries Act, 1927, to the extent that it provided that women were to be exempt from jury service but entitled to serve on application, was inconsistent with the Constitution and therefore of no force or effect. The effect of both Articles 40.1[56] and Article 41.2 was discussed.

O'Higgins C.J. dissenting from this finding referred to the second paragraph of Article 40.1 which permits the State to have regard in its laws to differences of capacity, physical and moral, and of social function. He stated that having regard to this Article and the special recognition of women and mothers in Article 41,

> ". . . It does not appear inappropriate that the State should in its laws give some preference to woman; particularly when the exercise of her right in relation to jury service also involves the acceptance of a burden."[57]

Walsh J. supporting the majority decision noted that Article 41.2

> "draws attention to and stresses the importance of woman's life within the home and makes special provision for the economic protection of mothers who have home duties" but that women also "fulfil many functions in society in addition to or instead of those mentioned in Sect. 2 of Article 41 . . . there can be little doubt that the Oireachtas could validly enact statutory provisions which could have due regard within the provisions of Article 40, to differences of capacity both physical and moral and of social function in so far as jury service is concerned . . . However, the provision made in the Juries Act, 1927, is undisguisedly discriminatory on the ground of sex only . . ." It "does not seek to make distinction between the different functions that women may fulfil and it does not seek to justify the discrimination on the basis of any social function. It simply lumps together half of the members of the adult population, most of whom have only one thing in common, namely, their sex. In my view, it is not open to the State to discriminate in its enactments between the persons who are subject to its

---

54. pp. 30–31 of judgement.
55. [1976] I.R. 38 (S.C.).
56. Article 40.1 of the Constitution states "All citizens shall, as human persons, be held equal before the law. This shall not be held to mean that the State shall not in its enactments have due regard to differences of capacity, physical and moral and of social function."
57. *Ibid* at p. 61. Whereas O'Higgins C.J. dissented from the majority opinion which held that the Act discriminated against women, together with the rest of the court, he held that a property qualification as a prerequisite to jury service was unconstitutional.

laws solely upon the ground of sex of those persons. If a reference is to be made to the sex of a person then the purpose of the law that makes such a discrimination should be to deal with some physical or moral capacity or social function that is related exclusively or very largely to that sex only."[58]

In *Murphy* v. *The Attorney General*[59] the Supreme Court while holding in favour of the plaintiffs on the grounds already discussed, rejected the argument that the taxation provisions challenged were contrary to Article 40.1. The court said that this Article

"is not a guarantee of equality before the law in all matters or in all circumstances. It is a qualified guarantee to all citizens as human beings that they will be held equal before the law. It therefore relates to those attributes which make us human: it is concerned with the essentials of human personality."[60]

Noting that the Article recognised that inequality may arise from differences of capacity or social function the court stated that the inequality in treatment for income tax purposes of married couples was "justified by the particular social function under the Constitution of married couples living together."[61]

It thus appears that under the Constitution married couples as a unit can be treated differently by legislation provided that the difference in treatment relates to the social function of married couples and is not such as to amount to a violation of the duty imposed on the State by Article 41 "to protect the family" and "to guard with special care the institution of marriage and to protect it from attack." Such differences in treatment, however, cannot be directed solely against one of the parties to a marriage, for example, the wife and be based only on the sex of the particular spouse.[62]

---

58. *Ibid* at pp. 70—71. As a consequence of this case the Juries Act, 1976, was enacted by the Oireachtas. See J. Connolly, 'The New Irish Jury' 110 I.L.T. & S.J. 119 *et seq.*
59. *Supra.*
60. p. 9 of judgement. For a detailed exposition of Article 40.1 see J.M. Kelly, *The Irish Constitution, supra,* p. 344 *et seq.*
61. p. 10 of judgement. In the High Court Hamilton J. had found that the provisions of the Income Tax Act, 1967, relating to the aggregation of the earnings of a married couple were in violation of both Articles 40.1 and 41. The Supreme Court relied solely on the latter Article in making its finding. In the High Court it had also been contended that income tax provisions which provided for a lower personal allowance to be allowed as a deduction against the taxable income of a married couple than that afforded to two single people, were unconstitutional. Hamilton J. rejected this argument on the ground that "the legislature was entitled to take into consideration the fact that when a husband and wife are living together certain expenditure is common to both." Rejecting the argument that this is also true of single people living together, he continued "there is a difference of social function between a husband and wife living together and single people living together . . . The husband and wife living together do so as a family recognised by the Constitution. The Law or the Constitution does not recognise or have regard to any other union or liaison between single persons." The Supreme Court, in its judgement, did not refer to the issue of income tax allowances. It is submitted with respect that the learned High Court Judge was incorrect. It is submitted that the difference in social function permits the State to treat a married couple differently to the manner in which it treats a single couple but that it does not permit the State by legislation to treat the married couple more oppressively. If it does so, the State is in breach of the duty imposed upon it by Article 41 as enunciated by the Supreme Court in its judgement of January 1980 in the same case.
62. See also *Somjee and Anor.* v. *The Minister for Justice and Anor., supra,* in which the constitutional validity of sections 8, 15, and 16 of the Irish Nationality and Citizenship Act were challenged. Under the Act an alien woman who marries an Irish citizen is automatically entitled to citizenship whereas an alien man is not. It was contended that the differentiation between the treatment afforded to alien men and alien women was contrary to Article 40.1. Dismissing the plaintiffs case, Keane J. held that the distinction made was not a discrimination based on sex. In the learned judges view "it should be regarded as conferring a form of privilege on female aliens rather than as being invidiously discriminatory against male aliens." See further p. 112.

Religious Rights

A leading commentator on Irish constitutional law writing in 1966 stated "Happily, in spite of the occasional public controversies on the subject of alleged Catholic intolerance or bigotry, it can fairly be said that tensions arising from religious differences play in the legal and political field at least, almost no part at all in Irish life."[63] It is not within the scope of this book to comment on the accuracy of this statement in relation to Irish politics, but as will be seen in the chapters that follow the statement is by no means accurate if it is intended to include family law within its compass. Certainly in the area of guardianship and custody of children, adoption, family planning and divorce, religious tensions have been, unfortunately, much to the fore.[64] Nevertheless only once since 1937 has a family law enactment been invalidated for being contrary to the guarantee contained in Article 44 of the Constitution.[65] Under this article freedom of conscience and the free profession and practice of religion are guaranteed to every citizen and the State pledges itself not to impose any disabilities or make any discrimination on the ground of religious profession, belief or status. Relying on this pledge the High Court, in *J. McG. and W. McG. v. An Bord Uchtála and the A.-G.*[66] held Sect. 12(2) of the Adoption Act, 1952, the effect of which was to prevent couples of mixed religions from adopting children, to be unconstitutional and thus invalid and of no effect.

---

63. J.M. Kelly, *Fundamental Rights, supra,* at p. 248.
64. See L. Beth, *Development of Judicial Review in Ireland,* p. 41 where he refers to Professor Kelly's statement as "remarkably complacent". See also J. White, *Minority Report,* Chapters 10 and 11.
65. Article 44:
    1.1. The State acknowledges that the homage of public worship is due to Almighty God. It shall hold His Name in reverence, and shall respect and honour religion.
    1.2. The State recognises the special position of the Holy Catholic Apostolic and Roman Church as the guardian of the Faith professed by the great majority of the citizens.
    1.3. The State also recognises the Church of Ireland, the Presbyterian Church in Ireland, the Methodist Church in Ireland, the Religious Society of Friends in Ireland, as well as the Jewish Congregations and the other religious denominations existing in Ireland at the date of the coming into operation of this Constitution.
    2.1. Freedom of conscience and the free profession and practice of religion are, subject to public order and morality, guaranteed to every citizen.
    2.2. The State guarantees not to endow any religion.
    2.3. The State shall not impose any disabilities or make any discrimination on the ground of religious profession, belief or status.
    2.4. Legislation providing State aid for schools shall not discriminate between schools under the management of different religious denominations, nor be such as to affect prejudicially the right of any child to attend a school receiving public money without attending religious instruction at that school.
    2.5. Every religious denomination shall have the right to manage its own affairs, own, acquire and administer property, movable and immovable, and maintain institutions for religious or charitable purposes.
    2.6. The property of any religious denomination or any educational institution shall not be diverted save for necessary works of public utility and on payment of compensation.
    The Report of the Committee on the Constitution (Stationery Office, Dublin, 1967) recommended the deletion of Articles 44.1.2 and 44.1.3, see p. 47–48 of their Report.
    In 1972, following a Referendum, the Fifth Amendment of the Constitution Act deleting these Articles came into force. See judgement of Walsh J. in *McGee* v. *Attorney General, supra,* where the effect of the deletion of these Articles is discussed.
    For a detailed account of Article 44, see J.M. Kelly, *The Irish Constitution, supra,* p. 525 *et seq.* See also Kelly, *Fundamental Rights,* Chapter 10; L. Beth, *Development of Judicial Review,* p. 139–143; A. O'Rahilly, *Thoughts on the Constitution,* p. 65–68; J.H. Whyte, *Church and State in Modern Ireland,* p. 53–61, 158–171, 349–350.
66. [1975] I.R. 81; (1974) 109 I.L.T.R. 62 (H.C.) See further p. 179 *infra.*

Conclusion

In the pages that follow many of the Constitutional matters touched on in this chapter are examined in greater detail. It was merely intended here to give an overview of the impact of the Constitution on Irish Family Law and to show how its tentacles have reached out to effect its development in a number of important areas. Whilst its influence has not been confined to Articles 41 and 42, it is these Articles that have arisen for consideration in the majority of Constitutional judicial pronouncements affecting this area of the law.

Articles 41 and 42 have been described both as "very long-winded, unnecessarily detailed and rather rhetorical",[67] and as formulating "first principles with conspicuous clarity of power".[68] In the past 44 years whilst their existence has not proved superfluous, neither has their influence been dramatic. On the one hand they can be criticised for rigidifying the law, for example by prohibiting divorce legislation, on the other they can be praised for encouraging and contributing to its development. Whilst they have acted as a catalyst to judicial creativity, they have failed as a general stimulant against legislative inertia. As shall be seen further on, the challenge they throw out to the Oireachtas to develop, within the limits they prescribe, a modern and humane law based on the needs of the family has not yet been accepted and acted upon.[69]

---

67. A. O'Rahilly, *supra* p. 6.

68. *In re Tilson, Infants* [1951] I.R. 1 at p. 14 per Gavan Duffy P.

69. See also Art. 45 of the Constitution which contains "Directive Principles of Social Policy", which are intended for the general guidance of the Oireachtas. This Article provides
"1. The State shall strive to promote the welfare of the whole people by securing and protecting as effectively as it may a social order in which justice and charity shall inform all the institutions of the national life.
2. The State shall, in particular, direct its policy towards securing
   i. That the citizens (all of whom, men and women equally, have the right to an adequate means of livelihood) may through their occupations find the means of making reasonable provision for their domestic needs.
4. 1° The State pledges itself to safeguard with especial care the economic interests of the weaker sections of the community, and, where necessary, to contribute to the support of the infirm, the widow, the orphan, and the aged.
   2° The State shall endeavour to ensure that the strength and health of workers, men and women, and the tender age of children shall not be abused and that citizens shall not be forced by economic necessity to enter avocations unsuited to their sex, age or strength."
The Article states that the application of the above principles "in the making of laws shall be the care of the Oireachtas exclusively, and shall not be cognisable by any Court under any provisions of this Constitution." Despite this Kenny J. interpreted subsection 2(i) above as indicating the existence of a right to an adequate means of livelihood which came under the protection of Art. 40.3 as one of the personal rights of the citizen—*Murtagh Properties* v. *Clery* [1972] I.R. 330 (H.C.). The provisions of Art. 45 were also relied on by the plaintiff in *McGee* v. *A.-G. supra.* In that case Fitzgerald C.J. stated at p. 303 that:
"Article 45 refers to principles of social policy which are intended for the general guidance of the Oireachtas in its making of laws and which are declared to be exclusively its province and not cognisable by any Court. In my opinion, the intervention by this or any other Court, with the function of the Oireachtas is expressly prohibited under this article. To hold otherwise would be an invalid usurpation of legislative authority."
No other members of the Supreme Court commented on the effect of this Article. However see comments of O'Keefe P. in the High Court at p. 291 where he suggested that the Article could be considered by the Courts in certain circumstances. Art. 45 has had little influence in the area of family law.

CHAPTER 2

THE FAMILY LAW JURISDICTION OF THE COURTS
AND RELATED MATTERS

In looking at the court system this chapter is only concerned with proceedings that can solely be classified within the category of Family Law, e.g. questions relating to marital breakdown, family maintenance, custody of children, decrees of nullity, etc. The jurisdiction of the courts over family law matters and the manner in which that jurisdiction is exercised is briefly examined. Questions relating to family law may, of course, arise in a variety of different categories of legal proceedings. For example, it may be necessary to determine whether a defendant's spouse is a competent or compellable witness in criminal proceedings or whether a husband is generally liable for a wife's debts. The jurisdiction of the courts in relation to such matters is not within the scope of this chapter.

THE JURISDICTION OF THE COURTS

The Jurisdiction of the Ecclesiastical Courts

In Ireland, as in England, the law relating to matrimonial causes and matters was formerly administered exclusively by the Ecclesiastical Courts of the Established Church. These courts had exclusive jurisdiction to hear suits for nullity of marriage, divorce *a mensa et thoro*, restitution of conjugal rights, and jactitation of marriage. They possessed no jurisdiction to dissolve a marriage (i.e. to grant a decree of divorce *a vinculo matrimonii*,) as the Church upheld the doctrine of indissolubility. This latter jurisdiction was exercised by Parliament.[1]

Up until the reign of Henry VIII the law administered by the Ecclesiastical Courts was based on the canon law of the Roman Catholic Church.[2] After the Reformation, the administration of the Ecclesiastical Courts passed from the Roman Catholic Hierarchy to that of the Established Church of England and Ireland, and canon law rules prevailed only insofar as they were unaffected by Acts of Parliament and the common law and custom of England.[3] The Ecclesiastical law administered by the Ecclesiastical Courts after the Reformation ceased to be affected by progress within the canon law of the Roman Catholic Church, and became known as the King's Ecclesiastical law.[4]

---

1. See *McM.* v. *McM.* and *McK.* v. *McK.* [1936] I.R. at pp. 187–190, (H.C.); see also *Mason* v. *Mason (otherwise Pennington)* [1944] N.I. 134, (K.B.D.).
2. *Ussher* v. *Ussher* [1912] 2 I.R. 445 at 458, (K.B.D.); *R.* v. *Millis* (1844) 10 Cl. & Fin. 534 at p. 678; 8 E.R. 844; (H.L.).
3. Lord Hale, *History of the Common Law*, Chapter 2; *McM.* v. *McM. supra*; S v S (July 1976), unreported, (S.C.). See judgement of Kenny J.
4. *McM.* v. *McM. supra*; *R. (Kelly)* v. *Maguire and others* [1923] I.R. 58; (1923), 57 I.L.T.R. 57 (K.B.D.); *Hunt* v. *Hunt* [1861] 4 De G.F. & J. 221 at p. 227; 45 E.R. 1168 (Chancery) *MacMahon* v. *MacMahon* [1913] I.R. 428, (C.A.); *Courtney* v. *Courtney* [1923] 2 I.R. 31; (1923) 57 I.L.T.R. 42 (C.A.).

The Irish Church Act of 1869 dissolved as from the 1st January 1871 the union of the Established Churches of England and Ireland and declared that the Church of Ireland should cease to be established by law. Section 21 of that Act provided that on or after the 1st January 1871, the jurisdiction of the Ecclesiastical Courts would cease. The latter's jurisdiction over matrimonial causes and matters was vested in the Court of Matrimonial Causes and Matters set up by the Matrimonial Causes and Marriage Law (Ireland) Amendment Act, 1870. Section 13 of this Act provides that:

> "In all suits and proceedings the said Court for Matrimonial Causes and Matters shall proceed and act and give relief on principles and rules which in the opinion of the said court shall be as nearly as may be comformable to the principles and rules on which the ecclesiastical courts of Ireland have heretofore acted and given relief."

Under the Judicature (Ireland) Act, 1877, this jurisdiction became vested in the permanent division of the Supreme Court of Judicature in Ireland described as Her Majesty's High Court of Justice in Ireland and was exercised by the Judge of the Probate and Matrimonial Division. On the establishment of Saorstat Eireann the jurisdiction passed to a new High Court of Justice created by the Courts of Justice Act, 1924.[5] Finally, in 1961 with the enactment of the Courts (Establishment and Constitution) Act it vested in the High Court established under the present Constitution.[6]

The Present Jurisdiction of the High Court

Under Article 34 of the 1937 Constitution, the High Court has full original jurisdiction in the administration of justice.[7] The law relating to matrimonial matters inherited by it from the Ecclesiastical Courts of the Church of Ireland is fundamentally the same as that formerly administered in those courts over one hundred years ago. In addition, the High Court has been conferred with jurisdiction over family law matters by the Married Woman's Status Act, 1957, the Family Home Protection Act, 1976, the Guardianship of Infants Act, 1964, the Adoption Acts, 1952–76, the Marriages Act, 1972, the Legitimacy Declaration Act (Ireland), 1868, the Succession Act, 1965, the Family Law (Maintenance of Spouses and Children) Act, 1976, and since the coming into force of the Courts Act, 1971, it can make orders under the Illegitimate Children (Affiliation Orders) Act, 1930.[8] The President of the High Court inherited the old jurisdiction of the Court of Chancery over wards of court.[9]

Jurisdiction of the Inferior Courts

1. *The Circuit Court*: The Circuit Court has both an original and an appellate

5. Sect. 17.
6. Sect. 2 of the Act of 1961.
7. Article 34.3.1[0] provides that "The Courts of First Instance shall include a High Court invested with full original jurisdiction in and power to determine all matters and questions whether of law or fact, civil or criminal".
8. To commence proceedings for a decree of divorce *a mensa et thoro*, nullity, restitution of conjugal rights, jactitation of marriage or for a declaration under the Legitimacy Declaration Act (Ireland), 1868 as amended, a petition must be filed in the Central Office of the High Court. See R.S.C. (S.I. No. 72 of 1962); the whole of Order 70 and Order 36, Rules 4 and 13 which relate to the above matrimonial causes; and Order 71 which concerns proceedings under the Act of 1868. Other family law matters coming before the High Court are commenced by special summons—Order 3, (10) and (13) and Order 38 *supra*.
See also E. Stewart, Recent changes in Irish Family Law: The Practice and Procedure (1979) I.L.T. & S.J. 41 *et seq*.
9. Courts (Supplemental Provisions) Act, 1961, Sect. 9.

jurisdiction in family law matters. Under its original jurisdiction the court may hear wardship proceedings,[10] proceedings under Part II of the Guardianship of Infants Act, 1964, the Married Women's Status Act, 1957, the Family Home Protection Act, 1976, the Legitimacy Declaration Act, (Ireland), 1868, the Succession Act, 1965 and the Family Law (Maintenance of Spouses and Children) Act, 1976, Sect. 22. Under its appellate jurisdiction it can hear and determine appeals from the family law matters within the jurisdiction of the District Court.

The Courts Bill, 1980, as initiated in Dáil Éireann, proposes to vest in the Circuit Court an original jurisdiction to hear proceedings for divorce *a mensa et thoro*, and an unlimited original jurisdiction in proceedings arising under Part III of the Guardianship of Infants Act, 1964, the Family Law (Maintenance of Spouses and Children) Act, 1976, and the Illegitimate Children (Affiliation Orders) Act, 1930.

2. *The District Court*: The District Court has a limited family law jurisdiction. It may hear proceedings under the Family Law (Maintenance of Spouses and Children) Act, 1976, the Family Home Protection Act, 1976, Sect. 9, the Illegitimate Children (Affiliation Orders) Act, 1931, as amended, the Children Acts, 1908–57, and the School Attendance Acts, 1926–67. The Children Act, 1908,[11] as amended requires the District Court when dealing with children under seventeen, to sit either in a different place or at different times, or at different days from those at which the ordinary sittings of the court are held. When such a special sitting of the court is taking place, the Act describes it as a juvenile court. The Courts of Justice Act, 1924, Sect. 80, provides for special court sittings in Dublin, Cork, Limerick and Waterford and such sittings are referred to as "Children's Courts". The only full time children's court is the Dublin Metropolitan Children's Court.

The Courts Bill, 1980, proposes to extend the jurisdiction of the District Court to enable the court to determine proceedings arising under the Guardianship of Infants Act, 1964.

PRIVACY

Article 34(1) of the Constitution states that "Justice shall be administered in courts established by law . . . and save in such special and limited cases as may be prescribed by law, shall be administered in public." Almost all family law court proceedings result in a disclosure by parties of various confidential details of their family life and personal relationships. In order to prevent unnecessary distress, it is particularly important for the protection of the parties and their families that such proceedings are heard in private. As a consequence, the great majority of such proceedings come within the "special and limited" category of cases envisaged in the above article from which the public may be excluded.

Section 45(1) of the Courts (Supplemental Provisions) Act, 1961 provides that

"Justice may be administered otherwise than in public in . . . matrimonial causes and matters . . . and minor matters."

The Act does not define the meaning of "matrimonial causes and matters" and

___

10. *Ibid.*, Sect. 22(1); See Third Schedule. Ref. No. 24 as amended by the Courts Act, 1971, Sect. 2(1).
11. Sect. 111 as amended by the Children's Act, 1941, Sect. 26.

it is uncertain as to whether its meaning is confined to those matters traditionally so called, over which the Ecclesiastical Courts had jurisdiction, or whether it has a wider application.

Proceedings that may be heard in private in reliance on this section are all proceedings formerly within the jurisdiction of the Ecclesiastical Courts,[12] proceedings under the Guardianship of Infants Act, 1964, the Adoption Acts, 1952–76 and wardship proceedings. Other family law matters may be heard in private in accordance with express legislative enactment. These include proceedings under the Married Women's Status Act, 1957 and the Family Home Protection Act, 1976 to determine proprietary disputes between spouses,[13] proceedings under the Family Law . . . Act, 1976,[14] proceedings dealing with children in the District Court when acting as a Juvenile or Children's Court under the Children Act, 1908[15] proceedings under the Illegitimate Children (Affiliation Orders) Act, 1930,[16] the Succession Act, 1965,[17] the Legitimacy Declarations Act (Ireland), 1868,[18] as amended, and applications under the Marriages Act, 1972[19] to be exempt from the prohibition to marry imposed on persons under 16 years of age or from the need to obtain a guardian's consent to marry.

The law as to hearing matters in private is not, under the above provisions, identical in all respects. In some proceedings the court merely has a discretion to hear matters in private, in others it must do so.[20] Further the language of the Acts permitting privacy varies. Thus proceedings may be heard "in private" or "otherwise than in public" or "in chambers".

---

12. See also Matrimonial Causes and Marriage Law (Ireland) Amendment Act, 1870, Sect. 14.

13. Sect. 12 (4) of the 1957 Act: "If either party so requests, the court may hear the application in private". Sect. 10 (6) of the Act of 1976: "Proceedings under or referred to in this Act in which each spouse is a party (whether by joinder or otherwise) . . . shall be heard otherwise than in public". Sect. 10 (7) provides that "Proceedings in the High Court and in the Circuit Court under or referred to in this Act in which each spouse is a party (whether by joinder or otherwise) shall be heard in chambers".

14. Sect. 25 (1) Proceedings under this Act shall be conducted in a summary manner and shall be heard otherwise than in public.

(2) Proceedings in the High Court and the Circuit Court under this Act shall be heard in chambers. See also District Court; Family Law . . . Act, 1976, Rules 1976; S.I. No. 96 of 1976, Rule 6—"Proceedings shall not be heard in public and only the parties, their legal representatives and witnesses shall be permitted to be present." See Nineteenth Interim Report of the Committee on Court Practice and Procedure, para. 48 which stated that "in maintenance proceedings the court should be given power to exclude witnesses until it is ready to hear their evidence". Witnesses may be excluded under existing rules of court. See The District Court Rules, 1948 (S.I. No. 431 of 1947) Rule 6(2); Rules of the Circuit Court, 1950 (S.I. No. 179 of 1950) Order 30, Rule 9.

15. Sect. III (4) of the Children Act, 1908, provides that "In a juvenile court no person other than the members and officers of the court and the parties to the case, their solicitors and counsel, and other persons directly concerned in the case, shall, except by leave of the court, be allowed to attend;

Provided that bona fide representatives of a newspaper or news agency shall not be excluded."

16. Sect. 3 (5) as amended by Sect. 28 (1) (d) of the 1976 Act *supra*. "Proceedings under this Act shall be conducted otherwise than in public".

17. See Sects. 56 (11), 119 and 122 of the 1965 Act, "All proceedings in relation to this part shall be heard in chambers".

18. See The Courts Act, 1971, Sect. 20 which provides that proceedings under the above Act "shall be heard in chambers".

19. Sect. 1 (3) (c) and Sect. 7 by which such application "may be heard in private".

20. If a court does not comply with a statutory requirement to exclude the public, the validity of the order made by the court will not necessarily be at risk. See *The State (Lee)* v. *Circuit Court Judge for Cork* (1947) 82 I.L.T.R. 22 (H.C.)—non-compliance with statutory provision that the judge "shall" exclude certain persons from the court held not to invalidate affiliation proceedings. The word "shall" held to be directory, not imperative.

THE PRESS

If the press is admitted to family proceedings, a limited amount of protection is afforded to parties by the Censorship of Publications Act, 1929 and by the Illegitimate Children (Affiliation Orders) Act, 1930 as amended.

Section 14 of the 1929 Act reads as follows:

(1) It shall not be lawful to print or publish or cause or procure to be printed or published in relation to any judicial proceedings—

(a) any indecent matter the publication of which would be calculated to injure public morals, or

(b) any indecent medical, surgical or physiological details the publication of which would be calculated to injure public morals.

(2) It shall not be lawful to print or publish or cause or procure to be printed or published any report, statement, commentary or other matter of or in relation to any judicial proceedings for divorce, nullity of marriage, judicial separation, or restitution of conjugal rights save and except all or any of the following particulars of such proceedings, so far as the same can be printed and published without contravening any other subsection of this section, that is to say:

(a) the names, addresses and occupations of the parties and witnesses,

(b) the court in which and the Judge before whom the proceedings were tried and the names of the solicitors and counsel professionally engaged in the proceedings,

(c) a concise statement of the charges, defences, and counter-charges in support of which evidence was given,

(d) particulars of any point of law raised and discussed in the proceedings and the decision of the court thereon,

(e) the summing-up of the Judge and the findings of the jury or the decision of the court and the observations of the Judge when pronouncing his decision.

(3) Nothing in this section shall apply:

(a) to the printing of any pleading, transcript of evidence, or other document for use in connection with any judicial proceedings or the communication thereof to persons concerned in the proceedings, or

(b) to the printing and publishing of any order, notice, or report in pursuance of the directions of the court, or

(c) to the printing or publishing of any matter in any separate volume or part of any *bona fide* series of law reports which does not form part of any other publication and consists solely of reports of proceedings in courts of law, or in any publication of a technical character *bona fide* intended for circulation among members of the legal or medical profession.

The Act of 1930 as well as providing that all proceedings under it "shall be conducted otherwise than in public" further provides in section 3(6)[21] that:

---

21. As amended by the Family Law ... Act 1976, Sect. 28 (1) (e).

"It shall not be lawful to print or publish or cause to be printed or published any material relating to proceedings under this Act which would tend to identify the parties to the proceedings".

Both Acts then provide that:[22]

> If any person being the proprietor, editor or publisher of any book or periodical publication or being a master printer engaged in the printing of such book or publication prints or publishes or causes, procures or permits to be printed or published therein in contravention of any of the (above) provisions . . . any matter, details, or particulars in relation to any judicial proceedings such person shall be guilty of an offence under this section and shall be liable on summary conviction thereof to a fine not exceeding five hundred pounds or at the discretion of the court to imprisonment with or without hard labour for any term not exceeding six months or to both such fine and such imprisonment.

In 1971, the six leading Irish national newspapers were fined in total over £23,000 in the only prosecutions ever brought for breach of the above sections of the 1929 Act.[23] The prosecution arose following their publication a year earlier of evidence given in a suit of divorce *a mensa et thoro*. The divorce proceedings reported by the papers had been held in open court.

In 1976, the editor of the Sunday World newspaper and a reporter of that paper were fined £600 and £300 respectively for contempt of court. The contempt arose out of the publication by that paper of an article concerning a case under the Guardianship of Infants Act which had been heard in private in the High Court and was under appeal to the Supreme Court. The newspaper in its report had revealed the names of the parties to the proceedings, published pictures of the mother and the children, and had given a gorssly inaccurate account of the High Court hearing.[24]

JURY ACTIONS

In the High Court, if a question of fact has to be determined in any of those matrimonial proceedings that were formerly within the jurisdiction of the Ecclesiastical Courts it may be determined by a jury. Either party can request a jury.[25] Even if such request is made the court is not bound to comply with it. It may decide, without the consent of the parties, that a matter of fact should be tried by a judge alone. In matrimonial matters the parties are not entitled as of right to a jury if they desire one. However, upon the court refusing an application for a jury, such refusal may be appealed to the Supreme Court.[26]

COSTS

It has been said in a number of cases that "one of the privileges of a husband

22. Sect. 15 of the 1929 Act, Sect. 3 (8) of the 1930 Act.
23. See *Irish Times*, 30th June 1971 and 7th July 1971.
24. *Re McCann and Kennedy* [1976] I.R. 382 (S.C.).
25. If the petitioner does not within 14 days from the filing of the last pleading, by motion on notice to the Master of the High Court apply to fix time and mode of trial, the respondent may do so. The Master, or the Court if the Master places the motion on the court list, fixes time and mode of trial.
26. See Sects. 15 and 27 of the Matrimonial Causes and Marriage Law (Ireland) Amend. Act, 1870 and R.S.C. (S.I. No. 72 of 1962), Order 36 Rules 4–7, Order 70 Rule 33; See also *B. (falsely called B.)* v. *B.* (1875) I.R. 9 Eq. 551 (Ct. for Mat. Causes). See further *Bradley* v. *Bradley* (Jan. 1971) unreported (H.C.), where Murnaghan J. stated that having regard to the above statutory provisions and rules of court there was some doubt as to whether in matrimonial matters the Master had power to order a trial by jury.

is to provide his wife with the sinews of war".[27] Put simply, a married woman is entitled to have the means required to employ a lawyer so as to obtain legal protection against violence or misconduct on the part of her husband.[28]

The Rules of the Superior Courts, Order 70, Rules 74—80 set down special rules as to costs which are applicable to those matrimonial causes and matters that come before the High Court.[29] Order 70 Rule 75 states

"After directions have been given as to the mode of hearing of trial of a cause, or in an earlier stage of a cause, where special circumstances are shown, the Court may, on the application by motion of a wife who is a petitioner or who has entered an appearance (unless the husband shall prove that the wife has sufficient separate estate or show other good reason) make an order directing him to pay her costs of the cause up to the date of such application, and her further costs *de die in diem* up to the trial or hearing, and directing the Taxing Master to tax such costs and at the time of such taxation (if directions as to the mode of hearing or trial have been given before such taxation) to ascertain and certify what is a sufficient sum of money to be paid into court or what is a sufficient security to be given by the husband to cover the costs of the wife of and incidental to the hearing or trial of the cause".

Order 70 Rule 78 states:

"When on the hearing or trial of a cause the decision of the Court or the verdict of the jury is against the wife, no costs of the wife of and incidental to such hearing or trial shall be allowed as against the husband, except such as shall be applied for, and ordered to be allowed by the Court at the time of such hearing or trial".

A husband will be held liable for all costs reasonably and properly incurred by his wife, whether she is petitioner or respondent, if she has no separate property of her own. This is so even if he succeeds against her[30] or if the trial is abortive,[31] or if the parties settle their differences and resume cohabitation after commencing proceedings.[32] If, however, she has some property of her own she may be held liable for all or part of her costs. If she possesses no property the court may only refuse an order for costs[33] if her action was vexatious, frivolous or without reasonable grounds and "where the attorney had the means of seeing before instituting the suit that it was one that ought not to be instituted".[34]

The duty imposed on a husband to pay a wife's costs arises both out of the former practice of the Ecclesiastical Courts to hold him so bound and from the common law duty of a husband to supply his wife with necessaries. Necessaries are said to include the necessary costs of obtaining legal protection against a

---

27. See *Bradley* v. *Bradley supra*.
28. *Robson* v. *Robson* (1891) 29 L.R. Ir. 152 (Matr. Ct.);*Mecredy* v. *Taylor* (1873) I.R.7 C.L. 256 (Exch. Cham.). (It is submitted that in this case the dissenting judgements are more convincing than the judgements for the majority); *Sullivan* v. *Sullivan* [1912] 2 I.R. 116, 125; (1911), 45 I.L.T.R. 198 (K.B.D.), (C.A.).
29. See also the Matrimonial Causes and Marriage Law (Ireland) Amendment Act 1870, Sect. 27 provides that the Court may make such order as to costs as "may seem just".
30. *Courtney* v. *Courtney supra*;*McM.* v. *McM. supra*.
31. *Bradley* v. *Bradley supra*; see also *Kemp-Welch* v. *Kemp-Welch* [1910] P. 233 (C.A.); *Sanders* v. *Sanders* [1911] P.D. 101, (C.A.).
32. *Ballance* v. *Ballance* [1899] 2 I.R. 128 (Matr.);*O'Neill* v. *O'Neill* (1908) 42 I.L.T.R. 281 (K.B.D.).
33. *Robson* v. *Robson supra*, *Cooney* v. *Cooney* (1947) 81 I.L.T.R. 131 (S.C.).
34. *Bradley* v. *Bradley supra*; *Carnegie* v. *Carnegie* (1885) 15, L.R. Ir. 513 (Mat. Ct.); *Flower* v. *Flower* (1873) L.R. 3 P & D. 132 (Ct. of P. & D.);*Sullivan* v. *Sullivan supra*.

husband's misconduct. Thus, as well as High Court matrimonial matters, a wife's right to obtain costs extends to costs arising from other necessary legal work done or proceedings brought to seek protection or obtain support from her husband.[35] However, if costs are recoverable from the husband but the wife's solicitors sue and recover costs from her, only to subsequently discover that she is unable to pay them, they are barred from proceeding against the husband.[36]

The law as to costs is based on the principle that if a husband was not obliged to discharge his wife's legal costs as many wives are financially dependent on their husbands they would be unable to obtain legal assistance when such assistance is required to resolve a family difficulty.[37] In reality, the help afforded to wives by this area of the law is not great. Many solicitors in private practice are unwilling to act for wives who are not in a position to discharge the legal fees incurred by them as even if a court order for costs is obtained against a husband it is often not possible to make the husband comply with the order made against him. However, where an award for costs is made in maintenance proceedings brought under the Family Law . . . Act, 1976, or the Guardianship of Infants Act, 1964, or in proceedings for alimony or proceedings under the Illegitimate Children (Affiliation Orders) Act, 1930, and the party against whom the award is made subsequently defaults in his maintenance alimony or affiliation payments, it is possible to secure payment of the costs by an attachment of earnings order, if such an order is made to enforce the maintenance, alimony or affiliation order.[38]

LEGAL AID

The most fundamental defect in the Irish legal system is the absence of a comprehensive statutory scheme of free legal aid and advice.[39] Whilst the State has by legislation provided free legal aid in limited circumstances for persons charged with criminal offences since 1962,[40] no legislation has been enacted to provide free legal aid and advice in civil matters, including family law, for those who cannot afford to pay for legal assistance. However, in December, 1979, the Minister for Justice laid before both Houses of the Oireachtas a booklet containing details of a non statutory scheme the Government intended to set up to provide civil legal aid and advice. On the 8th of September, 1980, the scheme formally came into operation.

The need for the State to provide free legal assistance in family law matters was clearly demonstrated by the work of the Free Legal Advice Centres (F.L.A.C.) in Dublin during the 1970's. This voluntary organisation in the period from the 1st of April, 1969 to the 1st of November, 1979, assisted 33,254 clients, 13,418

---

35. *Ottaway* v. *Hamilton* (1978) 3 C.P.D. 393 (C.P.D.); *Sullivan* v. *Sullivan supra*; *Wilson* v. *Ford* (1968) L.R. 3 Ex. 63; 37 L.J. Ex. 60 (Ct. of Exch.); *Mecredy* v. *Taylor supra*; *Turner* v. *Rookes* (1839) 10 Ad. & E. 47; 2 P. & D. 240; 113 E.R. 18 (Ct. of K.B.); *J.N. Nabarro* v. *Kennedy* [1954] 2 All E.R. 605; [1955] Q.B. 575 (Q.B.D.). See however the Family Law . . . Act, 1976, Sect. 26—"The costs of any proceedings under this Act shall be in the discretion of the court."
36. *Sullivan* v. *Sullivan supra*.
37. *Bradley* v. *Bradley supra*; *Flower* v. *Flower supra*.
38. See the Family Law . . . Act, 1976, Sect. 10 (4) (a). See also the Defence Act, 1954, Sect. 98 as amended by the Family Law . . . Act, 1976, Sect. 30 which provides a procedure for enforcing orders for costs made against a man of the Permanent Defence Force.
39. See F.L.A.C. Reports 1972, 1974, 1976, 1977, 1978.
40. Thus, children charged with a criminal offence may get free representation under the provisions of the Criminal Justice (Legal Aid) Act, 1962. See the recent case of *The State (Healey)* v. *Donoghue and Ors.* [1976] I.R. 325; (1976) 112 I.L.T.R. 37 (S.C.) in which the Constitutional right of a person to be informed of his entitlement to legal aid was enunciated by the Supreme Court.

of whom sought help with a problem classified as coming within the category of family law.[41] Despite the number of persons that sought its help, FLAC believed that it was only dealing with "a small proportion of the problems that arise within the particular areas of Dublin City where the centres operate."[42]

In December, 1977, the Pringle Report on Civil Legal Aid and Advice was published.[43] This report contained detailed recommendations for the establishment of a comprehensive state financed scheme of civil legal aid and advice. In relation to family law the Report stated

> "While in no way detracting from our view that a comprehensive scheme of legal aid and advice should be introduced at the earliest possible opportunity, we consider that family law cases merit immediate consideration because of the particular social problems which they present, the peculiar sensitivity of their nature and the consideration which must be given to the welfare of the children."[44]

In November, 1979, the European Court of Human Rights in the case of *Airey v. Ireland*[45] held the State to be in breach of Article 6(1) [46] and Article 8[47] of the European Convention for the Protection of Human Rights and Fundamental Freedoms, due to its failure to provide free legal aid in a family law matter. The applicant, Mrs. Airey, was unable to find a solicitor willing to represent her in proceedings for divorce *a mensa et thoro* (judicial separation) as she did not have the means to pay for legal representation. The Court held that the failure of the State to provide her with the necessary legal assistance constituted a denial to her by the State of an effective right of access to the High Court and a failure on the part of the State to respect her private family life.

The Court in its judgement stated

> "In Ireland, many aspects of private or family life are regulated by law. As regards marriage, husband and wife are in principle under a duty to cohabit but are entitled, in certain cases, to petition for a decree of judicial separation; this amounts to recognition of the fact that the protection of their private or family life may sometimes necessitate their being relieved from the duty to live together.
>
> Effective respect for private or family life obliges Ireland to make this

41. From figures supplied by F.L.A.C.
42. F.L.A.C. Report 1976. See also F.L.A.C. Report 1978 where the organisation stated that its statistics represented "only the tip of the iceberg".
43. *The Report of the Committee on Civil Legal Aid & Advice* (The Pringle Report) (December 1977, Dublin Stationery Office) (Prl. 6862).
44. *Ibid* at p. 47 para. 2.7.2.
45. See the judgements delivered by the court on the 9th October 1979 and on the 6th February 1981. In the latter judgement Mrs Airey was awarded £3,140 compensation. See also the Report of the European Commission on Human Rights adopted on the 9th March, 1978 (Application No. 6289/73).
46. Article 6 (1) provides "In the determination of his civil rights and obligations or of any criminal charge against him, everyone is entitled to a fair and public hearing within a reasonable time by an independent and impartial tribunal established by law. Judgement shall be pronounced publicly but the press and public may be excluded from all or part of the trial in the interests of morals, public order or national security in a democratic society, where the interests of juveniles or the protection of the private life of the parties so require, or to the extent strictly necessary in the opinion of the court in special circumstances where publicity would prejudice the interests of justice."
47. Article 8 provides "1. Everyone has the right to respect of his private and family life, his home and his correspondence. 2. There shall be no interference by a public authority with the exercise of this right except such as is in accordance with the law and is necessary in a democratic society in the interests of national security, public safety or the economic wellbeing of the country, for the prevention of disorder or crime, for the protection of health or morals or for the protection of the rights and freedom of others."

means of protection effectively accessible, when appropriate, to anyone who may wish to have recourse thereto. However, it was not effectively accessible to the applicant: not having been put in a position in which she could apply to the High Court . . . she was unable to seek recognition in law of her de facto separation from her husband."[48]

The Government had argued that Mrs. Airey was not deprived of access to the court as she was free to bring proceedings herself without legal assistance. In reply to this contention the Court stated that

"it is not realistic . . . to suppose that in litigation of this nature, the applicant could effectively conduct her own case . . . Litigation of this kind, in addition to involving complicated points of law, necessitates proof of adultery, unnatural practices or, as in the present case, cruelty; to establish the facts, expert evidence may have to be tendered and witnesses may have to be found, called and examined. What is more, marital disputes often entail an emotional involvement that is scarcely compatible with the degree of objectivity required by advocacy in court."[49]

Following the judgement of the European Court in the Airey case, the Government published details of the scheme of civil legal aid and advice which has now come into operation.[50] This scheme is considerably different to that proposed in the Pringle Report. Under this scheme, free legal assistance is provided through law centres only on a means tested basis. The scheme is administered by a Legal Aid Board whose duties include determining an applicant's eligibility for legal assistance and the establishment and provision of law centres with the Minister's consent. The addresses of the existing centres as at the 31st January, 1981, can be found in Appendix A. At the time of writing it is not certain how many law centres are to be provided under this scheme.

The scheme applies to most areas of family law. It does not apply, however, to actions for breach of promise to marry[51] or to any proceedings conducted before a social welfare tribunal.[52] Legal assistance under the scheme is confined to "the application of Irish law to any particular circumstances which have arisen in relation to the person seeking the assistance."[53] It thus appears that a person seeking advice about a family law matter to which the law of another country is relevant is unable to obtain such advice under ths scheme. There are a number of circumstances in which such advice may be required. For example, a wife living in Ireland whose husband is living in England may need advice about divorce proceedings instituted by the husband in England.[54]

A Legal Aid Certificate may not be granted under the scheme "where the

48. See Section 33 of judgement.
49. See Section 24 of judgement. See further S. Maidment, The Airey Case (1980) 10 Fam. Law 69.
50. See Scheme of Civil Legal Aid and Advice (Dublin Stationery Office) (Prl. 8543) laid by the Minister for Justice before each House of the Oireachtas, December 1979. For a critique of the Minister's scheme see It's Rough Justice With Legal Aid published by the Free Legal Advice Centre (Dublin, May 1980). The scheme has been amended on three occasions since December 1979. See Ministerial Policy Directives Nos. 1 and 2 of 1980 (22 July 1980) and Ministerial Policy Directive No. 3 of 1981 (1 February 1981).
51. Scheme of Civil Legal Aid and Advice, supra, December 1979, p. 38.
52. Ibid, p. 13. See Section 3.2 which confines the granting of a legal aid certificate to proceedings conducted in the District Circuit, High and Supreme Court. See the Pringle Report, supra, Section 2.8 which recommended that there should be legal aid to provide representation before tribunals.
53. Ibid, p. 12, Section 3.1.
54. See The Pringle Report, supra, Section 2.4 which made provision for legal advices in such circumstances.

Board is of the opinion that the application is not being made in the sole interest of the applicant or of a member of his family or other person for whom he has special responsibility but is of a kind commonly described as a test case."[55] Thus, an applicant wishing to bring a family law action which includes a constitutional challenge may also be excluded from assistance under the scheme.[56] Moreover, the Legal Aid Board cannot grant a Legal Aid Certificate in relation to any proceedings taken in a court other than the lowest court having jurisdiction in relation to those proceedings, unless an applicant is obliged by virtue of a decision taken by an unaided litigant to take or defend proceedings in a higher court. This provision, if strictly applied, may have the following consequences:

(a) It may result in a duplication of litigation. For example, a legally aided wife seeking maintenance for herself and her children under the Family Law . . . Act, 1976 and also claiming a proprietary interest in the family home under the Married Woman's Status Act, 1957, may have to institute proceedings in both the District Court and the Circuit Court instead of having both matters dealt with in one hearing in the High Court.

(b) A legally aided spouse may be prevented from instituting maintenance or barring proceedings in the High Court (or the Circuit Court, upon the enactment of the Courts Bill, 1980), and may be restricted to the more limited jurisdiction exercised by the District Court. A legally aided unmarried mother seeking an affiliation order may be similarly restricted.

(c) The independence of the lawyer representing a legally aided client may be infringed and the lawyer acting in a family law matter may be prevented from acting in the best interests of his client. For example, it may be clear from instructions obtained by a solicitor that if High Court maintenance proceedings are brought a wife will obtain a maintenance order for her own support in excess of the sum of £50 per week which is the maximum that the District Court can presently order. Nevertheless, under the scheme, a solicitor acting for a legally aided wife in such circumstances may be restricted to bringing proceedings in the District Court.

Finally, the scheme is non-statutory and does not confer a right to free legal assistance on those entitled to it. Thus, if an application for legal assistance is unsuccessful, the applicant has no right of appeal to the courts.[57]

CRITICISM AND SUGGESTED REFORMS

I. At the time of writing the Government's scheme of civil legal aid and advice

55. Scheme of Civil Legal Aid and Advice, *supra*, p. 14.
56. See the Pringle Report, *supra*, Section 2.7 where it is stated that if an interim scheme of legal aid is to be introduced which confines legal aid to particular categories of cases the order of priority should be (i) family cases; (ii) landlord and tenant cases, and (iii) consumer protection cases. The section concludes by stating "Constitutional actions arising under any of the three categories mentioned should also be included".
57. If the Legal Aid Board acts contrary to natural or constitutional justice or in excess of or without jurisdiction there may be a right to apply to the High Court to review a decision made by the Board. See *The State (Hayes)* v. *The Criminal Injuries Compensation Tribunal* (May 1977) unreported (H.C.) in which orders made by the Criminal Injuries Compensation Tribunal were held to be open to review by the High Court. This tribunal, like the Legal Aid Board, was set up by direct executive act and not as a result of any statutory provision or in pursuance of any direct statutory power. The Tribunal, in these proceedings however, accepted that its orders were open to such review.

has been in operation for only seven months. It is not possible within these pages to detail all the defects in the scheme. Some of these have been referred to briefly. There are many others. Whereas the scheme will undoubtedly provide legal assistance in the area of family law for some of those who cannot afford to pay for it, it is submitted that unless the scheme is substantially amended, it will not fully and properly meet the needs that exist in this area.

II. There is no logic or policy behind the way in which jurisdiction to entertain different types of family proceedings is distributed throughout the juridicial hierarchy. Family conflicts, particularly those that arise as a consequence of marital breakdown, frequently require the legal solution of a variety of issues, e.g. questions concerning maintenance, the matrimonial home, the right to live apart, guardianship and custody of children, may all need to be determined. At present different legal remedies may be sought in different courts, each matter being examined in isolation rather than as part of one family controversy.

The Committee on Court Practice and Procedure in its Twentieth Interim Report[58] recommended certain changes in the family law jurisdiction exercised by both the District Court and Circuit Court and the Courts Bill, 1980, as initiated, proposes to give effect to the Committee's recommendations. Although these recommendations, when implemented, will remove certain anomolies in the jurisdiction exercised by the two lower courts they will not, it is submitted, resolve all existing procedural and jurisdictional difficulties presently experienced and may lead to the creation of new ones.

Members of the High Court have had in recent years considerable experience in dealing with custody cases under the Guardianship of Infants Act, 1964, and a comprehensive case law has been built up. The District and Circuit Courts have had no such experience and considerable difficulties could be encountered in practise upon the Courts Bill, 1980, extending to the lower courts jurisdiction to determine custody proceedings under the 1964 Act.

The jurisdictional changes contained in the Courts Bill, 1980 will not remove all existing jurisdictional anomolies. For example, an unmarried mother seeking to regain custody of a child placed by her for adoption will be able to bring custody proceedings in the District or Circuit Court under the Guardianship of Infants Act, 1964, whereas the prospective adopters, if they wish to seek a court order under the Adoption Act, 1974, to dispense with the mother's consent to the making of an Adoption Order will still have to institute proceedings in the High Court. Further, if maintenance proceedings are commenced by a wife in either the District Court or Circuit Court under the Family Law . . . Act, 1976, and the husband alleges that he is not liable to maintain the wife because their marriage is a nullity, neither of the lower courts will possess jurisdiction to determine the latter issue and the husband will have to institute separate nullity proceedings in the High Court.

The principle reason given by the Committee on Court Practice and Procedure for their recommendations was the likely reduction that would result in the cost of family litigation. Undoubtedly, legal fees for representation before the lower courts in a family case are less than fees payable for representation before the High Court. This, however, is partly due to the simpler documentation required for instituting proceedings in the lower courts and the fewer procedural steps

---

58. Increase of Jurisdiction of the District Court and the Circuit Court (Dublin 1978, Stationery Office) (Prl. 7459). See also, Submission in Relation to the Twentieth Interim Report of the Committee on Court Practice and Procedure, (The Free Legal Advice Centres, Dublin 1979).

involved in such proceedings and due partly to the limited jurisdiction that the lower courts exercise in family matters resulting in shorter court hearings concerned with less complex areas of family law. Upon this jurisdiction being extended and the lower courts acquiring jurisdiction to deal with the additional matters proposed by the committee and contained in the Courts Bill, 1980, the legal costs of family cases in the lower courts will increase accordingly.

The Courts Bill, 1980, will in the short term ameliorate some of the difficulties that arise at present when family litigation takes place before the lower courts. In doing so, however, the Bill will also cause a further fragmentation of the courts' family law jurisdiction whilst leaving a variety of jurisdictional problems still unresolved. In the long term, the establishment of a unified system of family courts or tribunals throughout the country with original jurisdiction in all family matters would bring to an end all existing jurisdictional anomolies. The provision of a family court is further discussed later on in this chapter.

III. The statutory provision which permits jury actions in High Court matrimonial causes should be repealed. Juries serve no useful purpose in such proceedings and their presence can cause much unnecessary distress.

IV. All family law proceedings should be automatically heard in private. The right to privacy should extend to domestic disputes that result in the invocation of a court's criminal jurisdiction, e.g. proceedings in which a husband is prosecuted for assaulting his wife. Privacy however must not result in family law matters being shrouded in secrecy and mystique. Both the legal profession and the general public are entitled to information as to the manner in which family law is administered, interpreted and applied, by the courts. It is submitted that a central registry of family law judgements accessible to all persons desiring to obtain information about a family law matter should be set up. In order to protect the right to privacy of parties to proceedings there should be deleted from all family law judgements, the names and addresses of the parties and witnesses involved in a family law case.

Whether the press and other members of the media should be permitted to report family proceedings, provided the anonymity of the parties is preserved, is a matter that needs to be examined. Whereas their presence in certain types of proceedings may be harmful, their exclusion from all family proceedings may be equally detrimental, in so far as it would inhibit or prevent informed public discussion of the manner in which the law is administered and of the effect it has on the lives of those who look to it for assistance.

V. The judiciary that deal with family law matters are untrained in the specialised skills required to deal with family problems. In exercising their jurisdiction the courts do not always have to give a simple legalistic determination of opposing parties' rights and duties, but also in certain cases have to give their judgement on the basis of what is best for the welfare of a particular individual. This is particularly the case when a court is exercising its jurisdiction over children. In such cases a court should be required to obtain a welfare report from a welfare officer attached to the court before giving judgement. At present, only limited use is made of the probation service for this purpose.

The courts' role in family matters should not be viewed in isolation from the other social services available to parties with domestic problems. An efficient and formalised system of cooperation between the courts and other qualified persons working in these areas should be established. Further, judges adjudicating on disagreements arising from family conflict should themselves receive specialised training in family welfare problems, particularly in the areas of family breakdown and child care.[59] Equally, all those who intend to participate in the family judicial process should receive such training as part of a family law syllabus.

VI. Particularly in the area of family disputes and family breakdown the type of forum within which, and the way that, substantive rules are administered can have as far-reaching an effect on the lives of people as the content of the rules themselves. The courts that administer family law have been criticised on the grounds that they sometimes exhibit a great lack of sensitivity to the needs and feelings of those who use them. While the measures suggested above would to a limited extent improve the position it is submitted that a far more radical measure is required to bring Irish family law out of the nineteenth century, and into the twentieth century. What is required is a radical restructuring of the institutions and procedures by which family legislation is administered. The present splintered and sometimes overlapping court jurisdictions should be fused into a single jurisdiction exercisable by a family court or family tribunal. It should have jurisdiction over all aspects of family stress, i.e. child neglect and cruelty, juvenile crime, nullity, matrimonial property and financial disputes, judicial separations, guardianship and custody disputes, domestic assaults, questions of legitimacy, adoption and affiliation. Rather than jurisdiction over such matters being fragmented between several courts as at present, a family tribunal with specially trained personnel would provide an integrated and unified jurisdiction within which all such matters could be determined.

Such a court should employ, in so far as is possible, an inquisitorial rather than an adversorial system of justice. It should actively seek to resolve family conflicts in a manner that will generate the minimum of bitterness and recrimination between the parties. A court's ability to do this is, of course, largely dependent on the substantive rules which it has to administer upon its jurisdiction being invoked. Consequently this suggestion has to be placed within the context of many of the suggestions for reforming family law that are to be found in the chapters that follow.

There should be attached to such a court a conciliation service, from which parties with marital and other family problems, could obtain advice and assistance.[60] Use of this service should be voluntary and open to parties, who have not yet instituted legal proceedings.[61] Further it should be possible for the family court to refer parties to the service if of the opinion that there is a reasonable possibility of reconciliation or agreement between the parties.[62]

The service should co-ordinate its work with that of other agencies working in the same field and be able to refer parties to agencies operating in their own neighbourhood if they wish to be so referred. Although attached to the court, it should be independent of it. Confidences disclosed by one spouse should not be given in evidence in the court at a later date by a counsellor attached to the conciliation service.[63] Further, it is important that recourse to the service be

---

59. See the Australian Family Law Act, 1975, Sect. 22 which specifically provides that judges of the newly established Federal and State Family Courts in addition to having legal qualifications, must, by reason of training, experience and personality be suitable to deal with matters of family law. The Report of Committee on Non-Accidental Injury to Children (Stationery Office, Dublin 1976), recommended that judges dealing with children "should have some special training in the field of child care". See p. 21 of Report.
60. See the provisions of Part III of the Australian Family Law Act, 1975.
61. See Sects. 15, 16, 17 of the Australian Act.
62. See Sect. 14 of the Australian Act.
63. *Ibid.*, Sect. 19.

voluntary and not compulsory. If made compulsory, many parties using the service would regard an interview with a counsellor as a meaningless formality that has to be gone through before the institution of legal proceedings.

The policy of such a service upon a marriage breaking down should not be to reconcile couples at all costs. A counsellor should help parties to resolve their differences and seek to bring about a reconciliation if this is possible. If reconciliation is not possible, a counsellor should help the parties to deal with the consequences of the breakdown of their marriage and to part as amicably as possible without the necessity of first invoking the jurisdiction of the court. Such assistance would involve trying to get the parties to reach agreement on matters of custody, access to and education of children, maintenance, ownership and use of the matrimonial home, lawyers' fees and all other matters arising from the breakdown which call for decision. Upon an agreement being reached, it could be submitted to the court for approval to ensure that it is fair and reasonable in all the circumstances and properly protects the interests of the spouses and the welfare of their children.[64]

64. For reading material on family courts and conciliation services see particularly P.E. Nygh, *Guide to the Family Law Act, 1975*, (Butterworth-Sidney 1975) Chapter 3; J. Wade, The Family Court of Australia and Informality in Court Procedure, (1978) 27 I.C,L.Q. 820; S.M. Cretney, *Principles of Family Law*, Third Edition (Sweet & Maxwell, 1979) Ch. 27. K. Enderby, The Family Law Act, 1975 (1975) 49 A.L.J. 477. See also *Report of the Committee on One-Parent Families (The Finer Report)* (1974) H.M.S.O. Cmnd. 5629, Sects. 13 and 14; A. Samuels, Family Courts—The Future (1972) 122 N.L.J. 133–134; E.J. Griew, Marital Reconciliation—Contexts and Meanings (1972) 30 C.L.J. 294–315; A.H. Manchester, Reform and the Family Court (1975), 125 N.L.J. 984; A.H. Manchester and J.M. Whetton, Marital Conciliation in England and Wales (1974), 23 I.C.L.Q. 339, (the title of this article is misleading in that the authors also examine counselling provisions in legislation in the U.S.A., Canada, New Zealand and Australia at the date when the article was written). M.M. Mayo, Responsibility of the law in relation to family stability (1976), 25 I.C.L.Q. 409; P.T. Horgan, Family Court: The Need and the Obstacles (1976), 27 N.I.L.Q. 120; The Council for Social Welfare (A Committee of the Catholic Bishops Conference)–Statement on Family Law Reform chapters 3 and 8; J.P. Casey, The Judicial Power under Irish Constitutional Law (1975), 24 I.C.L.Q. 305. W. Duncan and J. O'Reilly, Marriage and the Law—Suggestions for Reform, *Irish Times*, 16th March 1974; Report of Committee on Non-Accidental Injury to Children, *Supra* p. 21.

CHAPTER 3

THE ENGAGEMENT

THE ACTION FOR BREACH OF PROMISE

The majority of couples become engaged to marry before they go through a marriage ceremony. An engagement normally involves parties exchanging promises to marry at some time in the future. Such an exchange of promises at common law constitutes a legally binding contract, breach of which, renders the party responsible liable to be sued in an action for breach of promise to marry.[1] The action for breach of promise reflects the general attitude of the law towards the matrimonial relationship in so far as it puts an agreement to enter into matrimony on the same legal level as a commercial agreement. The law does however, to a limited extent, recognise that engagement contracts are contracts of an extremely personal nature. While in general it can be said that the ordinary law of contract applies to them, they do possess certain distinguishing characteristics.

Proof of the Existence of the Contract

Like any other contract, a contract to marry must be supported by valuable consideration.[2] Reciprocal promises of marriage by the parties are sufficient to constitute such consideration. However, for a plaintiff to recover damages for breach of promise, by section 2 of the Evidence (Further Amendment) Act, 1869, his or her testimony must be corroborated by some other material evidence supporting the making of such promise. Such evidence need not establish the existence of the contract but must support the evidence tending to prove its existence.[3] For example in one case, evidence given by a sister of the plaintiff that she overheard a conversation in which the plaintiff said "You always promised to marry me, and you don't keep your word", and to which the defendant made no reply, was held to be sufficient corroboration.[4] However, evidence that a defendant did not deny an allegation of his having made a promise to marry the plaintiff will not in all circumstances be regarded as evidence supporting the making of the promise.[5] Much depends on the circumstances of

1. An action for breach of promise (or breach of contract to marry) may be brought against the person in breach whether that person is a man or a woman—*Harrison* v. *Cage* (1698) Carth 467; 90 E.R. 870 (K.B.).
2. *Kremezi* v. *Ridgway* [1949] 1 All E.R. 662; (K.B.D.); *Harvey* v. *Johnston* (1848) 6 C.B. 295; 136 E.R. 1265 (In this case D's promise to marry P. within a reasonable time of her arrival, if she would come to Lisahoppin in Co. Tyrone, was held to be a binding promise to marry, upon her in consideration, coming there from Toronto in Canada where she resided).
3. *Bessela* v. *Stern* (1877) 2 C.P.D. 265, (C.A.); *O'Shea* v. *Roche* [1952] 18 Ir. Jur. Rep. 11, (Cir. Ct.); in this case the judge remarked on the similarity of the corroboration required in this action, and that required by the Illegitimate Children (Affiliation Orders) Act, 1930.
4. *Bessela* v. *Stern supra*.
5. *Wiedemann* v. *Walpole* [1891] 2 Q.B. 534 (C.A.). D. had intimate relatios for a few

the particular case. The best type of corroborative evidence are statements contained in letters written by the defendant, or evidence by a third person either of overhearing the parties agreeing to marry,[6] or of the defendant stating himself to be engaged to the plaintiff. Evidence of third parties that the plaintiff and the defendant behaved like lovers is equivocal, its value being dependant on a consideration of all the circumstances, and the relationship of the parties.[7]

Unenforceable Promise: In two circumstances no action can be successfully maintained against a person who has resiled on a promise to marry:

I.   Infancy: At common law certain contracts made by an infant (i.e. a person under 21) were not binding upon the infant unless ratified by him upon his reaching 21 years of age. A contract to marry was one such contract. The Infants Relief Act, 1874, abolished a person's power to ratify this type of contract upon reaching his majority, and now no person can be sued on a promise to marry made during his infancy.[8] However, an infant may sue for breach by the other party if the other party was an adult when promises were exchanged.[9]

A new promise to marry, made after a person attains his majority (as opposed to confirmation or ratification of a previous promise), if supported by consideration, is enforceable. Application of this principle by the courts has illustrated how artificial the distinction can be in certain instances. Thus, a person who promises to marry when an infant and continues to treat himself as engaged after reaching full age is not liable for breach of promise, his behaviour being regarded at the most as "ratification" of his promise.[10] Alternatively, if a person after reaching his majority asks his fiancée to fix their wedding date[11] or says to her, "Now I may and will marry you as soon as possible, as I have obtained my father's consent"[12] the courts have held that there is sufficient evidence from which a new and independent promise may be inferred.

II.   Married Persons: The courts have taken the view that a person cannot be sued on a promise made when married, to marry another, it being contrary to public policy to permit an action to be maintained in such circumstances.[13] Thus if a married man promises a woman that he will marry her after the death of his wife and subsequently refuses to do so, the woman cannot succeed in an action for breach of promise. It seems, however, that if a married person promises to marry another and the latter does not know at that time that the former is married, the latter may subsequently sue on the promise.[14]

days with P. P. alleged he promised to marry her. She wrote a number of letters to him in which she said he had made such a promise. It was held that the fact that D. did not answer these letters did not constitute evidence corroborating the making of the promise. The court did not altogether rule out the possibility of the absence of a reply to such correspondence constituting corrobative evidence of a promise in a future case involving different circumstances.
6.   See *Hickey* v. *Campion* (1872) I.R. 6 C.L. 557, (Exch.).
7.   See *Wilcox* v. *Gotfrey* (1872) 26 L.T. 48 (Ct. of Exch.); *Cleeland* v. *M'Cune* (1908), 42 I.L.T.R. 201, (C.A.).
8.   *Coxhead* v. *Mullis* (1878), 3 C.P.D. 439, (C.P.D.).
9.   *Holt* v. *Ward* (1733) 2 Strange 937; 93 E.R. 954.
10.   *Coxhead* v. *Mullis supra.*
11.   *Ditcham* v. *Worrall* (1880) 5 C.P.D. 410, (C.P.D.).
12.   *Northcote* v. *Doughty* (1879) 4 C.P.D. 385, (C.P.D.).
13.   *Spiers* v. *Hunt* [1908] I K.B. 720, (K.B.D.); *Wilson* v. *Carnley* [1908] 1 K.B. 729, (C.A.); *Fender* v. *St. John-Mildmay* [1938] A.C. 1, (H.L. (E.)). However, if a person promises to marry another after obtaining a decree *nisi* of divorce but before the decree is made absolute, the promise may be sued upon.
14.   *Shaw* v. *Shaw and another* [1954] 2 Q.B. 429, (C.A.). (In this case Shaw had gone

Time for Fulfilment of Promise: Where no date has been fixed for the ceremony, a promise to marry is a promise to marry within a reasonable time.[15] A conditional promise to marry is perfectly valid and no action will lie until the time for its fulfilment has arrived. If, however, a party before the fulfilment of a condition, states he will not carry out his promise even if the condition is fulfilled, an action for breach of promise may be brought. A contract to marry may be the subject of an action for its anticipatory breach just as much as a commercial contract.[16]

Defences: The normal defences that are available to a defendant in any action for breach of contract may be used upon his being sued for breach of promise.[17] There are also certain special defences that are not normally available to a defendant. A defendant is afforded a defence if he can prove that the plaintiff is:

(a) A person of "unchaste conduct"[18] or of "bad character"[19] or,

(b) Is suffering from some mental or physical infirmity (e.g. impotence) which renders him unfit for marriage[20]

and that it was only after the engagement that any of the above facts came to the defendant's notice or that they had only arisen after the engagement.

through a ceremony of marriage with the Plaintiff, when unknown to her, he was a married man. Upon his death she discovered for the first time that she had never been legally married to him and successfully sued the administrator of his estate for damages for breach of contract to marry. A person could not, today in Ireland succeed in breach of promise proceedings brought after the death of the promisor as an action for breach of promise to marry, does not survive after the death of one of the parties to the contract to marry. See Civil Liability Act, 1961, Part II Sects. 6—9). See also *Wild* v. *Harris* (1849) 7 C.B. 999; 137 E.R. 395; *Millward* v. *Littlewood* (1850) 5 Ex. 775; 155 E.R. 339. On the question of bringing breach of promise proceeding where the promise was made by a party already married, see further, *Siveyer* v. *Allison* [1935] 2 K.B. 403 (K.B.D.) at p. 406 where Greaves, L.J. said that "a married man is incapable of legally contracting to marry, and the fact that an innocent person is persuaded into purporting to make such a contract does not give rise to any claim in contract, as where there is no contract there can be no breach"; see also *Wilson* v. *Carnley*, supra, where Vaughan Williams J. stated that the question as to whether the P. knew that the D. was married when he made the promise did not in his view have any bearing on the question of whether the promise could be sued upon. In this case however, the P. knew at the time of the making of the alleged promise that the D. was married.

15. *Cohen* v. *Sellar* [1926] 1 K.B. 536, (K.B.D.).

16. *Frost* v. *Knight* (1872) L.R. 7, Ex. 111, (Ct. of Exch. Cham.). Here D. having promised he would marry P. upon the death of his (D's) father, broke off the engagement and stated he would not fulfil his promise. P. was held entitled to succeed on her action although the marriage could not have taken place at the time when D. broke off the engagement, the father being then still alive.

17. See *Wharton* v. *Lewis* (1824) 1 CAR. & P. 529. A defendant who had been induced to promise marriage by the plaintiff's fraudulent misrepresentation of her financial prospects was held to have a good defence. By way of contrast, such facts would not justify annulment of an actual marriage. See Chapter 5. See also *Beachey* v. *Brown* (1860) El. Bl. & El. 796—the fact that the plaintiff unknown to the defendant was engaged to be married to another at the time she agreed to marry him did not afford a defence to the latter's subsequent breach of promise.

18. *Beachy* v. *Brown supra*; see also *Smith* v. *Woodfine* (1857) C.B. (N.S.) 670; 140 E.R. 272 (Ct. of C.P.).

19. *Baddeley* v. *Mortlock* (1816) Holt N.P. 15; 171 E.R. 195. It was emphasised that the defendant must prove the plaintiff to be of bad character. It is not enough to simply make an accusation on the basis of a rumour.

20. *Jefferson* v. *Paskell* [1916] 1 K.B. 57 (C.A.); As to whether a defendant can rely on his own supervening incapacity as a defence see *Hall* v. *Wright* (1859)El. Bl. & El. 765; 120 E.R. 695; (Exch. Ch.) (1858) El. Bl. & El. 746 (Q.B.) 120 E.R. 695. This case was decided before the modern doctrine of frustration had been properly developed and may no longer be good law. It is submitted that it is unlikely that a court would now hold that a party cannot rely upon his own mental or physical infirmity in order to justifiably terminate the contract. See also *Gamble* v. *Sales* (1920) 36 T.L.R. 427 (K.B.D.).

Damages: In determining the amount of damages in an action for breach of promise the judge or jury is not limited to mere pecuniary loss that the plaintiff may have suffered as a result of loss of the marriage. Damages may also be awarded for injury to the plaintiff's feelings, pride, reputation and matrimonial prospects.[21] The seduction of the plaintiff by the defendant is regarded as a matter of particular aggravation for which damages may be increased.[22]

ENGAGEMENT RINGS AND GIFTS

If a woman terminates an engagement or if an engagement is terminated by mutual consent the engagement ring must be returned.[23] If, however, a man unjustifiably refuses to perform his promise to marry he cannot demand the return of the ring.[24] Gifts given by a man to a woman so as to impress her or to introduce himself to her cannot be reclaimed if the man does not succeed in his ambitions.[25] Gifts, other than an engagement ring, given by one party on condition that the parties marry, may be reclaimed if no marriage takes place.[25a] Similarly gifts given by third persons by way of engagement or wedding presents are conditional on the parties' marriage taking place. If it does not take place, in the absence of any contrary intention expressed by the donor, such gifts must be returned.

CRITICISMS AND SUGGESTED REFORMS

The Episcopal Council for Social Welfare in their "Statement on Family Law"[26] in 1974 recommended that the action for breach of promise should be abolished. This recommendation was repeated by the Law Reform Commission in its fourth working paper published in 1978.[27] A number of arguments can be made in favour of or against abolition of the action.

In favour of retaining the action in its present form it can be said that:

1. The law should provide a remedy whereby a person can recover compensation for the hardship and distress suffered, and any pecuniary loss caused, as a result of the other party terminating an engagement.

2. The law should enable a person recover damages from another where the latter has agreed to marry the former, without possessing any real intention of doing so, but just so as to make unscrupulous use of the false relationship thereby created.

21. *Smith* v. *Woodfine supra*; *Berry* v. *Da Costa* (1866) L.R. 1 C.P. 331 (Ct. of C.P.); *Frost* v. *Knight* L.R. 7 Ex. 111, (Ct. of Exch. Cham.); see also *Morley* v. *Delaney*, *Irish Times*, 27th November, 1974 (H.C.). The P. was awarded £650. by O'Keeffe P. The award included £150. which she had lent to D. The P. had been engaged to the D. for 8 years. Soon after terminating the engagement he married someone else. The P. gave evidence that she did not think she would ever marry.
22. *Berry* v. *Da Costa supra*; see also *Smith* v. *O'Brien*, *Irish Times*, 21st October, 1969 (H.C.). £1,000. plus costs were awarded to a 22-year-old girl by Butler J. in the High Court. Part of the evidence was that the plaintiff had given birth to the defendant's child.
23. *Jacobs* v. *Davis* [1917] 2 K.B. 532, (K.B.D.); *Cohen* v. *Sellar* (1926) 1 K.B. 536, (K.B.D.).
24. *Cohen* v. *Sellar supra*.
25. *Jacobs* v. *Davis supra*.
25a. It is uncertain on the above authority, whether a party in default is entitled to recover gifts conditional on marriage given by the defaulter.
26. The Episcopal Council for Social Welfare (a Committee of the Catholic Bishops Conference) in the summer of 1974 published a Booklet entitled *A Statement on Family Law*, see page 7 of booklet.
27. The Law Relating to Breach of Promise of Marriage, The Law Reform Commission, Working Paper No. 4 (Dublin 1978).

3. It provides proceedings whereby a girl who becomes pregnant by her fiancee while engaged, can recover more from him upon his terminating the engagement than she could obtain by merely bringing affiliation proceedings.

In favour of abolishing the action it can be said that:

1. A law which renders a person liable in damages for terminating an engagement and refusing to marry is neither in the best interests of the parties to the engagement nor in the interests of society. Parties should be free to terminate engagements. The present law by threat of legal proceedings tends to push persons into marriages which they would not otherwise enter into, and which, as a consequence, are potentially unstable.

2. The action is one of many examples of a failure on the part of the law to show a realistic understanding of personal relationships. An agreement to marry is a purely social or domestic arrangement which should be outside the realm of contracts altogether.[28]

3. Affiliation proceedings are more suitable for the obtaining of support for an illegitimate child than are proceedings for breach of promise which cannot be brought by all mothers who give birth outside wedlock.

4. The present law gives an opportunity for claims of a gold-digging nature.

In place of the action for Breach of Promise the Law Reform Commission has recommended that a new procedure be provided for the determination of proprietry and financial disputes that arise upon the termination of an engagement. It has also proposed that certain reforms in substantive law be introduced to assist the Court in determining such disputes. The Commission has recommended[29] that

(a) gifts (including engagement rings) between parties to an intended marriage should be presumed to be conditional on marriage and thus returnable if the marriage does not take place, except where this is due to the death of the donor;

(b) there should be a presumption that wedding presents from third parties are intended to benefit both parties jointly and in the absence of a contrary intention should be returned if the marriage does not take place;

(c) where it appears that either party to an engagement to marry that has been terminated has been unjustly enriched by the other party or has been substantially and unjustly enriched by a third person, the Court should be empowered to make such order for restitution or compensation as appears to be just in all the circumstances;

(d) the Court should be empowered to award compensation to a jilted party for sizeable expenses and outlay thrown away because of the

28. See *Balfour v. Balfour* [1919] 2 K.B. 571 (C.A.)—Mutual promises made in the ordinary domestic relationship of husband and wife do not of necessity give cause for action on a contract.
29. Working Paper No. 4, pp. 40-48.

breach of promise, such as expenses incurred in a journey from a foreign country made by the jilted party during the engagement;

(e) where an agreement to marry is terminated any rule of law relating to the rights of husbands and wives in relation to property should apply in relation to any property in which either or both of the parties to the agreement had a beneficial interest while the agreement was in force;

(f) where either party to an engagement to marry contributes in money or money's worth to the purchase or improvement or maintenance of property (including any payments in respect of rent or in respect of a mortgage) in which or in the proceeds of sale of which either or both of them has or have a beneficial interest, the party so contributing should, if the contribution is of a substantial nature or increases the value of the property and subject to any agreement to the contrary between them, be treated as having acquired a share, or an enlarged share (as the case may be) in that beneficial interest of such an extent as may have been agreed or, in default of agreement, of such an extent as may in all the circumstances appear just to the Court for which the question of the existence or extent of the beneficial interest arises;

(g) where an agreement to marry is terminated, either party or any person concerned should be able to apply to the Court to determine the rights of the parties in relation to property in which either or both had a beneficial interest while the agreement was in force, provided that the application is made within three years of the termination of the agreement. It is implicit that the Commission envisages the procedure for making such an application to be similar to that available to married couples under the Married Women's Status Act 1957, sect. 12;[30]

(h) in making any determination the Court should not have regard to the question of the responsibility of either party for the termination of the engagement except where there has been "outrageous behaviour" by one of the parties: i.e. by committing acts of violence on the other party, or by acts of fraud or deceit such as seduction on the understanding of marriage.

In making the above proposals it appears that the overriding objectives of the Commission were to prevent the threat of legal proceedings being used as a lever to force a reluctant party enter into marriage, to simplify, as far as is possible, the law applicable to the resolution of property disputes between former parties to an engagement and to end the necessity for the courts to decide which party was at fault for the termination of an engagement in such proceedings. The proposals do not, however, fully achieve these objectives in so far as they propose to permit a "jilted party" seek compensation for sizable expenses and outlay "thrown away" as a result of the termination of an engagement and in so far as they enable courts when making a determination in any proceedings brought to have regard to "outrageous behaviour" by one of the parties. Nevertheless, it is submitted that the Commission's proposed reforms are to be welcomed. If implemented, they will simplify an unnecessarily complex area of law, in the vast majority of cases leave engaged parties free to decide whether to enter into marriage or not without fear of legal proceedings and provide a simplified procedure to determine any property disputes that arise between parties to a broken

30. *Ibid*, pp. 8, 12, 44 and 45.

engagement.

The Family Law Bill, 1981, as initiated before the Dáil, 20 February, 1981, when enacted will substantially implement the Commission's recommendations save that the Bill contains no specific provisions for a party to a broken engagement to obtain compensation due to "outrageous behaviour". See Appendix D for the text of the Bill.

CHAPTER 4

MARRIAGE

INTRODUCTION

Marriage Defined: The classic legal definition of marriage is that given by Lord Penzance in the case of *Hyde* v. *Hyde*[1]: "I conceive that marriage, as understood in Christendom may . . . be defined as the voluntary union for life of one man and one woman to the exclusion of all others."[2] This definition involves four conditions: a marriage must be voluntary; the parties must intend it to be for life;[3] it must be monogamous; it must be between parties of a different sex.

The Contract of Marriage: Marriage is both a contract and a relationship. For persons to become husband and wife in the eyes of Irish law they must comply with the conditions the law sets down for the entering into of a valid marriage contract. Firstly they must both possess the capacity to marry each other and secondly they must observe the necessary formalities. Generally speaking, capacity to marry is determined by the law of each party's pre-nuptial domicile, whilst the formalities to be observed are those required by the *lex loci celebrationis*, i.e. the law of the place where the marriage is celebrated.[4]

CAPACITY TO MARRY

For a person domiciled in Ireland to have capacity to contract a valid marriage he must comply with the following conditions:

Age: Section 1(1) of the Marriages Act, 1972, states that

"A marriage solemnised between persons either of whom is under 16 shall . . . not be valid in law."

This section did not come into force until 1st January, 1975[5] Prior to 1975, a valid marriage could be contracted in the case of a boy, when he reached the age of 14, and in the case of a girl when she reached the age of 12. Since the beginning of 1975 a person under 16 years of age who wishes to marry may

---

1. (1866) L.R. 1. P. & D. 130; [1861-73] All E.R. Rep. 176, (Ct. of P. & D.) cited with approval in *Griffith v. Griffith* [1944] I.R. 35, (H.C.)
2. (1866) L.R. 1. P. & D. 130, at p. 133.
3. *Nachimson v. Nachimson* [1930] P. 217, (C.A.).
4. *Sottomayor v. De Barros* No. 1 (1877) 3 P.D. 1, (C.A.). Dicey and Morris, *Conflict of Law*, 9th Edition. (Stephens & Sons Ltd. London 1973)—see Chapter 15 for a wide ranging discussion of the private international law rules concerning formalities of marriage and capacity to marry. See also *Du Moulin v. Druitt* (1860) 13 Ir. C.L.R. 212 (Q.B.); *Swifte v. A.G. for Ireland* [1912] A.C. 276 (H.L., Ir.); *Ussher v. Ussher* [1912] 2 I.R. 445 (K.B.D.).
5. See S.I. No. 324 of 1974.

apply to the President of the High Court (or a judge of that court nominated by the President) for exemption from the application of section 1(1). Such an application may be made informally through the Registrar of Wards of Court and is heard and determined in private. An exemption order can only be granted if "the applicant shows that its grant is justified by serious reasons and is in the interests of the parties to the intended marriage".[6] No fee is charged by the court for hearing the application.

In practice an application may be made to the Registrar either by letter or personally. The Registrar then sends the applicant a simple form which is designed to ascertain relevant information such as the age of the applicant and the name and address of the intended spouse and of both parties' parents or guardians. Copies of the parties' birth certificates are also sought. After this information has been received by the Registrar an appointment is made for the parties and their parents to meet the President of the High Court and separate interviews with the parties and their parents or guardians take place. If the parties are willing a report may be sought from other interested third persons such as a social worker. After the interviews have been completed and all information sought has been obtained an order granting or refusing exemption is made.[7]

From the 1st January, 1975 until the 31st December, 1979, 34 applications for exemption orders were made, 15 were granted, 13 were refused and 6 were withdrawn. As their are no reported cases on the exercise of this jurisdiction it is not known in what circumstances exemptions have been granted.[8]

If a person knowingly solemnises or permits the solemnisation of a marriage which, as a consequence of the provisions of section 1 is not valid or is a party to such marriage, he is guilty of a criminal offence and liable on summary conviction to a penalty not exceeding £50.[9]

Prohibited Degrees: Parties within the prohibited degrees of relationship cannot marry. Prohibitions are based either on consanguinity (blood relationship) or affinity (relationship by marriage).[10] Until 1835 a marriage within the prohibited degrees was merely voidable, but the Marriage Act (known as Lord Lyndhurst's Act) of that year made all such marriages void. The Act was amended in 1907 after much controversy, by the Deceased Wife's Sister's Marriage Act, which permitted a man marry his deceased wife's sister, and in 1921 by the Deceased Brother's Widow's Marriage Act, which permitted a woman marry her deceased husband's brother.[11]

6. Marriages Act, 1972, Sect. 1 (3).
7. See The Law Relating to the Age of Majority, The Age for Marriage and Some Connected Subjects, The Law Reform Commission Working Paper No. 2. 1977, at p. 39.
8. There are also no unreported written judgements setting out the facts of a case in which exemption was granted. In Australia the courts in exercising a similar jurisdiction have granted permission for under age marriages where the girl was pregnant, the parents consent and the maturity and compatibility of the parties make it probable that their marriage will succeed: Re K. (1963), 5 F.L.R. 38; Re W. [1968] Q.W.N. 45; Re Z (1970), 15 F.L.R. 420. The permission has been refused, however, where parties simply belong to a class of persons or ethnic group that customarily expects young girls to marry. Re S.G. (1968), 11 F.L.R. 326.
9. Marriages Act, 1972, Sect. 1 (6). See also Sects 1 (4) (5) & (7).
10. Affinity can only be created by marriage. See Wing v. Taylor (falsely calling herself Wing) 2 Sw. & Tr. 276; 164 E.R. 1002, (Ct. for Div. & Matr Causes).
11. For a critical examination of the law as to prohibited degrees in England see S.M. Cretney, Principles of Family Law 3rd ed. (Sweet & Maxwell, London 1979), p. 35—The comments made and reforms suggested are equally relevant to Irish Law.

Table of Prohibited Degrees

(The relationship of the half-blood is of the same effect as of the whole blood).

A Man may not Marry his

1. Grandmother.
2. Grandfather's Wife.
3. Wife's Grandmother.
4. Father's Sister.
5. Mother's Sister.
6. Father's Brother's Wife.
7. Mother's Brother's Wife.
8. Wife's Father's Sister.
9. Wife's Mother's Sister.
10. Mother.
11. Stepmother.
12. Wife's Mother.
13. Daughter.
14. Wife's Daughter.
15. Son's Wife.
16. Sister.
17. Son's Daughter.
18. Daughter's Daughter.
19. Son's Son's Wife.
20. Daughter's Son's Wife.
21. Wife's Son's Daughter.
22. Wife's Daughter's Daughter.
23. Brother's Daughter.
24. Sister's Daughter.
25. Brother's Son's Wife.
26. Sister's Son's Wife.
27. Wife's Brother's Daughter.
28. Wife's Sister's Daughter.

A Woman may not Marry her

1. Grandfather.
2. Grandmother's Husband.
3. Husband's Grandfather.
4. Father's Brother.
5. Mother's Brother.
6. Father's Sister's Husband.
7. Mother's Sister's Husband.
8. Husband's Father's Brother.
9. Husband's Mother's Brother.
10. Father.
11. Stepfather.
12. Husband's Father.
13. Son.
14. Husband's Son.
15. Daughter's Husband.
16. Brother.
17. Son's Son.
18. Daughter's Son.
19. Son's Daughter's Husband.
20. Daughter's Daughter's Husband.
21. Husband's Son's Son.
22. Husband's Daughter's Son.
23. Brother's Son.
24. Sister's Son.
25. Brother's Daughter's Husband.
26. Sister's Daughter's Husband.
27. Husband's Brother's Son.
28. Husband's Sister's Son.

Whereas a man may marry his deceased wife's sister and a woman her deceased husband's brother, the prohibition still remains if the first marriage comes to an end as the result of a divorce as opposed to a spouses' death, e.g. Joe Smith marries Mary Bloggs in Ireland and they go to live in England where they establish domicile. While domiciled there they obtain a divorce which is recognised in Ireland as terminating their marriage. Subsequently Joe returns to live in Ireland and marries Pat Bloggs who has lived in Ireland all her life and has an Irish domicile. Pat being Mary's sister, her marriage to Joe is invalid.

Monogamy: Marriage being a union between "one man and one woman" if at the time of the marriage ceremony either party is already lawfully married to a third party, the marriage is void.[12] In such a case it does not matter whether one or both of the parties knew of the continued subsistence of the first marriage

12. See *Johnson (falsely called Cooke) v. Cooke* [1898] 2 I.R. 130 (Q.B.D.).

at the time of the ceremony.[13] Further the fact that either or both of them may have a valid defence to a charge of bigamy, such as a mistaken but honest belief on reasonable grounds that the former spouse is dead, is immaterial. A person who has already contracted one marriage cannot validly contract another until the first spouse dies or the marriage is annulled or validly terminated.[14]

Sex: One party must be male and the other female. While this may seem almost a truism, the problem did arise recently in an English case.[15] A marriage ceremony had been performed between a man and a person who had been born with male characteristics, but had undergone surgery to give him all the external characteristics of a female. The latter had been issued with a national health card and passport appropriate to females and dressed as a woman. The court held however that this did not make him a female for the purpose of marriage. In doing so it stated that while a person may be of the female gender, the same person may be biologically male. It held that in determining a person's capacity to marry it is the biological sex that is important.

FORMALITIES OF MARRIAGE

Certain formalities are laid down by statute that parties wishing to enter into marriage in Ireland must observe. The general purpose of these formalities can be said to achieve the following: to ensure that the marriage ceremony is easily identifiable from the normal interaction of everyday life so that persons do not marry by accident; to facilitate the maintaining of public records of married persons; to enable persons easily prove that they themselves or others are married; and to prevent persons not free to marry from marrying.

The law as to formalities is complex and obscure, being contained in a labyrinth of statutes stretching from 1844 to 1972. There now follows a brief historical introduction and then a detailed examination of the formalities required under the present law for the celebration of a marriage to be lawful.

Historical Introduction:

Prior to the Reformation both Ireland and England were Roman Catholic countries and the formalities to be observed for a valid marriage ceremony were left by the common law to be determined by the canon law as decreed from Rome.[16] There were according to its rules three methods of contracting a valid marriage:

(a) *Sponsalia per verba de praesenti*; this was a simple declaration by the parties, in the present tense, agreeing to take each other as husband or wife.

(b) *Sponsillia per verba de futuro et copula*; this was a promise to marry in the future, the parties becoming husband and wife upon a subsequent consummation.

(c) *In facie ecclesiae*; this was a marriage contracted at the church door *per verba de praesenti* in the presence of a priest. Such a ceremony took

13. *Miles v. Chilton (falsely calling herself Miles)* (1849) I Robb. Ecc. 684; 27 Digest (Repl) 448; 163 E.R. 1178; *Hayward v. Hayward (orse Prestwood)* [1961] P. 152; [1961] I All E.R. 236, (P.D.A.).
14. See p. 57.
15. *Corbett v. Corbett (otherwise Ashley)* [1970] 2 All E.R. 33; [1971] P. 83 (P.D.A.).
16. See G.H. Joyce, *Christian Marriage*, Ch. 2.

place after the publication of banns, unless they were dispensed with by papal or episcopal licence.

By a decree of the Council of Trent in 1563, no marriage of a Roman Catholic was to be regarded as valid by the Church unless celebrated in the presence of a priest and at least two witnesses, but by this time the Reformation having taken place, the common law and the canon law had gone their separate ways. Thus, whilst this decree governs the question of the Roman Catholic Church's recognition of a marriage as valid, it is not relevant to the formalities required by the common law.[17]

The three above methods were accepted as valid means of contracting a marriage in Ireland until 1844. In that year, in the much criticised case of *R*. v. *Millis*,[18] it was decided by the House of Lords that at common law the presence of a clergyman in holy orders, either of the Roman Catholic or Protestant Episcopal Church, at the time of the solemnisation of the marriage was essential for the valid constitution of a marriage contract. This view was later confirmed by the House of Lords in 1861 in *Beamish* v. *Beamish*.[19]

As a consequence of the decision of *R*. v. *Millis*, the Marriages (Ireland) Act, 1844, which is at the foundation of our present law as to formalities of marriage, was passed.

Roman Catholic Marriages

The great majority of marriages that take place in the State are celebrated in accordance with the rites and ceremonies of the Roman Catholic Church— 20,088 out of a total of 20,864 marriages were so celebrated in 1979.[20] These marriages are generally unaffected by legislative enactments, the 1844 Act and subsequent amending legislation being largely inapplicable to them. In the main the formalities to be observed for a Roman Catholic marriage are left by the State to be determined according to the rites of the Church, whilst the question of the civil validity of such marriages is determined by the common law, i.e. the common law will regard them as valid if celebrated by an episcopally ordained clergyman.[21] There is, however, a limited amount of legislative interference in this area. The law lays down certain formalities that must be observed for the valid celebration of a mixed marriage. The main purpose of this legislation which was enacted in the second half of the last century, was to repeal the penal laws which prevented the valid celebration of such marriages by Roman Catholic clergymen. To facilitate the registration of Roman Catholic marriages, an Act of

17. See *Ussher v. Ussher* [1912] 2 I.R. 445; (1912) 46 I.L.T.R. 109, (K.B.D.).
18. 10 Cl. & Fin. 534; 8 Jur. 717; 8E.R. 844, (H.L.).
19. 9 H.L.Cas. 274; 11 E.R. 735; See also *Ussher v. Ussher supra*; See also W.J. Walshe "Two Famous Irish Marriage Cases" (1912), 31 *Irish Ecclesiastical Record*, 4th Series, 449-75; 579-605 and (1912) Vol. 32 10-30; 118-136.
20. From yearly summary of Births, Deaths and Marriages (1979) compiled by the Central Statistics Office.
21. See W.H. Faloon, *Marriage Law of Ireland*, p. 9. There the author writes "They (Roman Catholic marriages) might be celebrated privately or publicly, at any time or place, and in any form or manner the celebrating priest thought proper, without banns, licence, notice, residence or consent; and so far as the state is concerned this seems still the law;" This is no longer the case in respect of third party consents, see p. 51. See also J. Blanchard, *The Church in Contemporary Ireland*, p. 61. See also *Report of the Committee on the Constitution*, (Dublin, Stationery Office, December 1967), p. 45-46. The Committee suggests that the law in prescribing requirements that have to be complied with by parties to a non-Roman Catholic marriage, while not prescribing such requirements for a Roman Catholic marriage, may be unconstitutional, being contrary to Article 44.2.3 in that such provisions constitute discrimination on the grounds of religious profession or belief.

1863 imposes a duty on the husband in the case of all marriages celebrated by a Roman Catholic clergyman, to furnish the registrar of the district in which the marriage is solemnised with certain information after the marriage has taken place. Finally, the statutory provisions as to parental consent required for the lawful celebration of a marriage by a minor apply to all marriages celebrated in the State.

A Roman Catholic marriage may be celebrated by I. Episcopal dispensation; II. After publication of the banns; III. By ordinary licence; IV. On production of a Registrar's Certificate.

I. & II. The proceedings in these cases are regulated by the law of the Church. Both parties must be Roman Catholics.[22]

III: An ordinary licence can be granted by a person nominated by the bishop if either both or one of the parties are Roman Catholic. If only one of the parties is a Roman Catholic notice must be given to the licence issuer 7 days before the licence can be used, and he must send by post a copy of the notice to the clergyman who officiates at the places of worship where the parties have been in the habit of attending.[23] In this latter case the marriage must be solemnised in a Roman Catholic church or chapel with open doors in the presence of two or more witnesses.[24]

IV: For a Roman Catholic marriage to take place on production of a registrar's certificate one of the parties must be of a different persuasion than Roman Catholic.[25] The certificate, (or certificates, where the parties reside in different districts) must be given to the officiating clergyman at the time of the solemnisation of the marriage and the marriage must be solemnised in a Roman Catholic church or chapel in the district of the registrar who issued the certificate, with open doors and in the presence of two or more witnesses.[26] For the procedure to be followed to obtain a certificate see "Marriage in the Office of the Registrar."

Registration of Marriage celebrated by a Roman Catholic Clergyman: By the Registration of Marriages (Ireland) Act, 1863, Sect. 11, the parties to a Roman Catholic marriage are required to obtain from the registrar of the district in which the marriage is to take place, a certificate which they must produce to and which must be filled in by the clergyman celebrating the marriage. The certificate must contain the following particulars.[27]

22. See the Code of Canon Law, 1022-1028.
23. Matrimonial Causes and Marriage Law (Ireland) Amendment Act, 1871, Sect. 26. Under 19 Geo. II, c. 13 all marriages celebrated by a Roman Catholic priest, between a Protestant and a Roman Catholic were void. See *Thelwall v. Yelverton*, (1862), 14 I.C.L.R. 188, (Ct of C.P.). The Matrimonial Causes and Marriage Law (Ireland) Amendment Act, 1870, Sect. 39, repealed this Act in so far as it rendered all such marriages void, and Sect. 38 layed down the procedure to be followed whereby such a mixed marriage celebrated by a Roman Catholic priest would be valid. Under this section it is necessary for the certificate of the district registrar to be obtained for such a marriage to be valid. However, Sect. 27 of the Act of 1871 lays down that whenever a licence is issued for marriage pursuant to Sect. 25 of the same Act it is not necessary to obtain the registrar's certificate.
24. Under Sect. 27 of the Act of 1871 the licence is to have the same effect under the provisions of the Act of 1870 (i.e. Sect. 38 of that Act) as a certificate of the registrar would have had. See Sir Robert Edwin Matheson, *Digest of the Irish Marriage Law* (Dublin 1908).
25. Sect. 38 of the 1870 Act.
26. *Ibid.*, Sect. 38 as amended by Sect. 17 (1) (*e*) of the Marriages Act, 1972.
27. See Vital Statistics and Births, Deaths and Marriages Registration Act, 1952, Sect. 7 and S.I. No. 47 of 1956.

I. The date when married.

II. The name and surname of each party.

III. Their date of birth.

IV. Their status at time of marriage, i.e. whether bachelor, spinster, widow or widower.

V. Their occupation.

VI. The normal residence of each party before marriage.

VII. The name and surname of the father, and the name and maiden name of the mothers of both parties.

VIII. The place in which the marriage was solemnised.

IX. The intended future permanent residence of the parties.

The certificate must be signed by the parties married, the officiating clergyman and by two witnesses. It must be delivered or sent by post to the Registrar of the District in which the marriage was solemnised, within three days of the ceremony. Non compliance with the above provision in no way affects the validity of the marriage. It merely renders the husband liable to a penalty not exceeding £10.

In practice, however, the above described procedure is not followed. Normally it is the officiating clergyman that acquires the necessary certificate. He writes in the necessary information, has it signed as required, and returns it himself to the registrar.

Church of Ireland Marriages

Prior to the dis-establishment of the United Church of England and Ireland, the rules prescribed by the Rubric in the book of Common Prayer and the canons of the Church, except in so far as they were modified by the Act of 1844, determined the formalities to be observed in a marriage solemnised in that church. The Irish Church Act, 1869, brought about the dissolution of the union between the two churches and the dis-establishment of the Church of Ireland. As a consequence of that Act, the Matrimonial Causes and Marriage Law (Ireland) Amendment Acts 1870 and 1871 were passed. These acts, slightly amended, now regulate the formalities to be observed in a Church of Ireland marriage.

A Church of Ireland marriage may be celebrated by:

I. Special Licence; II. Ordinary Licence; III. After publication of the banns; IV. On Production of a Registrar's Certificate.[28]

I: A special licence may be granted by any Bishop of the Church of Ireland to marry at any convenient time in any place within his episcopal superintendence. Formerly both parties had to be Protestant Episcopalians but now only one of them need be.[29] "Protestant Episcopalian" is defined to mean a member of the Church of Ireland, the Church of England, the Episcopal Church of Scotland and any other Protestant Episcopal Church.[30] Parties to a marriage by special

---

28. Sect. 33 of the 1870 Act.
29. Sect. 36 of the 1870 Act as amended by Sect. 13 of the 1972 Act. The latter section makes provision for the granting of the above licence by a deputy, in the absence of the bishop.
30. Sect. 4 of the 1870 Act.

licence must give to the clergyman celebrating the marriage a certificate identical to that required for the registration of Roman Catholic marriages. The certificate must be filled in by the clergyman and the husband is under a duty to deliver or send it to the Registrar-General of Marriages (an tÁrd Chláraitheoir)[31] within three days of the ceremony. Failure on his part to do so renders him liable to a penalty not exceeding £10.[32]

II. An ordinary licence can be granted by a person nominated by the Bishop if either both or one of the parties to be married are Protestant Episcopalians. The marriage may be celebrated in any church or chapel in the licensor's district (a) in which Divine Service is performed according to the rites of the Church of Ireland and in which marriages could have been solemnised on 10th August, 1870, or (b) in any church or chapel of the Church of Ireland licenced since that date for the celebration of marriage by the bishop.

Before a licence can be issued, notice of the intended marriage must be given to the licensor (in person or in writing) by one of the parties who must have either (a) resided for not less than 7 days then next preceding in such licensor's district or (b) been for not less than three months then next preceding a member of the congregation of the church or chapel.[33] The notice to the licensor must state the church or chapel in which it is intended to solemnise the marriage. If the church or chapel is in a parish in which neither party resides at the time of the service of the notice, before a licence can be granted they must obtain the consent of the incumbent of the parish in which they reside to the celebration of the marriage in the place stipulated.[34] Before the licence can be given one of the parties must appear in person before the licensor and swear or affirm that there is no lawful impediment to the marriage; that one of the parties has had his or her usual place of abode for 14 days immediately before the day of the grant of such licence within the district attached to the church or chapel in which the marriage is to be solemnised, or for more than 3 months immediately preceding the day of the grant been a member of the congregation of such church or chapel; that they have both reached 21 years of age or if either is under 21, that the consent of the person or persons whose consent is required by law has been obtained, or that there is no person with authority to give such consent, or that the person under 21 is a widow or widower.[35]

The licensor is required to enter a copy of the notice in his "Marriage Notice Book", which must be open at all reasonable times for inspection by the public. A copy must also be sent to the officiating minister of the places of worship attended by the parties. On the expiration of 7 days from the service of the notice, the licence may be granted. If the licensor refuses to grant a licence the applicant can appeal to the bishop who appointed him or his successor.[36] If the marriage does not take place within three months from the date of the notice, the notice and licence become void.[37]

---

31. Vital Statistics Act, 1952, Sect. 3.
32. Sect. 22 of the 1871 Act as amended by the 1952 Act, Sect. 7 and S.I. No. 47 of 1956.
33. Sect. 35 of the 1870 Act, as amended by the 1972 Act, Sect. 12 (1) (b).
34. Sect. 35 of the 1870 Act as amended by the 1972 Act, Sect. 12 (1) (c). If the parties reside in different parishes the consent of the incumbents of both parishes must be obtained. Under this section every reference to an incumbent is said to include a curate in charge, and if there is no incumbent or curate in charge, it is to be construed as a reference to the bishop of the diocese.
35. Sect. 35 of the 1870 Act, as amended by the 1972 Act, Sect. 12 (1).
36. Sect. 35 of the 1870 Act.
37. Ibid.

III. The publication of banns is regulated in accordance with the rules of the Church of Ireland in force at the time when the parties seek to marry.[38] For marriage after publication of banns both parties must be Protestant Episcopalians.

IV. A certificate of a registrar can be used instead of banns, for the solemnisation of a marriage in a Church of Ireland church or chapel within the registrar's district.[39] For the procedure to be followed to obtain a certificate see "Marriage in the Office of the Registrar."

Solemnisation of Church of Ireland Marriages: Every marriage by ordinary licence, after publication of banns, or upon production of a registrar's certificate must be publicly solemnised in the presence of two or more witnesses and the officiating clergyman must immediately after solemnisation register the marriage in each of the Duplicate Marriage Register Books supplied to him by the Registrar-General.[40]

Presbyterian Marriages

Presbyterian marriages may be celebrated, **I.** By Special Licence; **II.** By Ordinary Licence; **III.** After Publication of banns.

I. By Section 37 of the Act of 1870 special licences to marry at any convenient time at any place in Ireland may be granted by any of the following persons:-

(a) The Moderator of the General Assembly of the Presbyterian Church in Ireland;

(b) The Moderator of the Remonstrant Synod of Ulster;

(c) The Moderator of the Presbytery of Antrim;

(d) The Moderator of the Synod of Munster.[41]

Formerly both parties had to be of the same religion as the Moderator who granted the special licence. Now only one of them need be.[42] Marriage by special licence is subject to the same rules concerning registration as apply to special licences issued by the Bishops of the Church of Ireland.

II. Marriage by ordinary licence takes place in a certified place of worship or church, pursuant to a licence granted by one of the authorised ministers of the church, specially appointed by the presbytery to issue such.[43] Such a licence can be granted if either both or one of the parties are Presbyterians. To obtain such a licence one of the parties must, 7 days prior to its issue, give to the licensing minister a certificate from the minister of the congregation of which he or she has been a member, stating that he has been a member for at least one preceding

---

38. Sect. 33 of the 1870 Act as amended by Sect. 11 of the 1972 Act.
39. Sect. 33 (1) of the 1870 Act; Sects. 13-16 of the 1844 Act; and Sects. 26-27 of the 1871 Act.
40. See Sects. 63 and 64 of the 1844 Act; Marriage Law (Ireland) Amendment Act, 1863, Sect. 6; Matrimonial Causes and Marriage Law (Ireland) Amendment Act, 1870, Sect. 33.
41. The 1972 Act, Sect. 14 (*e*) authorises a deputy appointed by one of the above persons to issue special licences in his absence.
42. Sect. 14 (*b*) and (*c*) of the 1972 Act.
43. Sects. 7 and 8 of the 1844 Act.

calendar month and that notice of the intended marriage has been entered in the congregation book kept for that purpose. The certificate also states the church or chapel in which it is intended to solemnise the marriage.[44]

Before the licence can be granted one of the parties must appear personally before the licensor and swear or affirm as to the same matters required to be sworn or affirmed before the grant of an ordinary licence for a Church of Ireland ceremony. The only matter of difference is that one of the parties must have had, for 15 days immediately preceding the grant, his or her usual place of abode in the Presbytery within which the marriage is to be solemnised.

The licensor is required to enter a copy of the certificate into his marriage notice book, which must be kept open at all reasonable times for inspection by the public. Any person may enter a caveat against the issuing of a licence. If upon examination of the matter stated in the caveat the licensing minister is satisfied that it ought not to obstruct his granting a licence, or if the caveat is withdrawn by the person who entered it, the licence may issue. But if the minister has any doubt he can refer the matter to the Presbytery for decision.[45]

If a licensing Minister for any reason refuses to grant a licence the applicant may appeal against the refusal to the Presbytery by which he was appointed.[46] On the expiration of 7 days from the delivery of the certificate the licence may be granted. If the marriage does not take place within a month from the date of the licence and within 3 months of the entry of the notice in the Marriage Notice Book, the notice and licence are void.[47]

III. For a marriage by publication of banns both of the parties to the marriage must be Presbyterians. Banns must be read on three consecutive Sundays preceding the solemnisation of the marriage by or in the presence of one Presbyterian Minister in the church of each congregation to which the parties belong. The marriage must be solemnised in a church in which the banns have been read. At least six days prior to the first reading of the banns the persons to be married must deliver or cause to be delivered to the minister or ministers by whom or in whose presence banns are to be read, a notice in writing stating their Christian name, surname, the congregation of which they are members, their respective abodes and the time during which they have resided in them.[48]

Solemnisation of Presbyterian Marriages: Every marriage by ordinary licence, or after publication of banns, must be publicly solemnised in the presence of two or more witnesses and the officiating minister must immediately after solemnisation register the marriage in each of the Duplicate Marriage Register Books supplied to him by the Registrar-General.

Protestant Marriages other than Church of Ireland or Presbyterian; and Marriages of any other Community of Christians not Roman Catholics who do not describe themselves as Protestants:

Other Protestant marriages may be celebrated by I. Special Licence; II. Registrar's Licence; III. Registrar's Certificate.

I. Special Licences to marry at any convenient time at any place in Ireland

44. *Ibid.*, Sect. 10.
45. *Ibid.*, Sect. 11.
46. *Ibid.*, Sect. 8.
47. *Ibid.*, Sect. 45.
48. *Ibid.*, Sects. 5 & 6.

may be granted by:[49]

(a) The Moderator of the Eastern Reform Presbyterian Synod;

(b) The Moderator of the United Presbyterian Presbytery of Ireland;

(c) The Moderator of the Secession Church in Ireland;

(d) The Moderator of the Reformed Presbyterian Synod of Ireland;

(e) The Chairman of the Congregational Union of Ireland;

(f) The Secretary of the Conference of the Methodist or Wesleyan Church in Ireland;

(g) The President or Head of the Methodist New Connexion Church;

(h) The President or Head of the Association of the Baptist Churches in Ireland.[50]

Formerly both parties had to be of the same religion as the person who granted the special licence. Now only one of them need be.[51] Marriage by special licences is subject to the same rules concerning registration as apply to special licences issued by the Bishops of the Church of Ireland.

II. & III. For the obtaining of a Registrar's licence or certificate see "Marriage in the Office of the Registrar".

Marriages by any other community of Christians other than Roman Catholics, and who do not describe themselves as Protestants may be solemnised by methods **II. & III.**[52]

Solemnisation: Every marriage by a registrar's licence or certificate must be solemnised by a minister of the Church or denomination to which the parties to the marriage or either of them belong, in the place of worship named in the notice with open doors and in the presence of two or more witnesses other than the person solemnising the marriage.[53] As in the case of marriages in accordance with the rites of religious denominations previously discussed all such marriages must be registered in the Duplicate Marriage Register Books.

Marriages in accordance with (a) the usages of The Society of Friends and (b) The Jewish religion:

Such marriages may be solemnised by I. Special Licence; II. Upon production of a Registrar's Certificate.

I. Special licences to marry at any convenient time or place in Ireland may be granted by the Clerk to the Yearly Meeting of the Society of Friends or by the Chief Rabbi of the Jewish Communities in Ireland.[54] One of the parties to whom such a licence is granted must be of the same religion as the person granting it.[55] Marriages by special licence are subject to the same rules concerning registration

49. Sect. 37 of the 1870 Act as amended by the 1871 Act, Sect. 21.
50. Sect. 14 (e) of the 1972 Act authorises a deputy appointed by one of the above persons to issue special licences in his absence.
51. Sect. 14 (b) and 14 (c) of the 1972 Act.
52. See Marriage Law (Ireland) Amendment Act, 1873.
53. Marriage Law (Ireland) Amendment Act, 1863, Sect. 7.
54. Sect. 37 of the 1870 Act as amended by the 1972 Act, Sect. 14 (a). Sect. 14 (e) authorises a deputy to issue special licences in the absence of the clerk or the Chief Rabbi.
55. Sect. 37 of the 1870 Act as amended by the 1972 Act, Sect. 14 (b) and Sect. 14 (c).

as apply to special licences issued by the Bishops of the Church of Ireland.

II. For the obtaining of a registrar's certificate see "Marriage in the Office of the Registrar". The certificate must be given to the registering officer of the place where the marriage is to be solemnised.

Solemnisation: Every marriage by a registrar's certificate must be solemnised according to the practice of the respective bodies, in the place named in the notice, with open doors in the presence of two or more witnesses.[56] All such marriages must be registered in the Duplicate Marriage Register Books by the registering officer. In the case of a Jewish marriage it must be registered by the Secretary of the Synagogue to which the husband belongs.[57]

Marriage in the Office of the Registrar:

The 1844 Act provided for the appointment of registrars with powers to solemnise marriages by civil contract after compliance with various conditions. A marriage may be solemnised in this way after parties have obtained a district registrar's certificate or licence. As we have already seen such a certificate or licence may be required not only for marriage in the office of the registrar, but also for marriage in accordance with the rites of the religious denominations previously discussed.

For a licence or a certificate to be issued, notice of the intended marriage must be given by one of the parties to the district registrar. If they reside in different districts the notice must be served on the registrar of each district.[58] The notice must state:[59]

(a) The name and surname of the parties;

(b) Their status, i.e. whether bachelor, spinster, widow or widower.

(c) Their rank or profession.

(d) Whether they are minors or of full age;

(e) The church, chapel or place of worship the parties or either of them usually attends;

(f) The parties' usual dwelling place, each having resided there for not less than 7 days;[60]

(g) The church, chapel or other place in which the marriage is to be solemnised. Except in the case of members of the Jewish faith, it must be within the district of the registrar, or one of the registrars to whom notice is given.[61]

(h) Whether the marriage is intended to be celebrated by virtue of the registrar's certificate or licence.

---

56. Marriage Law (Ireland) Amendment Act, 1863, Sect. 7.
57. Sect. 63 of the 1844 Act as amended by the 1972 Act, Sect. 4. This amendment provides for registration by a secretary's deputy. See also Sect. 5 of the 1972 Act, which concerns the Dublin Jewish Progressive Congregation.
58. Sect. 13 of the 1844 Act.
59. Marriage Law (Ireland) Amendment Act, 1863, Sect. 2.
60. By Sect. 6 of the 1972 Act, however, if there is not a church or building used by the religious denomination according to the rites of which the marriage is to be solemnised within the district where the parties have for the previous 7 days resided, the marriage may be celebrated in a church or building situate in another district.
61. Sect. 13 of the 1844 Act as amended by the 1871 Act, Sect. 28.

When the registrar is served with the notice he must[62]

1. File the notice and keep it in his Office Records;

2. Enter a true copy of the notice in the Marriage Notice Book which he must keep open for the inspection of all persons at all reasonable times without payment of fees.

3. On the day on which he receives notice or on the next day, send by post in a registered letter, a copy of the notice—

   (a) to the Minister of the church, chapel or registered place of public worship in which the marriage is intended to be solemnised;

   (b) to the Minister of the church, chapel or place of public worship which the parties to the marriage or either of them usually attend; or

   (c) To the Registering Officer of the Society of Friends, or to the Clerk of a branch of the Church of Christian Scientists[53] or to the Secretary of a Synagogue by whom the marriage is to be registered.

4. If the marriage is to be contracted in the registrar's office, then in addition to (b) he has to suspend a copy of the notice in some conspicuous place in his office, and keep it there (i) for 21 days if the marriage is to be celebrated by virtue of a certificate, or (ii) for 7 days, if it is to be celebrated by licence.

In the case of a marriage in the registrar's office, if the parties have no minister of a place of worship to which they ordinarily go, and are not Quakers or Christian Scientists or Jewish, the registrar must publish at the expense of the parties, once at least in 2 consecutive weeks after the receipt of the notice, a copy of the notice in a newspaper circulating in the district in which the marriage is to be solemnised. If there is no such newspaper, then in one circulating in the county in which such district is situated.[64]

Marriage by Licence: The party giving notice is required to declare in writing —that there is no lawful impediment to the intended marriage; that the parties have for one month preceding usually attended Divine Worship in the building named in the notice (if one is so named); that one of them has resided for 15 days in the district of the registrar on whom notice is served; and, in cases of minors, that the necessary consents have been obtained.[65] In cases where both parties reside in the same district a residence of 15 days is necessary for one party and not less than 7 days for the other. But if they reside in different districts a residence of 15 days in each is necessary at the time of the service of the notice.[66] The registrar may grant a licence after the expiration of 7 days from the date of entry of the notice.[67] The ceremony may then take place.

Marriage by Certificate: At the time of giving notice for marriage by certificate

62. Marriage Law (Ireland) Amendment Act, 1863, Sect. 3.
63. Sect. 10 (1) of the 1972 Act.
64. Sect. 41 of the 1870 Act, as amended by the 1972 Act, Sect. 10 (2).
65. Marriage Law (Ireland) Amendment Act, 1863, Sect. 4.
66. Ibid.
67. Ibid., Sect. 5.

a declaration similar to that required for marriage by licence must be made. The requirement of 15 days residence by one party is here replaced by a requirement that each party must reside within the registrar's district 7 days immediately preceding the giving of notice. Thus here the declaration is to 7 days residence.[68] After the expiration of 21 days from the entry of the notice, the registrar may issue his certificate and the ceremony can take place.

Caveats: Any person may enter a caveat with a registrar against the issuing of a certificate or licence to an applicant. Such a caveat must be signed by or on behalf of the person entering it and must state his address and the grounds for objection. No licence or certificate can issue until the Registrar has examined the matter of the caveat and is satisfied that it ought not to obstruct his issuing a certificate or licence or until it is withdrawn by the party who entered it. The registrar, if in doubt, can refer the matter to the Registrar-General to decide. If the registrar refuses to grant a certificate or licence the applicant may appeal to the Registrar-General.[69]

Registrar's Special Marriage Licence:[70] The Registrar-General may grant a special licence to marry on being satisfied that one of the persons to be married is, for health reasons certified by a doctor, unable to go to a registry office for a marriage ceremony. A marriage authorised by such a licence may be solemnised, in the presence of two witnesses, at any time and place by the registrar of marriages for the registration district in which that place is situated.

Solemnisation of Marriage: The following declaration must be made by both parties, in the presence of the registrar and witnesses, in the case of a marriage in a registry office or following the granting of a special licence by the Registrar-General.[71]

"I do solemnly declare that I know not of any lawful impediment why I, A.B. may not be joined in matrimony to C.D."

Each of the parties must say to each other

"I call upon these persons here present to witness that I, A.B. do take thee C.D. to be my lawful wedded wife (husband)."

Marriages in the registrar's office may take place between eight in the morning and five in the afternoon on any day except Sunday, with open doors in the presence of the registrar and two witnesses.[72]

NON-OBSERVANCE OF FORMALITIES

The general principle is that the non-observance of, or defect in, the formalities does not invalidate a marriage unless both parties were aware of it at the time of the ceremony. Only if the parties "knowingly and wilfully" disregard certain requirements will their marriage be void. Thus, a marriage is void if parties knowingly and wilfully marry (except in the case of a marriage celebrated by a Roman Catholic priest)[73]

---

68. *Ibid.*, Sects. 2 and 4.
69. Sect. 23 of the 1844 Act. See also Sect. 18.
70. Sect. 16 of the 1972 Act.
71. *Ibid.*, and Sect. 29 of the 1844 Act.
72. Sect. 30 of the 1844 Act as amended by the 1972 Act, Sect. 17 (2).
73. Sect. 49 of the 1844 Act.

(a) in any place other than the church or chapel in which the banns of matrimony between the parties were duly and lawfully published,[74] or

(b) in any place other than the church or chapel specified in the licence where the marriage is by licence; or

(c) in any place other than the church or chapel, registered building or office specified in the Notice and Registrar's Certificate; or

(d) without due notice to the registrar or without certificate of notice duly issued or without licence from the registrar where a notice or licence is necessary; or

(e) in the absence of a registrar where the presence of a registrar is necessary; or

(f) in any certified Presbyterian Church without publication of banns or any licence.

A marriage celebrated by a Protestant Episcopalian clergyman between a person who is a Protestant Episcopalian and a person who is not, or by a Roman Catholic clergyman between a person who is a Roman Catholic and a person who is not is void if the parties to such marriage knowingly and wilfully marry without[75]

(a) due notice to the registrar; or

(b) without certificate of notice duly issued; or

(c) without the presence of two or more witnesses; or

(d) in a building not set apart for the celebration of divine service according to the rights and ceremonies of the religion of the clergyman solemnising such marriage.

A marriage may also be void if not celebrated within three calendar months after notice has been given to the registrar. After the passage of such time the notice, certificate and any licence issued and all "other proceedings thereupon" are void.[76]

There are also certain specified defects, evidence of the existence of which can never be given so as to render a marriage void. Evidence may not be given[77]

(a) that any of the statutory requirements as to the residence of the parties prior to the marriage were not fulfilled; or

(b) that the consent of any third person required to be given was not so given;[78] or

(c) that either of the parties was not a Presbyterian in the case of a marriage solemnised in a Presbyterian church; or

(d) if the marriage was by licence, that the certificate required to be delivered to the Minister granting such licence had not been delivered, or that a certificate of the publication of banns had not been produced

---

74. See *Courtenay v. Miles* (1876) I.R. 11 Eq. 284 (Ct for Matr. Causes.) – The use of a false name in the publication of banns with the knowledge of both parties prior to the marriage for the purpose of deception or concealment was held to render the marriage void.
75. Sect. 39 of the 1870 Act.
76. See Sect. 25 of the 1844 Act.
77. Sect. 32 of the 1844 Act.
78. See "Consents of Third Parties" at p. 56 *infra*.

to the Minister by whom the marriage was solemnised where such production was required.

The Acts are silent as to the effect on the validity of a marriage, of non-observance of a number of other requirements, e.g. would a marriage be valid if celebrated by a registrar in his office without any witnesses present, or behind closed doors or after 5 p.m.? As a general rule it is submitted that unless a defect is said expressly to invalidate a marriage, the marriage is completely valid. Whilst the non-observance of certain formalities may not invalidate a marriage, as usually one of the parties has to make an oath or declaration, he or she may be rendered liable to prosecution for perjury or for the commission of an offence under the Statutory Declarations Act, 1938, Sect. 6. A person convicted under the latter provision is rendered liable to a fine not exceeding £50 and/or to a term of imprisonment not exceeding three months.

Lourdes Marriages

The Marriages Act, 1972, Sect. 2, provides that a marriage to which it applies "shall be, and shall be deemed always to have been valid as to form if it would have been so valid had it been solemnised in the State". The section is said to apply to marriages which were solemnised before the passing of the Act, solely by a religious ceremony in the department of Hautes Pyrenees, France, and were between "persons both or either of whom were or was citizens or a citizen of Ireland on the day of the marriage". The section further provides that the Registrar-General upon "production of such evidence as appears to him to be satisfactory" may cause such a marriage to be registered in a register to be maintained in his office. The need for section 2 arose out of the fact that a number of Irish Roman Catholic couples in previous years had gone to Lourdes to marry, and probably believing French law to be the same as Irish law had only gone through a religious ceremony while there. According to French law, however, a marriage ceremony must take place before an official of the State for it to be valid. The parties may then have their marriage celebrated according to the rites of their own religion. We have already seen that generally speaking the formal validity of a marriage is determined by the *lex loci celebrationis* i.e. the law of the place where the marriage is celebrated. Thus under both French and Irish law such Lourdes marriages, not being preceded by a civil ceremony, were invalid and of no effect. Section 2 was enacted so as to retrospectively validate all such marriages that took place prior to 20th December 1972, i.e. the date of the passing of the Act. Any marriages that have taken place in Lourdes since that date and that have not complied with French formalities are unaffected by the section, and are thus invalid.

There are a number of matters about this section worth noting:

I. Whereas the marriages to which the section applies are retrospectively validated in this country, the section cannot, and of course does not, affect the law of any other country. Generally speaking under private international law a marriage is only regarded as valid as to form if it complies with the formalities required by the country in which the marriage is celebrated. Thus if the parties to a marriage validated by Section 2 go to live in England, English law will test the validity of the marriage by looking to see whether the parties complied with the formalities required by French law. Upon making a finding that they did not, an English court would hold the marriage to be invalid under English law.

II. The section applies to marriages celebrated by a couple either or both of whom were Irish citizens at the time of the marriage. It is submitted that for a provision retrospectively validating in this State a marriage celebrated in another State, Irish domicile or at least residence at the time of the ceremony would have been a more appropriate connecting factor with this country. As the law stands at present Irish law regards as valid the marriages of Irish citizens to which the section applies irrespective of whether they were domiciled or resident in this country at the time of the celebration of the marriage, or at any other time.

III. In retrospectively validating such marriages the Act makes no provision for a person who having discovered the invalidity of his or her Lourdes ceremony, married another prior to section 2 coming into operation. In such circumstances having regard to the wording of the section it seems that the first marriage would be regarded as valid. Such a result could have particularly unjust consequences for a party's 'second' spouse.

IV. The section applies to marriages solemnised prior to the passing of the Act, i.e. prior to 20th December 1972. The provisions of the Act could not come into force until a ministerial order rendered them operative. Section 2 was not brought into force by such an order until 1st February 1973.[79] It is submitted that it would have been more appropriate for the section to have recognised marriages solemnised prior to the coming into operation of the section rather than prior to the passing of the Act.

Conflict between Church and State

There are a number of situations in which a marriage will be regarded as formally valid by the State but as invalid by the Roman Catholic Church. The most noteworthy are the following:

(a) A marriage of Roman Catholic parties celebrated by a Roman Catholic priest with no witnesses present is a valid civil marriage *per verba de praesenti* but is not valid in the eyes of the Church, such ceremony not being in compliance with the decree of the Council of Trent.[80]

(b) A marriage celebrated in a registry office between two Roman Catholics or between a Roman Catholic and a Protestant if the required formalities are properly observed is a valid marriage by the law of the State but is invalid according to the Church. Further it has not been unknown in the past for a Roman Catholic previously married in a registry office, to be married by a Roman Catholic priest to another person, and as a consequence convicted of committing bigamy.[81] In one such case, tried in Limerick in 1962, in the course of passing sentence the President of the Circuit Court, Judge Barra O'Briain, discussed the relationship between the canon law and the law of the State:

> "The position of a Judge who is called upon to administer the civil law that for historical reasons conflicts with the canon law which is binding upon the majority of the people of this State is ... unenviable. I do not intend to let that affect my interpretation of the criminal law or in any way to derogate from its effect. I might

79. S.I. No. 12 of 1973.
80. *Ussher v. Ussher supra.*
81. See *People (A.-G) v. Ballins* [1964] Ir. Jur. Rep. 14, (Cir. Ct.); *People (A.-G.) v. Hunt* (1945), 80 I.L.T. & S.J. 19, (C. C.C.).

add, however, that after 40 years of independence, it should be possible to amend the law here which for historical reasons now raises a grave problem of conscience among the majority of Irish citizens. It should be possible to amend the law without in any way creating a new problem of conscience for the majority, Protestants or otherwise."[82]

Where a person does marry bigamously any person who with knowledge of the circumstances persuades him to so marry may be convicted of bigamy as an accessory before the fact. Moreover any clergyman who with knowledge of the circumstances officiates at such a marriage may be convicted as a principal in the second degree. The bigamist, persuader and clergyman could all receive, if convicted, a maximum sentence of 7 years penal servitude.[83]

Criticisms of the Present Law:

In 1868 a Royal Commission, looking at Irish Marriage law stated that "a good general marriage law . . . ought to embrace the maximum of simplicity and the maximum of certainty". To say that the present law does not go near to doing so is to state the obvious. It is the product not of a systematic and coherent development but of piecemeal legislative action stretching across 140 years. In all that time no effort has been made by the legislature to clarify and simplify the general procedures that have to be followed by persons wishing to marry, or to codify or rationalise the extremely complex statutory position.

The confusing legal situation is exacerbated by the fact that there are a number of circumstances in which the State regards as formerly valid, a marriage between Roman Catholics that the Roman Catholic Church does not accept as valid, and *vice versa*. There are also circumstances in which a marriage between Roman Catholics solemnised in accordance with the formalities required by the Council of Trent, and thus valid in accordance with both the Civil law and Canon law, may be declared a nullity by the Matrimonial Tribunals of the Church. The civil law as to nullity, is discussed in a later chapter. Suffice it here to say that a declaration of nullity by a Church Tribunal does not affect the validity of a marriage in the civil law.

The fact that marriages celebrated in accordance with the rites of the Roman Catholic Church but subsequently annulled by the Marriage Tribunals of that church, may be regarded still as valid subsisting marriages under the civil law, has created confusion in the minds of the general public. Looked at simply, it seems that at one stage the State leaves the matter to the religious sphere and recognises its actions, while at another stage it refuses to do so.

The most obvious reform and solution to the present diverse statutory provisions would be to adopt the formula followed in many foreign countries and stipulate that a civil ceremony is the only legally effective way of contracting a marriage. The parties could then go through any religious ceremony they wish. Such a division of ceremonies would help to maintain in the public mind a distinction between the civil contract of marriage, and its effects under civil law, and the religious ceremony and its religious consequences. It would help to

---

82. *People (A.-G.) v. Ballins supra* at p. 15.
83. W. Conway, "Marriage in Ireland: Church and State", (1946), 68 *Irish Ecclesiastical Record* 361-6; D. Fennell, *The Changing Face of Catholic Ireland*, chap. 1; G.A. Lee, *Canon and Civil Marriage Law in Ireland*, (1946), 67 *Irish Ec. Record*, p. 154-58; "Family Law" by D. Barrington. (Society of Young Solicitors Lecture No. 33). C. Davitt, "Some aspects of the Constitution and the Law in Relation to Marriage", *Studies*, 1968 p. 6 (see also the comments by V. Grogan on p. 20 of the same edition of *Studies*).

instil in people the fact that the religious and civil spheres do not coincide and thus help to prevent confusion arising as to the effects in the civil law of a church decree of nullity, or of the church not regarding a marriage as validly celebrated. Moreover such a system by making the law both more simple and more certain would greatly facilitate the solution of any disputes that arise as to the formal validity of a marriage.[84] Such a reform of the law however may arouse very strong opposition from the various churches and religious bodies in the State.

REQUIRED CONSENTS OF THIRD PARTIES TO MARRIAGE

The basic policy of the law is that parental consent is required before a person under 21 is permitted to marry. This requirement, however, is by no means absolute and a marriage solemnised without such consent is regarded as valid. Consequently, the obtaining of consent is classified as part of the formalities, and not as a question concerning capacity.

Whose Consent is Required:

The requirements as to consents are set down in section 7 of the Marriages Act 1972. They are applicable to all marriages including those celebrated according to the rites of the Catholic Church. Section 7 taken in conjunction with the provisions of the Guardianship of Infants Act, 1964, sets down the following rules:

I. Where the minor is legitimate:

Circumstances:	*Person or persons whose consent required*:
(a) If both parents are living.	(a) Consent of both parents.
(b) If one parent dead and there is no other guardian.	(b) The surviving parent.
(c) If one parent dead and if a guardian has been appointed by deceased parent.	(c) Consent of both if acting jointly. If parent still sole guardian, consent of parent only.
(d) Where both parents dead and guardians or guardian appointed by deceased parents or by the court under the Guardianship of Infants Act, 1964.	(d) The guardian or guardians so appointed.
(e) Where both parents dead and no guardian has been appointed.	(e) The President of the High Court (or a Judge of that court nominated by the President).

II. Where the minor is illegitimate:

Circumstances:	*Person whose consent is required*:
(a) If the mother is alive.	(a) The mother.
(b) If the mother of the infant is	(b) The guardian so appointed.

84. See S. Ryan, "Irish Marriage Law: The need for Change", *Irish Times* 16th and 17th May 1973; A. Samuels, "Capacity and Formalities of Marriage" (1971), Fam. Law 118—Although the author is here writing about the English situation nearly all the comments made are equally applicable to the law of this country.

dead and a guardian has been
appointed by her or by the court.

(c) If mother dead and no guardian   (c) The President of the High Court
has been so appointed.   (or a Judge of that court nominated by the President).

If the minor is a widow or widower, the above consents are not required. In the
case of a ward of court, the consent of the court must be obtained.

Dispensing with Consent

The requirement of the consent of a guardian can be dispensed with if a
guardian:

(a) refuses or withholds consent; or

(b) is unknown; or

(c) is of unsound mind; or

(d) is of whereabouts which would be unreasonably difficult to ascertain.

and the President of the High Court (or a judge of that court nominated by him)
consents to the intended marriage.

An application to the President under section 7 of the 1972 Act can be made
informally through the Registrar of Wards of Court and is heard and determined
in private. No fee is charged by the court in respect of such an application and
the procedure is substantially the same as that used for determining applications
for exemption orders under section 1 of the 1972 Act. As there are no reported
cases on the exercise by the President of the High Court of the above jurisdiction,
it is impossible to say what reasoning is applied upon an application for dispensation of consent coming before him.[85] In making a determination under the
section, however, the court must regard the child's welfare as the paramount
consideration by virtue of section 3 of the Guardianship of Infants Act, 1964.

THE AGE FOR MARRIAGE – SUGGESTED REFORM

The law as to the minimum age for marriage and the necessity for parental
consent has recently been examined by the Law Reform Commission.[86] In its
second working paper the Commission having proposed that the age of majority
be reduced from 21 years to 18 years states:

"In most European States the age of majority is the same as the free age for
marriage (i.e. the age at which persons are free to marry without parental
consent) . . . when no question of principle is involved uniformity with
other legal systems, particularly those of the E.E.C., is desirable.

If it is correct to reduce the age of majority there seems to the Commission

---

85. There are also no unreported written judgements available setting out the facts of a
case and the decision reached. Australian law contains a similar provision permitting a
parent's consent to be dispensed with if unreasonably withheld. There, what amounts to an
unreasonable withholding of consent has been said to depend entirely on the circumstances
of the case. An objection will be held unreasonable if purely personal to the objector. Thus,
it has been held to be unreasonable to withhold consent because the proposed spouse is of a
different race or religion to that of the objecting parent—*Re B*. [1972] Q.W.N. 35, or
because it was not sought with proper respect—*Re An Infant* (1963), 6 F.L.R. 12, or because
the parent does not want to lose control over his child—*Re A Minor* (1964), 6 F.L.R. 129.

86. The Law Relating to the Age of Majority, The Age for Marriage and Some Connected
Subjects. The Law Reform Commission, Working Paper No. 2 (Dublin 1977). See also,
A. Shatter, 'What is the age of consent?', *Irish Times*, 2nd May, 1978.

to be no reason why a similar reduction should not be made in the free age for marriage. A person who is fit to manage his own affairs, who is fit to serve on a jury, to make a will, to vote, should, in the Commission's view, be responsible enough to enter into a marriage contract without acquiring the consent of any person or tribunal."[87]

The Commission accordingly recommends that the free age for marriage be reduced to eighteen years.

The Commission also proposes (a) that the minimum age for marriage should be the same as the "free age for marriage" i.e. eighteen years, *or* (b) that the minimum age for marriage should remain 16 years and that persons between 16 and 18 years should only be permitted to marry with the prior written consent of their parents or guardians or "with the consent of some other appropriate authority where there are no parents or guardians or where one or both of the parents or guardians refuse or withhold consent".[88] In addition it states that no person under sixteen years should be permitted to marry and that the present jurisdiction to grant exemptions to persons under sixteen years should be abolished.

The Commission states that if (a) is implemented all marriages of persons under eighteen years should be null and void and similarly if (b) is implemented all marriages of persons under sixteen years should be null and void as should marriages of persons between sixteen and eighteen years without the required consents.

It is submitted that proposal (a) has much to commend it. If, as a society, we believe that persons under eighteen years of age do not have sufficient experience and understanding of life to be able to enter into marriage on the basis of their own judgement, eighteen years should be the minimum age for marriage. Research has shown that teenage marriages are more at risk than older marriages and there is no evidence that the obtaining of parental consent reduces the risk.

In a study entitled "Age at Marriage and Marital Breakdown" written by Dr. Helen Burke contained in Appendix D of the working paper, Dr. Burke suggests that if the marriage of persons between sixteen and eighteen years is to be permitted both parental consent and judicial permission should be required before such a marriage could be validly celebrated. She states: "Judicial permission to marry is regarded as necessary in these cases as well as parental consent (a) to protect a couple from being pressurized into marriage by parents who might persuade them to marry to avoid the stigma of illegitimacy; (b) judicial consent, if it is tied in with a system of premarital counselling could provide a very positive service for underage couples"[89] The purpose of such premarital counselling is, she emphasizes "not to talk the couple out of marriage but rather to explore with them why they need to marry now and to help them to face more realistically what marriage involves."[90] Moreover a report from a marriage councillor would assist the court in its assessment of the couple's readiness for marriage.[91]

It is submitted that if the free age for marriage is reduced to eighteen years parental consent should not by itself be sufficient to enable persons between sixteen and eighteen years to enter into marriage. The concern of the law in

87. *Ibid.*, p. 48.
88. *Ibid.*, p. 50-51. See also pp. 79, 87.
89. *Ibid.*, p. 139.
90. *Ibid.*, p. 136.
91. *Ibid.*, p. 139-140.

establishing a minimum age for marriage should be to prevent minors from entering into precipitate and illadvised marriages. It should provide them with protection not only from their own actions but also from those of their parents. The need for such protection is clear. According to the Law Reform Commission's working paper, in 1975 there were nine applications to the President of the High Court for an exemption order to marry by persons under sixteen years of age. Eight of the applicants were girls, seven of whom were pregnant.[92] A law as to the age for marriage must protect minors from being forced into marriage by parents anxious to cover up the embarrassment of a daughter's premarital pregnancy.

If persons between the ages of sixteen and eighteen are to be permitted to marry, Dr. Burke's proposal should, it is submitted, be modified to permit such a person marry without parental consent if the parent or guardian whose consent is required

(a) is incapable of consenting by reason of mental disability; or

(b) cannot after reasonable enquiries be found; or

(c) is dead; or

(d) unreasonably withholds consent

and the court is satisfied that it is in the interests of the applicant's welfare that the marriage take place.

Finally, the proposal that, if permitted, marriages of persons between sixteen and eighteen years without the required consents should be null and void, is to be welcomed. If a person is regarded as too immature to make a proper judgement as to whether to enter into marriage or not and if the law only regards it correct to give effect to his decision upon his obtaining the consent of his parents or guardians or some other appropriate authority, a marriage without such consents should be null and void. As we have already seen, however, at present if persons under 21 years of age marry without first obtaining the necessary consents, the validity of their marriage is unaffected.[93]

---

92. *Ibid.*, pp. 40, 128. Three of the applications to marry were granted, three were refused and three were withdrawn.
93. Marriages (Ireland) Act, 1844, Sect. 32. See p. 46 *ante*.

CHAPTER 5

NULLITY OF MARRIAGE

As has already been seen the High Court inherited the matrimonial jurisdiction of the Ecclesiastical Courts over suits of nullity of marriage. By the Matrimonial Causes and Marriage Law (Ireland) Amendment Act, 1870, Section 13, in exercising this jurisdiction, it is to "proceed and act and give relief on principles and rules which in the opinion of the said Court, shall be as nearly as may be conformable to the principles and rules which the Ecclesiastical Courts of Ireland have heretofore acted on and given relief."[1]

The Courts' jurisdiction to grant nullity decrees is not affected by the constitutional prohibition on the dissolution of marriage. A decree of dissolution terminates a valid subsisting marriage; a decree of nullity determines that a marriage never came into being. Haugh J. in *Griffith* v. *Griffith* stated[2] that

"The question of nullity of marriage is best understood as part of the law of contract. A particular country may or may not permit of divorce; but in every country that treats of marriage . . . there must be a law of nullity, i.e. a law laying down the conditions under which the marriage contract is valid and binding."

Thus, in this chapter, we are concerned with discovering the conditions under which, what on the surface appears to be a valid marriage contract, may in fact be a nullity.

VOID OR VOIDABLE

A marriage may either be void or voidable. As Bromley has pointed out,

"A void marriage is strictly speaking a contradiction in terms, for it is no marriage at all; to speak of a void marriage is merely a compendious way of saying that, although the parties have been through a ceremony of marriage, they have never acquired the status of husband and wife owing to the presence of some impediment."[3]

Such a marriage will be regarded as never having taken place. Being void *ab initio* it does not need a decree to annul it. Any such decree can only be declaratory and cannot affect any change in status. A decree, however, may be sought if desired not only by the parties to the purported marriage, but also by any other interested persons, even after the death of the parties. Whereas a party to a void marriage may remarry without first obtaining a decree, such a decree is desirable

---

1. See chapter 2.
2. *Haugh J.* in *Griffith v. Griffith*, [1944] I.R. 35, at p. 41; (1943), 78 I.L.T.R. 95 (H.C.).
3. *Bromley's Family Law*, 4th Ed. (Butterworth's, London, 1971), p. 58. This statement can be found slightly modified in the 5th ed. (1976), p. 75.

in order to remove any doubt that may exist as to the validity of the former ceremony. In Irish law a marriage may be void because of:

I. Lack of Capacity;

II. Non observance of formalities;

III. Absence of Consent.

Impotence is the only ground on which a marriage is voidable. A voidable marriage is, for all purposes, a valid subsisting marriage until a decree of annulment is pronounced and the decree can only be made at the instance of one of the parties.[4] A decree cannot be granted after the death of one of the parties to the marriage. The effect of a decree is to retrospectively invalidate the marriage, the parties then being regarded in law as never having been married.[5]

There is a general presumption that once parties have gone through a marriage ceremony they have contracted a valid marriage. Thus the onus is on the petitioner (i.e. the party alleging invalidity) to rebut the presumption.[6] This onus was said by the court in *Griffith* v. *Griffith*[7] to be "severe and heavy". In *S.* v. *S.*[8] Kenny J. in the Supreme Court stated that "a petitioner must establish his or her case with a high degree of probability" or "must remove all reasonable doubt".

Frequency of Proceedings:

Nullity cases have arisen very infrequently in the courts in recent years.[9] In those that have arisen it has been emphasised that "the court must proceed with great caution before giving relief".[10] In the absence of such caution it is feared that "discontented spouses could find an easy road to circumvent, not only the law, but also the established public opinion which exists in this country against divorce and 'make their marriage vows as false as dicers' oaths' ".[11] Much stress has been placed on the fact that "it is not the function of the court

4. *A.* v. *B.* (1868) L.R. 1 P & D. 559 (Ct. of P & D.). See also *De Reneville v. De Reneville* [1948] 1 All E.R. 56, (C.A.) at p. 60 where Lord Greene M.R. stated: "A void marriage is one that will be regarded by every court in any case in which the existence of the marriage is in issue as never having taken place and can be so treated by both parties to it without the necessity of any decree annulling it; a voidable marriage is one that will be regarded by every court as valid subsisting marriage until a decree annulling it has been pronounced by a court of competent jurisdiction".
5. *Mason v. Mason (Otherwise Pennington)* [1944] N.I. 134 (K.B.D.).
6. *Griffith v. Griffith, supra; B. v. D.* (June 1973) (unreported) (H.C.); *S. v. S.* (November 1974) unreported (H.C.); (July 1976), unreported, (S.C.).
7. *Supra.*
8. *Supra.*
9.

Year	Number of High Court Nullity Petitions issued	Number of Nullity Decrees granted by High Court
1970	1	–
1971	4	2
1972	2	1
1973	3	2
1974	8	4
1975	8	–
1976	3	3
1977	11	1
1978	11	2
1979	9	3
1980 (up to 31st July)	8	8

See Dail Debates (7th June 1978) Vol. 307 Col. 606 and (18th June 1980) Vol. 322 Col. 56. 1980 statistic supplied by the Central Office of the High Court.
10. *B. v. D., supra.*
11. Hanna J. in *McM. v. McM.* and *McK. v. McK.* [1936] I.R. 177 at p. 185, (H.C.). See also *Griffith v. Griffith, supra.*

by the exercise of this important jurisdiction, to relieve parties from hasty and ill advised marriages".[12]

This cautious approach by the courts, taken together with the total absence of legislative intervention, has resulted until recently[13] in there being very little development of the law of nullity. It has, in the main, stagnated, its roots and principles remaining deeply embedded in 18th and 19th Century sociological and psychological canonical conceptions of the factors required to constitute a valid marriage.

GROUNDS FOR RENDERING A MARRIAGE VOID

I. **Lack of Capacity**

A: If parties go through a ceremony of marriage and

   (i) either party is at the time of the ceremony lawfully married to another person; or

   (ii) the parties are within the prohibited degrees of relationship; or

   (iii) are of the same biological sex

the ceremony is of no effect, and the marriage is void. See further chapter 4.

B: As we have already seen,[14] section 1(1) of the Marriages Act, 1972 which came into force on 1st January 1975,[15] states that a marriage between persons either of whom is under the age of 16 "shall not be valid in law" unless exemption from this subsection is obtained. Prior to the coming into force of this section, under the common law, a marriage by a boy under 14 or a girl under 12 although not valid, could be ratified by the continued cohabitation of the parties after both of them had attained the requisite age. Thus a marriage by parties under age prior to 1975 was in essence voidable and not void.[16] Ratification made the marriage irrevocably binding.

Having regard to the wording of section 1(1) and the power to obtain exemption from it prior to marriage, but not after marriage, a marriage between persons either of whom is under 16, it is submitted, is now void and cannot be subsequently validated. There is, however, no express statement to this effect to be found anywhere in the Act.[17]

---

12. *R.M. v. M.M.* (1941) 76 I.L.T.R. 165, (H.C.), per O'Byrne J. at p. 169.
13. See however *B. v. D.*, *supra*; *S. v. O'S*. (November 1978) unreported (H.C.).; *S. v. S.*, *supra*, particularly judgement of Kenny J.
14. See "Capacity to Marry", p. 38, *ante*.
15. S.I. No. 324 of 1974.
16. See Halsbury's *The Laws of England*, vol. 16, pages 281-282; see also *McM. v. McM.* and *McK. v. McK.* [1936] I.R. 177 at p. 215.
17. It is arguable that in the light of the fact that marriages celebrated by parties under age prior to the coming into operation of this section could be validated, that marriages of persons under 16 are under Sect. 1 (1) voidable, such marriages not being valid at the date of the ceremony but being capable of validation by the continued cohabitation of the parties after both have passed the age of 16. See the English Age of Marriage Act 1929, Sect. 1 (1) where marriages of persons under 16 were expressly declared void.
   Moreover, in the Act of 1929, it was thought necessary to state that the validity of a marriage celebrated prior to the passing of the Act would not be affected by the Act, see Sect. 1 (2). Thus, if the intention of Sect. 1 (1) of the 1972 Act is to render marriages of persons under 16 void, unless exempt, it is also arguable that marriages by persons under 16 that took place prior to the Act may now also be regarded as void, the section containing no provision excluding marriages already solemnised prior to it coming into force from its operation. Such a result would be preposterous and such an interpretation of the section highly unlikely.

II. Non-observance of Formalities.

That the parties have married in disregard of certain formal requirements relating to the marriage ceremony. See Chapter 4, page 51 *et seq.*

III. Absence of Consent.

Marriage being a contract entered into by the voluntary consent of the parties,[18] the absence of consent on principle should always render a marriage void. What on the surface appears to be a valid consent can be shown by, proof of the presence of insanity or unsoundness of mind, intoxication, mistake, misrepresentation, fear or duress to have been no consent at all. The possibility of an additional ground invalidating consent is discussed in D. below.

A. *Insanity*:[19] A person who has been certified as a lunatic or "a lunatic or person under a frenzy" whose person and estate have been committed to the care and custody of trustees under any statute is incapable of marrying until declared sane, by virtue of the Marriage of Lunatics Act, 1811. The marriage of such a person is absolutely void even if it takes place during a lucid interval.[20]

The question as to whether the marriage of a person to whom the above provisions do not apply, can be nullified on the ground of insanity, depends on whether at the time of the marriage he or she was capable of understanding the nature of the duties and responsibilities which marriage creates,[21] "free from the influence of morbid delusions upon the subject".[22] It has been said that the contract of marriage is a very simple one which does not require a high degree of intelligence to comprehend.[23] The onus of showing the absence of the necessary comprehension is on the party alleging it. It is not sufficient to show that a party has before or after the marriage suffered from insanity. It must be shown that at the time of the ceremony his state of mind was such that he was incapable of understanding the nature of the contract into which he was entering. Thus, unlike insanity under the 1811 Act, it is necessary to prove that the marriage did not take place during a lucid interval.[24]

B. *Intoxication*: A marriage contracted by a party so drunk as to be incapable of giving proper consent is invalid. Sir William Scott in the old case of *Sullivan* v. *Sullivan* stated[25] that:

> "Suppose three or four persons were to combine to effect such a purpose by intoxicating another, and marrying him in that perverted state of mind, this Court would not hesitate to annul a marriage on clear proof of such a cause connected with such an effect."

Similarly it is submitted that a marriage contracted by a party under the

18. See *Hyde v. Hyde* (1866), L.R. 1 P. & D. 130 (Ct. of P. & D.) cited with approval in *Griffith v. Griffith* [1944] I.R. 35.
19. "Mental Capacity and Marriage"–see (1964), 98 I.L.T. & S.J. p. 159-161.
20. This had already been the position in Britain: see 15 Geo. 2, C. 30. See judgement in *Turner v. Meyers (Falsely called Turner)* (1808) 1 Hag. Con. 414; 161 E.R. 600.
21. *Durham v. Durham* (1865), 10 P.D. 80; 1 T.L.R. 338, (P.D.A.).
22. *Hunter v. Edney (Otherwise Hunter)* (1885), 10 P.D. 93, per Sir J. Hannen P. at p. 95 (P.D.A.).
23. *Durham v. Durham, supra.* See also *In the Estate of Park Decsd.* [1945] P. 112, where it was held that although the deceased was "not of sound mind, memory and understanding" so as to execute a valid will, a different standard of capacity is required for entering into marriage, and that the consent given by him in a ceremony of marriage a few hours earlier was a valid consent, creating a valid marriage.
24. *B. (otherwise A.) v. B.* (1891) 27, L.R. Ir. 587 (Matr. Ct.).
25. 2 Hag. Con. 238; 161 E.R. 728 at p. 731 (Consistory Court).

influence of drugs or otherwise deprived of his capacity to consent is invalid. In all cases it is a question of whether a person is in "a state of disability, natural or artificial, which created a want of reason or volition amounting to incapacity to consent".[26]

C. *Mistake and Misrepresentation*: Both mistake and misrepresentation are given a very restrictive role in the annulment of marriages. In *Swift* v. *Kelly*[27] it was said that:

"...No marriage shall be held void merely upon proof that it had been contracted upon false representations and that but for such contrivances, consent never would have been obtained. Unless the party imposed upon has been deceived as to the person and thus has given no consent at all, there is no degree of deception which can avail to set aside a contract of marriage knowingly made".[28]

Thus if X marries Y believing him to be Z there is no valid marriage. On the other hand if X marries Y believing him to be rich and he turns out to have no money the validity of the marriage is not affected. When fraud is spoken of as a ground for avoiding a marriage it "does not include such fraud as induces a consent, but is limited to such fraud as procures the appearance without the reality of consent."[29] It is not the presence of fraud by itself, but the absence of consent that is a ground for a decree of annulment. Thus the fact that a woman concealed from her husband at the time of their marriage that she was then pregnant by another man did not invalidate their marriage.[30] Similarly, concealment by a man, from the woman he was marrying, of the fact that on the night immediately preceding their wedding he had slept with another woman was held not to render their marriage void.[31] If each party knows that he is going through a ceremony of marriage with the other, there is no evidence of mistake by which the marriage may be invalidated. However if one party did not know what the ceremony was that took place, then there is no marriage. Thus in *Ford* (*falsely called Stier*) v. *Stier*[32] a decree of nullity was pronounced upon the judge being satisfied that the petitioner believed she was going through a ceremony of betrothal and that she did not consent to marry the respondent.

D. *Intention not to fulfil a fundamental term of the marriage contract*: Following the recent Supreme Court judgement in *S.* v. *S.*[33] it is possible that such intention on the part of one party, without the knowledge of the other, at the

26. See *Legeyt v. O'Brien* (1834) Milw. Rep. 325 at p. 333 *et seq.* (Consistory Court). In this case it was alleged that the husband was of unsound mind at the date of the ceremony and incapable of consenting. The unsoundness of mind it was alleged was caused by his grossly drunken habits which caused delirium tremens. The court rejected the contention that the marriage was invalid on this ground, holding that the evidence did not prove incapacity at the time of the ceremony.

27. (1835) 3 Knapp 257; 12 E.R. 648, (P.C.) cited with approval in *Griffith v. Griffith*, *supra*.

28. *Ibid.*, 12 E.R. 648, per Lord Brougham at p. 661.

29. *Moss v. Moss* (*otherwise Archer*) [1897] P. 263 approved in *Griffith v. Griffith*; see also *Wakefield v. Mackay* (1807) 1 Hag. Con. 394; 161 E.R. 593; *Ussher v. Ussher* [1912] 2 I.R. 445; (1912), 46 I.L.T.R. 109, (K.B.D.).

30. *Moss v. Moss* (*otherwise Archer*), *supra*.

31. *S. v. S., supra*.

32. [1896] P. 1; see also *Valier v. Valier* (*otherwise Davis*) (1925), 133 L.T. 830; *Kelly* (*otherwise Hyams*) v. *Kelly* (1932), 49 T.L.R. 99, (P.D.A.); *Mehta v. Mehta* [1945] 2 All E.R. 690, (P.D.A.).

33. *Supra*.

time of the marriage ceremony has the result that the consent necessary for the existence of a valid marriage is absent, and that the marriage thus celebrated is void. For a full discussion of *S. v. S.* see section entitled "Impotence" further on in this chapter.

E. *Duress*: If a person is induced to go through a ceremony of marriage by fear, threats, intimidation or duress, such a marriage is invalid unless the fear caused is justly imposed. This principle was clearly laid down by Haugh J. in *Griffith* v. *Griffith.* [34] In this case the petitioner had married at the age of 19. Prior to the marriage he had been accused by the respondent and her mother of having unlawful carnal knowledge of the respondent (then under 17 years of age), and so causing her to become pregnant. They threatened him with criminal prosecution. This threat, with the consequent scandal and publicity to him and his family, along with a fear of conviction and of imprisonment, induced him to go through with the marriage. The petitioner had not in fact engaged in sexual intercourse with the respondent and the statement as to the paternity of the respondent's child was false. Haugh J. stated

> "That the consent to marry . . . given by the petitioner was in fact given not because of the usual inspirations caused by love and affection, but because of a real and grave fear inspired by an unjust and fraudulent misrepresentation on a very grave and vital matter, going to the root of his consent; and that it was this fear so unjustly imposed, that led to the marriage now impugned . . .
> . . . I feel bound to hold that a consent so obtained by this combination of fraud and fear, the first producing the second, is not a consent that binds the petitioner—and there being no real consent in law, there was accordingly no valid marriage." [35]

If in this case the allegation of paternity had been true and the petitioner had been induced by fear of prosecution to marry the respondent, Haugh J. made it clear that in such circumstances the marriage would have been valid.

> "Assuming that marriages have resulted from a fear so imposed, they are clearly valid and binding on both parties. The man is free to elect between the scandal and possible punishment on the one hand or the marriage to the girl he has wronged on the other". [36]

It is submitted that such a conclusion is contrary to the principle that marriage is a voluntary union entered into by the parties. A marriage entered into for fear of prosecution whether or not such fear is validly imposed, is not a marriage entered into voluntarily. [37]

The reasoning behind the above statement by Haugh J. is based on the belief that a man who makes a girl pregnant has responsibilities towards both her and the child. It is submitted, however, that in order for these responsibilities to be met it is not necessary for the parties to marry. For example, in the absence of agreement, the father can be forced to contribute towards the maintenance of such child by the bringing of affiliation proceedings. To regard such forced marriages as valid and binding should be contrary to public policy, in that it is

---

34. *Supra.*
35. *Supra* at p. 52.
36. *Supra* at p. 43.
37. See however *Buckland v. Buckland* [1968] P. 296; [1967] 2 All E.R. 300, (P.D.A.) which followed Haugh J's. judgement in *Griffith*; see also Marriage or Prison: The Case of the Reluctant Bridegroom, by A.H. Manchester in (1966), 29 M.L.R. 622. *Griffith* and *Buckland* are here discussed and criticised. Pre 1966 Irish and English authorities on duress are here discussed at length.

now generally accepted that so called "shot-gun" weddings have little chance of success.[38]

Duress can be imposed either by one of the parties to the marriage or by a third person[39] or external circumstances.[40] The amount of duress required to vitiate consent has been said to be "a question of degree" dependant on the facts of the particular case.[41]

In *B. v. D.*[42] the petitioner and respondent were both National School teachers and having known each other for 5 years, married in Dublin in August 1970. Throughout their relationship there was no evidence of any real affection between them. From the time they first met the respondent used the petitioner's car as if it was his own, spent most of his time gambling, and borrowed, (in the later stages demanded) money from her which he did not repay. Notwithstanding the petitioner telling her family two days prior to the ceremony that she did not wish to marry the respondent, she kept an arrangement to meet him and travelled to Dublin with him by car for the ceremony. On the way to Dublin the petitioner rang her sister and told her that the respondent was very aggressive and that she thought the best thing to do would be to drop him in Dublin and return home. However, she did not have the opportunity to carry out this intention and the ceremony took place. Murnaghan J. stated that having regard to the petitioner's age,[43] her social and educational standing it was very difficult to take any view other than that she consented to all that occurred. However, evidence was given that the respondent had a very domineering character. He went on:

> "I have very little doubt but that gradually from the first time they met, the petitioner found herself in her relationship with the respondent in a groove, which as time went on got deeper and deeper, and out of which she was constitutionally unable to extract herself, and in which perhaps she was prepared in the circumstances, if not content, to remain . . .
>
> I have . . . come to the conclusion after long consideration that the reasonable probabilities are that the degree of duress was such as to render the contract of marriage in this case one that the law should consider to be a nullity."

In *S. v. O'S.*[44] the petitioner and respondent having known each other for almost

38. In *Kelly v. Kelly* (Feb. 1971), unreported (H.C.), *Griffith v. Griffith* was expressly followed. In this case there was held to be no true marriage where a woman fraudulently induced a man to go through a marriage ceremony by falsely (unknown to him at the time) alleging she was pregnant by him and threatening that if he did not marry her she would inform his parents, his sister who was a nun, and that she would bring legal proceedings against him that would result in adverse publicity. The marriage was said to be "induced by fraud and fear to the point that his (the petitioner's) consent to the marriage was no true consent". The fact that the marriage was never consummated was regarded as an important indication of the petitioner's mental attitude to the marriage at the time of the ceremony.

See also Ralph Brown—*Marriage Annulment*, (Chapman, London 1971), p. 47. It seems that a Roman Catholic man forced to marry a Roman Catholic girl due to his being the father of her child, may obtain an annulment in the Marriage Tribunals of the Roman Catholic Church, such a marriage being regarded as being grounded on fear unjustly imposed. "It would be entirely unjust to impose marriage as a penalty for making a girl pregnant".

39. *Parojcic (orse Ivetic) v. Parojcic* [1959] All E.R. 1, (P.D.A.) (fear imposed by petitioner's father); *McLarnon v. McLarnon* (1968), 112 Sol Jo 419 (Parents threatened to send girl to convent if she did not marry, under the mistaken belief she was pregnant).

40. See *H. v. H.* [1954] P. 258; [1953] 2 All E.R. 1129; *Buckland v. Buckland supra*; *Szechter (orse. Karsov) v. Szechter* [1971] P. 286; [1970] 3 All E.R. 905; (P.D.A.).

41. In *Griffith v. Griffith supra*, at p. 52, Haugh J. said "Duress must be a question of degree and may begin from a gentle form of pressure to phsyical violence accompanied by threats of death . . ."

In *B. v. D., supra*, Murnaghan J. said "Duress must always be a question of degree. The degree of duress is a question of fact".

42. *Supra*.

43. She was over 27 at the date of the marriage.

44. (November 1978) unreported (H.C.).

one and a half years married in June, 1974. At the time of the marriage the petitioner was twenty two and the respondent was twenty five. Initially the parties had a normal courtship and planned to marry when the respondent, who was a medical student, completed his studies and finished his year's internship. One night during their courtship the petitioner went to a dance without the respondent. This act by the petitioner had a traumatic emotional effect on the respondent. He reacted by developing a condition known as Munchausen Periodic Syndrome. This condition consisted of projecting with elaborate detail bizarre sicknesses. The only cure for these alleged sicknesses, according to the respondent, was in the first instance the almost exclusive attention and physical presence of his fiancee, the petitioner, and secondly an early marriage. By May of 1974 the petitioner was persuaded by the respondent that if their marriage did not take place within six weeks she would be responsible for his rapid decline and death or his suicide. The petitioner in evidence admitted that she was totally taken in by the respondent and that she believed she would be responsible for his death if she refused to marry him. The psychiatric evidence established that at the time of the marriage she was "in the emotional bondage of the respondent". Holding the marriage to be void, Finlay P. stated:

> "Essentially, it seems to me that the freedom of will necessary to enter into a valid contract of marriage is one particularly associated with emotion and that a person in the emotional bondage of another person couldn't consciously have the freedom of will."

It is clear from the judgements delivered in *B.* v. *D.* and *S.* v. *O'S.* that the courts use a subjective test to determine whether duress has vitiated consent. The question the court must decide is not whether a reasonable person would have succumbed to the pressure imposed but whether the alleged pressure was such that it overbore the will of the particular petitioner in the particular case before the court. Thus, pressure sufficient to amount to duress in the case of one person may not be sufficient to do so in the case of another person of stronger character.[45]

The judgements in the above two cases provide a wider concept of duress than any of the previous Irish precedents. It remains to be seen whether the courts will be willing to further develop the law in this area and, in particular, if they will be willing to apply the notion of "emotional bondage" enunciated by Finlay P. in *S.* v. *O'S.* to different factual circumstances.

---

45. See *Scott (falsely called Sebright) v. Sebright* [1886] 12 P. D. 21 at p. 24 where Butt J. stated "It has sometimes been said that in order to avoid a contract entered into through fear, the fear must be such as would impel a person of ordinary courage and resolution to yield to it. I do not think that is an accurate statement of the law. Whenever, from natural weakness of intellect or from fear—whether reasonably entertained or not—either party is actually in a state of mental incompetence to resist pressure improperly brought to bear, there is no more consent than in the case of a person of stronger intellect and more robust courage yielding to a more serious danger."

It appears that the Irish courts will regard a marriage as invalid for duress on grounds less restrictive than those permitted by the English courts. See *Szechter (orse. Karsov) v. Szechter, supra, Singh v. Singh* [1971] P. 226; [1971] 2 W. L. R. 963, (C. A.) where it was held that there must be a threat of immediate danger to "Life, limb and liberty." There was no evidence that the petitioners in *B.* v. *D.* and *S.* v. *O'S.* were in such danger. Moreover, in *Szechter* and in *Buckland, supra* and *H.* v. *H.* [1953] 2 All E. R. 1229, the court was of the opinion that the fear must be reasonable. It is submitted that this approach by the English courts is wrong being contrary to precedent (See *Scott v. Sebright, supra, Cooper v. Crane* [1891] P. 369, and *Parojcic v. Parojcic, supra*). See further, J. O'Reilly, Fraud, Duress and Nullity [1972] 8 I. J. (n.s.) at p. 352–356.

GROUND RENDERING A MARRIAGE VOIDABLE

Impotence

If at the time of the solemnisation of a marriage either of the parties to it is impotent, the court may upon the petition of one of them pronounce a decree declaring it null and void. A marriage is only voidable and not void on this ground. A third person cannot sue for a decree of nullity on the ground of impotence, nor can the validity of the marriage be challenged on such a ground after the death of one of the parties.[46] Such a marriage is valid for all legal purposes during the lifetime of the parties, unless a decree of nullity is pronounced. If such a decree is pronounced, however, it is then regarded as void *ab initio.*[47]

The Meaning of Impotence: A decree for impotence is granted on the basis of a party's inability to consummate the marriage. A marriage is regarded as consummated once the parties have engaged in "ordinary and complete"[48] sexual intercourse after the solemnisation. A party's inability to engage in such intercourse is the basis for a decree. Thus it is essential to understand what is meant by "ordinary and complete" sexual intercourse.

The question to be considered is whether a party is capable of *vera copula* i.e. capable of the natural sort of coitus without the power of conception.[49] Inability to procreate or a party's sterility affords no ground for obtaining a decree of nullity. What has been said to be important in determining whether one or other party is impotent is the question of the "practical possibility" of full penetration by the male into the female.[50] It is not necessary to show that such penetration is physically impossible; it is sufficient to show that it is only possible under conditions to which a spouse would not be justified in resorting.[51] As the fertility of the spouse is irrelevant, so is the question of a spouse's ability to ejaculate.[52] Once "full and complete" penetration is achieved, a marriage is regarded in law as consummated and a petition on the ground of impotence cannot succeed.[53]

Impotence can arise from a number of causes. There may be some physical defect such as a total lack of sexual organs or a malformation of sexual organs rendering intercourse impossible. Alternatively, there may be some psychological or neurotic cause rendering it impossible for a perfectly formed individual to

46. *A. v. B.* [1868], L.R. 1 P. & D. 559 (Ct. of P. & D.);
47. See *Mason v. Mason* [1944] N.I. 134, (K.B.D.). Here H. married W. between the granting of a decree Nisi and a decree Absolute nullifying his first marriage. Upon a petition by W. seeking a declaration that their marriage was void, the H. being still married at the time of the ceremony, it was held that the effect of the decree Absolute was to retrospectively invalidate the first marriage to the date when it took place, and so the court was precluded from a finding that the H. was a married man at the date of his marriage to W.
48. *D-e v. A-g (falsely calling herself D-e)* [1845] 1 Robb. Eccs. 279; 163 E.R. 1039.
49. *Ibid.*
50. If the parties have not had intercourse, the birth of a child as a result of fecundation ab extra or artificial insemination will not amount to consummation—*Clarke (otherwise Talbott) v. Clarke* [1943] 2 All E.R. 540; *R.E.L. (otherwise R.) v. E.L.* [1949] P. 211 [1949] 1 All E.R. 141; (P.D.A.). As only full penetration by the male into the female is required, the fact that the husband used a contraceptive sheath does not prevent consummation from taking place, *Baxter v. Baxter* [1948] A.C. 274; [1947] 2 All E.R. 886, (H.L.). Similarly if the husband practises coitus interruptus consummation is not prevented—*White v. White* [1948] 2 All E.R. 151; [1948] P. 330, (P.D.A.). *Cackett (otherwise Trice) v. Cackett* [1950] 1 All E.R. 677; [1950] P. 253, (P.D.A.).
51. *G. v. G.* (1871) L.R. 2 P. & D. 287 (Ct. of P. & D.).
52. *R. v. R. (Otherwise F.)* [1952] 1 All E.R. 1194, (P.D.A.).
53. See *W. (otherwise K.) v. W.* [1967] 3 All E.R. 178, (P.D.A.). Husband able to enter wife but following entry his erection collapsed. Penetration held not to be "full and complete" and decree granted.

engage in the sexual act, i.e. a person may have an invincible repugnance to the sexual act resulting in a paralysis of the will,[54] or may suffer nervousness or hysteria.[35] A person's incapacity does not necessarily have to be general and may be *quoad hanc* or *quoad hunc* a particular spouse. i.e. a person may be unable to have sexual intercourse with the person he marries, but be able to with other persons.[56] Thus, in both *S. v. S.*[57] and *R. (otherwise W.)* v. *W.*[58] there was evidence that the impotent spouse was engaging in sexual intercourse with a third party although psychologically impotent *vis a vis* the other spouse.

Curability: The disability alleged must be incurable. Impotence will be regarded as incurable if the condition can be remedied only by an operation attended by danger, or if the spouse at fault refuses to submit to an operation. A spouse cannot compel the other spouse to have an operation and is only expected to use reasonable means of persuasion.[59]

Proof of Impotence: The onus of proof of impotence is on the party alleging it, and the impotence or "practical impossibility" of consummation must still exist at the date of the hearing.[60] This onus, as in all nullity petitions, is a heavy one. To succeed, "the petitioner must remove all reasonable doubt," as to the respondent's incapacity.[61]

The High Court has been much concerned to ensure that the onus of proof is fully discharged and that its jurisdiction to annul a marriage on the grounds of impotence is not used "to release ill-sorted spouses from a marriage bond because it has become irksome to one, if not both".[62] The degree of difficulty in establishing the onus of proof clearly depends on the nature of the impotence alleged. Where there is a physical deformity preventing consummation very little difficulty is likely to arise. In other cases where the impediment is psychological rather than physiological, the difficulty may be considerable.[63]

Wilful Refusal to Consummate: Until a recent judgement of the Supreme Court[64] wilful refusal of sexual intercourse has always been held to be insufficient to justify the court annulling a marriage.[65] In *McK.* v. *McK.*[66] the repeated attempts by a potent husband to consummate his marriage were repelled by his wife. It

---

54. *S. v. S.* (July 1976) unreported (S. C.); *R. (otherwise W.)* v. *W.* (February 1980) unreported (H.C.); *R.M.* v. *M.M.* (1941) 76 I.L.T.R. 165 (H.C., S.C.); *McM.* v. *McM.* and *Mc.K.* v. *McK.* [1936] I.R. 177 (H.C.); *G.* v. *G.* [1924] A.C. 349, (H.L. (Sc.).
55. *G.* v. *G.* (1871) *supra; S.* v. *A. (otherwise S.)* (1878) 3 P.D. 72 (P.D.).
56. *S.* v. *S., supra; R. (otherwise W.)* v. *W., supra; McM.* v. *McM., supra; R.M.* v. *M.M., supra; G.* v. *G. supra; C. (otherwise H.)* v. *C.* [1921] P. 399; [1921] All E.R. 268;
57. *Supra.*
58. *Supra.*
59. See *D-e* v. *A-g (falsely called D-e), supra; G.* v. *G.* (1871), *supra; L.* v. *L. (falsely called W.).* (1882) 7 P.D. 16. (P.D.A.); *G.* v. *G. (falsely called K.),* (1908) 25 T.L.R. 328; *S.* v. *S. (otherwise C.)* [1956] P. 1; (1954) 3 All E.R. 736, (Assize); *M.* v. *M. (otherwise B.)* [1957] P. 139; [1956] 3 All E.R. 769.
60. *S. v. S. (otherwise C.) supra.*
61. Per Lord Birkenhead in *C. (otherwise H.)* v. *C. supra*; approved by Kenny J. in *S. v. S.* (1976) *supra* and Hanna J. in *McM.* v. *McM.* and *McK.* v. *McK. supra*; see also *U. (falsely called J.)* v. *J.* (1867) L.R. 1 P. & D. 460, (Ct. of P. & D.).
62. *McM.* v. *McM.* and *McK.* v. *McK. supra* per Hanna J. at p. 187—see also *R.M.* v. *M.M. supra* at p. 169, where it was stated that "It is not the function of the Court . . . to relieve parties from hasty and ill advised marriages".
63. See *R.M.* v. *M.M. supra.*
64. See *S.* v. *S. supra* discussed further on p. 71 *et seq.*
65. *Napier* v. *Napier (Goodban)* [1915] P. 184, (C.A.); *McM.* v. *McM.* and *McK.* v. *McK. supra; R.M.* v. *M.M. supra.*
66. *Supra.*

was contended for the wife that she was neurotic and had an invincible repugnance to the husband amounting to a paralysis of her will, so that she was unable to consummate the marriage. On medical inspection she was found to be perfectly formed and *apta viro*; there was no suggestion of neurosis or hysteria or of any physical defect suggesting any kind of incapacity. It was stated to be a "difficult and delicate task to distinguish between impotence and wilful obstinacy" but such a difficulty "had to be faced and a determination come to". Hanna J. concluded that in his opinion the cause of the trouble was that the wife "had resolved from the first not to have any children" and that if the husband "had been a man of more determined and inconsiderate personality he would have succeeded in overcoming . . . the wilful and continued refusal on the part of the wife." Consequently the petition for nullity was refused.

In the later case of *R.M.* v. *M.M.*[67] the court also refused to grant a nullity decree. O'Byrne J. was satisfied that the wife was "genuinely shocked and disgusted" by attempts at consummation and that she had "a strong and real aversion to the sexual act". However, he was not satisfied that this aversion was of such an "invincible character as to produce a paralysis and distortion of the will". The marriage had not been consummated due to the wife's wilful refusal and he believed that he was fortified in his view by her statement that "she would never allow her husband or any other man to have sexual intercourse with her". On appeal, the Supreme Court affirmed this decision.

Since 1941 when the case of *R.M.* v. *M.M.* was decided, there have been considerable psychiatric advances in the understanding of psycho-sexual problems. It is questionable as to whether in the light of these developments *R.M.* v. *M.M.* would necessarily be decided today as it was in 1941.[68] It is certainly arguable that today the facts of the case would be regarded as involving a real impotence.[69]

The distinction between "real" incapacity to consummate and wilful refusal to consummate enunciated by the civil courts can be examined against the more enlightened approach adopted by the canon law of the Roman Catholic Church. By Canon 1119 an unconsummated marriage is a marriage *ratum sed non consummatum* and may be dissolved by the Holy See.[70] Mr. Justice Davitt, a former President of the High Court, in 1968 pointed out[71] that since 1941 the High Court has had to decide cases where the facts were almost identical to those in *R.M.* v. *M.M.* In some of these cases the parties involved were Roman Catholics and their marriages had been dissolved by Papal Dispensation. Thus they remained married according to civil law but were unmarried in the view of the Church.[72] Mr. Justice Davitt argued that a marriage in which one of the parties wilfully "refuses to accept and perform one of its fundamental obligations can hardly be regarded as in every sense a real marriage. The offending party has in one sense repudiated it. It would seem in the interests of justice, as well perhaps as in the interests of morality, that the unoffending spouse should be able to obtain relief".[73]

67. *Supra*.
68. See Article by Gerald Clarke in *Studies* 1968, p. 24—A response to an article in the same issue by the ex-President of the High Court, Mr. Justice Davitt.
69. See, in particular, the judgements in *S. v. S., supra* and *R. (otherwise W.) v. W., supra*.
70. See chapter 9.
71. See 1968 *Studies*, p. 6—"Some Aspects of the Constitution and the Law in Relation to Marriage".
72. See Jean Blanchard, *The Church in Contemporary Ireland* p. 70, where the unreported case of *Begley v. Begley* is cited as an example of a case involving parties who refused a civil annulment but were granted a canonical dissolution for impotence.
73. In England since the passing of the Matrimonial Causes Act, 1937, a marriage has

In the recent case of *S.* v. *S.*[74] Kenny J. in the Supreme Court appears to have adopted the above reasoning. In this case the husband and wife had known each other for two years prior to their marriage. During this two years they engaged in sexual intercourse on many occasions. After their marriage they went on honeymoon for eight days and then made their home in Dublin. Although the parties slept together both during their honeymoon and when living in the matrimonial home, they did not at any time after their marriage have sexual intercourse. When the wife discussed this matter with her husband he said that he did not like her, that she made him sick, that the marriage was a mistake and that he did not want any children. Six months after the wedding the husband left the wife and went to live with another woman. There was also evidence of the husband having sexual relations with this other woman immediately prior to the marriage.

Subsequent to his departure the wife, (the petitioner in the proceedings) obtained an annulment in the marriage tribunal of the Roman Catholic Church for the diocese of Dublin. Despite the fact that the church decree had no effect on the civil validity of her marriage, three days after obtaining it, she married another man in a Roman Catholic church. At the date of these proceedings she had had a child by her second husband. The Supreme Court, on appeal from the High Court,[75] granted the wife's petition for a decree of nullity on the ground of her husband's impotence. Two members of the court, while agreeing that the husband was obviously potent, concurred in holding that this was a case of relative impotence "i.e. *impotence quoad hanc*" and issued a decree of nullity on that ground. They both rejected the contention that the marriage was also invalid on the ground that the petitioner had been induced by fraud to marry her husband. Henchy J. in rejecting this ground stated that

"There is no doubt that the wife entered into the marriage on the inducement of a concealed falsity, but that falsity (by which I mean falsity as to emotional and sexual capacity on the part of the husband) may or may not have been known to the husband at the time of the marriage. For all we know, he may have genuinely believed or hoped that he would be able to make the marriage a success. Because of that, fraud must be discounted."

The above judgement leaves open the possibility of the marriage being annulled, due to absence of proper consent, upon proof that a party had an intention not to consummate at the date of the marriage ceremony. Henchy J. merely held that on the facts of the case non-consummation was due to the husband's real sexual incapacity in relation to his wife and not to a conscious decision by him prior to or at the time of the ceremony, not to consummate the marriage.

Kenny J. however in annulling the marriage did not agree that the husband had become impotent *vis a vis* his wife, but was of the opinion that at the date of the ceremony he had formed the intention not to have intercourse with her. He stated that

"Section 13 of the Act of 1870 did not have the effect of fossilising the law in its state in that year. That law is, to some extent at least, judge made and Courts must recognise that the great advances made in psychological medicine since 1870 make it necessary to frame new rules which reflect these . . . It

been voidable on the ground of wilful refusal to consummate. The present English law is contained in the Matrimonial Causes Act 1973, Sect. 12. See K. Hayes—*The Matrimonial Jurisdiction of the High Court.* (1973) 8 I.J. (n.s.) 55 at p. 69.
   74. (July 1976) unreported (S.C.).
   75. (Nov. 74) unreported (H.C.).

seems to me that the intention to have sexual intercourse is such a *funda-mental feature of the marriage contract*[76] that if at the time of the marriage either party has determined that there will not be any during the marriage and none takes place, and if the parties have not agreed on this before the marriage . . . a spouse who was not aware of the determination of the other is entitled to a declaration that the marriage was null. The intention not to have or permit intercourse has the result that the consent which is necessary to the existence of a valid marriage does not exist."

As a consequence of this case, despite earlier judicial pronouncements to the contrary, it seems that a marriage may now be annulled on the ground of a spouse's wilful refusal to consummate, provided the latter intended not to con-summate at the time when the marriage took place. However, it is only the judgement of Kenny J. that unequivocally supports wilful refusal as a ground. It remains to be seen whether this judgement will be followed in future cases.

Curiously, despite judicial assertions in cases prior to *S. v. S.* that wilful refusal to consummate will not afford a sufficient ground for the granting of a nullity decree, the Rules of the Superior Court seem to contemplate the granting of a decree on such a ground. Order 70, Rule 32(4) makes explicit provision for the medical inspection of parties "in proceedings for nullity on the ground that the marriage has not been consummated owing to the wilful refusal of the respondent to do so."

In practice there are great difficulties distinguishing between wilful refusal and psychological inability to consummate. The approach of Kenny J. lessens the importance of this distinction. However one essential difference does seem to exist. Impotence renders a marriage voidable. Proof of an intention not to consummate on the part of one spouse at the time of the wedding causes the consent necessary to constitute a valid marriage to be absent. As we have already seen, absence of consent renders a marriage void.

In conclusion, this judgement opens up the possibility of considerable judicial development of the whole law of nullity, particularly in relation to absence of consent as a ground of invalidity. Kenny J. stated that intention to have sexual intercourse with one's spouse was a fundamental feature of the marriage contract. Thus, he held the marriage to be void due to the fact that one spouse at the time of the ceremony intended not to fulfil a fundamental obligation of that contract i.e. he intended not to consummate the marriage. The question now arises as to whether a marriage may be declared void if a spouse intends not to fulfil any other fundamental term of the marriage contract at the date when the marriage is celebrated e.g. if a spouse intends not to live with the other spouse, or not to fulfil his or her obligation of support, or not to have any children. Whether judicial innovation will further develop the law in this direction is uncertain. It is, however, possible that the judgement of Kenny J. heralds the dawn of a less rigid and more compassionate approach by the Irish judiciary in the exercise of their nullity jurisdiction and is an indication that the courts are willing to move away from the narrow grounds for nullity of marriage laid down by the Ecclesiastical Courts and are willing to develop new grounds based on modern psychiatric thinking.

Medical Inspection:[77] It is the practice of the court, borrowed from the Ecclesiastical Courts, in a nullity suit for impotence to require a medical inspec-

---

76. Authors italics.
77. R.S.C. Order 70, Rule 32 (S.I. No. 72 of 1962).

tion of the parties. This is done by two medical practitioners experienced in gynaecology appointed from a rota of medical inspectors by the Master of the High Court. Either side can obtain a copy of the medical reports and the inspectors may be called as witnesses and cross-examined. Such an inspection is not obligatory and where a party refuses to submit to inspection, the court may nevertheless still grant a decree.[78] The fact that the marriage has not been consummated despite the co-habitation of the parties for a reasonable time, and the willingness of the petitioner to consummate, together with a refusal on the part of the respondent to undergo a medical examination can raise an inference of impotence on the part of the respondent.[79]

Petition of impotent spouse: As a result of the High Court decision in *McM* v. *McM*[80] it seems that a spouse cannot be granted a decree as petitioner on the ground of his own impotence unless he can satisfy the court that there has been conduct on the part of the other spouse which would prevent the latter from denying the "just cause" of the petition. An example of such conduct would be the latter's repudiation of the marriage contract and its obligaions.

Hanna J. stated:

> "The decree for nullity of marriage cannot . . . be granted to a petitioner on the ground merely of a petitioner's own impotence, but it is clearly established that if a petitioner can, in addition to proof of his own impotency, satisfy the Court that there had been, and is, conduct on the part of the respondent which has destroyed the *verum matrimonium* e.g., by a genuine and deliberate repudiation of the marriage contract and its obligations, the Court may *ex justa causa* grant the relief."[81]

In this case both parties were Roman Catholics. The petitioner, the husband in 1934 sought a decree on the ground of his own impotence. Three years earlier the respondent had left him and the court found that she would not return to him on account of his violence and neurasthenic condition over sexual matters. She refused to defend the proceedings and was content that he should obtain any redress to which he was entitled. However, her attitude was that she recognised the marriage until the Church dissolved it.

Hanna J. refusing to grant a decree of annulment stated that[82]

> "it would be contrary to reason and justice to hold that, where the respondent is a Roman Catholic, it is a repudiation of the status of wife and of her marriage contract for her to say to the Court: 'Though I have left him on account of his violence, and will not return for fear of violence, I shall take no part in the proceedings in the civil Court and shall adhere to my marriage until it is terminated by my Church'."

At the time of the court hearing the respondent had taken no steps to obtain a church dissolution or annulment. Rather than repudiating the marriage, as a matter of conscience and religious belief, she regarded it as still subsisting.

---

78. *E.M. v. S.M.* (1942) 77 I.L.T.R. 128; see also *S. (otherwise B.) v. S.* [1943] N.I. 87, (K.B.D.); *S. v. S.* (July 1976), unreported, (S.C.).

79. *S. (otherwise B.) v. S. supra; B (otherwise H.) v. B.* [1901] P. 39 (P.D.A.); *W. v. S. (orse. W.)* [1905] P. 231, (P.D.A.); see also *F. v. P. (falsely called F.)* (1869) 75 L.T. 192, where it was held that after a reasonable period of cohabitation during which one party was always willing to consummate, the court can draw an inference that something more than mere wilful refusal must have animated the other.

80. *Supra*.

81. *Ibid.*, at pp. 219, 220.

82. *Ibid.*, at p. 206.

In both the earlier case of *A.* v. *A.* (sued as *B.*)[83] and the recent case of *R.* (*otherwise W.*) v. *W.*[84] decrees of annulment were granted on the application of an impotent petitioner, the respondent in each case being held to have repudiated the marriage by seeking a decree of annulment in the Ecclesiastical Courts of the Roman Catholic Church. Finlay P. giving judgement in the latter case stated:

> "the parties were both Catholics at the time of the purported marriage and the marriage took place according to the rites of the Catholic Church. I have no doubt on the evidence that the respondent's immediate concern after the separation between the parties had become final and complete was to try and free himself of this marriage according to the law of the Church of which he was a member. There can be no other explanation of his very rapid institution of proceedings seeking a decree of nullity in the Ecclesiastical Courts. It is irrelevant to the issue at present before me that those proceedings have not been yet terminated since they are being persisted in by the respondent. That must, in my view, be a clear and unequivocal repudiation by him of the marriage and, therefore, in my view entitles the petitioner to a decree of nullity based on her own impotency."

In *R.* (*otherwise W.*) v. *R.* it was argued that a repudiation of the marriage is not required in all cases for the petition of an impotent spouse to succeed. The respondent's behaviour provided conclusive evidence of repudiation, however, and the learned judge reserved this question to be decided in a future case upon it arising.

It is difficult to understand why a spouse who upon marrying, discovers his own impotence should not be able to rely on it alone to obtain a decree of nullity, when such impotence can be relied upon by the other spouse to obtain a decree. The premise running through the decision in *McM.* v. *McM.* seems to be that an impotent spouse has committed some sort of wrong by marrying and that he should not be permitted to rely simply on his own wrong in order to terminate the marriage.

It is submitted that the court in *McM.* v. *McM.* fails to distinguish between two quite different situations. The first is the case of the person who marries fully aware of the fact that he is impotent, and knowingly deceives the other spouse. The second is the person who does not discover his own impotence until after the marriage has taken place.

Hanna J. admitted that the majority of commentators on the Canon Law were in favour of the proposition that a spouse can secure annulment on the grounds of his own impotence if he was unaware of it at the time of the marriage. In reaching the conclusion that a petitioner's impotence by itself is insufficient to ground a decree of nullity, he relied to a great extent on the case of *Norton* v. *Seton.*[85] He stated

> "In my opinion a fair reading of that judgement is that the learned Judge was of opinion that the petitioner could not maintain the claim solely on the ground of his own impotence."[86]

This, however, is not the basis of the decision in that case. In that case, Sir John Nicholl quoted the maxim that "No man shall take advantage of his own wrong" and it is evident that his judgement is founded on the belief that the husband

83. (1887), 19 L. R. (Ir.) 403. (Matr. Ct.).
84. (February 1980) unreported (H.C.).
85. (1819), 3 Phill. Ecc. 147; 27 Digest 266; 161 E.R. 1283.
86. *Supra* at p. 211.

entered marriage well knowing his physical defects and deceived the wife into marrying him. Whereas the decision of the Irish Court of Appeal in *A. v. A.* (sued as *B.*)[87] does support Hanna J.'s conclusion, two other cases he cites certainly do not. In *G. v. G. (falsely called K.)*[88] the Court of Appeal purporting to follow the previously mentioned case, decided that a decree of nullity can be granted at the suit of an impotent spouse and the Master of the Rolls did not deem it necessary for the other spouse to repudiate the marriage. Finally in *Davies (orse Mason) v. Davies*[89] Langton J. expressly refrained from deciding whether the court possesses jurisdiction to annul a marriage on the petition of an impotent spouse if there has been no repudiation by the other spouse.

McM. v. McM. itself was a case in which the spouse did not discover his impotence until after the marriage ceremony. It is submitted that the balance of authority is against the decision reached by Hanna J. and that the ratio of that case should be overruled upon a similar case arising.[90]

It is further submitted, however, that if a spouse enters marriage knowing himself to be impotent, the other spouse being unaware of his condition, it is only just that he should be denied relief. If he knew of his impotence at the time of the ceremony, he entered the marriage with a full realisation of the fact that it would not be consummated. His own impotence in such circumstances could make no difference to a situation which he had voluntarily accepted. In such a situation only the potent spouse should be permitted to petition the court. The present law, however, seems to be that if the potent spouse does some act repudiating the marriage, the impotent spouse can succeed on the grounds of his own impotence. It is difficult to understand why a spouse who enters a marriage fully knowing that it cannot be consummated due to his own incapacity, should be permitted to plead such incapacity to obtain an annulment in one situation —i.e. where the other spouse also repudiates the marriage—and be prevented from relying on it in another situation i.e. where there is an absence of such repudiation. In both situations the impotent spouse enters marriage knowing that it cannot be consummated and the principle cause of action is his own impotence. In such a situation only the other spouse should be permitted to petition.

---

87. *Supra.*
88. (1908), 25 T.L.R. 328 (C.A.).
89. [1935] P. 58, per Langton J., (P.DA.).
90. See *Harthan v. Harthan* [1949] P. 115; [1948] 2 All E.R. 639, (C.A.), in which *McM. v. McM.* is discussed on this point and disagreed with. It was held that the husband, who had been unable to consummate his marriage was entitled to succeed. In this case the husband petitioner clearly did not know of his impotence until after the celebration of the marriage; see also *J. (orse. S.) v. J.* [1947] P. 159; [1947] 2 All E.R. 43, (C.A.) and *Pettit v. Pettit* [1963] P. 177; [1962] 3 All E.R. 37, (C.A.); see also Webb and Bevan, *Source Book of Family Law*, (Butterworths, London 1964), p. 92–93; H.K. Bevan (1960), 76 L. Q.R. 267 "Limitations on the Right of an Impotent Spouse to Petition for Nullity".

BARS TO RELIEF[1]

Approbation of Voidable Marriage

As impotence renders a marriage voidable and not void it is well established that a party seeking a decree of annulment to such a marriage may be prevented by his own conduct from denying the validity of the marriage. It has been said that a party cannot both approbate and reprobate a marriage. In *G. v. M.*[2] Lord Selborne L.C., stated

"I think I can perceive that the real basis of reasoning which underlies that phraseology is this . . . that there may be conduct on the part of the person seeking this remedy which ought to stop that person from having it; as, for instance, any act from which the inference ought to be drawn, that during the antecedent time the party has, with a knowledge of the facts and of the law, approbated the marriage which he or she afterwards seeks to get rid of, or has taken advantages and derived benefits from the matrimonial relation which it would be unfair and inequitable to permit him or her, after having received them to treat as if no such relation had ever existed . . . that explanation can be referred to known principles of equitable and . . . general jurisprudence".[3]

Thus a judge will consider the conduct of the person seeking a decree and may on general equitable principles refuse to permit him to obtain it.

Sir Ignatius J. O'Brien L.C. in the Court of Appeal pointed out in *P. v. P.*[4]

"It is not an uncommon case that two very old people go through a form of marriage, knowing well that a true marriage cannot take place. Again, a woman may take large benefits under this supposed marriage, and may have allowed ten, twenty, or thirty years to have elapsed without making any complaint, in which case, having . . . approbated the marriage, to allow her to reprobate it in proceedings for a decree of nullity would not be in accordance with the public interest, nor in most cases with common justice".

Similarly, if a spouse with knowledge of the other's impotence agrees to adopt a child, he may be regarded as approbating the marriage and barred from successfully challenging its validity.[5]

The court in all cases in which non-consummation is alleged is said to have power to consider the general justice of the case. It may examine the surrounding facts of the parties' married life and marital relationship so that the conduct, as

---

1. For a more detailed exposition of the law as to Bars to Relief see J. Jackson, *The Formation and Annulment of Marriage*, 2nd ed. (London, Butterworths 1969), chapter 8. See further D. Lasok—Approbation of Marriage in English Law and the Doctrine of Validation (1963) 26 M.L.R. 249.
2. (1885) 10 App. Cas. 171 (H.L. (Sc.); see also *P. v. P.* (by amendment *McD v. P.*) [1916] 2 I.R. 400, 414; (K.B.D.) (C.A.); 50 I.L.T.R. 149.
3. *Supra*, p. 186.
4. *Supra* at p. 421–2; see also *G. v. G.* [1924] *supra; McM. v. McM. supra; R.M. v. S.M. supra.*
5. *W. v. W.* [1952] P. 152; [1952] 1 All E.R. 858, (C.A.). (Decree refused. Husband taken to know that the remedy of nullity was available to him before adoption order made); *Slater v. Slater* [1953] P. 235; [1953] 1 All E. R. 246, (C.A.) (Decree granted. Wife unaware that remedy of nullity available to her at time of adoption); See also *D. v. D.* [1979] Fam. 70 (Fam. D.); See further *Tindall v. Tindall* [1953] P. 63; [1953] 1 All E.R. 139, (C.A.), in which a spouse with full knowledge of her husband's impotence and the possibility of her obtaining a decree of nullity, having first brought proceedings in the Magistrates Court against him on which she relied on the validity of their marriage, subsequently alleged her husband's impotence as a ground for annulling their marriage. She was held to have approbated the marriage and it was said to be inequitable and contrary to public policy to allow her the decree sought.

well as the position of the parties can be properly considered.[6] Thus, for example, if parties live together for 20 years and then upon the impotent spouse becoming confined to bed, the other petitions for a decree of nullity, the court may hold it to be unjust and inequitable to grant a decree. This, however, can be seen as simply another branch of the doctrine of approbation. In the case, however, of the impotent spouse who only discovers his impotence after the marriage, if it is accepted that the repudiation of the other spouse is not required to permit him to petition, this doctrine can be important. Rather than a spouse being granted a decree as of right on the ground of his own impotence, it becomes necesary for the court to look at the whole of the circumstances including the other spouse's attitude and reaction to the situation created by the petitioner's impotence, in order to see whether it is just and equitable to grant a decree against a spouse in no way responsible for the non-consummation. In such a situation it should be recognised that both parties are aggrieved. Thus, in the case of an impotent husband who lives with his wife for many years and then when she is crippled and old brings proceedings for nullity on the ground of his own impotence, the court, on the above principles, could hold that to grant a decree would be unjust having regard to the length of time the parties have lived together and the incapacitated spouse's present vulnerable condition.

This would be different to the present position where the impotent spouse is regarded as having no cause of action unless the other spouse has repudiated the marriage. On the above suggestion the impotent spouse can sue and succeed unless in the circumstances of the case it is unjust that he should do so.[7]

Delay

Delay in presenting a petition on the ground of impotence is not an absolute bar to the remedy.[8] The reason for the delay is of the utmost importance, as a long delay may be proof of approbation of the marriage, or may render it inequitable that a decree be granted. Everything depends on the circumstances of the particular case.

By the very nature of the ground of impotence long delay will render it more difficult to establish the necessary proof and it has been said that following such a delay evidence to support the suit must be of the clearest and most satisfactory.[9] The objection of delay cannot be surmounted by the uncorroborated testimony of the petitioner.[10]

Long delay may throw so heavy a burden on a petitioner of proving the fact of incapacity that it may deprive him of his remedy. Thus in *B. (otherwise A.)* v. *B.*[11] despite the petitioner discovering her husband's impotence in 1873 she did not present a petition until 1891. The petitioner had lived apart from her husband since 1873 and had married another in 1874. There could be no medical evidence as to the condition of the wife and the husband refused to submit to medical examination. He denied being impotent at the time of the marriage, but the medical officer appointed by the court was satisfied as a result of his interview with him that he was impotent at the date of the interview. There was no excuse given by the petitioner for her delay in bringing proceedings. The court

---

6. *McM v. McM.* and *McK. v. McK. supra.*
7. See *Pettit v. Pettit* [1963] P. 177; [1962] 3 All E.R. 37, (C.A.).
8. *G. v. M. supra; B (otherwise A.) v. B. supra.*
9. *Castleden v. Castleden* (1861) 9 H.L. Cas. 186; *(otherwise A.) v. B. supra.*
10. *B. (otherwise A.) v. B. supra; U (falsely called J.) v. J.* (1867), L.R. 1 P. & D. 460, (Ct. of P. & D.).
11. *Supra.*

held that considering the length of time which had elapsed since the marriage and since the petitioner became aware of her husband's imperfection, in view of the lack of medical testimony (in that even if he was impotent in 1891 this did not necessarily mean he was in 1873) and the want of corroborative evidence, there was no sufficient or satisfactory proof that the respondent was impotent at the date of the marriage. A decree was refused.

When, however, there are valid reasons for a petitioner's delay and the im-' potence of the respondent can be adequately proved a decree will be granted.[12] Thus, in *G. v. R. (otherwise known as G.)*[13] a decree of annulment was granted on the grounds of the respondent wife's impotence seventeen years after the marriage had taken place. The parties had lived together continuously for the first fifteen years of the marriage. The petitioner in evidence stated that he only became aware of the possibility of instituting nullity proceedings when watching a programme on television a year prior to the court hearing.

Ratification of Void Marriages

At first sight the notion of validating or ratifying that which is void is strange. There is however some authority for the proposition that a marriage, void for lack of consent, may be ratified by the subsequent behaviour of the parties.[14] This doctrine of ratification is purely canonical in origin and cannot be explained on logical grounds. In the words of Lord O'Brien in *Ussher v. Ussher*[15]

> "how could the marriage be validated if it was altogether void? Such a proposition, it was contended, finds no support from 'reason'. I am afraid there are many things lying at the root, at the foundation, of the christian religion, mysteries of faith, for an elucidation of which we should appeal to 'reason' in vain."

The case law in support of this doctrine is sparse and it mainly rests on commentators' statements as to the principles applied by the Ecclesiastical Courts.[16] In effect, it renders the status of marriages void for lack of consent, similar to that of marriages voidable on the ground of impotence. In both cases a party can by his or her own conduct prevent such a marriage from being annulled.

A "void" marriage may also be rendered valid by statutory enactment. Thus as we have already seen the Marriages Act 1972 rendered valid certain marriages celebrated in Lourdes, that prior to its enactment were void.

Collusion: Order 70 Rule 4 of the Rules of the Superior Courts requires a petitioner seeking a decree of nullity to state in an affidavit filed with the petition that no collusion or connivance exists between the petitioner and

12. *G. v. M. supra; Castleden v. Castleden supra; Mansfield, (falsely called Cuno) v. Cuno* (1873) 42. L.J. (P. & M.) 65; *T. v. T. (otherwise J.)* (1963) 47 T.L.R. 629; H. *(falsely called C.) v. C.* (1860) 1 Sw. & Tr. 605; 164 E.R. 880 (Ct for Div. & Matr. Causes).

13. Decision of Barrington J. February, 1980. Record No. 1979/11M. There was no written judgement in this case.

14. See *Valier v. Valier* (1925) 133 L.T. 830 at p. 832; *Ash's Case* (1702) *Freem. Ch.* 259; Prec. Ch. 203; 22 E.R. 1196 (Chan.).

15. [1912] 2 I.R. 455 at p. 480. In this case no validation of the marriage was attempted. Validation was not however necessary. The parties to the marriage were both Roman Catholics. The marriage was celebrated by a Roman Catholic priest and was valid at common law, although invalid by the law of the Roman Catholic Church, only one witness being present at the ceremony.

16. See Tolstoy, Void and Voidable Marriages (1964), 27 M.L.R. 385, and The Validation of Void Marriages, (1968) 31 M.L.R. 656, and the authorities therein cited. See also J. Jackson *supra*, p. 357; Law Commission (Law Com. No. 33), *Family Law—Report on Nullity of Marriage*, (London–H.M.S.O. 1970), p. 4.

the respondent.

As has been seen the High Court has constantly reiterated the need to ensure that "discontended spouses" will not use the nullity jurisdiction to obtain release from the bonds of matrimony, and the courts have in a number of cases looked at the evidence presented to them to ensure that there is no suggestion of collusion between the parties.[17]

The exact effect of collusion in proceedings seeking a declaration of nullity is however uncertain. Whereas collusion between the parties may affect the veracity of their evidence and thus prevent the court granting a decree on the ground of impotence, if a marriage is void due, for example, to under age, prohibited degrees or prior marriage, collusion should not act as a bar to a decree. If it does so act, the doctrine is anomolous in that a void marriage will remain void even if a decree is refused on such a ground. There are no reported Irish cases in which a petition seeking a decree of annulment has been refused on the sole ground of collusion between the parties.[18]

THE CONSEQUENCES OF A DECREE OF NULLITY

If a marriage is void no legal consequences can flow from the relationship which in law did not exist. The parties have no succession rights or obligations of support vis á vis each other. Any children born to the parties are regarded as illegitimate, their mother being their sole guardian. Their father may however seek a court order of custody or access under the Guardianship of Infants Act 1964, section 11.

If a voidable marriage is annulled, the decree acts so as to retrospectively invalidate the marriage. It is then said to be void ab initio and the legal position of the parties is identical to that of parties to a void marriage. A decree annulling a voidable marriage retrospectively bastardises any children born to the parties.

Whilst a "wife" can obtain alimony pendente lite (pending the hearing of the case) from her husband, upon declaring a marriage to be a nullity, the court has no power to order the "husband" to contribute anything towards her future maintenance or the maintenance of their children. The only manner in which he can be compelled to give some financial support is if affiliation proceedings are subsequently brought to force him to contribute towards his children's maintenance.

CRITICISMS AND SUGGESTED REFORMS

I. Need to Extend Grounds

There has been in recent years some pressure for reform of the law of nullity.[19] This has arisen principally because of the considerable divergence between the

17. See for example Griffith v. Griffith supra, at p. 46, 50; R.M. v. M.M., supra at p. 169; Kelly v. Kelly (Feb. 1971) unreported, (H.C.), p. 3 of judgement; S. v. S. (July 1976) unreported, (S.C.), see judgement of Henchy J., p. 4. See also the old case of Pollard, falsely called Wybourn v. Wybourn (1828) 1 Hag. Ecc. 725; 162 E.R. 732 (Consistory Court).

18. See, however M. v. M. (May 1978) unreported (H.C.); (October 1979) unreported (S.C.). In the High Court, Murnahan J. refused to grant a decree of nullity on the grounds of impotence principally because he suspected collusion between the parties. On appeal, the Supreme Court granted the decree stating there was no evidence to support the trial judge's suspicions.

19. See "Some aspects of the Constitution and the Law in relation to Marriage" by Cahir Davitt, ex-President of the High Court and the replies to that article contained in 1968 Studies, p. 6; see also The Changing Face of Catholic Ireland, by D. Fennell, p. 18; "Some Aspects of Family Law", by Kenny J. (Society of Young Solicitors Lecture No. 46), F.L.A.C. Report, 1974, p. 11.

civil law of nullity and the canon law administered by the Marriage Tribunals of the Roman Catholic Church. By virtue of its jurisdiction over the marriages of Roman Catholics, the Church has always exercised the power to declare a marriage of a Roman Catholic to be a nullity according to Church or canonical law. Canon law has developed considerably in recent years, making it possible to obtain relief on grounds far wider than those entertained by the civil courts.[20] A canonical annulment, however, is not recognised by the State as having any legal effect. Thus, parties who obtain such annulments may still be regarded by the State as legally married,[21] while they themselves in accordance with their religious convictions feel free to remarry.[22] Yet if they do remarry they may render themselves liable to be prosecuted for bigamy and the second marriage will be invalid.[23]

At the end of August 1976 a discussion paper entitled "The Law of Nullity in Ireland", prepared in the Office of the Attorney General, was published.[24] In it, the Government's intention to reform the law of nullity is stated, suggested reforms are discussed, and a draft Nullity of Marriages Bill is set out. The Bill is both a codifying and reforming measure. It is intended here to briefly examine some of the reforms recommended in the Discussion Paper. The contents of the proposed Bill can be found in Appendix B.

The Discussion Paper notes the absence of developments in the law of nullity since 1871 and suggests three new grounds for rendering a marriage void, two of which are subsumed within the concept of absence of "true consent".

1. It recommends that a marriage should be void if either party at the time of the marriage was suffering (whether continuously or intermittently) from mental disorder of a kind or to an extent that rendered him or her unfitted for marriage.[25] "Mental disorder" is defined in the proposed Bill as "mental illness, arrested or incomplete development of mind or personality psychopathic disorder and any other disorder or disability of mind or personality". Psychopathic disorder within the above definition is said to mean "a persistent disorder (whether or not including subnormality of intelligence) which results in abnormally aggressive or seriously irresponsible conduct on the part of the person".[26]

This concept of mental disorder, rendering a person unfit for marriage, is a considerable extension of the present law. Under it, a person's mental incapacity

20. For a discussion on the present Canon Law on Nullity see, R. Brown—*Marriage Annulment* (Chapman, London 1971) and R. Brown, *Marriage Annulment in the Catholic Church—A Practical Guide* (Kevin Mayhew Ltd., Essex, England, 1977); See also 'Marriage Annulment in the Catholic Church', Vol. 72 (September, 1978) *The Gazette of the Incorporated Law Society of Ireland* p. 135 et seq.; *The Church's Matrimonial Jurisprudence, a Statement on Current Position*, The Canon Law Society Trust (Westminster 1975); L. G. Wrenn, *Annulments* (Canon Law Society of America, Connecticut 1972); An interesting case study illustrating the circumstances in which the church will annul a marriage is contained in *Matrimonial Jurisprudence, United States 1968—1971*, published by the Canon Law Society of America (1973). See further J.A. Coulter, 'The Pastoral Problem of Annulments', Vol. 29 (November 1978) The Furrow p. 680.

21. If a marriage is void no court decree if of course required. In such circumstances, parties who obtain a church decree may be regarded as single persons by the civil law. However, there may be doubts as to whether the facts surrounding their marriage were such as to render it void. For this to be certain a court decision is desirable.

22. See for example *S. v. S.* (July 1976), unreported, (S.C.) where the wife after obtaining a church decree of nullity remarried prior to the Supreme Court annulling their first marriage.

23. If however a party obtains a civil decree of nullity subsequent to a second marriage, as the first marriage is then retrospectively invalidated, the second marriage is then rendered valid—see *Mason v. Mason, supra*. See however *Wiggins v. Wiggins* [1958] I.W.L.R. 1013.

24. *The Law of Nullity in Ireland* (Stationery Office, Dublin, August 1976).

25. *Ibid.*, p. 6—8.

26. *Ibid.*, p. 34.

becomes a ground in itself, sufficient to invalidate a marriage. At present, mental incapacity renders a marriage invalid, when it prevents a person from giving a valid consent. It is inability to know to what you are consenting and not simply mental illness, that is all important.[27] Under the above recommendation, a person may have ability to consent and know to what he is consenting, but may still be regarded by the law as "unfitted for the institution of marriage".

2. The other new grounds for rendering a marriage void are, in the proposed Bill, subsumed within the concept of absence of true consent.[28] The Bill proposes that a marriage should be void if "the apparent consent to marry of either party was not a true consent". In deciding whether the "apparent consent" of a party was a true consent the court, it is recommended should take into account

"(a) mental incapacity or deficiency of the party at the date of the marriage, including a mental incapacity to appreciate the nature of the marriage contract and the responsibilities attached to marriage;

(b) a threat based on any financial or social obligation or liability of the party which existed, or was alleged by the threat to exist, or would have arisen, or it was alleged would have arisen, if the party had not married and which the court considers was in the particular circumstances a material inducement to the party to marry;

(c) deceit practised on the party by any person as regards a feature of the marriage which in the particular circumstances of the case the court considers the party reasonably regarded as fundamental and which induced, to a material extent, the marriage;

(d) duress or undue influence exercised over the party whether exercised by or on behalf of the other party or not;

(e) a mistake of either party to the marriage as to the identity of the other party, or as to the nature of the marriage ceremony."[29]

Factors (d) and (e) are merely a reiteration of two of the present factors that go to invalidate consent. Factor (b) would reform the existing law and permit a party to obtain a decree, if the marriage was brought about by threats justly imposed or not, if such threats destroyed the reality of a free consent. Under the present law, as we have seen, if a party is forced to marry by a threat "justly imposed", that party cannot challenge the validity of the marriage on the ground of absence of consent.

Factors (a) and to a lesser extent (c) constitute the new elements going to show absence of consent. (a) considerably widens the grounds for which a decree may be granted and it is examined further in the pages that follow.

(c) brings within its compass the additional factor suggested by Kenny J. in *S.* v. *S.*[30] as providing proof of absence of consent and extends its scope. Under it, deceit practised by any person, not merely the respondent, in relation to a fundamental feature of the marriage and which induced a party to marry, will invalidate consent. The deceit must be in relation to something the party reasonably regarded as fundamental. Thus, whilst the Report does not favour extending

---

27. Under the Marriage of Lunatics Act, 1811, it is the fact of lunacy that renders the marriage void. In practice however this Act is almost irrelevant.
28. See 4 (1) (i) and (2) of proposed Bill; see also p. 8–9.
29. See Sec. 4 (1) (h) of proposed Bill which makes second alternative a separate ground.
30. (July 1976) unreported (S.C.).

the grounds of nullity to wilful refusal to consummate,[31] a spouse who enters a marriage not intending to consummate, may be held to have induced the other party's consent by deceit as regards a fundamental feature of the marriage. Similarly, if a spouse, without the knowledge of the other spouse, is at the time of the marriage ceremony, sterile or has decided not to have any children, the other spouse's consent may be held to have been induced by deceit, if the court regards the procreation of children as a fundamental feature of marriage.

Other recommendations contained in the Discussion Paper, that if enacted would affect the grounds on which a decree of nullity may be granted, include:

(a) A spouse should be able to petition for a decree of nullity on the grounds of his own impotence and not only after the respondent has repudiated the marriage.[32]

(b) the distinction between void and voidable marriages should be abolished.

(c) the doctrine of approbation should apply except where a marriage is void due to (i) non-observance of formalities; (ii) lack of capacity, except in relation to under age marriages.[33]

(d) the doctrines of approbation and ratification should be codified and formulated so as to provide that if the respondent satisfies the court that (i) the petitioner, with knowledge that it was open to him to have the marriage declared null and void, so conducted himself in relation to the respondent as to lead the latter believe he would not do so, and (ii) in the circumstances of the case it would be unjust, to grant a decree, no decree should be granted.[34]

(e) so as to clarify the effects of collusion it is recommended that an agreement by virtue of which false evidence is given should be a punishable offence but should not necessarily bar the granting of a decree.[35]

(f) only parties to the marriage be entitled to bring proceedings for annulment in cases where a decree is sought on the ground of (i) impotence; (ii) lack of age; (iii) lack of consent; (iv) mental disorder.[36]

The proposal for a Nullity of Marriages Act is to be welcomed, in that a single statute containing all the grounds on which a nullity decree may be granted has never been enacted in this country. The enactment of such a measure, will to a certain extent, lessen public confusion as to the civil courts' powers in this area. While some of the proposed reforms of the grounds of nullity are also welcome in so far as they will, if enacted, lessen the rigidity of the law and its dependence on outmoded and anachronistic judicial pronouncements, a number of them call for further comment.

1. The discussion Paper notes that whether a marriage is void or voidable upon a decree being made by the court, it is regarded as always having been void. It states that the distinction between a void and voidable marriage is an artificial one and recommends that it should be abolished. In doing so, however, the

31. *Ibid.*, p. 10 see however p. 68 *ante*.
32. *Ibid.*, p. 9 see p. 70 *ante*.
33. *Ibid.*, p. 13.
34. *Ibid.*, p. 38, Sect. 6 of the proposed Bill.
35. *Ibid.*, p. 17, see however Sect. 6 (3) of the proposed Bill which, if enacted, would have the opposite effect of that intended by the recommendation.
36. *Ibid.*, p. 16, and Sect. 7 (4) and (5) of proposed Bill at p. 40.

Report recommends a new distinction—that between "void" marriages subject to such an impediment that no subsequent conduct can act as a bar to relief, and "void" marriages that can be validated by subsequent conduct. In the case of the latter, it is proposed that only parties to the marriage shall be entitled to bring nullity proceedings.

It is submitted that the concept of a voidable marriage, the validity of which parties cannot impugn because of their subsequent conduct (i.e. because of approbation), is far less artificial than that of a "void" marriage that may some time in the future be retrospectively validated by the behaviour of the parties. It is not the distinction between void and voidable marriages that is artificial, but the fact that upon a decree being granted in respect of a voidable marriage, the parties are held in law never to have been married, regardless of the length of time they have lived together as "husband and wife".

2. The new grounds proposed for the granting of a decree on the basis of "mental disorder" and absence of "true consent", if enacted, will bring about a radical change of emphasis in the nullity jurisdiction. As we have already seen, the jurisdiction of the court to annul a marriage is at present based on the contractual concept of marriage. It involves the court examining the circumstances existing prior to, and at the time of the marriage, in order to discover whether, as a result of the presence of a particular impediment, the parties did not or could not contract a valid marriage. Thus the parties' post-marital relationship is largely irrelevant to nullity proceedings,[37] whilst the existence or not of the marriage "contract" is all important.

The new grounds as proposed, lay particular emphasis on the relationship as opposed to the contractual concept of marriage.[38] Like the present nullity jurisdiction of the Marriage Tribunals of the Roman Catholic Church, the civil courts, if conferred with the jurisdiction proposed in the Discussion Paper, will be much concerned to discover, whether at the date of the marriage, both parties had the capacity to maintain a marital relationship, had the ability to understand the true implications of such a relationship, and the capacity and intent to carry out the responsibilities imposed by it.

Whilst a movement away from the formal contractual approach is to be welcomed, arguments can be made both in favour and against the concepts of "mental disorder", "mental incapacity" and "psychopathic disorder", as grounds for a granting of a nullity decree in the manner in which they are defined in the proposed Bill.

Advantages

A. In determining the validity of a marriage, the court will be able to look behind the consents of the parties to a greater extent than it can at present in order to decide whether, they possessed at the date of the ceremony, the personal elements essential to the creation of a marital relationship.

B. The above grounds take into account modern psychiatric and psychological learning as to the ability of parties to enter into a true marriage. This is

37. However under the present law, in the case of impotence evidence of failure to consummate after the ceremony is used to prove the existence of impotence at the time when the ceremony took place. Post marital conduct is also relevant in determining whether a party is barred from obtaining a decree.

38. This is not explicitly recognised in the Discussion Paper. See however references to marriage as an "institution" at p. 7.

particularly important in a country which regards a valid marriage as indissoluble.

C. These new grounds taken together with the other grounds that are intended to be included in the proposed Bill, will bring the civil law to a major extent into line with the law of nullity administered by the Marriage Tribunals of the Roman Catholic Church.[39] By so doing, it will greatly reduce the number of limping marriages i.e. marriages held to be null and void by the Church but valid by the State. The great majority of those who have had a decree of nullity pronounced by the Church Tribunals, will be able to have their position under civil law regularised.

D. In determining a person's capacity to marry, they permit the court to decide each case on its individual circumstances. In determining capacity, the court will be able to look at both the pre-marital and post-marital behaviour of the parties. Thus, where a marriage breaks down, proof of breakdown and the reasons for it may indicate an initial incapacity in one or both parties to enter into a valid marriage. Thus, many persons who are held bound by the law at present in an indissoluble union, may obtain legal release from their marriage, upon the court holding either of the parties to have lacked capacity at the date of the wedding, to enter into and maintain a marital relationship. For example, the battered wife should, in the great majority of cases, have little difficulty in satisfying the court that the assaults on her, by her husband constitute convincing evidence, that at the date of the marriage ceremony, he suffered from a psychopathic disorder, i.e. a persistent disorder which causes abnormally aggressive conduct.

Disadvantages

A. It should be possible to know with certainty, at the time of a party's marriage, whether it is valid or not. The concepts of mental disorder, mental incapacity and psychopathic disorder as used and defined in the proposed Bill, are vague and subjective notions. It will, in many instances, be impossible to determine at the date of the marriage, whether a party is free from all of these impediments. As a consequence, a doubt may exist as to the validity of a marriage for many years after it has been celebrated.

B. The law of nullity should not be concerned with events subsequent to the marriage ceremony. Under these grounds however, nearly all proceedings will be brought upon a marriage breaking down. Certainly, a party who is happily married will not seek a decree of nullity, alleging for example, that at the time of the ceremony, the other party lacked the mental capacity to appreciate the nature of the marriage contract and the responsibilities attached to marriage.

Upon breakdown taking place, parties will seek to relate the causes of breakdown to the possession, by either of them, of a personal defect at the time of their wedding. In many instances, the court will be placed in the impossible position of attempting to discover the mental condition of a party at the time of his or her marriage, some fifteen or twenty years after it has taken place. The validity of a marriage should not be placed in jeopardy by subjective assessments

---

39. In effect the proposed new grounds for the granting of a nullity decree, will, if enacted, to a large extent incorporate into the civil law, the gounrds of "lack of due discretion" and "inadequate consent" by which a marriage may be annuled in accordance with the modern jurisprudence of the Church. See footnote 20.

as to a party's mental condition at the date of marriage many years after that marriage has taken place.

C. Upon marital breakdown, in the great majority of cases, it is possible to discover something in a person's background and mental make-up, which can be regarded as a factor contributing to the breakdown. The Roman Catholic Church, by developing its nullity jurisdiction, may now annul many marriages which under the civil law of most States, could only be terminated by divorce. It is to a certain extent using nullity as a legal fiction for divorce. The desirability of the State employing such a legal fiction, so as to evade the Constitutional prohibition on divorce, is open to serious question.

D. The use of nullity as a legal fiction for divorce is going to unfairly penalise those who enter marriage with proper planning and a full understanding of what it involves. If parties to such a marriage grow apart and their relationship collapses, they will be held bound by the State in an indissoluble union. On the other hand, persons who enter into a marriage with no real insight of its meaning and totally unprepared, will be able to legally extracate themselves from their relationship, if they so wish.

E. Marital breakdown should be the concern of the law as to judicial separation and dissolution, and not the concern of the law of nullity. Upon a marriage breaking down, the fundamental question a court should ask is whether the relationship of the parties is still viable at the time when its jurisdiction is called upon. Its sole concern should not be to try to discover whether a party had a personal impediment at the time of the wedding which rendered the marriage invalid.

F. The use of the law of nullity in the marital breakdown situation rather than a law of separation or divorce based on irretrievable breakdown, will only exacerbate the bitterness of the parties and increase their distress. Rather than encouraging them to settle their differences in a dignified and humane manner, it will encourage the assignment of blame and require a finding of fault by the court, thus lessening the possibility of co-operation between the parties in the future. Such co-operation may be essential if the welfare of any children born to the parties is to be secured.

3. Although the Discussion Paper states, that it recommends no change in the law as to under age marriages,[40] further on it lists them amongst those "void" marriages, that may be approbated by the parties and recommends that their validity should only be questioned in proceedings between the parties to the marriage.

In its second working paper published in 1977 the Law Reform Commission stated that a marriage of parties below the minimum age for marriage or without required parental consents or judicial sanction should be void. It was also proposed that the present jurisdiction conferred on the President of the High Court to permit parties under 16 years to marry should be abolished. These proposals have already been discussed.[41] In making them, the Commission at no stage referred to the proposal contained in the Discussion Paper that it should be

40. At p. 6.
41. See p. 57 *ante*.

possible for parties to approbate and thus validate under-age marriage.

Even if the law as to the age for marriage is changed in accordance with the proposals contained in the Law Reform Commission's working paper a decision must also be made as to whether it should be legally possible for parties to approbate under age marriages. No reasons were given in the Discussion Paper for allowing them to do so.

In favour of the proposal it can be argued:-

(a) The reason for a minimum marriage age is that it is generally accepted that if parties marry at a very young age their marriage is likely to subsequently break down. If parties to such a marriage after a number of years still wish to remain together, there can be no social justification for holding their marriage to be invalid.

(b) A person may marry under-age without realising it. If parties have lived together for many years believing themselves to be married, great hardship may be caused upon a finding that the marriage is void. For example, a "spouse" may be denied maintenance, or succession rights or rights of guardianship.

Against the proposal it can be argued:-

(a) In effect this proposal would render marriages between under-age parties voidable and not void. If society believes that there is an age below which people should not be permitted to marry, to permit the validation of such under-age marriages at a later date renders the law meaningless.

(b) The proposal does not say at what age it would be possible for parties to approbate such a marriage but presumably approbation would not be possible until the parties reach the age of majority. If this is to be the case, it could be uncertain for a considerable period of time after a party celebrates his marriage whether it is valid or not. Thus, the status of children of such marriages would be unsure, as would parties' maintenance, property and succession rights.

(c) If under-age parties go through a marriage ceremony contrary to the law, it is open to them, if living happily together, to go through a further ceremony of marriage upon attaining the requisite age.

(d) The suggested hardships that may arise from a finding of invalidity are not a reason for varying the grounds of nullity, but merely for changing the consequences of a nullity decree.

It is submitted that the latter arguments are more convincing than the former and that marriages of under-age persons should be void and should not be open to the possibility of approbation.

4. As we have seen it is often very difficult to distinguish between "real" incapacity and "wilful refusal" to consummate. The proposals however reject the contention that wilful refusal to consummate should in itself be a separate ground for a decree of nullity.[42] However if a party enters marriage not intending to consummate, although capable of doing so, the other party could, as has been suggested, seek a decree alleging his consent not to be a "true consent", it being

---

42. At p. 15–16.

induced by deceit as to a fundamental feature of the marriage. It may, however, be particularly difficult to prove that the other party possessed an intention not to consummate at the date of the ceremony. As wilful refusal in the vast majority of cases results from psychological factors, dating back to a time before the celebration of a marriage, it is submitted that the proposed Nullity of Marriages Bill should provide, that if a party wilfully refuses to consummate, he is presumed to have had such an intention at the date of the ceremony.

Reforms of Consequences of a Decree of Nullity

The effects of a decree of nullity are unnecessarily harsh. The Discussion Paper states that "It is clearly desirable that the hardships which may result from a decree of nullity should be minimised as far as possible and, accordingly, it is recommended that powers be given to the Court to enable the Court to give financial relief to the parties of the marriage and to the children of the marriage so as to do justice between the parties and their children. The Court should be empowered to order that either party to the marriage should make to the other periodical payments or a lump sum; that a party to the marriage should make a payment for the benefit of a child of the marriage; that a party to the marriage should transfer to the other party, or to any child of the marriage, such property as may be specified in the order. Power to vary any ante-nuptial or post-nuptial settlement should also be given. The legislation should set out guidelines on which the discretion of the Court should be exercised, making it clear that the Court should take into consideration the income of the parties to the marriage, their financial needs, the standard of living enjoyed by the family, the age of each party to the marriage and any benefit accruing to the party which might result from the annulment of the marriage".

The Report also recommends that a child born of an annulled marriage should:

(a) be *treated* as a legitimate child of its parents,[43]

(b) have a right to share in the estate of both of his deceased parents.[44]

Whilst these proposals are to be welcomed, they are anomalous in so far as they propose to confer "rights" on parties to a marriage declared "void" greater than the rights possessed by parties to a valid marriage that breaks down. For example, under the present law a husband cannot be ordered by a court to pay a lump sum of money to his wife or to transfer to her property owned by him. A further anomaly is that a child will be treated as legitimate or be able to obtain a share in his father's estate if his parents have gone through a ceremony of marriage that is declared to be void by a court, but if they have merely lived together and were not parties to an invalid (i.e. non-existent) marriage, he will not be so treated or acquire any such succession rights. It is submitted that a more logical solution would be to abolish the concept of illegitimacy altogether and to base the legal relationship of parent and child, not on the fact of the celebration of a marriage ceremony, but purely on the biological link between the parties.[45] Finally, the proposals confer no rights of succession on a party to a void marriage. If it is deemed just to minimise the hardship that may arise from a decree of nullity during the lifetime of the parties, it is submitted that the hardship which may occur, upon a party discovering his or her marriage to be void after the death of the other, should also be minimised. Such a party should be empowered to apply to the court for a reasonable provision out of the deceased's estate.

43. At p. 15. The proposed Bill, however, fails to properly provide for this.
44. At p. 16.
45. See further Chapter 16.

CHAPTER 6

MARRIAGE AND THE LAW

Marriage creates a status to which the law attaches various rights and duties, which affect both the legal relationship of the parties between themselves, and with other people. The most fundamental right that marriage creates is the right that each party has to the other's company (consortium). The corollary of this right is the legal duty imposed on spouses to cohabit. In this chapter we discuss the legal means of enforcing the duty to cohabit and the remedies the law provides for loss of consortium. We then look to see how marriage historically affected the position of parties under various other categories of the law and the present day position. In conclusion we look at the procedure available whereby a person can obtain a declaration as to his marital status and the remedy available to prevent a person falsely asserting that he is another's spouse.

REMEDY TO ENFORCE DUTY TO COHABIT

Resitution of Conjugal Rights

The primary duty of a husband and wife under Ecclesiastical Law was the duty to cohabit. This duty was enforced by the Ecclesiastical Courts upon petition by a deserted spouse for a decree of Restitution of Conjugal Rights. This decree called upon the spouse in desertion, to resume cohabitation with the petitioner. If it was disobeyed, the respondent could be excommunicated. The power to excommunicate was abolished in England by the Ecclesiastical Courts Act, 1813, and replaced by a power to impose a six-month sentence of imprisonment. This Act did not apply to Ireland and until the abolition of the Ecclesiastical Courts in 1870 the power to excommunicate remained.[1] Today the jurisdiction to hear proceedings for restitution of conjugal rights is possessed by the High Court[2] and failure to comply with such an order of that Court would render a person liable to committal for contempt.[3] In order to obtain such a decree a petitioner must give evidence of the respondent having refused to comply with a

---

1. *Contra* K. Hayes, "Matrimonial Jurisdiction of the High Court", (1973) 8 I.J. (n.s.) 55.
2. See *Hood v. Hood* [1959] I.R. 225, (H.C.).
3. See *Bell v. Bell* [1922] 2 I.R. 103, 152 at p. 158; 56 I.L.T.R. 46; (K.B.D.); In England in 1884 the Matrimonial Causes Act (which did not apply in Ireland) abolished the courts power of attachment. From then on in England refusal to comply with a decree of restitution gave the other spouse a right to petition for a judicial separation, or until 1923, in the case of a wife, for divorce, if the husband had also committed adultery. See A. W. Samuels K.C., "Divorce Jurisdiction in Ireland", (1911), 45 I.L.T. & S.J. 6; also Westropp's Divorce Bill (1868), 11 A.C. p. 294n, (H.L.). Sect. 20 of the Matrimonial Proceedings and Property Act, 1970, abolished the action totally in England. By Sect. 120 (2) of Succession Act, 1965, a spouse who fails to comply with a decree for restitution of conjugal rights obtained by the deceased is precluded from taking any share in the estate of the deceased as a legal right or on an intestacy.

written demand to resume cohabitation and restore conjugal rights.[4] If at any time after the commencement of proceedings the respondent becomes willing to resume cohabitation, the petitioner may apply for an order to stay the proceedings.[5]

A defence to a petition for restitution is afforded by proof by the respondent that the petitioner has committed a matrimonial offence sufficient to ground an action for a divorce *a mensa et thoro*.[6] If a respondent succeeds in substantiating such a charge he or she is in turn able to obtain such a divorce decree.[7] Moreover evidence of matters of a less aggravated character than are sufficient to ground an allegation of cruelty or adultery for the purpose of *a mensa et thoro* decree may be held sufficient to justify a refusal to cohabit.[8] However, the fact that the petitioner has previously deserted the respondent without just cause, affords no answer to a suit for restitution, desertion not being a ground for *a mensa et thoro* decree.[9]

A decree for restitution of conjugal rights is the only lawful means whereby one spouse can force another to cohabit against the latter's will. In the case of *R. v. Jackson*[10] it was decided that a husband cannot resort to extra-judicial methods to enforce his right to his wife's consortium. In this case a wife who had gone to live with relations while her husband was away, refused to return to him and failed to comply with a decree for restitution of conjugal rights. One Sunday when she was leaving church the husband with two other men seized her, took her to his home and refused to permit her to leave. An application was made on her behalf for a writ of *habeas corpus*. The application was successful, the Court of Appeal holding that it was no defence that the husband was merely attempting to enforce his right to consortium.

Mr. A.W. Samuels, K.C. in giving evidence on Irish Marriage Laws before the Royal Commission on Divorce in 1910[11] referring to the power to make an order of restitution, stated

"This is a peculiar jurisdiction exercised by the divorce tribunal, by which it purports to compel two people who detest one another to live together. It would be a very difficult thing to discover a case in which the husband or wife was by the promptings of affection urged to bring a suit for the restitution of conjugal rights. To quote the words of Lord Hannen in *Marshall v. Marshall*[12] 'I must observe that so far as suits for restitution of conjugal rights from being in truth and in fact what theoretically they purport to be, proceedings for the purpose of insisting on the fulfilment of the obligation of married persons to live together, I have never known an instance in which it has appeared that the suit was instituted for any other

4. See Order 70, Rule 4 of the Rules of the Superior Courts.
5. *Ibid.*, Order 70, Rule 58.
6. *Ruxton v. Ruxton* (1880), 5 L.R. Ir. 19, 455 (P. & M.)., (C.A.); *D'Arcy v. D'Arcy* (1887) 19 L.R. Ir. 369, (P. & M.).
7. *Seaver v. Seaver* (1846), 2 Sw. & Tr. 665; 164 E.R. 1156 (Consistory Ct).
8. *Carnegie v. Carnegie* (1886), 17 L.R. Ir. 430, (P. & M.); *Sopwith v. Sopwith* (1860), 2 Sw. & Tr. 168; 164 E.R. 954; *Russell v. Russell* [1895] P. 315, (C.A.); [1897] A.C. 395, (H.L.) affirming C.A.; *Manning v. Manning* (1873) I.R. 7 Eq. 520; (1872) I.R. 6 Eq. 417; (1873) I.R. 7 Eq. 365 (Ct. of App. in Ch.).
9. *Dunne v. Dunne* [1947] I.R. 277; (1947) 81 I.L.T.R. 80, (H.C.); *Manning v. Manning, supra*.
10. [1891] 1 Q.B. 671, (C.A.); see also *R. v. Reid* [1972] 2 All E.R. 1350 (C.A.)—in this case a husband was convicted of kidnapping his wife; see further (1972) 2 Fam. Law 135.
11. See (1911) 45 I.L.T. & S.J. 6.
12. (1879), 5 P.D. 19, (P.D.A.), at p. 23.

purpose than to enforce a money demand'."

Today such proceedings are not even necessary for this latter purpose as a wife who is not supported by her husband can bring maintenance proceedings in either the High Court or the District Court so as to compel her husband to properly maintain her and their children.

Even if one spouse is genuinely desirous of a reconciliation a court order directing the other to cohabit is hardly an appropriate method of effecting one. It is accepted that an order of specific performance cannot issue to enforce personal services. One wonders what strange logic regards as beneficial the availability of what can be described as a matrimonial order of specific performance to enforce the most personal services of all. The action for restitution of conjugal rights is rarely used today, the last reported case being in 1959. It is a valueless anachronism and should be abolished.[13]

REMEDIES FOR INTERFERING WITH THE RIGHT TO WIFE'S SOCIETY AND SERVICES

Action for loss of Society and Services (per quod servitum et consortium amisit)

In the eyes of the common law a husband has a proprietary or at the very least a quasi proprietary interest in the society and services of his wife. As a consequence, if he is deprived of her society or services as a result of a wrong[14] committed against her by a third person, he has a right of action against that person. The husband's action is quite distinct from any claim which the wife may have, and his claim is not affected by any contributory negligence on her part.[15] There is no analogous right in the wife to sue for the loss of her husband's society or companionship.[16]

Damages may be recovered for loss of her services or society or both. The usual damages recovered for loss of services are for the cost of providing an alternative housekeeper to look after the husband and children while the wife was in hospital, together with medical expenses. Damages are also recoverable for the cost of domestic assistance that the husband may have to obtain in the future by reason of his wife's incapacity to carry out her domestic duties.[17] Where a husband has suffered any loss of earnings in order to be with his wife during her illness, he is able to recover these earnings to the extent that they were incurred in order to mitigate the damage flowing from the loss of consortium.[18]

Damages can be recovered for the total loss of a wife's society or consortium but they cannot be recovered for an impairment of consortium. Thus in *Spaight* v. *Dundon*[19] whereas a husband could recover damages for the total loss of his wife's companionship during the period of one year which she had to spend in

13. See "Matrimonial Jurisdiction of the High Court", K. Hayes, *supra*, Esp. 74—77.
14. The wrong is usually a tort, but such a claim may arise from a breach of contract. In *Jackson v. Watson & Sons* (1909) 2 K.B. 193, (C.A.)—A husband was held entitled to sue for compensation the vendor of bad salmon which his wife ate and which caused her death by food poisoning.
15. See the Civil Liability Act, 1961, Sect. 35 (2) as amended by the Civil Liability Act 1964, Sect. 4. See also *Mallet v. Dunne* [1949] 2 K. B. 180 (K.B.D.).
16. *Best v. Samuel Fox* [1952], A.C. 716, (H.L.).
17. *Spaight v. Dundon* [1961], I.R. 201; 96 I.L.T.R. 69, (S.C.).
18. *McNeill v. Johnstone* [1958] 3 All E.R. 16 (Q.B.D.). Moreover, if in his employment, a husband is particularly dependent on his wife's presence or assistance, and it is reasonable for him to refuse employment while she is incapacitated, he may be able to recover damages for his loss of earnings—*Behrens v. Bertram Mills Circus Ltd.* [1957] 2 Q.B. 1 (Q.B.D.); see, however, *Kirkham v. Boughey* [1958] 2 Q.B. 388, (Q.B.D.) in which the authority of the previous case was doubted.
19. *Supra*.

hospital, he was not entitled to be compensated because she was disfigured or because her temperament or mental outlook might be affected. In *O'Haran* v. *Divine*[20] it was said that consortium is "the sum total of the benefits which a wife may be expected to confer on her husband by their living together–help, comfort, companionship, services and all the amenities of family and marriage. If by the negligent action of the defendant a husband was deprived of all these, even for a limited period he was entitled to recover damages; but if the deprivation was merely of one or more elements of consortium while other elements continued to be engaged no action lay".[21] The fact that a husband may visit his incapacitated wife in hospital is not regarded as preventing him from recovering for loss of consortium.

This action has been condemned by both the English and Irish judiciary as an anachronistic survival of a medieval outlook. When it was argued in the English case of *Best* v. *Samuel Fox Ltd.*[22] that it was anomalous to permit a husband to bring such an action while denying the wife a similar right, the House of Lords replied that the real anomaly was the husband's right of action in the first place, and that the action should not be extended. The Supreme Court in *Spaight* v. *Dundon* agreed with this opinion of the House of Lords, stating that the action would not be extended and that damages for loss of consortium should not be too generous.[23]

Harbouring a Wife

This action, like the previous one, is based on the notion that a husband has a proprietary interest in his wife. Where a person provides accommodation for another's wife and after receiving notice from the husband not to do so, permits her to remain on, he is liable in the tort of harbouring.[24] But if a wife is received from "principles of humanity" such an action cannot succeed. Thus if a wife is being ill-treated by a husband, such ill-treatment, or reasonable belief of such ill-treatment affords a defence to the person granting her protection.[25]

In the 18th Century harbouring was considered objectionable because it interfered with the economic process by which a wife, refused food and shelter elsewhere than in the matrimonial home, would eventually be forced to return to it. This action, like the one previously discussed, cannot be brought by a wife against a person "harbouring her husband".[26]

---

20. (1966), 100 I.L.T.R. 53, (S.C.).
21. *Per* Kingsmill Moore J. at p. 55. See also *Cutts v. Chumley* [1967], 2 All E.R. 89, (C.A.), where damages were given for impairment of consortium, but what was regarded as an impairment of consortium on the facts of that case–the total incapacitation and institutionalisation of the wife–would be regarded on the basis of the decision in *O'Haran v. Divine* as a total loss of consortium. There "a healthy companion and helper was reduced to a condition where she had to be separated from her husband" and "all the innumerable advantages, pleasures and consolations of married life were brought to an end–save a limited measure of communication–" (1966), 100 I.L.T.R. at p. 56; see also *Lawrence v. Biddle* [1966], 2 Q.B. 504, (Q.B.D.). See further the Law Relating to Loss of Consortium and Loss of Services of a Child, The Law Reform Commission, Working Paper No. 7 (Dublin 1979) at p. 2 *et seq.*
22. *Supra*.
23. See however the Law Reform Commission, Working Paper No. 7, *supra*, at p. 4 *et seq.* where it is suggested that the courts may now extend the actions so as to enable a wife sue for loss of consortium.
24. See *Winchester v. Fleming* [1958], 1 Q.B. 259, (Q.B.D.), [1957], 3 All E.R. 711.
25. *Philp v. Squire* (1791), 1 Peake 114; 3 R.R. 659, (Nisi Prius).
26. *Winchester v. Fleming, supra.* See The Law Relating to Criminal Conversation and the Enticement and Harbouring of a Spouse, The Law Reform Commission, Working Paper No. 5 (Dublin 1978) at p. 15 where it is suggested that the courts may extend the action to enable a wife sue for the harbouring of her husband. The Law Reform (Miscellaneous

Enticement

Any person who "procures, entices or persuades" a spouse to leave the other is liable in this tort.[27] Unlike other remedies for interference with the right to services and consortium, a wife as well as a husband may as plaintiff sue a third party for enticement.[28] As in the case of harbouring if such enticement is justified by "principles of humanity" an action cannot succeed. In deciding whether a person has been enticed away by another, the court may look not only to the words used by the defendant but also to his or her relationship with the spouse alleged to have been enticed. Advice is not sufficient to render a defendant liable. There must be some element of persuasion. It is not, however, necessary for the plaintiff spouse to prove that the will of the other spouse was overborne.[29]

Criminal Conversation

An action for criminal conversation may be brought by a husband against a person who commits adultery with his wife.[30] The basis of this action is derived from the principle that anyone having sexual intercourse with a wife is violating a property right of her husband. A wife has no corresponding right of action against another woman who commits adultery with her husband.[31] Damages in this form of action can only be compensatory. They cannot be punitive or exemplary. They are awarded for the loss and injury suffered by a husband as a consequence of his wife's adultery.[32]

Mere proof of adultery, without proof of any consequent loss or injury does not entitle a husband to damages. In the leading case of *Maher* v. *Collins*[33]

Provisions) Act. 1970 abolished in England actions for harbouring.

27. *Place v. Searle* [1932], 2 K.B. 497, (C.A.).
28. *Best v. Samuel Fox and Co. Ltd.* [1952] A.C. 716; *Gray v. Gee* (1923), 39 T.L.R. 429, (K.B.D.).
29. The Law Reform (Miscellaneous Provisions) Act, 1970 abolished such actions in England. There are no cases of enticement to be found in any of the modern Irish Law reports, but see *The Gazette of the Incorporated Law Society of Ireland*, Vo. 69, No. 2 (March 1975), p. 43–44, where the case of *Keating v. O'Driscoll* (17th January 1975), (H.C.), is reported. In this case a Cork jury awarded a husband £12,000. for the enticement of his wife.
30. For meaning of adultery see p. 116. In *Morrow v. Morrow* [1914] 2 I.R. 183, (K.B.D.), it was said that in criminal conversation proceedings there is no rule of law precluding a jury from acting on the uncorroborated evidence of the plaintiff's wife, as to acts of adultery committed with the defendant. In an action of criminal conversation there must be strict proof of the spouses marriage ceremony—*McCarthy v. Hastings* [1933] N.I. 100, (C.A.).
31. *Newton v. Hardy and Ano.* [1933], All E.R. Rep. 40;(1933), 149 L.T. 165, (K.B.D.). See, however, the Law Reform Commission, Working Paper No. 5, *supra*, at p. 6 *et seq.* where it is suggested that the courts may extend the action to enable a wife to sue for criminal conversation.
32. *Maher v. Collins* [1975] I.R. 232, (S.C.);*Butterworth v. Butterworth and Eaglefield* [1920], P. 126; [1920] W.N. 96, (P.D.A.).
33. In *Maher v. Collins* a Jury award of £15,000 in the High Court was overturned by the Supreme Court as being "grossly excessive". A new trial was directed. In this case the plaintiff had suffered no pecuniary loss as a result of his wife's adultery, nor was there any loss of consortium, as he was living in England at the time. In relation to injured feelings it was said that he received the news of his wife's infidelity "rather philosophically and was prepared to concede that his own conduct may have contributed to what had happened". The court went on to say that he went back to live with his wife and they lived together since.
Juries seem inclined to make large awards in such cases. (It is to be noted however that until *De Burca v. A.-G.* [976] I.R. 38 (S.C.) juries in practice nearly always had an all male composition). See also *Braun v. Roche* Irish Times 22nd June 1972 (H.C.). Mrs. Braun had changed her name by deed poll to Mrs. Roche and was living with the defendant. An award of £12,000 damages was made in favour of her husband.

O'Higgins C.J. set down the matters which must be considered by a judge or jury when assessing damages. He stated

"Regard should be had to (a) the actual value of the wife to the husband and (b) the proper compensation to the husband for the injury to his feelings, the blow to his mental honour and the hurt to his matrimonial and family life". The value of a wife can be considered on two aspects "(a) the pecuniary aspect in relation to which her fortune and her assistance in her husband's business and such allied matters are relevant and (b) the consortium aspect in relation to which the wife's general qualities as a wife and mother and her conduct and general character are relevant."[34]

In relation to damages for the injured feeling of the husband, moderation rather than undue severity was said to be the principle. Further, in assessing damages, the character and conduct of not only the defendant but also of the husband and wife is relevant. In relation to the defendant it was said

"Any feature of treachery, any grossness of betrayal, any wantonness of insult, may deeply add to the husband's sense of injury and wrong and therefore, call for a larger award—not as exemplary damage but as appropriate compensation."[35]

Ignorance on the defendant's part that the plaintiff's spouse was married at the date when sexual relations took place does not afford a good defence but may reduce the damages.[36]

Until 1922 the above action, apart from securing damages for an aggrieved husband, had another purpose. Before a husband could obtain a parliamentary dissolution of his marriage on the ground of his wife's adultery, he had first to sue the alleged adulterer for criminal conversation. As the Oireachtas no longer has the power to pass a Divorce Bill, these proceedings are no longer relevant for this purpose.[37]

REMEDIES FOR INTERFERING WITH RIGHT TO CHILDREN'S SERVICES

Just as a husband at common law has a right to his wife's services, a parent is regarded as having a legal right to the services of his unmarried children under twenty-one years who ordinarily live at home.[38] If a third party wrongfully deprives a parent of such services, for example by enticing, harbouring,[39] or seducing a child,[40] the parent acquires a right of action against the former, in which, if he is successful, he can obtain damages.[41] In practice, the great majority of such actions are brought by a parent for the seduction of his daughter. Although in theory such an action is brought for loss of services, this is little more than a legal fiction. In reality, the action is for a wrong done to the honour

34. [1975] I.R. at p. 237.
35. *Ibid.*, at p. 238. As for costs see *Sheehan v. Sheehan* (1944), 78 I.L.T.R. 119, (H.C.).
36. *Lord v. Lord and Lambert* [1900] P. 297
37. In England the action of criminal conversation was abolished by the Matrimonial Causes Act, 1857, which substituted under Section 33 of that Act a power in the Divorce Court to award damages for adultery to a petitioning husband. The right to claim such damages was abolished in 1970 by the Law Reform (Miscellaneous Provisions) Act.
38. *Lough v. Ward* [1945] 2 All E.R. 338, (K.B.D.).
39. *Lough v. Ward, supra.*
40. All reported cases of seduction relate to the seduction of a girl. See cases cited in the following footnotes.
41. See the interesting case of the *People (A.-G) v. Edge* [1943] I.R. 115 (S.C.), in which the Supreme Court held that the defendant could not be convicted of the criminal offence of kidnapping, following his taking a boy of fourteen and a half years of age away from his parents, with the boy's, but without the parents', consent.

and feelings of the parent.[42]

Loss of services: The legal basis of the action is loss of services and not the familial relationship between a parent and child.[43] Thus, if a child is too young to give any services,[44] or is in the service of another and not living with his parents,[45] a parent cannot obtain damages for a wrong committed against his child. However, it is possible for a child to remain in the service of a parent, although also employed by another,[46] whilst if a child quits another's service a parent's right may revive.[47] A parent may obtain damages without proving that a child in fact renders any services. If the child lives with the parent and is old enough to provide services the law will conclusively presume that service is given.[48] Such an action can be brought by any parent living with his child whether the parent is married or unmarried,[49] or whether the child is the natural or adopted child of the parent.[50]

In the old case of *Hamilton* v. *Long*[51] it was held that if both parents are alive and living together with their child, the latter's services are owed exclusively to the father as master of the household. The court held that the mother could not sue for loss of services arising out of her daughter's seduction during the father's lifetime. Now that it is accepted that a mother has the same constitutional rights[52] with respect to a legitimate child as the father, it is submitted that she must have the same rights as the father to recover damages for loss of her child's services.

Damages: The court in such proceedings has no power to order a child to return to a parent. It may, however, as well as awarding damages, restrain the defendants by way of injunction from harbouring a child or otherwise depriving a parent of the child's services.[53] Damages are not limited to the financial worth

42. A parent may of course have a right to the service of a child over twenty one years. However such a right is presumed in relation to a child under twenty one but will not be presumed in relation to an older child—see *O'Reilly* v. *Glavey* (1893) 32 L. R. (Ir.) 316 (Ex. Div.); *Farrelly* v. *Donegan* (1931) 65 I.L.T.R. 102 (Cir. Ct.); *Beetham* v. *James* [1937] 1 K. B. 527 (K.B.D.). See also *Murray* v. *Fitzgerald* [1906] 2 I.R. 254 (C.A.) where a brother successfully claimed damages for the seduction of his older sister. Both were over twenty one years. The brother managed the family farm while the sister performed the domestic chores around the house. In *Clements* v. *Boyd* (1894) 28 I.L.T.R. 44 (C. Ct.) and *Brennan* v. *Kearns* (1943) 77 I.L.T.R. 194 (Cir. Ct.) similar actions were unsuccessful. See further W. Binchy, 'Seduction and the Irish Law' (November 1977) Vol. 71 Gazette of the Incorporated Law Society of Ireland 187.
43. *Grinnel* v. *Wells* (1844), 7 Man & G. 1033; 135 E.R. 419, (Ct. of C.P.); *Beetham* v. *James, supra*.
44. *Hall* v. *Hollander* (1825), 4 B. & C. 660; 107 E.R. 1206, (K.B.) (Accident-son).
45. *Hedges* v. *Tagg* (1872), L.R. 7 Ex. 283, (Ct. of Ex.) *Gladney* v. *Murphy* (1890) 26 L.R. Ir. 651 (Q.B.D.); *Kearney* v. *M'Murray* (1894) 28 I.L.T.R. 148 (C. Ct.); *Barnes* v. *Fox* [1914] 2 I.R. 276 (C.A.). All these cases are concerned with the seduction of a girl and establish that for a parent to obtain damages for loss of services he must show a right to his daughter's services both at the time of the seduction and during her confinement. See however *Long* v. *Keightley* (1877) I.R. 11 C. L. 221 (Com. Pleas); *Connell* v. *Noonan* (1883) 17. I.L.T.R. 103 (C. Ct.) in which it is held that it is not necessary for a daughter to remain in the plaintiff's service during the confinement. See further 1877 I.L.T. & S.J. at pp. 402 and 428 where the case of *Long* v. *Keightley* is discussed.
46. *Dent* v. *Maguire* [1917] 2 I.R. 59 (Appeal).
47. *Terry* v. *Hutchinson* (1868), L.R. 3, Q.B. 599, (Q.B.).
48. *Ibid.*
49. *Beetham* v. *James, supra*.
50. *Peters* v. *Jones* [1914] 2 K.B. 781, (K.B.D.).
51. [1903] 2 I.R. 407, (K.B.D.) affirmed [1905], 2 I.R. 552, (Appeal), *Thompson* v. *Fitzpatrick* (1920) 54 I.L.T.R. 184 (K.B.D.); *O'Donnell* v. *Neely* (1940) 70 I.L.T.R. 120 (Cir. Ct.); see also *Peters* v. *Jones, supra; Beetham* v. *James, supra*.
52. See p. 210 *infra*.
53. *Lough* v. *Ward, supra*, (Young girl entered religious society without parental con-

of the services lost, which in the majority of cases is not very great, but may also be awarded as compensation for the damage done to the pride and honour of the parents. They may further include all reasonable and necessary expenses incurred as a consequence of the defendant's actions. Thus, if a baby is born as a result of the dependant's seduction, it has been held that the costs of maintaining such a child may be taken into account.[54] However, the behaviour of the parents[55] or the child[56] may be such as to mitigate damages, whilst the behaviour of the defendant may be such as to justify the award of exemplary damages as an indication of the court's disapproval of his conduct.[57]

PROPOSALS FOR REFORM

The case for reforming this area of the law has been extensively examined by the Law Reform Commission in three separate working papers.[58]

Working Paper No. 5

In its Working Paper No. 5 the Commission recommends that the action for harbouring a spouse be abolished, that the action for criminal conversation be replaced by a new family action for damages for adultery and that the action for enticement be retained as a family action for damages with certin amendments to the existing law. Both actions would have the following characteristics in common:[59]

(a) The actions would be available to either spouse for the benefit of members of the family unit (to be defined as comprising each spouse and the children, including adopted children and children to whom either spouse is in loco parentis).

(b) Damages could be awarded (in part or in whole) to the plaintiff's children and to the adulterous or enticed spouse, the court being required to assess the damages payable to each member of the family.

(c) The court would have a discretion as to the amount of the damages (if any) to be awarded to the plaintiff spouse where he or she has condoned or connived at or by wilful neglect or misconduct conduced to the adultery, in the case of an action for adultery, or the enticement, in the case of an action for enticement.

(d) In the action for damages for adultery a rebuttable presumption that the defendant was aware that the plaintiff's spouse was married would be introduced; the presumption would be rebutted only where the defendant showed that he or she neither knew nor had any reasonable

sent.)

54. *Flynn v. Connell* [1919] 2 I.R. 427, (K.B.D.).

55. *Beetham v. James, supra*, (unmarried parents cohabiting); see also *Reddie v. Scoolt* (1795), Peake 316; 170 E.R. 169 (Nisi Prius)—where it was held that a father who permitted a married man to make visits to his daughter, could not maintain an action against him for seduction.

56. *Verry v. Watkins* (1836), 7 Car. & P. 308; 173 E.R. 137, (Nisi Prius), (Child sexually promiscuous).

57. *Lough v. Ward, supra*.

58. The Law Relating to Criminal Conversation and the Enticement and Harbouring of a Spouse, The Law Reform Commission's Working Paper No. 5 (Dublin 1978); The Law Relating to Seduction and The Enticement and Harbouring of a Child, The Law Reform Commission's Working Paper No. 6 (Dublin 1979); The Law Relating to Loss of Consortium and Loss of Services of a Child; The Law Reform Commission's Working Paper No. 7 (Dublin (1979).

59. Working Paper No. 5, see pages 72 and 73.

cause to believe that the spouse was married.[60]

The Law Reform Commission's arguments in favour of retaining the action for enticement and for replacing the action for criminal conversation with an action for adultery as described above can be summarised as follows:

(1)   The law should "provide a buttress for stable marital relationships and stable family life" and the action for damages for adultery and the proposed amendments to the action for enticement would "effectively assist this purpose".[61]

(2)   The actions would deter persons from intruding into other people's marital relationships.[62]

(3)   The actions would give effect to public policy towards marriage as enunciated by the Constitutional Prohibition on Dissolution of Marriage and give practical effect to Article 41 of the Constitution in that it protects the privacy of family relations.[63]

(4)   Total abolition of the actions might lead to anti-social acts of revenge.[64]

(5)   The action serves the desirable policy end of giving the injured spouse necessary financial assistance in attempting to rear his or her children in what normally will have become a single parent family unit.[65]

It is difficult to support the Commission's reasoning. The following arguments can be made against its proposals:

(1)   If the law seeks, as it should, to buttress or assist marriages such actions are not an appropriate means to use, as they are only concerned with the symptoms and not the causes of marital breakdown. Moreover, the issuing of such proceedings could militate against a reconciliation between spouses whose marriage has run into temporary difficulties by driving a further wedge between the spouses. The law by permitting proceedings even when spouses continue to reside together may further destabilise marriages already at risk.

(2)   The State cannot by legislation compel spouses to be compatible and make marriages viable. Marriage is a relationship that can only function properly with the co-operation of both parties. When that co-operation breaks down, that relationship cannot be helped but can only be demeaned by such proceedings.

(3)   There is no evidence that the existing actions deter would-be adulterers and the Commission acknowledges that it is unlikely that the existence of a right of action is a major deterrent.[66]

(4)   The proposed actions have no relevance to the Constitutional prohibition on dissolution of marriage. The sole effect of the prohibition is that it prevents a spouse who is a party to a broken marriage from re-marrying.

(5)   The actions, rather than protecting a spouse's privacy, will provide spouses with an incentive to spy on each other if their marriage breaks down rather than deal realistically with the effects of breakdown. The principle

---

60. Logically a similar presumption should be introduced in the action for enticement.
61. Working Paper No. 5, pp. 56–57.
62. *Ibid*, pp. 53,67.
63. *Ibid*, pp. 53, 55, 66.
64. *Ibid*, p. 54.
65. *Ibid*, p. 55.
66. *Ibid*, pp. 53, 67, 71.

beneficiaries of the Commission's proposed actions will be private detectives.[67]

(6) The actions proposed are illogical. For example, why should the action for damages for adultery, be confined to adultery? In order to establish adultery in law a plaintiff's spouse must prove that the other spouse has engaged in voluntary sexual intercourse with a third party. Sexual intimacy falling short of adultery between a spouse and a third person can provide just as great a "threat" within the Commission's reasoning to a marriage, as can other extra marital sexual relationships e.g. a homosexual or lesbian relationship.

(7) There is an undue emphasis on adultery at a time when the law has already recognised that adultery is a symptom of marital breakdown (see for example the Family Law . . . Act, 1976, Sect. 5(3) and 6(4).[68]

(8) Logically the proposed action for adultery should lie against the plaintiff's spouse if the purpose of the action is to protect marriage. In many cases it is the "guilty spouse" who "makes the running". At the very least the defendant should have a right to counter claim against or seek a contribution from the adulterous spouse upon a claim being made against him.[69]

(9) There is no evidence that in other jurisdictions when similar actions have been abolished there has been an upsurge in "acts of revenge". It is stretching credibility to its limits to believe that a husband intent on assaulting a third person for committing adultery with his wife makes a rational decision as to whether he should physically attack or sue the offender.

(10) The actions provide a means whereby one spouse can blackmail the other into returning to the family home without the parties coming to terms with the cause of their marital difficulties. As a result, the future welfare of children of such spouses may be seriously jeopardized.

(11) The actions give the opportunity for claims of a "gold-digging" nature and provide unscrupulous spouses with a means of blackmailing third parties.[70] For example, even if an action is spurious, the publicity attached to it could ruin a defendant's reputation and put his marriage at risk. Thus, many defendants may prefer to settle such actions rather than withstand the pressures generated by a court hearing.

(12) The financial assistance given to single parent families would produce further anomolies. For example, a husband whose wife commits adultery could receive such assistance whereas a battered and deserted wife living alone with her children could not.

(13) The Commission proposes that there should be "a right of compensation for the children for injury to the family and for the mental and emotional distress to which they have been subjected". It is submitted that this proposal, if implemented, will encourage spouses to embroil children in marital conflicts rather than discourage such behaviour, as the courts do at present.

It is submitted that the arguments against the actions proposed by the Commission are overwhelming and that the actions for criminal conversation, enticement and harbouring should simply be abolished and not replaced. The

---

67. And possibly lawyers.
68. See Working Paper No. 5, pp. 50–52.
69. *Ibid*, p. 49.
70. *Ibid*, p. 49.

Family Law Bill, 1981, as initiated before the Dáil on 20 February 1981, proposes the total abolition of all three actions and contains no provisions for their replacement. Under the terms of the Bill, upon its enactment "no action shall lie for criminal conversation, for inducing a spouse to leave or remain apart from the other spouse or for harbouring a spouse". This provision will not, however, effect any action commenced before the Bill's enactment.

Working Paper No. 6

In its working paper No. 6 the Law Reform Commission recommends that the existing action for seduction of a child should be abolished and replaced by a single family action for seduction. It further recommends that the actions for enticing and harbouring a child be retained, subject to certain amendments. All these actions would have the following characteristics in common:[71]

(a) The actions would be in the nature of single family actions for the benefit of all members of the family unit to be defined as comprising the parents and their children[72] and the requirement of a service relationship would be abolished.

(b) The child's right of action would be merged in the family action, allowing her to be awarded damages where the circumstances so warrant.

(c) The actions would be limited to cases of unmarried children under eighteen years of age and in the case of an action for seduction, the child must not be married either at the time of the seduction or at the time of the court hearing[73] and the seduction must have resulted in pregnancy.

(d) The present law as to damages would be retained and in the case of actions for enticement and harbouring, in assessing damages or granting discretionary relief, the court would be required to have regard to the welfare of the child as the paramount consideration. The Commission gives no explanation as to why this requirement should not apply in an action for seduction.

It is submitted that the Commission's recommendations are misconceived and that the actions for seduction, harbouring and enticement of children should simply be abolished. If a parent does not wish a child to associate with a third party, it is submitted that the welfare of the child can be better protected by bringing wardship proceedings or proceedings under section 11 of the Guardianship of Infants Act, 1964. Moreover, if a baby is born as a result of such an association, the mother may bring affiliation proceedings. Undoubtedly, a number of reforms are required in our affiliation laws but the Commission did not deal with that area of law in its recommendations.

In the case of the action for seduction, the Commission itself acknowledges that in countries where it is available "it has no significant deterrent effect on behaviour".[74] Moreover, there is no evidence that the existing actions that are

---

71. Working Paper No. 6, see pages 73–75.
72. Children are said to include legally adopted children and children to whom either parent is in loco parentis.
73. Thus if a child marries prior to the action being heard damages could not be obtained. It would be more logical if this bar merely applied if the child married the alleged seducer. Such a provision could however, give rise to further problems for example, it could encourage so called "shot gun" marriages.

available in this country have had any deterrent effect whatsoever. Indeed the rarity of such actions is indicative of their irrelevance to modern social relationships.

The Law Reform Commission in this Working Paper and in Working Paper No. 5 has exhibited a total lack of understanding of intra-family relationships. The seduction of a young girl or the departure from home of a young child is in the great majority of instances a symptom or consequence of a deep family malaise. The Commission's proposals merely deal with some of the symptoms and fail to suggest a method to help parents come to terms with or understand the causes. (For example, by the establishment of a statutory family counselling service funded by central government). In practice the proceedings proposed could aggravate rather than ameliorate family difficulties by further alienating from the family the child in respect of whom such proceedings are instituted.

Working Paper No. 7

In its Working Paper No. 7 the Law Reform Commission discusses the existing actions for loss of the services and society of a wife and for loss of the services of a child. It recommends that these actions be replaced by a single family action for the benefit of all members of the family unit residing together. The family unit would be defined as being parents and their children.[75] Damages which would be without monetary limitation (i.e. at large) would cover

(a) All reasonable expenses and other financial losses incurred by the members of the family of the victim;

(b) Mental distress resulting to the members of the family;

(c) Damage to the continuity, stability and quality of the relationships between members of the family.[76]

The Commission further recommends that only one action should be capable of being brought and the court should be empowered to award such damages to each member of the family unit as it considers fit. It also states that the defence of contributory negligence should be available to the defendant in such proceedings.[77]

These recommendations by the Commission are to be welcomed. The new proposed action would remove the medieval foundations on which the present law is based by extending the action to all members of the family unit and no longer requiring proof of a service relationship. It would end artificial distinctions between total and partial loss of consortium and concentrate on the consequences to the family unit of an injury to one of its members. It would also remove the existing legal anomaly whereby damages for mental distress can be obtained for the death of a spouse, child, or parent as a result of a deliberate or negligent act by a third party but cannot be obtained for their permanent incapacitation.

The expenses incurred by a family as a result of one of its members being wrongfully injured can give rise to considerable hardship. The proposed action would enable members of the family to recover reasonable expenses properly incurred in consequence of the injury. Such expenses could include loss of earnings, costs of visits to hospital and costs of any domestic help required as a

74. Working Paper No. 6, p. 58.
75. Children are said to include legally adopted children and children to whom either parent is in loco parentis.
76. Working Paper No. 7, p. 44.
77. *Ibid.*

result of such injury.[78]

DEATH OF A RELATION

The case of *Baker* v. *Bolton*[79] in 1808 layed down that at common law "in a civil court the death of a human being could not be complained of as an injury".

Thus, whereas a husband could recover damages for the loss of his wife's consortium and services if she suffered an injury at the hands of another, if the injury caused her death he could not recover for the permanent deprivation suffered as a result of her death. The legislature intervened to ameliorate the position by the passing of the Fatal Accidents Acts. The present law is set down in Part IV of the Civil Liability Act, 1961.[80] By its provision dependants of a deceased may recover damages where his death is caused by the wrongful act of another, if the act was such as would have entitled the deceased, but for his death, to maintain an action and recover damages against the other.[81] If during the deceased's lifetime he has accepted full compensation from the defendant in respect of the injury no action can be brought as a result of his death.[82]

The relatives whose interests are protected are the wife, father, mother, grandfather, grandmother, stepfather, stepmother, son, daughter, grandson, granddaughter, stepson, stepdaughter, brother, sister, half-brother and half-sister. An adopted child is to be considered as the legitimate child of the adopter or adopters, an illegitimate person, if not adopted by another, is to be considered as the legitimate child of his mother and reputed father,[83] and a person *in loco parentis* to another is considered as the parent of that other.[84]

In order for any of the above persons to recover damages it must be shown that they suffered injury or mental distress as a result of the deceased's death. Only one action may be brought against the same person and such action is to be for the benefit of all the dependants.[85]

The action is to be brought by the deceased's personal representative but if at the expiration of 6 months from the death there is no personal representative, or no action has been brought by a personal representative, all or any of the dependants may sue. The plaintiff must provide the defendant with particulars of the person or persons for whom and on whose behalf the action is brought, and of the nature of the claim in respect of which damages are sought.[86] The action must commence within 3 years after the death.[87]

---

78. Earnings lost or expenditure incurred by a spouse or parent as a result of a tort committed against the other spouse or against his child may be recoverable in an action brought by the injured spouse—*Cunningham v. Harrison* [1973] Q.B. 942 (C.A.)—or the injured child—*Donnelly v. Joyce* [1974] Q.B. 454 (C.A.); *Taylor v. Bristol Omnibus Co. Ltd.* [1975] 2 All E.R. 1107 (C.A.). In the first case it was suggested that the plaintiff held any such damages recovered for the spouse who rendered the services—per Lord Denning, M.R. at p. 952.

79. (1808) 1 Camp 493, (Assize); 170 E.R. 1033.

80. See "Some Aspects of Damages Under the Civil Liability Acts of 1961 and 1964" Michael Knight, 1966, 1 I.J. (n.s.) 35; see also Article in (1962–63) Vol. XXVIII–XXIX, I.J. 30, "Assessment of damages in Fatal Injury cases" by V. T. H. Delany.

81. Sec. 48 (1); also see *Malone v. C.I.E.* (1953), 94 I.L.T.R. 179, (S.C.).

82. See *Swords v. St. Patrick's Copper Mines Ltd.* [1965], Ir. Jur. Rep., 63, (S.C.). (The Workmens Compensation Acts, 1934–55 therein referred to, were repealed by the Social Welfare (Occupational Injuries) Act, 1966).

83. See *O'Mahoney v. E.S.B.* (1959), 93 I.L.T.R. 4, (S.C.).

84. Sect. 47 (1) and (2); see also *Waters v. Cruikshank* [1967] I.R. 378, (1963), 103 I.L. T.R. 129, (S.C.).

85. See *Swords v. St. Patrick's Copper Mines Ltd., supra*.

86. Sect. 48 (5).

87. Sect. 48 (6).

Assessment of Damages[88]

Damages are recoverable for injury, mental distress and for funeral and other expenses.

I. Injury: Injury is measured solely by reference to the financial loss suffered by a claimant as a result of a person's death. The loss is estimated by reference to the actual pecuniary loss incurred, together with any reasonable expectation of benefit (either money or money's worth) the claimant would have had, whether as of right or otherwise, if the life had continued,[89] set off against any pecuniary benefit and any reasonable expectation of such benefit the claimant has as a result of the death.[90] The court requires information showing as accurately as possible the net pecuniary loss sustained by each dependant in consequence of the death. The courts have constantly stated that there must be affirmative evidence of the extent of the loss. Damages will not be awarded merely on a basis of guesswork.[91] Any damages given are purely by way of compensation and are not of a punitive nature. If the deceased was guilty of contributory negligence, the damages awarded may be reduced proportionately.[92]

II. Mental Distress: Since the enactment of the 1961 Act[93] "reasonable compensation"[94] has been recoverable for mental distress caused to a dependant as a result of a death. Prior to the coming into force of the Act no such damages were recoverable.[95] Whereas the amount of damages for "injury" suffered by a dependant may be assessed by a jury, damages for purely mental distress are to be assessed solely by a judge. Moreover the total amount awarded for such distress may not exceed one thousand pounds.

In determining the amount of damages to be awarded Walsh J. stated in *Dowling* v. *Jedos Ltd.*[96]

"The correct approach is for the judge to make a notional award in the sum which he would on the evidence be justified in giving to each of the

88. See Sect. 49 of Act.
89. *Gallagher v. E.S.B.* [1933], I.R. 558, (S.C.); *Horgan v. Buckley* (No. 1) [1938] I.R. 115, (S.C.); *Byrne v. Houlihan and Ano.* [1966], I.R. 274, (S.C.). *Murphy v. Cronin* [1966] I.R. 699 (S.C.) *O'Sullivan v. C.I.E.* [1978] I.R. 409 (H.C., S.C.).
90. *Byrne v. Houlihan and Ano., supra; Murphy v. Cronin, supra; O'Sullivan v. C.I.E., supra.*
91. *Hull v. Great Northern Railway Co. of Ireland* (1890), 26L.R. Ir. 289, (Ex. Div); *Appelbe v. West Cork Board of Health* [1929], 1 I.R. 107, (S.C.); *Horgan v. Buckley, supra; Gallagher v. E.S.B., supra; Byrne v. Houlihan, supra.*
92. *McCarthy v. Walsh* [1965] I.R. 246, (S.C.); *Murphy v. Cronin, supra.*
93. Now see Civil Liability (Amendment) Act, 1964.
94. See *McCarthy v. Walsh, supra,* on the meaning of reasonable compensation and for criticism by Lavery J. of the £1,000, limit put on such damages. The Minister for Justice at the time of the passing of the 1964 Act, Mr. Haughey, explained that the reason for the limitation to £1,000, was that damages for mental distress were new to the law. He promised that the figure would be reviewed from time to time with regard to the fall in the value of money—see Seanad Debates Vol. 57, col. 1391. See however, Dáil Debates Vol. 282, Col. 879 (June 1975). The then Minister for Justice Mr. Cooney in answer to a question asking whether he will increase the present maximum of £1,000 stated "The limit of £1,000 . . . was fixed on the basis that it contained a substantial allowance for future inflation. I have no proposals at present for the introduction of legislation that would provide for an increase in the limit". In answer to supplementary questions arising out of the reply the Minister stated that he was not aware that the courts felt their hands tied by being limited in the amount they can award for mental distress. On this see comments of Lavery J., *supra.* The Courts Bill, 1980, proposes to increase the maximum that can be awarded to £5,000.
95. *Gallagher v. E.S.B., supra.*
96. (March 1977) unreported (S.C.).

persons who suffered mental distress without taking into account at that stage that the maximum possible total is £1,000. When the notional figures have been arrived at and if their total exceeds £1,000 then as the ratio between them is already known they should be scaled down proportionately so that the total is reduced to £1,000."

As for the meaning of mental distress, Lavery J. in *Cubbard* v. *Rederij Viribus Unitis & Another*[97] stated

"Mental distress is something very different from being moved or affected by the death of a relative. Everyone is moved or affected by the death of a relative or a friend . . . The view I take of the section is that it is not intended to provide monetary compensation for every member of the family. If it were there would be no end to it. It would mean that there would be damages recovered by a group of people that ordinarily would be very large. I think the section must be considered in the light of some real intense feeling or being grievously affected by the death."

In *McCarthy* v. *Walsh*[98] it was decided that the fact that a relative could not show a financial loss arising from the death entitling him to damages for "injury", was not a bar to his obtaining damages for mental distress.

The Courts Bill, 1980, as initiated, proposes to increase the total amount that can be awarded for mental distress to £5,000.

III. Funeral & Other Expenses: Damages may also be recovered for funeral and other expenses incurred by the deceased, the dependants or personal representative by reason of the wrongful act. "Other expenses" could include medical expenses incurred before death and wages or salaries lost by a dependant as a result of the deceased's injury and subsequent death.

Finally section 50 of the Act provides that in assessing damages no account is to be taken of any sum payable on the death of the deceased under any insurance contract, or any pension, gratuity or other like benefit payable under statute or otherwise in consequence of the death of the deceased.[99] However, in assessing damages for funeral expenses account is to be taken of any death benefit granted under Part II Chapter 5 of the Social Welfare Consolidation Act, 1981, in respect of such expenses.[100] Finally the rights conferred by Part IV of the 1961 Act are in addition to the rights conferred by Part II of the Act, under which certain causes of action vested in the deceased at the time of his death survive for the benefit of his estate.[101] There cannot, however, be a duplication of damages.

97. (1965), 100 I.L.T.R. 40, at p. 40, (H.C.).
98. *Supra.*
99. See, for example, *Murphy* v. *Cronin supra*—sum payable to widow from deceased husband's superannuation fund a "gratuity" and not to be taken into account in assessing damages.
100. See Sect. 68 of 1981 Act: See also article entitled "The Occupational Injuries Act: Some Reflections" by J. Casey, (1969), 4 I.J. (n.s.) 234 (particularly pages 242–246). See article by M. Knight, *supra*; see also "Ten years of the Civil Liability Act", by Earnán P. de Blaghd, (1972) 106 I.L.T. & S.J. 206, 211, 219.
101. See Part II of the 1961 Act, Sects. 6–10. Under Sect. 8 certain causes of action subsisting against the deceased at the time of his death also survive against his estate.

MARRIAGE AND THE LAW AS TO FAMILY PLANNING

The decision of the Supreme Court in *McGee* v. *Attorney General*[1] recognised the existence of a constitutional right to marital privacy which conferred on married couples a right to obtain contraceptives for their own use. The Health (Family Planning) Act, 1979, which came into operation on the 1st November 1980[2] makes provision for family planning services and for the availability, importation, manufacture, sale, and advertisement of contraceptives. It also amends the grounds upon which the Censorship Board may ban a publication.

Family Planning Service: A family planning service is defined in the Act as a service for the provision of information, instruction, advice, or consultation in relation to one or more of the following: (a) family planning; (b) contraception; (c) contraceptives[3]. A family planning service as defined does not include within its functions the provision or supply of contraceptives.

The Act imposes a duty on the Minister for Health to secure the orderly organisation of family planning services, and to provide a comprehensive natural family planning service, that is, one that is concerned with methods of family planning that do not involve the use of contraceptives.[4]

A Health Board is bound by the regulations made under the Act to make available "a family planning service",[5] but it appears that if a Health Board makes available a natural family planning service alone, this will be sufficient for the purpose of the duty imposed on it by the Act. A Health Board itself does not have to provide the service. It may make such a service available by way of an arrangement with another person or body.[6] A family planning service established by a person other than a Health Board and which gives advice or instruction about contraceptives can only operate with the consent of the Minister for Health and any such service must operate under "the general direction, and supervision" of a doctor.[7] However, a natural family planning service can operate without the necessity of obtaining any such consent.[8] Moreover, there is a statutory obligation imposed on a Health Board or any other person providing a service that gives advice as to the use of contraceptives also to give advice about methods of family planning that do not involve the use of contraceptives. The Act does not, however, prevent a doctor "in his clinical relations with a patient" or a chemist selling contraceptives from giving advice as to their use.[9]

The Sale of Contraceptives

The Act defines a contraceptive as "any appliance, instrument, drug, preparation or thing, designed, prepared, or intended to prevent pregnancy resulting from sexual intercourse between human beings".[10] Under section 4 of the Act contraceptives can only be supplied by way of sale, and the only person authorised to sell contraceptives to the general public is a chemist "who keeps open shop

---

1. [1974] I.R. 284; (1973) 109 I.L.T.R. 29 (S.C.). see p. 9 *ante*.
2. See the Health (Family Planning) Act, 1979, (Commencement Order) 1980 (S.I. No. 247 of 1980).
3. Health (Family Planning) Act, 1979, section 1.
4. *Ibid*, section 2.
5. Health (Family Planning) Regulations, 1980 (S.I. No. 248 of 1980) para 3 (1).
6. *Ibid*, para 3 (2).
7. Health (Family Planning) Act, 1979, section 3 (3) and 3 (4) see also Health (Family Planning) Regulations, 1980, *supra*, para 4.
8. Health (Family Planning) Act, 1979, section 3 (2).
9. *Ibid*, section 3 (6).
10. *Ibid*, section 1.

for the compounding and dispensing of medical prescriptions in accordance with the provisions of the Pharmacy Acts, 1875 to 1977" or his servant or agent. Moreover, the sale must be made "at the place where he keeps open shop" or in connection with the service provided by the chemist "in keeping such open shop at a place where family planning services are made available".[11] The sale of contraceptives is restricted to the person named in a doctor's written prescription or authorisation, and prior to issuing any such prescription or authorisation a doctor must be satisfied that the person seeking it, requires contraceptives "for the purpose bone fide, of family planning, or for adequate medical reasons and in appropriate circumstances".[12] Where a prescription indicates that contraceptives are to be given for the purposes of the Act, the section states "it shall be conclusively presumed" that the person named in it is a person who in the opinion of the doctor required contraceptives for the purpose or reasons stated in the Act.[13] A prescription or authorisation can be issued for any period up to one year, but its validity cannot extend beyond one year.[14] Section 4 also permits a licensed importer or manufacturer to sell contraceptives to a chemist, his servant or agent.[15]

Paragraph 6 of the regulations provides that a sale of contraceptives under section 4 "shall not be made unless the quantity sought to be purchased is not such as to indicate they are not solely for the purchaser's own use". Neither the Act nor the regulations provide any criteria by which a chemist can determine whether "the quantity sought" is for a purchaser's own use. Moreover, this regulation applies to all sales of contraceptives under section 4 of the Act, and it appears that an importer or manufacturer selling contraceptives to a chemist for re-sale to the general public is bound by it!

Importation and manufacture of contraceptives: Under section 5 of the Act a person may import contraceptives if "they are part of his personal luggage accompanying him when he is entering the State, and if their quantity is not such as to indicate they are not solely for his own use".[16] As in the case of paragraph 6 of the regulations, the Act lays down no test for determining whether contraceptives imported are solely for a person's own use. Moreover, a person who so imports contraceptives does not require a prescription. The section also provides for the granting of licenses for the importation of contraceptives by chemists or by persons for sale to chemists. The Act does not permit a person to import contraceptives by post for his own use.

Section 6 of the Act provides for the granting of licenses for the manufacture of contraceptives by chemists or by other persons for sale to chemists.

Advertisements and publications: Advertisements concerning contraception or contraceptives may only be published or displayed in relation to family planning services authorised under the Act, and in the case of a family planning service provided by a person other than a Health Board, the publication or display must accord with any consent given by the Minister to operate a family planning service that provides information about the use of contraceptives.

An advertisement relating to contraception or contraceptives can also be

11. *Ibid*, section 4 (1) (b) (i).
12. *Ibid*, see sections 4 (1) (b) (ii). and section 4 (2).
13. *Ibid*, section 4, (2).
14. Health (Family Planning) Regulations, 1980, para 5 (1) (e).
15. Health (Family Planning) Act, 1979, section 4 (1) (c).
16. *Ibid*, section 5 (1) (a).

published for the purpose of providing information for

(i) Persons providing family planning services in accordance with the Act;

(ii) Registered medical practitioners;

(iii) Registered pharmaceutical chemists and registered dispensing chemists and druggists;

(iv) Persons registered in the Register of Nurses;

(v) Persons who are in training with a view to becoming a member of any of the classes of persons specified in (ii) to (iv).

Publication of advertisements may also be arranged by or on behalf of the Minister for Health.[17]

Section 12(3) of the Act removes the powers conferred on the Censorship Board by the Censorship of Publications Act, 1946, to ban a book or a periodical publication on the ground that it advocates or advocated the unnatural prevention of conception. A book may now only be banned if the Board is of the opinion that

(a) it is indecent or obscene, or

(b) it advocates the procurement of abortion or miscarriage or the use of any kind of method, treatment or appliance for the purpose of such procurement.

Periodical publications may be banned on similar grounds.[18]

Abortion: Section 10 provides that nothing in the Act shall be construed as authorising the procuring of abortion or the doing of any other thing which is prohibited under Sections 58 or 59 of the Offences Against the Persons Act, 1861 (which sections prohibit the administering of drugs or the use of instruments to procure abortion or the supplying of drugs or instruments to procure abortion) or sale, importation to the State, manufacture, advertising or display of abortifacients.

Consciencious objectors: Section 11 provides that nothing in the Act shall be construed as obliging any person to take part in the provision of a family planning service, the giving of prescriptions or authorisations for the purposes of the

---

17. See Health (Family Planning) Act, 1979, sections 7, 12 (1) and 12 (2) and the Health (Family Planning) Regulations, 1980, para 8.

18. See further *Irish Family Planning Association Ltd and Anor. v. Ryan and Ors.* [1979] I.R. 295 (S.C.) in which an order made by the Censorship Board banning a book entitled *Family Planning*, which contained information about different methods of contraception, on the ground that it was "indecent or obscene" was declared null and void. Section 6 of the Censorship of Publications Act, 1946, conferred power on the Board when examining a book to communicate with its author, editor or publisher and to take into account any representations made in relation to the book. The Board did not communicate with the plaintiffs prior to making its order and from evidence given by the secretary in the High Court it was clear that prior to the date of these proceedings it had never so communicated prior to banning a book or periodical publication. The Supreme Court held that the Board had acted "unjustly" and that prior to banning the book it should have communicated with the plaintiffs who were responsible for its publication. Its failure to do so was a violation of the right to natural justice and in particular, the obligation imposed on the Board to observe the rule of Audi Alteram Partem. The Court also expressed considerable doubt as to whether the book could have been lawfully banned as being "indecent and obscene" had the Board correctly observed the duty imposed on it. O'Higgins C.J. in his judgement (at p. 315) stated that "Far from being pornographic or lewdly commercial or pandering to prurient curiosity, it simply aimed at giving basic factual information on a delicate topic as to which there is genuine concern."

Act or the sale, importation into the State, manufacture, advertising or display of contraceptives.

Offences: Contravention of the provisions contained in the Act or the regulations made under it constitutes a criminal offence, punishable in the first instance, by a fine not exceeding £500 and/or imprisonment for a term not exceeding six months. A second or subsequent offence renders a person liable to a fine not exceeding £5,000 together with, in the case of a continuing offence, a fine not exceeding £250 each day or part of a day for which the offence is continued and/or to a term of imprisonment not exceeding 12 months.[19]

Commentary: The Act does not confine the availability of contraceptives to single persons as has been suggested by some commentators. It is clear that any person, single or married, may import contraceptives for his own use in his luggage under the provisions of section 5 of the Act. It is also clear that a doctor may give a prescription for contraceptives to a single person, if he is satisfied that the contraceptives are required for the purpose, bone fide, of family planning or for adequate medical reasons and in appropriate circumstances. Moreover, it appears that if such a prescription is issued it is not open to a chemist to challenge the doctor's conclusions. A chemist may however require proof of identity from the person tendering the prescription.

Doubt must exist as to the constitutional validity of the provisions of the Act concerned with the supply of contraceptives. In the context of married couples, it is arguable that the Act is an invasion of the constitutional right to marital privacy first enunciated in the McGee case. It is worth noting that it again renders it unlawful for a spouse to import contraceptives by post for his or her own use. In *McGee* v. *The Attorney General* it was the constitutional right of Mrs. McGee to import contraceptives by post for her own use that was asserted by the Supreme Court.[20] It is submitted that a married couple who wish to obtain contraceptives in this way, without the necessity of discussing matters concerning their private sexual relations with a doctor in order to obtain a prescription or authorisation for contraceptives, would have good grounds for asserting that the Act is unconstitutional in that it constitutes an invasion of the right to marital privacy and that it also fails to protect, defend or vindicate the constitutional right of a married couple to determine how many children they wish to have without outside interference.[21]

MARRIAGE AND THE LAWS OF EVIDENCE

At common law a party's spouse was generally incompetent as a witness for, or against him, in both civil and criminal proceedings. The only important exception to this rule arose in the case of a criminal charge involving personal violence by one spouse against the other. The incompetence of a spouse resulted from fear as to the trustworthiness of the evidence of a spouse and also out of recognition that undesirable consequences might follow if one spouse was compelled to give evidence against the other and perhaps forced to break matrimonial confidences.

The rule as to the incompetency of spouses in civil cases was abolished by the Evidence Amendment Act, 1853, which rendered spouses competent and compellable witnesses for any party to an action. The position in criminal cases was

19. Health (Family Planning) Act, 1979, section 14.
20. See p. 10 *ante*.
21. *Ibid*.

changed by the Criminal Justice (Evidence) Act, 1924. By section 1(e) the spouse of a person charged may be called as a witness upon the application of the person charged. Whereas such a spouse is now competent to give evidence he/she is not generally compellable.

A spouse is normally an incompetent witness for the prosecution. There are, however a number of exceptions to this rule. Section 4(1) of the 1924 Act states that the spouse of a person charged with an offence under any of the enactments listed in the Schedule of that Act may be called as a witness, either for the prosecution or defence, without the consent of the person charged.[22] A spouse while competent is not compellable in such proceedings. The Act did not affect the case where the spouse of a person charged with an offence could at common law be called as a witness without the consent of that person.[23] The principle example of the latter that arises in practice is a charge involving personal violence by one spouse against the other. Until recently the balance of authority favoured the view that under common law a person who suffered violence at the hands of their spouse was not only a competent but also a compellable witness for the prosecution. However, in a recent English decision the House of Lords held that a wife is not a compellable witness against her husband in such proceedings.[24]

By virtue of section 1(d) of the 1924 Act and section 3 of the Act of 1853, neither a husband nor a wife are compellable to disclose in either criminal or civil proceedings any communication made by one to the other during the marriage. This privilege as to revealing the content of a communication between spouses is the property of the spouse being questioned in the witness box. Thus, if the spouse being questioned wishes to reveal what the other spouse has previously communicated, there is nothing the other spouse can do, to prevent disclosure. The communication itself is not privileged and if a spouse refuses to reveal its contents, there is nothing to prevent a third party giving evidence as to what information it contained.[25] This of course is subject to the rules as to

22. Since the coming into force of the 1924 Act the enactments referred to in the Schedule have been added to and some have been repealed and replaced. The offences now included in the Schedule under which a wife can give evidence for the prosecution include offences under the Prevention of Cruelty to Children Act, 1904; offences under Sects. 48, 52, 53, 54, so far as unrepealed, and 55 of the Offences Against the Person Act, 1861, (see Criminal Law Amendment Act, 1935, Sects. 6 & 20); see also Sect. 9 of Married Women's Status Act, 1957, repealing and replacing Sects. 12 & 16 of Married Women's Property Act, 1882.

Also see *McGonagle v. McGonagle* [1951] I.R. 123, (S.C.); [1952] Ir. Jur. Rep. 13, (S.C.).. The appellant was convicted for that having the custody of a child aged six years he did "wilfully neglect said child in a manner likely to cause said child unnecessary suffering and injury to its health" contrary to Sect. 12 of the 1908 Children Act. By Sect. 1 it is provided that in any proceedings against any person for an offence under Part II of the Act (including Sect. 12) or for any offences mentioned in the First Schedule of the Act, a spouse of the accused shall be competent but not compellable to give evidence. It was contended that as the 1908 Act was not listed in the Schedule to the 1924 Act that Sect. 133 (28) was repealed and the spouse of the accused was not a competent witness. The Supreme Court noted that *per incuriam* the legislature overlooked the fact that a great deal of the Act of 1904 had been repealed and re-enacted in the Act of 1908; that one of the sections repealed in 1904 Act was Sect. 1 whereby a spouse of an accused may be called as a prosecution witness without the consent of the party charged; that provisions substantially the same as those in Sect. 1 were re-enacted in Sect. 12 of the 1908 Act, and that as a consequence there was a clear intention expressed by the legislature that a spouse of the accused should be a competent witness and this provision of the 1908 Act was unaffected by the Act of 1924. See also p. 253 *et seq.*

23. Sect. 4 (2). The Act also did not affect the Evidence Act, 1877, under which a spouse is both competent and compellable as a witness for a limited class of offence.

24. *Hoskyn v. Metropolitan Police Commissioner* [1978] 2 W.L.R. 695; [1978] 2 All E. R. 136 (H. L.). See also (1978) 94 L. Q. R. 321.

25. *Rumping v. D.P.P.* [1964] A.C. 814, 822, (H.L.), where Sect. 1(d) of the English

inadmissibility of hearsay evidence.

Finally, in *E.R. v. J.R.*[25a] it was held that communications made by spouses consulting with a priest as marriage counsellor are privileged, "that the privilege is that of the people consulting" and that if both spouses have participated "the privilege must be waived clearly and unequivocally by both" before evidence can be given in matrimonial proceedings revealing the content of the communications. The court expressly reserved the question as to whether the privilege can arise where the counsellor is not a minister of religion.[25b]

MARRIAGE AND THE CRIMINAL LAW

1. Bigamy[26]

Bigamy is the only crime that cannot be committed by an unmarried person.[27] Originally it was only an ecclesiastical offence but it was declared to be a capital felony by statute in 1603.[28] The present law is contained in section 57 of the Offences Against the Person Act, 1861. Bigamy is committed when a person who is a party to a valid subsisting marriage goes through a ceremony of marriage with another. It is a defence to a charge of bigamy that the first marriage was void or voidable and has been validly annulled by the civil courts,[29] or that it has been validly dissolved.[30] It is no defence to such a charge to show that the first marriage was not recognised by or has been annulled by a Matrimonial Tribunal of the Roman Catholic Church.[31] Thus, where a Roman Catholic, having been told that her marriage in a Registry Office was regarded as having no effect according to church law, went through a ceremony of marriage with another man in a Roman Catholic church, she was convicted of bigamy.[32]

A defence to the charge is also afforded by an accused proving that the first spouse has been continuously absent for seven years and has not been known by the accused to be living within that time. Such absence for seven years merely provides a defence to a charge of bigamy and does not dissolve the first marriage. Thus if the first spouse is alive, even though an accused may be held to be innocent of bigamy, his "second marriage" is still a complete nullity. It is also a defence that the accused believed on reasonable grounds that his or her spouse was dead, although he or she has not been absent for seven years;[33] or that his

---

Criminal (Evidence) Act, 1898 was discussed. This section corresponds to Sect. 1 (d) of the Irish Act of 1924.

25a. (February 1981) unreported (H.C.).

25b. See also *Cook v. Carroll* [1945] I.R. 515 (H.C.). In *E.R. v. J.R., supra*, Carroll J. stated "confidential marriage counselling . . . is protection of the most practical kind . . . a guarantee of confidentiality which will not be breached by giving evidence in court is an important element in building up confidence . . . The family as such, i.e. both parents and children, benefit by successful counselling. Therefore . . . any benefit which could be gained in litigation by having the evidence available does not outweight the possible injury to the relationship if disclosure can be compelled." It is submitted that the privilege will be extended by the courts to apply to marriage counsellors who are not ministers of religion. The "right to marital privacy" first enunciated in *McGee v. A.-G.* [1974] I.R. 284 (S.C.) may also be utilised by the courts in this context.

26. For a more detailed discussion of the criminal law as to Bigamy see Smith & Hogan *Criminal Law*, 4th (London, Butterworths, 1978) Ch. 18.

27. An unmarried person can of course be convicted as an accessory or for aiding and abetting.

28. 1 Jac 1, c.11.

29. See Chapter 5.

30. See Chapter 10.

31. *People (A.-G.) v. Hunt* (1945), 80 I.L.T.R. & S.J. 19, per Haugh J., (C.C.C.); *People (A.-G) v. Ballins* [1964] Ir. Jur. Rep. 14 (Cir. Ct.).

32. *People (A.-G.) v. Ballins, supra*.

33. *R. v. Tolson* (1889), 23 Q.B.D. 68, (C.C.R.).

first marriage was void[34] or that his first marriage was dissolved.[35]

2. Coercion

There is a rebuttable presumption of law that a misdemeanour or a felony, other than treason or murder committed by a wife in the presence of her husband is committed under his coercion or duress. It is for the prosecution to rebute this presumption.[36]

3. Conspiracy

Arising out of the notion of the unity of husband and wife, spouses cannot be convicted of conspiring together. Both can, however, be charged with conspiring with other people.[37]

4. Rape

By marriage a wife implicitly consents to having sexual intercourse with her husband. He cannot be convicted of raping her during the subsistence of the marriage, even if he forces her to have sexual relations with him against her will. But if she obtains a divorce *a mensa et thoro* or there is a separation agreement binding the spouses, her implied consent is withdrawn, and he may be liable to a charge of rape.[38] Moreover, if a husband undertakes to a court not to "assault, molest or interfere with his wife" he may be charged with raping her.[39] It is to be assumed that the courts will hold that a husband can be convicted of raping his wife if he has been barred by court order from entering the place in which his wife is residing under sect. 22 of the Family Law . . . Act 1976. Even though a husband has a right to marital intercourse, he is not entitled to use force or violence, for the purpose of exercising that right. If he does so he may render himself liable to other criminal charges such as assault.[40] Moreover the use of undue force may enable a wife petition for a divorce *a mensa et thoro* on the ground of cruelty or obtain a barring order under section 22 of the 1976 Act.

5. Larceny

At common law neither spouse could steal from the other. This rule was

34. *R. v. King* [1964], 1 Q.B. 285, (C.C.A.).
35. *R. v. Gould* [1968], 2 Q.B. 65; [1968] 1 All E.R. 849, (C.A.). This case overruled *R. v. Wheat and Stocks* [1921], 2 K.B. 119, (C.C.A.), in England which regarded bigamy as an offence of strict liability. Despite a *dicta* of Kenny J. in *Counihan v. Counihan* (July 1973), (H.C.), unreported, citing *Wheat & Stocks* as being the law, it is submitted that *Gould* will be followed in Ireland.
36. G. Williams, *Criminal Law: The General Part*, 2nd. ed. (Stevens & Sons Ltd., London, 1961) Section 249. See particularly *R. v. Caroubi* (1912) 7 Cr. App. Rep. 149 (C.C.A.); *R. v. Smith* (1916) 12 Cr. App. Rep. 42 (C.C.A.); *R. v. Torpey* (1871) 12 Cox C.C. 45 (C.C.C.); see also *R. v. Hallet* (1911) 45 I.L.T.R. 85 (K.B.D.) (the headnote to this report is misleading); *The People v. Murray* [1977] I.R. 360 (C.C.A.) (S.C.)—see judgement of O'Higgins C.J. in Court of Criminal Appeal at p. 367.
37. *Mawji v. R.* [1957] A.C. 126; [1957] 1 All E.R. 385, (P.C.) See Smith & Hogan *Criminal Law*, 3rd edition, p. 180, (Butterworths, London 1973). See also *Midland Bank Trust Co. Ltd. v. Green* [1979] 2 W.L.R. 594 (Ch D); F. Graham Glover, 'Conspiracy as between husband and wife (1979) 9 Fam. Law 181.
38. *R. v. Clarence* (1888), 22 Q.B.D. (C.C.R.); *R. v. Clarke* [1949] 2 All E.R. 448; (Assize). *R. v. Miller* [1954] 2 Q.B. 282, (K.B.D.); [1954] 2 All E.R. 529. A husband may be prosecuted for aiding and abetting the rape of his wife—see *D.P.P. v. Morgan* [1975] 2 All E.R. 347, (H.L.). See also *R. v. O'Brien* [1974] 3 All E.R. 684—grant of decree nisi of divorce revokes wife's implied consent. For criticism of the present law see P. English, 'The Husband Who Rapes His Wife' (1976) 126 N.L.J. 1223, M.D.A. Freeman, 'Rape By A Husband?' (1979) 129 N.L.J. 332; P. Matthews, 'Marital Rape' (1980) 10 Fam. Law 221.
39. See *R. v. Steele* [1977] Crim. L.R. 290 (C.A.).
40. *R. v. Jackson* [1891], 1 Q.B. 671, (C.A.); *R. v. Miller, supra*.

modified by the Married Women's Property Act, 1882, Sect. 12 and by the Larceny Act, 1916, Sect. 36. The present law is to be found in the Married Women's Status Act, 1957, Sect. 9. It provides that criminal proceedings may be brought against either spouse for the protection and security of a spouse's property, but forbids such proceedings being brought while they are living together, or while they are living apart concerning any act done by a spouse while living with the other, unless property was wrongfully taken by one of the parties when leaving or deserting or about to leave or desert the other. If criminal proceedings, to which this section relates, are brought against a spouse, the other spouse may be called as a witness for the prosecution or the defence without the consent of the spouse charged.[41]

6. Assaults

Until recently the only District Court remedy available to a battered wife wishing to obtain protection from the assaults of her husband was a summons for assault and breach of peace. The Family Law . . . Act, 1976, Sect. 22 has now provided an alternative remedy in that it confers jurisdiction on the District Court to make an order barring a spouse from the matrimonial home. The powers of the court to make such an order are discussed in a later chapter. Suffice it to say here that there are a number of defects in the procedure for bringing such proceedings that may render the assault summons a more efficient means of obtaining protection in certain circumstances.

Upon being assaulted a wife herself may issue a summons against her husband or it may be issued by a Garda. Ironically, a wife who issued a summons for assault against her husband could not before February 1981 obtain State free legal aid, being the prosecutor, whilst her husband, being the accused, was able to do so, provided he was eligible in accordance with the provisions of the Criminal Justice (Legal Aid) Act, 1962. A husband may still obtain legal aid under the 1962 Act whilst a wife may now obtain legal aid under the civil Legal Aid Scheme.[42] If a Garda issues the summons he is then the prosecutor and the wife merely a witness in the proceedings, and she does not require legal representation.

When such cases arise in the District Court most district justices adjourn the proceedings to obtain a report from a probation officer or court welfare officer before deciding on what course of action to take. However if the assault charged is a particularly vicious one, or if a husband has been convicted of assaulting his wife previously, he may be imprisoned without further inquiries being made by the court. A remedy frequently employed by justices in such cases is to discharge the husband without proceeding to conviction upon his entering into a recognisance to be of good behaviour and to comply with such conditions as the court stipulates for a period of time not exceeding three years.[43] The court may also place the husband under the supervision of a probation officer.[44] If a husband fails to observe any of the conditions of his recognisance and for example again assaults his wife, she may so inform the court, which is empowered to issue a warrant for his arrest. By such behaviour the husband renders himself liable to

41. Sect. 9 (5).
42. See Scheme of Civil Legal Aid and Advice (Stationery Office, Dublin 1979) laid before each House of the Oireachtas by the Minister for Justice in December, 1979. A wife bringing criminal proceedings against her husband was not originally entitled to legal aid or advice under the scheme but following an amendment made to section 3.1 of the Scheme on 1st February 1981 she may be granted legal aid for such proceedings.
43. Probation of Offenders Act, 1907, Sect. 1.
44. *Ibid.*, Sect. 2.

conviction and sentence.[45] An alternative means used by the courts to protect a wife from further violence is an order binding a husband to keep the peace and be of good behaviour for a specified period of time.[46]

MARRIAGE AND THE LAW OF TORT

At common law a husband had to be joined as a party to an action either brought by a wife in respect of a tort committed against her or brought by a third party in respect of a tort committed by the wife before, or during the marriage. If the wife was a plaintiff the husband could recover the damages; whilst if she was the defendant he was liable for them.

The necessity of joining the husband as a co-plaintiff was abolished by the Married Women's Property Act, 1882, which permitted a wife to retain damages and the Acts of 1874 and 1882 while not affecting his liability for torts committed during coverture, limited his liability for ante-nuptial torts to the amount of the property that he became entitled to on marriage. Now under section 2(1)(c) of the Married Woman's Status Act, 1957, a married woman is liable in tort, and a husband by reason of only being her husband, cannot be sued or made a party to any legal proceedings brought, nor be made liable for any tort committed by her, by reason of the fact that she is his wife.[47]

Until 1865 no action in tort could be brought by one spouse against the other. The Married Women's Property (Ireland) Act of that year enabled a wife, deserted by her husband or separated from him by a decree of divorce *a mensa et thoro*, to sue him in tort. Her rights were further extended by the Act of 1870 by which she could bring an action to recover her separate property against anyone including her husband.[48] This remained the position until the Act of 1957, which permits a spouse to bring any action in tort against the other spouse.[49] Thus if a husband uses force or violence against his wife she may, if she wishes, bring a civil action for assault to recover compensation for the damages inflicted. At present, many civil actions are brought by wives against husbands and *vice versa*, for damages for injuries due to the negligent driving of a motor vehicle. The named defendant is the spouse; the real defendant is that spouse's insurance company.

MARRIAGE AND THE LAW OF NATIONALITY AND CITIZENSHIP[50]

Section 6 of the Irish Nationality and Citizenship Act, 1956, provides that every person born in Ireland is an Irish citizen from birth. Moreover, a person is an Irish citizen if either his father or mother is an Irish citizen at the time of his

---

45. *Ibid.*, Sect. 6 (1).
46. On the power of the District Courts to make such orders see J.F. Crotty, *Practice and Procedure in the District Court* (Cork University Press, Cork, 1960) p. 171 *et seq.*
47. Sect. 2 (1) (c).
48. See Sect. 11. He may of course under the general law of tort be vicariously liable on other grounds.
49. Sect. 2 (2).
50. Article 9 of the Constitution provides:-
    1.1.   On the coming into operation of this Constitution any person who is a citizen of Saorstat Eireann immediately before the coming into operation of this Constitution shall become and be a citizen of Ireland.
    1.2.   The future acquisition and loss of Irish nationality and citizenship shall be determined in accordance with law.
    1.3.   No person may be excluded from Irish Nationality and citizenship by reason of the sex of such person.
    2.   Fidelity to the nation and loyalty to the state are fundamental political duties of all citizens.
For a detailed discussion of these provisions see J.M. Kelly, *The Irish Constitution*, Chapter 9.

birth. However, section 7 of the Act provides that if a person is born outside Ireland and if the father or mother from whom citizenship derives was also born outside Ireland, that person does not acquire Irish citizenship unless (a) his birth is registered in a foreign births entry book kept in an Irish diplomatic mission or consular office; or (b) the father or mother from whom citizenship derives is at the time of the birth resident abroad in the public service.

A foundling, unless the contrary is proved, is deemed to be an Irish citizen and a child, whose father died before his birth, will acquire Irish citizenship from his father, if he would have acquired such citizenship from the father if the latter had been alive at the time of the child's birth.[51] An adopted child, if it is not an Irish citizen, automatically acquires Irish citizenship when adopted, if the adopter or where the adoption is by a married couple, either spouse, is an Irish citizen.[52] In addition, a person born in Northern Ireland, who is not otherwise an Irish citizen, may acquire Irish citizenship by declaring himself to be an Irish citizen upon attaining full age or upon his being so declared by his parent or guardian.[53]

Under the nationality laws of some countries, a woman upon marrying automatically acquires her husband's nationality. By section 8 of the Act of 1956, a woman who is an alien at the date of her marriage to an Irish citizen does not automatically become an Irish citizen by virtue of her marriage. In order to do so, she must lodge a prescribed declaration with the Minister for Justice, or with any Irish diplomatic mission or consular office, either before or at any time after the marriage, accepting Irish citizenship as her post-nuptial citizenship. If such a declaration is lodged prior to the marriage, she becomes an Irish citizen from the date of her marriage. If it is lodged after the marriage, it takes effect from the day of lodgement. If a man who is not an Irish national marries an Irish citizen he cannot avail of a similar procedure to acquire Irish nationality. He may however acquire a certificate of naturalisation.[54] Finally, a person who marries an alien does not cease to be an Irish citizen, whether or not he or she acquires the nationality of the alien.[55]

MARRIAGE AND THE LAW AS TO PASSPORTS

The Ministers and Secretaries Act, 1924, Section 1(xi) provides that the Department of External Affairs (now called the Department of Foreign Affairs) shall "comprise the administration and business generally of public services in connection with . . . the granting of passports and of visés to passports and all powers, duties and functions connected with same." Apart from the provisions of the now defunct Spanish Civil War (Non-intervention) Act, 1937, this provision is the only statutory reference made to the issuing of passports in any legislation enacted since the foundation of the State.

No legislative provisions define or identify those persons who are entitled to

51. See Sections 9 and 10 of the Act of 1956.
52. See Section 11 of the Act of 1956.
53. See Sections 2 and 7 (1) of the Act of 1956.
54. See Part III of the Act. In *Somjee and Anor. v. The Minister for Justice and Anor.* (December 1979) unreported (H.C.) the constitutional validity of section 8 of the Act of 1956 was upheld, Keane J. holding that the section did not violate Articles 9.1.3. or 40.1 of the Constitution. In the learned judges view the distinction made "conferred a form of privilege on female aliens" but did not invidiously discriminate or sexually discriminate against male aliens. The legislation merely provided "a diversity of arrangements" for the obtaining of citizenship. This decision was not appealed and it respectfully submitted that until the issue is determined by the Supreme Court some doubt must still exist as to the constitutional validity of section 8.
55. Sect. 23.

Irish passports or lay down any conditions or criteria that must be complied with by an applicant for a passport. Moreover, no statute states the circumstances in which a parent or non parent is entitled to have a minor included in his or her passport or when a minor is entitled to obtain his own separate passport.

It is clear from the questions asked on passport application forms that the Department of Foreign Affairs has developed its own rules in connection with the issue of passports but the content of these are unknown and have no statutory force. Having regard to the practices followed by that Department, it appears that an individual Irish citizen, single or married, who is no longer a minor may be granted a passport provided the applicant's identity and signature is certified by a witness to whom the applicant has been personally known for one year. The witness must also certify that to the best of his knowledge and belief the particulars supplied on the application form are true and correct in every detail and that the applicant is "a fit and proper person" to hold an Irish passport. In practice Irish citizens over 21 years experience little real difficulty in obtaining passports for themselves. An area of some difficulty and confusion relates to passports for minors.

As a general rule, if a parent wishes his legitimate child to be included on his passport, the written consent of the other parent is sought. If an application is made for a legitimate child to have his own separate passport, the written consent of both parents is sought. There is no statutory provision which stipulates that the Department of Foreign Affairs must ensure that both parents agree to their legitimate child being granted passport facilities prior to their provision by the Department but the Department appears in this area to have regard to the fact that in law parents are joint guardians of their legitimate children and has taken upon itself to enforce this provision in this way.

If one of the parents is deceased this can be certified by the person witnessing the passport application, if the latter is in a position to confirm this fact. Alternatively, the death certificate of the deceased parent may be submitted. An illegitimate child will be included on its mother's passport, on the mother's application and only the mother's consent is required for such a child to obtain its own separate passport. A passport when granted remains in force for a period of ten years. If a minor is included in a parent's passport, the minor's inclusion remains valid until either the parent's passport loses its validity or until the minor obtains his own passport or attains his majority.

In practice, difficulties are frequently experienced by spouses whose marriages have broken down when they seek passports for children in their custody. If in a deed of separation one spouse has consented to the other spouse obtaining passports for the parties' children or if a court order has specifically stated that a spouse may obtain such passports or have the children included on his or her own passport, little difficulty arises. If, however, one spouse has merely departed and his whereabouts are unknown and if no such court order has been obtained or no agreement containing such a consent concluded, the approach of the Department is unclear. In practice, it has not been unknown for the Department to refuse to grant any passport facilities for a minor in such circumstances without the applicant parent first obtaining a court order authorising the issuing of the requested passport. On other occasions, the Department has refused to grant a passport valid for a ten year period but has merely granted a temporary passport, whilst on some occasions the Department has granted a passport valid for ten years on foot of a court order or agreement granting the applicant parent custody but silent as to the question of passports.

There is one statutory provision indirectly of relevance to the issue of passports for minors. Section 40 of the Adoption Act, 1952, prohibits the removal from the State of a legitimate child under seven years of age who is an Irish citizen unless such removal is by or with the approval of a parent, guardian or relative of the child. A person who contravenes this section or causes or permits its contravention is guilty of an offence and liable to imprisonment for up to twelve months and/or to a fine not exceeding one hundred pounds. It is thus clear that a civil servant in the service of the Department of Foreign Affairs cannot issue a passport to enable a legitimate child under seven years of age to be removed from the State if he knows such removal will contravene this section. If, however, a parent wishes to take his or her legitimate child outside the State, whether the child is under or over seven years of age, this section does not provide any statutory authority for the Department's practice of seeking the other parent's consent before it will issue a passport for the child. It also does not provide the statutory justification for the different approaches adopted by the Department when a separated parent seeks a passport for one of his children.

Section 40 of the 1952 Act also prohibits the removal from the State of an illegitimate child under seven years unless such removal is by or with the approval of the child's mother, guardian or a maternal relation.[56] In *The State (K.M. & R.D.)* v. *The Minister for Foreign Affairs and Ors*,[57] a further provision in this section relating to illegitimate children was held to be unconstitutional. The provision in question prohibited the removal from the State of an illegitimate child less than a year old except for the purpose of residing with its mother or a maternal relative. The judgement delivered by the High Court, contains the first detailed examination by the Irish Courts of the law as to passports and, in particular, of the question as to whether an Irish citizen has a constitutional right to a passport.

In this case, the Department of Foreign Affairs refused to grant a passport for a two and a half month old illegitimate child upon the mother's application. The child's mother was an Irish national and the natural father a Nigerian national. Both of the child's parents wished to send the child to Nigeria to be brought up by the natural father's parents, pending the natural father's return to that country upon the completion of his studies. Finlay P. formed the view that the proposals of the natural parents were consistent with the child's welfare. He then considered whether the child had a constitutional right to travel. He held that a citizen has the right to travel as one of the unenumerated personal rights of Article 40.3 of the Constitution and stated that "subject to the obvious conditions which may be required by public order and the common good of the State the right to a passport," which latter right is "inextricably intertwined" with the right to travel. In the case of a child, this right is exercisable

> "by the choice of its parent, parents or legal guardian subject always to the right of the courts by appropriate proceedings to deny that choice in the dominant interest of the welfare of the child."[58]

He stated that the above provision failed to defend and vindicate the child's personal right to travel and held it to be unconstitutiona. He concluded stating that unless the Department of Foreign Affairs are in a position to bring wardship proceedings as a result of which the court decides that "it is contrary to the child's welfare for it to travel out of Ireland . . . the child has a constitutional right to a passport."

56. See sections 3 and section 40 (1) and 40 (3). of the 1952 Act.
57. [1979] I.R. 73 (H.C.).
58. *Ibid.*, at p. 81.

In the later case of *Cosgrove v. Ireland & Ors.*[58a] the father of two legitimate children brought proceedings against the State claiming damages. Passports had been issued by the Department of Foreign Affairs to the plaintiff's wife for the parties' two children, contrary to the plaintiff's express objections communicated to the Department. The wife took the children to Holland and did not return to Ireland, so depriving the plaintiff of regular contact with them.

McWilliam J. stated that as parents are joint guardians of their legitimate children "neither parent may deprive the other of his or her children without an order of the court". In this case, he continued, the mother was aware of the father's opposition to her obtaining passports for their children and she ought to have made an application to the court for permission to take them out of the country. Referring to the Department of Foreign Affairs' practice of normally seeking the written consent of both parents for the issue of passports to legitimate minors, he stated:

> "This is a very prudent practice to adopt, but there is no statutory provision requiring it and I am not satisfied that there is any duty imposed on the State or the Department by the Constitution or otherwise to take any particular steps to protect rights which they have no reason to suppose are being infringed.
>
> Here, the passport office was notified by the plaintiff that he was objecting to the issue of the passports after forms had been issued which the plaintiff had failed to sign. Under these circumstances the Department was put on notice that the plaintiff was exercising his rights as joint guardian under the Guardianship of Infants Act, and I am of opinion that the passports should not have been issued without an application to the court being made by the wife and that this should have been told to the wife."

In holding against the State, the learned Judge adjourned for argument at a later date the question of what damages, if any, in the circumstances the plaintiff was entitled to receive from the State.

As a result of the above two judgements it appears that if a parent applies to have a minor placed on his or her passport or consents to a minor obtaining a separate passport, the minor has a constitutional right to have the passport facilities sought afforded to him. If the minor is legitimate and one parent objects to the issue of passports, the Department may not issue a passport and has a duty to advise the spouse seeking it that before a passport can be issued the spouse must apply to the appropriate court under the Guardinahsip of Infants Act, 1964, and obtain an order permitting the spouse to apply for a passport and to take the children out of the country. If, however, the Department is unaware of any objection to the issue of a minor's passport, it must issue the passport and can only deny the minor passport facilities by bringing wardship proceedings and establishing to the satisfaction of the court in those proceedings that it is contrary to the welfare of the particular minor to permit it to travel outside Ireland. It is, of course, open to a spouse who fears that the other spouse may remove children from the jurisdiction without the former's consent to apply to the High Court under the 1964 Act for an injunction to prevent the other spouse doing so. In practice, many such injunctions have been granted.[58b]

In relation to married couples, both of whom are Irish citizens, it is clear from the judgement delivered in the *State (K.M. & R.D.)* v. *The Minister for Foreign Affairs & Ors.* that each spouse has an independent right to a pass-

58a. (December 1980) unreported (H.C.).
58b. See further pp. 224, 227, *infra*.

port. However, in relation to this right, Finlay P. stated:

"There are obvious and justified restrictions, the most common being the existence of some undischarged obligation to the State by the person seeking a passport or seeking to use his passport—such as the fact that he has entered into a recognisance to appear before a Criminal Court for the trial of an offence."[59]

The question arises as to whether the restrictions referred to by the learned judge will be extended by the courts to prevent a spouse leaving the jurisdiction in order to renege on his obligation to maintain his spouse and children. Having regard to the constitutional protection afforded to the family, the courts may be willing to restrict the right to travel and the right to use or obtain a passport in such circumstances.

It is submitted that legislation should be enacted to clarify this whole area of the law. It should clearly set out the duties imposed on the Department of Foreign Affairs in relation to the issue of passports and the manner in which these duties are to be exercised. In particular, such legislation should clearly specify the circumstances in which parental consents are required for the issuing of a passport for a minor and should provide a simple and inexpensive court procedure for dispensing with the consent of a parent, where to do so is in the interests of a minor's welfare. In addition, the legislation should state the circumstances in which the Department may refuse to issue a passport and the circumstances in which the courts may place restrictions on the issuing or use of passports in the interests of "public order" and the "common good".

DOMICILE

Many problems in family law are intimately bound up with the concept of domicile. These include questions relating to a person's capacity to marry, the question of recognition of foreign decrees of divorce, and questions concerning a person's status, e.g. whether he is legitimate or illegitimate. Put simply a person's domicile is said to be that of the country in which he has his permanent home.[60] However, as will be seen the rules for determining domicile often require a far more complex enquiry than one simply to discover the location of an individual's home. Moreover it is not strictly accurate to equate the concept of domicile with that of a country. Domicile strictly signifies a separate law district, i.e. a territory subject to a single system of law. Thus whilst the equation is accurate for example in the case of the Republic of Ireland or England, in the case of the U.S.A. it is not. There, each State is a separate law district, and persons are not domiciled in the U.S.A. as such, but in one of its states.[61]

The two basic rules as to domicile are that nobody can be without one and that no person can have more than one domicile, at the same time, for the same purpose.[62]

Domicile of Origin

Every person is deemed at birth to have a domicile of origin. The domicile of

59. [1979] I.R. at p. 81.
60. *Whicker v. Hume* (1858), 7 H.L. Cas. 124 at p. 160, (H.L.); see comments of Budd J. in *In re Adams* [1967], I.R. 424, (H.C.). Nationality and domicile may often coincide but they are not necessarily the same. Thus, a person of Irish nationality, may have an English or French domicile under Irish law, providing he acquires it in accordance with one of the rules under Irish Law for the acquisition of domicile.
61. Dicey and Morris, *Conflict of Law*, 9th edition, p. 12–13; Cheshire & North, *Cheshires Private International Law* 10th Edition, p. 163.
62. See Cheshire & North *supra*, p. 162–165.

a legitimate child born during his father's lifetime, is that of the domicile of the father at the time of his birth. The domicile of a legitimate child born after his father's death or of an illegitimate child is that of his mother. The domicile of a foundling is in the country where he is found. Thus domicile of origin, as can be seen, in no way depends on the intention or actions of the person who acquires it.

Domicile of Choice

Every person over the age of 21, apart from a married woman, or a person of unsound mind, can acquire a domicile of choice. To do so a person must leave the country of his domicile of origin and take up residence in another country, with the intention of continuing to reside there permanently or at least indefinitely.[63] A person may lose his domicile of choice by ceasing to reside there and abandoning his intention to reside there.[64] Upon abandoning a domicile of choice a person may acquire a new domicile of choice. Alternatively, he may abandon his domicile of choice without having any definite intention as to where to set up a home. In such circumstances his domicile of origin revives.[65]

Domicile of Dependency

Neither married women, nor minors (persons under 21), nor persons of unsound mind can acquire a domicile of choice. They have what is known as a domicile of dependence.

Married Women

The domicile of a husband is communicated to a wife immediately upon solemnisation of the marriage and during the subsistence of the marriage she is unable to acquire an independent domicile of her own. This applies even if spouses are living apart, whether or not they are doing so in pursuance of a separation agreement or a decree of divorce *a mensa et thoro*.[66] Thus if a husband deserts his wife and goes to live in England acquiring an English domicile of choice, even though the wife never sets foot in England she also acquires under Irish law, an English domicile. It has been suggested by Walsh J. in *Gaffney* v. *Gaffney* that the rules as to a wife's dependent domicile may be unconstitutional.[67]

Upon the valid dissolution of her marriage, or the death of her husband, a wife is free to acquire a domicile of choice of her own.[68] Until she does so, however, she continues to retain her husband's domicile.[69] Upon the pronouncement of a decree annulling a voidable marriage a wife is also free to acquire her

---

63. Rule 10, Dicey and Morris, *supra*; see *In re Joyce, Corbet v. Fagan* [1946] I.R. 277, (S.C.); *In re Sillar, Hurley v. Wimbush* [1956] I.R. 344 (H.C.); *In re Adams, supra; Revenue Commissioners v. Shaw and Talbot Crosbie* (April 1977) unreported (H.C.); *Gaffney v. Gaffney* [1975] I.R. 133 (S.C.). See also *Sproule v. Hopkins* [1903] 2 I.R. 386 (K.B.D.); *Revenue Commissioners v. Iveagh* [1930] I.R. 386 (S.C.); *Revenue Commissioners v. Z* (1967) 101 I.L.T. & S.J. 492 (Sp. Com.); *J.W. v. M.W.* (July 1978) unreported (H.C.); *L.B. v. H.B.* (July 1980) unreported (H.C.).
64. Rule 13, Dicey and Morris *supra*; see *Sproule v. Hopkins, supra, Revenue Commissioners v. Matthews* (1958), 92 I.L.T.R. 44 (S.C.); *In re Adams, supra*.
65. *Udny v. Udny* (1869), L.R. 1 Sc. & Div. 441 at p. 450, (H.L.); see Cheshire and North *supra*, p. 177–178 where he criticises the doctrine of revival—The doctrine of revival can result in a person being domiciled in a country with which he has little or no connection and even upon which he has never set foot.
66. *A.-G for Alberta v. Cook* [1926] A.C. 444, (P.C.).
67. *Gaffney v. Gaffney* [1975] I.R. 133, (S.C.).
68. *In re Scullard deceased*, [1957] Ch. 107, (Ch. Div.); see P.B. Carter—Domicile of a Widow, (1957) 33 B.Y.I.L. 329–332.
69. *In re Wallach deceased*, [1950], 1 All E.R. 199, (P.D.A.).

own domicile of choice. If she is party to a void marriage, she never becomes a dependent person, and so retains her independent domicile.[70]

Minors

A person is a minor until he reaches the age of 21. As we have seen a legitimate infant acquires the domicile of his father, if born during the latter's lifetime, and of his mother if not. An illegitimate child acquires his mother's domicile, and if legitimated his father's. However, in the latter circumstances the mother's domicile is the domicile of origin and his father's, the domicile of choice. An adopted child acquires the domicile of his adopters. The generally accepted rule is that a minor is incapable of acquiring a domicile of choice of his own, the only exception being that a female minor acquires the domicile of her husband. A domicile of choice, however, may be acquired for him by the act of one of his parents.

The domicile of an infant follows any change which occurs in the domicile of his father. In the Northern Ireland case of *Hope* v. *Hope*,[71] it was said that this rule is based "on the authority and responsibility that a father has to act for his child".[72] If a father abjures his responsibility by conduct which results in the marriage being dissolved by a competent court, and the custody of the infant is given to the mother, it is the mother who has the authority and responsibility to act for the infant, and a change in the mother's domicile results in a corresponding change in the infant's domicile.[73]

Upon the death of a father, an infant's domicile becomes dependent on and will, prima facie, change with that of his mother. This power to change her infant's domicile is said to be vested in a mother, to be exercised for the welfare of the infant. It was decided in *In re Beaumont* that if a mother changes her own domicile, she may abstain from changing that of her child provided she does so without fraudulent intention and with the child's welfare in mind.[74]

All the classical writers affirm that a father is incapable of conferring on his infant a domicile different to his own. The Irish case of *Spurway* v. *Spurway*[75] is frequently relied on to support this principle. However, anything said in that case about the respondent's domicile as an infant, was purely *obiter*.[76] There is no logical reason why a mother should be able to confer a domicile on her infant different to her own and a father prevented from doing so. Moreover *In re Beaumont*, although decided a year prior to *Spurway* was not mentioned in the latter case.[77]

Under the present law, if a male married prior to attaining his majority and

---

70. *In Gray v. Formosa* [1963] P. 259, (C.A.)—The rule of dependent domicile of a married woman was said to be "the last barbarous relic of a wife's servitude",—Per Lord Denning M.R. at p. 267. The rule was abolished in England by the Domicile and Matrimonial Proceedings Act, 1973, Sect. 1. In Ireland this is only one of the many "barbarous relics" of servitude that still exist.
71. [1968] N.I. 1, (Q.B.D.).
72. *Supra* at p. 10, per Lord MacDermot, L.C.J.
73. See however, the contrary decision of *Shanks v. Shanks* in 1965, S.L.T. 330, per Lord Fraser.
74. [1893] 3 Ch. 490, (Ch. Div.).
75. [1894] 1 I.R. 385, 401; (1893), 28 I.L.T.R. 2, (C.A.).
76. See W. R. Duncan "The Domicile of Infants", (1969), 4 I.J. (n.s.) 36.
77. See *Stephens v. M'Farland* (1845), 8 Ir. Eq. Rep. 444 (Rolls Ct.) and the comments thereon by Duncan *supra*—However note that the parent in M'Farland was the mother, although the Master of the Rolls does not mention that fact in his judgement. In England, Sects. 1, 3 and 4 of the Domicile and Matrimonial Proceedings Act have lowered the age of minority for the purpose of domicile of dependency to 16. The rules as to which parent a minor's domicile is dependent on have also been radically changed. There is a need for a similar reform of the law in this country.

sets up home in Ireland, and if his parents emigrate to Australia, while he is still under twenty-one, he and his wife and their children automatically acquire an Australian domicile. It is possible, however, that under the principle laid down in *Beaumont's* case the court would hold that the parents could abstain from changing a son's domicile in such circumstances.

Criticisms and suggested reforms

The law as to domicile is badly in need of reform.

(a) There is no valid reason for retaining the notion of revival of domicile of origin. Upon a person leaving a domicile of choice he should retain that domicile until he settles down in a new domicile.

(b) The rule of dependant domicile of a married woman should be abolished. A wife should be able to establish an independent domicile.[78]

(c) The rule of dependant domicile of a minor should be changed to permit a minor acquire an independent domicile upon attaining the age at which he acquires capacity to marry. Under the present law this would be sixteen years but the Law Reform Commission has recently suggested raising the age for marriage to eighteen years.[79]

At the time of writing the Law Reform Commission is preparing a report on the law of domicile.

JACTITATION OF MARRIAGE

In 1871 the High Court inherited the old jurisdiction of the Ecclesiastical Courts to hear proceedings in which application is made for a decree of Jactitation of Marriage.[80] A petition in a suit for jactitation of marriage is designed to prevent a person (the respodent) from making false assertions that he or she is married to the petitioner.[81] Upon the court being satisfied that the parties to the proceedings are not married it makes a declaration to that effect together with an order forbidding the respondent from repeating the assertion. The declaration that the parties are not married does not bind third parties and is not therefore in any way equivalent to a decree of nullity.[82] There are three defences to the suit:

(a) A denial that the assertion was made;[83]

(b) An admission that it was made together with a statement as to its truth.[84]

---

78. See M. Mathews, 'Dependent Domicile of Irish Wives' (1977) 111 I.L.T. & S.J. 17. See however A. Shatter, "The Mixed Blessing of an Independent Domicile", Irish Times 30 Nov. 1976.

79. See p.

80. The word "jacitation" is derived from the Latin "jacitare" meaning to boast.

81. *Goldstone v. Smith* (1922), 38 T.L.R. 403, (P.D.A.).

82. *Duchess of Kingston's Case* (1776), 20 State Tr. 355; 168 E.R. 175, (H.L.). In this case, the Duchess, in a prosecution for bigamously marrying the Duke of Kingston, relied by way of defence on a decree of jactitation in respect of her first marriage to another man, but it was held the decree could only bind the parties to the suit and therefore was not binding the Crown.

Further, it seems that it is not even conclusive as between the parties, but that the case can be reopened upon the respondent showing on new evidence that the parties were married.

83. *Hawke (Lord) v. Corri* (1820), 2 Hag. Con. 280; 161 E.R. 743, (Consistory Ct.).

84. *Lindo v. Belisario* (1794), 1 Hag. Con. 216; appeal at, (1796), 1 Hag. Con. 7; 161 E.R. 530, 636, (Consistory Arches Cts.); *Hawke v. Corri, supra; Bodkin v. Case* (1835) Milw. Rep. 355, (Consistory Ct.); *Thompson v. Rourke* [1893], P. 70, (C.A.); *Goldstone*

(c) Proof that the assertion was authorised or acquiesced in by the petitioner.[85]

If the court upholds the respondent's claim that he or she is validly married to the petitioner, the court can make a declaration that the parties are validly married.[86]

There are no cases of suits for jactitation of marriage to be found in any of the modern Irish law reports. The remedy seems to have fallen into general disuse. It does, however, provide a useful procedure to enable a person stop another from causing him embarrassment by pretending in public to be married to. him. A defect in the remedy is that it does not enable the court to make an order to silence or prevent third parties from making false statements as to a person's marital status, nor does it enable a husband or wife to obtain a court order to prevent a third party from claiming to be married to his or her spouse or to prevent such third party from assuming their spouse's name.[87]

MARRIAGE AND DECLARATORY JUDGEMENTS

A spouse may petition the High Court for a declaration that his marriage is valid under the provisions of the Legitimacy Declaration (Ireland) Act, 1868. The Attorney General must be joined as a respondent to any petition. A declaration made under the Act is binding on all persons given notice of, or made parties to the proceedings (including the State) and anyone claiming through them. However, a decree proved to have been obtained by fraud or collusion has no binding effect on anyone.[88] A second way in which a declaration may be obtained was discussed in the Court of Appeal in England in *Har-Shefi* v. *Har-Shefi*.[89] Here it was held that the court had jurisdiction to make an order declaratory of the parties' status under Order 25, Rule 5 of the English Rules of the Supreme Court. The English Order corresponds exactly with Order 19, Rule 29 of the Irish Rules of the Superior Courts which states that

"No action or pleading shall be open to objection on the ground that a merely declaratory judgement or order is sought thereby, and the court may if it thinks fit, make binding declarations of right whether any consequential relief is or could be claimed or not."

The jurisdiction of the High Court to give a declaratory judgement on the general question of a person's marital status could be a particularly useful method of testing the validity of foreign decrees of divorce under Irish law before a question as to the validity of such a decree arises in other proceedings. The jurisdiction of the court has not as yet, been used for such a purpose.

---

v. Smith, supra; Schuck v. Schuck (1950), 66 T.L.R. 1179, (P.D.A.); *Igra v. Igra* [1951], P. 404, (P.D.A.).

85. *Thompson v. Rourke* [1893], P. 11, (P.D.A.).
86. *Goldstone v. Smith, supra.*
87. See Working Paper No. 34 of the English Law Commission; see also Working Paper No. 48 of the same body.
88. See Order 71 of the R.S.C. (S.I. No. 72 of 1962).
89. [1953], P. 161; [1953], 1 All. E.R. 783, (C.A.). The tendency in recent English decisions has been to limit the scope of this jurisdiction—See P. M. Bromley, *Family Law* 5th Ed. (London, Butterworths 1976), p. 67.

CHAPTER 7

SEPARATION AGREEMENTS

"Whereas unhappy differences have arisen between the husband and the wife."

So traditionally commences the most depressing of all legal contracts, the Separation Agreement. When parties to a marriage no longer wish to cohabit a separation agreement affords the means whereby they can regularise their affairs without recourse to a court.

Prior to the Reformation marriage was regarded both by the Church and the law as a sacrament. The duty of cohabitation was the fundamental matrimonial duty and a contract made for giving effect to voluntary separation was regarded as *contra bonos mores* and of no effect. After the Reformation although such contracts were not regarded as contrary to common law, the Ecclesiastical Courts still refused to recognise them. It was not until the middle of the last century that the validity and enforceability of separation agreements was finally established.[1] In upholding the validity of separation agreements the courts recognised the desirability of estranged spouses settling their differences in private, rather than in open court.

It is now settled law that a contract between a husband and wife to live separate and apart and to regulate their respective legal rights is valid and enforceable. However, a contract by spouses living together, providing for a future separation, is void and inoperative as contrary to public policy.[2] The one exception to this arises if an agreement is made by spouses not cohabiting, providing for their resuming cohabitation and containing provisions to regulate their position if they should again separate.[3]

Form

A separation agreement need not be in any particular form, provided each spouse gives valuable consideration it will be valid and enforceable. Mutual oral promises simply not to cohabit, if intended to have legal effect, are enforceable.[4]

---

1. *Wilson v. Wilson* (1848) 1 H.L. Cas. 538, (H.L.).
2. *Westmeath (Marquis of) v. Westmeath (Marchioness of)* (1830), 1 Dow & Cl. 519; 6 E.R. 619, (H.L.). See also *Brodie v. Brodie* [1917] P. 271, (P.D.A.), ante-nuptial agreement of non-cohabitation, void.
3. *MacMahon v. MacMahon* [1913] 1 I.R. 154, 428 (M.R., App.); *Purser v. Purser* [1913] 1 I.R. 422, 428 (Ch.D., App.).
4. *Courtney v. Courtney* [1923] 2 I.R. 31; (1923), 57 I.L.T.R. 42, (C.A.). See judgement of Dodd J. at p. 37 where he suggests mutual oral promises to live apart are not sufficient to create a binding agreement. See, however, judgement of Ronan C.J. at p. 42 where he states that such an agreement would be enforceable provided that the parties intended it to have legal consequences. As for the need for intention to creat legal relations, see *Balfour v. Balfour* [1919] 2 K B. 571, (C.A.); *Gould v. Gould* [1970] 1 Q.B. 275, (C.A.); *Merritt v. Merritt* [1970] 1 W.L.R. 1211, (C.A.).

Generally, however, an agreement is much more complicated making provision for maintenance and custody of children, maintenance of the wife, division of matrimonial property, non-molestation of one spouse by the other, etc. In such a case it will usually be put in writing and is generally embodied in a deed. Formerly owing to a married woman's inability to contract it was necessary to join trustees to such an agreement to contract on behalf of the wife. Since the coming into force of the Married Women's Property Act, 1882 (now replaced by the Married Women's Status Act, 1957) this has not been necessary. A separation agreement is subject to the ordinary law of contract. If obtained by fraud or duress such an agreement will be voidable.[5] Whereas if it is entered into by unmarried parties, thinking themselves to be married, it is void.[6]

Terms that may be included in an agreement

The following are the terms more usually found in separation agreements.

Agreement to Live Apart: This is the fundamental provision in every separation agreement. By it, each spouse is released from the duty of cohabiting with the other. However this provision should be regarded with caution. If a deserted spouse consents to living apart, the desertion automatically comes to an end. Under the Family Law . . . Act, 1976, a deserting spouse is barred from claiming maintenance for his or her own support. Thus, by signing a separation agreement a deserted spouse may render himself liable to contribute to the maintenance of the spouse in desertion.[7] Similarly, a deserted wife by agreeing to separate may render herself ineligible for deserted wife's benefit or allowance, a social welfare payment she might otherwise receive in the event of her husband failing to maintain her. Where the parties are not agreed on a separation but are agreed on financial and other arrangements subsequent to desertion by one, of the other, a "maintenance" or other type of agreement may be more appropriate than a "separation" agreement. Whereas a separation agreement normally recites that the parties "have agreed to live apart from each other" a maintenance or other agreement would contain merely the factual statement that they "are living apart from each other" or that a named spouse has deserted the other spouse.

Non-Molestation Clause: There is generally a term that neither spouse will "molest, annoy, disturb or interfere with the other". Molestation must be some act done by the wife or husband, or on his or her authority, with the intent to annoy the other and in fact be an annoyance to him or her. A covenant not to molest is not broken by the subsequent bringing of a *bona fide* matrimonial action.[8] Neither adultery by a wife, nor adultery followed by the birth of an illegitimate child, is a breach of such a covenant, though if a wife held out such a child to be the legitimate child of her husband it would amount to molestation.[9] Behaviour in breach of such a clause may be restrained by an injunction.

Custody of Children: At common law any agreement whereby a father divested himself of the custody of his children was regarded as contrary to public policy and void. Now by the Guardianship of Infants Act, 1964, Sect. 18(2)

5. See *V.W. v. J.W.* (April 1978) unreported (H.C.) in which the plaintiff failed to have an agreement declared void.
6. *Galloway v. Galloway* (1914), 30 T.L.R. 531, (K.B.D.)., (D.C.).
7. See further p. 272, *et seq.*
8. *Courtney v. Courtney* [1923], 2 I.R. 31; (1923), 27 I.L.T.R. 42, (C.A.).
9. *Fearon v. Earl of Aylesford* (1884), 14 Q.B.D. 792, (C.A.).

"A provision contained in any separation agreement made between the father and mother of an infant shall not be invalid by reason only of its providing that one of them shall give up the custody or control of the infant to the other."[10]

However, if provision is made in a separation agreement for the custody of, or for access to a child and subsequently proceedings are brought, the court will not enforce the provision if enforcement is contrary to the child's welfare.[11]

The spouse who does not obtain custody of a child is usually given reasonable rights of access to it. Such rights normally include as a minimum the right to visit and take out the child on one day each week and in addition, to have the child either reside with or go on holidays with such parent for part of the school holidays. It is also usual to state the circumstances in which a child may be taken outside the jurisdiction by either parent e.g. whether the other parent's consent is required, how much notice must be given etc. The exact agreement reached as to access varies and is dependent upon the individual circumstances and the ages of the parties' children. To avoid dispute at a later date a separation agreement should also state whether it is agreed or not that a passport be obtained for a child or that a child's name be placed on the passport of either parent.

Maintenance Clause: Usually a husband agrees to pay maintenance to his wife, and if she obtains custody of the children, part of the maintenance is usually set down as being for the benefit of the children. This may be done in a number of ways. The agreement may provide for payment of one lump sum[12] or for a yearly or monthly sum. The more usual arrangement, however, is for the husband to make weekly payments. Payment may be secured or unsecured. It can be payable directly to a wife, to her agent, or to a District Court clerk, if the agreement is made a rule of court under section 8 of the Family Law . . . Act, 1976. It is important to note however, that if an agreement is ruled under the latter section, the maintenance provision in it does not become a maintenance order, the maintenance merely becomes payable through the District Court and enforceable as if it were a maintenance order. Thus, if at a future date, the person receiving maintenance seeks a sum larger than that provided in the agreement, maintenance proceedings have to be brought. It is not sufficient to simply apply to the court to vary the maintenance provision as if it is a maintenance order.[13]

Prior to the coming into force of the Family Law . . . Act, 1976, it was not unusual for a separation agreement to contain a clause whereby a wife, in receipt of a weekly sum of maintenance or in receipt of a lump sum by way of final settlement, covenanted not to apply to the courts at any future time for a maintenance order. It is now clear that even if a wife does so covenant, she is

---

10. This section in effect re-enacts Sect. 2 of the Custody of Infants Act, 1873; see also the article in (1883) 17 I.L.T. & S.J. 473–4 entitled, "The Right to the Custody of Children".

11. See Sect. 3 of the 1964 Act. See further Chapter 13, particularly p. 225.

12. See *Lett v. Lett* [1906], 1 I.R. 618, 630, (M.R., App.).

13. See, however, *J. H. v. C. H.* (July 1979) unreported (H. C.) in which Keane J. suggested, that upon an Agreement being made a Rule of Court under Section 8 the defendant husband could apply to the court for a Variation Order if he considered the maintenance provisions in the agreement excessive. The judgement does not however fully reveal the contents of the settlement and it is possible that it contained a term permitting the husband to make such an application in such circumstances. If it did not do so it is submitted, with respect, that the learned judge was incorrect. For further reference to Section 8 of the Family Law . . . Act, 1976, see p. 280.

not excluded from obtaining a maintenance order under the provisions of the Family Law . . . Act, 1976.

In *H.D.* v. *P.D.*[14] proceedings brought by the applicant wife against her husband seeking a divorce *a mensa et thoro* had been settled in 1973. A written consent signed by the parties had been received and filed in court. In accordance with its terms the respondent husband had paid to the wife a sum of £10,000 which was stated in the consent to be "in full satisfaction of all claims in the petition". In 1977, the wife issued further proceedings against her husband seeking a maintenance order under section 5 of the Family Law . . . Act, 1976, for the support of herself and two of her children.

It was contended on behalf of the husband that the wife was estopped from seeking maintenance by reason of the consent. The court however held that despite the covenant contained in the consent the claim fell within the provisions of section 5 of the Family Law . . . Act under which a maintenance order may be made if it appears to the court that a spouse has failed to provide "such maintenance as is proper in the circumstances."

Walsh J. delivering the judgement of the court, held that the consent "was in effect a separation agreement" and went on to state

> "The operation of the (Family Law) Act cannot be affected by a separation agreement or other document in the nature of the consent in this case entered into before the passing of the Act unless there is an express provision to the contrary in the Act. It is clear from the whole structure of the Act that its purpose is to deal with the situation of the parties at the time the proceedings were brought under the Act and that the primary function of the Act is to ensure that proper and adequate maintenance will be available in accordance with the provisions of the Act to spouses and children. The basic question to be decided is whether at any given time there is a failure by one spouse to provide reasonable maintenance for the support of the other spouse and for any dependent children of the family of the spouses. In my view it is not possible to contract out of the Act by an agreement made after the Act came into force or by an agreement entered into before the legislation was enacted."

As for agreements entered into after the Act came into force and made rules of court under section 8 of the Act he continued

> "a provision in any such agreement for periodical maintenance payments is not final and there is nothing to prevent the spouse receiving the payments from subsequently applying for a maintenance order if the circumstances have changed."

Curiously, Walsh J. did not refer in his judgement to section 27 of the Act which provides that a provision in an agreement, in so far as it would have the effect of excluding or limiting the operation of any provision of the Act, is void. His judgement is however wholly consistent with the intent of this provision.

The Act of 1976 does not affect the jurisdiction of the High Court to make an alimony order. The question now arises as to whether a wife can bar herself in an agreement from applying for alimony if, at some later date, she petitions

---

14. (May 1978) unreported (S.C.) See further G. McGann, 'Maintenance Agreements and the Family Law (Maintenance of Spouses and Children) Act 1976,' vol. 72 (1979) *Gazette of the Incorporated Law Society of Ireland* 115.

the High Court for a decree of divorce *a mensa et thoro*. Judicial pronouncements in the first half of this century held that she could, and that she is held bound by such a clause unless a state of things arises not contemplated by her when signing the agreement i.e. unless she subsequently discovers her husband to be guilty of gross misconduct of a nature completely different from that known to her when entering into the agreement (e.g. incestuous adultery).[15]

However in 1929 in the English case of *Hyman* v. *Hyman*[16] Lord Atkin stated that

> "In my view no agreement between the spouses can prevent the court from considering the question whether in the circumstances of the particular case it shall think fit to order some reasonable payment to the wife ... The wife's right to future maintenance is a matter of public concern which she cannot barter away."

It was pointed out that if a wife was prevented from seeking alimony the State might have to become responsible for her support.

In *Courtney* v. *Courtney*[17] discussed in the next section, it was emphasised that there is nothing to prevent a spouse challenging a clause in an agreement on grounds of public policy. The question of whether a covenant by a wife not to seek alimony is contrary to public policy has never been determined by an Irish Court. It is submitted that the reasoning in *Hyman*, which was a case of divorce *a vinculo*, is equally applicable to an award of alimony subsequent to a decree of divorce *a mensa et thoro*.[18] If, however, the High Court holds a wife to be bound by a clause in an agreement not to sue for alimony, there is nothing to prevent her from seeking maintenance under the Act of 1976.

It has been usual in the past to make provision in agreements for variation of the amount payable by way of maintenance if the circumstances of the parties change. Although a spouse in receipt of inadequate maintenance under a separation agreement may now apply for a maintenance order under the Act of 1976, regardless of the terms in the agreement, parties may still wish to obviate the necessity of going to court unless it is absolutely necessary.

There are numerous types of variation clauses that may be inserted in an agreement to ensure that it keeps step with the requirements and resources of the parties to the agreement. For example at the end of each year an agreement may provide for

(a) a fixed annual percentage increase in the maintenance payments e.g. 10 per cent. *or*

(b) an annual percentage increase based on the increase in the cost of living,

---

15, See *Morrall* v. *Morrall* (1881), 6 P.D. 98, (P.D.A.); *Gandy* v. *Gandy* (1882), 7 P.D., 77 (P.D.A.); on appeal, (1882), 7 P.D. 168 (C.A.); *Lett* v. *Lett, supra; Rose* v. *Rose* [1908]. 2 I.R. 339 (K.B.D.); *Lewis* v. *Lewis* [1940] I.R. 42 at p. 50; (1939), 74 I.L.T.R. 170, (H.C.).

16. [1929] A.C. 601, (H.L.). The law in England has since been affected by statute. See S.M. Cretney, *Principles of Family Law*, 2nd ed. (Sweet & Maxwell, 1979) p. 369 *et seq*., P.M. Bromley, *Family Law*, 6th ed. (Butterworths 1976) pp. 503–509. See also the recent cases of *Minton* v. *Minton* [1979] 1 All E.R. 79; [1979] 2 W.L.R. 31 (H.L.) and *Jessel* v. *Jessel* [1979] 3 All E.R. 645 (C.A.).

17. *Supra*.

18. See *Dempsey* v. *Dempsey* [1943], Ir. Jur. Rep. 47, (H.C.), in which Haugh J. did not disagree with a statement by counsel that "Permanent alimony for a judicially separated wife is and always has been inalienable". This case was however concerned with the question whether a court having awarded alimony after granting a divorce *a mensa et thoro* could be prevented from making or varying the order for alimony at some future time by an agreement, assignment or release entered into by the spouses concerned, by which the wife deprived herself of the right to it. It was accepted that such an agreement only had binding force if made a rule of court.

or

(c)   a fixed sum increase e.g. £5 per year, *or*

(d)   an increase proportionate to the annual increase in the husband's income, *or*

(e)   a variation of the maintenance payable in the light of changes in either spouses' financial circumstances at the end of each year.

Each of the above methods has advantages and disadvantages. Methods (a), (b) and (c) are preferable to (d) and (e) in so far as they avoid annual arguments between the parties as to their true earnings. Further, they lessen the pressure on the parties to 'spy" on each other and thus prevent any further unpleasantness that such behaviour can cause. The main disadvantage of methods (a) and (c) is that in times of extreme inflation, despite such a provision, a wife's income in real terms would decline. Alternatively, in a more stable monetary situation her income could as a result increase in real terms, but such an increase could be beyond the means of her husband. Method (b) avoids many of the above difficulties. It is disadvantageous however in so far as it may give rise to uncertainty, in that the parties may not know until a short time before payment is due, the exact amount of the annual increase. Further it does not make any allowance for change in the financial circumstances of each party unconnected with cost of living increases. It is submitted that the best compromise clause is one that provides for an annual increase based on the cost of living[19] together with provision for either party to serve notice on the other proposing an alternative sum payable "upon the occurrence of a fundamental change" in the financial circumstances of either. In the event of the parties failing to agree there is nothing to prevent the party receiving maintenance from applying under the Act of 1976 for a maintenance order.[20]

Covenant not to bring "Mensa et Thoro" proceedings for matrimonial misbehaviour prior to Deed: A covenant in a separation agreement not to bring *Mensa et thoro* proceedings against a spouse for behaviour prior to the execution of the agreement will be upheld by the court. In *Courtney* v. *Courtney*[21] a wife petitioned for a divorce *a mensa et thoro* from her husband on the ground of cruelty. Some time prior to the petition an agreement had been made by the parties whereby the wife returned her ring and a watch to the husband and he in turn gave her £150. Upon receiving the money she signed the following receipt: "Received from Mr. Michael Courtney the sum of one hundred and fifty pounds (£150), being in full discharge of all claims of every nature and kind by me against the said Michael Courtney".

The court held that the consideration from the wife was that if the husband agreed to the terms she would abstain from bringing proceedings for separation or for alimony. It was contended that if there was no express covenant not to sue, no agreement not to sue was to be implied. To this Dodd, J. stated

"If parties who are free to contract do in fact contract for the settlement of an action or for the abandonment of claims which might terminate in

---

19.   The *Irish Statistical Bulletin* issued by the Central Statistics Office sets down the annual increase in the consumer price index. It gives quarterly figures on the 21st February, 21st May, 21st August and the 21st November in each year.

20.   For a discussion of the relevance of the law of taxation to maintenance payments under a separation agreement see, M. V. O'Mahony—The Drafting of Separation Agreements, S.Y.S. Lecture No. 93.

21.   *Supra.*

legal proceedings, can it be contended that the settlement having been entered into and completed by one party complying with it, the other party can keep the money and go on with the action?"

Parties to a binding contract

"who agree so to settle a matrimonial controversy must be taken to contract that they will not go behind the settlement, and cannot be listened to saying that they did not make an express stipulation not to sue. The decision here must be kept within its legitimate limits, and is not to be taken to extend to contracts that are against the public policy".[22]

Dum Casta Clause: Such a clause may be included in an agreement, limiting a spouse's obligation to maintain the other in accordance with the provisions of the agreement only so long as the latter shall lead a chaste life. In the absence of such a clause, it has long been held that no term can be implied into a contract that the parties are to live in chastity.[23] The position was not changed by the family provisions in the 1937 Constitution and this was clearly stated in two cases in the 1940's.

In *Lewis* v. *Lewis*[24] a husband had covenanted under a separation deed to pay his wife a monthly sum for her maintenance. There was no clause making the continuance of its operation dependant on the wife's living single and chaste. The payment fell into arrears, but before the claim for arrears was heard the husband obtained a decree of divorce *a mensa et thoro* on the ground of his wife's adultery. On the hearing of the wife's claim, it was held by Hanna J. that, in the absence of a *dum casta* clause in the deed, she was entitled to recover arrears. As to whether it is contrary to public policy in this country to permit a wife, living an adulterous life, to recover under a deed, he went on:

"To distinguish the public policy in Eire from that in England, reliance has been placed upon the provisions of Art. 41 of our present Constitution . . . In my judgement the provisions of our Constitution do not help on the question of public policy in Ireland, which I have to decide, as regards a separation deed without a *dum casta* clause. I can find no public policy that I could legally rely upon as a guide upon this matter".[25]

In the similar case of *Ormsby* v. *Ormsby*[26] it was argued that a *dum castus* clause must be implied in every separation deed since it would be against Irish public policy as expressed in Art. 41 that a wife should have to support her husband while he maintained an adulterous household. This argument was rejected by the Supreme Court, Sullivan C.J. saying:

"Art. 41 of the Constitution has satisfied me as being the law of this country as it existed prior to the Constitution".[27]

If maintenance payments for the support of a spouse are to cease upon that spouse engaging in a sexual relationship with another person this must be clearly stated in the agreement. Modern agreements more usually state that maintenance

22. See also *Rose v. Rose* (1883), 8 P.D. 98, (C.A.).
23. *Fearon v. Earl of Aylesford, supra*.
24. [1940] I.R. 42 (H.C.).
25. *Ibid.* at pp. 51, 52.
26. Here the wife under the deed was to pay the husband maintenance and it was the husband who was living in adultery (1945), 79 I.L.T.R. 97, (S.C.).
27. *Ibid.* at p. 102.

will cease to be payable for the support of a spouse if that spouse and another "co-habit as husband and wife" for a continuous specified period or upon the spouse entitled to receive maintenance going through a ceremony of marriage with another "whether or not such ceremony creates a valid and recognisable marriage under Irish Law." This latter provision is designed to deal with the position of the spouse who "remarries" after obtaining a decree of annulment from the Marriage Tribunals of the Roman Catholic Church or after obtaining a foreign decree of divorce that is not recognisable under Irish Law.

Even if maintenance ceases to be payable under the terms of a separation agreement a spouse is, of course, still free to seek a maintenance order by issuing proceedings under the Family Law . . . Act, 1976.

Clauses relating to property: The property provisions in a separation agreement vary according to the circumstances and wishes of the parties concerned. Their content totally depends on the amount of property owned by the spouses and the terms upon which agreement is reached. Thus it may be agreed between spouses that the family home be sold and the proceeds divided in agreed proportions between them. Alternatively, it may be agreed that the home be transferred from one spouse to the other, or that a spouse be granted sole right of residence in the home, the other spouse agreeing not to enter or approach the home without the former's consent. If the family home is held in or transferred into the sole name of one spouse, the other spouse may give a general consent to the sale of the said home at any future date for the purposes of the Family Home Protection Act, 1976, so as to obviate the necessity of the former spouse having to seek such a consent many years after the parties have separated prior to a sale taking place.

Agreement may also be reached as to which spouse is to discharge the mortgage repayments on the family home and to repay bank loans or other moneys owed by the parties. Provision may also be made for the manner in which the contents of the family home and other property is to be dealt with. If spouses jointly own a business, the agreement may specify the terms upon which it is to be wound up or the manner in which their interests are to be divided. Spouses may also renounce their succession rights under Part 9 of the Succession Act, 1965.[28] Finally the parties to the agreement may exclude section 21 of the Family Law . . . Act, 1976, from applying to any property purchased or money saved by one spouse out of any allowance payable to that spouse by the other under the provisions of any clause in the separation agreement.[29]

Medical Clause: Many separation agreements require the spouse who is obliged to pay maintenance to also discharge medical and dental expenses incurred by the dependent spouse and children of the family. For example, a husband may covenant to insure his wife and children with the Voluntary Health Insurance Board for inpatient private or semi private hospital treatment. Liability to insure the children would normally end when the obligation to pay maintenance for their support ceases under the agreement.

Indemnification Clause: It is usual for both the husband and the wife to indemnify each other from liability for all future debts incurred by either of them. Additionally, a deed may specifically provide that the sole financial obligations owed

28. See p. 348.
29. See p. 340.

by each spouse to the other are those set down in the agreement. Such a clause will not prevent either seeking maintenance under the 1976 Act at a future date.

DISCHARGE OF SEPARATION AGREEMENT

An agreement may be discharged by the subsequent agreement of the parties, or in accordance with a term in the original agreement.[30] Alternatively there may be a repudiation of the agreement by one party, giving the other the right to treat it as discharged if he so wishes. Whether there is such a repudiation is purely a question of fact. Continued failure on the part of a husband to pay maintenance might be regarded as such.[31] Again a fundamental breach of the contract may entitle the other party to regard himself as discharged from its obligations.[32] Non-observance of one particular covenant, however, is unlikely to be sufficient to entitle the other party to regard himself as so discharged. The fact that one party does not observe one covenant in a contract will not entitle the other party to renege from obligations arising under another covenant, unless they are so phrased as to be interdependent.[33]

A separation agreement entered into in order to determine the rights of the parties while living apart is put to an end by reconcilement and renewed cohabitation. However, covenants in an agreement may be phrased so as not to be dependent on the parties living apart and may still remain binding after cohabitation has resumed, unless the parties agree to discharge them. Thus financial provisions or a settlement made in the deed for the benefit of a wife and children may still be effective. Everything, however, depends on the construction of the particular deed.[34]

Finally, covenants in a separation agreement can still be held binding after a decree of divorce *a mensa et thoro*[35] or *a vinculo*[36] or it seems after a decree of nullity[37] for a voidable but not a void marriage.[38] In the case of the latter the agreement is regarded as having no effect, being made as a consequence of mistake, the parties at no time being married.

REMEDIES FOR BREACH OF AN AGREEMENT

Ordinary damages are always obtainable for breach of an agreement, specific performance is available to force a spouse to carry out a covenant, for example, to transfer property to trustees to be used for the benefit of his wife,[39] and the remedy of injunction is available to restrain a party from breaching a non-molestation[40] or non-interference clause or a promise not to bring proceedings

30. *Newsome v. Newsome* (1871), L.R. 2, P. & D. 306, (Ct. of D. & M. Causes). Here the wife promised to be bound only if her husband "remained true to her". It was held that his subsequently committing adultery terminated the agreement.
31. The innocent spouse is not bound to inform the spouse in breach that he has accepted the repudiation. It is sufficient if there is evidence that upon repudiation he treated the contract as a dead letter. See *Pardy v. Pardy* [1939] 3 All E.R. 779; [1939] P. 288, (C.A.).
32. *Besant v. Wood* (1879), 12 Ch. D. 605, (M.R.); *Morrall v. Morrall, supra.*
33. *Fearon v. Aylsford, supra.*
34. *Negus v. Forster* (1882), 46 L. T. 675, (C.A.); *Ruffles v. Alston* (1875), L.R. 19, Eq. 539, (V.–C.M.); *Nicol v. Nicol* (1886), 31 Ch. D. 524, (C.A.). See Article entitled "Agreements for Separation followed by Re-cohabitation", (1886), 20 I.L.T. & S.J. 295–6.
35. *Gandy v. Gandy, supra.*
36. *May v. May* [1929] 2 K.B. 386, (C.A.); *Charlesworth v. Holt* (1873), L.R. 9 Exch.38. See Article "Dissolution of Marriage–Effect on Separation Agreements", (1941), 75 I.L.T. & S.J., 289–90; 295–97.
37. *Adams v. Adams* [1941] 1 K.B. 536, (C.A.); *Fowke v. Fowke* [1938] 2 All E.R. 638; [1938] Ch. 774, (Ch. Div.).
38. *Galloway v. Galloway, supra.*
39. *Lurie v. Lurie* [1938], 3 All E.R. 156; 159 L.T. 249; (Ch. Div.).
40. *Sanders v. Rodway* (1852), 16 Beav. 207; 20 L.T.O.S. 122; 51 E.R. 757, (Rolls Ct.).

for past misconduct.[41] Further, periodical payments of maintenance provided for in an agreement may be payable to a District Court clerk, and enforceable by an order for attachment of earnings if the agreement is made a rule of court in accordance with the provisions of section 8 of the Family Law . . . Act, 1976.[42]

THE NEED FOR REFORM

It is submitted that when marital breakdown occurs and spouses agree to resolve their differences by the conclusion of a separation agreement, the law should seek to achieve four objectives. It should ensure that the welfare of any children of the spouses is properly protected, that proper provision in relation to support and housing is made for the dependent spouse and children, that in so far as is possible the necessity for future litigation between the spouses is obviated and seek to encourage spouses to reorganise their lives and plan for the future with a degree of security and certainty. In order to achieve the latter three objectives some spouses wish to conclude 'once and for all' financial settlements, by which, more usually, the husband is to pay a lump sum to the wife and/or transfer property owned by him into the wife's sole name, in consideration for the wife waiving her rights to future maintenance. However, as a result of the Supreme Court's decision in H.D. v. P.D.[43] estranged spouses are no longer able to conclude permanent and binding settlements of this nature as there is no existing legal mechanism to protect the husband from future claims for maintenance by the wife.

To a husband this type of settlement is advantageous only if it terminates what is otherwise an open-ended legal obligation to support his wife and if it enables him to plan his future with a degree of financial certainty. To a wife such a settlement is advantageous if she is to receive a sum of money sufficiently large or property sufficiently valuable as to enable her to become financially independent of her husband and free of the problems that can be experienced by a wife in receipt of weekly maintenance payments, such as the fear that if the husband leaves the jurisdiction she may be left with no means of support other than social welfare payments.

It is submitted that amending legislation should provide that if a permanent financial settlement is concluded between spouses, under the terms of which a lump sum payment is to be made and/or property is to be transferred to the dependent spouse and (a) both spouses extinguish their rights to future maintenance, and (b) such settlement is approved by the High Court as properly protecting the interests of all the parties to it and their dependent children, and (c) is made a rule of court, such settlement is binding on the parties to it and is an absolute bar on either party applying for maintenance for his or her support at any future date. It is further submitted, however, that in order to properly fulfil the first objective, this provision should only apply to spouses' maintenance and should not extend to children's maintenance. The overriding public interest in protecting the welfare of children requires that the courts be in a position to vary all orders and agreements made in relation to children when circumstances change and financial orders and agreements relating to children should be open to such variation.

---

41. *Lett v. Lett, Supra.*
42. See p. 280.
43. *Supra.*

CHAPTER 8

DIVORCE A MENSA ET THORO[1]
(Judicial Separation)

By virtue of the Matrimonial Causes . . . Act, 1870, the High Court has in-herited the jurisdiction of the Ecclesiastical Courts to grant a decree of divorce *a mensa et thoro*.[2] The Courts Bill, 1980, as initiated, proposes to confer juris-diction also on the Circuit Court to hear and determine such proceedings.

The remedy is in a sense misleadingly named in that it does not amount to a divorce in the popular meaning of the term but only to a judicial separation of the spouses. In order to distinguish it from a divorce *a vinculo matrimonii* which the Irish courts have no power to grant, and for convenience sake, this remedy will, in the pages that follow, be occasionally referred to as a decree of judicial separation. As in the case of other jurisdiction inherited from the Ecclesiastical Courts, the court has to exercise its jurisdiction to grant such a decree on principles and rules "which shall be as nearly as may be comfortable to the principles and rules on which the Ecclesiastical Courts acted". Thus its powers to give relief are as limited as the powers possessed and exercised by the Ecclesiastical Courts in the first half of the 19th century.

The only grounds for which relief can be granted are cruelty, adultery or unnatural practices.[3] The latter ground arises so rarely that it is not discussed further in the text. The authorities for its existence are in footnote 3 below.

Effect of Decree

A decree of divorce *a mensa et thoro* does not dissolve a marriage so as to permit the parties to remarry. It merely relieves a spouse from the duty of cohabiting with the other. It can be said that it suspends the cohabitation obligation of marriage. The obligation is not terminated for all time, as if at some future date a reconciliation takes place and the parties again wish to cohabit, the decree may be discharged and the obligation thus revived.

It is intended first to examine the grounds on which a decree can be obtained,

---

1. For the procedure to be followed to bring such proceedings see R.S.C. Order 70 (S.I. No. 72 of 1962).
2. *A mensa et thoro*—Latin for "from bed and board".
3. See Shelford's *Law of Marriage*, (1841), p. 364. See also Kisby, *The Law and Practice of the Court on Matrimonial Causes and Matters*, (Dublin (1871), p. 5. This ground has been relied on in very few cases. See *Bromley v. Bromley*, (2) Burns Ecc. Law 499 n; 2 Add 158 n. In this case a woman founded her claim and was granted a divorce *a mensa et thoro* on the ground that her husband had been found guilty of assaulting another with intent to commit an unnatural act with him for which he was sentenced to two years imprisonment.

See also *Mogg v. Mogg* (1824), 2 Add 292; 162 E.R. 301, (Arches Ct.). The wife sought a decree on the grounds of cruelty and unnatural practices. The evidence for the latter ground was that her husband had been convicted of assaulting another with the intent of engaging in homosexual conduct.

and the various bars to the obtaining of relief, and then to set out a number of criticisms and recommendations for reform.

ADULTERY

Adultery may be defined as voluntary sexual intercourse between two persons of whom one or both are married but not to each other. In a suit for divorce *a mensa et thoro* on this ground, the only parties to the proceedings are the two spouses. The person with whom a spouse is alleged to have committed adultery is never a party but will usually be called as a witness.

Nature of the Act

For the commission of adultery it is not necessary for the complete act of sexual intercourse to have taken place, but there must have been at least some penetration of the female by the male organ.[4] Sexual play falling short of penetration does not constitute adultery.

In order to be guilty of adultery a person must have consented to sexual intercourse. Thus the rape of a wife does not constitute adultery on her part.[5] Moreover a spouse who is mentally ill may be regarded as incapable of giving the requisite consent.[6] Rarely will there be direct evidence of the fact of adultery.[7] "The fact is inferred from circumstances that lead to it by fair inference as a necessary conclusion".[8]

A confession by the adulterous spouse has been held not to be sufficient evidence by itself. It must be corroborated by other testimony or by the evidence of the surrounding circumstances in order to prevent a decree being granted as the result of collusion.[9]

Standard of Proof

In *Loveden* v. *Loveden*[10] Sir William Scott stated that

> "The only general rule that can be laid down on the subject is that the circumstances must be such as would lead the guarded discretion of a reasonable and just man to the conclusion . . ."

It has been said that this standard is more stringent than that required of a plaintiff in other civil actions which may be determined on a mere balance of probability, but less stringent than the standard of proof "beyond reasonable

---

4. *Dennis v. Dennis (Spillett cited)* [1955], P. 153; [1955], 2 All E.R. 51, (C.A.); *Sapsford v. Sapsford and Furtado* [1954], P. 394; [1954], 2 All E.R. 373, (Assize).
5. *Redpath v. Redpath and Milligan* [1950], 1 All E.R. 600, (C.A.), where it was said that once the act of intercourse is established, the burden is on the wife to show that the act was forced against her will.
6. *Long v. Long and Johnson* (1890), 15 P.D. 218, (P.D.A.); *Yarrow v. Yarrow* [1892], P. 92, (P.D.A.); *Hanbury v. Hanbury* [1892], 8 T.L.R. 559, (C.A.).
7. *Loveden v. Loveden* (1810), 2 Hag. Con. 1; 161 E.R. 648, (Consistory Ct.); *Allen v. Allen and Bell* [1894], P. 248, (C.A.); *Grant v. Grant* (1839), 2 Curt. 16; 163 E.R. 322 (Arches Ct.).
8. *Loveden v. Loveden, supra*, 161 E.R. at p. 648; *Chambers v. Chambers* (1796), 1 Hag. Con. 440; 161 E.R. 610 (Consistory Ct.).
9. *Burgess v. Burgess* (1817), 2 Hag. Con. 222; 161 E.R. 723, (Consistory Ct.); *Noverre v. Noverre* (1846), 1 Rob. Ecc. 428; 163 E.R. 1090, (Eccles. Ct); *Owen v. Owen* (1831), 4 Hagg. Ecc. 259; 162 E.R. 1441, (Consistory Ct.). See also *Robinson v. Robinson & Lane* (1859), 1 Sw. & Tr. 362; 164 E.R. 767, (Consistory Ct.), and the comments thereon in Kisby, *Matrimonial Causes and Matters*, p. 10–11.
10. *Supra.*, 161 E.R. at pp. 648–9.

doubt" which is required in criminal cases.[11]

It is submitted that the standard of proof should be the same as that required in all civil cases, i.e. simply the balance of probability. This is the standard required for proof of cruelty, when alleged as a ground for a decree.

The matter is, however, complicated by the common law rule that the presumption of legitimacy can only be rebutted by evidence putting the matter beyond reasonable doubt.[12] Thus, if the standard of proof for adultery is less, a court could find itself in a position whereby, arising from identical evidence, it would regard adultery as proved, but a child conceived around the time when the adultery was committed to be legitimate. This is not however as incongruous as it may at first appear. Proof of a wife's adultery does not imply that a child conceived by her, close to the time when the adulterous act was committed, is of necessity illegitimate. It is perfectly possible for a woman to have sexual relations with her husband while also having an affair with another man. In such circumstances although she may be guilty of adultery, it is also possible for her child to be the legitimate offspring of her marriage.[13]

CRUELTY

Cruelty on the part of either spouse is a ground for a decree *a mensa et thoro*. What constitutes cruelty depends on the facts of each individual case. Conduct which may plainly amount to cruelty in one case may not do so in another. Much depends on the nature of the conduct, the attitude of the spouses and their physical and mental weaknesses.[14] Cruelty cannot be measured by a fixed invariable standard. It is relative to age, to strength, to health and to capacity of endurance upon the part of the sufferer. [15]

Nature of the Conduct

The courts have consistently refused to lay down a comprehensive definition of cruelty. However it is established that no conduct amounts to legal cruelty unless it causes injury to life, limb or health, bodily or mental or a reasonable apprehension of such.[16]

It has been frequently stated that it is not necessary to wait until a person's health is impaired for a decree to be granted.[16a] It is sufficient if the conduct is such as to give rise to a reasonable apprehension of personal injury.[17] Whilst

11. *Lyons v. Lyons* [1950], N.I. 181, (K.B.D.); see also *Ginesi v. Ginesi* [1948], P. 179, [1948], 1 All E.R. 373, (C.A.); *Blyth v. Blyth and Pugh* [1966], A.C. 643, [1966], 1 All E.R. 524 (H.L.); *Bastable v. Bastable and Sanders* [1968], 3 All E.R. 701, (C.A.).

12. See Chapter 11; see also *Morris v. Davies* (1837), 5 Cl. & Fin. 163; 7 E.R. 365, (H.L.); *Bosvile v. A.-G* (1887), 12 P.D. 177 (D.C.); *Preston-Jones v. Preston-Jones* [1951], A.C. 391; [1951], 1 All E.R. 124, (H.L.); *Bastable v. Bastable, supra; F. v. F.* [1968], 1 All E.R. 242; [1968], P. 506, (P.D.A.).

13. See (1949), 65 L.Q.R. 220, "Standard of Proof of Adultery", by J. A. Coutts.

14. *Gollins v. Gollins* [1964], A.C. 644; [1963], 2 All E.R. 966, (H.L.).

15. *Russell v. Russell* [1897], A.C. 395, (H.L.); *D'Aguilar v. D'Aguilar* (1794), 1 Hagg Ecc. 733; 162 E.R. 748; *Evans v. Evans* (1790), 1 Hag. Con. 35; 161 E.R. 466, (Consistory Ct.); *Westmeath (Earl of) v. Westmeath (Countess of)*, (1827), 2 Hagg. Ecc. Supp. 1, 148; 162 E.R. 992, 1043, (Consistory Ct.); *Milford v. Milford* (1866), L.R. 1 P. & D. 295, (P. & D.).

16. *Evans v. Evans, supra; M'Keever v. M'Keever* (1876), I.R. 11 Eq. (Ct. for Matr. Causes); *Russell v. Russell, supra; Gollins v. Gollins, supra; Jamieson v. Jamieson* [1952] A.C. 525; [1952], 1 All E.R. 875, (H.L.), (Sc.); see also *Ward v. Ward* [1948], N.I. 60, (K.B.D.); *Bradley v. Bradley* (11th December 1970), *Irish Times*, in which the address of Murnaghan J. to the jury is reported.

16a. See for example the old Irish case of *Carpenter v. Carpenter* (1827), Milw. Rep. 159, heard in the Consistory Court of Dublin.

17. See e.g. *Evans v. Evans, supra; Kirkman v. Kirkman* (1807), 1 Hag. Con. 409; 161

the main question to be determined is whether X's conduct in fact gave rise to Y fearing such injury (the test thus being subjective) it has been said that "it must not be an apprehension arising merely from an exquisite and diseased sensibility of mind".[18] Thus if Y's fear of X has arisen as a result of abnormal hypersensitivity a decree may be refused.[19]

The character of the conduct must be "grave and weighty"[20] before a decree will be granted. In the face of such conduct the court grants a decree on the basis of it being impossible for the unoffending spouse to carry out her (his) marital duties in "a state of dread".[21]

Physical Violence: Where physical violence is involved there is generally little difficulty in proving injury or a reasonable apprehension of injury to a person's health. Thus, in *Murphy* v. *Murphy*[22] the wife obtained a decree against her husband, the particulars of cruelty set out in her petition against her husband referring to assaults, beatings, woundings, threats, locking out from the home, the use of demanding and insulting language and refusing to support and maintain her and her children of the marriage.

There does not have to be proof of one individual act of cruelty, proof of an aggregate of acts, each of which individually are insufficient to obtain relief, may when taken together be sufficient.[23] If the violence alleged is trivial or was perpetrated in self-defence as the result of provocation it may be excusable.[24] However provocation will only afford a defence if it bears a direct relation to the subsequent violence.[25] The violence of a wife will only justify such force by the husband as is necessary to restrain her. In *Holden* v. *Holden*, Sir W. Scott said:[27]

> "It is not necessary that the conduct of the wife should be entirely without blame. For the reason which would justify the imputation of blame to the wife will not justify the ferocity of the husband . . . If the passions of the husband are so much out of his own control, as that it is inconsistent with the personal safety of the wife to continue in his society, it is immaterial from what provocation such violence originated".

Mental Cruelty: In the 19th century the courts expressed extreme unwillingness to grant a decree for "mental cruelty". Thus in *Evans* v. *Evans* it was said

---

E.R. 598, (Consistory Ct.).
    18. *Evans v. Evans, supra*, 161 E.R. 466 at p. 468, per Sir William Scott.
    19. *Jamieson v. Jamieson, supra.*
    20. *Evans v. Evans, supra* per Sir William Scott at p. 467; *Russell v. Russell, supra.*
    21. *Milford v. Milford, supra*, per Lord Penzance at p. 299. See also *Evans v. Evans, supra*, where Sir William Scott (later Lord Stowell) stated at p. 467, "The causes must be grave and weighty, and such as to shew an absolute impossibility that the duties of the married life can be discharged. In a state of personal danger no duties can be discharged; for the duty of self-preservation must take place before the duties of marriage which are secondary both in commencement and obligation . . . "
    22. [1962–63] Ir. Jur. Rep. 77 (H.C.); see also *M'Keever v. M'Keever* (1876), I.R.II Eq. 26, (Ct. for Matr. Causes).
    23. *D'Arcy v. D'Arcy* (1887), 19 L.R. Ir. 369 (Ct. for Matr. Causes); *Cochrane v. Cochrane (Royce intervening)* (1910), 27 T.L.R. 107, (P.D.A.).
    24. *Waring v. Waring* (1813), 2 Hag. Con. 153; 161 E.R. 699; 2 Phill Ecc. 132; 161 E.R. 1098, (Consistory Ct.).
    25. In *O'Reardon v. O'Reardon* (February 1975), unreported, (H.C.), in his direction to the jury Finlay P. stated "In order for cruelty to be justified there must be a reasonable relationship between the cruelty and the provocation . . . you have to relate the provocation to the extent of the cruelty".
    27. (1810), 1 Hag. Con. 453; 161 E.R. 614 at p. 616 (Consistory Ct.); see also *Stick v. Stick* [1967], 1 All E.R. 323, (Assize).

that

"What merely wounds the mental feelings is in few cases to be admitted, while unaccompanied with bodily injury either actual or menaced. Mere austerity of temper, petulance of manners, rudeness of language, a want of civil attention and accommodation, even occasional sallies of passion if they do not threaten bodily harm do not amount to legal cruelty".[28]

However, acts which one hundred years ago would not have been regarded as causing injury or reasonable apprehension of injury, would today with greater medical understanding of mental ill health and its causes be more readily accepted as having such an effect.

Standard of Proof

Cruelty must be proved on the balance of probabilities by the person alleging it. It is a question of whose version of the facts is "the more probable".[29] Thus the standard required is less than that required for adultery. It is not essential to show that the respondent intended to injure the petitioner. It is sufficient if having regard to all the circumstances a person's conduct can fairly be called cruel. Proof of intention however may be an important element in a particular case, especially where mental cruelty is alleged.[30]

Conduct Constituting Cruelty

A wide variety of different types of conduct apart from the application of physical violence by one spouse against the other has been held to constitute cruelty. These include nagging,[31] threats,[32] abuse,[33] spitting on a spouse,[34] wilful communication of venereal disease,[35] uncontrollable fits of drunkenness,[36] refusal of sexual intercourse[37] and the use of contraceptives or the practice of coitus interruptus against the other's wishes.[38] Desertion by itself however is not cruelty[39] and does not afford a ground for granting a decree. Moreover cruelty to the children may be cruelty to the other spouse. Thus cruelty to the children in the presence of the mother has been held sufficient ground for a decree.[40]

28. 161 E.R. 466 at p. 467, per Sir William Scott. See also *Harris v. Harris* (1813), 2 Hag. Con. 148; 161 E.R. 697 (Consistory Ct.); 2 Phill. Ecc. 111; 161 E.R. 1093 (Consistory Ct.); *Le Brocq v. Le Brocq* [1964], 3 All E.R. 464, (C.A.).
29. *O'Reardon v. O'Reardon, supra.*
30. See *Gollins v. Gollins, supra; Williams v. Williams* [1964], A.C. 698, (H.L.); *Jamieson v. Jamieson, supra;* in *Holden v. Holden* (1810), 1 Hag. Con. 453; 161 E.R. 614 (Consistory Ct.), per Sir W. Scott at p. 616, "It is not necessary . . . to inquire from what motive such treatment proceeds, it may be from turbulent passion, or sometimes from causes which are not inconsistent with affection . . ."
31. *Atkins v. Atkins* [1942], 2 All E.R. 637, (P.D.A.).
32. *Carpenter v. Carpenter, supra; Bostock v. Bostock* (1858), 1 Sw. & Tr. 221; 164 E.R. 701, (Ct. for Div. & Matr. Causes).
33. *Harris v. Harris, supra; Kelly v. Kelly* (1869), L.R. 2 P. & D. 31 and, on appeal, (1870), L.R. 2 P. & D. 59, (Ct. for Div. & Matr. Causes).
34. *Saunders v. Saunders* (1847), 1 Rob. Ecc. 549; 163 E.R. 1131, (Consistory Ct.); *O'Reardon v. O'Reardon, supra.*
35. *Brown v. Brown* (1865), L.R. 1 P. & D. 46, (Ct. for Div. & Matr. Causes); *Durant v. Durant* (1825), *supra; Browning v. Browning* [1911], P. 161; 104 L.T. 750, (P.D.A.).
36. *Power v. Power* (1865), 4 Sw. & Tr. 45 and 173; 164 E.R. 1483, (Ct. for Div. & Matr. Causes); *Baker v. Baker* [1955], 1 W.L.R. 1011, (Assize).
37. *Sheldon v. Sheldon* [1966], P. 62; [1966], 2 All E.R. 257, (C.A.); *Slon v. Slon* [1969] P. 122; [1969], 1 All E.R. 759, (CA.).
38. *Knott v. Knott* [1955], P. 249; [1955], 2 All E.R. 305, (Assize); *Forbes v. Forbes* [1956] P. 16; [1955], 2 All E.R. 311, (P.D.A.).
39. *Evans v. Evans, supra,* at p. 496.
40. *Suggate v. Suggate* [1859], 1 Sw. & Tr. 489, 492, 497; 164 E.R. 827, 828, 830, (Ct. for Div. & Matr. Causes); *Wright v. Wright* [1960], P. 85; [1960] All E.R. 678, (C.A.).

No conduct or act carries with it an inherent quality of cruelty. The essential question is "whether this conduct by this man to this woman or *vice versa* is cruelty". The answer to this question depends on the particular facts of the case and the temperament and character of the spouses concerned.

BARS TO RELIEF

Condonation

It is a complete defence to a charge of cruelty or adultery that the petitioner has condoned the matrimonial offence of the respondent. Condonation is effected by the voluntary forgiveness and reinstatement of the erring party to the marriage by the wronged spouse with knowledge of the offence of the former.[41] In the case of cruelty the question of the petitioner's knowledge of the acts of cruelty will hardly arise. In the case of adultery it is necessary to show that the act or acts of alleged condonation were done with knowledge of the other's adultery.

Condonation may be express or implied. The best evidence of the latter is the continuance or resumption of sexual intercourse, or the fact that the parties continued to live or have resumed living in the same house. But such evidence is not conclusive.[42] For example a wife who remains in the home with the adulterous spouse may do so simply because she has nowhere else to go and no means of her own. Mere delay in bringing a petition after a spouse's misconduct does not necessarily amount to condonation, but if the delay is very long and there is no good excuse it may bar a remedy. Much depends upon the validity of the reason for the delay. If it is due to a hope of reconciliation, or a lack of means to bring a suit, or a desire to avoid upsetting a close relation it should not be an obstacle to obtaining relief.[43] As a wife was regarded by the Ecclesiastical Courts as being under the power of her husband, condonation has been said not

It has been suggested that cruelty by a mother to her child cannot ground a petition by the father. "It may well be that violence practised on a child in its mother's presence, would be injurious to the health of a woman, gifted as most women are, with tender sensibility when their offspring suffers, but men are supposed to be made of sterner stuff;". *Manning v. Manning* (1873), I.R. 7 Eq. 520, (Matr. Causes). It is submitted that the question of the effect of such behaviour on the father and whether it is such as to amount to legal cruelty must depend on the facts of the particular case. It is unlikely that a court would today refuse to regard violence practiced on a child by its mother, in the father's presence as cruelty to the father.

41. *D'Aguilar v. D'Aguilar* (1794) *supra; Turton v. Turton* (1830), 3 Hagg. Ecc. 338; 162 E.R. 1178, (Consistory Ct.); *Burch v. Burch* [1958], 1 All E.R. 848; [1958], 1 W.L.R. 480, (P.D.A); *Swan v. Swan* [1953], P. 258, [1953], 2 All E.R. 865, (P.D.); *O'Reardon v. O'Reardon* (Feb. 1975), unreported, (H.C.) in his direction to the jury, Finlay P. stated "If one of the parties to a marriage commits an offence against the marriage, and if with knowledge of that offence, the other party resumes or continues ordinary marital relations then the act condones the marital offence". If P. condones D.'s adultery with X. not knowing that D. has also committed adultery with Y. the former condonation in relation to X. is not avoided. *Bernstein v. Bernstein* [1893], P. 292, (C.A.); see also *Inglis v. Inglis and Baxter* [1968], P. 639, (P.D.A.); *Wells v. Wells* [1954], 1 W.L.R. 1390, (C.A.).

42. If a husband has sexual intercourse with his wife knowing that she has committed adultery, the husband's act in consenting to intercourse amounts to condonation. On the other hand a wife's sexual intercourse with a husband after he has committed a matrimonial offences does not automatically establish that she condones his conduct. *Henderson v. Henderson* [1944], A.C. 49, (H.L.); see also *Mackrell v. Mackrell* [1948], 2 All E.R. 858, (C.A.); *Blyth v. Blyth* [1966], A.C. 643, (C.A.).

43. *Coode v. Coode* (1838), 1 Curt. 755; 163 E.R. 262, (Consistory Ct.); *Newman v. Newman* (1870), L.R. 2 P. & D. 57, (P.D.); *Durant v. Durant* (1825), 1 Hagg. Ecc. 733; 162 E.R. 734, (Arches Ct.); *Turton v. Turton* (1830), 3 Hagg. Ecc. 338; 162 E.R. 1178, (Consistory Ct.); *Beeby v. Beeby* (1799), 1 Hagg. Ecc. 789; 162 E.R. 755, (Consistory Ct.); *Kirkwall (Lady) v. Kirkwall (Lord)* (1818), 2 Hag. Con. 277; 161 E.R. 742, (Consistory Ct.).

to be presumed as a bar so readily against her as it is against the husband.[44]

The forgiveness and reinstatement of the guilty spouse is subject to an implied condition that the injury shall not be repeated, and that the unoffending spouse shall in every respect be "treated with conjugal kindness".[45] Subsequent matrimonial misconduct revives condoned cruelty or adultery.[46] The principle being that "much less is sufficient to destroy condonation than to found an original suit".[47] Thus intimacy falling short of adultery, or misbehaviour insufficient in itself to found a suit for cruelty, is sufficient to revive condoned adultery and cruelty.[48] After condonation an offence can be revived by an act not *eiusdem generis*. Thus cruelty can revive adultery and vice versa.[49]

A spouse who condones another spouse's offence and subsequently commits an offence of his own, may be divorced by the other in the absence of a revival of the condoned offence.[50] Finally in the case of *Rose* v. *Rose*[51] it was held that an agreement between spouses not to take proceedings against each other in respect of any offence already committed, precluded either spouse from obtaining relief on the ground of such offence, and further that any matrimonial wrong committed after the date of the agreement would not, if the parties had so agreed, revive the offence 'condoned' by the agreement.[52]

Recrimination

A plea of recrimination provides a complete answer to a suit whether brought by the husband or wife. Thus if the petitioner alleges and proves adultery on the part of the respondent, the respondent may answer that the petitioner has also committed adultery. Proof of the latter's allegations may be established by evidence less than that necessary to prove an original suit.[53]

In order for a plea of recrimination to succeed it is not necessary that the misconduct of the petitioner should have occurred prior to that of the respondent.[54]

44. *Durant v. Durant, supra*, per Sir John Nicholl at p. 744; *Beeby v. Beeby, supra*.
45. *Durant v. Durant, supra*, per Sir John Nicholl at p. 744; see also *Dent v. Dent* (1865), 4 Sw. & Tr. 105; 164 E.R. 1455, (Ct. for Div. & Matr. Causes).
46. *Durant v. Durant, supra; Dent v. Dent, supra*; see also *Murphy v. Murphy, supra; O'Reardon v. O'Reardon, supra*.
47. *Cooke v. Cooke* (1863), 3 Sw. & Tr. 126; 164 E.R. 1221 at p. 1226, (Ct. for Div. & Matr. Causes); *M'Keever v. M'Keever, supra; Westmeath v. Westmeath, supra; Bostock v. Bostock, supra*.
48. *M'Keever v. M'Keever, supra; Westmeath v. Westmeath, supra; Winscom v. Winscom* (1864), 3 Sw. & Tr. 380; 164 E.R. 1322, (Ct. for Div. & Matr. Causes); *Bramwell v. Bramwell* (1831), 3 Hagg. Ecc. 618; 162 E.R. 1285, (Consistory Ct.); *Worsley v. Worsley* (1730), 1 Hagg. Ecc. 734; 162 E.R. 735, (Consistory Ct.); *Gardiner v. Gardiner* [1949], N.I. 126 (K.B.D., N.I.); *Cooke v. Cooke* [1948], N.I. 46 (K.B.D., N.I.).
49. From Finlay P.'s direction to jury in *O'Reardon, supra. Bramwell v. Bramwell supra; Durant v. Durant, supra*.
50. *Anichini v. Anichini* (1839) 2 Curt. 210; 163 E.R. 387, (Consistory Ct.); *Beeby v. Beeby, supra; Seller v. Seller* (1859), 1 Sw. & Tr. 482; 164 E.R. 823; see also *Everett v. Everett and McCullum* [1919], P.D., 298, (C.A.).—If a petitioner is still committing the condoned or connived at offence, he or she cannot get a decree on the basis of the misconduct of the other spouse.
51. (1883), 8 P.D. 98; [1881—85], All E.R. Rep. 141, (C.A.).
52. See also *Courtney v. Courtney* [1923], 2 I.R. 31; (1923), 57 I.L.T.R. 42, (C.A.), discussed at p. 111. In this case there was no evidence of the commission of a matrimonial offence after the date of the agreement.
53. *Forster v. Forster* (1790), 1 Hag. Con. 144; 161 E.R. 504, (Consistory Ct.); see however *Chettle v. Chettle* (1821), 3 Phill. Ecc. 507, 161 E.R. 1399, (Arches Ct.). It seems from this case that for a plea of recrimination to succeed in reply to a petition on the ground of adultery, the respondent must allege and prove adultery on the part of the petitioner. On the other hand adultery on the part of the petitioner may afford a good defense to the petitioner's allegation of cruelty.
54. *Proctor v. Proctor* (1819), 2 Hag. Con. 292; 161 E.R. 747; (Consistory Ct.); *Beeby v. Beeby, supra*.

Moreover, it is possible upon proof of the charge of recrimination, and failure on the part of the petitioner to prove his original charge, for the Court to pronounce a decree *a mensa et thoro* in favour of the respondent.[55]

Connivance

Connivance on the part of the petitioner to the respondent's adultery constitutes a complete bar to his alleging such adultery as a ground for a divorce *a mensa et thoro*.[56] Mere negligence or inattention on the part of the unoffending spouse is not sufficient, there must be proof that it was his intention that adultery should take place or continue.[57] Once evidence of the presence of such "corrupt intention" has been given it is not necessary to prove "express" or "active" consent, mere passing acquiescence being sufficient to raise the implication of consent.[58] Such consent must be freely given; the principle on which connivance is based being *volenti non fit injuria*.[59] Connivance by its very nature must be precedent to the occurrence of the adultery alleged.[60] Moreover there must be a distinct connection between the connivance and subsequent acts of adultery. Even if such connection did exist at one stage, it seems that it may be held to have "spent". This may occur where subsequent to the act of connivance there has been a complete reconciliation between the parties, or where considerable time has elapsed before the commission of a further matrimonial offence.[61] A spouse who keeps watch or hires a private detective to keep watch on the other spouse whom he suspects of adultery is not guilty of connivance.

"A man who suspects his wife of adultery is allowed to keep watch on her with suitable witnesses, so that he may give proof of her adultery; for that is not conniving at her sin, but discovering her guilt so that he can get his remedy. It is one thing to request, counsel, or commend evil to be done; that is not allowed, but it is quite another thing to permit, or not to interfere with the doing of evil. That is sometimes allowed as being the greater good".[62]

The evidence to establish connivance is generally, as in the case of condonation, circumstantial, and if the facts are equivocal there is a presumption against the presence of the requisite corrupt intention.[63] The petitioner in all *mensa et thoro* cases must swear in an affidavit, filed with his or her petition, that there is no connivance or collusion between the petitioner and the other spouse.

Collusion

Collusion can be looked on as another aspect of connivance. It is an absolute

---

55. *Harris v. Harris* (1829), 2 Hagg. Ecc. 376; 162 E.R. 894, (Consistory Ct.); *Kenrick v. Kenrick* (1831), 4 Hagg. Ecc. 114; 162 E.R. 1389, (Consistory Ct.).
56. *Harris v. Harris, supra; Forster v. Forster, supra.*
57. *Rix v. Rix* (1777), 3 Hagg. Ecc. 74; 162 E.R. 1085, (Arches Ct.); *Hoar v. Hoar*, (1801) 3 Hagg. Ecc. 137; 162 E.R. 1108, (Consistory Ct.); *Gipps v. Gipps and Hume* (1864), 11 H.L. Cas. (H.L.); *Rogers v. Rogers* (1830), 3 Hagg. Ecc. 57; 162 E.R. 1079, (Arches Ct.); see also *Harris v. Harris, supra; Phillips v. Phillips* (1844), 1 Rob. Ecc. 144; 163 E.R. 993, (Consistory Ct.).
58. *Moorsom v. Moorsom* (1792), 3 Hagg. Ecc. 87; 162 E.R. 1090, (Consistory Ct.).
59. i.e. a person cannot complain of an act to which he has freely consented. *Rogers v. Rogers, supra; Moorsom v. Moorsom supra; Harris v. Harris, supra; Reeves v. Reeves* (1813), 2 Phill. Ecc. 125; 161 E.R. 1097, (Arches Ct.); *Douglas v. Douglas* [1951], P. 85; [1950], 2 All. E.R. 748, (C.A.).
60. *Churchman v. Churchman* [1945], P. 44; [1945], 1 All E.R. 190, (C.A.).
61. See *Godfrey v. Godfrey* [1965], A.C. 444; [1964], 3 All E.R. 154, (H.L.).
62. *Timmings v. Timmings* (1792), 3 Hagg. Ecc. 76 at p. 82; 162 E.R. 1086; *Phillips v. Phillips, supra; Douglas v. Douglas, supra.*
63. *Rogers v. Rogers, supra; Kirkwall v. Kirkwall, supra; Turton v. Turton* (1830), 3 Hagg. Ecc. 338; 162 E.R. 1178, (Consistory Ct.).

bar to the obtaining of a decree. In order for there to be collusion it is not necessary for there to be an agreement between the parties for one to commit a matrimonial offence so as to enable the other to bring separation proceedings. In *Churchward* v. *Churchward*[64] it was stated that

"If the initiation of a suit be procured, and its conduct (especially if abstention from defence be a term) provided for by agreement that constitutes collusion, although no one can put his finger on any fact falsely dealt with, or withheld".

Collusion today has no practical importance, as, if spouses agree to separate, there is no sense in their colluding to bring proceedings for a divorce *a mensa et thoro*. They can simply enter into a separation agreement.

Ancillary Relief

In proceedings for a judicial separation, the court has ancillary power to determine a husband's liability to pay alimony to his wife[65] and to make a declaration that the spouse, by reason of whose misconduct the decree is made, is unfit to have custody of any children of the marriage.[66] In addition, the court has jurisdiction, since the coming into force of the Family . . . Law Act, 1976, to make an order barring a spouse from the place where the other spouse resides.[67] Injunctions may also be granted by the court in appropriate cases, for example, the court may by way of injunction prevent a violent husband from entering, attending at or approaching a place where his wife carries on business. A decree of divorce *a mensa et thoro* also automatically deprives the guilty spouse of his or her right to a share in the estate of the other spouse, either as a legal right or on intestacy under the Succession Act, 1965.[68]

The court does not possess jurisdiction to determine any other disputes between the spouses and may not make any other orders in relation to the family home or other family property, nor can it grant custody of a child to a particular parent or resolve other disagreements between the parties over a child's upbringing.[69] It cannot order the payment of maintenance for the support of children or of a husband and orders for alimony are limited to ordering periodical payments, the court being unable to make lump sum orders in favour of a spouse.

So as to circumvent the limited jurisdiction of the court and to avoid duplication of litigation, the practice has grown up in recent years of simultaneously instituting and attempting to have tried together, special summons proceedings claiming whatever other relief is required to finalise all matters in dispute between spouses. The latter proceedings may contain claims under all or any of the following enactments—the Married Women's Status Act, 1957, the Guardianship of Infants Act, 1964, the Family Law Protection Act, 1976 and the Family Law . . . Act, 1976. Although this manœuvre saves spouses the expenses of a second and completely new court hearing, the necessity to use two totally separate sets of proceedings results in much unnecessary paper work, expense and duplication.

---

64. [1895], P. 7 at p. 30, (P.D.).
65. See p. 281 *infra*.
66. See p. 226 *infra*.
67. See p. 335 *infra*.
68. See p. 355 *infra*.
69. A. W. Samuels K. C. in 1910 criticised this limitation on the jurisdiction of the court. See 'Divorce Jurisdiction in Ireland' (1911) I.L.T. & S.J.6.

CRITICISMS AND SUGGESTED REFORMS[70]

Since the inception in 1970 of the Scheme of Social Welfare Payments for deserted wives over 11,150 applications have been made by wives seeking support for themselves and their children.[71] Between 1st April 1969 and the 1st November 1979 the Free Legal Advice Centres operating in limited areas of Dublin assisted 13,418 clients with marital problems.[72] The District Court which serves the Metropolitan District Court area in Dublin heard 540 applications for maintenance in 1971-73 inclusive under the limited provisions of the now repealed Act of 1886.[73] The same court dealt with 1,778 applications under the wider jurisdiction conferred on it by the Family Law . . . Act, 1976, in the first four years of its operation.[74] In the period 1976-1979 inclusive 657 Special Summonses seeking maintenance were issued in the High Court. In the same period, 764 Special Summonses were issued in the High Court under the Guardianship of Infants Act, 1964.[75] Despite this, since 1970 there has only been an average of 5 decrees of divorce *mensa et thoro* a year granted by the High Court.[76]

In recent years *mensa et thoro* proceedings have become increasingly irrelevant due to the anachronistic nature of the proceedings themselves and the courts limited power to make ancillary orders. The expense involved in bringing such proceedings has also been a major deterrent although this may not be the case in future years, as a result of the provision by the State of civil legal aid.

In practice, *mensa et thoro* proceedings are only instituted when one or both spouses are relatively wealthy, as the possibility of a court decree terminating

70. See generally J. Dominian, *Marital Breakdown* (1968); the F.L.A.C. *Report* 1972; K. O'Higgins, *Marital Desertion in Dublin* (E.S.R.I. 1974); *Statement on Family Law* by the Council for Social Welfare. A Committee Of The Catholic Bishops Conference (Dublin 1974). Kenny J., "Some Aspects of Family Law", S.Y.S. Lecture No. 48 (Cork 1970). W. Duncan, "Desertion and Cruelty in Irish Matrimonial Law" (1972), 7 I.J. (n.s.) 213 particularly 237–239; M. Viney, *The Broken Marriage*, (Irish Times Publication, Dublin 1970), N. Fennell,*Irish Marriage How are Ye!* (Mercier Press, Dublin 1974);*Putting Asunder: A Divorce Law for Contemporary Society*, Report of a group appointed by the Archbishop of Canterbury in January 1964 (S.P.C.K., 1966); English Law Commission, *Reform of the Grounds of Divorce: The Field of Choice* (1966, Cmnd. 3123). W. Duncan, *The Case for Divorce*, (Irish Council for Civil Liberties, Dublin, 1979).
71. Dail Debates Vol. 320 (29th April, 1980) col. 120.
72. From statistics supplied by the Free Legal Advice Centres.
73. Nineteenth Interim Report of the Committee on Court Practice and Procedure— Desertion and Maintenance, p. 11.
74. See Dail Debates Vol. 322 (10th June, 1980) cols. 53 and 54. In the period the 6th May, 1976 to the 31st May, 1978 1,501 District Court Maintenance Summonses and 797 District Court Barring Summonses were issued for the hearing of such proceedings outside the Dublin Metropolitan District Court Area.
75. See Dail Debates Vol. 322 (10th June, 1980) cols. 52 and 54.

76.

Year	Number of Petitions issued for a Divorce a mensa et thoro	Number of Decrees granted
1970	40	11
1971	27	5
1972	30	9
1973	26	2
1974	51	10
1975	43	4
1976	37	3
1977	29	5
1978	40	1
1979	34	2

Total for ten year period = 357 petitions issued and 52 decrees granted.

See Dáil Debates Vol. 307 (7th June, 1978) col. 607 and Dáil Debates Vol. 322 (10th June, 1980) col. 52. By way of comparision, in 1979, 263 High Court Special Summonses were issued seeking maintenance under the Family Law Act, 1976. See Dáil Debates Vol. 322 col. 54.

the "guilty" spouse's succession rights while the petitioner's are retained, confers on the petitioning spouse a major advantage in any negotiations that may take place to settle the proceedings. The possibility of a jury trial with the attendant publicity also puts pressure on a respondent not to proceed to a full court hearing. The action has rightly been described as a "privilege" of the richer members of society.[77]

Mr. Justice Kenny in a speech to the Society of Young Solicitors in 1970 stated that:[78]

"One of the most serious failings of our legal system is the absence of an expeditious, cheap method of hearing separation proceedings. The cases involve petitions, answers, applications for alimony, settlement of issues before the Master, motions to fix the amount of security to be given by the husband and finally a jury trial lasting three or four days. It is a risk which a husband cannot insure against and if he has to pay the costs of both sides, the result is usually financial ruin. So never bring a separation action if any other method is available of procuring a reasonable financial settlement."

It is submitted that even if the court procedures were simplified or if the legal costs were reduced the present remedy would still be totally inadequate.

The Role of the Law: It is submitted that the proper role of the law of judicial separation is (a) to function in a manner that encourages voluntary reconciliation between estranged spouses, and (b) to provide a dignified release from the matrimonial obligation of cohabitation and to protect those likely to be adversely affected by the estrangement, when reconciliation is not possible.

Upon a court being of the opinion that a marriage has irretrievably broken down it should possess jurisdiction to afford judicial recognition to the factual collapse of the marital relationship by the granting of a decree of separation. Further, the court should be empowered to make ancillary orders to properly and efficiently regulate the consequences of marital breakdown without the parties having to institute further proceedings. Such jurisdiction should empower the courts to make ancillary orders so as to provide financial protection for the economically dependent spouse and any children of the parties, to determine property rights between the parties and to make property transfer orders where desirable, to ensure a spouse physical protection from molestation or attack by the other spouse and to determine any disputes as to guardianship or custody of the children of the spouses.

Matrimonial offence: As has been seen, the present law is based not on the concept of marital breakdown, but on the notion of the matrimonial offence. In exercising its jurisdiction to grant a decree, the court is much concerned with assigning 'fault' and trying to discover whether a party is guilty of behaviour inconsistent with the obligations of matrimony. If one party is 'guilty' a decree will be granted in favour of the 'innocent' spouse. If both are guilty no decree may be granted at all. There is in the law "a tacit assumption that where there is family failure, the failure is in some way culpable and merits redress or punishment".[79]

Instead of encouraging, the law actively discourages reconciliation between estranged spouses. The bars to relief encourage a spouse to stand his ground

77. F.L.A.C. Report 1972 at p. 23.
78. Kenny J., *supra*, p. 5.
79. The Council for Social Welfare, *supra*, p. (iv).

upon the other stepping outside the matrimonial bond, as if an attempted reconciliation fails, the latter may find himself barred from relying on the former's offence. The law by insisting on labelling parties are guilty or innocent tends to perpetuate and exacerbate family conflict, rather than promote future harmony.

The Free Legal Advice Centres have strongly attacked the whole basis of the present law. In a report published in 1972 they wrote that "The idea that marriages break up because only one party has committed an offence against the other is unreal. In the vast majority of cases both parties are at fault in varying degrees. To permit divorce only where some matrimonial offence has been committed is to put the emphasis on the symptoms of the breakdown rather than the breakdown itself".[80]

The doctrine of the matrimonial offence is based on the contractual concept of marriage. The court offers a remedy to a spouse when the other breaks the contract of matrimony. The fact that marriage is a personal relationship which cannot function without the cooperation of the parties is ignored.

Irretrievable breakdown: The Council for Social Welfare in a statement on family law wrote that "where a marriage has broken down the parties should separate as amicably as possible".[81] Both they and F.L.A.C. have recommended that irretrievable breakdown should be the basis for judicial intervention rather than the commission of a matrimonial offence. F.L.A.C. stated[82] that "A law founded on the doctrine of breakdown would accord with social realities and would have the merit of showing up divorce or separation for what in essence it is—not a reward for marital virtue on one side and a penalty for marital delinquency on the other, not a victory for one spouse and revenge for the other, but a defeat for both—a failure of a relationship in which both members were involved, however unequal their responsibility".

Reconciliation: Intrinsically embodied in a law of separation based on the notion of breakdown would be the question of the possibility of the reconciliation of the spouses. The present law simply asks whether a matrimonial offence has been committed? A law based on marital breakdown would ask whether despite the commission of a matrimonial offence, the relationship has any possibility of remaining viable? The fact that one or both of the parties are in court seeking a separation will in the great majority of cases give a "no" answer to such question. However, the present legal inhibitions to attempted reconciliation prior to going to court would be effectively eliminated. In fact an attempt at reconciliation, rather than endangering the obtaining of relief, would be encouraged by a doctrine of marital breakdown, in that evidence of an attempted reconciliation that failed, would provide almost conclusive proof of the breakdown of the marriage.

80. F.L.A.C. Report 1972 at p. 24.
81. *Supra*, p. 9.
82. F.L.A.C. Report 1972 at p. 25.

CHAPTER 9

DIVORCE A VINCULO MATRIMONII

Article 41.3.2.⁰ of the Constitution states "No law shall be enacted providing for the grant of a dissolution of marriage".

The Irish courts have never possessed jurisdiction to pronounce a decree of divorce *a vinculo matrimonii* (for brevity referred to simply as divorce in the following pages) so as to dissolve a valid marriage and permit the parties to remarry. In England prior to the Reformation marriage was regarded as a sacrament and indissoluble. Whilst after the Reformation a marriage could be dissolved by an Act of Parliament, the Ecclesiastical Courts still adhered to the doctrine of indissolubility and the jurisdiction that they passed on to the High Court in 1870 has never been extended so as to enable it to pronounce a decree of divorce.

In Ireland before the Act of Union divorce proceedings could take place in the Irish Parliament. Prior to the dissolution of the Irish Parliament there were nine divorce Bills passed and one rejected. Thereafter, the jurisdiction was transferred to the Imperial Parliament.

In 1857, the Matrimonial Causes Act set up the Court of Divorce and Matrimonial Causes in England and jurisdiction was conferred upon it to grant decrees *a vinculis*. This Act, however, did not apply to Ireland and until 1922 a marriage of spouses domiciled in Ireland could only be validly dissolved, according to Irish Law, by a Bill of Divorce passed by the British Parliament.[1]

A husband could obtain a Bill on the ground of his wife's adultery. Adultery alone would not suffice in the case of a Bill submitted on behalf of the wife. She had ɔ show that the adultery was accompanied by some other matrimonial offence, such as bigamy, incest or an unnatural offence. Although the Act of 1857 and the subsequent Matrimonial Causes Act, 1884, did not apply to Ireland, it was decided that in so far as they set down grounds for divorce,[2] the Acts were to apply to Parliamentary divorces sought by persons domiciled in Ireland.[3] As a consequence, following their enactment, a husband could present a petition for divorce on the ground of his wife's adultery; whilst a wife could petition on the grounds that her husband had committed incestuous adultery, adultery with bigamy,[4] adultery with cruelty, adultery coupled with a failure on the husband's

---

1. See generally J. Roberts, "Divorce Bills in the Imperial Parliament", (Dublin, 1906) See also W. Duncan, "Desertion and Cruelty in Irish Matrimonial Law" (1972) 7 I.J. (n.s.) 213–216. *Mayo-Perrott v. Mayo-Perrott* [1958], I.R. 336, (S.C.); *Bank of Ireland v. Caffin* [1971], I.R. 123, (H.C.).
2. See Sect. 27 of the Act of 1857, and Sect. 5 of the Act of 1884.
3. *Westropp's Divorce Bill* (1886), 11 App. Cas. 294 (H.L.); *Parker's Divorce* [1922], 2 I.R. 154n (H.L.); see also *Bell v. Bell* [1922], 2 I.R. 103, 152; (1922), 56 I.L.T.R. 46, (K.B.D.).
4. i.e. he had married another after marrying the petitioner. If the petitioner was a party to the second "marriage" such marriage would be void, and there would be no necessity to obtain a divorce.

part to comply with a decree of restitution of conjugal rights,[5] rape, sodomy, or bestiality.

Before a petitioner could successfully bring parliamentary divorce proceedings he or she had to bring proceedings for divorce *a mensa et thoro* in the Irish High Court.[6] Moreover a husband alleging his wife's adultery was required to bring an action of criminal conversation against the adulterer or to provide a satisfactory reason for not having done so. As a consequence of the enormous costs involved in bringing such divorce proceedings they were completely outside the reach of the great majority of people.[7]

1922 and after

The Constitution of the Irish Free State contained no prohibition against divorce legislation. By the beginning of 1925 three bills for divorce *a vinculo* had been deposited in the Private Bill Office of the Oireachtas. In February, 1925 the Dáil without a division passed the following resolution:

> "That the Joint Committee on Standing Orders relative to Private Business be requested to submit additional Standing Orders regulating the procedure to be adopted in connection with Private Bills relating to matrimonial matters other than Bills of divorce *a vinculo matrimonii*, and to propose such alterations in the Standing Orders as will prevent the introduction of Bills of Divorce *a vinculo matrimonii*; and that a message be sent to the Seanad requesting its concurrence in this resolution".[8]

In his speech introducing this motion, Mr. W.T. Cosgrave[9] said:

> "I have no doubt but I am right in saying that the majority of people of this country regard the bond of marriage as a sacramental bond which is incapable of being dissolved. I personally hold this view. I consider that the whole fabric of our social organisation is based upon the sanctity of the marriage bond and that anything that tends to weaken the binding efficacy of that bond to that extent strikes at the root of our social life".[10]

On the resolution coming before the Senate, the Cathaoirleach ruled that the proposal was *ultra vires* the Constitution, inasmuch if divorce *a vinculo* was to be prohibited it could be done only by legislation and not by standing orders.[11] In June 1925 the Seanad proposed an alternative method by resolution that such bills should be read a first time in each House before being proceeded with in the

---

5. *Parker's Divorce, supra.*

6. *Sinclair's Divorce Bill* [1897], A.C. 469, (H.L.); see also *Sinclair v. Sinclair* [1896], 1 I.R. 603, (Ch. Div.).

7. See A.W. Samuels, "Evidence to the Royal Commission on Divorce" in 1910 reported in (1911) 45 I.L.T. & S.J. 6, or see "Reports of the Royal Commission on Divorce and Matrimonial Causes" Vol. III 1912–13 Cmnd. 6481, xx 455, Samuels, although he referred to the exorbitant costs involved in obtaining a Divorce Bill, was adamant that public opinion in Ireland would be totally against the introduction of a court to deal with full dissolution of marriage in this country; see also M.J. Roberts evidence to the same commission in Reports Commissioners, Vol. III, 1912–13 XX.

8. Dáil Debates, Vol. X cols, 156 and 182; see also D. O'Sullivan, *"The Irish Free State and Its Senate"*, 161–5; J.H. Whyte, *"Church and State in Modern Ireland 1923–1970"*, (Gill and Macmillan, Dublin 1971), p. 36–37; C. Davitt, Some Aspects of the Constitution and the Law in Relation to Marriage, 1968, Studies at p. 16; M. Nolan, "The Influence of Catholic Nationalism on the Legislation of the Irish Free State" (1975) 10 I.J. (n.s.) 128 at pp. 133–137.

9. W.T. Cosgrave led the Government of the Irish Free State from 1922–1932. Eamon de Valera led the Free State Government from 1932–1937.

10. Dáil Debates, Vol. X, col. 158.

11. Seanad Debates, Vol. IV, cols. 929 to 945.

Senate. However, the Dáil rejected this proposal, the Seanad rescinded its previous resolution, and there the matter ended.[12] Thereafter until the enactment of the present Constitution there were no Standing Orders providing for private bills of divorce and no legislation on the subject.[13]

The 1937 Constitution

Mr. de Valera in his introductory speech on the second stage of the Draft Constitution in the Dáil said in relation to Article 41:

"We pledge the State to protect the family in its constitution and its rights generally. This is not merely a question of religious teaching; even from the purely social side, apart altogether from that, we would propose here that we should not sanction divorce. Therefore no law can be passed providing for divorce".[14]

Later on he said:

"With regard to the question of divorce in general there is no doubt that sometimes there are unhappy marriages, but from the social point of view, without considering any other point of view, the obvious evil would be so great, and it has been proved to be so great in other countries that I do not think any person would have any difficulty—at least I would not—in making a choice in this matter".[15]

There was little discussion in the Dáil of the social significance of Article 41.3.2°. Indeed during the debate in Committee on Article 41 the House had on two occasions to be counted to see whether a quorum of 20 deputies was present.

Article 41.3.2° has since its enactment been the subject of frequent criticism. It has been especially criticised as being an imposition by Roman Catholics of their religious convictions on the non-Roman Catholic minority in the State.[16] Mr. de Valera justified its enactment on both religious and social grounds. It is now intended to examine how closely Article 41.3.2° reflects Roman Catholic teaching on marriage and then to discuss the validity of the social premise on which the Article is based.

THE CANON LAW OF THE ROMAN CATHOLIC CHURCH

Under the Canon Law of the Roman Catholic Church a valid sacramental and consummated marriage between two Christians is indissoluble and remains

---

12. Seanad Debates, Vol. V, cols. 426 to 482 (434 to 443 reports a famous speech by W.B. Yeats in defence of the right to divorce) and cols. 820 to 824 and 933 to 938; Dáil Debates Vol. XII, cols. 1563 to 1572; see also *McM. v. McM.* and *McK. v. McK.* [1936], I.R. 177 at pp. 187—189; see also J. White, *Minority Report*, (Gill and Macmillan, Dublin 1975), pp. 116—118.
13. See J.H. Whyte, *supra*, p. 57—60 where he discusses the Protestant opposition to the Dáil's attitude to divorce and other legislation. For an invaluable insight into attitudes to divorce in the 1920s, see, *correspondence regarding divorce in the Irish Free State (24 Jan 1923—1 Aug 1929)* File No. S.4127—Cabinet Papers, State Records Office, Dublin Castle.
14. Dáil Debates, Vol. 67, col. 63.
15. Dáil Debates, Vol. 67, col. 1886.
16. Kenny J. in "Some Aspects of Family Law" (Society of Young Solicitors Lecture 46; 22nd March, 1970) stated that "In his view ... the great majority of non-Roman Christians in the Republic and Northern Ireland are as strongly opposed to divorce laws as Roman Catholics and do not regard the absence of a divorce law as an imposition of the views of others on them". On the other hand see J. White, *Minority Report*, 114—120; J.H. Whyte, *Church and State ...*, *supra* 51—53. Report of the Committee on the Constitution, (Dec. 1967), 43—4. See also footnote 30 below.

in force throughout the lifetime of the parties.[16a] Thus a civil decree of dissolution granted by the State would not be recognised by the Church. The Church can however in specific limited circumstances itself dissolve a marriage.[17] These are described below.

I. **Non-consummation**: According to Roman Catholic doctrine the rite of marriage is a sacrament. The union between husband and wife is representative of the union between Christ and the Church. It is symbolic of the inseparable alliance between the Son of God and mankind. This symbolism is only found fully in the consummated marriage however. A validly celebrated[18] marriage of a Roman Catholic only becomes indissoluble when the husband and wife have in fact become "one flesh". For centuries the Roman Pontiffs have exercised power to dissolve an unconsummated marriage so permitting the parties to remarry. Such a dissolution can be granted upon the request of both parties or one of them. Dissolution will be granted as of right where the marriage is unconsummated and one party has made a definite choice to enter religious life. In the absence of either party having such intention dissolution will be granted providing there is "a just cause", e.g. if it appears that the marriage will result in discord and misery for the parties concerned or if one of the parties wishes to marry another within the Church and to lead a normal family life.[19]

II. **Dissolutions in favour of the faith**

(a)   *Pauline Privilege*: A marriage between two unbaptised persons is regarded by the Roman Catholic Church as a true marriage but as lacking the sacramental character attached to a Christian marriage.[20] By virtue of the Pauline Privilege[21] the Church is able to dissolve such a marriage if one of the parties becomes a baptised Roman Catholic[22] and the other refuses to live peacefully with the former and does not wish to convert.[23] Provided these three conditions can be

16a. Canon 1118 of the Code of Canon Law (1917).

17. For an interesting discussion from the point of view of Roman Catholic theology of the basis for the continuous assertion by Catholic theologians and philosophers of the indissolubility of marriage see "The Indissolubility of Marriage in Natural Law", by Liam Ryan (1963), 30 *Irish Theological Quarterly*, 293–310 and I.T.Q. 62–71; W.J. Harrington, "Jesus' Attitude Towards Divorce" (1970) 37 I.T.Q. 199, and "The New Testament and Divorce" (1972), 39 I.T.Q. 199. For a recent critique of the Church's attitude to civil divorce see P.J. McGrath, "Marriage Annulments: A Second Look" (Nov. 1975) Vol. 1. *Maynooth Review* 45.

18. "Validly celebrated" here means validly celebrated according to Roman Catholic doctrine.

19. Canon 1119; see also G.H. Joyce, S.J., *Christian Marriage*, Chapter X; Bouscaren, Ellis and Korth, *Canon Law – A Text and Commentary*, 4th Edition, (U.S.A. 1963) chap. XVIII, p. 612–614; R. Brown, *Marriage Annulment*, (London 1971) chap. 6 and *Marriage Annulment in the Catholic Church* (Kevin Mayhew, England, 1977) chap. 7; Davitt, *Studies*, 1968, p. 16–17.

20. The Roman Catholic Church regards the marriages of all baptised Christians as sacramental unions. Thus the marriage of two members of The Church of Ireland would be so recognised by the Roman Catholic Church and could not be dissolved by means of the Pauline Privilege. Alternatively a marriage of two members of the Jewish faith is not regarded as possessing this sacramental character and could be dissolved.

21. See Canon 1120 to 1126; Passage in 1 Corinthians VII, 12–15. See also *Christian Marriage, supra*, Chapter XI; *Canon Law, supra*, ch. XVIII, p. 614–628; See also Dáil Debates, Vol. 67, col. 251, the divergence between civil law embodied in Art. 41.3.2⁰ and Canon Law in relation to the Pauline Privilege was pointed out by Deputy James Dillon to Mr. de Valera in the debate on the 1937 Constitution.

22. Valid baptism outside the Roman Catholic Church is sufficient foundation for the use of the privilege. But there would be practical difficulties in the procedure unless the person became a Roman Catholic, see *Canon Law, A Text and Commentary*, by Bouscaren, Ellis & Korth, p. 615.

23. It must be clearly established that the couple cannot live together. See R. Brown, *Marriage Annulment in the Catholic Church, supra*, p. 98.

properly established the convert is permitted by the local Bishop to proceed to a new marriage.[24] The former valid marriage subsists until the moment when the second marriage, valid by reason of the Pauline Privilege, takes place, i.e. the first marriage is dissolved by the exercise of the Pauline Privilege.

(b) *Petrine Privilege*:[25] A marriage between a baptised and a non-baptised person may be a valid marriage in the eyes of the Church,[27] but also lacks the sacramental character of the marriage of two baptised persons. Such a marriage can be dissolved by the Pope upon the baptised party[28] wishing to marry a Roman Catholic.

In the case of both the Pauline and Petrine privileges a dissolution is said to be granted *in favorem fidei* i.e. in favour of the faith.

Just as the State will not recognise a Church decree of nullity it will not recognise a Church dissolution. Whereas a dissolution in "Favour of the Faith" is of little importance in the Irish context in that it rarely occurs, a dissolution for non-consummation is of major importance. We have already seen that a civil decree of nullity can be obtained for impotence. However, the canonical concept of "non-consummation" is far wider than the legalistic civil concept of "impotence". Thus, many persons who could get their marriages dissolved by the Church on the former ground are unable to obtain civil release from their bond, the State holding it to be indissoluble.

Whereas the civil prohibition on dissolution is an accurate reflection of the Church's general attitude to marriage, in specific instances it is stricter, in that it holds marriages indissoluble that the Church itself exempts from such categorisation. The State not only refuses to dissolve marriages that the Church regards as dissoluble, but also regards as indissoluble marriages that the Church has annulled and marriages that it does not recognise as having taken place, e.g. those celebrated by Roman Catholic parties in registry offices.

1967 DÁIL COMMITTEE ON THE CONSTITUTION

Art. 41.3 was examined by the all party committee on the Constitution whose report was published at the end of 1967.[29] The Committee pointed out that the prohibition on divorce has been criticised for ignoring "The wishes of a certain minority of the population who would wish to have divorce facilities and who are not prevented from securing divorce by the tenets of the religious denominations to which they belong".[30] It drew attention to

"the more liberal attitude now prevailing in Catholic circles in regard to the

---

24. There is no intervention by the Pope or any other ecclesiastical authority other than the local Bishop who verifies the necessary conditions.

25. See Canon 1127; see also R. Brown, *Marriage Annulment*, ch. 7 and *Marriage Annulment in the Catholic Church*, Chap. 8.

27. By the impediment of disparity of cult a marriage between a person baptised as a Roman Catholic and a non-baptised person is invalid, unless the necessary dispensation is obtained. This only applies to Roman Catholics and does not affect the status (in the eyes of the Roman Catholic Church) of a baptised non-Catholic who marries an unbaptised person, see R. Brown, *Marriage Annulment*, p. 71.

28. If the non-baptised party becomes baptised subsequent to the marriage, for a dissolution to be granted, it must be established that the couple did not live together as man and wife after the baptism.

29. See Report of the Committee on the Constitution, (Dec. 1967), 43–45.

30. See also "The Constitution" a report of a working party of the Irish Theological Association, (June 1972), 23, The Furrow 374. The Committee recommended the deletion of Article 41.3.2.⁰ on the ground that it is religiously divisive in so far as it has been interpreted as representing the Roman Catholic position on dissolution of marriage.

rites and practices of other religious denominations, particularly since the Second Vatican Council"

and noted as shown above that the present law

"deprives Catholics also of certain rights to which they would be entitled under their religious tenets. There are several circumstances in which the Catholic Church will grant dissolutions of valid marriages or will issue declarations of nullity . . . The absolute prohibition in our Constitution has therefore the effect of imposing on Catholics regulations more rigid than those required by the law of the Church".[31]

The Committee suggested the replacement of the present article by one such as the following:-

"In 'the case of a person who was married in accordance with the rite of a religion no law shall be enacted providing for the grant of a dissolution of that marriage on grounds other than those acceptable to that religion."

They went on to state that

"This wording would . . . meet the wishes of Catholics and non-Catholics alike. It would permit the enactment of marriage laws acceptable to all religions. It would not provide any scope for changing from one religion to another with a view to availing of a more liberal divorce regime. While it would not deal specifically with marriages not carried out in accordance with the rites of a religion, it would not preclude the making of rules relating to such cases".

According to J.H. Whyte[32] no religious leaders of any denominations were consulted as to the content of this recommendation. Upon its publication, it met instant opposition from Cardinal Conway, the Roman Catholic Archbishop of Armagh and from both Archbishops of the Church of Ireland. Leaders of other

31. See also "Church & State in the Constitution of Ireland", Rev. E. McDonagh, (1961), 28 I.T.Q. 131.
32. See *Church and State in Modern Ireland*, 1923–1970, by J.H. Whyte, pp. 347–349; see also *The Changing Face of Catholic Ireland*, D. Fennell, p. 187. The Catholic Bishops particularly condemned it as being the first step on the way to permitting civil divorce for the whole population. Cardinal Conway stated "The proposal would involve the setting up of divorce courts in the Republic. In the beginning they would be limited in scope but, inevitably, this would only be the first step. Everyone knows how these things spread once the gates are opened. Already, within 24 hours, one national newspaper has suggested that there should be divorce for all.
One must have the greatest possible respect for the tenets of our fellow-Christians. Yet, in fact, comparatively few of them believe in divorce, and still fewer of them want it. Even these few have little difficulty in securing a divorce elsewhere, and many of them have done so. One may ask whether what inconvenience there is, affecting very few, would justify such a radical and far-reaching break with our national traditions.
One thing is certain. Once the first divorce law has been introduced it will only be a matter of time till it is extended to apply to everybody. I am sure that Irish husbands and wives will ponder very carefully on what the committee's proposal to open the gates to divorce will almost inevitably lead to in terms of family life". Irish Times, 15th December, 1967 p. 1.
The then Bishop of Dublin, Dr. McQuaid, two months later said "Civil divorce, as a measure which purports to dissolve a valid marriage, is contrary to the law of God. The experience of other countries has proved that civil divorce produces the gravest evils in society. The effort, even if well-intentioned, to solve hardships within marriage by civil divorce has invariably resulted for society in a series of greater sufferings and deeper evils". Irish Times, (26th February, 1968), p. 9.
See also comments of Dr. Daly, the Roman Catholic Bishop of Ardagh and Clonmacnois, Irish Times, (December 21st, 1967); and see "Socio-Political Aspects of Divorce", by Rev. (now Bishop) Jeremiah Newman, (1969), 23 Christus Rex p. 5.
The Church of Ireland Archbishop of Dublin, Dr. Simms, and the Church of Ireland

Protestant denominations gave the Committee's recommendation a reserved welcome.[33]

In discussing Art. 41.3.2.º the Committee failed to make a distinction that is central to the whole controversy surrounding the Article; that is, the distinction between the civil contract of marriage and its effects under civil law and the religious ceremony and its religious effects. It is a distinction that tends to get blurred and confused in debates concerning nullity and divorce. As we have seen the annulment or dissolution of a marriage by the Church is not recognised by the State and *vice versa*. There is similar non-recognition of each other's competence over the marriage bond between the State and other religious denominations. Thus, it does not matter whether the State permits dissolution on grounds either consistent or inconsistent with the religious tenets of the parties seeking the dissolution. Irrespective of the grounds on which a decree is granted, the marriage will be regarded as unaffected in the religious sphere. It is only the civil contract of marriage over which the State has jurisdiction and for which it may legislate.

Leaving aside the question of whether the laws of the State should seek to enforce the various religious teachings on marriage in the manner suggested by the Committee,[34] the above recommendation if implemented would create more problems than it would resolve. If implemented, the Irish Courts would find themselves embroiled in complex assessments of the matrimonial doctrines of the various religious denominations, and couples who changed their religion subsequent to their marriage would find themselves bound by the doctrines of a religion they no longer adhered to.[35] Moreover the recommendation gives no guidance as to the circumstances in which State legislation ought to permit the grant of a divorce in accordance with the tenets of a person's religion, e.g. it is certainly arguable that it would not be good public policy for the State to permit Roman Catholics to obtain a divorce under the civil law in accordance with the Petrine Privilege or Pauline Privilege. Nor does it give guidance as to the grounds for which a divorce should be permitted in the case of parties married other than in accordance with the rites of a religion, i.e. in a registry office. The Committee reached a unanimous decision to permit a limited measure of divorce, a measure that is both undesirable and impossible to implement, without considering the one question that is fundamental in reaching a decision as to whether divorce legislation should be permitted and enacted, i.e. whether such legislation is socially desirable.[36]

Archbishop of Armagh both stated that their church upheld the indissolubility of the marriage bond. The latter, however, stated that he also wished to respect the rights of others who do not accept the principle of indissolubility. See Irish Times, (16th December, 1967) p. 1.

See also Editorial of Church of Ireland Gazette reprinted in Irish Times, (27th December, 1967), p. 9. "If there is to be freedom to divorce it is a freedom that ought to be open to all so far as the state is concerned. What the churches may lay down as a discipline to be accepted by their members is a different matter altogether. If it is right that divorce should be available to those whose consciences allow them to avail of it, then it should be left to their consciences to decide".

33. See Irish Times, (16th December, 1967), p. 1 and 6.

34. See "Revision of the Constitution; Religion and Marriage", by J.M. Kelly, Irish Times, (5th January, 1968).

35. See further, W. Duncan, *The Case for Divorce*, p. 40.

36. See P. Hannon "Catholics and Divorce", Vol. 27, The Furrow, p. 470, (Aug. 1976). In discussing whether divorce legislation should be introduced the author writes that the question should be regarded "not as a religious but as a socio-legal one . . . To consider it in terms of the respective rights of religious majorities and minorities is confusing and likely to obscure the real question. That question is how best is the state through legislation to cope with the fact that some marriages break down irretrievably?"

THE SOCIAL ARGUMENT

To Mr. de Valera "from the social point of view" divorce was an "obvious evil" and it had been proved to be such in other countries. No countries were named nor facts produced by him to substantiate this statement.[37] The Constitutional prohibition is based on the assumption that the existence of divorce facilities will be detrimental to the stability of marriage and cause marital breakdown. However, it has been seen in the previous chapter that without such legislation, there is already much evidence of a substantial marital breakdown problem in this country.[38] It is submitted that it is the factual breakdown of a marriage relationship and not the availability of divorce proceedings that constitutes a social evil. The collapse of a relationship may cause parties to seek a dissolution of the legal tie. The existence of a means of obtaining such a dissolution does not cause the relationship to collapse.[39]

The role played by divorce proceedings is not very different from the role played by separation proceedings. They are merely alternative remedies to deal with the problems that arise upon breakdown occurring. The sole difference is that the former permit parties to a broken marriage to marry someone different during the lifetime of the other party, whilst the latter do not.[40]

A right to divorce? Kenny J. in a speech to the Society of Young Solicitors stated that he was convinced that there is no such thing as "a right to divorce ... How can there be a right to convert a joint tenancy for life into a tenancy at will? How can there be a right to break a contract which the parties have entered into to last for their lives? Our law has always repudiated the idea that there is a right to break a contract."[41]

To this it can be replied, that marriage is something more than a commercial contract, it is a personal relationship. The question that should be posed and discussed is not whether there is a "right" to divorce or not, but in what way should legislation seek to deal with the human problems that arise upon the irretrievable breakdown of a marital relationship? It is submitted that, when a marriage becomes a marriage in name only, no social advantages can be gained by insisting on the preservation of a meaningless legal tie and condemning estranged spouses to a matrimonial limbo in which they are single in reality but married in law.[42]

Divorce legislation cannot be introduced without first, the majority of the population in a referendum voting either in favour of the deletion of Art. 41.3.2.°

37. G. Sheehy in "Studies", (Spring 1968) on p. 30 makes a similar statement in a reply to the article by Davitt, as does Dr. McQuaid in the above quotation. Neither cite any evidence to substantiate their statements.
38. See also W. Duncan, *The Case for Divorce, supra*, chap. 1.
39. See F.L.A.C. *Report* 1972, p. 24 where the organisation stated "Divorce does not cause family breakdown, it is the inadequacy of the families and the incompatability of the spouses that lead to divorce. Where one spouse deserts another or obtains a decree of judicial separation, or obtains a maintenance order, or an order for custody and maintenance of children under the Guardianship of Infants Act, or they simply part or sign a separation agreement, the marriage may be just as irretrievably broken down as if there has been a divorce". See also C. Murphy, "Divorce Irish Style", Irish Times, (21st Nov., 1975), p. 12.
40. See W. Duncan, *The Case for Divorce, supra*, p. 22.
41. J.M. Kelly, Irish Times, *supra*, stated "An ordinary commercial contract confers rights on both parties but not—except in cases recognised by the legal order—the right to avoid or rescind the contract. The same goes for the contract of marriage and it is nonsense to talk, at any level except an emotional level of a 'right' to 'divorce' "; for comment on the speech of Kenny J. see M. Viney "Broken Marriage", (Irish Times publication, Dublin 1970), p. 25 *or* see Irish Times, 26th-30th Oct., 1970.
42. See F.L.A.C. *Report* 1972, p. 24; AIM Group *Report* Number Two—"Legal Separation in Ireland", (Dublin 1976), p. 36. W. Duncan, *The Case for Divorce, supra*, chap. 4.

or for the enactment of a new Constitution not containing a prohibition on divorce. An ex-President of the High Court, Cahir Davitt, has emphasised the importance of making any decision as to the retention or deletion of the article on the basis of an understanding of all the factors involved. Upon an investigation being undertaken he suggested that it might "transpire that the number of marriages which have broken down beyond hope of redemption is much greater than is generally suspected and presents a really serious social problem. Is it practical politics or is it an ideal impossible of realisation", he asked "that the people should be put in a position to compare the social harm which can result from the availability of divorce *a vinculo* with that which can result from the existence in the community of many broken marriages, and freely to decide whether it is in the interest of the common good to accord to the victims of such unions what many of them may regard as simple justice?"[43]

Today, there is considerable evidence of the existence of a large number of marriages that have irretrievably broken down. Evidence that did not exist or was not available to the general public when Mr. Justice Davitt wrote the article from which the above passage was taken. The social problem referred to by the learned judge is now exacerbated by spouses whose marriages have broken down seeking to use other mechanisms and legal forms as a substitute for divorce. These include

(a) Marrying another person in a Roman Catholic Church after first obtaining a marriage annulment in the Church that is not recognised by the State.

(b) Marrying another person either in Ireland or outside Ireland after obtaining a non-recognisable foreign decree of divorce.[44]

(c) Executing a deed poll whereby a woman changes her surname to correspond with that of a man with whom she is residing, where one or both of them are already married to somebody else.

There are no available statistics as to the number of people who are living together having resorted to using one of the above forms of "remarriage" The parties to such "remarriages" in law are merely co-habitees and none of the protections that the law provides for spouses and their children extend to them. There is little doubt that if divorce was available in Ireland, the great majority of such co-habitees would obtain a divorce and remarry under Irish law. It is ironic, as one writer has remarked, that the very absence of divorce facilities is contributing to the growing phenomena of cohabitation outside legal marriage, when divorce is prohibited by Article 41 on the basis of a philosophy of providing support for family life based on marriage.[45] It is submitted that the deletion of Article 41.3.2 from the Constitution and the enactment of legislation to afford legal recognition to the social reality of dissolved marriages now requires serious consideration by both legislators and the general public.

---

43. "Studies", (Spring 1968), p. 18.
44. For the Law as to the Recognition of Foreign Divorces, see chapter 10.
45. W. Duncan, "Second Marriages After Church Annulments — A Problem of Legal Policy" (1978) vol. 72, *The Gazette of the Incorporated Law Society of Ireland*, p. 203. See also W. Duncan, "Supporting the Institution of Marriage in Ireland" (1978) 13 I.J. (n.s.) 215 at p. 227, where the author states that "There are signs that the absence of divorce is giving rise to practices of evasion and avoidance which characterised pre-divorce Italy".

CHAPTER 10

RECOGNITION OF FOREIGN DECREES OF DIVORCE A VINCULO[1]
ARTICLE 41.3.3.° AND ITS INTERPRETATION

The law relating to the recognition in this country of foreign decrees of divorce *a vinculo matrimonii* is governed by Art. 41.3.3.° of the Constitution. This article states that:

"No person whose marriage has been dissolved under the civil law of any other State but is a subsisting valid marriage under the law for the time being in force within the jurisdiction of the Government and Parliament established by this Constitution shall be capable of contracting a valid marriage within that jurisdiction during the lifetime of the other party to the marriage so dissolved".

The 1922 Constitution contained no article corresponding to Art. 41.3.3.° Its meaning was first judicially considered in *Mayo-Perrott* v. *Mayo-Perrott*.[2] The plaintiff had obtained a divorce *a vinculo matrimonii* in England, where she and her husband had been domiciled. Having been awarded the costs of the petition by the English court she sought to recover the sum remaining unpaid in the Irish courts, her former husband having come to reside within the jurisdiction of the Irish courts. The Supreme Court on appeal, however, refused to enforce the order for costs partly on the ground that the cause of action was of such a character that it could not have supported an action in this country and partly that to enforce an order which assisted the obtaining of a divorce decree was contrary to public policy.[3] Kingsmill Moore J. stated:[4]

"Our law will [not] give active assistance to facilitate in any way the effecting of a dissolution of marriage in another country where the parties are domiciled . . . [The law] would fail to carry out public policy if by a decree of its own Courts it gave assistance to the process of divorce by

---

1. See generally, C. Jones "The Non-Recognition of Foreign Divorces in Ireland" (1968), 3 I.J. (n.s.) 299; W. Duncan "The Future for Divorce Recognition in Ireland", 2 D.U.L.R. (No. 1) 1970; G. Lee: "Irish Matrimonial Law and the Married Status", 16 N.I. L.Q. 385; J.M. Kelly, *Fundamental Rights in the Irish Law and Constitution*, 2nd Ed. (1967), p. 199–204; J. O'Reilly "Recognition of Foreign Divorce Decrees" (1971), 6 I.J. (n.s.) 293; W. Duncan "Desertion and Cruelty in Irish Matrimonial Law", (1972), 7 I.J. (n.s.) 213; W. Duncan "Foreign Divorces Obtained on the Basis of Residence and the Doctrine of Estoppel", (1974), 9 I.J. (n.s.) 59; A.W. Kerr, "The Need for a Recognition of Divorces Act," (1976) 1 D.U.L.J. 11. P.M. North, *The Private International Law of Matrimonial Causes in the British Isles and the Republic of Ireland* (North Holland Publishing Company, 1977), p. 372–386; J.M. Kelly, *The Irish Constitution* (Jurist Publishing Co.Ltd., Dublin, 1980), p. 487–492.
2. [1958], I.R. 336, (S.C.).
3. See judgement of Kingsmill Moore J. and O'Daly J. especially.
4. *Supra* at p. 350.

entertaining a suit for the costs of such proceedings".[5]

However, while the courts will do nothing to facilitate the bringing of divorce proceedings, this does not of necessity mean that they will not recognise the change of status brought about by the grant of a decree of divorce. The meaning of Art. 41.3.3.° and the question as to whether the Irish courts will recognise a divorce granted by the courts of a foreign country was discussed by Maguire C.J. and Kingsmill Moore J.[6] Maguire C.J. regarded the article as

"clearly . . . designed to double bar the door closed in sub-s.2. Far from recognising the validity of a divorce obtained outside the country it seems to me expressly to deny to such a divorce any recognition for it prohibits the contracting of a valid marriage by a party who has obtained a divorce elsewhere. The sub-section says as plainly as it could be said that a valid marriage which is dissolved under the law of another State remains in the eyes of our law a subsisting valid marriage. It may be that the Constitution recognises that a decree of dissolution of marriage elsewhere may be valid in the country where it has been obtained, but to my mind as I have said, it denies it any validity here".[7]

Kingsmill Moore J. disagreed with the above interpretation. He reviewed a number of pre-1922 English and Irish decisions,[8] and on the basis of these, concluded that prior to that date the Irish courts would have recognised a divorce decree granted by a foreign court within the jurisdiction of the common domicile of the parties. The law was not affected by the enactment of the 1922 Constitution, nor by the coming into force of the 1937 Constitution. Art. 41.3.3.°, he stated, only denied recognition to divorces

"where, under the law for the time being in force within our jurisdiction (i.e. the jurisdiction of the Irish courts), the original marriage is regarded as valid and subsisting or in other words, where, by that law the divorce is regarded as not being effectual to put an end to the original valid marriage.[9]

---

5. See also *N.M. v. E.F.M.* (July 1978) unreported (H.C.) in which Hamilton J. held that the enforcement in this country of a maintenance order made in and consequent to English divorce proceedings could not be said to assist in or facilitate the process of divorce. See also J.M. Kelly, *The Irish Constitution, supra*, at p. 488 where the author refers to two further cases. These are Ex p. Minister for External Affairs: *Hovells v. Hovells* (1962) unreported (S.C.) in which the Supreme Court on the application of the Minister for External Affairs, on appeal from the High Court, ordered the examination within the jurisdiction of the courts of the Republic of Ireland of a witness in divorce proceedings then pending before a foreign court and *Heffernan v. Heffernan* (1955) unreported (H.C.) in which the High Court refused to make a similar order. The latter decision was not appealed. There are no detailed written judgements available in either case.
6. The Chief Justice found it "not easy to construe" whilst Kingsmill Moore J. stated the words to be "not without difficulty".
7. *Supra* at 344.
8. *Shaw v. Gould* (1868), L.R. 3, H.L. 55; *Le Mesurier v. Le Mesurier* [1895], A.C. 517; (P.C.); *Bater v. Bater* (1906), P. 209 (P.D.A.); *Sinclair v. Sinclair* [1896], 1 I.R. 603, 613, (Ch.D.). See also *Maghee v. M'Allister* (1853) 3 Ir. Ch. Rep. 604 (Ct. of Ch.) which was not referred to by the learned judge.
9. Further on as an example of a divorce decree that would not be recognised in Ireland he suggested the case of one granted to persons not domiciled in the place where the divorce is granted. He went on to state however that whereas such persons "shall not be capable of contracting a valid marriage within that jurisdiction" (within Ireland) there is nothing to stop them remarrying elsewhere. "The words do not declare that such a person cannot *anywhere* contract 'a marriage valid within our jurisdiction' but merely prohibit the contracting *within our jurisdiction* of a valid marriage", (at p. 349). Kingsmill Moore J. went on to say that there is nothing to make such a marriage invalid if contracted elsewhere. Undoubtedly such a second marriage contracted in a foreign country which recognised the divorce would be valid in that country, but if the parties to such a marriage entered Ireland, as the divorce would not be recognised, it is difficult to see how the second marriage would not be regarded as invalid and perhaps even bigamous here.

No doubt the Oireachtas could pass a law that no dissolution of marriage, wherever effected, even where parties were domiciled in the country of the court pronouncing the decree, was to be effective to annul[10] the pre-existing valid marriage. If it did so then by the law for the time being in force, the first marriage would still be valid and subsisting within our jurisdiction. But the Oireachtas has not done so". Thus, "the law for the time being in force" is "that a divorce effected by a foreign court of persons domiciled within its jurisdiction was regarded as valid in our jurisdiction".

Further there was nothing contained in the Constitution to invalidate the remarriage of such persons.[11]

The sub-section next came up for judicial pronouncement in the English case of *Breen* (*orse Smith*) v. *Breen.*[12] Mr. Justice Karminski, considering whether the Irish courts would recognise a divorce decree granted by the English courts, to a couple of English domicile, favoured the construction given by Kingsmill Moore J. He stated

> "I am bound to say that I do not understand the section to say either plainly or at all that a valid marriage dissolved by the court of another State remains in the eyes of the Irish law a subsisting valid marriage"[13] Later he added, "The principle of recognising the validity of a decree pronounced by the court of the domicile has been long established, and indeed forms an essential part of the comity of nations . . . If the article intended to depart from this established principle it could no doubt have done so; but it would have expressed the intention in clear and unequivocal terms".[14]

In 1971 in the High Court, in *Bank of Ireland* v. *K. Caffin and Y. Caffin,*[15] Kenny J. followed the reasoning of Kingsmill Moore J. and expressly disagreed with Maguire C.J. Stating the purpose of Art. 41.3.2.º was to deprive the National Parliament of its power to pass legislation dissolving a marriage, or the courts of jurisdiction to grant a divorce, he went on

> "The recognition of orders of divorce made by the courts of another country where the husband and wife had their domicile has no logical connection with the power of the Oireachtas to dissolve a marriage; and the restrictions imposed on it by the Constitution do not involve a general principle that the Courts should not, or cannot, recognise orders for the dissolution of a marriage made by the courts of another country when the parties to the marriage were domiciled in that country at the time of the court proceedings. This gets support from the words 'under the law for the time being in force within the jurisdiction of the Government and Parliament established by this constitution' for they give the National Parliament jurisdiction to decide by legislation that some decrees of dissolution made by the courts of other states are to be recognised by our courts".[16]

The Oireachtas has not so legislated, and so he held the pre-1937 law prevailed.

Kenny J. also rejected the argument that the court should refuse to recognise the English divorce because it was given on the ground of desertion which

10. "Dissolve" would have been more appropriate.
11. *Supra* at p. 348.
12. [1964], P. 144; [1961], 3 All E.R. 225, (P.D.A.).
13. *Supra* at p. 149.
14. *Supra* at p. 152.
15. [1971] I.R. 123 (H.C.).
16. *Supra* at p. 129.

was not a ground on which divorce *a vinculo* could have been granted to those domiciled in Ireland by the Imperial Parliament before 1921. As Mr. C. and Y. were domiciled in England the grounds upon which a divorce *a vinculo* could be granted were to be determined by English law. For the purpose of deciding whether a foreign divorce is to be recognised or not, the grounds on which such a divorce are granted are irrelevant.[16a] The sole question to be determined is whether in the eyes of Irish law the foreign court could exercise jurisdiction over the parties.[17]

The court consequently recognised the English divorce of H., the testator, and Y. his first wife which was granted when they were domiciled in England. It further held that K., his wife by a second marriage was thus entitled to one half of the deceased's estate under the provisions of the Succession Act, 1965.[18]

In two decisions in 1973 (*Counihan* v. *Counihan, Gaffney* v. *Gaffney*),[19] Kenny J. reiterated the principle that a divorce *a vinculo* if granted by a court of the parties common domicile is recognised as valid in this country. In 1975, giving judgement on appeal in *Gaffney* v. *Gaffney*, a majority of the Supreme Court accepted this as a correct statement of the law.[20]

The Intent of the Drafter: In deciding whether the interpretation of the sub-section enunciated by Kingsmill Moore J. and Kenny J. or that enunciated by Maguire C.J. is what was intended by the original drafter of the Article. It is interesting to look at Mr. de Valera's explanation of it, when introducing it to the Dáil.

The sub-section in its original form read

"No person whose marriage has been dissolved under the civil law of any other State shall be capable of contracting a valid marriage during the life-time of the other party to the marriage so dissolved".

16a. See, however, *L.B.* v. *H.B.* (July 1980) unreported (H.C.) *infra*.

17. See *In re Adams, Bank of Ireland Trustee Co. Ltd.* v. *Adams* [1967], I.R. 424, (H.C.), it is the court of the forum which must determine whether the foreign court had jurisdiction.

18. Sect. 111 of the Act states that "if the testator leaves a spouse and no children the spouse shall have a right to one half of the estate". Also see article entitled "Recognition of Foreign Divorce Decrees" by J. O'Reilly (1971), 6 I.J. (N.S.) 293. He suggests that Kenny J. in *Caffin* by recognising K. as the wife of Caffin for the purpose of the Succession Act was not only recognising the divorce decree but enforcing it. Thus he suggests Kenny's judgement was inconsistent with the judgement of the Supreme Court in *Mayo-Perrott* in which the court would not enforce the decree for costs made in favour of the plaintiff. It is submitted that the author confuses the concepts of "enforcement" and "recognition" of a decree (See Dicey & Morris "Conflict of Law", edition 9, p. 985–987). Kenny J. was not enforcing the divorce decree between Caffin and Y. his first wife, he was merely recognising the change of status brought about by the decree, which resulted in Caffin being able to enter into a valid marriage with K. On this see also W. Duncan "Desertion and Cruelty in Irish Matrimonial Law", (1972), 7 I.J. (n.s.) 213 esp. 231–235.

19. *Gaffney* v. *Gaffney* [1975], I.R. 133, (H.C., S.C.); *Counihan* v. *Counihan* (July, 1973), unreported, (H.C.). See also *In re McComisky; Gibson* v. *Patterson* [1939], I.R. 573, (H.C.), where Gavan Duffy J. held on the construction of a will that Mrs. Cottu did not die "unmarried" but she did die without a surviving husband. Dr. Cottu the person to whom she was married was alive at her death but he said "I must take Dr. Cottu to have been domiciled in England at . . . the dissolution of the marriage, and in the absence of an Irish law in-validating that decree, the law of his domicile must determine whether he is married or not, when that question arises on a claim of which a marriage is the foundation".

20. See judgements of Walsh J., O'Higgins C.J. and Parke J. Griffin J. in his judgement seems to accept that a decree will be recognised if granted in the place of the parties' common domicile. However, he concludes (at p. 159) stating, "For the purposes of the present case, it is not necessary to decide whether and to what extent, if at all, the recognition of a decree of divorce *a vinculo* made by a foreign court is inconsistent with or repugnant to any of the Articles of the Constitution, and I express no view on this question." Henchy J. expressed no opinion on the matter.

Maguire C.J.'s interpretation seems undoubtedly to apply to this. However, the sub-section was amended to its present form on the motion of the Government, Mr. de Valera explaining

"The purpose of this amendment is to see that the mere fact that a marriage was dissolved in another State would not of itself, by itself, prevent a person from being married in this country. I think everybody will agree that if the marriage is, according to the laws of this country, a subsisting valid marriage, one of the partners to that marriage—even if it were dissolved by the civil law of another State—should not come here and get married".[21]

While this statement is less than unambiguous it seems to favour the Kingsmill Moore/Kenny interpretation.

Divorces Granted in Jurisdiction Other than that of Common Domicile

The question which now arises is whether the Irish courts will recognise a foreign divorce decree if the parties who obtain such decree are not domiciled within the jurisdiction of the foreign court that grants it. In *Caffin*,[22] Kenny J. expressly left to be decided at a future time the question of whether a divorce granted to a person who was resident, but not domiciled, within the foreign court's jurisdiction would be recognised here. In June of 1973 in *Gaffney* v. *Gaffney*,[23] the facts of which are given further on, his judgement on the matter was equivocal. While stating that he again expressly reserved this question he also stated that

"the court of the domicile of the husband and wife is the only court which the courts in the Republic of Ireland recognise as having jurisdiction to grant a divorce *a vinculo*".[24]

A month later, in *Counihan* v. *Counihan*[25] the matter arose for direct consideration. The plaintiff was seeking a maintenance order in the High Court on the grounds of her husband's constructive desertion. Since 1965 the parties had been living apart. In 1968 the wife went to England to reside and to obtain employment. In October 1971 she brought proceedings in the English High Court for a divorce *a vinculo* and obtained an order which was made absolute in January, 1972. The petition seeking divorce contained a statement that the husband and wife were domiciled in England or alternatively that the husband was not domiciled in "the U.K. or in the Channel Islands or in the Isle of Man and that the wife had been ordinarily resident in England for three years immediately preceding the presentation of the petition," such period of residence in English law at that time being sufficient to confer on the court jurisdiction to hear a wife's petition for divorce.[26] Thus, the question of the recognition of the English divorce decree in Ireland had to be determined as, if the divorce was recognised as valid in Irish law, the wife was no longer married and could not succeed in a maintenance action.

Kenny J. stated

21. See 68 Dáil Debates, 224—5.
22. *Supra.*
23. *Supra.*
24. *Supra* at p. 137.
25. *Supra.*
26. Under Sect. 40 (1) b. of the Matrimonial Causes Act, 1965 now repealed and replaced by the Domicile & Matrimonial Proceedings Act, 1973, Sect. 5 (2) of which confers jurisdiction on the English court to entertain divorce proceedings if either of the parties to the marriage
(1) is domiciled in England at the date when the proceedings are begun (the wife in

"The domicile of a wife is that of her husband until their marriage is validly terminated by a divorce *a vinculo*, and as the husband was at all times domiciled in the Republic of Ireland, the courts in this country do not recognise the divorce in England as having the effect of dissolving the marriage. While a divorce given by the courts of the country in which the husband and wife are domiciled will be recognised ... a divorce granted to a wife who was resident in England against a husband who is domiciled in the Republic of Ireland does not have the effect ... of dissolving the marriage. I know that the courts in England now have jurisdiction under legislation to grant divorces to wives who have been resident for 3 years in England but this jurisdiction did not exist in 1921 and the doctrine of comity of Courts does not require that the courts in the Republic of Ireland should recognise this divorce. No legislation has been passed by the National Parliament giving recognition to divorces granted to a wife resident in England who is domiciled in the Republic of Ireland, and in my opinion, the husband and wife are, under our law, married".

Almost two years later in *Gaffney* v. *Gaffney*[27] the Supreme Court seemed to rule out any remaining possibility that existed of recognition being afforded to foreign divorce decrees granted by any court other than that of the parties common domicile. Walsh J. stated:

"The courts here do not recognise decrees of dissolution of marriage pronounced by foreign courts unless the parties were domiciled within the jurisdiction of the foreign court in question".[28]

In this case, however, there was no question of either party to the divorce being resident or domiciled in a foreign jurisdiction at any time.

Doctrine of Estoppel and Foreign Decrees of Divorce

In *Gaffney* v. *Gaffney*, the question arose as to whether "a spouse domiciled in one State who obtains an invalid divorce in another State is estopped in the State of the domicile from establishing that the divorce was invalid."[29] The facts of *Gaffney* v. *Gaffney* were as follows: The plaintiff and her husband were both resident and domiciled in the Republic of Ireland until the husband's death in 1972. Despite the plaintiff not wanting a divorce, her husband instructed a firm of solicitors in Manchester in 1957 to prepare a petition by her seeking a divorce *a vinculo* from him. By threatening her with physical violence he forced the plaintiff to swear an affidavit stating that he resided in Blackburn and that they were both domiciled in England. Believing that he would assault her if she did not do what he demanded, she flew to Manchester with him on the morning of the divorce proceedings. Upon arriving at the court they were coached by the husband's solicitors as to what they were to say, and the case was concluded in the court in a few minutes. On the same day she returned to Dublin. In January 1959 the English court granted a decree absolute. In April 1959 the husband married the defendant, his second wife, in a Registry Office in Blackburn. They then came to live in Dublin.

English law can now acquire a separate domicile to that of her husband, Section 1 (1) of the same Act) or
(2) was habitually resident in England throughout the period of one year ending with that date.
27. *Supra.*
28. *Supra* at p. 150.
29. *Supra* per Kenny J. at p. 141.

The husband died intestate in 1972. Upon his death, the plaintiff successfully brought proceedings claiming that she was his widow for the purpose of succession, and that she was entitled to obtain a grant of Letters of Administration to his estate. Kenny J. held that the divorce proceedings had not validly dissolved the marriage in the eyes of Irish law because:

1. The parties were at all times domiciled and resident in Ireland and the courts in this country will only recognise decrees of dissolution pronounced by a court of the parties common domicile.

2. The decree was procured by the fraudulent invocation of the English court's jurisdiction, neither party being domiciled or resident in England when the court's jurisdiction was invoked. If the English court had itself known of the true position it would not have pronounced a decree, and further if today the true facts were made known there, the decree could be set aside.

3. The Plaintiff had obtained the decree under duress.

The Supreme Court confirmed that the decree was invalid on grounds 1 and 2.

In this case, however, the respondent further contended that the wife being the petitioner in the divorce proceedings could not now give evidence that the divorce was improperly obtained, i.e. she could not deny the validity of such proceedings having instituted them herself. Kenny J. pointed out the extraordinary consequences that would result if she was estopped from establishing the invalidity of the divorce; e.g. whereas the spouse who obtained the divorce would be prevented from proving its invalidity, if the other spouse remarried he or she might be successfully prosecuted for bigamy.[30] If there were children of such second marriage, upon the husband dying intestate, the first wife could not dispute their legitimacy, but her children could do so. On grounds of public policy such estoppel was undesirable. It was held and confirmed by the Supreme Court that estoppel did not apply either to the question of the existence of a valid marriage, or in relation to determining property rights between the spouses. Walsh J. giving judgement in the Supreme Court stated:

"Apart from other legal incidents in this country, certain constitutional rights may accrue to a woman by virtue of her being a wife which would not be available to her if she were not. The matter cannot, therefore, by any rules of evidence be left in a position of doubt nor could the Courts countenance a doctrine of estoppel, if such existed, which had the effect that a person would be estopped from saying that he or she is the husband or wife, as the case may be, of another party when in law the person making the claim has that status".[31]

In the above case the plaintiff was not a free agent, but even if she had been, her application to the courts in England would not have estopped her contesting the validity of the divorce. In *Counihan* v. *Counihan*[32] the fact that the plaintiff had voluntarily invoked the jurisdiction of the English courts and there obtained

---

30. Even more extraordinary would be the result that whilst the spouse who petitioned for the divorce would be prevented from asserting its invalidity, if she remarried she would be liable to a charge of bigamy.
31. [1975] I.R. 133 at p. 152. See further Duncan (1974), 9 I.J. (n.s.) 59, *supra*. See also E.M. Clare Canton, "Duress and Estoppel in Matrimonial Causes" (1978) 94 L.Q.R.15.
32. *Supra.*

a divorce was not held to estop her from asserting in the Irish courts that the English divorce decree lacked validity in this country.[33]

Thus a person domiciled in Ireland, whether he be the petitioner or respondent in a foreign divorce case, is never estopped from establishing the invalidity of such a divorce, under Irish law. The fact that parties consent to using the foreign jurisdiction to obtain a divorce is irrelevant. Persons by consent, cannot confer a jurisdiction on a foreign court, that in the eyes of Irish law, it does not possess.[34]

Further Grounds on which a Foreign Decree may be Refused Recognition

(a) *Fraud*: As we have already seen one of the grounds on which validity was denied to the English decree in *Gaffney* was that it was procured by the fraudulent invocation of the jurisdiction of the English court, i.e. the parties had fraudulently misrepresented facts (domicile) in order to lead the court to believe it had jurisdiction. But whereas fraudulent invocation of jurisdiction will overthrow a foreign decree, fraud as to the merits of the petition will be ignored[35] unless such fraud constitutes a "substantial defeat of justice".[35a]

(b) *Duress*: Kenny J. further denied recognition to the divorce decree in *Gaffney* because the plaintiff had acted under duress. She had only gone to Manchester because of "genuine and reasonable fear of immediate physical danger if she refused"[36] to go. He stated that

> "It is established law that a marriage may be declared null if it is entered into because of duress and, in my view, a similar principle applies to an application for a decree of divorce. There is no reason in logic or in principle why, if the doctrine of duress applies to contracting a marriage, it should not apply to its termination by divorce".[37]

Walsh J. in the Supreme Court, however, suggested that if the divorce court had possessed jurisdiction and the facts as to coercion still existed, in order to successfully assert her status as wife the petitioner may have had to apply to the court that granted the decree to set it aside.[38]

33. See also the old case of *Maghee v. M'Allister, supra*, in which the court held that a husband who had applied for and obtained a divorce from a Scottish Court was not estopped from impugning the validity of the divorce decree.

34. Walsh J. in *Gaffney*, stated "Consent cannot confer jurisdiction to dissolve a marriage where that jurisdiction does not already exist" (*supra* at p. 152). See also the Nullity case of *Addison (otherwise McAllister) v. Addison* [1955], N.I. 1, (Q.B.D.), "In cases involving status jurisdiction cannot be conferred by the submission of a party to the jurisdiction of the court". See also *Papadopoulos v. Papadopoulos* [1930] P. 55 (P.D.A.) and Cheshire and North's *Private International Law* 10th Edition, p. 389.

35. *Bonaparte v. Bonaparte* [1892] P. 402, (P.D.A.); *Bater v. Bater* [1906] P. 209, (C.A.); *Crowe v. Crowe* [1937], 2 All E.R. 723, (1937) 157 L.T. 557, (P.D.A.); *Middleton v. Middleton* [1967], P. 62, (P.D.A.), there a divorce granted in Illinois was denied recognition by the English courts on the ground that the husband petitioner had fraudulently invoked the jurisdiction of the Illinois court. It was denied recognition despite the fact that it would have been recognised in Indiana where the petitioner was domiciled. This fraud as to jurisdiction intervened so as to prevent recognition on the *Armitage v. A.-G.* rule (see further on). See J. Unger (1966), 29 M.L.R. 327; P.B. Carter (1966), 41 B.Y.I.L. 445.

35a. See p. 160 *infra*.

36. *Supra* at p. 139.

37. *Supra* at p. 139; agreeing with the views expressed by Bagnall J., *In re Meyer* [1971], P. 298; [1971], 1 All E.R. 379, (P.D.A.). See also *Hughes v. Hughes* (1932), 147 L.T. 20, (P.D.A.).

38. See *In re Meyer, supra*. There was no doubt that the German Court had in the eyes of English law, jurisdiction to grant a decree. The decree was denied recognition in England as the petitioner had been overborne by extreme duress into seeking the divorce. The duress was said to be such that when seeking the divorce decree the petitioner "was overborne by a genuine and reasonably held fear caused by present and continuing danger to life, limb or liberty arising from external circumstances for which [she] was not responsible"—Per Bagnall J. at p. 307. See further Clare Canton, *supra*.

(c) *Denial of Justice*: Finally it has been said that a divorce decree will be refused recognition if granted in circumstances which amount to a denial of substantial or natural justice. This ground for refusing recognition has had very limited application in England[39] and has on only one occasion been relied upon by an Irish Court.

In *L.B.* v. *H.B.*[39a] the parties in 1958 when domiciled in France obtained a divorce decree from the French courts. For the purpose of obtaining the decree they had employed French lawyers to manufacture evidence to present to the court and at the date of the proceedings, the parties' circumstances were such that no real grounds existed upon which either party could obtain a divorce. Both during the divorce proceedings and after the granting of the divorce decree the parties continued to reside together. They subsequently came to live in Ireland and in 1979 the wife issued proceedings in the Irish High Court seeking a maintenance order and certain other orders against the husband. In these proceedings the wife submitted that the divorce should not be recognised in Ireland as it had been obtained by collusion and constituted a substantial denial of justice. Evidence was given that had the French court been aware of the collusive nature of the proceedings in 1958, it would have dismissed them but that the French court would not now set aside the divorce decree.

Barrington J. finding in favour of the wife's submission stated:

> "I have no doubt whatsoever that the divorce was a collusive divorce . . . it represented the worst form of collusion as the evidence on which the court decided the case was manufactured to achieve that precise result"

He stated that under the principles of private international law as stated in *Re Caffin, decsd.* and *Gaffney* v. *Gaffney* the divorce decree was entitled to recognition as it was granted by a court of competent jurisdiction to people domiciled within its jurisdiction. However, he continued:

> "in the present case . . . I am satisfied that there was such a measure of collusion between the parties in the proceedings before the French Court as to amount to a fraud upon that court. I am also satisfied that if the French Courts had known of the collusion it would have rejected the (divorce) petition . . ."

This was not one of those cases, he stated, in which

> "one of the parties has committed a fraud, or suppressed the truth, or where there has been collusion between the parties about peripheral matters. Clearly matters which have been fully heard and determined before a competent tribunal should not lightly be reopened . . . (Here) the entire suit was manufactured and conducted in such a way that it amounted to a fraud upon the French court . . ."

Whilst there was no fraud or substantial denial of justice as between the parties

---

39. See *Pemberton v. Hughes* [1899], 1 Ch. 781, (C.A.); *Middleton v. Middleton* [1967], P. 62, (P.D.A.); *Qureshi v. Qureshi* [1972], Fam. 173 at p. 201, (P.D.A.). See also the nullity cases of *Gray (orse Formosa) v. Formosa* [1963] P. 259, (C.A.); *Lepre v. Lepre* [1965], P. 52, (P.D.A.); *Macalpine v. Macalpine* [1958], P. 35; [1957], 3 All E.R. 134, (P.D.A.); *Rudd v. Rudd* [1924], P. 72, (P.D.A.); *Igra v. Igra* [1951], P. 404, (P.D.A.); *Wood v. Wood* [1957], P. 254, [1957] 2 All E.R. 14, (C.A.); *Viswalingham v. Viswalingham* (1980) 1 F.L.R. 24, (C.A.). Cheshire 8th Edition p. 655–658. Dicey 9th Edition p. 1033, *supra*. In England the law is now governed by the Recognition of Divorces and Legal Separations Act 1971, Sect. 8. See further, *Kendall v. Kendall* [1977] Fam. 208 (Fam. D.); *Newmarch v. Newmarch* [1978] Fam. 78, (Fam. D.).
39a. (July 1980) unreported (H.C.).

"The collusion . . . between the parties was such that the entire proceedings became a charade and the French court was unwittingly led to a conclusion which had been pre-determined by the parties. There was a substantial defeat of justice for which the parties and not the court bear the responsibility . . . it is accordingly no disrespect to the French court if (this court) refuses to recognise a divorce obtained in such circumstances. Indeed, once this court has been fixed with knowledge of what happened in the French divorce proceedings it is hard to see how it could recognise the validity of the divorce and at the same time observe the constitutional duty of the State to uphold the institution of marriage."

Having refused to recognise the French divorce decree, Barrington J. concluded making a maintenance order against the husband under the Family Law . . . Act, 1976, and holding the home in which the parties resided to be a "family home" within the meaning of the Family Home Protection Act, 1976. The learned judge's decision has been appealed to the Supreme Court and whether it will be upheld on appeal remains to be seen. In the meantime, a considerable degree of uncertainty has been introduced into this area of the law by the denial of recognition to the French divorce decree on the ground that recognition of the divorce would have constituted "a substantial defeat of justice", a concept that was at no stage fully defined in the judgement delivered by the court.

Statement of Present Law

The present law as to the recognition of foreign divorce decrees may be summarised as follows:

I. A foreign divorce will be recognised in this country if at the date of the institution of the divorce proceedings[40] both parties were domiciled within the jurisdiction of the court that granted it.[41] However, even if a divorce is obtained in the parties' common domicile, if the petitioner was overborne by duress into seeking the divorce, the Irish courts may regard it as null and refuse to recognise it. A divorce may also be denied recognition on the ground that it was obtained by a fraudulent invocation of the foreign jurisdiction or that it constitutes a substantial defeat of justice.

II. If a divorce is obtained in a jurisdiction other than that of the parties' common domicile, it will not be recognised.

III. In *Caffin*, Kenny J. left to be determined at a future time the question of whether a divorce granted by the courts in Northern Ireland to persons domiciled there will be recognised by our law. As we have already seen domicile merely signifies a territory which is a separate law district. Northern Ireland is such a

---

40. The date of the institution of the proceedings is the relevant time for determining domicile. It does not matter if the domicile of the parties has changed between that time and the date of the decree. See *Mansell v. Mansell* [1967], P. 306; [1966], 2 All E.R. 391, (P.D.A.).

41. Under the rule in *Armitage v. A.-G.* [1906], P. 135, (P.D.A.), a foreign decree will also be recognised if it would be recognised by the courts of the country where the parties were domiciled. In this case a divorce decree granted to W. in South Dakota after 90 days residence there was recognised as validly dissolving the marriage by the English Courts as the law of New York, the place of the parties domicile would recognise the validity of the decree.

law district with an established legal system different to that of the Republic of Ireland. It is recognised as such in Art. 3 of the Constitution[42] and in various legislative enactments; see, for example, the Maintenance Orders Act, 1974. Moreover, in *The State* (*Gilsenan*) v. *District Justice McMorrow*[43] the Supreme Court unanimously held Northern Ireland to be a jurisdiction separate to that of the Republic of Ireland. It is now settled law that the Republic's courts recognise divorce decrees granted by courts within the jurisdiction of the parties' common domicile and it is submitted that there is no reason why such decrees granted by the courts in Northern Ireland should be treated any differently to decrees granted elsewhere. It is worth noting that the Supreme Court in *Gaffney* v. *Gaffney* made no reference to the existence of an obstacle to the recognition of Northern Ireland decrees.

IV. Either party to a foreign divorce decree may challenge the validity of the divorce in the Irish courts regardless of whether they were petitioner or respondent.

CRITICISMS OF PRESENT LAW

The present law can be criticised on a number of grounds:

I. A justification for confining recognition to decrees granted by the courts of the parties' common domicile has been said to be that the courts by so doing may prevent the creation of limping marriages, i.e. marriages that are regarded as valid and subsisting in one country and as dissolved and terminated in another. Griffin J. in *Gaffney* quoted with approval[44] a passage from the judgement of Lord Watson in *Le Mesurier* v. *Le Mesurier* in which the latter stated *inter alia* that

> "the domicile for the time being of the married pair affords the only true test of jurisdiction to dissolve their marriage"

and further on continued saying that

> "honest adherence to this principle . . . will preclude the scandal which arises when a man and a woman are held to be a man and wife in one country, and strangers in another".

It is submitted that the opposite is true, i.e. that the courts by confining recognition of divorce decrees to those granted by the place of the parties' common domicile are contributing to, rather than preventing, the creation of limping marriages. Foreign courts assume jurisdiction to dissolve marriages not only on grounds relating to the parties' domicile but also on the basis of residence and nationality. Moreover some of the countries that use domicile as a jurisdictional ground have a less exacting definition of domicile than that used by the Irish courts. The only manner in which limping marriages can be prevented is if

---

42. Article 3 states "Pending the reintegration of the national territory and without prejudice to the right of the Parliament and Government established by this Constitution to exercise jurisdiction over the whole of that territory, the laws enacted by that parliament shall have the like, area and extent of applications to the laws of Saorstat Eireann and the like extra territorial effect."

43. (January 1978) unreported (S.C.). Henchy J. stated "In my opinion the courts are bound to take judicial notice of the expression "Northern Ireland" as connoting the part of this island which is outside the functioning jurisdiction of the State which has been given the statutory description of "The Republic of Ireland" (by the Republic of Ireland Act, 1948)."

44. *Supra* at p. 158.

all countries agree to co-ordinate the grounds on which courts will regard themselves as possessing jurisdiction to grant a decree and the grounds on which a decree will be recognised. In the absence of such agreement a refusal to recognise any decree unless granted by the place of the parties' common domicile can only contribute to the creation of limping marriages.

II. Under the present law a deserted wife is in a particularly anomalous position. If her husband deserts her and goes to England and obtains an English domicile, either herself, or her husband may obtain an English divorce that will be recognised in this country. If, on the other hand, her husband forces her out of the matrimonial home (or she deserts him) and she goes to England, if her husband remains domiciled in Ireland, there is no way in which she can obtain a divorce that will be recognised here. Her domicile being dependent on that of her husband, in the first instance, she acquires an English domicile, even though she may never have set foot in England, whilst in the second instance she remains domiciled in Ireland although she is living in England and may never intend to return to this country. To further confuse matters the Department of Social Welfare will still give Deserted Wife's Allowance or Benefit to a person who is according to Irish law validly divorced and no longer a wife. Up until April 1973 all claims to D.W.A. from divorced women were disallowed by the Department. Since that date, the practice has been to allow a claim for the allowance where desertion by a husband preceded the granting of a divorce decree.

III Lord Watson in the passage approved by Griffin J. stated that

"the differences of married people should be adjusted in accordance with the laws of the community to which they belong".[45]

On the basis of this statement our courts should recognise a decree granted by the courts of the country in which a person has lived for a long period or with which he has a substantial connection. However, under the present law this does not always happen, for example:

(a) if a woman lives all her single and married life in England and after twenty years of marriage her husband deserts her and becomes domiciled in Ireland, if she commences divorce proceedings in England after her husband has acquired Irish domicile and if she succeeds in obtaining an English divorce it will not be recognised in this country. Although she has lived in England all her life the Irish courts will not regard the English courts as having jurisdiction to grant a decree, the wife being held under our law to have acquired an Irish domicile, her domicile being dependant on that of her husband.

(b) Similarly if an Irish couple live in England for all their married life but never have the intention to remain there permanently and thus retain their Irish domicile, the Irish courts will not recognise a divorce granted to them by the English courts, even though such divorce could be said to be granted "in accordance with the laws of the community to which they belonged".

IV. The limitation by the Irish courts of recognition to the present narrow ground can be attributed to a desire on the part of the Irish courts to prevent or discourage forum shopping, i.e. to prevent or discourage persons living in Ireland from seeking a divorce in a more favourable jurisdiction. Such an approach in the

45. [1895] A.C. 517 at p. 540, (H.L.).

light of Art. 41.3.2.° is understandable. It is to be expected that the courts will do nothing to facilitate persons avoid Irish public policy as therein expressed.[46] On the other hand it has been stated that that article in no way affects the courts' power to recognise foreign decrees. Further, it is arguable that the stage when recognition is sought is not the appropriate stage at which to discourage forum shopping. At that stage the forum shopping has already taken place and the real problem is the creation and existence of limping marriages.

V. If a foreign court assumes jurisdiction on a ground other than domicile and in accordance with its own domestic law validly dissolves the marriage of parties domiciled in Ireland, although the divorce is not recognised as valid in this country, if one of the parties then lives in a jurisdiction where the decree is recognised he/she will usually be free and able to marry another.[47] If, however, the other spouse remains in this country he or she will not be similarly free to marry. From the point of view of Irish law both parties are still validly married. Looking at the social reality of the situation one spouse is held in the bonds of a marriage to which there is no other party. Having regard to public policy and common sense there is something very wrong with a law which fosters such a situation.

The Possibilities of Reform

The present law is the law as it was developed by the courts prior to 1922. In England, the courts having had their own jurisdiction to grant divorces extended, as a consequence extended recognition to foreign divorce decrees granted in a place other than the parties' domicile, provided facts existed upon which the English courts would themselves have assumed jurisdiction.[48] In Ireland there can be no similar development, the courts possessing no divorce jurisdiction of their own.

In 1967 the House of Lords,[49] further extended the circumstances in which the English courts would recognise a foreign divorce decree. In so doing it was influenced by a desire to avoid the creation of limping marriages. It established that where there was a real and substantial connection between the place granting the divorce and either the petitioner or the respondent, the English courts could recognise it as valid. In deciding on what amounted to a real and substantial connection, the English courts looked principally to the domicile, residence and nationality of the parties.[50]

---

46. See *Gaffney v. Gaffney, supra*, in the High Court where Kenny J. cited with approval a passage of Lord Westbury in *Shaw v. Gould* ((1868), L.R. 3, H.L. 55) in which he stated "No nation can be required to admit that its domiciled subjects may lawfully resort to another country for the purpose of evading the laws under which they live".
47. See however *Dicey & Morris, supra*. Rule 34 and Exceptions 2, 3, 4.
48. *Travers v. Holley* [1953], P. 246, (C.A.); *Carr v. Carr* [1955], 2 All E.R. 61, (P.D.A.); *Robinson-Scott v. Robinson-Scott* [1958], P. 71, (P.D.A.); *Indyka v. Indyka* [1969], A.C. 33, (H.L.); *Tijanic v. Tijanic* [1968], P. 181, (P.D.A.).
49. *Indyka v. Indyka, supra*.
50. See Cheshire & North, *Private International Law*, 8th Edition, 362–368 and cases there discussed. Dicey & Morris, *Conflicts of Law*, 9th Edition, p. 316–319 and cases cited therein; see Duncan in D.U.L.R. article *supra*. Indyka has been followed in Australia–*Nicholson v. Nicholson* (1971), 17 F.L.R. 47; and in Canada–*Kish v. Director of Vital Statistics* (1973), 35 D.L.R. (3d.) 530; *Mac Neill v. Mac Neill* (1974), 53 D.L.R. (3d.) 486; *La Carte v. La Carte* (1975) 60 D.L.R. (3d.) 507; *Holub v. Holub* (1976) 71 D.L.R. (3d.) 698; *Keresztessy v. Keresztessy* (1976) 73 D.L.R. (3d.) 347; *Siebert v. Siebert* (1978) 82 D.L.R. (3d.) 70; *Clarkson v. Clarkson* (1978) 86 D.L.R. (3d.) 694; *El-Sohemy v. El-Sohemy* (1979) 89 D.L.R. (3d.) 145.
English law on recognition has now changed. See the Recognition of Divorces and Legal

What are the possibilities of a similar development in Irish law? Change in the present law can be brought about either (a) by judicial development or (b) by legislation.

Judicial Development: There seems little likelihood of the courts in the near future extending the grounds on which a foreign decree will be recognised. However, although the judiciary seems intent on confining recognition within its present boundaries, the few pronouncements of the Supreme Court that can be regarded as relating to the possibility of a judicial extension of the grounds of recognition are all *obiter dicta*. Although Kingsmill Moore in *Mayo Perrott* regarded recognition as dependent upon the parties being domiciled within the jurisdiction that granted the decree, there was no question of the parties being domiciled elsewhere in that case. In *Gaffney* there was no question but that both parties were domiciled and resident in Ireland at all relevant times. Thus in neither case was recognition refused to a decree granted by a jurisdiction with which either party had a "real and substantial connection".

The decision in *Gaffney* is not as major an obstacle to judicial change of the law as it first appears for a number of other reasons:

(a) Counsel for the appellant submitted to the court himself that the divorce would only be recognised if the parties were both domiciled in England at the time the petition was presented. He did not suggest that a real and substantial connection test should be used. (If such test had been used in that case the decree would still not have been recognised.)

(b) The appeal was only based on one point—that the court should not have heard evidence from the wife denying the validity of the divorce.

(c) Walsh J. suggested[51] that the law whereby a wife's domicile is dependent on her husband may "some day . . . be challenged on constitutional grounds in a case where the wife has never phsyically left her domicile of origin and where a deserting husband may have established a domicile in another jurisdiction". If the rule as to dependent domicile is unconstitutional, as Walsh J. seems to suggest, and a wife is held at some future date to be capable of having a domicile independent to that of her husband, the courts may as a consequence evolve different rules as to recognition for the situation in which a husband is domiciled in one jurisdiction and a wife in another.[52]

(d) Both Kingsmill Moore and Kenny J. seem to have interpreted the Constitution on the basis that it permitted recognition of divorce decrees that would have been recognised by the law at the time of the passing of the Constitution (i.e. in 1937) and that it denied recognition to divorce decrees if the original marriages would have been regarded as still subsisting in Ireland in 1937. Walsh J. however emphasised that the law as to recognition was part of the common law and that

"Neither Art. 73 of the Constitution of Saorstát Éireann nor Art. 50 of the

Separations Act, 1971 and the Domicile and Matrimonial Proceedings Act, 1973; see also Cheshire and North, *supra*, 10th Edition, p. 369–389; also Dicey and Morris 9th Edition, *supra*, p. 315–331 and the supplement to that edition; see I.G.F. Karsten (1972), 35 M.L.R. 299, for a note on the Recognition of Divorces and Legal Separations Act, 1971. For the present Australian law as to recognition, see the Australian Family Law Act, 1975, Sects. 104–106.
51. *Supra* at p. 152.
52. Alternatively, the circumstances in which a foreign divorce decree will be recognised may be reduced. See A. Shatter, "The Mixed Blessing of an Independent Domicile," *Irish Times* 30th Nov. 1976.

present Constitution could be construed as freezing our common law, or other non-statutory law in the condition in which it was found at the coming into force of the Constitution of 1922 so that it could never be departed from save by enactment of the Oireachtas".[53]

The common law was created by the judges and can be modified by them.

To this it can be added that Art. 41.3.3° speaks of a person being incapable of contracting a valid marriage if his first marriage has been dissolved by the laws of another jurisdiction but is a subsisting valid marriage under Irish "law for the time being in force". It is for the courts to determine what is "the law for the time being in force", and in the absence of a parliamentary prohibition on the recognition of divorce decrees on grounds other than domicile, it is open to the courts to develop the law in this area.

Even if the Irish courts were to establish a "real and substantial connection test" the number of people living in this country who are parties to a limping marriage is likely to steadily increase as a result of the enactment by the Westminster parliament of the Domicile and Matrimonial Proceedings Act, 1973. This Act abolishes a wife's dependent domicile in English law and states that the English courts shall have jurisdiction to entertain proceedings for divorce if either of the parties to the marriage are domiciled in England, at the date when the proceedings are begun, or if either is habitually resident in England, throughout the period of one year ending with that date.[54] Even if the Irish courts were to adopt the "real and substantial connection test" as a basis for recognition, it is unlikely that one year's residence in a foreign country by itself would be regarded as such a connection.

Legislation: Having regard to the record of the Oireachtas in enacting legislation to reform non-controversial areas of family law, there is probably little likelihood of it in the near future extending the grounds for recognition of foreign decrees of divorce *a vinculo*. The only substantial reference made in recent years by either House of the Oireachtas to the need to change the law in this area was that made by the 1967 Dáil Committee on the Constitution. In their report,[55] they recommended the deletion of Art. 41.3.3° because of the confusion existing at that time as to its precise meaning. Upon its deletion they stated "the recognition of divorce decrees will be a matter for determination in accordance with private international law, the principles of which have been fairly well established". However, at the time when the report was issued the law as to recognition was by no means "fairly well established", different countries acting on different principles.

The position has now been changed by the Hague Convention on the Recognition of Divorces and Legal Separations[56] which sets out the principles to be applied by the countries who are party to the Convention in relation to recognition. Ireland has not, as yet, ratified this Convention.

---

53. *Supra* at p. 151.
54. Similarly the Act abolishes a wife's domicile of dependency in Scotland and Northern Ireland and confers jurisdiction on the courts there to grant a divorce on the basis of either spouses domicile or one year's habitual residence.
55. Report of the Committee on the Constitution, December, 1967, paragraph 127, p. 44–45.
56. See A.E. Anton, "The Recognition of Divorces and Legal Separations" (1969), I.C.L.Q. 620. On pages 658 to 664 of the same edition the terms of the Draft Convention are set out. The Convention came into force in 1975.

CONCLUSION

Due to the inability of the Irish Courts to pronounce a decree of divorce *a vinculo* it is generally accepted that there has been, in recent years, an increasing number of persons domiciled in this country, making use of the divorce jurisdiction of the courts of the United Kingdom and elsewhere. Many of these have subsequently returned to Ireland and re-married. The non-recognition of a foreign decree dissolving a first marriage means that in this country,

1. The first marriage is still subsisting.

2. The spouse of the first marriage may retain their succession rights[57] and rights to maintenance.[58]

3. A second marriage is void if celebrated during the lifetime of the first spouse.

4. The celebration of such a second marriage may render the person acquiring a second spouse liable to a charge of bigamy.

5. A void second marriage means that the parties to it acquire no rights of succession or maintenance *vis à vis* each other.

6. The children of a void marriage are illegitimate.

In future years this area of the law is going to prove a lawyer's paradise and a social nightmare. It seems that in the immediate future, change is unlikely. If however, the courts do decide to develop the law, such a development is necessarily slow and piecemeal. Also, change by judicial innovation by its very nature creates considerable uncertainty as to the actual state of the law. Without doubt, there is a need for the Oireachtas to examine this whole area and to consider the desirability of extending and clarifying the jurisdictional grounds of recognition. If at some future date legislation is thought desirable, The Hague Convention could provide a useful blueprint of what is required.[59]

57. See *Gaffney v. Gaffney, supra.*
58. See *Counihan v. Counihan, supra.*
59. See however articles 7 and 20 of the Convention. Article 7 states "contracting states may refuse to recognise a divorce when at the time it was obtained, both the parties were nationals of states which did not provide for divorce and of no other State". Article 20 states "contracting States whose law does not provide for divorce may, not later than the time of ratification or accession, reserve the right not to recognise a divorce, if at the date it was obtained, one of the spouses was a national of a State whose law did not provide for divorce . . ."
If effect was given to these two provisions in our domestic law recognition would be refused in the case of a number of divorce decrees to which it is afforded at present.

CHAPTER 11

LEGITIMACY AND LEGITIMATION

Under Irish law the biological link between parents and their children does not, by itself, decide the legal consequences of the parental relationship. These are based not simply upon the fact of parenthood, but upon the concept of legitimacy which is determined by reference to the existence of a valid marriage of the parents.

In this chapter we consider the circumstances in which a child is regarded as legitimate and propose a number of reforms. In a later chapter the position of the illegitimate child is examined and it is argued that in so far as it is possible, all legal distinctions between legitimacy and illegitimacy should be abolished.

The Common Law

At common law no child can be legitimate unless his parents are married at the time of his conception or at the time of his birth. The usual case of a legitimate birth involves both conception and birth during the parents marriage. However, by this rule, a child conceived during marriage, but born after the marriage has been ended by the husband's death, or a child conceived in pre-marital intercourse, but born during marriage, is also legitimate. The only circumstance in which it has been suggested that a child may be legitimate at common law although his parents were married neither when he was conceived nor when he was born, is the case of the child conceived by pre-marital intercourse, his parents then marrying but his father dying before his birth.[1]

Legitimation per Subsequens Matrimonium

In 1931 the Legitimacy Act modified the common law rules by introducing the principle of legitimation into Irish law. Now an illegitimate person is legitimated upon the subsequent marriage of his parents, provided the father is domiciled in this country at the time of such marriage, and both he and the mother could have been lawfully married to each other at the time of the birth or at some time during the period of ten months preceding the birth.[2] Thus if the father of an illegitimate child is married to another, who dies a week before the child is born, and after the child's birth he marries its mother, that child is

---

1. *Bromley's Family Law*, 5th Edition, (Butterworth, London 1976), p. 280.
2. Legitimacy Act, 1931, Sect. 1. For the position where the father is domiciled in another country at the date of the marriage see Sect. 8 of the Act. Generally speaking if the law of the country of the father's domicile legitimates an illegitimate child upon his parents subsequently marrying, provided the child was not a *filius adulterinus* (Sect. 1 (2) Irish law will regard the child as legitimated. For conflict of law problems that arise under Legitimacy and Legitimation see Dicey & Morris, 9th Edition *The Conflict of Law* (Stevens & Sons Ltd., London 1973), chapter 19, p. 428 and the supplement to that edition.

legitimated. However, if the father is married to another, and she dies a week after the illegitimate child's birth and he subsequently marries the mother, the child remains illegitimate.

If the parents of an illegitimate child married prior to 1931 the child is only legitimated as and from the commencement of the Act, i.e. 1st July, 1931.

Effects of Legitimation[3]

In *In re J.*[4] Henchy J. stated:[5]

"I find it impossible to distinguish between the constitutional position of a child whose legitimacy stems from the fact that he was born the day after his parents were married, and that of a child whose legitimacy stems from the fact that his parents were married the day after he was born. In the former case the child is legitimate and a member of the family from birth by operation of the Common Law; in the latter case, by operation of the statute, from the date of his parents' marriage. The crucial fact in each case is that the child's legitimacy and consequent membership of the family are founded on the parents' marriage".[6]

Thus there is no difference between the constitutional position of the legitimate or legitimated child.

Whereas a person when legitimated has substantially the same legal rights and duties as a legitimate person,[7] there still remains some distinction between the effect of common law and statutory legitimacy. The Act does not give a child who is legitimated the right to succeed to any dignity or title of honour or to any property which devolves with a dignity or title, where he would not have succeeded to it prior to the passing of the Act.[8] A legitimated child cannot take an interest as a legitimate child, under any disposition[9] which came into operation prior to the date of legitimation or by descent under an entailed interest created before that date. A child's seniority for inheritance purposes only dates from the time of his legitimation and not from the date of his birth. Thus if X was born illegitimate in 1929 and his parents married in 1930 and gave birth to Y in that year, Y would be regarded as the senior child, X not having been legitimated until 1931. As between children legitimated on the same date their seniority ranks in accordance with their age.

Death of Child before Parents' Marriage

By section 5 of the Act if an illegitimate person dies after the coming into

---

3. For the law as to the re-registration of the birth of a legitimated child—see the Schedule to the Legitimacy Act, 1931.

4. [1966], I.R. 295, (H.C.).

5. *Supra* at p. 306.

6. In the English case of *In re Lowe, Stewart v. Lowe* [1929], 2 Ch. 210 (Ch. D.) decided shortly after legitimation by law was made possible in England, Romer J. stated (at p. 212—3) "Legitimacy is a question of status . . . This status of legitimacy can be obtained by being born legitimate or by being legitimated by virtue of the provisions of the Act. The Plaintiff had attained that status, and it is an irrelevant consideration whether she attained it in one way or in the other".

7. The 1931 Act does not expressly confer upon a legitimated person any specific right in respect of grants of Probate and Administration but in *In re P.* [1945], Ir. Jur. Rep. 17, (H.C.) it was stated that such a person is entitled on the death intestate to apply for and obtain a grant of letters of Administration to the deceased in equal priority with the children of the deceased who were born during wedlock.

8. Sect. 3 (3) of the 1931 Act.

9. Disposition is defined in Sect. 11 of the Act as "an assurance of any interest in property by any instrument whether *inter vivos* or by will". A will comes into operation upon the death of the testator.

force of the Act and before the marriage of his parents if (i) he would have been legitimated by their subsequent marriage; (ii) they do subsequently marry; (iii) he is survived by a wife, children or remoter issue, the provisions of the Act

> "with respect to the taking of interests in property by, or in succession to, the spouse, children and remoter issue of a legitimated person . . . apply as if such person as aforesaid had been a legitimated person and the date of the marriage of his parents had been the date of legitimation".

Declarations of Legitimacy

The question as to whether a person is legitimate or illegitimate may arise in a number of different circumstances. If the matter is determined, however, in one set of proceedings, for example upon a claim by a person to an interest in property, it does not mean that the question is settled for all time. Such a judgement only operates *inter partes*. Thus if in a different set of proceedings with another party the matter again arises, proof of status must be again given. The desirability of having a procedure to settle for all circumstances disputes over a person's status, resulted in the enactment of the required legislation in the second half of the last century.

By the Legitimacy Declaration (Ireland) Act, 1868, as amended,[10] application may be made to the Circuit or High Court by a child or his parents for a declaration of legitimacy or legitimation.[11] Further under this legislation, any person may petition for a declaration that he, or his parents, or grandparents are, or were, validly married.

The Attorney-General must be joined as a respondent to any petition.[12] A declaration is binding on all persons given notice of, or made parties to the proceedings, and anyone claiming through them. A decree proved to have been obtained by fraud or collusion however, has no binding effect on any one.[13]

Presumption of Legitimacy

There is a legal presumption that a child born to a married woman is legitimate, her husband being the father of the child.[14] This presumption applies even

10. See the Legitimacy Act, 1931, Sect. 2 and the Courts Act, 1971, Sect. 20.
11. See *In re Duane* [1936], Ir. Jur. Rep. 60, (Cir. Ct.) where the Circuit Court declared a person who became legitimated upon the coming into operation of the Legitimacy Act, 1931, to be a legitimated person. The proceedings were brought due to the fact that the Petitioner wished to re-register in the Register of Births and Marriages pursuant to Para. 1(c) of the Schedule to the 1931 Act. See also the interesting case of *Swifte v. Attorney-General for Ireland and Anor.* [1912] A.C. 276 (H.L., Ir.) in which the applicant sought a declaration that he was legitimate. His father, who was a Protestant, had married a Roman Catholic in a Roman Catholic Church in Austria in 1833. In 1845 while his first wife was still alive his father married the applicant's mother. The court refused to make the declaration sought. It held that Sect. 1 of 19 Geo 2, c. 13 (Ir.) (repealed in 1870) which enacted that any future marriage between a Papist and a Protestant celebrated by a Popish Priest was null and void was not extra territorial in its operation and did not affect a marriage between a domiciled Irish Protestant and an Austrian Roman Catholic celebrated in Austria. The second marriage was therefore bigamous and the applicant illegitimate.
12. See *A.B. v. A.-G and Others* (1869–70), I.R. 4 Eq. 56, (Prob); *King v. A.-G. and others* (1869–70), I.R. 4 Eq. 464 (Prob). The court held that it had no power to award the A.-G. costs in such proceedings if they are successful but it may award costs to the A.-G. when a petition is dismissed.
13. See the *Ampthill Peerage Case* [1976], 2 All E.R. 411, (H.L.), where the meaning of fraud and collusion is discussed in connection with the English Legitimacy Declaration Act, 1858.
14. *Russell v. Russell* [1924], A.C. 687, (H.L.), for the sequel to this case see the *Ampthill Peerage Case, supra. Banbury Peerage Case* (1811), 1 Sim & St. 153; 57 E.R. 62, (V.-C. Ct.) *Morris v. Davies* (1837), 5 Cl. and Fin. 163; 7 E.R. 365 (H.L.) *Cope v. Cope* (1833), 5 Car & P. 604; 172 E.R. 1119 (Nisi Prius); *Yool v. Ewing* [1904], 1 I.R. 434 (M.R.); *Mulhern v. Clery* [1930], I.R. 649, (S.C.) *In re Goods of Shellew* (1949), 83 I.L.T.R. 190, (H.C.).

in the case of a child born within two or three months of the marriage of the mother as where "a man marries a woman who at the time of marriage is in a state of pregnancy, the presumption of paternity from that mere fact is very strong".[15]

Thus the burden of rebutting the presumption is thrown on to the person denying legitimacy. Only proof beyond reasonable doubt will suffice. Lord Lyndhurst in *Morris* v. *Davies* stated the

"presumption of law is not lightly to be repelled. It is not to be broken in upon, or shaken by mere balance of probability; the evidence for the purpose of repelling it must be strong, distinct, satisfactory, and conclusive".[16]

The presumption can be rebutted by showing either

(a) that the husband and wife did not engage in intercourse at a time when the child could have been conceived;[17] or

(b) that the child is not the issue of the husband's intercourse.

(a) Proof that the husband did not have intercourse with his wife is complicated by what is known as the Rule in *Russell* v. *Russell*.[18] This prohibits the mother and her husband from personally giving evidence of not having intercourse so as to bastardise a child born in wedlock. In this case it was said in the House of Lords by Lord Birkenhead that "deeply seated domestic and social policy renders it unbecoming and indecorous that evidence should be received from such a source; upon such an issue; and with such a possible result".[19] The rule, however, does not apply if a child is born so soon after marriage that it must have been conceived prior to it. In that circumstance a spouse can give evidence that intercourse did not take place before marriage.[20]

Thus, normally if a husband wishes to rebut the presumption that he is the father of a child conceived by his wife in wedlock, he must prove non-access to his wife by evidence from a source other than his wife or himself. In the Northern Ireland case of *Smyth* v. *Smyth and Gray*[21] evidence was given by an army Colonel establishing that the husband was overseas at all times when the wife could have conceived her child. This rule does not apply simply to cases between a husband and wife but to every case in which for any purpose, it becomes necessary to determine the question whether a child born of the wife during the marriage is the child of the husband.[22]

(b) If the husband had access to his wife at any time when the child could

---

15. Cairns L.C. in *Gardner v. Gardner* [1877], 2 App. Cas. 723, at p. 729, (H.L.) quoting Lord Gifford in the Court of Session, Fourth Series, vol. iii, p. 721.

16. *Morris v. Davies* (1837), 5 Cl. & Fin. 163; 7 E.R. 365 at p. 404; *Yool v. Ewing supra*, at p. 441 the Master of the Rolls said the presumption "is of enormous strength".

17. See *Banbury Peerage Case, supra*; *Piers v. Piers* (1849), 2 H.L. Cas. 331; 9 E.R. 1118, (H.L.).

18. *Supra.*

19. *Supra* at p. 699. See, however, *O'Connell v. Broderick* (February 1977) unreported (H.C.) where the plaintiff, a married woman, obtained an affiliation order for the support of her fifth child. The court does not appear to have considered the rule in *Russell v. Russell*.

20. *Poulett Peerage Case* [1903], A.C. 395; 19 T.L.R. 644, (H.L.).

21. [1948], N.I. 181, (K.B.D.).

22. *Russell v. Russell supra*; *Poulett Peerage Case, supra*; *R. v. Kea* (1809), 11 East 132; 103 E.R. 954, (K.B.); *R. v. Sourton* (1836), 5 Ad. & E. 180; 111 E.R. 1134, (K.B.); *Goodright d. Stevens v. Moss* (1777), 2 Cowp. 591; 98 E.R. 1257, (K.B.). See also *Mulhern v. Clery supra* — if trying to discover whether persons were married or not, evidence of one of them tending to bastardise a child is admissible; see also *In re Darcys'* (1860), 11 I.C.L.R. 298, (C.P.)

have been conceived it is very difficult to disprove legitimacy. Proof that a wife committed adultery by itself is not sufficient to rebut the presumption. Such proof merely establishes that either the husband or the adulterer could be the father and the presumption still works in favour of the husband.[23]

In order to help determine a child's status or prove paternity, blood testing and tissue testing may be carried out. By the use of blood tests, it can be established that a man cannot be the father of a particular child but, as many people have the same blood group, it cannot be positively established by such tests that a man is the father of a particular child. It can only be shown that he could be the father. Tissue tests are of greater assistance in proving paternity and it is now possible to establish with a high degree of probability whether a particular man is or is not the father of a child. However, if the parties in dispute will not voluntarily participate in such testing, the courts appear to have no power to require them to do so under existing law.[24] It is submitted that when such an issue arises for determination before the courts, statutory provision should provide for the necessary testing to be carried out.

Restrictions on Presumption: If spouses are living apart under a decree of divorce *a mensa et thoro*, and a child is born to the wife on such a date that it must have been conceived after the date of the decree, the presumption is reversed, and the child is *prima facie* illegitimate.[26] The spouses are presumed to have obeyed the court decree, and if a spouse wishes to establish its legitimacy, he cannot personally give evidence that they had intercourse by which the child may have been conceived. In all other circumstances the presumption of legitimacy applies, even if at the date of conception the parties are living apart under a separation agreement,[27] or one of the spouses is in desertion.

Children of Void and Voidable Marriages

Children born of a void marriage are illegitimate. The fact that such a child's parents never seek a court decree to declare their marraige void is irrelevant, such a decree being merely declaratory.

At present a marriage is voidable only on the ground of impotence. It is possible for there to be children of such a marriage in three circumstances, i.e. children born prior to the marriage, as a result of fecundation *ab extra*, or artificial insemination.[28] Upon a decree being granted annulling the marriage

23. See *Park v. Park and McBride* [1946], N.I. 151, (K.B.D.).
24. Under Sect. 3 of Guardianship of Infants Act, 1964, the "welfare of the infant" is the paramount consideration in proceedings relating to an infant. Is it possible that under this provision in proceedings to determine the legitimacy or illegitimacy of an infant the court may order blood tests when such tests would be in the best interests of the infant? On this see English cases of *W. v. W.* No. 4 [1964], P. 67; [1963], 2 All E.R. 841, (C.A.); *B. (B.R.) v. B. (J.)* [1968], P. 466; [1968], 2 All E.R. 1203, (C.A.); *B. v. B. and E.* [1969], 3 All E.R. 1106, (C.A.); *S. v. S.*; *W. v. Official Solicitor* [1970], 3 All E.R. 107, (H.L.). See also *Re J.S. (a minor)* [1980] 1 All E.R. 1061 (C.A.).
25. See P.T. Horgan, "The Financial Support of Illegitimate Children" (1976), 11 I.J. (n.s.) 59 at p. 73 *et seq*. See also the English Family Law Reform Act, 1969, Part III Sect. 20 (1). The court in England may now direct blood tests to be taken. If a person refuses to comply with such a direction the court may draw such inferences as the circumstances properly warrant. See 1968 Law Com. No. 16: English Law Commission Report on Blood Tests and the Proof of Paternity.
26. *The Parishes of St. George and St. Margaret Westminster* (1706), 1 Salk 123; 91 E.R. 115, (K.B.).
27. *Morris v. Davies, supra*; *Ettenfield v. Ettenfield* [1940], P. 96; [1940], 1 All E.R. 293, (C.A.).
28. *Dredge v. Dredge* [1947] 1 All E.R. 29. (P.D.A.) (pre-marital intercourse); *Clarke v. Clarke* [1943], 2 All E.R. 540, (P.D.A.) (Fecundation ab-extra); *L. v. L.* [1949], P. 211; [1949], 1 All E.R. 111 (P.D.A.); (artificial insemination).

any such children would be restrospectively bastardised. Of course, if no decree is sought or obtained the children would remain legitimate.

CRITICISMS AND PROPOSALS FOR REFORMS[29]

It is suggested further on that the legal concepts of legitimacy and illegitimacy should be abolished, and that for the determination of rights and duties *vis à vis* children, the parental link should be the only matter of relevance. If we are, however, to continue with the present legal distinctions between legitimate and illegitimate children the following reforms are required:

I. The presumption of legitimacy undoubtedly exists so as to protect a child's interests, by preventing the father escaping from his legal obligations by simple denials of paternity. The presumption as it stands at present, however, renders it unnecessarily difficult to disprove paternity. A child's interests are unlikely to be furthered by holding, on a presumption of legitimacy that his mother's husband is his father when the latter is firmly convinced that he is not. It is submitted that the presumption should be rebuttable by a person proving on the balance of probability that he was not the father of his wife's child. This is the position in England under Sect. 26 of the Family Law Reform Act 1969.

II. The rule in *Russell* v. *Russell* serves no useful purpose and should be abolished. If a husband is firmly convinced that he is not the father of his wife's child he should be able to give evidence personally in court of not having sexual intercourse with his wife. The giving of such evidence will in no way help husbands to falsely disprove paternity, as there will still be a heavy burden on them to provide sufficient corroborative evidence to rebut the presumption of legitimacy.

III. The courts should be given explicit power to direct persons to undergo blood tests and tissue tests and upon their failing to comply with such a direction be entitled to draw an inference adverse to their case. Such a power would greatly assist the courts in all proceedings in which the paternity of a child was at issue. A former Minister for Justice, Mr. Patrick Cooney, in 1974 referring to current English legislation concerned with blood testing and which permits the English courts to draw such an inference, said it was "a very happy compromise, enabling the court to avail itself of the technical resources at its disposal whilst at the same time not invading the right to bodily integrity of the parties concerned".[30]

IV. The 1931 Act seeks to prevent the legitimation of a *filius adulterinus*. The reason usually put forward for so limiting the law on legitimation is that if such a child could subsequently be legitimated the institution of marriage would be in some way threatened or weakened.[31] However, at present it is possible for a *filius adulterinus* to be legitimated.

If at any time during the ten months prior to the child's birth it's adulterous parent's marriage is terminated, as a result of a valid dissolution or the death of the other spouse, such child is legitimated if its natural parents marry subsequent to its birth, and is legitimate if they marry immediately prior to its birth. Further, even if an adulterous parent's marriage subsists from the time of a child's con-

---

29. See particularly Cherish Booklet—Conference on "The Unmarried Parent and Child in Irish Society", (Dublin 1974). Cherish is an association of unmarried parents.
30. *Ibid* p. 5–10. See footnote 25 *supra*.
31. See Morton Commission, Cmnd. 9678, paras. 1172–1183.

ception until a number of years after its birth it is still possible for the child to escape from the status of illegitimacy. If at some future date the natural parents are both free to marry and enter into a valid marriage they may jointly apply to the Adoption Board to adopt their own child, and upon an adoption order being made in their favour the child is placed in the same legal relationship as a legitimate child born to married parents.

It is submitted that to still classify a child as illegitimate after its parents have married, while regarding its brothers and sisters subsequently born in wedlock as legitimate, is totally unjust. To place married parents in a position in which they feel it to be necessary to adopt their own child is a superfluous use of the adoption process. To suggest that legally stigmatising children for their parents' "sins" protects the status of marriage is little short of ludicrous. In all circumstances upon natural parents of a child validly marrying the child should be legitimated.

V. Where a voidable marriage is annulled the legitimacy of the children of such a marriage should be preserved.[32] The retrospective bastardisation of such children is inhumane and unnecessary.

VI. As a void marriage is no marriage at all it is logical that any children born to the parties of the marriage should be regarded as illegitimate. Such a rule, however, can be unjust and unnecessarily harsh. Parties may be married and rear children for many years, before discovering that they are within the prohibited degrees of relationship. Alternatively a person may marry believing a former spouse to be dead, and only discover ten or 20 years later that he is still alive. In both instances any children born to such parties are regarded by the law as illegitimate. In order to avoid the harsh consequences of a void marriage there should be enacted into Irish law the doctrine of the "putative marriage". By this doctrine the children of a void union are regarded as legitimate if the parties reasonably believed their marriage to be valid.[33]

---

32. See "Statement on Family Law Reform", by the Council for Social Welfare (A Committee of the Catholic Bishops Conference), (Dublin 1974), p. 17, the Committee states "Children of a void or voidable marriage should not be bastardised but should continue to be regarded as legitimate offspring of the parties following a decree of nullity".
33. See "The Law of Nullity in Ireland", (Dublin Stationery Office, Aug. 1976), p. 15 where it is recommended that "a child born of a marriage which is annulled should be *treated* as the legitimate issue of its parents." The proposed Nullity of Marriages Bill fails to properly provide for this.

CHAPTER 12

ADOPTION

INTRODUCTION

Under the common law there could be no irrevocable transfer of the rights and duties of a parent to a stranger.[1] Whereas a stranger could be in *loco parentis* to a child his legal position was always precarious, as a parent or a legally appointed guardian could always assert his legal rights and reclaim the child. The execution of an "adoption deed" by which a parent or parents expressly surrendered all rights and duties to their child to a stranger made no difference. Such agreements had absolutely no effect in law being regarded as contrary to public policy.[2] The only way in which the claim of the parent could be defeated was to prove in court that it would definitely not be in the interests of the child to be removed from the person in *loco parentis*.[3]

The legislatures of most European countries provided for legal adoption in the years between the two World Wars. "The 1914–18 War gave the first great fillip to adoption by creating a vast number of orphans and illegitimate children. In other ages, perhaps, people would have been content simply to take the children into their homes, but modern life consists largely of social insurances, passports, identity cards, a thousand and one compulsions which require an unambiguous civil status. A legal form giving recognition to adoption had therefore to be created or re-created in every country".[4] In England and Wales, legal adoption was introduced in 1926, in Northern Ireland in 1929 and Scotland in 1930.

However in Ireland it was not until the late 1940's that agitation developed on any large scale for the introduction of such a law here. In 1948 the Adoption Society, a multi-denominational body, was founded. It vigorously pressed for adoption legislation and obtained a great deal of public support. Finally in 1952 an adoption bill introduced by the then Minister for Justice, Mr. Boland, was enacted by the Oireachtas.[5]

The reluctance of the law to recognise adoption and of the legislature to provide for it was based on a number of grounds. There was a fear that parents would simply give away or abandon their children to inadequate people, or that

---

1. *In re O'Hara* [1900] 2 I.R. 232; (1899), 34 I.L.T.R. 17, (C.A.); per Holmes L.J.– "But English law does not permit a parent to relieve himself of the responsibility or to deprive himself of the comfort of his position" ([1900] 2 I.R. at p. 253). Per Fitzgibbon L.J.–"English law does not recognise the power of bindingly abdicating either parental right or parental duty".
2. *The State (Williams) v. Markey* [1940], I.R. 421; (1939), 74 I.L.T.R. 237, (S.C.); *In re Cullinane, an Infant* [1954], I.R. 270, (H.C.).
3. See p. 228 *et seq*.
4. M. Kornitzer, *Legal Adoption in the Modern World*, p. 318.
5. See J.H. Whyte, *Church and State in Modern Ireland*, p. 183–193 and 274–277.

they would have children in order to sell them. There was a belief that the Catholic Church opposed adoption, and that if it was permitted it could result in an increase in proselytism. Further, it was argued that the adoption of a child would interfere with another child's lawful inheritance rights. The Minister for Justice in 1951, Gen. MacEoin, stated that a law that would compel a mother to waive for all time her rights to her child "would be against charity and against the common law of justice".[6] After 1937 it was suggested that a law permitting adoption might be unconstitutional, being contrary to Articles 41 and 42, in that it would permanently deprive parents of their inalienable and imprescriptible rights to their child.

The Adoption Act, 1952, reflected some of the above fears and attempted to provide safeguards against them. This Act, thrice amended (1964, 1974 and 1976) contains our present law on adoption.

THE MAKING OF ADOPTION ORDERS

The 1952 Act provides for the creation of an Adoption Board, An Bord Uchtála, the chairman of which must have legal training (so far he/she has always been a District Justice) and six voluntary members appointed by the Minister for Justice.[7] An adoption society registered by the Adoption Board or a Health Board may handle and process adoptions[8] and the Adoption Board has the power to make adoption orders on the application of the person or persons who wish to adopt a child.[9] In the period 1953-1979 inclusive 27,059 adoption orders were made.[10]

Welfare of the Child

Prior to 1974 the Adoption Acts were continually criticised for being "mother-centred" as opposed to "child-centred".[11] Father James Good wrote in 1971[12] that "an Adoption Act should be child-centred while not neglecting the rights of other parties like parents, adopters and the community . . . adoption is not a technique of getting children for childless marriages, nor for relieving unmarried parents of their responsibility or even for saving the State the cost of keeping children in an orphanage. Adoption should be primarily and above all else a process for finding a home and family for the homeless and familyless child, but when we look at our Adoption Act . . . right through the Act the dominant idea is that the child is the property of the mother and that short of killing or physically maltreating it she can do just what she likes with it".

To meet such criticism, section 2 of the 1974 Act states that

"In any matter, application or proceedings before the Board or any court

6. Irish Times, 8th February, 1951.
7. Adoption Act, 1952, Sect. 8. The present Chairman of the Board is District Justice Agnes Cassidy. The Adoption Act, 1974, (Sect. 7) empowers the Government to appoint one of the ordinary members to Deputy Chairman, if such person is qualified to be appointed Chairman. The Deputy Chairman may act as Chairman in the latter's absence.
8. See Part IV of the Adoption Act, 1952.
9. Adoption Act, 1952, Sect. 9.
10. Report of An Bord Uchtála for Year Ending 31st Dec. 1979 (Stationery Office, Dublin), p. 4.
11. See Rev. J. Good, "Legal Adoption in Ireland" in "Child Adoption" No. 3 of 1971. See also 15th Joint Seminar of Society of Young Solicitors Lecture No. 68 by Sen. M. Robinson "The Status of Children under the Adoption Acts". Also from the same seminar Lecture No. 67 "An Outsider's View—Reform in the Law relating to Children—by Dr. Paul E. McQuaid. See also "Adoption—The Way Ahead"—by Barry Desmond, T.D., The Irish Times, 2nd May, 1973.
12. Child Adoption No. 3 of 1971.

relating to the arrangements for or the making of an adoption order, the Board or the court, in deciding that question, shall regard the welfare of the child as the first and paramount consideration".[13]

Who may be Adopted

An adoption order can only be made in respect of a child who is an orphan, illegitimate,[14] or who has been legitimated by virtue of the Legitimacy Act, 1931, but whose birth has not been re-registered under the Act.[15] The child must be resident in the State and not less than six weeks old.[16] If a child is over seven years of age at the date of the application for his adoption, the Board are under a statutory duty to give due consideration to the wishes of the child, having regard to its age and understanding.[17] No person can be adopted upon reaching the age of 21.

Who may Place a Child for Adoption

In general only a registered adoption society or a health board can lawfully make arrangements for the adoption of a child. (See Appendix B for names and addresses of registered adoption societies.) However, the parent of a child can herself place it with a third party for adoption, or a child can be placed for adoption by a third party, if the person who intends to adopt the child is a relative or the spouse of a relative of the child.[18] For the purposes of the Adoption Acts a relative means a grandparent, brother, sister, uncle or aunt. Relationships to an illegitimate child are traced through the mother only.[19]

Who may Adopt

An adoption order may not be made unless the applicant or applicants are either a married couple living together, the mother, natural father, or a relative of the child or a widow.[20] A widower can only adopt if he has another child in his custody and if the child to be adopted was placed in the care of his wife and himself, and the former died after the application for adoption had been made but before the making of the order.[21] No such stipulations are made in respect of a widow.

It is submitted that the Adoption Acts should permit an adoption order to be made in favour of a widower, if he is in a position to take proper care of a child. Under the present law if a child has been placed with a couple for adoption and the wife dies, if the couple have no other child, the husband cannot adopt. The law is illogical and inhumane. There is no reason why the existence of another child should in such circumstances be of fundamental importance in determining whether the widower should be permitted to adopt. There is no valid reason for the existence of different requirements for a widower than for

13. See *G. v. An Bord Uchtála* (1978) 113 I.L.T.R. 25 (S.C.). judgement of Henchy J. at p. 53 and Walsh J. at p. 45–46 for judicial comment on the scope of application of this section.
14. Adoption Act, 1952, Sect. 10(c).
15. Adoption Act, 1964, Sect. 2.
16. Adoption Act, 1974, Sect. 8.
17. See Sect. 10 of the 1952 Act as amended by Sect. 3 of the 1964 Act as amended by Sect. 11 of the 1974 Act.
18. Adoption Act, 1974, Sect. 6 replacing Sect. 34 of the 1952 Act.
19. Adoption Act, 1952, Sect. 3.
20. Adoption Act, 1952, Sect. 11 (1).
21. Adoption Act, 1974, Sect. 5.

a widow. In all cases the question should be simply whether it is in the interests of the child's welfare that an adoption order be made.

An order may not be made in favour of more than one adopter except in the case of a married couple, where both may adopt jointly.[22] In the *State (A.-G.)* v. *An Bord Uchtála*[23] an adoption order was quashed as the purported adopting father was unaware of the application for adoption made by his wife in their joint names. He was led to believe that the child was his own. Lavery J. stated that as the order stood

"a person had thrust upon him the obligations of a father. It makes no difference that now he might be willing to accept these obligations. The order is bad".[24]

In *S.W., Applicant*,[25] the High Court held, in a Case Stated by the Board, that under section 11 of the 1952 Act a married man or woman was not precluded from having an order for the adoption of a child by him or her made by the Board merely by reason either of the non-joinder of the spouse in the application, or of the fact that the applicant and the spouse are not living together. This question arose as the result of an application by a married woman, separated from her husband, to adopt her own illegitimate child.

The adoption by a mother of her own illegitimate child usually stems from a desire on her part to have removed from the child the social stigma and legal disadvantages associated with illegitimacy. By using the expedient of adoption she can have the child placed in the same legal relationship to her as a child born within marriage. We have already seen that married parents of an illegitimate child, where marriage has not resulted in the legitimation of their child, may apply for an adoption order both for the same reason and so as to produce the same result.

Age Requirements

Age is an important matter in deciding a person's eligibility to adopt. In the case of a widow, widower or a married couple, each of them must have attained the age of 30.[26] However, an adoption order may be made in favour of a married couple each of whom has attained the age of 25 and have been married to each other for at least three years.[27] Where the applicants are a married couple and the wife is the mother of the child, only one of them need to have attained 21,[28] whilst if one of them is the natural father or a relative of the child each spouse must have attained 21.[29] In order for the mother, natural father or a relative to adopt by themselves they must have attained 21.[30] Although the Acts do not do so, in practice most adoption societies fix an upper age limit of 40 or so, though this is not always rigidly adhered to. Much depends on the circumstances of the applicants who seek an adoption order.

---

22. Adoption Act, 1952, Sect. 11 (2).
23. [1957], Ir. Jur. Rep. 35, (S.C.).
24. *Ibid.*, at p. 36.
25. [1957], I.R. 178, (H.C.).
26. Adoption Act, 1952, Sect. 11 (3) (a).
27. Adoption Act, 1964, Sect. 5 (1).
28. Adoption Act, 1952, Sect. 11 (3) (c).
29. *Ibid.*, Sect. 11 (3) (d).
30. *Ibid.*, Sect. 11 (3) (b).

Religious Requirements

Section 12, sub-section (2) of the 1952 Act was the most controversial provision in the adoption laws. By virtue of that section no adoption order could be made unless the applicant or applicants were of the same religion as the child and his parents, or if the child was illegitimate, its mother. A child's religion was said to be that religion in which he was being brought up. This section was undoubtedly conceived originally to remove the bogey of proselytism. It not only prevented Protestant parents from adopting Roman Catholic children and *vice versa* but also totally prohibited parties to a mixed marriage[31] from adopting a child and prevented the adoption of an orphan child born of parents of a mixed marriage. In an ecumenical age, apart from the unfortunate consequences it produced in the mixed marriage situation, the provision was out of place and an unnecessary anachronism.

In May 1974 the constitutional validity of section 12(2) was challenged in the High Court.[32] A husband and wife wished to jointly adopt the wife's illegitimate son.[33] The husband was a Roman Catholic and the wife was a member of the Church of England. The wife had cared for her child since its birth. The child had been baptised in the Church of England but since the plaintiffs' marriage had been brought up as a member of the Roman Catholic faith. The couple's application to the Adoption Board for an order for the adoption of the child was rejected on the ground that the provisions of section 12(2) of the Adoption Act, 1952, were not satisfied; the couple not being of the same religion could not be said to be of the same religion either of the child or of his mother and similarly the mother could not adopt her own child as she was not of the same religion as the child.[34]

Upon their application to the High Court challenging the constitutional validity of the decision of the Adoption Board the sub-section was declared unconstitutional by Pringle J. accepting the contention of the couple's counsel that it imposed a disability and made a "discrimination on the ground of religious profession or belief" contrary to Art. 44.2.3.º of the Constitution.[35]

The present law is contained in section 4 of the 1974 Act. This states that an adoption order shall not be made unless every person whose consent is required knows the religion (if any) of the applicant or of each of the applicants when he gives consent. Whether this provision will more readily facilitate or will hinder adoption by parties to a mixed marriage will depend to a great extent on the attitude of the various adoption societies. As practically all of them are denominationally based, the societies by restricting placements for adoption to couples of one religious denomination could, in effect, render the law irrelevant and the situation not very different in practice from that which existed prior to the above case. It is too early yet to assess the full impact of section 4. It can be noted that in the period 1975 to 1977 inclusive, out of 3,674 adoption orders made, 52 were made in favour of adopters of mixed religion, 3,553 in favour of Catholic adopters and 69 in favour of adopters of a religion other than Catholic.[36]

31. Apart from the exceptions set out in Sect. 12 (3).
32. *J. McG. and W. McG. v. An Bord Uchtála & A.-G.* (1974), 109 I.L.T.R. 62 (H.C.); *M. v. An Bord Uchtála* [1975], I.R. 81—although differently entitled these citations refer to the same decision.
33. The husband was not the father of the child.
34. Under subs. 5 "A child's religion shall be taken to be that in which he is being brought up".
35. Following *Quinns Supermarket v. A.-G.* [1972], I.R. 1 (S.C.); and *Mulloy v. The Minister for Education & A.-G.* [1975], I.R. 88, (S.C.).
36. See Reports of An Bord Uchtála for Years Ending 31st December, 1975, 1976, and

Other Matters

For an adoption order to be made the applicant must be ordinarily resident in the State and have been so resident during the year ending on the date of the order.[37]

Finally the Board cannot make an adoption order unless satisfied that the applicant is of good moral character, has sufficient means to support the child and is a suitable person to have parental rights and duties in respect of the child.[38]

Consents required for Making of Order

An adoption order cannot be made without the consent of the child's mother or guardian or any person having charge or control over the child.[39] In the case of a legitimated child the consent of the natural father is necessary.[40]

A consent is not valid unless it is given after the child has attained the age of six weeks and not earlier than three months before the application for adoption.[41] Thus, in *In re J*,[42] an adoption order was quashed as the mother had signed a consent only one month after the birth of her illegitimate child. A consent must be given in writing and can be withdrawn at any time before an adoption order is made.[43] The withdrawal of consent prevents the making of an adoption order unless a court order dispensing with consent is obtained.

Under section 15(2) of the 1952 Act, the Board prior to making an adoption order is under a duty to "satisfy itself" that every person whose consent is necessary and has not been dispensed with, has given consent, and understands the nature and effect of the consent, and of an adoption order.[44] Further by section 39 of the above Act, before accepting a child for adoption, an adoption society is obliged to furnish the mother or guardian who proposes to place the child at its disposal, with a statement explaining the effect of an adoption order upon the rights of a mother or guardian and the provisions of the Act relating to consents. The society must ensure that the person understands the statement and signs a document to that effect.[45]

Until the Supreme Court decision in *McL*. v. *An Bord Uchtála and the A.-G.*[46] the forms used by the Board and the adoption societies to comply with the above provisions failed to inform a person, placing a child for adoption, of his or her right to withdraw his consent prior to the making of an order.[47] In this

1977. (Stationery Office, Dublin). The 1978 and 1979 Reports do not identify the religion of adopters in each of those years. No reason is given for the omission from these Reports of information contained in the earlier Reports.
37. Adoption Act, 1964, Sect. 5 (2).
38. Adoption Act, 1952, Sect. 13 (1).
39. *Ibid.*, Sect. 14 (1). See Form 4a of the Schedule to the Adoption Rules 1976 (S.I. No. 216 of 1976).
40. Adoption Act, 1964, Sect. 2.
41. Adoption Act, 1974, Sect. 8 amending Sect. 15 of the 1952 Act.
42. [1966], I.R. 295, (H.C.).
43. Adoption Act, 1952, Sect. 14 (5) and (6).
44. These provisions were formerly in Sect. 15 (3) of the 1952 Act. However the original Sect. 15 was amended by the Adoption Act, 1974, Sect. 8 and the contents of the original Sect. 15 (3) are now contained in Sect. 15 (2). Thus, where Sect. 15 (3) is mentioned in judgements discussed further on in the text, for the sake of clarity I have referred to it as Sect. 15 (2).
45. See Form 10 in the Schedule of the Adoption Rules 1976 (S.I. No. 216 of 1976).
46. [1977] I.R. 287 (S.C.). (This case is reported as *M. v. An Bord Uchtála and the A.-G.* but in order to distinguish between it and the case reported in [1975] I.R. I have preserved the name used in the first edition of this book).
47. The court order perfected in July 1976 does not contain a declaration as to custody although the majority of the Supreme Court made such a declaration when delivering judgement. See also footnote 102 further on.

case the natural parents of an illegitimate child sought and were granted declarations that the adoption order made in relation to their child was null and void; that as a consequence the child was legitimated by their subsequent marriage and they were entitled to an order of custody.[48] The facts were as follows:

A mother having placed her child for adoption expressed considerable reluctance to consent to the making of an adoption order. She finally signed the affidavit of consent 11 months after her child had been placed with the adopters. Between the time when she signed the consent and the making of the order—two weeks approximately—the mother and the father of the child agreed to marry. The father had always been opposed to the child being adopted, but was at that time under the impression that the adoption process had been completed. The mother gave evidence that having signed the consent she was under the impression that it was final and irrevocable, and that if she had known she could have reclaimed her child before the order was made, she would have done so. Further, although the mother of a child is entitled to be heard by the Adoption Board, she was not informed of the date when the application for adoption was listed for hearing. Declaring the adoption order to be null and void O'Higgins C.J. stated that

> "section 15(2)[49] imposes a statutory obligation on the Board to be satisfied that not merely has the formality of a written consent been observed, but that it is a genuine and real consent in the sense that its nature and effect are fully understood by the person consenting[50] . . . Not only is there no evidence that the Board took any steps so to satisfy itself but all the evidence indicates that once the written consent . . . was obtained by the Board no further action . . . was taken to involve the mother in the adoption process. This meant that this mother not only did not understand the true nature of the consent she had given but that the Board took no step whatsoever to inform her".[51]

As a consequence of this case the Adoption Act, 1976, was passed. The Act renders valid all consents given and orders made prior to its enactment in so far as they might be invalid by reason of the defects existing in *McL*'s case.[52] The act further expressly provides, that a person whose consent is necessary, is to be informed before or "as soon as may be" after giving consent, of his right to withdraw it at any time prior to the making of the order, and of his right to be heard on the application for the order.[53] Further, upon giving consent, a person must be asked to state in writing whether he wishes

(a) to be informed of the date on which the Board will, if he wishes to be heard, hear him *or*

(b) to be otherwise consulted in relation to the order.[54]

If a person does not wish to be heard by the Board or to be consulted again in relation to the order, the Board does not have to inform or consult him.[55] As

---

48. Adoption Rules, 1965, (S.I. No. 19 of 1965) see e.g. Forms 4 (a) and 10.
49. As the case commenced prior to the coming into force of the 1974 Act, the Chief Justice in fact referred to Sect. 15 (3). See footnote 44 *supra*.
50. [1977], I.R. at p. 294.
51. [1977] I.R. at p. 295.
52. Adoption Act, 1976, Sect. 2.
53. *Ibid*., Sect. 3 (1) (a).
54. *Ibid*., Sect. 3 (1) (b).
55. *Ibid*., Sect. 3 (2).

the Supreme Court layed down that to comply with section 15(2) it was not sufficient for the Board to have before it a sworn affidavit of consent, the Act provides that the Board may authorise a suitable person to make enquiries on its behalf to ensure a person understands the nature and effects of a consent and an adoption order.[56]

Dispensing with Consent

Under the 1952 Act the Board can only dispense with the consent of a person if satisfied that that person is incapable by reason of mental infirmity of giving consent or cannot be found.

In *In re F., an Infant*,[57] a mother having given birth to a baby in an institution disappeared. The child was placed by an adoption society for adoption, but before an adoption order could be made a letter was received from the baby's mother saying she had accommodation in England, she did not want the child adopted and wanted to know how to get custody of the child.

Nothing more was heard of the mother and upon a subsequent application for adoption the Board stated a case for the High Court. The Court said that if the Board was satisfied that all reasonable efforts had been made to trace the mother they could make the order sought notwithstanding the mother's previous opposition.

The limited power of dispensation conferred by the 1952 Act was the subject of much criticism. It did nothing to provide a remedy for any of the following problems: (a) the problem of the mother whose whereabouts are known agreeing to her child being placed with prospective adopters but subsequently refusing to sign a final consent to the making of an adoption order although unwilling to reclaim and provide for the child herself; (b) the problem of the mother who on a number of occasions signs a final consent to the making of an adoption order only to withdraw it each time before the adoption order is made; (c) the problem of the child who is placed in an orphanage or in fosterage for all or most of its infancy but whose mother will not permit it to be placed for adoption, the whereabouts of the mother being known.

Section 3 of the 1974 Act sought to deal with some of the above difficulties. It provides as follows:

> (1) In any case where a person has applied for an adoption order relating to a child and any person whose consent to the making of an adoption order relating to the child is necessary and who has agreed to the placing of the child for adoption either—
>
> (a) fails, neglects or refuses to give his consent, or
>
> (b) withdraws a consent already given,
>
> the applicant for the adoption order may apply to the High Court for an order under this section.

> (2) The High Court, if it is satisfied that it is in the best interests of the child so to do, may make an order under this section—
>
> (a) giving custody of the child to the applicant for such period as the Court may determine, and

56. *Ibid.*, Sect. 4.
57. (April 1972), unreported, (H.C.).

(b) authorising the Board to dispense with the consent of the other person referred to in subsection (1) of this section to the making of an adoption order in favour of the applicant during the period aforesaid.

(3) The consent of a ward of court shall not be dispensed with by virtue of a High Court order under this section except with the sanction of the Court.

Up to October, 1980, out of the eight applications that had been made under section 3 to dispense with a required consent, six were granted, one was refused and in the remaining case the court deemed that an application under the section was inappropriate.[58] In only two cases, *G.* v. *An Bord Uchtála and Ors.* [59] and *S.* v. *E.H.B. and Ors.*,[60] have written judgements been delivered.

It is clear from the judgements delivered in both of these cases that for the section to operate two conditions must be satisfied. Firstly, a person whose consent is necessary to the making of an adoption order must have "agreed to the placing of the child for adoption". Secondly, that person must have either failed, neglected or refused to consent to an adoption order being made or have withdrawn a consent already given. If these two conditions have been complied with, the court must make it's decision solely having regard to the best interests of the child. Thus, a valid agreement to place must exist before the court can consider whether it is in the best interests of a child that a consent be dispensed with.

"Agreed to the placing of the child for adoption"

In *G.* v. *An Bord Uchtála* a majority in the Supreme Court held that the rights of the mother of an illegitimate child are personal rights protected by Article 40.3.1 of the Constitution and that these rights include the right to care for and to have custody of her child.[61] The Court further held that there is nothing in Article 40 to prevent a mother surrendering, abdicating or transferring her rights. O'Higgins C.J. stated:

"They can be alienated or transferred in whole or in part and either subject to conditions or absolutely, or they can be lost by the mother if her conduct towards the child amounts to an abandonment or an abdication of her rights and duties.[62]

Further on, referring to section 3 of the 1974 Act, he continued:

"The words 'who has agreed to the placing of her child for adoption' must contemplate a mother who has so agreed and acted in such a manner as to abrogate her constitutionally recognised rights to the custody of her child. This requires a free consent on the part of the mother given in full knowledge of the consequences which follow upon her placing her child for adoption".[63]

---

58. (21st October 1980) Dáil Debates Vol. 323 Cols. 247–248.
59. (1978) 113 I.L.T.R. 25 (H.C., S.C.).
60. (February 1979), unreported, (H.C.).
61. See the judgements of O'Higgins C.J., Walsh J., and Parke J. Henchy J. and Kenny J. did not agree with the approach of the majority and held that the mother of an illegitimate child does not have a constitutional right to its custody. In Mr. Justice Henchy's opinion "The mother's rights in regard to the child although deriving from the ties of nature, are given a constitutional footing only to the extent that they are founded on the constitutionally guaranteed rights of the child". (*Supra* at p. 52).
62. *Supra* at p. 35. See also the judgement of Walsh J. at pp. 42 and 45 and of Parke J. at p. 59.
63. *Supra* at p. 36.

Dealing with the same matter, Walsh J. in the course of his judgement stated:

"There is no definition in any of the Acts of the phrase 'the placing of a child for adoption'. However, I think one may reasonably assume that it means either the handing over of the child for the purpose of it's being adopted or even, if the mother retains the child, the giving of a clear and unambiguous indication that it is her desire to surrender her natural rights in respect of the child and that it be adopted. I am satisfied that having regard to the natural rights of the mother, the proper construction of the provision in section 3 of the 1974 Act is that the consent, if given, must be such as to amount to a fully informed, free and willing surrender or an abandonment of these rights. I am, however, also of the opinion that such a surrender or abandonment may be established by her conduct when it is such as to warrant the clear and unambiguous inference that such was her fully informed free and willing intention. In my view a consent motivated by fear, stress or anxiety or consent or conduct dictated by poverty or other deprivations does not constitute a valid consent."[64]

Dealing with the particular facts of the case Parke J. said:

"On the evidence and on the facts found by the learned President there is no doubt that during the interview which the mother had with the social worker immediately before she signed the consent to the placing for adoption, the full implications and legal consequences of what she was doing were explained to her and that she understood them. In particular she was made aware that although she could refuse her Consent to an Adoption Order at any time before such Order was made, if she did so, the proposed adopting parents could apply to the Court under section 3 of the Adoption Act, 1974, for an Order dispensing with her consent if the Court considered that it would be in the best interests of the child so to do. In these circumstances I am satisfied that she waived or abandoned her rights so as to leave the matter to be decided under section 3 . . ."[65]

In essence, for a mother to validly alienate her constitutional rights so as to

64. *Supra* at p. 45.
65. *Supra* at p. 59. Both O'Higgins C.J. and Parke J. formed the view that the criteria for entry into a valid agreement to place had been complied with. Walsh J., holding that a valid agreement to place had not been entered into, stated "Before anybody may be said to have surrendered or abandoned his constitutional rights it must be shown that he is aware of what the rights are and of what he is doing. Secondly, the action taken must be such as could reasonably lead to the clear and unambiguous inference that such was the intention of the person who is alleged to have either surrendered or abandoned the constitutional rights. The facts of the present case cannot support any such conclusion." He referred to the "great trauma and the medical, physical and psychological effects of the birth of a child on an unmarried mother", to the fact that her parents were unaware of the birth of the child and to "the isolated position of the plaintiff and to her extreme youth" and stated that "In so far as the evidence goes she was not made aware of the possibilities which exist for aiding persons in her position or of the several excellent societies which exist for the purpose of enabling a woman who finds herself in the position she did to retain her child and at the same time carry on her life as normally as is possible in the circumstances. By the time the plaintiff did sign the form it may be that she was no longer confused but that is very far from saying that she was a completely free agent or that she was aware of the result if she withdrew her consent. All the circumstances indicate that she was not a free agent. The evidence discloses a reluctance and an anxiety on her part throughout the transaction; and the matter which appears to have been operating mostly on her mind was her desire to maintain secrecy over the whole affair". Henchy J. and Kenny J. having denied that an unmarried mother has a constitutional right to the custody of her child, both went on to hold that the "best interests of the child" did not require that the mother's consent be dispensed with. Neither referred to the criteria that must be complied with to enter into a valid agreement to place.

confer power on the court to make an order under section 3, an agreement to place must be freely made by her, with full knowledge of the consequences and under circumstances where neither advice received from those involved in the adoption process nor the surrounding circumstances deprive the mother of the capacity to make a fully informed, free decision.[66]

The agreement to place must still subsist at the date of the hearing of the proceedings. In *S.* v. *E.H.B. & Ors.* Finlay P. stated:

> "I am bound to giving a meaning to the word 'agreed' in this section. It is to me of significance that the word 'consent' elsewhere used in the section is not used in this context and whilst it appears inappropriate to construe this with the full meaning, consequences and characteristics of a legal agreement it seems to me to incorporate the concept of an arrangement between at least two parties. Having regard to the provisions of the section which deal only with the situation where there are applicants for an adoption order in respect of the child it would seem to me to follow that the agreement concerned must be construed as an agreement between the mother of the child and the applicants for its adoption inevitably made through some agency acting as agents for an undisclosed principal. If I am correct in this view of the interpretation of the word 'agreed' it follows in my opinion that it is an agreement capable of mutual rescission."[67]

He went on to state that an agreement to place entered into in this case by the mother in December 1977 had been rescinded upon the prospective adopters returning the child to its mother at the latter's request, the child being physically handed to the mother by the adoption society's social worker acting as an intermediary.

Finlay P. further on continued:

> "If the agreement is to be construed not as an agreement between the other and the prospective adoptive parents but rather an agreement in the facts of this case between the mother and the adoption society permitting that society to place the child at their discretion with any adoptive parent then the intervention of the society in those events through the social worker concerned would constitute a mutual rescission of that agreement between the mother and the adoption society."[68]

He concluded that upon the child being returned to its mother, the mother "was no longer within the meaning of section 3 a person who has agreed to the placing of the child for adoption".

In *S.* v. *E.H.B. & Ors.*, two weeks after the child had been returned by the adopters, the mother changed her mind and requested that the child again be placed with the original adopters and signed a final consent to the making of an adoption order. Sixteen days later, the mother withdrew her consent, but this time the adopters refused to return the child. Upon the adopters making an application under section 3, it was contended that a new agreement to place should have been executed by the mother, rather than a final consent, for the section to be brought into operation. Finlay P. rejected this contention stating

> "The form of the consent does not, in my view, affect the question as to whether it constituted an agreement to place for adoption within the section

---

66. See *S. v. E.H.B. and Ors., supra,* judgement of Finlay P. at p. 18.
67. See p. 21 of judgement.
68. See p. 22 of judgement.

or not. The final consent is, in effect, a misnomer for the Act provides and it was fully understood by the plaintiff at the time of these transactions that she could still, before final adoption, withdraw that consent."[69]

The learned judge had earlier held that the mother fully understood the nature and effect of an agreement to place.

"Best interests of the child"

If the two stipulated conditions have both been complied with, the court is bound to determine a section 3 application, O'Higgins C.J. stated in *G.* v. *An Bord Uchtála,*

"On the sole test as to what is in relation to the granting or refusing the order sought in the "best interests of the child . . ." I interpret section 3 as giving to the child the statutory right to have her (his) interests considered without regard to the clashing claims and competing rights of others. Further I conceive it to be the clear duty of this court to ensure that this right is both recognised and protected."[70]

In *G.* v. *An Bord Uchtála*, the plaintiff, having placed her illegitimate child for adoption, changed her mind and sought to have the child returned to her custody but the prospective adopters refused to do so. She brought proceedings against the Adoption Board seeking custody of her child and the prospective adopters, having been added as notice parties to the proceedings, sought an order under section 3 of the 1974 Act.

The child had been born on the 14th November, 1977. The mother's parents were unaware of the birth of the child and following her leaving hospital, she placed the child in a nursery. She sought the advice of an adoption society and had four interviews with its director. Finally on the 6th January, 1978, having had a further interview with a social worker attached to the society, she signed an agreement to the placing of her child for adoption. Prior to her signing the agreement, the legal consequences of her so placing the child were fully explained to her. On the 22nd January, 1978, the child was placed with the prospective adopters.

At the end of January the mother informed her parents of the birth of her child. Rather than reacting adversely, as she had feared, they expressed a willingness to help her bring up the child, if she wished to keep it. On the 11th February, 1978, she wrote to the adoption society, informing them she had changed her mind. The prospective adopters refused to return the child and on the 11th May, 1978, the mother instituted custody proceedings.

On the 14th September, 1978, the President of the High Court ordered that the child be returned to the mother. On the 19th December, 1978, the latter's order was affirmed by the Supreme Court, rejecting the adopters' appeal. A majority of the Supreme Court found that a valid agreement to place had been entered into but held that the "best interests of the child" were consistent with its being returned to the custody of its mother.

Kenny J. stated:

"The blood link between the applicant and the child means that an instinctive understanding will exist between them which will not be there if the child

69. See p. 24 of judgement.
70. *Supra* at pp. 36 and 38.
71. Walsh J. held the agreement to place to be invalid.

remains with the adopting parents. A child's parent is the best person to bring it up as the affinity between them leads to a love which cannot exist between adopting parents and the child. The child is now 12 months old and children of that age are infinitely adaptable."[72]

Walsh J. and Henchy J. also found that the child's best interests coincided with its being returned to its mother.

O'Higgins C.J. and Parke J. however dissented from this finding. At first instance Finlay P., in ordering the return of the child to its mother, had placed considerable reliance on the mother's constitutional rights and had based his judgement on the premise that these rights continued to subsist after she had agreed to place her child for adoption.

O'Higgins C.J. stated that:

"While he dealt with the welfare of the infant, having regard to the circumstances of each of the parties, he does not appear ever to have considered the one question which arises under section 3, namely what was 'in the best interests of the child'."[73]

The Chief Justice and Parke J., in the minority, both stated that the case should be remitted to the High Court for that question to be determined.[74]

In S. v. E.H.B. and Ors. the court found that it was in the child's best interests to remain with the prospective adopters. The plaintiff having given birth to an illegitimate child on the 3rd June, 1977 in St. Patrick's Home in Dublin, remained in the home for ten days and then resumed employment. She regularly visited the child until August, 1977 and was encouraged to make a decision as to what future arrangements should be made for the child's upbringing. Her visits ceased from August until December, 1977, when she agreed to the child being placed for adoption. The child was so placed on the 19th December, 1977. In April of 1978, upon the child being returned to her by the adopters at her request, she retained the child in her custody for only three days and then placed it in another children's home as she was unable to cope.

On the 2nd May, 1978, the mother signed a consent to the making of an adoption order and the child was returned at her request to the original adopters. Sixteen days later she withdrew her consent. The child was still residing with

---

72. *Supra* at p. 58. The learned judge's approach is open to serious question. He gave no explanation as to how he formed the view that there is "an instinctive understanding between a natural parent and child as a result of the 'blood link' ". Neither did he explain the reasoning behind his conclusion that there is an affinity between a child and its natural parent that leads to a love which cannot exist between a child and its adoptive parents. Recent studies in this area have emphasised that psychological rather than biological parenthood is what is important. See J. Goldstein, A Freud, A.J. Solnit, *Beyond the Best Interests of the Child* (The Free Press, New York, 1973) particularly ch. 2; M. Rutter, *Maternal Deprivation Reassessed* (Penguin Books Ltd., England, 1972); see also J. Rowe, "Parents and Substitute Parents" (Spring 1977) Children First Newsletter No. 7, p. 27; F. Bates, "Beyond the Best Interests . . . in the American Courts" (1978) 8 Fam. Law 46; W. Binchy, "The American Revolution in Family Law" (1976) 27 N.I.L.Q. 371 at p. 410 *et seq.*; G. McGann, "*G. v. An Bord Uchtála*—the best interests of the child and constitutional rights in adoption" (1979), vol. 73 *The Gazette of the Incorporated Law Society of Ireland* 203.

73. *Supra* at p. 37.

74. Finlay P. in the High Court *supra* at p. 32 stated "If the issue in this case was an analogous to that arising where contending parents who have separated are each seeking the custody of a child of a marriage then I would be forced to the conclusion that the welfare of the child would be marginally better fitted by remaining with her present custodians in the event of their obtaining an adoption order concerning her than it would be by being returned to the custody of her mother and into the family home consisting of her grandmother, her grandfather and her aunt.

the adopters early in 1979 when the case was heard.

The Court held that it was in the best interests of the child that it remain with the adopters and that the mother's consent be dispensed with. Finlay P. stated that he accepted, on the evidence, that the child had integrated into the adopters' family, that the separation in April of 1978 had had an injurious effect on the child's development which had taken some months to repair and that it was presently developing normally and well. Referring to the psychiatric evidence, he stated,

> "That he was satisfied that this child is essentially a child who has significantly suffered in its emotional and psychiatric development by the first period of six months in which it remained in St. Patrick's Home ... It has the badges of an institutional child and ... there are very real dangers to its ultimate intellectual and emotional development unless a continuity of an existing caring custody is maintained. My view is not that the child would particularly suffer from now being transferred to the custody of its mother but rather that the child would be most likely seriously to suffer now from being transferred from the custody of the applicants for adoption."[75]

As a result of the coming into force of section 3 of the 1974 Act, some of the difficulties concerning consents no longer exist. An order can be made under this section to meet the problems outlined in (a) and (b) on page 181. However, it appears from the judgement of Finlay P. in *S.* v. *E.H.B. & Ors.* that if in either circumstance the mother requests the return of her child and the prospective adopters comply with her request, even if the mother subsequently proves incapable of caring for her child, the court has no power to dispense with her consent unless she signs a new agreement to place or a consent to the making of an adoption order which she subsequently withdraws.[76] Section 3 also fails to meet the difficulties referred to in (c) on the same page. It is submitted that if a person unreasonably refuses to agree to the placing of a child for adoption, the court should be empowered to dispense both with the need for that person's agreement to place and with the requirement of obtaining that person's consent prior to the making of an adoption order, if it is in the best interests of a child's welfare that it be adopted.

Finally the court itself does not make the adoption order in proceedings brought under section 3 of the 1974 Act. It merely dispenses with a required consent and the power to make the adoption order still rests with the Adoption Board.[77]

Procedure for the Making of an Adoption Order

As has been seen, before accepting a child for adoption an Adoption Society is obliged to furnish the mother or guardian, who proposes to place the child

---

75. See pp. 25 and 26 of judgement.

76. As in *S. v. E.H.B. and Ors., supra.*

77. In proceedings brought under section 3 of the 1974 Act the courts seek to ensure that the natural mother and adopters remain unaware of each other's identity. A date is fixed for hearing the evidence of the natural mother and her witnesses in the absence of the prospective adopters but in the presence of their lawyers. A separate date is fixed for hearing the evidence of the prospective adopters and their witnesses in the absence of the mother but in the presence of her lawyers. The full names of parties are also excluded from affidavits that each party receives from the other side and a reserved judgement is delivered by the court in the absence of both parties to the proceedings. See *G. v. An Bord Uchtála, supra,* judgement of Finlay P. This procedure was approved by the Supreme Court in that case. See also G. McGann, *supra.*

at its disposal, with a statement explaining the effect of an adoption order upon the rights of the mother or guardian, and the provisions of the Act relating to consents. The Society must ensure that the person understands the statement and signs a document to that effect.[78] This document has a dual function. It is both a receipt for the explanatory statement and a written agreement to the placing for adoption of the child. The child is then placed with prospective adopters. Prior to the Adoption Board making an adoption order the final consent to the making of such an order must be obtained by the society. If no such consent is forthcoming, an adoption order cannot be made unless the consent is dispensed with in accordance with the provisions described earlier.

Section 9 of the 1974 Act empowers the Adoption Board to prescribe a period during which a child must be in the care of the applicants before an order can be made. The Board, however, has not at the time of writing yet made an order under the powers conferred by this section. In practice, however, in the absence of very special circumstances it requires a child to be in the care of the applicants for a minimum of six months before it will make an order.

Upon an adoption application being made the Board is empowered to hold an oral hearing, can summon witnesses, examine on oath, and require any witness to produce to the Board any document in his power or control. The Board may make whatever enquiries it thinks necessary to fulfil its function. A member or officer of the Board may visit the homes of the child, the guardian of the child, the applicants and the person to whom custody of the child has been given under an interim order.[79] Unless a person whose consent is required informs the Board that he does not wish to be heard, the Board must inform that person of a date on which he will be heard by it.[80] It must also ensure that such person properly understands the nature and effect of giving consent and of an adoption order.[81]

The following persons are entitled to be heard on an application for an adoption order:[82]

(a) the applicants;

(b) the mother of the child;

(c) the guardian of the child;

(d) a person having charge of or control over the child;

(e) a relative of the child;

(f) a representative of a registered adoption society which is or has been at any time concerned with the child;

(g) a priest or minister of religion (or, in the case of any such religion which has no ministry, an authorised representative of the religion) where the child or a parent (whether alive or dead) is claimed to be or to have been of that religion;

(h) an officer of the Board;

(i) any other person whom the Board, in its discretion, decides to hear.

---

78. Adoption Act, 1952, Sect. 39.
79. See First Schedule to the Adoption Act, 1952. For interim orders see further on p. 173.
80. See Adoption Act, 1976, Sect. 3, *ante* p. 170.
81. See p. 181 *ante*.
82. Adoption Act, 1952, Sect. 16 (1).

If the application is in respect of a legitimated child whose birth has not been re-registered under the Legitimacy Act, 1931, the natural father of the child is also entitled to be heard.[83]

Any of these persons may be legally represented.

As has been seen the Board may state a case for the determination of the High Court on any question of law arising out of an application for an adoption order and such a case may be heard in camera.[84] If the Board has been notified that custody proceedings are pending in regard to the custody of a child in respect of whom an application is before the Board, it can make no order until the proceedings have been disposed of.[85]

Administrative Duties of the Adoption Board and of Adoption Societies

The Board must produce a yearly report stating the number of applications for adoption and the decisions thereon, the names of the registered societies concerned in the applications, the number of applications for registration of societies and the decisions of the Board thereon, and the name and address of each registered society or of the societies whose registration has been cancelled.[86]

An Adoption Societies Register is kept by the Board and no body can be entered into the register unless it exists only for the purpose of promoting charitable, benevolent or philanthropic objects and the Board is satisfied that it is competent to discharge the obligations imposed on adoption societies.[87] A registered adoption society must furnish the Board with whatever information it requires in regard to its constitution, membership, employees, organisation and activities. It must also permit the Board to inspect all books and documents relating to adoption in the possession of the society.[88] The Board may cancel the registration of a society on any ground which would entitle them not to register the society or if it appears to the Board that the requirements of the Act are not being complied with by the society or its members.[89] The Board does not however have a statutory power to set down a minimum code of practice for adoption societies. Although it did in 1970 produce some guide lines for the societies, these are not mandatory. The absence of power to issue such statutory regulations has been the subject of criticism.[90]

In *McL.* v. *An Bord Uchtála & A.-G.*[91] the applicants sought a declaration that the making of an adoption order was not the exercise of a limited judicial power or function and that accordingly section 9 of the 1952 Act which confers such power on the Board was repugnant to the Constitution.[92] Butler J. in the High Court dismissed this contention, holding that the Board exercises an administrative and not a judicial function. On appeal, the Supreme Court left the matter

83. Adoption Act, 1964, Sect. 2 (2).
84. Adoption Act, 1952, Sect. 20.
85. *Ibid.*, Sect. 16 (4).
86. See *Ibid.*, First Schedule.
87. *Ibid.*, Sect. 36.
88. *Ibid.*, Sect. 38.
89. *Ibid.*, Sect. 37.
90. See V. Darling, "Statutory Regulations for the Operation of Adoption Societies". Children First Newsletter No. 1, (Dublin 1975), p. 9.
91. (October 1974), unreported, (H.C.); [1977] I.R. 287 (S.C.).
92. Article 37.1 of the Constitution provides "Nothing in this Constitution shall operate to invalidate the exercise of limited functions and powers of a judicial nature, in matters other than criminal matters, by any person or body of persons duly authorised by law to exercise such functions and powers, notwithstanding that such person or such body of persons is not a judge or a court appointed or established as such under this Constitution." For a detailed discussion of this article see J.M. Kelly, *Irish Constitutional Law*, p. 280.

undecided, holding that the adoption order was invalid for reasons already discussed.

In *G. v. An Bord Uchtála*,[93] Walsh J. also stated that the Board was exercising an administrative and not a judicial function. The other members of the Supreme Court, however, expressly reserved their opinion on the issue as it did not arise for consideration and had not been argued before them.

On the 5th of July, 1979 following the holding of a Constitutional Referendum, the Sixth Amendment of the Constitution (Adoption) Act, 1979, became law and the following provision was inserted into Article 37 of the Constitution as Article 37.2.

"No adoption of a person taking effect or expressed to take effect at any time after the coming into operation of this Constitution under laws enacted by the Oireachtas and being an adoption pursuant to an order made or an authorisation given by any person or body of persons designated by those laws to exercise such functions and powers was or shall be invalid by reason only of the fact that such person or body of persons was not a judge or a court appointed or established as such under this Constitution."

As a result of the addition of this provision to the Constitution, adoption orders made by the Board are no longer open to challenge on the ground that the Board is exercising a judicial function.

Interim Orders:[94] On an application for an adoption order the Board is empowered to adjourn the application and make an interim order giving the custody of the child to the applicant for a probationary period of not more than two years. Conditions as to the maintenance, education and supervision of the welfare of the child can be attached to such an order, and the order can be revoked by the Board under its own initiative or at the request of the person to whom custody of the child has been given or of the mother or guardian of the child.

The Position of the Natural Father of an Illegitimate Child

For the purpose of the Adoption Acts the role of the father of an illegitimate child is only given limited recognition. Whereas he is one of those who are eligible to apply to adopt the child, he is not regarded as a parent or as a relation of the child. Relatives under the Act, are traced through the mother only. The only instance in which the consent of a natural father is required before the making of an adoption order is when a child has been legitimated by the subsequent marriage of his parents. In all other cases the feelings and views of the natural father are irrelevant.

The natural father as such is not one of those entitled to be heard by the Board in an oral hearing prior to determining whether an order to adopt should be made. He may of course acquire a right to be heard as an applicant for adoption, as a person having charge or control over the child, or as the guardian of the child.[95] The Board may also hear him in exercise of their discretion to

93. *Supra.*
94. Adoption Act, 1952, Sect. 17.
95. Guardianship of Infants Act, 1964, Sect. 11 (4) confers on the natural father of an illegitimate child the right to apply to the Circuit or High Court for the custody of such child. Thus if the father of an illegitimate child does not wish it to be adopted he may strengthen his hand by making such an application. Even if he does not succeed in getting custody he will at least delay the making of an order by bringing such proceedings. This Act

hear "any other person".[96]

In the *State* (*Nicolaou*) v. *An Bord Uchtála*[97] the constitutional validity of the Adoption Act, 1952, was challenged on the ground that it violated the constitutional rights of the natural father of an illegitimate child by enabling the Board to make an adoption order without hearing his views.

Nicolaou, a Greek Cypriot of Greek Orthodox faith and English domicile, was the father of the illegitimate child of a Catholic Irishwoman with whom he had lived in London. The child was born on 23rd February, 1960 and on 16th June, 1960, the mother returned to Dublin with the child and on the 23rd September, 1960, she left it in the custody of the Catholic Protection and Rescue Society for adoption. Towards the end of September, Nicolaou learnt that the child was being put forward for adoption, and on 7th October, 1960 his solicitors wrote to the Adoption Board stating that they had been instructed to institute proceedings in the High Court to prevent the adoption of the child and that they were putting the Board on notice in accordance with section 16 of the Act. Nothing more was done by Nicolaou or his solicitors and in September 1961 the mother signed the papers necessary for the adoption to take place and an order was made for the child's adoption by a married couple.

At all times Nicolaou had been willing to marry the mother but she would not agree to a marriage unless he became a member of the Catholic Church. In mid 1963 Nicolaou learnt that the child had definitely been adopted and having been refused a conditional order of Habeas Corpus directed to the registrar of the Board and the secretary of the adoption society, he sought to have the adoption order quashed by an order of certiorari. One of the arguments on his behalf was the contention that the Adoption Act discriminated against him by according a status to the mother which was not accorded to the father contrary to Article 40.1. In reply to this, Walsh J. delivering the judgement of the court, said:

> "In the opinion of the court each of the persons described as having rights under S. 14, sub-s. 1, and S. 16, sub-s. 1, can be regarded as having, or capable of having, in relation to the adoption of a child a moral capacity or social function which differentiates him from persons who are not given such rights. When it is considered that an illegitimate child may be begotten by an act of rape, by a callous seduction or by an act of casual commerce by a man with a woman, as well as by the association of a man with a woman in making a common home without marriage in circumstances approximating to those of married life" (*the latter was the situation here*—Author.) "and that, except in the latter instance, it is rare for a natural father to take any interest in his offspring, it is not difficult to appreciate the difference in moral capacity and social function between the natural father and the several persons described in the sub-sections in question."[98]

In reply to this it can be asserted that it takes two people to conceive a child and that unless all women are to be regarded as mindless creatures incapable of fending off the sexual passions of the dominant male, except in the case of rape, there is no reason why a natural father should not have the same natural or constitutional rights as the mother of an illegitimate child. Undoubtedly the

---

was not in force at the time when Nicolaou commenced the proceedings discussed further on.

96. Adoption Act, 1952, Sect. 16 (1) (i).
97. [1966], I.R. 567, (S.C.).
98. *Supra* at p. 641.

man who commits rape has a different physical, moral and social capacity than the poor unsuspecting victim, but it is difficult to understand how in other circumstances the status of a woman who engages in sexual relations outside marriage can be differentiated from that of the man by whom she conceives. It is also difficult to understand the reason why a relative of the illegitimate child or a priest of the religion in which the child is being brought up should be regarded as having a moral and social function in relation to the child, superior to that of the father by whom the child was conceived.

Finally, the court also held in *Nicolaou* that the Act was not contrary to Article 40.3 as, on the evidence presented, the father had no "personal rights" in relation to the child, nor was it contrary to Articles 41 and 42 as these articles related solely to a family and parenthood based on marriage.[99]

Invalid Orders

The Supreme Court decision in *McL.* v. *An Bord Uchtála & A.-G.*[100] caused considerable public controversy. At the date when the judgements were delivered the 'adopted' child was six years old and had been in the custody of its adoptive parents since the age of three months, its mother having placed the child with an adoption society within five weeks of its birth. A year after the making of the order the natural parents married and went to live in West Africa. It was not until the child was four years old that the parents commenced the proceedings that resulted in the court holding the adoption order to be invalid and the natural parents entitled to custody of the child.[101]

Section 5 of the 1976 Act, enacted as a result of the above case, provides that an adoption order shall not be declared invalid if the court is satisfied

"(a) that it would not be in the best interests of the child concerned to make such a declaration, and

(b) that it would be proper, having regard to those interests and to the rights under the Constitution of all persons concerned, not to make such a declaration".

In making an order of custody in *McL*, the Supreme Court failed (wrongly in the author's opinion) to have regard to section 3 of the Guardianship of Infants Act, 1964, which requires that the child's welfare be the paramount consideration in all custody disputes. Further, it granted custody to the natural parents although the adoptive parents were not parties to the proceedings and had no opportunity to present their case.[102] The Adoption Act, 1976, Sect. 6 now provides that if an adoption order is declared invalid at the request of a person who does not have custody of the child subject to the order, the court cannot make an order of custody unless

---

99. See also *G. v. An Bord Uchtála* (1978), 113 I.L.T.R. 25 (S.C.); *S. v. E.H.B. and Ors.* (February 1979), unreported, (H.C.); *The State (K.M. and R.D.) v. The Minister for Foreign Affairs and Ors.* [1979], I.R. 83, (H.C.); *McNally v. Lee* (Jan. 1970), unreported, (H.C.). See further p. 3 *ante* and p. 320 below.

100. *Supra.*

101. See footnotes 47 *ante* and 102 *infra*. See also dissenting judgement of Henchy J.

102. Subsequent to the Supreme Court decision, the adopters commenced proceedings seeking a declaration that they were not bound by the Supreme Court order as they were not afforded any opportunity to be heard, and sought an order that the child remain in their custody. The natural parents sought an order of Habeas Corpus requiring the adopters to return their child to them. On 6th Oct. 1976, it was announced to the President of the High Court that the actions had been settled. A consent was executed by the parties in which they agreed that the child be made a ward of court and remain in the custody and care of the adopters. See the *Irish Times* 24th July and 7th Oct., 1976.

(a) such an order is sought and

(b) any person having custody of the child is joined in the proceedings and

(c) it is in the interests of justice that the question of custody be determined, without the necessity of bringing separate proceedings.

If the court decides to determine the question of custody, the section makes it clear that it is bound by section 3 of the Act of 1964.

The persons in whose favour an adoption order is made can only be heard in proceedings where the validity of an adoption order is challenged with the consent of the court. In deciding whether to give consent the court may hear submissions from the Board or any other interested person relating to the identification of the person or persons concerned or to any other relevant matter.[103]

THE LEGAL CONSEQUENCES OF THE MAKING OF AN ADOPTION ORDER

The effect of an adoption order is to establish the legal relationship of parent and legitimate child between the adopter and the adopted child. Section 24 of the 1952 Act states:

"Upon an adoption order being made—

(a) the child shall be considered with regard to the rights and duties of parents and children in relation to each other as the child of the adopter or adopters born to him, her, or them in lawful wedlock;

(b) the mother or guardian shall lose all parental rights and be freed from all parental duties with respect to the child."

The child thus attains the same status as if born in lawful wedlock to the adopters and the legal rights and duties arising from the relationship between the child and his natural mother or guardian automatically cease. Any affiliation order or any agreement by the father of an illegitimate child to make payments for its benefit is discharged unless the mother is an adopter.[104] Similarly a court order under the Children Act, 1908, committing a child to the care of a fit person, ceases to have effect.[105] The child obtains the same property and succession rights as a child born in lawful wedlock.[106] Further, he is placed in the same position as the latter in respect of his right to claim damages under Part IV of the Civil Liability Act, 1961.[107] If the adopter is an Irish citizen and the child is not, it becomes an Irish citizen.[108] The adoption of a child is not affected by the subsequent marriage of its natural parents and the Legitimacy Act of 1931 will not apply to the child unless the adoption order is set aside.[109] Where the child has been adopted by one of his natural parents who subsequently marries the other parent, the 1931 Act is applicable, and the child can be legitimated and his name removed from the Adopted Children Register.[110]

In *Nicolaou* the submission, that the 1952 Act, by permitting the adoption of a child by the parents of an existing family and by enacting that the child shall

---

103. Adoption Act, 1976, Sect. 6 (2).
104. Adoption Act, 1952, Sect. 31 (1).
105. Adoption Act, 1952, Sect. 31 (2) and Sect. 33.
106. Adoption Act, 1952, Sect. 26 and see also Sect. 110 of the Succession Act, 1965.
107. Adoption Act, 1952, Sect. 28; see also Part IV of the Civil Liability Act, 1961.
108. Adoption Act, 1952, Sect. 25 and the Irish Nationality and Citizenship Act, 1956, Sect. 11.
109. Adoption Act, 1952. Sect. 29 (1). See also *In re J. supra*; *McL. v. An Bord Uchtála and the A.-G., supra.*
110. Adoption Act, 1952, Sect. 29 (2).

be considered as one born in lawful wedlock, in some way infringed the guaranteed rights of the family and its members under Article 41, was rejected.

Walsh J. stated that

"The adoption of a child by the parents of a family in no way diminishes for the other members of that family the rights guaranteed by the Constitution. Rights of succession, rights to compensation for the death of a parent and such matters may properly be the subject of legislation and the extension of such legal rights by legislation to benefit an adopted child does not encroach upon any of the inalienable and imprescriptible rights guaranteed by the Constitution to the family or its members or upon the natural and imprescriptible rights of children referred to in Sect. 5 of Article 42."[111]

Finally where an Act of the Oireachtas passed after July 1976 refers to a child of a person unless there is a contrary intention the reference is to be construed as including a child adopted by that person.[112]

CRITICISM OF THE PRESENT LAW ON ADOPTION AND SUGGESTED REFORMS[113]

The present law on adoption can be criticised on the following grounds:

(a) Under existing legislation, there are no circumstances in which a legitimate child who is not an orphan can be adopted. A number of different circumstances arise in which it would clearly be in the best interests of such a child if it could be adopted, for example, a child permanently abandoned by its parents or a child destined to spend all or most of its childhood in care as a result of the disintegration of its family unit or due to the inadequacy, neglect or cruelty of its parents. Some children taken into care are placed with foster parents but many remain in residential institutions. As they are unadoptable, they have at present little, if any, prospect of experiencing a normal family upbringing.[114]

Two Private Members Bills have sought to extend adoption to legitimate children. The Adoption Bill, 1971, empowered the Adoption Board where it was "satisfied that in the particular circumstances of the case it is desirable to do so, to make an adoption order in respect of a child who is neither illegitimate or an orphan." The Sixth Amendment of the Constitution Bill, 1978, sought to deal with constitutional objections raised to the adoption of legitimate children by amending Articles 41 and 42 of the Constitution and by the addition of a section to Article 41 expressly conferring power on the State to transfer "parental rights to substitute parents" in certain specified circumstances. Neither of these measures, however, became law.

---

111. *Supra* at p. 645.

112. Sect. 8 of the 1976 Act.

113. For a comprehensive survey of the problems that arise under the English Adoption laws: See "Report of the Departmental Committee on the adoption of children" (The Houghton Report) 1972, (H.M.S.O. 1972), (Cmnd. 5107). Many of the problems discussed and recommendations made are equally applicable in the Irish context. Various proposals of the Houghton Committee are implemented in the Children Act 1975; on this see S.M. Cretney, "Children Act 1975" in (1976), 126 N.L.J. 7–8, 29–31, 57–59. The most recent comprehensive discussion of the reforms required in the Irish adoption process is contained in "Children First", Second Submission to the Task Force on Child Care Services, (Dublin, February 1976). See also Children First Newsletter, No. 7, "Proceedings of the Children First Conference on Substitute Parenting" (Dublin, Spring 1977).

114. See Rev. J. O'Mahony, "Key Issues Facing Adoption Today", Children First Newsletter, No. 7, *supra*, p. 35. See also Children First, "Second Submission . . .", *supra*, pp. 3 and 9.

Successive Ministers for Justice have stated that legislation permitting the adoption of legitimate children who are not orphans would be unconstitutional. The question thus arises as to whether a constitutional amendment is required prior to the enactment of any such legislation to ensure its constitutional validity. Moreover, as there is no difference between the constitutional position of a legitimate and a legitimated child, it is possible that section 2 of the Adoption Act, 1964, which permits the adoption of legitimated children is also unconstitional.[115]

The constitutional objection derives from Articles 41 and 42 of the Constitution under which both the family and parents are stated to possess inalienable and imprescriptible rights. It is argued that if parental rights are inalienable, they cannot be totally extinguished by an adoption order.[116] These Articles do not apply to the relationship existing between an illegitimate child and its parents[117] and thus present no obstacle to the adoption of illegitimate children. The courts have expressly stated that the rights of the mother of an illegitimate child, which fall to be protected under Article 40.3.1 of the Constitution can be alienated or transferred.[118] Moreover, no constitutional problem is created by the natural parents of an illegitimate child marrying subsequent to its adoption. By section 29(1) of the Adoption Act, 1952, upon such a marriage taking place, if an adoption order has previously been made, the Legitimacy Act, 1931, has no application and the child is not legitimated unless the adoption order is set aside.[119]

In chapter 13, which deals with the law as to guardianship and custody of children, it is noted that in the first edition of this book it was argued that to give the welfare of a child primacy over parental rights in determining a dispute between its parents and a stranger as to custody is in accordance with and not contrary to basic constitutional principles. This view is further supported by judgements recently delivered by members of both the High Court and the Supreme Court, who have clearly stated that children as well as parents have rights under the Constitution and that the exercise of parental rights can be controlled to afford protection to the rights of the child.[120] Thus, it is submitted that legislation permitting the adoption of a legitimate child in circumstances in which such a child has been abandoned or neglected by its parents would not be contrary to the Constitution. This view is clearly supported by the judgement of Walsh J. in *G. v. An Bord Uchtála*. As this judgement contains the first detailed examination of this issue by a member of the Supreme Court, it is quoted in extenso. Walsh J. stated:

115. *In re J. supra*; see article by Fr. James Good, "Are the Adoption Acts Unconstitutional?" *Irish Times* 25 August 1973.
116. See W. Duncan, "Substitute Parenting and the Law", Children First Newsletter, No. 7, *supra*, p. 9 and see also speech delivered in March, 1977 by the then Minister for Justice, Mr. P. Cooney at the Children First Conference on Substitute Parenting reported in the same newsletter at p. 5; M. Staines, "The Concept of the Family under the Irish Constitution" (1976) 11 I.J. (n.s.) 223. See further The Irish Council for Civil Liberties, Report No. 2, *Children's Rights under the Constitution* (Dublin 1977).
117. *The State (Nicolaou) v. An Bord Uchtála, supra; G. v. An Bord Uchtála, supra; The State (K.M. and R.D.) v. The Minister for Foreign Affairs and Ors., supra; S. v. E.H.B. and Ors., supra*.
118. See, in particular, *G. v. An Bord Uchtála, supra; S. v. E.H.B. and Ors., supra*.
119. See *In re J., supra*, in which an adoption order was set aside as the mother had given her consent too soon, and *McL. v. An Bord Uchtála, supra*, in which an adoption order was set aside upon the mother's consent being held to be invalid. In both cases the natural parents had married after the adoption order had been made. Upon the adoption order being set aside the child in each case was legitimated.
120. See especially *G. v. An Bord Uchtála, supra*, in particular judgement of Walsh J; *J. v. D. and Ors.* (June 1977), unreported, (S.C.) in particular judgement of Kenny J.; *P.W. v. A.W.* (April 1980), unreported, (H.C.).

"In my view, there is nothing whatever in the Constitution to prevent a member of a family passing out of that family . . . I do not see any impediment in principle to a child's passing out of one family and becoming a member of another family in particular circumstances[121] . . . parents are the natural guardians of the children of the family. Guardianship may be surrendered or abandoned provided that doing so does not infringe any constitutional rights of the child and is not inimical to the welfare of the child[122] . . . Article 42.5 of the Constitution speaks of the case where parents for physical or moral reasons fail in their duty towards their children and provides that the State as *guardian* of the common good, by appropriate means shall endeavour to supply the place of the parents, but *always with due regard for the natural and imprescriptible rights of the child*. The State, under this section, may very well by legislation provide for the failure of the parents and it may very well in appropriate cases extend the law beyond simple provisions for a change of custody. A parent may for physical or moral reasons decide to abandon his position as a parent or he or she may be deemed to have abandoned that position, and a failure in parental duty may itself be evidence of such an abandonment[123] . . . where there is a complete abandonment of the parental right and duty, the State may be justified in taking measures by statute or otherwise to protect the rights of the child. These measures may include the enactment of adoption legislation."[124]

As for the inalienability of parental rights, Walsh J. noted

"It is also to be borne in mind that some inalienable rights are absolutely inalienable while others are relatively inalienable."[125]

It is clear that in this judgement the learned judge was referring to both legitimate and illegitimate children. Whilst the above cited passages are merely obiter dicta with reference to the position of legitimate children, they are a clear indication that the adoption of such children is constitutionally permissible in certain specified circumstances.[126]

(b) As already stated there is no valid reason for rendering it more difficult for a widower to adopt than a widow. It is submitted that the provisions of the Adoption Acts in this respect are unconstitutional being contrary to Article 40.1. In *De Burca and Anderson* v. *The A.-G.*[127] Walsh J. stated

"it is not open to the State to discriminate in its enactments between the persons who are subject to its laws solely upon the ground of the sex of those persons" and that if a reference is made to a person's sex "the purpose of the law that makes such a discrimination should be to deal with some physical or moral capacity or social function that is related exclusively or

---

121. *Supra* at p. 43.
122. *Supra* at p. 45.
123. *Supra* at p. 47.
124. *Supra* at p. 48.
125. *Ibid.*
126. See however, Dáil Debates Vol. 311, Cols. 556–587 in which the present Minister for Justice, Mr. G. Collins proposed the second reading of The Sixth Amendment of the Constitution (Adoption) Bill, 1978, (it became an Act of 1979). In his speech, the Minister made it clear that he was opposed to legislation permitting the adoption of legitimate children on social grounds; see particularly cols. 585–587. For a discussion of different aspects of the Minister's speech see Children First Newsletter No. 15 (Spring 1979) pp. 1–3. See further Children First Newsletter No. 16 (Summer and Autumn 1979) pp. 1–5.
127. [1976], I.R. 39 (S.C.) at p. 71.

very largely to that sex only."

Clearly some functions of necessity depend on sex, e.g. a male cannot give birth to a child. However, once a child has been born, the great majority of the functions performed by a mother can also be carried out by a father. If the law permits a widow with no children to adopt a child, it is submitted that it is contrary to the Constitution to prevent a widower with no children from adopting. In so far as each in their role of adoptive parent would also have to perform functions normally performed by the absent parent, their functions are for all practical purposes, identical. Further it is arguable that the present law is unconstitutional in that it gives rise to unlawful discrimination between widowers with a single child and those with no children.

(c) If a person unreasonably refuses to agree to the placing of a child for adoption and refuses to consent to the making of an adoption order, the court should be empowered to dispense with the need for an agreement or a consent, if such dispensation is in the best interests of the child.[128]

(d) It is submitted that an adoption law should seek to minimise the risk of uprooting a young child who has already been placed and lived with prospective adopters for a number of months. At least six months normally pass from the time when a mother agrees to the placing of her illegitimate child for adoption until the Adoption Board makes an adoption order. Following the placing of her child a mother (or father in the case of a legitimated child) may refuse to sign a final consent to the making of the adoption order, or having given such consent, may revoke it before the order is made.

The fear of a change of mind on the part of the person placing the child for adoption adds unnecessary uncertainty to the adoption process and can cause considerable anxiety to the applicants. In turn such anxiety can have a harmful effect on the development of a relationship between the child and the adoptive parents. This could be avoided if the agreement to place and the further requirement of a consent to the making of an adoption order were amalgamated into a single authorisation to the placing of a child for adoption and the making of an adoption order, with such authorisation becoming irrevocable on an exact number of days or weeks after being given, for example, in Australia a consent to the making of an adoption order is irrevocable after thirty days have elapsed.[129] Alternatively adoption could be arranged in two stages:

(i) a relinquishment stage, in which the parent would irrevocably relinquish her rights over the child and vest them in the adoption agency.

(ii) an adoption stage, in which the child is placed for adoption.[130]

(e) The natural father, when known, should be informed that a child is to be placed for adoption, and should be entitled to a hearing before the Board. The fact that he cannot directly intervene in the adoption process, but can do so indirectly by an application for custody is particularly unsatisfactory.[131]

128. See p. 188 *ante*.
129. See F. Bates, "Adoption in the Context of Children's Rights: Some Reflections from Australia" (1977), 12 I.J. (n.s.), 261 at p. 276.
130. See H.M.S.O., *Report of the Departmental Committee on Adoption of Children* (The Houghton Report) 1972, Recommendations 37–44 and the English Children Act, 1975, Sect. 14. See also Children First, "Second Submission . . ." *supra*, para. 3.19; Goldstein, Solnit, Freud, *Beyond the Best Interest of the Child, supra*, p. 36.
131. See Guardianship of Infants Act, 1964, Sect. 11 (4).

(f) Vivienne Darling, in her evaluation of the workings of the Adoption Acts, states that "fifty per cent of the personnel employed in adoption work have no training in social work".[132] Adoption work is an extremely skilled process. The responsibility of placing children for adoption calls for a high level of knowledge and decision making and should only be undertaken by properly qualified personnel.

(g) There is a total lack of uniformity in the practices of the Adoption Societies. Miss Darling in her study states that the assessment procedure leading to selection of adopters in many instances is merely superficial. "In some cases there is little to suggest that much thought has been given to the actual placement and indeed it sometimes appears as if there is a most casual approach to the arrangements for handing over of the baby to its new parents." Moreover, once the child has been placed "it seems as if supervision is often regarded merely as an opportunity for checking that nothing is amiss and social workers do not see it as their role to use this period in a more positive way of helping the adopters to integrate the baby into their family . . . Adopters experience a high degree of anxiety in the time which elapses between the placement and the making of the Adoption Order and one of the supervisory tasks should be to provide a supportive help during this period."

It is submitted that the Adoption Board should be statutorily required to set down basic minimum standards in a code of adoption practice to be binding on Adoption Societies and Health Boards. The code should lay down amongst other things, the minimum number of visits that a representative of an agency must make to applicants before an order can be made, the minimum number of qualified personnel required by an agency to avoid individuals carrying too large a caseload, minimum qualifications to be possessed by personnel, the nature of pre-placement enquiries and post-placement supervision.[133]

(h) Adoptions by relatives are mainly adoption by grandparents.[134] As such in the case of an illegitimate child they can create more problems than they solve, both for the child and the mother, especially if the mother still resides at home. The Houghton Report points out that "Adoption by relatives severs in law, but not in fact, an existing relationship of blood or of affinity, and creates an adoptive relationship in place of the natural relationship, which in fact, though not in law, continues unchanged".[135] The new relationship created distorts the natural relationship. In such a situation the Report suggests "that guardianship should normally be the appropriate means of recognising the position of relatives who seek to care for a child and of conferring legal security".

Houghton envisaged a modified form of guardianship, more akin to our concept of custody. It is submitted that upon an adoption application being made by a relative, a custody order rather than adoption order should be made. Further it should be possible both for a relative and a non-relative looking after a child to seek an order of custody under sect. 11 of the Guardianship of Infants

132. V. Darling, "Adoption in Ireland" (C.A.R.E. Discussion Paper No. 1) (Dublin 1974), p. 19.
133. See also Vivienne Darling "Statutory Regulations for the Operation of Adoption Societies"; also Children First, Second Submission . . . p. 5–6; Children Deprived, The Care Memorandum on Deprived Children and Children's Services in Ireland, (Dublin 1972), p. 61; Rev. J. O'Mahoney, *supra*.
134. *Adoption in Ireland, supra*, p. 45.
135. H.M.S.O. Adoption of Children–Working paper of Houghton Committee published in 1970, p. 27 par. 81.

Act, 1964. At present, foster parents may make an application under the latter act to be appointed guardians of an illegitimate child in their care, if the child's mother is dead.[136] If however she is alive, foster parents can obtain some legal security only if they succeed in having the child made a ward of court and the court grants them custody.[137] It should not be necessary to invoke the wardship jurisdiction for this purpose.[138]

(i) Third party placements are prohibited by section 6 of the 1974 Act. There are, however, exceptions to this prohibition. A third party may place a child if it is placed with a relative or a spouse of a relative of a child. Moreover, a mother may place her illegitimate child for adoption. It is submitted that these exceptions should not exist. It is totally undesirable that a child should be placed for adoption without the applicants' suitability for adoption being first assessed by an adoption society or a Health Board. The Adoption Board should be prohibited from making an order unless a placement has been made through one of the above agencies. Where a parent desires a child to be placed with a particular person or a relative wishes to adopt, there is nothing to prevent their approaching an adoption society, requesting a particular placement and asking the society to do the necessary assessment. Such a procedure is necessary if the welfare of the child is to be properly protected.[139]

(j) Finally, there is a need to re-examine a number of other matters relating to the adoption process, e.g. the right of adopted children to obtain information relating to their natural parents,[140] the role of natural fathers and the desirability of giving them greater say, the functions of the Adoption Board and whether it should play a greater role in public discussion on the workings of the Adoption Acts.

---

136. See the Guardianship of Infants Act, 1964, Sects. 6 (4) and 8 (1).

137. If a mother herself brings proceedings against foster parents to regain custody of the child, it is open to the court in her proceedings to make a custody order in favour of the foster parents.

138. See English Children Act 1975, Sects. 33—35 which provides for "Custodianship Orders". A grandmother could apply for the custody of her illegitimate grandchild under these provisions. If she were to seek adoption it seems likely that the court in England would now prefer to make a custodianship order; Sect. 37. See also M.D.A. Freeman "Custodianship—New Concept, New Problems", (1976), 6 Family Law 57.

139. See Children First, Second Submission . . . ibid., para. 5.8.

140. See J. Triseliotis In Search of Origins (Routledge and Keegan Paul, London 1973). See also Children First, Second Submission . . . p. 10.

CHAPTER 13

GUARDIANSHIP AND CUSTODY OF CHILDREN

INTRODUCTION

There are two concepts central to any discussion of the law as to parent and child. These are "guardianship" and "custody".

Guardianship: Parents have both rights and duties in respect of the upbringing of their children, e.g. a duty to maintain and rights to make decisions as to education. This whole relationship, both rights and duties, is one of "guardianship". Persons other than parents can be a child's guardian. Thus, as we shall see in the pages that follow, a person may be appointed guardian either by a parent under a deed or will, or by a court of competent jurisdiction.

Custody: Custody essentially means the right to physical care and control. Thus, a parent deprived of custody is not prevented from having any further say in the upbringing of his child. The right to custody is merely one of the rights that arise under the guardianship relationship. It is the enforcement of this right that has given rise to the greatest amount of litigation and with which the courts in recent years have been mainly concerned. Consequently, the pages that follow concentrate on the law as to determination of disputes concerning the custody of children.

The law as to guardianship and custody of children is governed by the Guardianship of Infants Act, 1964. The Act gives statutory expression to the equitable rule that all matters concerning guardianship and custody of children should be decided on the basis of the welfare of the child and to the constitutional principle[1] that parents have equal rights to, and are the joint guardians of their children.[2]

Part II of the Act sets down the equality of rights as between parents as the joint guardians of their children and confers jurisdiction on both the High Court and Circuit Court to determine disputes between parents or guardians on matters affecting a child's welfare. The Courts Bill, 1980, as initiated, proposes to extend this jurisdiction to the District Court.

Part III of the Act is concerned with the enforcement of a right to custody of a child, a matter over which only the High Court has jurisdiction. However, the Courts Bill, 1980, proposes to vest this jurisdiction also in both the District and Circuit Courts.

It is intended to first deal in detail with the development of the law up to the

---

1. See *B. v. B.* [1975], I.R. 54, (S.C.) particularly the judgements of O'Dalaigh C.J. & Walsh J.
2. An infant or child under the Act is a person under 21.

present day in the area of rights and the determination of disputes between parents as to the custody and upbringing of their legitimate children and then similarly to deal with the position between parents and strangers.

DISPUTES BETWEEN PARENTS

Methods of Resolving Disputes: Formerly such disputes were resolved upon an application for a writ of Habeas Corpus by which one parent sought to obtain custody from the other. Today such disputes are usually determined upon an application to the court by special summons under section 11 of the 1964 Act. It is also possible for a parent to have a child made a ward of court so as to enable the court resolve a parental dispute over a child, but this is rarely done in practice.

History of Parental Right

At common law a father was the sole guardian of his legitimate child and his right to the custody[3] of such child until the age of 21 was almost absolute, forfeited only in those exceptional cases where he had been guilty of such grave misconduct as was likely to cause physical or moral harm to the child. This paternal right to custody was a corollary to the paternal duty to protect and maintain one's legitimate minors, but whereas the former right was enforceable by the father, the machinery for enforcing the duties was almost wholly ineffectual.

Equity, on the other hand, derived from the prerogative of the Crown a jurisdiction to act as supreme parent to all children and took a far broader view of the jurisdiction it exercised over children and parents. Stressing the welfare of the child as the paramount consideration, it showed greater willingness to deprive the father of his right to custody, even exceptionally where he had been guilty of no misconduct.

Whilst *prima facie* the father's rights were to be enforced, upon their exercise being shown to be clearly contrary to the child's welfare, they were pushed aside. After the passing of the Judicature Act, 1877, the equitable rule stressing the importance of the child's welfare prevailed in all courts.[4]

During the father's lifetime the mother possessed no real power, but on the death of the father without having appointed a testamentary guardian,[5] she was entitled to the custody of her infant children and acquired all the father's rights and responsibilities. But where a testamentary guardian had been appointed, a mother as such had no right to interfere with him. Even if in a deed of legal separation, the father voluntarily gave up his rights to his children, the courts held that such a provision was void in so far as it deprived the father of his powers over his children or provided that the mother should have possession of them to his exclusion.

In the first half of the 19th century a number of factors combined to bring about a gradual reform of the law by limiting the exclusive powers of the father by statute. The development of the Chancery jurisdiction on the basis of the welfare of the child resulted in a gradual judicial realisation of the anomalous

---

3. See "The Right to the Custody of Children" (1883), 17 I.L.T. & S.J. 417–8, 431–2, 445–6, 459–60, 473–4, 483–4.

4. *R. v. Gyngall* [1893], 2 Q.B. 232, (C.A.); *In re O'Hara, an Infant* [1900], 2 I.R. 232; (1899), 34 I.L.T.R. 17, (C.A.); *In re Kindersley an Infant* [1944], I.R. 111; (1943), 78 I.L.T.R. 159, (S.C.).

5. A testamentary guardian could be appointed by the father under the Tenures Abolition Act, 1662.

and unequal position of the mother, and a growing judicial concern about the restrictive nature of the common law courts' jurisdiction over children. Much publicity was also given to extreme cases where mothers were deprived of their children's custody in situations where such a decision seemed contrary to the child's benefit and this helped to bring about pressure for reform.[6]

Talfourds Act of 1839 which conferred on the mother the right to seek custody of her children until they reached the age of seven, was the first of a number of 19th century Acts which gradually whittled down the paternal authority and power. This Act specifically provided that no custody order was to be made in favour of the mother if she had been guilty of adultery. The Custody of Infants Act, 1873, empowered the court to give the mother custody until the child reached the age of 16 and omitted the provision relating to adultery. The Act also rendered enforceable a provision in a deed of separation whereby a father surrendered custody of his children to their mother "except where the court might deem it contrary to the benefit of the child to enforce it". The Guardianship of Infants Act, 1886, enabled the mother to obtain custody of her children until they reached 21 and for the first time in a statute stated that such an application was to be decided having regard to the welfare of the infant, as well as the conduct and wishes of both parents. A father could no longer defeat a mother's rights after his death by appointing a testamentary guardian, for if one was appointed she was to act jointly with him. The mother was also empowered in the Act to appoint a guardian to act after both her and her husband's death and one to act after her death jointly with the father "if it be shown to the satisfaction of the court that the father is for any reason unfitted to be the sole guardian of his children".[7]

Disputes as to Custody between Parents from 1886 to the Present Day

Effect of Act of 1886: Despite the fact that the 1886 Act was described as "essentially a mother's Act"[8] it did not result in the stage being reached whereby it could be said "that the respective rights of the parents of a child are equal". Thus in *In The Matter of N.P. An infant*[9] it was said that whilst the primary question is the welfare of the child

> "The father is the head of the household and is liable to contribute to the cost of maintenance of his wife and family. If the circumstances show that he has not disentitled himself I rather lean in favour of conceding to him a greater claim than to the mother.[10] This, however, is subject to an important exception, namely, that where the child is of very tender years her claim is substantially increased".[11]

But if she was regarded by the court as being primarily responsible for the breaking up of the family she was denied custody irrespective of the age of the child.[12]

6. See *Children in English Society*, Vol. II by I. Pinchbeck & M. Hewitt, (Routledge & Kegan Paul, London 1973), Ch. XIII.
7. Now under the Guardianship of Infants Act, 1964, both parents have identical powers of appointment of testamentary guardians (see p. 207).
8. Per Lord Justice Lindley, *In re A. & B., (Infants)* [1897], 1 Ch. 786, (C.A.).
9. *In the matter of N.P. an Infant*, (1943), 78 I.L.T.R. 32, (H.C.).
10. *In re McNally, an Infant* (1949), 84 I.L.T.R. 7, (H.C.). "If the conditions are equal *prima facie* the father is entitled to the custody of the child". Per Haugh J. at p. 8. See also *In re Kindersley an Infant, supra*.
11. *Supra* per Maguire J. at p. 34.
12. *In re Mitchell*, [1937], I.R. 767, 776, (S.C.). In which a mother was denied custody of her three year old child because she returned to her home in Dublin leaving her husband

A considerable number of parental disputes as to custody involved a dispute as to the education and particularly the religious education[13] of the children of the marriage. At common law not only was the father's right to custody fundamental, but he also had an absolute right to determine a child's education and in particular its religious upbringing. These rights could of course be overridden by equity and by all the courts after 1877 upon their exercise being proved contrary to the child's welfare.[14]

In disputes as to the religious upbringing of a child the courts constantly stated that they would never attempt to adjudicate between the merits of different faiths.[15] They did, however, regard it as a matter of great importance that a child should be brought up in some religion.[16] The courts, moreover regarded it as essential that such belief as a child was taught should not be disturbed by controversy "the result [of which] may be to unsettle the foundations of belief in the mind, and substitute a scepticism fatal to the existence of any religious faith whatever".[17] "The child must be taught dogmatically that the religion in question is true. The child must soon learn that there are other religions, but must be taught that its own is the true one. The religious belief of a child is not the result of a consideration of arguments as to which is the true religion."[18] The father's authority over a child's religion was such that his wishes were still to be adhered to after his death, despite the fact that the mother who had custody of the child, did not agree with them. Ante-nuptial agreements that children should be brought up in a religion different from that of the father were held not to be binding.[19]

Although wishing to ensure that children should be educated in the religion of their father, the courts constantly reiterated that the law was not so rigid as to compel them to order children to be so educated regardless of the consequences to themselves.[20] Thus, if it was clearly contrary to the child's welfare the

in Glasgow, because of homesickness. See also *In re McNamara, Infants* (1948), 86 I.L.T.R. 75, (H.C.)–In which a father was denied custody on the grounds of his responsibility for breaking up the family; see also *In re Kevin Isherwood, An Infant* (1948), 82 I.L.T.R. 85, (H.C.).

13. For a dispute as to a child's educational upbringing but not his religious education see *In re Kindersley, an Infant, supra*.

14. *In re Kindersley, an Infant, supra*–however, in this case it was emphasised that in the case of a dispute as to a child's education in determining what course is best for the child's welfare "greater weight should be attached to the view of the father".

15. *In re Grimes* (1877), I.R. 11 Eq. 465, (Chancery) Ball L.C. stated "of religious systems how far true, how far in error it (the court) pronounces nothing; it neither favours nor condemns any; and views the claims and rights of all with perfect impartiality." In *In re Connor* [1919], 1 I.R. 361, 367, (M.R.) (C.A.), Ronan L.J. stated "We are bound to treat the Catholic and Protestant religions as equally beneficial to the minor. We are prohibited from considering the respective merits of the two religions, and therefore from saying that as between the two religions, as such, it is more for the welfare of the minor that he should be brought up in one of them than in the other". See also *In re Story, Infants* [1916], 2 I.R. 328; (1916), 50 I.L.T.R. 123, (K.B.D.).

16. See *In re Greys* [1902], 2 I.R. 684; (1902), 36 I.L.T.R. 170, (K.B.D.); see also *Shelley v. Westbrooke* (1817), Jacob 266n.; 37 E.R. 850, (Chancery). In this case the poet Shelley was denied custody of his children on the grounds of his declared atheism.

17. *In re Grimes, supra* per Ball L.C. at p. 471.

18. Ronan L.J., *In re Connor, an Infant, supra* at p. 389.

19. *In re Browne* (1852), 2 Ir. Ch. Rep. 511 (Rolls); *In re Meades, Minors* (1871), 2 I.R. 5 Eq. 98, (Chancery); *Andrews v. Salt* (1873), 8 Ch. App. 622, (C.A. in Ch.); *Agar-Ellis v. Lascelles* (1878), 10 C. Div. 49, (C.A.); *In re Kevin Isherwood, an infant, supra.; In re Story, Infants, supra*–see however statement by Dodd J. at p. 352 that "A promise by a father to bring up his children in his wife's religion though it is not a promise that can be enforced in law or equity, . . . still is a circumstance to which weight, and perhaps even great weight, should be attached".

20. *In re Meades, Minors, supra; In re M'Grath (Infants)* (1893), 1 Ch. 143, (C.A.); *In re Story, Infants, supra; The State (Kavanagh) v. O'Sullivan* [1933], I.R. 618; (1931), 68 I.L.T.R. 110, (S.C.).

parental right was not enforced.[21]

The Influence of the 1937 Constitution

The court's right to deprive a mother of the custody of her children in order to ensure that they should be educated in their deceased father's religion was challenged in *In re Frost, Infants*.[22] It had been agreed in an ante-nuptial agreement that the children should be brought up as Catholics; after the marriage and before the father's death, the mother under pressure of economic circumstances agreed to their being placed in one of Mrs. Smyly's homes, "the Bird's Nest" in Dún Laoghaire, a Protestant institution. The decision of the High Court resulted in the mother getting custody of the two youngest children, but not of the others. The mother contended that the court must regard the family as a unit by virtue of Article 41.1 of the Constitution, the control and management of which is vested in both parents while they are both living and, on the death of either of them, in the parent who survives. This the court stated as a general proposition was unquestionable. It was also contended however that "So long as either parent is alive, the court has no power to interfere with the education, religious or otherwise of the children, contrary to the parents' wishes, except for the special reasons set out in Article 42 of the Constitution; nor should a surviving mother's right be displaced merely because the court is of opinion that the welfare of the children requires a religious education other than that which the mother proposes to provide".

Sullivan C.J. in answer to this stated:

> "I cannot, however, accept . . . that the rights of the parents, or of the surviving parent, are absolute rights, the exercise of which cannot in any circumstances be controlled by the Court. That a child has natural and imprescriptible rights is recognised by the Constitution (Article 42.5), and if . . . (this) proposition were accepted, it would follow that the Court would be powerless to protect those rights should they be ignored by the parents. I am satisfied that the Court has jurisdiction to control the exercise of parental rights, but in exercising that jurisdiction it must not act upon any principle which is repugnant to the Constitution. The Constitution does not define the respective rights of the parents during their lifetime. Where as in the present case, the parents could not agree on the particular religion in which their children should be brought up and educated, the children should not be deprived of all religious education. If that be so then the only alternative is that one or other of the parents should have the legal right to determine the religion in which the children shall be educated. The rule which the courts both in this country and in England have consistently followed, is that the father has that legal right, and that when that right has been exercised by him, the children must be educated in the religion which he has chosen, by his wife should she survive him. In my opinion that rule is not inconsistent with any Article of the Constitution, and the Courts are entitled to act upon it."[23]

---

21. *Ward v. Laverty* [1925], A.C. 101, (H.L.); see also [1924], 2 I.R. 19, (C.A.).

22. *In re Frost, Infants* [1947], I.R. 3; (1945), 82 I.L.T.R. 24, (S.C.). See also *In re Keenan, Infants* (1949), 84 I.L.T.R. 169, (H.C.). (This case also involves children being brought up in the Bird's Nest in Dún Laoghaire).

23. *Supra* at pp. 28—9; Sullivan J., also said at p. 29 that "it is not necessary in this case to consider the question whether the provisions of the Constitution affect what had been the established law as to the validity and effect of ante-nuptial agreements. In respect of the religion of children, in view of the fact that subsequent to their marriage the parents agreed

A case which illustrates the extreme lengths to which the courts would go to ensure that a child would be brought up in his father's religion is that of *In re Corcoran, Infants.*[24] In this case, the applicant, the mother, after a short and unhappy marriage finally left her husband on 11th November, 1943, being unable when leaving to bring her child of two and a half years with her. On 24th December upon visiting her husband's residence to see the child, she discovered that the child had been brought by her husband to her mother-in-law's residence in Bishopswood, Dundrum, Co. Tipperary. The child remained in the custody of the mother-in-law, the respondent, until the date of an application for Habeas Corpus by the mother on 18th November, 1949.

Prior to this application, the mother stated that she had frequently tried to persuade her husband to bring the child back to England where the parties lived before separating. This he denied. In 1947 the applicant's husband instituted proceedings against her in England for divorce, grounded on alleged desertion on her part. The applicant cross-petitioned for divorce on the grounds of cruelty, and a decree of dissolution was granted on the ground alleged by her. The English High Court granted her custody of the child but the husband refused to comply with the order and was eventually lodged in Winchester Gaol because of his refusal. The mother applied for an order of Habeas Corpus to obtain custody of the child from the grandparents. The court accepted that the grandparents were merely an instrument in the case and that in reality it was a dispute between parents. The mother in this case was a Protestant and the father a Catholic. Prior to the marriage the mother had signed an undertaking to bring up any children of the marriage in the Catholic religion and did not contend in this application that the child should be brought up in any other religion. The High Court decided that the child should remain in its grandparents' home on the grounds that it would be contrary to the child's welfare and happiness to be removed from her paternal grandmother's home and sent to live in England with her mother in strange surroundings, since she had from the earliest age lived apart from her, and also that if the child went to England the court could not guarantee that the child would be brought up a Roman Catholic as the mother had promised.

On Appeal, the majority judgement of the Supreme Court, given by Murnaghan J., affirmed the High Court decision. He stated that the father "apart from his temper and violence"[25] was "hardworking and industrious". He went on "I do not, however, overlook the consideration that the character of the father is always an important element in any case involving the custody of a child", but there is no rule that "cruelty to a wife should deprive the father of the custody of his child". Murnaghan J. suggested that the notion that the welfare of the child was the paramount consideration was unconstitutional and concluded that the child should not go outside the jurisdiction, as if it did the court could not be certain that it would be educated as a Catholic.

Black J. in a remarkable dissenting judgement criticising the decision and reasoning of those who found in the father's favour, stated:

> "the learned judges who held against the mother in the High Court left the 'important factors of living space, hygiene and income, out of consideration altogether in forming their view of the child's welfare . . . I should have

that their children should be educated in a different religion from that stated in the ante-nuptial agreement". See also *In re Keenan, Infants, supra.*
    24. (1950), 86 I.L.T.R. 6, (S.C.).
    25. *Ibid.*, at p. 17.

thought that without giving due and great weight to all of them it would be impossible to arrive at a wise and balanced opinion as to the child's welfare'. A weightier matter is 'the supreme asset of a loving mother's intimacy and care—in sickness and in health, in happiness and in trouble—a blessing which I had thought was recognised by all mankind as unique, irreplacable and priceless' ".[26]

As to the father's rights in relation to religious upbringing

"This religious (or as I think it would be more accurate to call it, sectarian) dictatorship of the father is often referred to as his absolute right ... The extremity, fanatical as it seems to me, to which the 'right' of the father has been carried is shown by the rule that it must be upheld even if the father has induced the mother to marry him on the faith of a solemn undertaking that he will renounce the right in question and let the children be brought up in the mother's religion. The law is that even that solemn undertaking is unenforceable."

"The father has the right to have the child brought up in his religion ... When I speak of his religion I mean the religion for which he professes zeal ... Such zeal may, for all I know, co-exist with intolerable cruelty, but I wonder whether it can exist in the soul of an individual who, like this man, does his best to get a divorce *a vinculo* which would set him free to re-marry and might lead his wife to do so, knowing well that such a divorce is contrary to the most solemn inhibitions of his professed religion."[27]

He concluded by holding that in his opinion custody should be awarded to the mother and that she should be trusted to keep her undertaking to continue the child's education in the Roman Catholic faith.

In 1950 shortly after *In re Corcoran, Infants*, the whole question of the paternal supremacy to determine a child's religious upbringing and the validity of ante-nuptial agreements was re-examined in the light of Irish public policy and the 1937 Constitution. The case of *In re Tilson, Infants*,[28] came before the High Court and on an appeal, the Supreme Court, and gave rise to considerable public interest and controversy.

Tilson, a Protestant, having signed an ante-nuptial undertaking that any children of the marriage would be brought up as Catholics, had married a Catholic woman in a Catholic Church in Dublin in 1941. They had four children, all boys, who were baptised as Catholics. Differences having arisen between the spouses, Tilson removed the three elder children from the home of his wife's parents (where the whole family was then living) and took them to live with his parents; he subsequently removed them to Mrs. Smyly's home "The Bird's Nest" in Dún Laoghaire. The eldest child was eight at the time. The mother obtained a conditional order of Habeas Corpus against the trustees of the institution and on her motion to have the order made absolute, Gavan Duffy J. held that it was for both the spiritual and temporal welfare of the children to be returned to their mother's custody. He considered at length the basis of the rule against enforcing ante-nuptial agreements, noting that the marriage could not have been celebrated in a Catholic Church without the parties having reached such an agreement. In reply to the argument that to enforce such an agreement against the father's wishes was contrary to public policy he stated:

---

26. *Ibid.*, at p. 19.
27. *Ibid.*, at p. 21.
28. [1951], I.R. 1; (1950), 86, I.L.T.R. 49, (S.C.).

"The plea implies that the paternal trust is more sacred in the eyes of the law than a man's sacred ante-nuptial agreement; . . . I have the temerity to prefer a principle of public policy that would imperatively require a man to keep faith with the mother whom he has induced to wed him by his categorical engagement to respect her convictions in the supernatural domain of her children's creed, at least when that promise is shown to have been of grave importance to her, as it must be to a Catholic . . .[29] The doctrine of Articles 41, 42 and 44 of the Constitution appears to me to present the ante-nuptial agreement of the parties upon the creed to be imparted to their future children in a new setting and, subject to the welfare of the particular infants concerned, to invite recognition of the agreement in our Courts as a compact that serves the social order in Ireland, because the agreement, far from conflicting in any way with those Articles, is consonant with their spirit and purpose and tends directly (a) to safeguard a marriage which cannot be dissolved; (b) to safeguard the harmony of the projected family; and (c) to safeguard the innate and imprescriptible right of the child to religious education, its most precious inheritance in the eyes of a Christian state."[30]

He remarked that he thought it possible that a man might estop himself in law by signing an ante-nuptial agreement subsequently acted upon, but that he proposed to decide the issue on other grounds.

"In my opinion, an order of the Court designed to secure the fulfilment of an agreement peremptorily required before a mixed marriage by the Church whose special position in Ireland is officially recognised as the guardian of the faith of the Catholic spouse, cannot be withheld on any ground of public policy by the very State which pays that homage to that Church."[31]

Pointing out that the Tilson children had not been long enough in the "Bird's Nest" to have acquired fixed Protestant views he concluded that:

"There is no question here of any attempt (such as no Court would entertain) to coerce into the Church of Rome any young person who by a Protestant education, in disregard of an ante-nuptial agreement, has in fact acquired Protestant convictions; the Church itself would condemn any such attempt."[32]

He held that for the boys' spiritual and temporal welfare they should remain with their mother.

The decision of Gavan Duffy J. was upheld in the Supreme Court by a majority of 4 to 1. The judgement of the majority was delivered by Murnaghan J. and was based primarily upon the court's interpretation of Article 42.1.

"This article includes among 'Fundamental Rights' the inalienable right and

---

29. [1951], I.R. at p. 12.
30. *Ibid.*, at p. 17.
31. *Ibid.*, at p. 19; Gavan Duffy J. is here referring to Article 44.1.2.° which stated "The State recognises the special position of the Holy Catholic Apostolic and Roman Church as the guardian of the faith professed by the great majority of the citizens". This Article together with the one following it, was deleted from the Constitution following a Referendum held in 1972. See footnote 38, p. 10 *ante.*
Murnaghan J. delivering the majority judgement in the Supreme Court stated (at p. 35) that "It is right . . . to say that the Court in arriving at its decision, is not now holding that the last mentioned Articles (44 & 41) confer any privileged position before the law on the Roman Catholic Church . . . and Black J. stated (at p. 44) "Unequivocally" that the "constitution does not confer any such privileged position before the law upon members of any religious denomination whatsoever".
32. [1951], I.R. at p. 21.

duty of parents to provide according to their means for the religious and moral, intellectual, physical and social education of their children. Where the father and mother of children are alive this article recognises a joint right and duty in them to provide for the religious education of their children. The word 'parents' is in the plural and naturally should include both father and mother. Common sense and reason lead to the view that the mother is under the duty of educating the children as well as the father and both must do so according to their means."[33]

Later on in the judgement, Murnaghan, J. stated:

"The parents—father and mother—have a joint power and duty in respect of the religious education of their children. If they together make a decision and put it into practice it is not in the power of the father—nor is it in the power of the mother—to revoke such decision against the will of the other party. Such an exercise of their power may be made after marriage when the occasion arises; but an agreement made before marriage dealing with matters which will arise during the marriage and put into force after the marriage is equally effective and of binding force in law."[34]

Having regard to the views expressed by him in *In re Corcoran Infants*, Black J. surprisingly dissented from the majority judgement. While regarding it as desirable to construe Article 42.1 as altering the common law, which was in this area described by him as

"an archaic law and a relic of barbarism—a law derived from another law, that of the serfdom of women, which . . . emanated from the cave-men, long ages before the art of writing was discovered",[35]

he thought it did no more than reflect an already existing paternal right and duty.[36]

Seven years later in *In re May, Minors*[37] the law as established in *In re Tilson* was applied where no express agreement had been made between parents as to their children's religious upbringing. Mr. and Mrs. May were both Roman Catholics and had been married in a Roman Catholic Church. There were five children of the marriage who, for over 10 years had been brought up as Roman Catholics and no differences of any kind had previously arisen as to their religious upbringing. In 1954 Mr. May became a follower of the beliefs of the Jehovah's Witnesses and a year later attempted to interfere with his children's religious upbringing. Davitt J. held that as both parents had for many years followed the Catholic faith there was an implied agreement between the parties as to the children's religious upbringing and as the children had been educated in that faith, that agreement had been exercised and could not be abrogated by the unilateral act of one of the parties. Mr. May could not change the children's religion without Mrs. May's consent.

33. *Ibid.*, at p. 32.
34. *Ibid.*, at p. 34.
35. *Ibid.*, at p. 37.
36. The judgement in the Tilson case caused considerable controversy at the time—see J. White,—*Minority Report*, p. 125—128. J.H. Whyte,—*Church and State in Modern Ireland 1923-1970*, p. 169—171; V.T.H. Delaney, "The Custody and Education of Children" 18 I.J. 17; J.M. Kelly,—*Fundamental Rights*, p. 229—230; P.C. Moore,—*Support and Custody of Children*", (the international Bar Association of Ireland 1968), p. 11—14.
37. 92 I.L.T.R. 1, (H.C.).

1964 AND AFTER

The Tilson case in 1951 firmly established that the rights and duties of parents in relation to their children under the Constitution are equal. This equality was finally given statutory expression in the Guardianship of Infants Act, 1964. Section 6(1) of the Act provides that "the father and mother of an infant shall be guardians of the infant jointly". This section has since been said to be "no more than a reiteration of the principles enunciated in Article 42 of the Constitution".[38] Each parent now has the same rights in relation to the person of their child, i.e. to custody, to determine the child's upbringing and education, both secular and religious, and the same powers to appoint a testamentary guardian.

Section 11 of the 1964 Act provides that

(1) "Any person being a guardian of an infant may apply to the court for its direction on any question affecting the welfare of the infant and the court may make such order as it thinks proper".[39]

(2) "The court may by an order under this section—

(a) give such direction as it thinks proper regarding the custody of the infant and the right of access to the infant of his father or mother.

(b) order the father or mother to pay towards the maintenance[40] of the infant such weekly or other periodical sum as having regard to the means of the father or mother, the court considers reasonable."

An order can be made under section 11 on the application of either parent, even if they are still living together.[41] However, an order under sub-s. (2) is not enforceable while they continue to do so and ceases to have effect if the parties continue to reside together for three months after it is made.

---

38. O'Dalaigh C.J., *B. v. B.* [1975], I.R. 54, (S.C.) at p. 58. Although not reported until 1975 judgement was in fact delivered by the Supreme Court in this case in April 1970. Walsh J. in the same case stated: "The main purpose of the Guardianship of Infants Act, 1964 was to give both parents of an infant equal rights in guardianship matters. In doing so it provided a statutory expression of the rights already guaranteed by the Constitution". See J.M. Kelly,—*Fundamental Rights*, p. 229 where the author remarks that "it is very difficult to read in Article 42.1 the intention that paternal supremacy is to be replaced by joint parental authority". See also "Private Law Aspects of the Irish Constitution", by J. Temple Lang (1971), 6, I.J. (n.s.) 237 where the author points out in a section on Family Law that "if parents have equal rights over their children's upbringing, they presumably have equal duties, and responsibilities in relation to it. This suggests that a father having custody of children would have the same right to be financially supported by a wealthy wife, as a wife would have if the situation were reversed". On this point see The Report of the Committee on Court Practice & Procedure entitled "Desertion & Maintenance". See now Family Law (Maintenance of Spouses and Children's) Act, 1976, Sect. 5, discussed on p. 242 *et seq.*

39. An application can be made to the court under section 11 (1) for directions with regard to the administration of the assets or estate of an infant on the application of the guardian or guardians. See *In re Meade, Applicant* [1971] I.R. 327, (H.C.). See, however, *In the Matter of J.S. an infant* (1977), 111 I.L.T.R. 146, (H.C.) where Finlay P., expressing a preference for such applications being made under the Wards of Court procedure, stated "Whilst it is not possible nor desirable to attempt an exclusive or comprehensive classification of the cases which might be appropriate for directions concerning the estates or assets of minors under Section 11 (1) rather than by the Wardship of Court procedure, in general it would appear that they are appropriate only where one or at most two or three applications would be necessary and where a fixed and final straightforward scheme not requiring variations and not requiring the continued supervision of the Court is appropriate in the interests of the children".

40. Maintenance is said to include education—Sect. 2 of the 1964 Act.

41. See *J. O'C. v. M. O'C.* (Aug. 1975) unreported (H.C.); *O'D. v. O'D.* (June 1976) unreported (H.C.).

Whilst prior to 1964 the courts stressed that the most important factor in parental disputes concerning children was the welfare of the child, it was not until that date that statutory force was given to the equitable principle that the child's interests are paramount. Section 3 states

"Where in any proceedings before any court the custody, guardianship or upbringing of an infant, or the administration of any property belonging to or held on trust for an infant, or the application of the income thereof, is in question, the court in deciding that question, shall regard the welfare of the infant as the first and paramount consideration."

It has been stated that this requirement means "More than that the child's welfare is to be treated as the top item in a list of items relevant to the matter in question". It connotes "a process whereby, when all the relevant facts, relationships, claims and wishes of parents, risks, choices and other circumstances are taken into account and weighed, the course to be followed will be that which is most in the interests of the child's welfare as that term has now to be understood. That is the first consideration because it is of first importance and the paramount consideration because it rules on or determines the course to be followed".[42]

Welfare in relation to an infant is said to comprise its religious and moral, intellectual, physical and social welfare.[43]

The great majority of disputes heard under the Act are disputes as to the custody of children. In reaching a decision the court must take into account all the factors comprised in the concept of welfare. The matter, Walsh J. has stated, is

"not . . . to be decided by the simple method of totting up the marks which may be awarded under each of the five headings . . . all the ingredients which the Act stipulates . . . are to be considered globally . . . It is the totality of the picture presented"[44]

that the court must consider and on which it must make its decision. Often the court has an almost impossible task in determining which parent should be awarded custody.

The Conduct of the Parents

Whilst prior to 1964 it was extremely unlikely that the spouse responsible in the eyes of the court for a marriage breaking down would obtain custody of the children of the marriage,[45] the courts have since that date constantly reiterated that

"An award of custody is not a prize for good matrimonial behaviour".[46]

42. Per Lord MacDermott, *J. v. C.* [1970], A.C. 668 (H.L.) at p. 710–711 adopted by the Supreme Court in the judgement of Henchy J. (with whose judgement Kenny J. expressed agreement) in *MacD. v. MacD.* (April 1979) unreported, (S.C.); see also *E.K. v. M.K.* (July 1974), unreported, (S.C.) judgement of Henchy J.; *O. v. O.* (May 1979), unreported, (H.C.).
43. Guardianship of Infants Act, 1964, Sect. 2.
44. *M.B. O'S. v. P.O. O'S.* (1974) 110 I.L.T.R., 57 (S.C.) *per* Walsh J. at p. 61. See also judgements of Walsh J. and Budd J. in *E.K. v. M.K., supra*, and judgement of Griffin J. in *MacD. v. MacD., supra*.
45. See *In re Mitchell, supra; In re McNamara, supra; In re Kevin Isherwood, an Infant* (1948), 82 I.L.T.R. 85, (H.C.). Unless the child was being educated in the religion of the spouse so responsible, the parties being of different faiths—see *In re Corcoran, Infants* (1950), 86 I.L.T.R. 6, (S.C.); on the other hand see *In re Story, supra.*
46. Kenny J. in *J.J.W. v. B.M.W.* (1971), 110 I.L.T.R. 45, (H.C.) at p. 47. See also *M.O'B. v. P.M. O'B.* (Jan. 1971), unreported, (H.C.).

"So far as the custody of the children is concerned . . . evidence (as to which of the parties contributed to or caused the breakdown of the marriage) was relevant only to the character of the respective parents with a view to deciding whether the welfare of a particular child would best be served by its being left in the custody of one parent rather than the other."[47]

Thus the fact that a husband (or by analogy a wife) must bear the bigger share of the blame does not mean that he "has by his conduct forfeited the right to have the custody of the children if it be found that it is in the best interests of any one or more of the children to be placed in his custody".[48] "The conduct, wishes and needs of the parents are irrelevant except in so far as such considerations bear on the welfare of the children."[49] However,

"Where a marriage has broken down, whether temporarily or permanently, it may be possible to show that the welfare of the children requires that one or other parent should by reason of character or conduct be excluded from consideration, as being a person unfit to have custody . . . The courts should always be reluctant to reach such a conclusion, because the welfare of the children will rarely be advanced by a verdict of condemnation of one or other of the parents".[50]

Such a condemnation will only be made in the most extreme cases, for example where a parent is likely to be an extreme danger to the physical or moral welfare of his children.

It is now intended to examine in detail the matters that the courts have regard to in reaching a determination on the basis of the child's welfare. However, it is to be remembered that the importance of any given factor depends on the circumstances of each individual case. Thus a decision in any one case cannot be completely relied upon to give an accurate prediction of the outcome of any other case.

Physical Welfare of the Child

Physical welfare primarily appears to be concerned with the health, bodily comfort, nourishment and hygiene of children with the qualification that their health may be affected by emotional or psychiatric disturbances which are also of relevance to their intellectual welfare.[51] Mothers are regarded by the courts as

---

47. Fitzgerald J. in *B. v. B., supra.* See also Hamilton J.—"The Guardianship of Infants Act 1964 and Recent Decision in Relation Thereto", S.Y.S. Lecture No. 91 (Nov. 1975), p. 10. See further section on moral welfare below.

48. Budd J. in *B. v. B., supra,* at p. 66. Similarly Kenny J. in *B. v. B.* (January 1969), unreported, (H.C.) stated "A hot tempered, emotional difficult incompetent wife may be a much more suitable person to have custody of young children than a cold, unsympathetic self-righteous and very able husband". See also *M.B. O'S. v. P.O. O'S., supra,* (S.C.) at p. 65, judgement of Griffin J. "If this were a contest simpliciter between the wife and the husband . . . and if only the right and interests of the parents were to be considered . . . the wife would be entitled to custody". He went on to hold, however, that the welfare of the children being paramount, they should remain in the custody of the father. In *MacD. v. MacD., supra,* Henchy J. stated "If custody of children could be granted as a badge of moral approval, the father, who has been steadfast as a husband and a father would come first. But the right to custody may not be determined in that way". He went on to grant custody in this case to the wife.

49. Henchy J. in *MacD. v. MacD., supra.* See however, dissenting judgement of Griffin J. where he states "the conduct of the parents is relevant in so far as inferences can be drawn from it to show where the priorities of the parents lie in relation to the children, as this is an important factor to consider in relation to their welfare".

50. O'Dalaigh C.J. in *B. v. B.,* [1975] I.R. 54 (S.C.) at p. 59.

51. See judgement of Finlay P. in *MacD. v. MacD.* (February 1979), unreported, (H.C.). Although the decision of the High Court in this case was reversed on appeal, the Supreme

prima facie the best persons to minister to the physical and emotional needs of young children[52] and all things being equal a mother will normally be given custody of children under twelve years of age.[53] The availability of the mother in the home during the day has been one of the factors that has influenced the courts to favour mothers on the ground that a father working outside the home cannot give to young children the time and attention which their welfare requires.[54] As children get older, the courts take the view, especially in the case of boys, that they have more need of the father. There are, however, no hard and fast rules and everything depends on the circumstances of the particular case. Thus, in *J.J.W.* v. *B.M.W.*[55] three young girls (aged nine, seven and three years) were placed in their father's custody, and in the recent case of *H.* v. *H.*[56] a boy aged two and a half was placed in his father's custody.

As all orders as to custody are interlocutory and not final, the court can vary its orders and it is possible for a child to be given into its mother's custody until it reaches a certain age and then given into its father's custody. Thus, in *M. O'S.* v. *M. O'S.* a boy was given into his mother's custody until he reached 12½ years of age and then given into the custody of his father.[57]

The court has, however, stated that it is essential that children of a broken marriage should establish roots and not be constantly moved from place to place, from parent to parent and from school to school.

> "The main psychological need for children if they are to become happy citizens is a feeling of security, a conviction that people care for them and about them and a feeling of continuity. They should have a chance of putting down roots and should not have the fear that they will be moved around."[58]

The fact that one parent is financially better off does not necessarily mean that that parent will get custody. In the majority of cases the husband will be better off financially than the wife, and where this is the case, the making of a

Court did not disagree with the learned trial judge's definitions of the different factors comprised in the concept of welfare.

52. See *MacD.* v. *MacD.* (April 1979), unreported, (S.C.), judgements of Henchy J. and Kenny J.

53. In *J.J.W.* v. *B.M.W.*, Fitzgerald J. said "children of tender age and particularly girls would ... other things being equal, be better in the custody of their mother". (1971), 110, I.L.T.R. 45, 49, at p. 52, (S.C.). See also judgement of Walsh J. in *E.K.* v. *M.K.* (July 1974), unreported, (S.C.) and judgement of Griffin J. in *MacD.* v. *MacD.* (April 1979) unreported (S.C.). See further *O'D.* v. *O'D.* (June 1976) unreported (H.C.); *J.W.* v. *M.W.* (July 1978), unreported, (H.C.).

54. See particularly judgement of Henchy J. in *MacD.* v. *MacD., supra*, (S.C.). See also *E.* v. *E.* (February 1977) unreported (H.C.) in which the plaintiff wife was granted custody although she suffered from depression.

55. Fitzgerald J. "The circumstances in the present case are by no means equal as regards either the character of the respective parents or the benefits which they are in a position to provide for any of the children"–*ibid*. See also *W.* v. *W.* (Dec. 74), unreported, (S.C.)–see however p. 203 below.

56. (Feb. 1976), unreported, (H.C.). See also *J. O'C.* v. *M. O'C.* (Aug. 1975) unreported (H.C.); *MacC.* v. *MacC.* (Jan. 1976), unreported (H.C.); *O'.* v. *O'.* (May 1979) unreported (H.C.) and (June 1979) unreported (H.C.). See also *B.* v. *B.* [1975] I.R. 54, (S.C.) in which a boy of almost ten years old and a girl eight and a half years old were placed in their father's custody and the children's brother who was six and a half years old was placed in the mother's custody.

57. (April 1970), unreported, (H.C.). See also *M. O'S.* v. *M. O'S.* (April 1972), unreported, (H.C.).

58. Kenny J. in *M. O'S.* v. *M. O'S.* (April 1970), unreported, (H.C.); in *W.* v. *W.* (April 1972), unreported, (H.C.), Kenny J. stated "They (the children) should be given an opportunity to put down roots somewhere, because a sense of security is essential for children's happiness". See also *J.J.W.* v. *B.M.W.* (1971), 110 I.L.T.R. 49, (S.C.). In his judgement, Walsh J. also spoke of the need for stability in the lives of children.

maintenance order by the court can ensure that the children, if given into the wife's custody, will not suffer any great material disadvantages. Moreover, it has been persistently reiterated that it is the happiness of the child and not its material prospects with which the court is concerned.

A parent who frequently employs corporal punishment to discipline his children may find it particularly difficult to obtain an award of custody. In *J. O'C.* v. *M. O'C.*[59] four children (two boys aged 12 and 6½ and two girls aged 9½ and 8½) were placed in their father's custody. Kenny J., in the course of his judgement stated

> "I am satisfied that the wife has consistently inflicted severe corporal punishment on the children, has humiliated them before each other and that the position now is that all the children are very frightened of her. Each husband and wife have their own standards and their own theories about bringing up children and it may be necessary on some rare occasions to punish them but severe corporal punishment administered consistently to young children and particularly to girls is certain to cause emotional trouble. The parents who use corporal punishment on young children may think that it is for their good but civilized human beings have long since abandoned this barbaric practice."

When a marriage has broken down the courts regard anything which may tend towards preserving the unity of the family as being for the welfare of the children. It was suggested in *B.* v. *B.* that where the custody of a number of children was in question one parent should not be totally deprived of custody as this might lead to further ill-feeling and be a "major stumbling block to any worthwhile type of reconciliation between the parents".[60]

Whereas it is always desirable to bring about a reconciliation between estranged spouses, there is a danger in such an approach that children will be regarded merely as tools or instruments to re-unite their parents. It is submitted that a child's welfare is more likely to be protected if it is living with a single parent in a stable, peaceful and loving home environment than with both parents in a warring, embittered and tension-filled situation. An important factor in maintaining some sort of family unity is to preserve the unity of the children. Children should not be separated unnecessarily. Any spirit of comradeship that exists between them, should be fostered, not extinguished.[61]

Intellectual and Religious Welfare

Intellectual welfare is concerned with the emotional security, settled affections and psychiatric stability of children, with plans for their education and intellectual development, the manner in which their environment and their parents contribute to this aspect of their development and with ensuring that children can take the maximum advantage of the educational opportunities available to them. If a child has a particular gift or aptitude the courts will often seek to ensure that the child has an opportunity of developing it.[62]

The religious welfare of children is concerned with their education in and

59. *Supra.*
60. [1975] I.R. 54, per Budd J. at p. 69.
61. See *B.* v. *B.* [1975] I.R. at p. 59 where O'Dalaigh C.J. states: "After the separation of the parents, there remains two lesser points of unity around which one would wish, if possible to build: the first of these is the unity or comradeship of the three children and the second is the family home where these children have grown up together." See also *E.* v. *E. supra.*
62. See particularly judgement of Finlay P. in *MacD.* v. *MacD., supra.* (H.C.).

practice of the religion in which they are being brought up.[63] It also involves ensuring, in so far as is possible, that the arrangements made for the custody of a child will not jeopardise the child's religious education.

As has already been seen, a great number of pre-1964 disputes as to custody between parents involved the question as to which parent should determine the children's education and in particular the religious education. Until *Tilson*'s case the courts permitted the father alone to dictate his children's religious upbringing and secular education. The 1964 Act expressly replaced paternal supremacy with joint parental authority. Now a mother and father have an equal say in the upbringing and education of their children and where agreement has been reached between parents as to a child's education, religious or secular, one parent cannot deviate from that agreement,[64] without the assent of the other.[65] If in a custody case today there is a dispute as to a child's religious upbringing the court would hold any agreement previously reached by the parties as binding, unless contrary to the child's welfare.[66]

It is arguable, however, that a remnant of paternal supremacy still survives. Whereas both parents have the "right and duty" to determine their children's education and religion, it was stated in *In re May, Minors,*[67] that in the absence of agreement the father's wishes are still to prevail. Thus in a dispute between a couple of a mixed marriage, who have never come to any agreement[68] as to their children's religious education, it seems that it is the father's wishes that will prevail. Certainly the court could not decide that the practice of one religion was better for the welfare of a child rather than another.[69] On the other hand the court may not regard itself as bound by *In re May* and simply decide that it is for the child's welfare to be educated in the religion of that parent in whose custody it is for its welfare to be placed. The latter seems the more likely and desirable solution.[70]

If there is still a remnant of paternal religious dictatorship it could arise in another situation. Both the *Tilson* and *May* cases were concerned with express and implied agreements that were acted upon by the parties. There was no clear statement as to what the position would be if having made an agreement one of the parties renounced it before there was an opportunity to act upon it, i.e. before any children of the marriage were born. Would this be a case of "disagreement", and as a consequence the old common law rule of paternal supremacy could prevail or would the parties be held bound by the unexercised agreement? Upon a dispute arising following the birth of a child to the parties, Gavan Duffy J. undoubtedly would have enforced such an agreement upon grounds of public

---

63. *Ibid.*
64. As we have seen such an agreement can be either express, (*In re Tilson, supra*) or implied (*In re May, Minors supra*). See *H. v. H.* (Feb. 1976), unreported, (H.C.) where Parke J. expressly followed *In re May.*
65. That third parties cannot coerce parents into educating their children in the religion that the third party favours has been laid down in a number of cases. See *Burke and O'Reilly v. Burke and Quail* [1951] I.R. 216, (H.C.); (1950), 84 I.L.T.R. 70; *In re Blake, decd.* [1955] I.R. 89, (H.C.).
66. *Cullen v. Cullen* (May 1970), unreported, (S.C.). See O'Dalaigh, C.J. part V of judgement.
67. *In re May, Minors*, (H.C.), *supra.*
68. Express or implied.
69. See comments of Parke J. in *H. v. H.* (Feb. 1976), unreported, (H.C.).
70. This would not, however, solve the problem where parents intended to continue to cohabit but could not agree on their child's religious upbringing and made an application to the court for a direction under Sect. 11 (1). Such a problem, however is unlikely to arise, as if such a dispute between parents reached the stage where they applied to a court for its determination it is unlikely that they would continue to live together and thus the question of custody would also arise.

policy[71] and whereas Murnaghan J. and Davitt J. spoke primarily of an agreement acted upon, Murnaghan J. stated

"I cannot accept the contention . . . that where a joint agreement has been made by a father and mother entitled under the Constitution to make it, the father at his mere wish can substitute an arrangement of his own".[72]

In the light of this statement and section 6(1) of the present Act such an unexercised agreement would more than likely be held to bind the parties and to be enforceable.

Prior to the 1964 Act the courts were very unwilling to grant custody to a parent of a religion different from that in which the child was being brought up.[73] Since that date there have been few written judgements delivered in cases involving disputes between parents of different religions. Certainly, the fact of a parent being of a religion different to that of his or her children has not in practice been a major obstacle to a parent succeeding in an application for custody.[74] In such circumstances, however, it is a frequent condition of an award of custody, that a child will continue to receive proper instruction in a particular faith. In a number of cases discussed in the next section the interaction between the concepts of religious and moral welfare are examined. As shall be seen, in deciding disputes as to custody, the courts have been much influenced by the fact that the parent was living or intending to live in a manner condemned by the religion in which he proposed to bring up his children, that is, he was or was going to be, a party to an adulterous liaison.

Social and Moral Welfare

Social Welfare has been said to mean "the type of welfare which is to be judged by what is best calculated to make them (the children) better members of the society in which they live."[75] Social Welfare is concerned with enabling the children to grow up to be "good citizens"[76] and well integrated members of society.[77] It is much concerned with ensuring that the child will be inculcated with "correct values" and imbued with a "proper" outlook on life. It is in fact a nebulous concept, difficult to pin down, its importance and influence in an

---

71. See *In re Tilson, Infants* [1951] I.R. 1. (H.C., S.C.).
72. *Ibid.*, at p. 35.
73. See *In re Keenan, Infants* (1949), 84 I.L.T.R. 169, (H.C.). *In re Corcoran, Infants* (1950), 86 I.L.T.R. 6, (S.C.); alternatively see *In re Begley, Infants*, (1949), 82 I.L.T.R. 89, (H.C.).
74. *B. v. B.* [1975] I.R. 54 (S.C.) and *B. v. B.* (July 1972), unreported, (H.C.); *MacD. v. MacD., supra*, (S.C.); *Healy v. Healy* (July 1969), unreported, (H.C.); *S. v. S.* (May 1978), unreported, (H.C.); In *Cullen v. Cullen, supra* the fact that the mother had ceased to practise her religion did not prevent her being awarded custody of her youngest son (5½) upon her giving assurances that he would receive proper religious instruction. In *H. v. H.* (Feb. 1976), unreported, (H.C.) both parents were Catholics and married in accordance with the rites of the Church. The husband was found by the judge to drink heavily and to have previously assaulted his wife. Subsequent to the husband's assaults, the wife formed a liaison with an English man (Mr. G.) of the Jewish faith. She sought to have the marriage dissolved in England and intended to convert to Judaism and marry Mr. G. The court refused to grant custody of her 2½ year old son to the wife. Much weight was given to the wife's desire to change her son's religion and to the fact that she could not constitutionally do so without the father's consent. The question of her educating the boy in the Catholic religion was not considered.
75. *M.B. O'S. v. P.O. O'S., supra* (S.C.), per Walsh J. at p. 61. See also *H. v. H.* (Feb. 1976), unreported, (H.C.).
76. *E.K. v. M.K.* (May 1974), unreported, (H.C.) Kenny J.
77. *M.B. O'S. v. P.O. O'S., supra*, (S.C.) Henchy J.–Social welfare taken to mean "well-being as members of society". He went on to state that the children lead "an active, normal well-integrated existence".

individual case being much dependent on the subjective assessment of the facts by the individual judge.

Moral Welfare is concerned with the moral example given by a parent to his child, with the influence that the behaviour of the parent may have on the child's development and the manner in which the parent's conduct is likely to affect the child's religious, intellectual and social welfare.[78] The danger of the moral corruption of a child as a result of a parent's adulterous conduct has been a matter of particular concern to the courts and has given rise to a variety of conflicting judicial opinions and approaches in the application of the welfare principle.

In *J.J.W.* v. *B.M.W.*[79] the parties lived in England and were both Roman Catholics. The wife left the husband in 1969 and went to live with L. There were three children of the marriage, all girls, aged nine, seven and three. When the wife left home she took the two youngest girls with her but the husband regained custody of the children.

The husband came to live in his parents' house in Dublin with the children. His parents being elderly, three children were too much for them and as a result the two eldest were placed in a school run by nuns of the Poor Clare Order. They were visited at weekends by their father and spent their holidays with him and their grandparents.

In 1971 the wife, who was then living in England in a large flat with L,[80] came to Dublin and with the help of her parents, brought the two eldest children back to England. She brought divorce proceedings in England and asked the English court to give her custody. The English court decided that the custody of the children was a matter to be decided by the Irish courts and directed her to return the children to her husband. Subsequently proceedings were brought in the High Court in Dublin.

Kenny J. decided that the religious, moral and intellectual welfare of the children would be better promoted by leaving them with the father. They would get a good secular and religious education in Ireland. They had been in school in Dublin for two years and it was not in their interests to be moved from school to school. Also, he stated,

"They will not have the corrupting example of their mother living with a man to whom she is not married".

However, these were not the only considerations.

"In my view the ages of the children, their sex, the certainty that they would be happier if they were living at home rather than in a school and the necessity that they should grow up together . . . makes it so desirable that they should be with their mother that these elements should be held to outweigh the arguments based upon the moral, religious and intellectual aspects".[81]

Accordingly the judge awarded custody of the three children to the mother.

However, the Supreme Court reversed Kenny J.'s decision and granted custody of all three to the father. His conclusions as to the religious, moral and intellectual welfare of the children were accepted. The fact that the father was

---

78. See judgement of Finlay P. in *MacD.* v. *MacD.*
79. (1971), 110 I.L.T.R. 49, (S.C.). See also (1971), 110 I.L.T.R. 45, the High Court judgement of Kenny J. delivered in May 1971.
80. Who had by this time been divorced by his wife.
81. *Supra*, at p. 49.

compelled by circumstances to keep two of the children in boarding school for the greater part of the year and was therefore unable to let them all grow up together in one household, whereas the mother could do so, was not such a decisive factor as should give the mother custody. Walsh J. stated

> "As matters stand at the moment the children are leading a stable existence ... the school in question specialises in catering for children from broken homes" and "the evidence does not disclose that the children are not happy . . . the present position of their mother offers no such stability and there is nothing to suggest that in the immediate future any such stability will be available".[82]

Fitzgerald C.J. stated

> "The fact is that the home which she has to offer to her children is one in which she continues an adulterous association with a man who has deserted his own wife and his own two children. A more unhealthy abode for the three . . . children would be difficult to imagine".[83]

The fact that Mr. L. had divorced his wife and that Mrs. W. had obtained a decree nisi for divorce in the English Courts against her husband was regarded as irrelevant. The learned judge stated that even if Mrs. W. had entered into marriage with L. "her status in relation to her own children would not appear to me to be thereby in any way advanced".[84]

In *M.B. O'S.* v. *P.O. O'S.*[85] the moral welfare of the children was again considered. Here the husband P. left his wife B. and with her agreement kept their three young children in his custody. They lived for a year and a half with P.'s married sister, then for half a year with P.'s mother and finally coming to Dublin to live in a large house with P. and a woman with whom he was living, and who had assumed his name by deed poll. A year later B. instituted proceedings to obtain custody of the children intending to live with them in her parents' house in Cobh.

Kenny J. in the High Court held that the intellectual, physical and social welfare of the children would best be served by the father retaining custody, but that

> "having regard to my obligation to follow *J.J.W.* v. *B.M.W.* I have no doubt whatever that I should award the custody of the three children to the wife . . . The moral welfare of the children would not be promoted by the fact that their father is with a lady to whom he is not married and by whom he has had one child. As the children grow up they will be taught the virtues of chastity and the importance of marriage and they will be living in a household where each of them will be aware that the lady with whom their father is living is not his wife."[86]

On appeal the Supreme Court, by a majority decision, held that the father should retain custody. There was no principle in *J.J.W.* v. *B.M.W.* which Kenny J. was obliged to follow.

> "[*J.J.W.* v. *B.M.W.*] was decided on the facts in that case, as indeed must all cases of this unhappy nature."[87]

---

82. *Ibid.*, at p. 50.
83. *Ibid.*, at p. 52.
84. See the contrasting approach of McWilliam J. in *MacC.* v. *MacC.*, *supra*, (H.C.).
85. (1974), 110 I.L.T.R. 57 (H.C., S.C.).
86. *Ibid.*, at pp. 58, 59.
87. *Ibid.*, per Griffin J. at p. 65.

The majority referred to the dangers of again uprooting the children[88] and to the fact that all aspects of their welfare including their religious welfare was being properly attended to. Griffin J. stated that

"In my view, the moral danger to the children does not outweigh the other advantages to them in living with their father."[89]

The majority emphasised the fact that the father's relationship with the second Mrs. O'S. had all the appearances of being a permanent union and that, as such, the children would have to come to terms with it. Henchy J. stated that

"Beyond the mere fact that the father and the stepmother are living together in an unmarried state there is nothing in the evidence to suggest that the children do not live in a healthy moral atmosphere."[90]

Walsh J. dissenting stated that

"The Constitution recognises the family as the natural primary and fundamental unit group of society; that is the keystone of the social structure which the Constitution undertakes to maintain. The household in which these children now reside with their father is not a family in that sense . . . These three children would in my view, be far more of a family unit if they lived with their mother instead of residing with their father in the mixed menage in which they now find themselves . . . So far as the social, moral and religious aspects are concerned the present atmosphere in which they are found . . . is one which is a manifest repudiation of the social and religious values with which they should be inculcated at this stage of their lives . . . The welfare of the children requires that they should be returned to their mother to form the natural family unit from which, unfortunately, only the father is missing but in which there is no element alien or hostile to ordinary family life."[91]

In *E.K.* v. *M.K.*[92] the Supreme Court in a majority decision (3-2) granted custody of two children, a boy aged five and a half years and a girl aged three and a half years, to the father. In the High Court the mother had been granted custody.

In the High Court both parties agreed that their marriage had irretrievably broken down. Evidence was given that a year prior to the parties separating the wife had committed "an act of adultery" with one of her husband's employees but it was not alleged that this act by the wife had been a major factor in the breakdown of the marriage. The parties separated and agreed that the children would reside with the wife. However, a short time later, the wife became friendly with a Mr. M. and the evidence established that M. and Mrs. K. had engaged in sexual intercourse on many occasions in the latter's home after the children had

---

88. Henchy J. thought that their intellectual welfare "would be retarded by the emotional disturbance that the change would cause and by the rupture of the continuity of their schooling" *ibid.*, (at p. 62). The children when interviewed by the court gave evidence that they dreaded the prospect of being removed to Cobh where the mother lived.

89. *Ibid.*, at p. 66.

90. *Ibid.*, at p. 64. He further stated that "Where the Supreme Court differed from the High Court in, [*J.J.W.* v. *B.M.W.*] was in holding that in spite of the fact that the father had to keep two of the children in a boarding school, it was to their intellectual and social welfare that he should retain custody . . . [*J.J.W.* v. *B.M.W.*] is a decision on its own facts". See also *M. O'B.* v. *P.M. O'B.* (January 1971), unreported (H.C.).

91. *Supra*, at p. 61. See also *H.* v. *H., supra*.

92. (July 1974), unreported, (S.C.). In this case both parents accepted that their marriage was "irretrievably broken down". The court regarded the mother responsible for the breakdown.

gone to bed. It was also established that M. was well known to the children, was liked by them and was referred to by them as "uncle". There was no suggestion that the wife's association with M. commenced before the Ks. separated. Walsh J., awarding custody to the father, stated that

"a removal of the children from the custody of their mother at such an age would be justified only when it has been found that the mother has been so greatly wanting in her duty to her children that the removal would be warranted."

Having regard to the mother's behaviour such removal was justified. The life she was leading Walsh J. stated was

"a manifest repudiation of the social and religious values with which the children should be inculcated and which she believes she can teach them while at the same time clearly repudiating them herself in the sight of her own children."[93]

In the later case of *W.* v. *W.*[94] the Supreme Court affirmed a High Court order to transfer the custody of two boys (14 and 11) from their father to their mother. Two years earlier the High Court had granted custody of the boys to their father. While they were in his custody, the father was found to have committed acts of adultery, one of which took place when the children were present in the house. It was stated that

"such misconduct would have a devastating effect on the moral standards of the children at their present age."

Six months later, however, the High Court transferred custody back to the father. Mrs. W. had brought proceedings to commit her husband to prison for breach of the previous order of the court. Contrary to the court's order, the boys had returned to live with their father. Upon being interviewed by Kenny J., the boys were adamant that they wished to remain with their father and stated that if the court placed them in their mother's custody they would run away. Stating that

"when children of this age express . . . a strong preference for living with one of their parents, the court should give effect to it,"

Kenny J. granted custody to the father. A year later, the Supreme Court affirmed this latter order.[95]

The most recent case in which the Supreme Court has had to consider the concept of moral welfare is that of *MacD.* v. *MacD.*[96] The parties had married in 1969 in a Roman Catholic Church, the husband being Roman Catholic and th wife a member of the Church of Ireland. At the date of the proceedings they had two children, a girl aged six and a half years and a boy aged four and a half years. By the beginning of 1975 a relationship had developed between the wife and D. who was a divorcee. When the husband learned of the relationship, the

---

93. The majority judgements were delivered by Walsh J., Budd J. and Fitzgerald C.J. Dissenting judgements were delivered by Henchy J. and Griffin J. It is interesting that in this case the dissenting judgements were given by the two judges in the majority in the earlier case of *M.B. O'S.* v. *P.O. O'S.* in which only a three man Supreme Court sat.

94. (December 1974), unreported, (S.C.). The members of the Supreme Court in this case were Walsh J., Henchy J. and Griffin J. and the decision was unanimous.

95. Four unreported written judgements were delivered by Kenny J. in the High Court in *W.* v. *W.* (April 1972, July 1974, Oct. 1974, June 1975). No written judgement was delivered by the Supreme Court in July 1976 when affirming the June 1975 High Court decision.

96. (February 1979), unreported, (H.C.); (April 1979), unreported, (S.C.).

marriage had broken up and in January 1977 a deed of separation was concluded which provided that the husband was to have custody of the children. In December 1977 the wife issued proceedings seeking custody of the children. In April, 1978 these proceedings were settled and a further agreement concluded, under the terms of which the wife obtained custody and neither child was "to come into contact with D."

In December, 1978 the wife took up residence in D.'s home with the two children. The husband re-entered the proceedings and sought custody. He proposed that the children should reside with him and stated that he would retain a housekeeper during the day to look after them when he was at work.

In the High Court, Finlay P., granting custody to the father, held that the children's physical and intellectual welfare would be equally safeguarded by both parents but that their moral, social and religious welfare would be better protected by the father. He stated,

> "It seems to me clear on the evidence that at present at least the household of the father of these children is one based upon the importance, sanctity and integrity of the family carrying no hint of approval of any permissive standards with regard to the sanctity of marriage."

As for the mother, her behaviour, he stated "is a firm and clear repudiation both of the fundamental integrity of the family as a unit and of these moral standards with regard to the sanctity of marriage and condemnation of adultery."[97]

The Supreme Court, on appeal, reversed the order of the High Court and in a majority decision granted custody to the mother.[98] The age of the children and the fact that the mother would be available during the day to look after them, whereas the father would be at work, greatly influenced the majority in holding that it was in the interests of the children's physical, social and intellectual welfare that the mother be granted custody. As for the children's religious and moral welfare Henchy J. stated

> "The mother's relationship with D. is already an accomplished fact in the children's lives . . . The mother has given evidence (which has not been doubted in cross examination and which is supported by her conduct when she already had custody), that she is prepared to bring up the children as Catholics . . . In other words, she is prepared, so far as in her lies, to look after the religious and moral welfare of the children . . . The unfortunate extra-marital situation in which she finds herself, which cannot be regularised so as to acquire constitutional propriety, detracts considerably from her willingness and ability to satisfy the religious and moral welfare of the children. But so long as she is ready as a loving and caring mother to do her best to see to that welfare, the obvious need of these young children for her as a mother should weigh heavily in the balance in favour of her claim to be given custody."

In conclusion, he emphasised that

> "custody is awarded not as a mark of approbation or disapprobation of parental conduct but solely as a judicial determination of where the welfare of the children lies.[99]

---

97. See also *S. v. S.* (May 1978), unreported, (H.C.) judgement of Finlay P.; *N. O'D. v. M. O'D.* (November 1977), unreported, (H.C.) judgement of McMahon J.; *H. v. H.* (February 1976), unreported, (H.C.) judgement of Parke J.
98. Henchy J. and Kenny J. A dissenting judgement was delivered by Griffin J.
99. Kenny J. stated that "an award of custody must not be used as a method of punish-

The case law in this area lacks coherence and is difficult, if not impossible, to reconcile. The fact that a spouse is engaged in an adulterous relationship without doubt renders it more difficult for that spouse to succeed in any application for custody. It is, however, impossible to predict with accuracy the likely outcome of such proceedings having regard to the varying judicial opinions as to the likely damage to the welfare of a child if it is placed in the custody of an adulterous parent. Nevertheless, it is clear from existing authorities that a less serious view of the "moral danger" is taken in the case of the spouse who has formed an adulterous liaison some time after his or her marriage has broken down and separation has occurred, than in the case of the spouse who commits adultery while still living with the other spouse and who leaves the family home to set up home with a third party. In both circumstances, but particularly in the latter one, the adulterous parent's chances of success will improve if the children whose custody is sought are aware of the adulterous relationship and have resided with the adulterous parent and third party for a period prior to the matter arising for judicial decision. Moreover, a parent who can prove that an adulterous association has terminated will further increase his or her chances of success. Thus, in *Cullen* v. *Cullen*[100] a mother held to be the parent responsible for the breakdown of the marriage was granted custody of her youngest child on the condition and subject to the understanding that her association with her former lover was at an end.

In a society whose courts possess no jurisdiction to dissolve the matrimonial bond upon the breakdown of a marital relationship, the number of cases coming before the courts in which one or both parties to a broken marriage are engaged in an adulterous relationship is likely to increase. In such circumstances the application of the "welfare" principle is particularly difficult. This difficulty is exacerbated by the Supreme Court's failure to clearly enunciate the principles applicable in deciding such cases.[101]

Access

Where parents can agree between themselves about duration, frequency and circumstances of access, the court will not usually interfere. If they cannot agree and if custody is granted to one parent, the other will normally be given access by the court to the child if he wants it, and frequently access includes the right to have the children for a proportion of their school holidays. Where a parent is living in an adulterous relationship with another, a condition of access may be that the other person must not be present when the parent has access to the children.[102] This, however, depends very much on the circumstances of the case.

In determining a dispute as to access the welfare of the child is the first and paramount consideration. The court is reluctant to refuse a parent access but it will do so if the child's welfare demands it. In *B.* v. *B.*[103] the behaviour of the

ing the wife for her adultery". He also stated that he reserved "for future consideration by a full court the questions of whether the decisions of this court in (*J.J.W.* v. *B.M.W.*) and (*E.K.* v. *M.K.*) were correct". See also the decision of the English Court of Appeal in *S.* (*B.D.*) v. *S.* (*D.J.*) [1977] Fam. 109; [1977] 2 W.L.R. 44 referred to with approval by Henchy J. See further *K.* (*Minors*) (*Wardship*) [1977] 1 All E.R. 647 (C.A.).

100. (May 1970), unreported, (S.C.).

101. See J. O'Reilly, "Custody Disputes in the Irish Republic: the Uncertain Search for the Child's Welfare" (1977) 12 I.J. (n.s.) 37.

102. Thus in *Braun v. Braun* (December 1973), unreported, (H.C.) the mother was permitted to have access to her children in the house in which she was living on condition that R. the person with whom she was living would not be present at the time. See also the judgement of Fitzgerald J. in *J.J.W.* v. *B.M.W., supra.*

103. See Kenny J.'s judgement of July 1974, unreported, (H.C.).

father almost resulted in such a refusal. In this case the parents were living apart and the father having been given custody of two of his three children, used his children to spy on their mother, and place microphones in her bedroom. He turned both the children completely against their mother engaging in "violent verbal onslaughts" against her in their presence. Upon a new application by both parents to the High Court, the mother was granted custody of all three children and the father's access was curtailed to once a month.

In *M. v. M.* the English Court of Appeal stated that access to a child by a parent is a basic right of the child rather than of the parent. Wrangham J. stated that

"No court should deprive a child of access to either parent unless it is wholly satisfied that it is in the interests of that child that access should cease, and that is a conclusion at which a court should be extremely slow to arrive."[104]

The Child's Wishes

Formerly, Chancery frequently consulted a young child not for the purpose of obtaining the child's agreement or consent to being put into a particular parent's custody but in order to help the court determine for itself what was for a child's welfare. At common law a boy was regarded as reaching the age of discretion at 14 and a girl at 16 and the court regarded itself as bound by the wishes of the children when they reached the above ages. After 1877 the court exercised both jurisdictions and where a boy of 14 or girl of 16 wished to be in the custody of a particular parent the court regarded itself as being under an obligation to respect the child's wishes, even if it believed that the implementation of them would be contrary to the child's welfare.[105]

In applications brought under section 11 of the 1964 Act, interviews of children have been undertaken by both the High Court and Supreme Court where appropriate. Such interviews are of an extremely informal nature.[106] The court, however, has to be on its guard as to what a child says, as it may have been coached by one of its parents.[107] Whether the court would uphold the wishes of a 14 year old boy or 16 year old girl today if it believed them totally contrary to the child's welfare and long-term interests is uncertain.[108] It is to be hoped that it would not do so. If it did, it is certainly arguable that any such decision would be contrary to section 3 of the Act. On the other hand it has been recognised that it would be impractical to transfer the custody of a 17½ year old girl from her mother to her father against the girl's own wishes.[109] Upon

104. [1973] 2 All E.R. 81 at p. 85, Fam. D., (D.C.). At p. 88 in the same case Latey J. stated: "I do not accept that . . . a parent should have access to the child although such access is contrary to the child's interests". This case was cited by Kenny J. but not commented on in *Braun v. Braun* (December 1973), unreported, (H.C.). See also *M. v. J.* (1977), 121 S.J. 759 (D.C.).
105. *State (Meagan) v. Meagan* (1942), I.R. 180, (H.C.). See also *R. v. Gyngall, supra*; *In re Elliott, an Infant* (1893), 32 L.R. Ir. 504, (C.A.); *In re O'Hara, an Infant, supra*; *In re Kevin Isherwood, an Infant, supra*; *In re Frost, Infants, supra*. Statutory authority was given to the practice of the courts interviewing the child in Habeas Corpus proceedings in the Custody of Children Act, 1891. See now Sect. 17 (2) of the 1964 Act.
106. See e.g. *M. O'S. v. M. O'S.* (April 1972), unreported, (H.C.) where Kenny J. describes how he met the child for lunch and strolled around the boat-show at the R.D.S. and then went into the jumping enclosure.
107. In *B. v. B.* (January 1969), unreported, (H.C.) Kenny J. said that he did not interview the children as he thought it would be of no assistance, and might upset them. He also complained that in another case he had interviewed a child obviously coached by his father. On the other hand the Supreme Court on appeal did interview the children.
108. See *In re S. Infants* [1967], 1 All E.R. 202 (Ch.D.).
109. See *Cullen v. Cullen* (May 1970), unreported, (S.C.) See also *W. v. W.* (June 1975), unreported, (H.C.), discussed on page 203 *ante*.

a child reaching such an age, in the absence of grave danger to its welfare, it is very unlikely that its wishes will not be complied with.[110]

Effect of Award of Custody

The fact that a parent is deprived of his right to custody does not mean he has no further say in the upbringing of his child. Such a parent is still a guardian of the child, and is entitled to be consulted on all matters affecting the child's welfare. As seen earlier, this applies to all matters that comprise the religious, moral, intellectual, physical and social welfare of the child. "Section 6 of the Act stated the equality of the parents and recognised them as the guardians of the infant and there is nothing in any provision of the Act which purports to confer upon any court or other body the power to displace either one or both of the parents from the position of guardian or guardians."[111]

Custody and Parental Kidnapping

A problem that has become more frequent in recent years is that of the parent who seeks to resolve a dispute as to the custody of children by removing them unilaterally from one jurisdiction to another without the consent of the other parent. Such behaviour is commonly described as parental kidnapping although it is not usually kidnapping in the criminal sense. It is proposed first to deal with the parental kidnapping of children living in this jurisdiction and then to look at the problem of children brought to Ireland from other jurisdictions.

Kidnapping within the jurisdiction: a parent who fears that the other parent may seek to remove a child from this jurisdiction can in proceedings brought under Section 11 of the 1964 Act obtain an order prohibiting the latter from removing the child from the jurisdiction without either the consent of the parent seeking the order or, in the alternative, the consent of the court. The court in making such an order may also require the parent against whom it is made hand into court any passport issued in respect of the child, that is in his possession.

If a parent has already kidnapped a child, an ex parte application can be made to the High Court by the other parent seeking an immediate order prohibiting the removal of the child from the jurisdiction. In such circumstances it is also usual for the court to make an order authorising the solicitor acting for the applicant to notify by 'phone and telegram the Commissioner of the Gardai and all points of departure from the State of the content of the order. The court would also usually order the kidnapping parent to produce the child before the court within one or two days. If the whereabouts of the kidnapping parent are unknown, the court may further authorise the publication of a notice in a national or local newspaper containing the court order to bring it to the attention of the kidnapping parent. In practice, in an emergency, the High Court has granted such orders upon hearing the evidence of a parent even before proceedings have been drafted and issued.

If a parent knowingly breaks an order prohibiting the removal of a child from

---

110. An example of a circumstance in which the court would not agree to comply with the wishes of such a child would be perhaps where a parent was engaging in incest with the child. Here, despite the child's desire to remain with the parent, it is highly unlikely that such a parent would be permitted to retain custody.

111. Walsh J. in *B. v. B.* [1975], I.R. 54, (S.C.). In *J.J.W. v. B.M.W. supra*, (S.C.) Walsh J. stated: "The award of custody does not affect the rights which accrue to the parents as guardians of the children". See also *W. v. W.* (December 1974), unreported, (S.C.).

the jurisdiction, or if a third party knowing that such an order has been made, assists a parent to break it, he is guilty of contempt of court.[112]

Kidnapping outside the jurisdiction: in cases in which a parent has unilaterally brought a child to Ireland from another jurisdiction in which it has had its home, without the consent of the other parent, the Irish courts have in practice been reluctant to engage in a comprehensive examination of all the issues involved in a dispute as to custody and have generally approached the matter on the basis that the proper courts to determine such disputes are those of the home jurisdiction. Thus, in *A.* v. *H.*[113] the High Court peremptorily ordered that an illegitimate child just over two years of age be returned to the custody of its mother stating that any dispute as to its custody should be determined by the courts of Northern Ireland. Five days earlier the child, which was residing with its mother in Belfast, had been kidnapped by the father and brought to Dublin. In *O'D.* v. *O'D.*[114] the High Court ruled that the proper forum to determine a dispute as to the custody of three legitimate children kidnapped by their father from Alberta in Canada was the Supreme Court of Alberta. Two months prior to these proceedings the plaintiff had been residing with her children in Alberta and prior to her instituting proceedings in Ireland she had successfully applied to the Supreme Court in Alberta for custody.

To date, no written judgement has been delivered by the Irish courts in this particular area. It is clear that in dealing with such cases the court is bound by the welfare principle as stated in section 3 of the 1964 Act. The law will, however, only be clarified upon there being delivered a detailed judgement setting out the exact manner in which the welfare principle is to be interpreted and applied in the determination of such proceedings.[115]

Agreements as to Custody

As has been seen, at common law, as in the case formerly of an agreement by a father to curtail his rights to determine a child's education, any agreement by which he purported to assign the custody of his minor to another, was contrary to public policy and void. As a consequence of this, section 2 of the Custody of Infants Act was enacted in 1873. This section was re-enacted in Section 18(2) of the 1964 Act and reads:

"A provision contained in any separation agreement made between the father and mother of an infant shall not be invalid by reason only of its providing that one of them shall give up the custody or control of the infant to the other."

112. See *D. v. D.* (April 1974), unreported, (H.C.).
113. 1978 No. 484 Sp. Decision of D'Arcy J. 23rd August, 1978. There was no written judgement in this case.
114. See (July-August, 1979) Vol. 73 *Gazette of the Incorporated Law Society of Ireland*, "Recent Irish Cases" in which there is a summary of this case. No written judgement was delivered.
115. For an excellent discussion of English law see Lowe & White, *Wards of Court* (London, Butterworths 1979). See also G. Ritche, "Wardship and Kidnapping" (1979), 129 N.L.J. 873; N.V. Lowe, "Wardship and Kidnapping—A Reply" (1980), 130 N.L.J. 584; D.W. Fox & A.N. Khan, "Kidnapping Ones Own Child" (1979), 9 Fam. Law 68. See in particular the following cases: *Re H. (Infants)* [1966] 1 W.L.R. 381, (C.A.); *Re E. (An Infant)* [1967], Ch. 287; [1967] 1 All E.R. 329, (Ch.D.); [1967] 2 All E.R. 881, (C.A.); *Re T. (Infants)* [1968], Ch. 704, (C.A.); *Re A. (Infants)* [1970], Ch. 665, (C.A.); *Re L. (Minors) (Wardship: Jurisdiction)* [1974] 1 W.L.R. 250, (C.A.); (Pet. Dis.) [1974] 1 W.L.R. 266, G. (H.L.);*Re M.-R. (A Minor)* (1975) 5 Fam. Law 55 (C.A.);*Re C. (Minors) (Wardship: Jurisdiction)* [1978] Fam. 105 (C.A.).

If any agreement made is contrary to a child's welfare it will not be enforced by the courts.[116] An agreement between parents and strangers is unaffected by this sub-s. and is still void, though it might be evidence of a parent having abandoned his parental rights.[117]

Effect of a Mensa Et Thoro Decree

Section 18(1) of the 1964 Act states:

"In any case where a decree for divorce *a mensa et thoro* is pronounced, the court may thereby declare the parent by reason of whose misconduct the decree is made to be a person unfit to have the custody of the children (if any) of the marriage or of any children adopted under the Adoption Act, 1952, by the parents jointly; and in such case, the parent so declared to be unfit shall not, on the death of the other parent, be entitled as of right to the custody of the children."

This sub-section is in essence a re-enactment of section 7 of the Act of 1886. The effect of such a declaration is not to award custody of a child to a particular parent. Upon a petition for a decree of divorce *a mensa et thoro* the court has no jurisdiction to do so. Its effect is to put an onus on the parent against whom a declaration is made, to show, if and when the question of the custody of the child arises, that he has so altered his mode of conduct from what it was before the declaration was made, to have become a fit and proper person to be entrusted with the care of his child.[118] In exercising its discretion to declare such a parent unfit, the court must be guided by the paramount consideration of the welfare of the child. As the welfare of the child is the paramount consideration, the parents' conduct, as in the case where no *mensa et thoro* action has been brought, should only be relevant in assessing their character as parents, not as spouses. It has been constantly stated that an award of custody is not a prize for good matrimonial behaviour. It is submitted that in *mensa et thoro* proceedings the court is more concerned with the parents' character as spouses and that in the absence of jurisdiction to examine their character as parents, the court cannot properly decide whether such a declaration would be in the interest of a child's welfare or not. As yet no order has been made under this section. The section is anomalous and should be repealed.

Appeals/Variations

If the case is first heard in the Circuit Court an appeal lies to the High Court. If the case is first decided in the High Court an appeal lies to the Supreme Court. The Supreme Court has stated that if it is necessary or desirable further evidence not presented in the High Court can be examined by it on appeal. Whilst if new evidence was produced it would be a better course to refer the matter back to the High Court, if necessary a whole new trial of the action could take place in the Supreme Court.[119] Any order made by the Court under Part II of the Act is not final, and may be varied upon the application of either party to

---

116. See *Cullen v. Cullen, supra* where O'Dalaigh C.J. stated "the courts duty in considering the interests of the children transcends the agreement of the parents as to the custody of the children". Also see *In re Besant* (1879), 11 Ch. D. 508, (C.A.).
117. See p. 228 *et seq*.
118. See *Carey v. Carey* [1935] N.I. 144, (C.A.).
119. *B. v. B.* [1975] I.R. 54, (S.C.). See, however, *E.K. v. M.K.* where the Supreme Court refused to hear medical evidence that had not been heard in the High Court. See in particular judgement of Henchy J.

the High Court upon a change in circumstances occurring.[120]

Guardianship and Custody on Parents' Death

By section 6 of the 1964 Act, on the death of either parent, the surviving parent is guardian of any infants of the marriage. Both parents have the power to appoint a testamentary guardian to act after their death, and if one is appointed, he acts jointly with the surviving parent. If the surviving parent objects to the testamentary guardian or the testamentary guardian considers the surviving parent unfit to have the custody of the infant, the latter may apply to the Circuit or High Court. Upon such an application the court may decide that the parent is to be the sole guardian, that both parent and testamentary guardian are to act jointly or that the latter is to act as guardian to the exclusion, so far as the court thinks proper, of the surviving parent. If the last decision is made the court must make an order as to custody and access to the infant and may order the parent to pay a reasonable sum to the guardian for the maintenance of the infant.[121]

A parent may appoint a guardian by either deed or will.[122] A court has power to appoint a guardian also if a deceased parent has not done so or if the appointed guardian or guardians are dead or refuse to act.[123] Any person interested in a child's welfare can apply to the court to be appointed guardian.[124] The court has a general power to remove from office any guardian appointed by will or deed or by order of the court.[125] It may appoint another guardian in place of one so removed or in place of a guardian appointed by court order who dies.[126]

A guardian appointed to act jointly with a surviving parent continues to act upon the death of such parent.[127] Where guardians are appointed by both parents, after the death of the surviving parent they act jointly.[128] Finally, where two or more persons are appointed to be guardians, on the death of either of them, the survivor continues to act.[129]

Generally speaking a guardian has the same rights and duties *vis-à-vis* a child as a parent. However, in relation to a child's education, secular or religious, he must observe the wishes of the child's parents unless they are contrary to the child's welfare. In relation to any property belonging to the child over which he has control, he is regarded as a trustee.

The guardian or guardians, as we have already seen, can apply to the court for its direction on any question affecting the welfare of the infant.[130] The court in reaching a determination must give paramount consideration to the welfare of the infant.[131] The guardians' duties automatically terminate upon a child becoming 21 years of age, or upon the death of the child.

120. Guardianship of Infants Act, 1964, Sect 12–see particularly *B. v. B.* (Dec. 1974), unreported, (H.C.) this case was the subject of continual application for variation over a period of six years.
121. Guardianship of Infants Act, 1964, Sect. 7.
122. *Ibid.*, Sect. 7 (1) and Sect. 7 (3).
123. *Ibid.*, Sect. 8 (2). See *J. v. D. and others* (Jan. 1977), unreported, (H.C.); (June 1977), unreported, (S.C.).
124. *Ibid.*, Sect. 8 (1).
125. *Ibid.*, Sect. 8 (4).
126. *Ibid.*, Sect. 8 (5).
127. *Ibid.*, Sect. 8 (3).
128. *Ibid.*, Sect. 9 (2).
129. *Ibid.*, Sect. 9 (1).
130. *Ibid.*, Sect. 11 (1). See *In re Meade, Applicant* [1971] I.R. 327, (H.C.). For the limitation on such applications see *In the Matter of J.S. an Infant* (1977) 111 I.L.T.R. 146, (H.C.).
131. *Ibid.*, Sect. 3.

Part III of 1964 Act

Part III of the 1964 Act, Sects. 14 to 17, in effect re-enact the provisions of the Custody of Children's Act, 1891. These provisions apply to habeas corpus applications to the High Court and primarily relate to disputes between parents and strangers.[132] They may also apply to a dispute between parents[133] if either parent brings habeas corpus proceedings against the other to enforce a right of custody, but in practice such a dispute is normally resolved upon an application being made under section 11 of the Act.[134] It is thus intended to discuss Part III in the following section.

DISPUTES BETWEEN PARENTS AND STRANGERS [135]

Methods of Resolving Custody Disputes

If a parent wishes to regain custody over his child from a stranger he can bring Habeas Corpus proceedings, proceedings under section 11 of the Act of 1964, or wardship proceedings. Alternatively, if a stranger wishes to bring a custody action against a parent he will have to commence proceedings to have the child made a ward of court and himself awarded custody.[136] Wardship proceedings are dealt with in the next section. This section is concerned with the bringing of either of the first two above mentioned proceedings by a parent so as to enforce the parental right to custody.

History of Parental Right

At common law the general rule was that a parent had an absolute right, unless guilty of extreme misconduct, as against a stranger to the guardianship and custody of his children. Any agreement between a parent and a stranger whereby a parent deprived himself of custody of his children was absolutely ineffective and the parent could at any time resume control over them. However, if a parent did relinquish control after 1877, the courts were governed by the Chancery rule that if they were satisfied that to return the child to the custody of its parent would be harmful to its welfare, then, even though the parent was guilty of no misconduct, they could refuse to do so. However, the

132. In practice, both the High Court and the Supreme Court have referred to the provisions in Part III of the Act when determining custody disputes between parents and strangers in proceedings instituted by parents under section 11 of the Act. See for example, *J. v. D. and Ors.* (January 1977), unreported, (H.C.); (June 1977), unreported, (S.C.); *S. v. E.H.B. and Ors.* (February 1979), unreported, (H.C.); *P.W. v. A.W. and Ors.* (April 1980), unreported, (H.C.).
133. See e.g. *In re Story, Infants, supra.* See however *Campbell v. Campbell* [1956], S.C. 285, (Ct. of Sess.) in which it was held that these provisions of the Act of 1891 only applied to disputes between a parent and a third party and not as between parents; see also Halsbury—"Law of England", 3rd Edition, Vol. 21 (Butterworth, London 1957), 196.
134. See, however, *Donnellan v. Donnellan, Irish Times* 22nd and 27th Oct. 1976. Mrs D. was granted custody of her five year old daughter by the High Court. Four months later, Mr D. disappeared with the child when exercising his right of access to it. Upon the wife's application, a conditional order of Habeas Corpus was granted, requiring Mr D. to produce the child in Court. Upon him failing to do so, a warrant was issued for his arrest.
135. A stranger in the pages that follow refers to a person who is neither a parent nor a legally appointed guardian of the child in question.
136. It has been held, however, that upon an application for custody by a parent in proceedings brought against a stranger, the court may make a custody order in favour of the stranger. See *J. v. D. and Ors., supra.* See *P.W. v. A.W. and Ors., supra.* See also *Re J.L. (a Minor)* (March 1978), unreported, (H.C., P.) in which Finlay P. stated: "I would be prepared to hold that the powers conferred by Sections 14 and 16 of the Act of 1964 to deprive a parent of the custody of its child must imply as a necessary corollary a power to place the child in the custody of another".

attitude of the courts was that, *prima facie*, it was contrary to a child's welfare to remove it from the custody of its natural parents and to place it in the custody of persons with no natural relationship to it, that "generally speaking, the best place for a child is with its parents".[137]

The Act of 1964 and Disputes as to Custody

Today the principle laid down in section 3 of the Guardianship of Infants Act, 1964, that the welfare of the child is to be regarded as the first and paramount consideration governs all disputes as to the custody of a child. Thus, the matters previously discussed as comprising the various elements in a child's welfare, are equally applicable in disputes between parents and strangers.

Sections 14 to 16 of the 1964 Act are of particular relevance in custody disputes between parents and strangers. They read as follows:

14.—Where a parent[138] of an infant applies to the court for an order for the production of the infant and the court is of opinion that that parent has abandoned or deserted the infant, or that he has otherwise so conducted himself that the court should refuse to enforce his right to the custody of the infant, the court may in its discretion decline to make the order.

15.—Where, upon application by a parent for the production of an infant, the court finds—

(a) that the infant is being brought up at the expense of another person,[139] or

(b) that at any time assistance has been provided for the infant by a health authority under section 55 of the Health Act, 1953,

the court may, in its discretion, if it orders the infant to be given up to the parent, further order that the parent shall pay to that person or health authority the whole of the costs properly incurred by the person or health authority in bringing up or providing assistance for the infant or such portion thereof as the court considers reasonable, having regard to all the circumstances of the case, including, in particular, the means of the parent.

16.—Where a parent has—

(a) abandoned or deserted an infant, or

(b) allowed an infant to be brought up by another person at that person's expense, or to be provided with assistance by a health authority under section 55 of the Health Act, 1953, for such a length of time and under such circumstances as to satisfy the court that the parent was unmindful of his parental duties,

the court shall not make an order for the delivery of the infant to the parent unless the parent has satisfied the court that he is a fit person to have the custody of the infant.

---

137. Lord Esher in *R. v. Gyngall, supra*, at p. 243.
138. Under Part III, "Parent" includes a guardian of the person and any person at law liable to maintain an infant or entitled to his custody—Sect. 13 of the 1964 Act.
139. "Person" includes any school or institution; *ibid.*

The provisions of sections 14 and 16 are essentially inter-related. A parent found to have misbehaved in a manner described in section 16 must satisfy the court that he is "a fit person" to have custody before an order for custody can be made in his favour. However, even if he so satisfies the court, the court may by virtue of the discretion conferred upon it by section 14, refuse to grant custody to the parent, if the court when having regard to the child's welfare concludes that it is in the interests of the child's welfare that a different order as to custody be made.[140] If the court is of the opinion that a parent ought not to have custody of a child, it may make such order as it thinks fit to ensure that the child is brought up in the religion in which the parent or parents desire it to be-brought up. The court is given statutory authority to consult the wishes of a child in considering what order ought to be made and any right which the child possesses to exercise his own free choice is said not to be diminished by the 1964 Act.[141]

Sections 14-16 of the 1964 Act basically re-enact the statutory provisions contained in the Custody of Children Act, 1891. It is thus intended to examine a number of leading pre-1964 cases in which the provisions of the 1891 Act were discussed and interpreted and then to look at more recent cases, and discuss the effects of the Constitution on the present Act. As will be seen in the pages that follow, a number of the cases that precede the coming into force of the Adoption Act, 1952, involve parents attempting to regain custody of a child some time after concluding an "adoption agreement" with a third party, whilst many of those after 1952 concern natural parents seeking to regain custody of a child in respect of whom an invalid adoption order has been made. Where a section of the 1891 Act is referred to in the text that follows, the corresponding provision in the 1964 Act is set down in the footnotes.

The case which is at the foundation of the modern law in this area is *R.* v. *Gyngall*.[142] In this case a widowed Roman Catholic mother was refused custody of her 15 year old daughter, who had been brought up for a number of years in a Protestant institution. The Court of Appeal found that the mother had been "obliged to earn her living by moving from place to place, and from country to country", and had not been able herself to bring up the child, the child being placed with other people for long periods. It was thought likely that if she was granted custody within a short time the girl would be again institutionalised. The court was satisfied that the mother had been guilty of no misconduct or fault but as the overriding consideration was the child's welfare and happiness, taking into account her age, her wish to stay where she was, the fact that she now entertained Protestant views and that she would very shortly be in a position to earn her own living, it held that the mother's natural right must be superseded.

In the Irish Court of Appeal in *In re Elliott an Infant*[143] the court followed the principle layed down by the Divisional Court[144] in Gyngall's case. In 1884 Mary Elliott when only six years old with her mother's assistance or connivance was committed to nine years in an industrial school by the Thurles magistrates. Mary's mother was a Catholic and the industrial school was under the charge of Roman Catholic nuns. Upon the termination of the nine years her uncle, who was a Protestant, attempted to obtain custody of Mary. The mother, who had remarried and was living in England, permitted her name to be used in an appli-

---

140. See *S. v. E.H.B. and Ors.* (February 1979), unreported, (H.C.).
141. See Sect. 17 of the 1964 Act, and see p. 223 *ante*.
142. *Supra.*
143. (1893) 32 L.R. Ir. 504, (C.A.).
144. 9 Times Rep. 47.

cation for a writ of Habeas Corpus. Holmes J.[145] noted that the mother was not seeking custody for herself:

"I would not consider this, taken by itself, as a very important element in the case, for I think that a mother, if she is not possessed of means herself, may select a relative who has means, and who is willing to undertake to stand in her place as the custodian of her child, but it withdraws from our consideration such topics as the cultivation of filial affection and the personal association of the parent with a child, to which great weight ought to be given. Secondly, the education of this girl has been hitherto conducted in the industrial school upon a definite and distinct plan, leading to a definite and distinct end, namely, to placing her in a position in life where she would be able to earn a respectable livelihood by her own exertions; and if she be now removed from the nuns' care this plan will be broken in upon".[146]

Having interviewed the girl the court was satisfied "that as far as she herself is concerned she wishes to remain with the nuns, in the belief that her material prospects, and her hopes of becoming independent will be more advanced by this course". The court regarded her views as sound and reasonable and also bore "in mind the fact that this application comes before us within six weeks of the time when the child, having attained 16 years of age will be able to select her own place of residence".[147]

In re O'Hara, an Infant,[148] was the first Irish case in which the Custody of Children's Act, 1891 was discussed. On the 5th October 1897 an agreement in writing was entered into between the mother and one McMahon, whereby she agreed to give her nine year old daughter to McMahon and to have no more claim on her, and McMahon agreed to adopt the child. The child had resided in an orphanage since she was two years of age due to her mother's poor circumstances following the death of her husband, the child's father. In May, 1898 the mother married a small farmer. In the beginning of 1899 she demanded the return of her daughter from McMahon who refused to give her back unless he was paid £8.50 expenses for her support and maintenance. The High Court refused to return the child to the mother, one of the reasons being the child's expressed desire to remain with the McMahons. Fitzgibbon L.J. in the Court of Appeal, while approving of the practice of ascertaining the views of a young child, commented that

"the parent's *prima facie* right must also be considered and the wishes of a child of tender years must not be permitted . . . to subvert the whole law of the family, or to prevail against the desire and authority of the parent, unless the welfare of the child cannot otherwise be secured".[149]

Referring to the agreement signed by the mother, he stated that the law did "not recognise the power of bindingly abdicating either parental right or parental

---

145. Stating (at p. 508) the question to decide was "what order will be best for the moral, mental and material welfare of the infant"?
146. *In re Elliot, an Infant, supra*, at pp. 507, 508.
147. *Ibid.,* p. 508; Holmes J. also stated at p. 509 that "the question of religion . . . has not affected our decision. At her age and after nine years of conventual instruction Mary Elliot has now received fixed religious convictions if her mind is capable of them, and her uncle disclaims any inclination to interfere with them. On the one hand, it is much too late to have her instructed in her father's religion. On the other hand, we would not be justified in refusing this application on the grounds that the relatives, with whom her mother wishes her to live, are Protestants".
148. [1900] 2 I.R. 232; (1899), 34 I.L.T.R. 17, (C.A.).
149. [1900] 2 I.R. 232 at p. 240.

duty".[150]

As for the general principles applicable in determining proceedings of this nature, he noted that since the Judicature Act the court was bound by the chancery jurisdiction under which "the main consideration was the welfare of the child" and continued,

"In exercising the jurisdiction to control or to ignore the parental right (to custody) the court must act cautiously . . . and (act) in opposition to the parent only when judicially satisfied that the welfare of the child requires that the parental right should be suspended or superseded . . . It appears to me that misconduct or unmindfulness of parental duty or inability to provide for the welfare of the child must be shown before the natural right can be displaced. Where a parent is of blameless life and is able and willing to provide for the child's material and moral necessities . . . the court is, in my opinion, judicially bound to act on what is equally a law of nature and of society and to hold . . . that 'the best place for a child is with its parent.' Of course I do not speak of exceptional cases . . . where special disturbing elements exist, which involve the risk of moral or material injury to the child, such as the disturbance of religious convictions or of settled affections, or the endurance of hardship or destitution with a parent, as contrasted with solid advantages offered elsewhere. The court, acting as a wise parent, is not bound to sacrifice the child's welfare to the fetish of parental authority, by forcing it from a happy and comfortable home to share the fortunes of a parent, however innocent, who cannot keep a roof over its head, or provide it with the necessaries of life."[151]

Referring to section 3[152] of the 1891 Act, he continued

"The phrase in the Act which most nearly fits the present case is that which speaks of a parent having 'allowed his child to be brought up by another person at that person's expense'; but that phrase occurs in connection with abandonment and desertion and is qualified by the words 'for such a length of time and under such circumstances as to satisfy the Court that the parent *was unmindful of his parental duties*'. On the construction of the Act I hold that the surrender of a child to an adopted parent as an act of prudence or of necessity, under the pressure of present inability to maintain it, being an act done in the interest of the child, cannot be regarded as abandonment or desertion or even as unmindfulness of parental duty within the meaning of the Act."[153]

Holmes J. felt that the provisions of the 1891 Act gave "little or no assistance" in determining the application for custody. The court, he stated, must decide

"(1)   whether the mother by her conduct has disabled herself from making the application; and, if she has not

---

150. *Ibid.*, at p. 241.
151. [1900] 2 I.R. 232 at pp. 239, 240, 241.
152. The equivalent of Sect. 16 of the 1964 Act.
153. *Ibid* at p. 244. See also *Re Hyndman, Infants,* (1905) 39 I.L.T.R. 191 (K.B.D.); *In the matter of M.E. Bell, an Infant* (1909) 43 I.L.T.R. 35 (K.B.D.). On the other hand, see *In re Boyd* [1918] 2 I.R. 98 (K.B.D.)—In this case, a mother claimed the custody of her 13 year old son who had resided with her sister for six years. The Court being of the opinion that it was for the child's benefit to remain with the sister, refused the mother's application for a writ of habeas corpus. See also article "The Custody of Infants" in (1918), 52 I.L.T. & S.J. p. 295—6.

(2) whether it is more for the welfare of the child that she should remain
in the house and under the care of the McMahons".[154]

Further on he stated,

"A mother entitled *prima facie*, as guardian by nurture, to the custody of
her child may fail to make good her right to such custody, by reason of her
own conduct or, where no valid objection can be taken thereto, for reasons
connected with the welfare of the child."[155]

He went on to hold, as did the other members of the court, that the mother
had not misconducted herself and that it was in the interests of the child's welfare that she be returned to her mother's custody.

That a parent forced by economic circumstances to give custody of his children
to a stranger was not guilty of abandonment or unmindful of his duties was
further stated in the *State (Kavanagh)* v. *O'Sullivan.*[156] Kavanagh's wife after
the birth of their three children became mentally ill and was confined to a
mental home. Kavanagh was a Protestant and the children with their mother's
agreement had been baptised and brought up as Protestants. The mother was a
Catholic. Kavanagh lived in a tenement house and sometimes worked nights.
With no one to mind the children in his absence, he got heavily in debt and,
wishing to prevent their starvation, agreed to their being admitted to a Catholic
institution whose main pre-condition was that the children be baptised Roman
Catholic. A year and a half later he obtained a writ of Habeas Corpus to regain
custody of the children. In the action it was alleged that he was not a fit person
to have their custody by virtue of sub-s. (b) of section 3 of the 1891 Act.[157]

To this contention, Kennedy C.J. said

"So far from deserving censure for his action or being driven from a defence
of his parental rights to the setting up under the Act of 1891 of his fitness
as a parent to have custody of his children, he is rather to be commended
for that, anxious for the well-being of his children, on the failure of his
attempt to continue to carry on anything like a home . . . he took the most
prudent action, the action best calculated in his unhappy situation to
secure their welfare and to afford them protection against the danger
surrounding them during the absence of their mother".[158]

If a parent has been unmindful of his duties or abandoned his child, the Act
gives him an opportunity of showing that notwithstanding the abandonment he
is a fit person and that it is in the interests of the child's welfare that he be
entrusted with its custody.

Thus in the *State (Williams)* v. *Markey*[159] the Supreme Court gave parents
custody of their child, their having previously given it to another couple for
fear that the wife's mother would discover that its birth took place within five
months of the parents being married. It held that in the circumstances the
abandonment of the child was understandable and it did not indicate that the
parents were unfit to have custody. Having regard to the parents' better financial
circumstances, their desire to regain custody and to the fact that a "cloud of
suspicion always darkens the life of a child where the circumstances of its

154. [1900] 2 I.R. at p. 251.
155. *Ibid.*
156. [1933] I.R. 618; (1931) 68 I.L.T.R. 110, (S.C.).
157. The equivalent of Sect. 16 (b) of the 1964 Act.
158. [1933] I.R. 618 at p. 636.
159. [1940] I.R. 421; (1939) 74 I.L.T.R. 237, (S.C.).

adoption are obscure"[160] it was for the welfare of the child that it should return to the custody of its parents.

Alternatively, in *In the Matter of M. Skeffington*[161] the court refused to grant a writ of Habeas Corpus to a father so as to force his child's grandmother to return the child to his custody. The child had been in the custody of the grandmother from the age of three and was 11 years old at the date of the application. The parents had had an unhappy marriage having been separated and reconciled on numerous occasions. At the time of the application to the court they were again living together. The court held that the father had allowed the child to be brought up at another's expense and had been unmindful of his parental duties. Further, having regard to the history of the marriage it felt that there was "nothing in the nature of permanency in the home",[162] and that consequently the father was not a fit person to be granted custody, having regard to the interests of the child.[163]

In the recent case of *S.* v. *E.H.B. and Ors.*[164] the court held that the mother of an illegitimate child had not abandoned her child by leaving it in a children's home. The child had been born in June 1977 and the mother regularly visited it in the home until August. From August until December 1977 she did not visit and made no contact with the home. Referring to sections 14 and 16 of the 1964 Act, Finlay P. stated

"Abandonment in these two sections must, in my view, be construed as total neglect, the leaving of an infant with the knowledge that there is nobody to care for it or look after it."

There was no abandonment in this case as there was no possibility that those in charge of the home would fail to care for the child. However, the mother was held to have deserted her child, as "she took no steps of any description to ascertain its welfare, to provide for its welfare or to engage the services of others who would provide for its welfare". In particular during that period she refused to communicate with the authorities of the children's home and that "must be viewed in the light of the fact that some urgent question of the welfare of the child might have required to be dealt with ... Her conduct was prompted to a large extent by an escapism and one which is understandable. Desertion however does not necessarily mean heartless or wanton desertion."

Finlay P. concluded on the evidence that the mother was, at the date of the proceedings, a fit person to have custody stating "that finding constitutes a finding only that there is nothing in her make-up arising from her personality or from any physical, emotional or psychiatric abnormality which would prevent her from being capable of caring for a young infant."

Nevertheless, having regard to the best interests of the child the court made an order dispensing with the mother's consent to the making of an adoption order, as sought by the prospective adopters with whom the child had been placed. The child at the date of the proceedings was 20 months old and had

160. [1940] I.R. 421 at p. 437 per Meredith J.
161. (1908) 43 I.L.T.R. 245, (K.B.D.). See also *In re Boyd, supra.*
162. *Supra* at p. 246 per Palles L.C.B.
163. See further *O'N. v. O'B. and Ors.* (January 1980) unreported (H.C.) in which Finlay P. returned to the mother's custody a child that had been in the custody of the mother's parents for six years.
In *In re Cullinane, an Infant* [1945] I.R. 270 (H.C.), a case involving a dispute as to the custody of an illegitimate child, the limitations of the 1891 Act were demonstrated. Here, the court stated that the *wishes* of a mother as to who should have custody of her child were not to be disregarded, even if she had let it be brought up at another's expense for so long as to satisfy the court that she had been unmindful of her parental duties. As she was not seeking custody, the section was said to have no application to the proceedings.
164. (February 1979), unreported, (H.C.). See also p.

resided continuously with the adopters since the age of 6 months save for a two week break.

THE 1937 CONSTITUTION AND THE WELFARE PRINCIPLE

Since the enactment of the 1937 Constitution there has been discernible in some judicial decisions a change of emphasis on the part of the courts. In making reference to the provisions of Articles 41 and 42 of the constitution greater stress has been placed on parental rights and the parental position appears to have been strengthened *vis-à-vis* other individuals and the state.[165] This strengthening of parental authority and emphasis on parental rights has given rise to the expression of doubts as to the constitutional validity of section 3 of the 1964 Act, in so far as the section requires the courts to regard a legitimate child's welfare as the first and paramount consideration in the determination of custody disputes between parents and strangers.[166]

Since 1964 in only three cases involving a dispute as to the custody of a legitimate child between parents and strangers have written judgements been delivered in which the affect of the family provisions of the Constitution on section 3 of the 1964 Act has been directly discussed. In addition, a number of other written judgements have been delivered to which this issue is of relevance. It is now intended to examine these.

In *In re J.*[167] an unmarried mother gave birth to a child in November 1964 and a month after its birth signed a written consent to its adoption. Less than a week later, the child was placed with prospective adopters and in July 1965 an adoption order was made. One and a half weeks after the making of the order the mother married the child's father. In February 1966 the adoption order was quashed as the mother's consent was invalid, being given in breach of a statutory provision. The natural parents sought custody of the child and obtained a conditional order of Habeas Corpus. At the hearing it was submitted that the infant had been legitimated[168] and that they were entitled to have custody of the infant as its parents, because they, with the infant, constituted a family within the meaning of Articles 41 and 42 of the Constitution. The adopters submitted that they could provide a more secure financial background for the child, that the child would be harmed by a change in custody and that the court should regard the welfare of the infant as the first and paramount consideration.

Henchy J. first held that the father, mother and child constituted a family for the purpose of Articles 41 and 42.[169] He further said that the case was not one

---

165. See *In re Art. 26 and the School Attendance Bill* 1942 [1943] I.R. 334; (1943) 771 I.L.T.R. 96, (S.C.); *In re Doyle, an Infant* [1956] I.R. 213, (H.C.); (21st December, 1955), unreported, (S.C.); see also J.M. Kelly, *Fundamental Rights*, p. 211 and *The Irish Constitution*, p. 498 *et seq*; "Children's Rights Under the Irish Constitution", Irish Council for Civil Liberties Report No. 2 (Dublin, January 1977); M. Staines, "The Concept of 'The Family' under the Irish Constitution" (1976) 11 I.J. (n.s.) 223.

166. *In re Corcoran, supra*—Murnaghan J. referring to the English Guardianship of Infants Act, 1925 suggested that a law which did not allow the rights and claims of a parent to the custody of his child to be considered except in their relation to "considerations affecting the welfare of the child" would be inconsistent with the Constitution. *In re O'Brien* [1954] I.R. 1; (1953), 87 I.L.T.R. 156, (S.C.), Byrne J. stated that the court assumed without deciding that Sect. 3 of the Custody of Children Act, 1891 was consistent with the Constitution. See also *In re Blake*, deceased, [1958] I.R. 89, (H.C.); *In re Doyle, an Infant, supra*. See further (1956) 90 I.L.T. & S.J. pp. 53–55, "Some Observations of The Children's Act 1941"; M.V. O'Mahony, "Legal Aspects of Residential Child Care" (1971), 6 I.J. (n.s.) 217; *Burke and O'Reilly v. Burke and Quail* [1951] I.R. 216; (1950) 84 I.L.T.R. 70, (H.C.).

167. [1966] I.R. 295, (H.C.), see also p. 169 and p. 180 *ante*.

168. By virtue of Legitimacy Act, 1931; see Chapter 11.

169. See p. 169 *ante*.

that could be brought within Article 42.5, there being nothing culpable on the part of the parents, and that it would be impossible to give effect to the parents' right and duty of education if they were deprived of custody. Henchy J. went on

"If I am correct in my application of the Constitution to the facts of this case, the parents' right to the custody of the child is conclusively established without looking further than Articles 41 and 42. But counsel for the adopters say that S. 3 of the Guardianship of Infants Act, 1964 requires that in deciding the question of custody we must regard the welfare of the infant as the first and paramount consideration . . . Having regard to the inalienable right and duty of parents to provide for the education of their children and their right in appropriate cases to obtain custody of the children for that purpose, I consider that S. 3 must be interpreted in one or other of the following ways: first by regarding it as unconstitutional, or secondly, by reading it in conjunction with Articles 41 and 42 as stating, in effect, that the welfare of the infant in the present case coincides with the parents' right to custody . . . I expressly reserve an opinion (counsel not having raised the matter) as to whether it was competent for the Legislature to provide that in a case such as this, where the parents are jointly seeking custody of their child for the purpose of giving effect to their inalienable right and duty to provide for its education, the Court should be bound to decide the question of custody by regarding the welfare of the infant as the first and paramount consideration."[170]

Teevan J. stated that it was well established that the child has an excellent home[171] and it would be "a sad parting and one that *must*[172] deeply affect the child, with the undoubted prospect of some permanent effect".[173] He stated however that the parents' right to custody was absolute until forfeited in a way already well defined in many authoritive cases and in section 14 of the 1964 Act

"Nothing has been or can be urged to suggest their unfitness for their responsibilities and duties as parents . . . In such circumstances the court must presume that restoration to her parents is the best thing for the child's welfare".[174]

As for section 3 and the argument that the child's welfare would be more secure in the adopters' home he went on

"To be valid it would have to be shown that S. 3 . . . effects a change in the law as it stood prior to that enactment, and that the section purports to diminish or curtail the rights of parents to the absolute control over their children. If it does then . . . a question of its constitutionality might arise. We are not however, confronted with any such question in this case."[175]

In *McL.* v. *An Bord Uchtála and the A.-G.*[176] no reference was made either to section 3 of the 1964 Act or its constitutionality. The Supreme Court granted declarations that an adoption order made five years earlier, in 1971, was null and void, and that as a consequence the child in respect of whom the proceedings

170. *Supra* at p. 308.
171. With the adopters.
172. Author's italics.
173. *Supra* at p. 302.
174. *Ibid.*, at p. 304.
175. *Ibid.*, at p. 303.
176. [1977] I.R. 287 (S.C.). See also p.

were brought was legitimated by its natural parents' marriage in 1972. The natural parents also sought an order directing that the child be placed in their custody. The child, who was by this time six years old, had never known its natural parents and had been in the care of its adoptive parents since the age of three months. The Supreme Court in granting custody to the natural parents made no mention of the provisions of the 1964 Act and in particular omitted to refer to the fact that the court, in custody proceedings, is bound to regard the welfare of the infant "as the first and paramount consideration". The court seems to have presumed, wrongly in the author's opinion, that once the adoption order was invalid, an order of custody had to be made. It failed to realise that the question as to whether the natural parents should be granted custody was a separate issue. Further, it determined the question of custody in the absence of the adopters. As they were not parties to the proceedings, they had no opportunity to oppose the natural parents' application for custody.[177]

In *J. v. D. and Ors*,[178] the plaintiff sought custody of his four children (three girls aged 14, 12 and 5 years and a boy aged 8½ years) following the death of his wife. The parties had married in 1961 and resided together in England. Twelve years after their marriage the parties separated and in July, 1973, the plaintiff's wife, who was Irish, came to live in her father's home in Ireland with her children. Shortly afterwards, the plaintiff formed a relationship with another married woman, who subsequently was divorced. On the evidence, the court found that in the period that followed, the plaintiff showed no interest in his wife and children and made no contact with them. In October, 1975, the wife died. The children remained in Ireland residing with their maternal aunts and their husbands.

In July, 1976, the plaintiff issued proceedings under section 11 of the 1964 Act and in December, 1976, he married the woman with whom he had been having a relationship. At the date of the hearing of the proceedings the two eldest girls were residing with one of the aunts and the youngest girl and the boy were each residing with a different aunt.

The plaintiff was unsuccessful in both the High Court and, on appeal, to the Supreme Court. It was held on the evidence that the plaintiff's failure to properly support his wife and children following their return to Ireland resulting in their being supported by his wife's sisters, his failure to defray even a portion of their expenses either before or after his wife's death and his failure to maintain contact with them amounted to an abandonment of his children. The maternal aunts were granted custody of each of the children in their care and were appointed guardians of them jointly with the plaintiff.

O'Higgins C.J. stated

"In my opinion in this case the welfare of each infant is best served by refusing the order sought by the plaintiff. For this reason alone in accordance with the provisions of Section 3 of the Act I would feel compelled to decide against the plaintiff ... I must add, however, that in my view the plaintiff's claim ought to fail both under Section 14 and under Section 16 of the Act. In my view, the plaintiff's conduct in relation to the infants would justify the court in declining to make an order under each of these sections."[179]

---

177. See however p. 180 ft. 47 and p. 193 ft. 102 *ante*.
178. (January 1977), unreported, (H.C.); (June 1977), unreported, (S.C.).
179. See p. 10 of judgement. The reference to Art. 41 section 2 is mistaken. It is submitted that the learned judge in fact intended to refer to Art. 41.1.2.

Earlier in his judgement, he stated

"Neither in this court nor in the High Court, has any question been raised
as to the validity of the Guardianship of Infants Act or any part thereof
having regard to the provisions of the Constitution. It falls therefore to this
court to decide this appeal in accordance with the provisions of the Act
and without regard to the difficult problems which could arise had its
compatibility with the provisions of Article 41 of the Constitution been
raised."[180]

Kenny J. in his judgement stated

"I agree . . . that the welfare of all the children to whom this case relates
requires that they should remain where they are now. It would be monstrous
to hand them over to their father: they have roots, a settled way of life and
a feeling of security where they are now . . . I have no doubt that giving
them to their father would cause permanent psychological damage to
them."[181]

As for the contention that "there is a *prima facie* parental right to custody" he
continued

"I deny that there is any natural or *prima facie* right of a parent to custody
of his children: there is a rule of prudence that in most cases the best place
for a child is with its parent".[182]

In disputes relating to custody the principles applicable, he continued, had not
altered from those stated by Holmes L.J. in *Re O'Hara*, that is, a parent may be
deprived of custody of a child "for reasons connected with the welfare of the
child" even when a parent's conduct has been unobjectionable. In the learned
judge's opinion

"The Constitution has not . . . altered this. Article 41 deals with the Family:
the children are part of that unit and the authority of the family referred to
in Article 41, Section 2, is that of the parents and children considered as a
unit."[183]

However, in *G.* v. *An Bord Uchtála and Ors.*[184] Kenny J. again referring to the
family provisions in the Constitution appeared to acknowledge that parents do
have a constitutional right to the custody of their legitimate children. He stated,

"While the Constitution deals with the rights of parents of legitimate
children and 'the natural and imprescriptible rights' of the child, it says
nothing about the custody of legitimate or illegitimate children. As Article
42 acknowledges that the family is the primary and natural educator of the
child and guarantees to respect the inalienable right and duty of parents to
provide, according to their means for the religious and moral intellectual,
physical and social education of their children, it inferentially gives those
who have married and are living together a constitutional right to the custody
of their children."[185]

180. See p. 4 of judgement.
181. See p. 1 of judgement.
182. See p. 2 of judgement.
183. See p. 4 of judgement.
184. (1978) 113 I.L.T.R. 25 (S.C.).
185. *Ibid.* at p. 57.

In the same case Henchy J. stated

"The Constitution does not pronounce specifically on rights of custody, but it is necessarily inherent in the (constitutional) provisions I have cited that in the case of children whose parents were or have become married, the primary right to custody is vested in the parents."[186]

In *G. v. An Bord Uchtála* the majority held that the natural mother of an illegitimate child has a constitutional right to the custody of her child which falls to be protected under Article 40.3. Both Henchy J. and Kenny J. dissented from this finding and denied that the mother of an illegitimate child has any such constitutional right. It is submitted, however, that it is clear that all members of the Supreme Court in this case were of the view that the parents of a legitimate child have such a constitutional right arising under Article 42 of the Constitution. This right is not, however, an absolute right. Walsh J., emphasising that the rights of both legitimate and illegitimate children are also protected by the Constitution, stated

"There is nothing in the Constitution to indicate that in cases of conflict the rights of the parent are always to be given primacy."[187]

Further on in his judgement he continued

"Where the Guardianship of Infants Act, 1964 defines 'welfare' it is, as has been previously remarked in other cases, following the wording of the Constitution itself. It is also to be borne in mind that some inalienable rights are absolutely inalienable while others are relatively inalienable."[188]

In none of the above cases was the question of the constitutionality of section 3 an issue. The various judicial statements made merely confirmed that a question mark hangs over the constitutionality of the section and are illustrative of conflicting judicial approaches to the application of the welfare principle in the determination of disputes between parents and strangers. The statements are also clearly indicative of some judicial confusion as to the historical development of the law as to custody. In *In re J.* it is clear that the court held the view that prior to 1964, in the absence of fault on the part of parents, parental rights could not be curtailed and that a parent was automatically entitled to custody of his legitimate child unless he had done something culpable or committed some wrong in relation to the child. This, however, is not so. It is clear from decided cases that since the Judicature Act, 1877, the courts have deprived parents of custody when to do so has been in the interests of the child's welfare, even when the parent has not been culpable or guilty of any misconduct. On the other hand, contrary to the view expressed by Kenny J. in *J. v. D.*, it is also clear that in the absence of parental fault, the courts regarded it as *prima facie* in the interests of a child's welfare for it to be in its parents' custody.[189] In essence, the courts took the view, that a child should be in its parents' custody unless judicially satisfied that the welfare of the child required that the wishes of the parents be overruled.[190]

---

186. *Ibid.*, at p. 51.
187. *Ibid.*, at p. 47.
188. *Ibid.*, at p. 48. See also *O'N. v. O'B. and Ors.*, *supra*, where Finlay P. stated that in deciding a dispute as to custody between a mother and grandparents "I can only do so looking at the problem from the dominant view of the welfare of the child" (p. 18 of judgement).
189. See *R. v. Gyngall*, *supra*; *In re O'Hara, an Infant*, *supra*; *State (Williams) v. Markey*, *supra*; *In re Kindersley, an Infant*, *supra*; See also *J. v. C.* [1970] A.C. 668; [1969] 2 W.L.R. 540 (H.L.) in particular the judgement of Lord MacDermott. The learned judge's summary of the law was subsequently approved of in *E.K. v. M.K.* (July 1974), unreported, (S.C.) and *MacD. v. MacD.* (April 1979), unreported, (S.C.).
190. See *B. v. B.* [1975] I.R. 54 (S.C.) judgement of Walsh J. at p. 62.

In the first edition of this book it was contended that a statutory requirement that a child's welfare be regarded as the paramount consideration in the determination of custody disputes between parents and strangers is not contrary to but in accord with the provisions of the Constitution. It was noted that the Supreme Court had rejected the contention that the rights of parents are absolute rights and that it had pointed out that the Constitution recognised that a child has natural and imprescriptible rights of his own.[191] It was also noted that the inalienable and imprescriptible rights of the family under Article 41 attach to each member of the family, including the children.[192] It was submitted that the only way that the "inalienable and imprescriptible" (Art. 41) and "natural and imprescriptible" (Art. 42.5) rights of the child can be protected, a child possessing a different "capacity, physical . . . moral and . . . social function (Art. 40.1) to that of his parents, is by the courts regarding the welfare of the child as the paramount consideration in all disputes as to its custody. In conclusion it was argued that under Art. 40.3 one of the personal rights that arise from "the Christian and democratic nature of the State"[193] is the personal right of a child to have his welfare regarded as the paramount consideration in any court determination of a dispute as to custody.

In *P.W.* v. *A.W. and Ors.*[194] the constitutionality of section 3 finally arose for direct consideration. The facts of the case were found by the court to be as follows: The husband (P.W.) and wife (A.W.) had married in July, 1963, and had four children. Since 1971 the wife had been in ill health, primarily due to a psychiatric illness and had required both in-patient and out-patient hospital treatment. Shortly after the fourth child's birth, in March, 1974, due to A.W.'s inability to cope, the child went to live with the husband's sister (M.) and her husband. Originally, this was a temporary arrangement and the intention was that the child would return to reside with A.W. when she had sufficiently recovered her health. However, A.W. continued to be unwell and when the child was a few months old she "gave" the child to M. permanently. The child then continued to reside with M. In 1976 P.W. and A.W. separated. In November, 1976, the High Court granted A.W. custody of the three eldest children and granted custody of the youngest child to M. In December, 1977, the court provided for A.W.'s access to the child and the court was advised by her counsel that she wanted a further hearing relating to the child's custody. This hearing took place in April, 1978, but no judgement was delivered, the court indicating that it wished to seek further assistance from a child psychiatrist who had given evidence at the hearing. The child continued to reside with M. and further access arrangements were made. The case came on for a final hearing in November, 1979. By that date the child was 5½ years of age and the court found that she regarded M. and her husband as her parents.

Ellis J., holding that the child's welfare required that it remain in the custody of M., stated

"There is no natural or prima facie right of a parent to custody of his or her children but . . . there is a rule of prudence that in most cases the best

---

191. In addition to the judgements already referred to in this section see judgement of O'Sullivan C.J. in *In re Frost, Infants* [1947] I.R. 3 at p. 28. See also *Landers v. A.G.* (1973) 109 I.L.T.R. 1 (H.C.).
192. *The State (Nicolaou)* v. *An Bord Uchtála & A.-G.* [1966] I.R. 567 (S.C.); *In re J. supra; McGee v. A.G.* [1974] I.R. 284; (1973) 109 I.L.T.R. 29, (S.C.). For the rights that the courts have enunciated as vesting in children, see further p. 4, 8-9, 196-97, 241-2, 358-61.
193. See *Ryan v. A.G.* [1965] I.R. 294 (H.C., S.C.); *O'Brien (an Infant)* v. *Keogh* [1972] I.R. 144 (S.C.); *Landers v. A.G., supra*.
194. (April 1980), unreported, (H.C.).

place for a child is with its parents, but that there can be circumstances varying with each case, (not necessarily amounting to intentional misconduct or misbehaviour) to which valid objection can be taken in the interests of the welfare of a child, whereby the parent can lose custody of the child not only to another contending parent but to a stranger . . . [195] A removal now from the home and environment which Mr. and Mrs. M. have been providing for (the child) continuously since she was a few weeks old baby and the sundering of the relationships and the continuity which existed and had been built up between (the child) and M. over these most formative years in a mother and child existence would in my view be prejudicial to her welfare as would placing her in the changed custody of A.W. where no such mother and child relationship has existed in the true sense and where she would be exposed to and endangered by physical and emotional risks and potential if not actually present domestic conflicts . . . (this child) has now a sense of security and a feeling of protection with the Ms. which she would lose if given to A.W."[196]

The learned judge then went on to consider the submission made on behalf of the wife that under the Constitution she was entitled to be granted custody of her child even if the child's welfare under section 3 requires that she should remain in the custody of M. He also dealt with the further submissions that

(i)   in so far as section 3 impinged on A.W.'s constitutional rights it was incompatible with and repugnant to the Constitution;

(ii) a stranger can only take the place of parents in the exceptional cases referred to in Art. 42.5 of the Constitution where the parents for physical or moral reasons failed in their duty towards their children;

(iii) that A.W. and her child formed part of a family unit under the Constitution, that the natural and imprescriptible rights of the child can only be found within the inalienable rights of the family which rights emanate from the same source and cannot be in conflict and that therefore the rights of the family should prevail by the child being returned to it.

Due to the importance of the constitutional issues involved, it is intended to quote in extenso from the judgement of Ellis J. Dealing with the submissions made on behalf of A.W., he stated

"In my opinion, I am not necessarily concerned with nor do I have to determine an issue of conflicting constitutional rights either as between (the child) and her mother A.W. or between (the child) in the custody of M. and the constitutional recognition of the family . . . I am concerned to protect and uphold the infant's constitutional rights. In finding this can best be achieved in the custody of M. I do not think I am trespassing on the constitutional rights of A.W. or on the W. family. As already mentioned in the judgement of Walsh J. in *G. v. An Bord Uchtála*, there is nothing in the Constitution to indicate that in cases of apparent or alleged conflict the rights of a parent are always to be given primacy . . . the natural (and constitutional) rights of A.W. in respect of (the child) are preserved by her

---

195. See p. 17 of judgement.
196. See p. 43 of judgement. There was evidence given in the proceedings of disagreements occurring on a number of occasions between the husband and the wife when the husband exercised his rights of access to the three children in the custody of the wife.

retention of her natural and statutory rights as (the child's) guardian, even if custody is given to M. . . .

If, however, there is a conflict between the constitutional rights of a legitimate child and the prima facie constitutional right of its mother to its custody I am of opinion that the infant's rights which are to be determined by regard to what is required for its welfare should prevail, even if its welfare is to be found in the custody of a "stranger" if for good and justifiable reason, to be ascertained on the facts and in the circumstances of any particular case, valid objection can be taken to the mother's inability to provide for her child's welfare, either emanating from the mother herself or for reasons connected with the child's welfare and not necessarily confined to failure by the parents (here A.W.) of their duty towards their children for physical or moral reasons, whereby the parents or as here the mother's custody would or could not vindicate, protect or be compatible with the child's constitutional rights including its welfare.

Having regard to these conclusions I do not think it necessary for me to make a finding under Art. 42.5 of the Constitution. If, however, such a finding may be regarded as necessary or material to the issues involved I hold that this is an exceptional case. I also hold that in so far as it was or is the duty of the parents (and in the circumstances of this case, the duty of A.W.) to provide for the requirements of (the child) specified in Art. 42.1 or generally, that A.W. has failed in such for physical reasons. In my view the word physical as used in Art. 42.5 need not include intentional or purposeful reasons and would include reasons of health . . . which have combined to prevent and render her (A.W.) unfit or unable to carry out her required duty or duties towards (the child) . . ."

The learned judge then referred to the similarity in the wording of Art. 42.1 of the Constitution when compared to the definition of "welfare" in section 2 of the 1964 Act and continued

"Such similarity accords with the view that the welfare of the child under the Act was intended to be of similar paramount consideration under the Constitution."

He concluded stating

"Finally . . . it was held in *In Re Frost Infants* . . . that the rights of parents are not absolute rights and that a child also had natural and imprescriptible rights of its own and further that to afford protection to the rights of the child the court regarded itself as having jurisdiction to control the exercise of parental rights. In my opinion, the inalienable and imprescriptible rights of the family under Art. 41 of the Constitution attach to each member of a family including the children. Therefore, in my view, the only way the "inalienable and imprescriptible" and "natural and imprescriptible" rights of the child can be protected is by the courts treating the welfare of the child as the paramount consideration in all disputes as to its custody, including disputes between a parent and a stranger. I take the view also that the child has the personal right to have its welfare regarded as the paramount consideration in any such dispute as to its custody under Art. 40.3 and that this right of the infant can additionally arise from "the Christian and democratic nature of the State."[197]

197. See pp. 69—74 of judgement.

He concluded directing that the child should remain in the custody of M.

In essence, the court held that section 3 of the 1964 Act, in so far as it requires the court to regard the welfare of a legitimate child as the first and paramount consideration in custody disputes between parents and strangers, is not unconstitutional. This decision has been appealed to the Supreme Court but at the time of writing the appeal has not been heard or determined.

WARDS OF COURT

The jurisdiction over wards of court is vested in the President of the High Court and in the Circuit Court.[198] This jurisdiction historically originates in the feudal obligation of the Soveriegn, as *parens patriae*, to protect the person and property of his subjects particularly those unable to look after themselves, including infants or minors. The courts' jurisdiction to make a minor a ward of court is in the majority of instances invoked where it is necessary to protect the property interests of the minor. Today, if parties wish to make use of the wardship jurisdiction and a minor has no proprietory interest, it is common to settle a small sum, e.g. £50 on the minor in order to commence proceedings. In practice, however, minors have been taken into wardship without the use of this expedient[199] and the President of the High Court has stated that he is satisfied that he has proper jurisdiction to take a minor into wardship when no property matter is involved, if to do so is in the interests of the minor's welfare.[200]

Wardship proceedings differ from proceedings under the Guardianship of Infants Act, 1964, in that they can be commenced by a third party even though the parents or guardians of a child are alive. Proceedings under the Act of 1964 can be initiated by a third party only if a child has no guardian or if a deceased parent or guardian has failed to appoint a testamentary guardian.[201] It is by bringing wardship proceedings that a third party can seek custody of a child against a parent,[202] or seek to obtain protection for a child against the actions of a parent.[203] Alternatively a parent seeking to regain custody from a third

---

198. Courts (Supplemental Provisions) Act, 1961, Sect. 9 (The President may assign another judge of the High Court to exercise the jurisdiction on his behalf). See also R.S.C. (S.I. No. 72 of 1962) Order 65.
 The Circuit Court has jurisdiction in proceedings for the wardship of infants and the care of infants' estates where the property (a) in so far as it consists of personality does not exceed £5,000 in value; (b) in so far as it consists of land does not exceed the ratable valuation of £100—Courts (Supplemental Provisions) Act, 1961, Sect. 22 (1) as amended by Courts Act, 1971, Sect. 2 (1). See Third Schedule, Ref. No. 24 of the 1961 Act.
199. See, for example, *Re J.L. (A Minor)* (March 1978), unreported (Finlay P., H.C.). See also *In re Meades Minors*, (1871) I.R. 5 Eq. 98 (Ch. L.C.) at p. 114 where it is stated that exercise of the wardship jurisdiction is not dependent on the existence of property. See further T.W. Bell and R. Armstrong, *Minor Matters* (Dublin 1886) at p. 2.
200. Stated after delivering his written judgement in *Re Lynch (A Minor)*, *supra*. Unfortunately this statement is not contained in the judgement.
201. See Sect. 8 of the 1964 Act. A third party or non-guardian cannot in any circumstances issue proceedings under Sect. 11 of the 1964 Act.
202. See *Re J.L. (A Minor)*, *supra*. See also *Re Farrell (Minors)*, Orders dated October 1977 and January 1978; (Gannon J., H.C.) *Re Williams (Minors)*, order dated August 1978. (D'Arcy J., H.C.). No written judgements were delivered in the last two mentioned cases. In the former, two children were made wards of court although the maternal grandmother and aunt who made the application failed to obtain custody of them. The court granted joint custody to their mother with another aunt who was not originally a party to the proceedings. In the latter case, on the application of Leeds City Council 3 children who had been kidnapped by their mother and brought over to Dublin were made wards of the Irish High Court and subsequently returned to England. Prior to the Irish proceedings, the English Courts had placed the children in the care of the City Council.
203. In recent English case *Re D. (a minor)* [1976] Fam. 185 (Fam. D.) in a novel application a mentally retarded child of 13 years was made a ward of court on the application

party can commence proceedings under section 11 of the 1964 Act or bring Habeas Corpus proceedings. Parents and guardians of a minor may of course themselves commence wardship proceedings in various circumstances.

When a minor is made a ward of court all matters affecting the ward's upbringing become the responsibility of the court. The court may determine in whose care and custody the minor should be placed, the manner in which his property should be managed, and may make orders relating to the residence, education and holidays of the minor.[204] The court may also order maintenance to be payed for the benefit of the minor out of funds held on his behalf.[205] Further, the minor may not marry without the consent of the court.

The paramount consideration in all questions brought before the court is the ward's welfare.[206] The court exercises a continuing supervisory function and any person in whose custody the ward is placed must comply with the directions of the court. The power of the court to give directions on matters affecting a ward's welfare is unfettered by statute and has been held to be more extensive and flexible than that conferred by the Guardianship of Infants Act, 1964.[207]

Upon a minor attaining 21 years of age the court will make an order of discharge from wardship. Failure to comply with an order of the court constitutes contempt of court and may result in the committal to prison of the person held in contempt.[208] In the case of such behaviour on the part of a person granted custody of the ward it can also result in the loss of such custody. The court may also enforce its orders by injunction.

Circumstances in which Wardship Jurisdiction may be used

I Where parents seek to prevent a teenage son or daughter from marrying,[209] leaving home, or associating with undesirable persons, they may apply to have him/her made a ward of court.

II If a child is placed with or is living with relations, foster parents, potential adopters or any other persons who wish to retain custody of the child, contrary to the wishes of the natural parent or parents, the former may apply for a custody order under the wardship jurisdiction.[210]

---

of a third party so as to prevent her mother having a sterilisation operation carried out on her. For a discussion of this case see A.L. Polak–"Sterilisation of a minor", (1976), 6 Fam. Law. 37.

204. See *In re Westby, Minors*, (No. 2) [1934] I.R. 311, (S.C.); *Re J.L. (A Minor)* *supra*. See also *In re Gills' Minors*, (1891) 27 L.R.Ir. 129 (Ch. L.C.)–a female infant ward of court should not become a novice in a convent without the consent of the court.

205. See for example in *in re Birch's Trusts* (1885) 15 L.R. Ir. 380 (Ch. M.R.); *In the Matter of R.J. Duddy & A.M. Duddy, Minors*, [1925] 1 I.R. 196, (C.J.).

206. Guardianship of Infants Act, 1964, Sect. 3. See *J. v. C.* [1970] A.C. 668 (H.L.); *Re H. (A Minor) (Wardship Jurisdiction)* [1978] Fam. 65, (C.A.).

207. See *In the Matter of J.S., an Infant* (1977) 111 I.L.T.R. 146 (Finlay P., H.C.); *Re J.L. (A Minor)*, *supra*.

208. See *In re McLorinan, a Minor*, [1935] I.R. 373 (S.C.)–The court may not punish a ward in contempt by placing restrictions on her rights of ownership of property to which she is entitled upon discharge from wardship.

209. A teenager of course requires parental consent to marry unless a court order is obtained dispensing with consent–Marriages Act, 1972, Sect. 7; where the marriage of a ward takes place without the court's consent the parties to the marriage and any person who helps to bring about the marriage commits contempt of court–see *In Re H.'s settlement H. v. H.* [1909], 2 Ch. 260 (Ch. Div.).

210. See *Re J.L. (A Minor)*, *supra*. In this case the court took a child of eight and a half years into wardship and made the child's mother and a Miss M. joint guardians of the person of the child. The application had been made by F., a widower, whose household consisted of three sons and Miss M., who looked after the family and assisted F. in his business. The child had resided in F.'s household since the age of fifteen months. The

III A Health Board, Local Authority or other such agency may apply to have a child whose welfare is threatened made a ward of court[211] and seek orders enabling it to have the child assessed or supervised in its place of residence or taken into care.

IV To restrict the removal of a minor from the jurisdiction[212] or to have a minor returned to the jurisdiction from where he was brought. Thus, the wardship jurisdiction may be invoked by an estranged spouse upon the "kidnapping" of a child by the other spouse.[213] If it is in the best interests of a ward of the Irish Court to leave this jurisdiction, permission will be granted by the court.[214]

V To determine a dispute between spouses as to their child's upbringing.[215] It is however more appropriate normally to use the provisions of section 11 of the Act of 1964 for this purpose.

VI The most common circumstance in which a minor is made a ward is where it is thought desirable to obtain independent protection for a minor's property interests.[216]

mother originally resided in F.'s home but had not done so for almost four years prior to these proceedings. At the date of the proceedings, the child was under the belief that Miss M. was her mother and she had no relationship with the real mother. The court placed the child in the custody of Miss M. See further *J. v. C. supra.*

211. See *Williams (Minors) supra*, footnote 202. In this case, prior to the children being returned to Leeds, the court placed them under the care of the Eastern Health Board.

212. See *The State (K.M. and R.D.) v. The Minister for Foreign Affairs and Ors.* [1979] I.R. 73 (H.C.) where the constitutional "Right to Travel" was enunciated. It is clear from this judgement that if parents wish a child to travel outside the jurisdiction, the child has a constitutional right to a passport and if the Dept. of Foreign Affairs and the Passport Office believe that it is contrary to the interests of the child to issue a passport, it must bring wardship proceedings and prove its case. See further p. 114-115 *ante*.

213. For example, see the cases cited in footnote 115, *supra*.

214. *In re Westby, Minors, supra*, see also the English case of *Re R, a Minor* (1974), 4 Fam. Law 153; see also *In re Kindersley*, [1944] I.R. 111; (1943), 78 I.L.T.R. 159, (S.C.). This case concerned a Habeas Corpus application on behalf of the father to have his son taken out of his mother's custody and sent to a school in England, i.e. sent outside the jurisdiction. The boy had previously been made a ward of court in England.

215. See *In re May, Minors* (1957), 92 I.L.T.R. 1, (H.C.).

216. See *In the Matter of J.S., an Infant, supra*, in which Finlay P. held that if directions of the court are sought concerning the estates or assets of minors, as a general rule such directions should be sought by use of the wardship procedure. Such applications should only be made under Section 11 (1) of the Guardianship of Infants Act, 1964, when very few court applications are necessary and "where a fixed and final straightforward scheme not requiring variations and not requiring the continued supervision of the court is appropriate in the interests of the children". See further *In re Meade* [1971] I.R. 327 (H.C.).

THE CHILDREN ACT, 1908, AND RELATED LEGISLATION

It is not within the scope of this book to give a comprehensive account of the law relating to children. It is however intended to briefly examine circumstances other than those already discussed in which a parent may be deprived of the custody of his or her child. As will be seen in the pages that follow, this may happen either when a child is charged with or is found guilty of a criminal offence or is held to be in need of care and attention.

The Children Act, 1908, is at the foundation of the statutory provisions discussed in this section. Other relevant legislative enactments are the Children Acts, 1934, 41, the Children (Amendment) Acts, 1949 and 57, the Health Act, 1953, the School Attendance Acts, 1926-67.

For the purposes of the Children Acts, 1908 to 1957 a child is defined as a person under the age of 15 years and a young person as a person who is 15 years or upwards and under the age of 17 years.[1] Reference to a child or young person in the following pages thus refers to persons defined as such under the above legislation unless otherwise indicated.

Criminal liability[2]

A child may be held criminally responsible for his acts from the age of seven. Under common law there is an irrebuttable presumption that a child below that age cannot commit a criminal offence, in that such a young child could not distinguish between right and wrong. From the age of seven to 14 years there is a rebuttable presumption of innocence,[3] i.e. a presumption that a child lacks

1. Children Act, 1908, Sect. 131 as amended by the Children Act, 1941, Sect. 29.
2. Under the Summary Jurisdiction over Children (Ireland) Act, 1884, as amended by the Children Act, 1941, Sect. 28, a child or young person charged with an indictable offence other than homicide may be dealt with by a court of summary jurisdiction, if the parent or guardian does not object. The court of summary jurisdiction that hears such cases is the District Court, sitting as a juvenile or children's court (see p. 14). In practice the great majority of criminal charges whether of a minor or serious nature, brought against children are dealt with by the District Courts. Although a child has a right to a jury trial for a non-minor offence—(see Articles 38.2 and 38.5 of the Constitution) in practice the number that opt for jury trial is small. See further footnote 84 below.
3. See cases cited in footnote 5 below. See further *Monagle v. Donegal Co. Council* [1961], Ir. Jur. Rep. 37, (H.C.)—"The law does not presume children under the age of seven to be responsible for their acts and there is a rebuttable presumption that children under fourteen years are not so responsible" per Murnaghan J. at p. 39. See also *Goodbody v. The Mayor of Waterford* [1954], Ir. Jur. Rep. 39, (H.C.); J.F. Crotty, *Practice and Procedure in the District Court* (Cork University Press, Cork 1960), p. 44.

However in recent years a number of District Justices have accepted the contention that it applies until a child's fifteenth birthday. See *Reformatory and Industrial Schools Systems Report*, (The Kennedy Report), (Stationery Office, Dublin 1970), p. 68 where the presumption is said to apply to children "from the age of seven to fifteen". See also E. Stewart, "Young Offenders: Children and the Criminal Law" (1976) 110 I.L.T. & S.J. pp. 279, 286, 291, 297, 303, at p. 292 where it is also stated that the presumption applies from "the age of seven years to fifteen years". The Children Act, 1941, Sect. 28 is relied upon to support this contention. However, that provision merely amends the definition of child for the purposes of the Summary Jurisdiction Over Children (Ireland) Act, 1884. The latter Act says nothing about the age of criminal responsibility.

criminal capacity or is *doli incapax*.[4] To override this presumption it must be established that at the time of committing the act charged, the child knew it was wrong.[5] Unfortunately, in practice the necessity to prove such knowledge is often ignored.

The decided cases are unclear as to the exact meaning of "knowledge of wrongfulness".[6] Does the requirement of knowledge of wrong refer to legal wrong or moral wrong; or may a child be convicted if he knew that his act belonged to either class of wrong? No definite answer has yet been given by the courts to this question.

It has been held that in order to prove the requisite knowledge, evidence that the child committed the act in question is not sufficient.[7] Evidence of a child's home background, however, may determine the matter. Thus, proof that a boy, nearly nine years of age, came from a respectable home and had been properly brought up was held sufficient to establish knowledge of wrongfulness in respect of a charge of breaking and entering.[8] Evidence that an eight year old upon being accused of "stealing" a cash box and money, admitted it, has also been held to rebut the presumption.[9] In this case, evidence as to a child's "home background and all his circumstances" was said to be "highly material to the question of whether a child knows what he is doing is wrong and should be admitted in spite of the risk that it will disclose information highly prejudicial to him".[10] Moreover, in a recent case, the English Court of Appeal held that evidence of previous convictions may be given provided such evidence is relevant to the issue of the child's capacity to know good from evil.[11] However, such evidence may only be introduced if it has a bearing on the latter issue. If it does not, it will generally be excluded due to the prejudicial effect of such evidence. Finally, a boy under 14 years of age cannot be found guilty of rape or certain other sexual offences, there being an irrebuttable legal presumption that all boys under that age are physically incapable of committing such offences.[12]

---

4. For criticism of the use of the phrase *doli incapax* see G.L. Williams, "The Criminal Responsibility of Children", 1954 Crim. L.R. 493. The author states that the use of this phrase suggests that proof of fraud or intention on the part of a child is sufficient to rebut the presumption. However, a child may intend to do the act in question, without knowing that it is wrong. It is knowledge by a child of the wrongfulness of his act that is required to rebut the presumption.

5. *R. v. Owen* (1830), 4 Car. & P. 236; 172 E.R. 685 *(Nisi Prius); R. v. Manley* (1844), 1 Cox C.C. 104 (Assizes); *R. v. Smith* [1845] 1 Cox C.C. 260, 393 (Assizes). See also *R. v. Vamplew* (1862) 3F & F. 520; 176 E.R. 234 *(Nisi Prius); R. v. Kershaw* (1902), 18 T.L.R. 357 (Assizes); *R. v. Gorrie* (1918), 183, J.P. 136, *W. (An Infant) v. Simpson* [1967], Crim. L.R. 360, (Q.B.D.); *B. v. R.* (1960) 44 Cr. App. Rep. l., sub nom. *X v. X.* [1958] Crim. L.R. 805, (Q.B.D.); *F. v. Padwick* [1959] Crim. L.R. 439 (Q.B.D.). (The minimum age at which a child could be convicted of an offence was raised in England to 8 in 1933 and to 10 in 1963).

6. See G.L. Williams, *supra.* See also N. Osborough, "Rebutting The Presumption of Doli Incapax" (1975) 10 I.J. (n.s.) 48.

7. *R. v. Owen, supra; R. v. Smith, supra; R. v. Kershaw, supra.*

8. *B. v. R., supra.*

9. *F. v. Padwick, supra.*

10. *Ibid.*, at p. 440.

11. *R. v. B.* [1979] 3 All E.R. 460 (C.A.). See also J.S. Fisher, "Rebutting the Presumption of a Child's Criminal Incapacity" (1980) 130 N.L.J. 752.

12. See e.g. *R. v. Groombridge* (1836), 7 Car. and P. 582; 173 E.R. 256 *(Nisi Prius); R. v. Brimilow* (1840), 2 Mood. 122; 169 E.R. 49 (Crown Cases); *R. v. Eldershaw* (1828), 3 Car. & P. 396; 172 E.R. 472, (Assizes); *R. v. Philips*, (1839), 8 Car. & P. 736; 173 E.R. 695, *(Nisi Prius); R. v. Waite* [1892], 2 Q.B. 600, (C.C.R.). Although this rule rests on the principle that such a young child is physically incapable of committing a sexual offence, no evidence is admissable to prove that the particular child charged was capable—*R. v. Philips, supra; R. v. Jordan* (1838), 9 Car. & P. 118; 173 E.R. 765, *(Nisi Prius); R. v. Waite, supra.* However he may be convicted of indecent assault—*R. v. Williams* [1893], 1 Q.B. 32, (C.C.R.).

Pre-trial detention

A child or young person charged with an offence may be released on bail pending trial or held in custody.[13] The relevant legislation is contained in Part V of the Act of 1908. Section 94[14] provides that

"Where a person apparently under the age of seventeen years is apprehended with or without warrant, and cannot be brought forthwith before a court of summary jurisdiction, a superintendent or inspector of police, or other officer of police of equal or superior rank or the officer in charge of the police station to which such person is brought, shall inquire into the case and may in any case, and shall

(a) unless the charge is one of homicide or other grave crime; or

(b) unless it is necessary in the interest of such person to remove him from association with any reputed criminal or prostitute; or

(c) unless the officer has reason to believe that the release of such person would defeat the end of justice,

release such person on a recognizance, with or without sureties, for such an amount as will, in the opinion of the officer, secure the attendance of such person upon the hearing of the charge, being entered into by him or by his parent or guardian".

Where a person under 17 is not released under the above provision he must be held in a place of detention provided under Part V of the Act[15]

"until he can be brought before a court of summary jurisdiction, unless the officer certifies—

(a) that it is impracticable to do so; or

(b) that he is of so unruly a character that he cannot be safely so detained; or

(c) that by reason of his state of health or of his mental or bodily condition it is advisable so to detain him;

and the certificate shall be produced to the court before which the person is brought".[16]

Section 97 provides that

"(1) A court of summary jurisdiction, on remanding or committing for trial a child or young person who is not released on bail, shall instead of committing him to prison, commit him to custody in a place of detention provided under this Part of this Act and named in the commitment, to be there detained for the period for which he is remanded or until he is thence delivered in due course of law:

Provided that in the case of a young person it shall not be obligatory on the court so to commit him if the court certifies that he is of so unruly a character that he cannot be safely so committed, or that he is of so depraved a character that he is not a fit person to be so detained.

---

13. As for the general circumstances in which bail may be refused see *People (A.G.) v. O'Callaghan* [1966], I.R. 501, (S.C.).
14. As amended by the Children Act, 1941, Sect. 24.
15. See Children Act, 1908, Sect. 108. There is, at the date of writing, only one place of detention in Ireland, St. Laurence's School in Finglas, Dublin.
16. Children Act, 1908, Sect. 95, as amended by Children Act, 1941, Sect. 25.

(2) A commitment under this section may be varied or, in the case of a young person who proves to be of so unruly a character that he cannot be safely detained in such custody, or to be of so depraved a character that he is not a fit person to be so detained, revoked by any court of summary jurisdiction acting in or for the place in or for which the court which made the order acted, and if it is so revoked the young person may be committed to prison".[17]

Consequences of conviction[18]

A child cannot be sentenced to imprisonment and neither a child nor a young person can be sentenced to death or penal servitude.[19] If a child or young person is convicted of an offence punishable with penal servitude and if the court considers that the imposition of a period of detention is the only suitable punishment to impose, it may commit the child or young person to a place of detention for such term as may be specified in the order but in no case exceeding one month.[20] A young person can only be imprisoned for the commission of an offence if the court certifies that he is of so unruly a character that he cannot be detained in a place of detention, or that he is so depraved a character that he is not a fit person to be so detained.

In the *State (Hanley)* v. *Governor of Mountjoy Prison*[21] the court certified that the applicant was of so unruly a character that he could not be detained in a place of detention in safety, and he was sentenced to one month's imprisonment in Mountjoy Prison. No express evidence was adduced to show unruly character and at the time of conviction no place for detention after sentence[22] existed for the Dublin Metropolitan District in which the applicant had been tried.[23] On

17. See the *State (Ward and others)* v. *Superintendent of the Bridewell Garda Station, Irish Times* 24th & 25th Jan. 1975. The High Court granted an order of Habeas Corpus in respect of six children between the ages of 9 and 13 who had been remanded in custody in the Bridewell Garda Station in Dublin. The Bridewell was not a scheduled place of detention as provided under Part V of the Act of 1908 and there was no evidence of the children being unruly. Consequently, their detention was unlawful. No order was made in relation to two other children in respect of whom the application was also made, as they had been detained in St. Lawrence's School in Finglas, which was a place of detention provided under Sect. 108 for the purpose of detaining children and young persons on remand. See also *The State (fifteen year old girl)* v. *Deputy Governor of Mountjoy Prison, Irish Times* 27th Feb. 1975. An order of Habeas Corpus was granted in the High Court in respect of a fifteen year old girl held in Mountjoy Prison on remand.

18. It is intended here to briefly look at the consequences of the conviction of children under 16. A child over 17 may be sentenced in the same manner as an adult whilst a child of 16 years or over may also be detained in St. Patrick's Institution or Shanganagh Castle. For a full discussion of the history of, and the law applicable to these institutions see N. Osborough, *Borstal in Ireland*, (I.P.A., Dublin 1975).

A person under 16 cannot be sent to St. Patrick's—see (*Two Limerick girls*) v. *Limerick Circuit Court Judge*. The *Irish Times* 23rd Jan. 1975—The High Court held an order sentencing a girl under 16 to St. Patrick's Institution to be invalid. See also D.C. Mitchell, A Report on the Law and Procedure Regarding the Prosecution and Disposal of Youthful Offenders (Commissioned by the Director of Public Prosecutions, Dublin, 1977), p. 63—67. See further *The People v. Howard, Irish Times*, 1 April 1977, where the Court of Criminal Appeal in confirming a sentence of ten years penal servitude imposed on the defendant held that in relation to determining sentence, the relevant age was the defendant's age at the date of sentence and not at the date of the commission of the offence. The defendant was seventeen years old when sentenced.

19. Children's Act, 1908, Sect. 103 and 102(1) and (2). See also the *State (O)* v. *O'Brien* [1973] I.R. 50, (S.C.).

20. Children Act, 1908, Sect. 106.

21. (1974) 108 I.L.T.R. 102, (H.C.).

22. As envisaged under the Children Act, 1908, Sect. 108.

23. St. Laurence's in Finglas was at that time only a place of detention for the purpose of detaining young persons on remand. See footnotes 17 *supra* and 27 *infra*.

an application for Habeas Corpus, it was held by Finlay J. that since the crimes to which the applicant pleaded guilty involved, in part, crimes of violence, this in itself amounted to some evidence of unruly character. However, he granted the application on the ground that a District Justice could not certify a person as being unsuitable to detain in a place of detention when no such place existed.

In the later case of the State (Holland) v. District Justice Kennedy and Another,[24] Hamilton J., in the High Court, making absolute a conditional order of Certiorari stated that

> "It is the duty of the Courts to protect the rights of citizens and in particular the rights of 'young persons' within the meaning of the Children's Act, 1908 . . . very definite and specific evidence of the unruly nature of the general character of a convicted young person would be necessary before he was committed to prison rather than to a place of detention . . . the Court must conduct an enquiry as to the general character of the convicted young person and the convicted young person should have the right to challenge and rebut any evidence given".[25]

As no such inquiry had been made by the District Justice, an order made by her certifying the applicant to be of so unruly character that he could not be detained in a place of detention and sentencing him to one month's imprisonment in Mountjoy Prison, was quashed. The Supreme Court, on appeal, affirmed the decision of Hamilton J. The Court held that the word "character" means "nature or disposition". Henchy J. stated that the relevant provision of the 1908 Act requires that a District Justice must be satisfied that a young person

> "is of so unruly a character (not that he has been so unruly) that he cannot be (not that he ought not to be) detained in the provided place of detention".[26]

Thus, proof of the committal of a particular offence is not sufficient by itself. The court must fully examine the young person's antecedents and behavioural pattern in so far as that is possible. The mere conviction of Holland for assault without further enquiries being made as to his character was not sufficient to support the ruling of the District Justice.[27]

---

24. [1977] I.R. 193 (H.C., S.C.).
25. Ibid., at pp. 197, 198.
26. Ibid., at p. 200.
27. The ground on which the applicant was successful in Hanly's case could not be relied on by Holland as by the time the District Justice made her order St. Laurence's in Finglas had been designated as a place of detention for young persons after sentence. On the question of the imprisonment of young persons see also Sect. 123 (1) of the 1908 Act as amended by Sect. 27 of the 1941 Act which provides
> "Where a person whether charged with an offence or not is brought before any Court otherwise than for the purpose of giving evidence and it appears to the Court that he is a child or young person the Court shall make due enquiry as to the age of that person and for that purpose shall take such evidence as may be forthcoming at the hearing of the case but an order or judgement of the Court shall not be invalidated by any subsequent proof that the age of that person has not been correctly stated to the Court and the age presumed or declared by the Court to be the age of the person so brought before it shall for the purposes of this Act be deemed to be the true age of that person and where it appears to the Court that the person so brought before it is of the age of 17 years or upwards the person shall for the purposes of this Act be deemed not to be a child or young person".
In the State (Kenny) v. D.J. O'hUadhaigh [1979] I.R. 1 (H.C.), Finlay P. made absolute a conditional order of Certiorari quashing three District Court convictions for which the applicant had been sentenced to six months imprisonment. The applicant should have been dealt with under the Children Acts as she was only fifteen at the date of the District Court hearing, but she had told the District Justice and the arresting guard that she was 18 years of age and had been treated as an adult. No inquiry as to her age had been made when she was

In *The State* (*Donohue*) v. *District Justice Kennedy*[28] the High Court again made absolute a conditional order of certiorari quashing an order of the District Justice certifying that the applicant, who was fifteen years of age, was a person of unruly character and remanding him in custody in Mountjoy Prison. At the date when the district court order was made there was no sworn evidence given to the court of unruly behaviour, the District Justice basing her decision on an assessment report received by her from the Child Assessment Centre in St. Laurence's School, Finglas. Neither the applicant nor his solicitor saw or read the report and the solicitor had not objected to the District Justice reading it at the District Court hearing.

Giving judgement in favour of the applicant, Finlay P. stated:

"I have come to the conclusion that a decision to certify a young offender as of unruly character is of the same status as any other decision in a criminal proceeding and as such can only be reached by a court upon sworn evidence properly admissible before it the accused having an opportunity through his solicitor to cross-examine the witnesses deposing to the facts concerned. I am therefore satisfied that the procedure which was operated . . . notwithstanding the willingness of the District Justice to let the report be read by the solicitor for the prosecutor was not in accordance with natural justice and that therefore the order of remand in custody must be quashed."

In the same case Finlay P. referred to the desirability of assessment reports being made available to the courts dealing with young offenders and stated:

"A District Justice should be in a position having received an appropriate report from the Social Workers and other persons concerned at the Remand Centre to obtain as a matter of practicality the consent of the solicitor representing the young offender to the reading of those reports making them available to the solicitor and hearing any submissions or comments he should make upon them. For such a procedure it would be necessary presumably for the reports to be received but not read by the District Justice until he or she has obtained the consent of the solicitor for the young offender. This procedure would in my view not only be lawful but is most desirable so as to prevent the District Justice dealing with young offenders from being deprived of the valuable recommendations and observations of persons concerned with the Children's Centre."

It is clear that in the absence of the necessary consent being forthcoming the court may not read or take into consideration the contents of any such report.

A child under 12 years of age convicted of an offence punishable in the case of an adult by penal servitude or a lesser punishment, may be sent by the court to an industrial school[29] if the court is satisfied "that it is expedient so to deal with him".[30] A child of 12 years or upwards but less than 17 years of age convicted of a similarly punishable offence may be sent to a reformatory school.[31]

giving evidence on oath. Finlay P. stated that the proper construction of the above quoted section imposes "upon the Court an obligation to take some evidence on oath with regard to the question of the age of the person before it". As no such evidence as to age had been obtained the convictions could not stand.
28. (July 1979), unreported, (H.C.).
29. An "industrial school means a school for the industrial training of children, in which children are lodged, clothed and fed, as well as taught"–Children Act, 1908, Sect. 44 (1).
30. Children Act, 1908, Sect. 58 (2).
31. *Ibid.*, Sect. 57 (1) as amended by the Children Act, 1941, Sect. 9 (1). A "reformatory school" means a school for the industrial training of youthful offenders in which youthful offenders are lodged, clothed and fed as well as taught. Children Act, 1908, Sect. 44 (1).

A child who has reached 12 years of age and is under 15 years of age, however, with no previous conviction, may be sent to an industrial school, if having regard to the special circumstances of the case the court is satisfied he should not be sent to a reformatory. The court must be satisfied that "the character and antecedents of the child are such that he will not exercise an evil influence over the other children" in the school and that the manager of the school is willing to accept the child.[32]

A number of alternative options are available to the court other than detaining a child or young person who commits an offence.[33]

(a) ˙The court may (i) dismiss the information or charge;*or*(ii) may discharge the child or young person conditionally on his entering into a recognisance with or without sureties to be of good behaviour and to appear for conviction and sentence when called on at any time during a specified period not exceeding three years. In the case of (ii) the court may impose a further condition that he be placed on probation under the supervision of any person named in the order.[34]

(b) The court may fine the child or young person or order him to pay damages and the costs of the proceedings. The maximum amount a child can be required to pay in respect of each is two pounds.

(c) If a child or young person is charged with any offence for the commission of which a fine, damages, or costs may be imposed, and the court is of opinion that the case would be best met by the imposition of a fine, damages, or costs, whether with or without any other punishment, the court may in any case, and shall if the offender is a child, order that the fine, damages, or costs awarded be paid by the parent or guardian of the child or young person, unless the court is satisfied (a) that the parent or guardian cannot be found or (b) that he has not conduced to the commission of the offence by neglecting to exercise due care of the child or young person.[35]

(d) Where a court thinks that a charge against a child or young person is proved, it may make an order on the parent or guardian for the payment of damages or costs or requiring him to give security for good behaviour, without proceeding to the conviction of the child or young person.[36]

(e) The court also has a general power to order a parent or guardian to give security for the good behaviour of a child or young person.[37]

(f) The court may make a fit person order.[38]

Finally, a child who commits an offence of a minor nature may not be brought

---

32. *Ibid.*, Sect. 58 (3) as amended by Children Act, 1941, Sect. 10 (2).
33. See generally the Children Act, 1908, Sect. 107.
34. See the Probation of Offenders Act, 1907, Sects. 1 and 2, as amended by the Criminal Justice Administration Act, 1914. Under the provisions of Sect. 1 a justice may dismiss the charge or information or conditionally discharge the offender without proceeding to conviction if the court thinks the charge is proved; "but is of opinion that, having regard to the character, antecedents, age, health, or mental condition of the person charged, or to the trivial nature of the offence, or to the extenuating circumstances under which the offence was committed, it is inexpedient to inflict any punishment or any other than a nominal punishment, or that it is expedient to release the offender on probation". See also the Summary Jurisdiction Over Children (Ireland) Act, 1884, Sect. 7.
35. Children Act, 1908, Sect. 99 (1).
36. *Ibid.*, Sect. 99 (3).
37. *Ibid.*, Sect. 99 (2).
38. For the circumstances in which such an order can be made see p. 256 *infra*.

into court at all, but may simply come under the supervision of a juvenile liaison officer.[39]

Children in need of care and attention

Section 58 of the 1908 Act as well as enabling a child who has committed an offence to be sent to an industrial school, also confers on a District Court power to send a child under 15 years who has not committed an offence to such a school if the child

(a) is found begging or receiving alms (whether or not there is any pretence of singing, playing, performing, offering anything for sale, or otherwise), or being in any street premises or place for the purpose of so begging or receiving alms;[40] or

(b) is found not having any home or settled place of abode, or visible means of subsistence, or is found having a parent or guardian who does not exercise proper guardianship;[41] or

(c) is found destitute, not being an orphan and having both parents or his surviving parent, or in the case of an illegitimate child his mother, undergoing penal servitude or imprisonment;[42] or

(d) is under the care of a parent or guardian who, by reason of reputed criminal or drunken habits is unfit to have the care of the child;[43] or

(e) is the daughter, whether legitimate or illegitimate, of a father who has been convicted of an offence under Section 4 or 5 of the Criminal Law Amendment Acts, 1885 to 1935, in respect of any of his daughters, whether legitimate or illegitimate;[44] or

(f) frequents the company of any reputed thief, or any common or reputed prostitute;[45] or

(g) is lodging or residing in a house or the part of a house used by any prostitute for the purpose of prostitution, or otherwise living in circumstances calculated to cause, encourage, or favour seduction or prostitution of the child;[46] or

(h) is under the care of a parent or guardian who has been convicted of an offence under Part II of this Act or mentioned in the First Schedule to this Act[47] in relation to any of his children, whether legitimate or

39. See P. Shanley, "The Formal Cautioning of Juvenile Offenders", (1970), 5 I.J. (n.s.) 262; "*Children Deprived—The CARE Memorandum on Deprived Children and Children's Services in Ireland*", (Dublin 1972), p. 21.
40. Children Act, 1908, Sect. 58 (1) (a).
41. *Ibid.*, Sect. 58 (1) (b) as amended by the Children Act, 1941, Sect. 10 (1) (b).
42. *Ibid.*, Sect. 58 (1) (c) and Sect. 133 (17).
43. *Ibid.*, Sect. 58 (1) (d) as amended by Children Act, 1941, Sect. 10 (1) (c).
44. *Ibid.*, Sect. 58 (1) (e).
45. *Ibid.*, Sect. 58 (1) (f).
46. *Ibid.*, Sect. 58 (1) (g).
47. The offences under Part II of the Act are as follows: Sect. 12 (1) of 1908 as amended by Sect. 4 of 1957 provides that it is a criminal offence "If any person over the age of seventeen years, who has the custody, charge, or care of any child or young person, wilfully assaults, ill-treats, neglects, abandons, or exposes such child or young person, or causes or procures such child or young person to be assaulted, ill-treated, neglected, abandoned, or exposed, in a manner likely to cause such child or young person unnecessary suffering or injury to his health (including injury to or loss of sight, or hearing, or limb, or organ of the body, and any mental derangement)". See *McGonagle v. McGonagle* [1951], I.R. (S.C.), see further p. 97 *ante*. See also *Re Arkins* [1966] 3 All E.R. 651 (Q.B.D.) in which the court refused to grant an order of habeas corpus and upheld a magistrate's order that the applicant

illegitimate;[48] or

(i) is uncontrollable by his parent or guardian,[49] or

(j) if a public assistance authority satisfied the court that a child maintained in a county home is refractory or is the child of parents either
of whom is convicted of an offence punishable with penal servitude
or imprisonment and that it is desirable that the child be sent to an
Industrial School.[50]

A child may not be treated as coming within (f) above if the only prostitute
whose company the child frequents is the child's mother, and she exercises
proper guardianship and care over the child.[51] If an application is made under
(i) above, the court may, instead of sending the child to an industrial school,
place him under the supervision of a probation officer.[52]

A child found to come within one of the categories of neglect or ill-treatment
listed in section 58(1)—i.e. within one of those listed in (a) to (h) above—may,
as an alternative, be placed in the care of a fit person.

"Any person" may bring a child before a district court, to apply for a care
order on any of the above grounds, other than (i) and (j).[53] Under (i) an application is brought by a parent or guardian. Moreover, there is a duty imposed on
the Garda Siochana to take such proceedings in relation to any child who
appears to come within one of the descriptions mentioned in section 58(1),
unless—(i) the case is one in which the local school attendance committee are
beinging proceedings; or (ii) proceedings are being taken by some other person;
or (iii) the gardai are satisfied that the taking of proceedings is undesirable in the

be extradited from England to Ireland to answer a charge made against him under Section
12 (1).
    Sect. 13 provides that "Where it is proved that the death of an infant under three years
of age was caused by suffocation (not being suffocation caused by disease or the presence of
any foreign body in the throat or air-passages of the infant) whilst the infant was in bed
with some other person over sixteen years of age, and that that other person was at the time
of going to bed under the influence of drink, that other person shall be deemed to have
neglected the infant in a manner likely to cause injury to its health within the meaning of
this Part of this Act".
    Sect. 14 makes it an offence for a person to cause or procure a child or young person in
their custody or care to beg. Sect. 15 makes it an offence for a person not to properly protect a child under 7 years of age in their custody or care against the risk of being burnt so
that the child is killed or suffers serious injury. *Sect. 16 makes it an offence for a person
to allow a child or young person under 17 in their custody or care reside in or frequent a
brothel. *Sect. 17 makes it an offence for a person to cause or encourage the seduction or
prostitution of a girl under 17 in their custody or care".
    *Both these sections were amended by the Criminal Law Amendment Act, 1935, Sect. 11.
    The offences set down in the first Schedule to the Act consist of: Any offence under
sections twenty-seven, fifty-five or fifty-six of the Offences Against the Person Act, 1861,
and any offence against a child or young person under sections five, forty-two, or sixty-two
of that Act, or under the Criminal Law Amendment Acts, 1885 to 1935.
    Any offence under the Dangerous Performances Acts, 1879 and 1897.
    Any other offence involving bodily injury to a child or young person.
    48. *Ibid.*, Sect. 58 (1) (i) as appended by Children Act, 1941, Sect. 10 (1) (d). See *In re
Doyle, an Infant* (Dec. 1955), unreported, (S.C.) in which the whole of Sect. 10 (1) (d) and
(e) was held to be repugnant to the Constitution and invalid, with the exception of only
the introductory words and paragraph (i) in subs. 1 (d).
    49. Children Act, 1908, Sect. 58 (4).
    50. *Ibid.*, Sect. 58 (5) as amended by the Public Assistance Act, 1939, Sect. 89 (2). See,
however, the Social Welfare (Supplementary Allowances) Act, 1975, Sect. 24. Under this
provision Section 89 (2) of the 1939 Act is repealed but not replaced. In practice provision
(j) in the text is obsolete.
    51. Children Act, 1908, Sect. 58 (1).
    52. *Ibid.*, Sect. 58 (4).
    53. *Ibid.*, Sect. 58 (1).

interests of the child.[54]

The requirement in section 58(1) to bring the child before the court has been interpreted by some district justices to mean that the child must be physically present in the court throughout the hearing of an application brought under that sub-section. The presence of a child in court during the hearing of such proceedings, particularly if the application is contested by the child's parents, must be extremely traumatic both for the child and parents and place at considerable risk the welfare of the child. It is submitted that it is sufficient for the purposes of this provision if the child is identified to the court and that it is not necessary for a child to be kept in court throughout the hearing.

Today, the majority of proceedings under Section 58 are brought by social workers employed by the Health Boards and the principle ground upon which such applications are made is that of the failure of a guardian or parent to exercise "proper guardianship".[55] An application on this ground gives the court an opportunity to examine in detail all matters of relevance in determining what action, if any, should be taken to protect a child's welfare. The court, in determining such application is bound by section 3 of the Guardianship of Infants Act, 1964, to "regard the welfare of the infant as the first and paramount consideration".

The Handicapped Child

If a child or youthful offender has "a mental or physical defect", rather than sending him to an ordinary industrial or reformatory school, the court may order that the child be detained in a school "where special provision is made for the training of youthful offenders or children suffering from such defect."[56]

Temporary Detention and Assessment

A detention order may take effect immediately, or at a later date. The court may make such order as it thinks fit having regard "to the age or health of the youthful offender or child".[57] If—

(a) a detention order is made, but is not to take effect immediately; or

(b) at the time specified for the order to take effect the youthful offender or child is unfit to be sent to a reformatory or industrial school; or

(c) the school to which the youthful offender or child is to be sent cannot be ascertained until inquiry has been made,

the court may make an order committing him either to custody in any place to which he might be committed on remand under Part V of the 1908 Act, or to the custody of a relative or other fit person, until he is sent to a reformatory or industrial school in pursuance of the deterntion order.[58]

(c) above is the provision which may be utilised by the court if it wishes to send a child to an assessment centre prior to determining where he should be detained.

54. *Ibid.*, Sect. 58 (8).
55. See D. Greene, "The Child and the Law", Vol. 73 (September 1979) *Gazette of the Incorporated Law Society of Ireland* 143 and "Legal Aspects of Non-Accidental Injury to Children", Vol. 74 (September 1980) *Gazette of the Incorporated Law Society of Ireland* 152.
56. Children Act, 1908, Sect. 62 (2).
57. *Ibid.*, Sect. 61.
58. *Ibid.*, Sect. 63.

Fit person orders

Under the Children Act, 1908, section 58[59] the court may place a child under 15 in the care of a "fit person" if the child is refractory,[60] or beyond control[61] or convicted of his first offence[62] (or of any offence if under 12 years[63]) or if the child comes within any of the categories of neglect or ill-treatment listed in section 58(1). Under section 59 a person of 15 years may also be so placed if so circumstanced that if he were a child within the meaning of the Act (i.e. a person under 15) he would come within one of the categories of neglect listed in section 58(1).

Section 21 of the Act provides for the making of a fit person order in respect of a child or young person following the criminal conviction of such person's parent or guardian. It provides in sub-s. 1 that

"Where a person having the custody, charge, or care of a child or young person has been—

(a) convicted of committing in respect of such child or young person an offence under this Part of this Act or any of the offences mentioned in the First Schedule to this Act;[64] or

(b) committed for trial for any such offence; or

(c) bound over to keep the peace towards such child or young person,

by any court, that court, either at the time when the person is so convicted, committed for trial, or bound over, . . . or at any other time, and . . . may, if satisfied on inquiry that it is expedient so to deal with the child or young person, order that the child or young person be taken out of the custody, charge, or care of the person so convicted, committed for trial, or bound over, and be committed to the care of a relative of the child or young person, or some other fit person, named by the court (such relative or other person being willing to undertake such care), until he attains the age of sixteen years, or for any shorter period, and that court or any court of like jurisdiction may of its own motion, or on the application of any person, from time to time by order renew, vary, and revoke any such order".

Sub-s. 2 provides that

"If the child or young person has a parent or legal guardian, no order shall be made under this section unless the parent or legal guardian has been convicted of or committed for trial for the offence, or is under committal for trial for having been, or has been proved to the satisfaction of the court making the order to have been, party or privy to the offence, or has been bound over to keep the peace towards the child or young person, or cannot be found."

Sub-s. 4 provides that

"Where an order is made under this section in respect of a person who has been committed for trial, then, if that person is acquitted of the charge, or if the charge is dismissed for want of prosecution, the order is rendered

59. Subs. 7.
60. See Sect. 58 (5).
61. See Sect. 58 (4).
62. See Sect. 58 (3).
63. See Sect. 58 (2).
64. Sect. 21 is in Part II of the Act. For the offences under Part II and those listed in the Schedule see footnote 47.

void, except with regard to anything that may have been lawfully done under it."[65]

In practice a fit person order is only made in relation to a child under section 21 after the parent or guardian has been convicted of one of the offences mentioned in the section.

As will be seen in the section that follows, a fit person order may also be made under Section 24 of the Act of 1908 subsequent to the court making a place of safety order.[66]

A fit person under the Act may be a friend or relation or "any society or body corporate established for the reception or protection of poor children or the prevention of cruelty to children.[67] Clearly the I.S.P.C.C. comes within this definition. In practice, fit person orders are often made in favour of health boards, although no express authority is conferred on them by the Health Acts to act as "fit persons". Section 5(1) of the Health Act, 1970, does however provide that a health board is a "body corporate", and as, undoubtedly, part of a board's function is to "provide for the reception or protection of poor children",[68] it is submitted that the health boards properly come within the concept of fit person as defined in the 1908 Act.[69]

Finally, where a fit person order is made under section 58 or 59 of the Act, the court may, in addition, make an order placing the child or young person under the supervision of a probation officer.[70]

Place of safety order

Section 20 of the Act of 1908 empowers a member of the Garda Siochana, or any person authorised by a justice, to take to a place of safety, any child or

65. Children Act, 1908, Sect. 21 (4).
66. We have already seen that a child or young offender may be placed with a fit person temporarily (see previous section). See also the Employment of Children Act, 1903, Sect. 5 which provides that a child under sixteen years of age convicted of contravening any bye-law as to "street trading made under the Act" is liable in the case of a second or subsequent offence to be sent to an industrial school or to be "committed to the charge and control of some fit person".
67. Children Act, 1908, see Sects. 38 (1), 58 (7) and 59.
68. See the Health Act, 1953, Sect. 55.
69. It could, however, be argued that to come within the above definition, a body must be established *solely* for the above stated purposes. If such an argument was upheld, health boards would have no authority to act as fit persons. The power to perform certain functions under the Children Act, 1908, is expressly conferred on health boards by the Health Act, 1970. Sect. 6 (2) (g) provides for the performance by health boards of functions which previously were performed by local authorities under "Part I of the Children Act, 1908 and Sections 2 and 3 of the Children (Amendment) Act, 1957". These provisions do not apply to the making of fit person orders.
70. 1908 Act, Sect. 60. The following are the number of fit person orders made in each of the years 1970 to 1979 by the Dublin Metropolitan Children's Court.

Year	Orders Made
1970	–
1971	–
1972	1
1973	9
1974	6
1975	7
1976	34
1977	20
1978	18
1979	43

No statistics are available as to the orders made by the District Courts outside the Dublin Metropolitan area. See (10th June 1980) Dáil Reports Vol. 322 Col. 56.

young person in respect of whom an offence under Part II of the Act or any offence mentioned in the Schedule to the Act has been, or there is reason to believe, has been committed.[71]

A child or young person taken to a place of safety, or seeking refuge in one may be kept there until he can be brought before the District Court. The court may make such order as the circumstances require until the charge against the person alleged to have committed the offence is determined. Where it appears to the court that such an offence has been committed and that it is in the interests of the child that an order be made, the court may make "such order as circumstances require for the care and detention of the child or young person" until a reasonable time has elapsed for a charge to be made, and if one is made within that time, until the charge is determined. In the case of a person being convicted on such charge, the child may be kept in care for a further 21 days.[72] These provisions are essentially of a 'holding' nature. They are designed to ensure that where there is a possibility that a person has committed an offence against a child, the child may be taken out of the offender's custody until the matter is determined.

Section 24 of the Act of 1908, provides that if it appears to a District Justice, upon information on oath being laid by any person acting in the interests of a child or young person

"that there is reasonable cause to suspect—

(a) that the child or young person has been or is being assaulted, ill-treated, or neglected . . . in a manner likely to cause the child or young person unnecessary suffering, or to be injurious to his health; or

(b) that an offence under this Part of this Act or any offence mentioned in the First Schedule to this Act, has been or is being committed in respect of a child or young person,

the justice may issue a warrant authorising any constable named therein to search for such child or young person, and if it is found that he has been or is being assaulted, ill-treated, or neglected in manner aforesaid, or that any such offence as aforesaid has been or is being committed in respect of the child or young person, to take him to and detain him in a place of safety, until he can be brought before a court of summary jurisdiction, or authorising any constable to remove the child or young person with or without search to a place of safety and detain him there until he can be brought before a court of summary jurisdiction; and the court before whom the child or young person is brought may commit him to the care of a relative or other fit person in like manner as if the person in whose care he was had been committed for trial for an offence under this Part of this Act."

As in the case of proceedings brought under section 58(1) this provision has been interpreted so as to require the child or young person to be physically present in court at that portion of the court hearing concerned with determining whether or not a fit person order should be made. It is again submitted that this is not required by the section.

A child can be removed to a place of safety under section 24 and ultimately be the subject of a fit person's order even if no offence has been committed against him. The section confers a wider discretion on the court to make orders

---

71. *Ibid.*, Sect. 20 (1).
72. *Ibid.*, Sect. 20 (2) and (3).

to protect a child at risk than does section 20 and it is section 24 that is used most often in practice.[73]

The Health Act 1953

Section 55(1) of this Act empowers Health Boards to have a child cared for in one of three ways: by boarding him out or fostering; by sending him to a school approved by the Minister for Health, or if the child is over 14 by placing him in employment.[74] A Health Board may so act in relation to any child eligible for institutional assistance under section 54 of the same Act, and who is

(a) a legitimate child whose parents are dead or who is deserted by his parents or (where one of them is dead) by the surviving parent, or

(b) an illegitimate child whose mother is dead or who is deserted by his mother.[75]

Further with the approval of the Minister for Health, a Health Board may assist any person eligible for general assistance within the meaning of the Public Assistance Act, 1939,[76] by having any child such person is liable to support, cared for in one of the above stated ways with that person's consent.[77]

When a child is boarded out the Health Board pays the foster parents an allowance for the child's maintenance. If a child is subsequently adopted by the person or persons to whom it was boarded out the Health Board may continue to make such payments.[78] The Kennedy Report noted that the main reason for distinguishing between committed children and Health Board children is the channels through which they arrive in industrial schools rather than their background.[79] An important difference however is that in relation to the latter there is no obstacle to such children leaving a school if a more suitable place can be found for their upbringing or if their parent or parents are again able to care for them.

The School Attendance Acts 1926-67[80]

The School Attendance Act, 1926, Section 17 provides for

(i) the issue of a warning notice to parents who fail to send a child to school

(ii) the fining of parents who fail to comply with such a warning,

(iii) the commital of a child to an industrial school or to the care of a fit person.

---

73. See D. Greene, *supra*.

74. See however School Attendance Act, 1926 (Extension of Application) Order, 1972 (S.I. No. 105 of 1972) which raised the school leaving age from 14 to 15 years.

75. Health Act, 1953, Sect. 55 (2). Sect. 54 (2) provides that "a person who is unable to provide shelter and maintenance for himself or his dependants shall, for the purposes of this section, be eligible for institutional assistance". Sect. 54 (1) states "institutional assistance" to mean "shelter and maintenance in a county home or similar institution".

76. The 1939 Act was repealed and replaced by the Social Welfare (Supplementary Welfare Allowances) Act, 1975.

77. Health Act, 1953, Sect. 55 (3).

78. *Ibid.*, Sect. 55 (9) (c).

79. Reformatory and Industrial Schools Systems, Report 1970 (The Kennedy Report), (Stationery Office, Dublin), p. 112.

80. See also the School Attendance Act, 1926 (Extension of Application) Order 1972, *supra* which provides that "the provisions of the School Attendance Act, 1926 . . . shall extend to children who have attained the age of fourteen years and have not attained the age of fifteen years".

The District Court may act under (iii) above if a parent, in proceedings brought against him satisfies the court that "he has used all reasonable efforts to cause the child to whom the proceedings relate, to attend school or the parent is convicted for a second time or for subsequent offence in respect of the same child.[81]

Period of detention

The period for which a child or young person may be detained in an industrial school or a reformatory, is called the period of detention and is determined by the court. Under section 65 of the 1908 Act, the period of detention in an industrial school is to be for such time as seems proper to the court, for the teaching and training of the child but may not extend beyond the child's 16th birthday.[82] The Minister for Education however may extend the period until the child reaches 17 years of age "for the purpose of the completion by the child of any course of education or training" provided the consent of the child's parents, surviving parent, mother (in the case of an illegitimate child) or guardian is obtained.[83] The above provision applies irrespective of the reason why a child was first sent to an industrial school, i.e. whether he was sent to the school for the commission of an offence or simply because he was in need of care and attention. A youthful offender may be detained in a reformatory for not less than two years and not more than four years, but not beyond the time when he attains 19 years of age.[84]

Finally, a child or young person convicted of murder, manslaughter, or attempted murder or wounding, may be detained for such period as is specified

81. School Attendance Act, 1926, Sect. 17 (4). This subsection provides that Part IV of the Children Act, 1908, so far as applicable, shall apply if the court thinks fit to send a child to an industrial school, whilst Part II of the same Act shall apply in so far as applicable to a fit person order. See further D. Mitchell, *supra*, at pp. 84—90.

82. Children Act, 1908, Sect. 65 (b).

83. Children Act, 1941, Sect. 12. In the case of a girl sent to St. Anne's school, Kilmacud, it seems that the Minister may make such an order without the consent of her parents—see the Children (Amend.) Act, 1949, Sect. 6.

84. Children Act, 1908, Sect. 65 (a) as amended by Children Act, 1941, Sect. 11. As we have already seen the great majority of criminal charges against children are dealt with in the District Court. Article 38.5 of the Constitution provides that "no person shall be tried on any criminal charge without a jury." Article 38.2 however makes an exception in relation to minor offences. One of the indications of the seriousness of an offence is the severity of the punishment which it may attract. See *Melling v. Mathghamhna* [1962], I.R. 1; 96 I.L.T. & S.J. 29, (S.C.); *Conroy v. A.-G.* [1965], I.R. 411, (S.C.); *The State (Sheerin) v. Kennedy* [1966] I.R. 379, (S.C.); *In re Haughey* [1971] I.R. 379 (S.C.); *Cullen v. A.-G.* [1979] I.R. 394, (H.C.); *Kostan v. Ireland and the A.-G.* (February 1978), unreported, (H.C.). It is arguable that the above discussed provisions of the 1908 Act are unconstitutional in relation to the length of the periods of detention that they permit the District Court to impose. See *The State (a ten year old boy) v. District Justice H. McCay*—in this case the applicant was sentenced to be detained in an industrial school for five years and eight months. Kenny J. granted a conditional order of certiorori on the ground that the District Justice had no power to impose such a sentence under the Constitution, the imposition of such sentence indicating the offence to be of a non-minor nature. See the *Irish Times*, 18th September, 1974. An absolute order was granted upon the respondent failing to show cause.

Even where parties opt for a District Court trial (see f.2) if the offence is one of a non-minor nature it seems that the District Court has no jurisdiction to deal with it. See *De Burca and Anderson v. A.-G.* [1976] I.R. 38 (S.C.) at p. 66 where Walsh J. stated "The wording of this constitutional provision relating to the trial of criminal cases with a jury is in mandatory terms. Trial with a jury is thus not simply an option open to the accused but is a system imposed by the Constitution subject only to the exceptions referred to" in the Constitution. (As well as minor offences the Constitution permits trial by military court and special courts in specific circumstances). See also the Criminal Procedure Act, 1967, Sect. 13 which permits the District Court to deal summarily with various indictable offences upon the person charged wishing to plead guilty. The maximum penalty the court can impose is a fine of £100 and a 12 month term of imprisonment.

by the court.[85]

Release

A child or youthful offender may be released prior to completing the period of detention laid down by the court in the following ways.

(1) *By Order of discharge*: The Minister for Education may at any time order a child or youthful offender to be discharged from an industrial school or reformatory with or without conditions. If a discharge is conditional the Minister may revoke the discharge if a condition is breached.[86] If an application is made to the Minister for Education by a parent or guardian for the release of a child committed to an industrial school under section 58, if the Minister is satisfied

    (a) that the circumstances which led to the making of the committal order have ceased and are not likely to recur upon the release of the child, and

    (b) that the parent or guardian is able to support the child,

he may either discharge the child or refer the application to the court. If the court is satisfied as to (a) and (b) above it may order the discharge of the child.[87]

(2) *Release on licence*:[88] A youthful offender or child detained in an industrial school or reformatory may be released on licence by the manager of the place where he is detained,

    (a) at any time with the consent of the Minister for Education, *or*

    (b) after six months without any consent.[89]

A licence permits a child to live with any "trustworthy and respectable person" named in the licence willing to receive and take charge of him. Unless the licence is revoked, a child remains on licence until such time as his period of detention would have expired. The Kennedy Report noted that this system is rarely used.[90]

(3) *Leave of absence*: At any time during the period of detention the manager of an industrial school or reformatory may give a child or youthful offender leave to be absent. A child is granted leave to be placed in the charge "of such person and for such period" as the manager shall think fit, *or* "to attend a course of instruction at another school, either as a boarder or a day pupil". During leave of absence a child is deemed to be still in detention and under the manager's care. The latter may at any time require the child to return to the reformatory or industrial school.[91]

---

85. See Children Act, 1908, Sects. 103 and 104 and the *State (O) v. O'Brien, supra*. See also *R. v. Fitt* [1919], 2 I.R. 35; 53 I.L.T.R. 7, (Cr. Ca. R.) in which it was held that for the purpose of sentencing a youthful offender the relevant time for determining his age is when he is being sentenced by the court and not when he commits the offence.
86. Children Act, 1908, Sect. 69.
87. Children (Amendment) Act, 1957, Sect. 5.
88. Children Act, 1908, Sect. 67 as amended by Children Act, 1941, Sect. 15. Strictly speaking a person released under the circumstances described in this section is released under a supervision certificate. However the word "licence" has been preserved here so as to distinguish it from release on supervision discussed further on.
89. Children Act, 1908, Sect. 67 as amended by Children Act, 1941, Sect. 13 (a).
90. *Supra*, p. 76.
91. Children Act, 1957, Sect. 6 (1).

(4) *On supervision*: A youthful offender sent to a reformatory school whose period of detention has expired remains under the supervision of the managers of the school up to the age of 19.[92] Further, if the Minister for Education directs that "it is necessary for the protection and welfare of the youthful offender" the supervision period can be extended until he reaches 21 years of age.[93] A child sent to an industrial school remains under the supervision of the managers of the school from the expiration of the period of detention until he reaches 18 years of age.[94] Further, as in the case of a reformatory school, the Minister can extend supervision until a child reaches 21 years of age. A child detained in an industrial school for the purpose of enforcing an attendance order however, upon release, is not subject to such supervision,[95] Where a supervision certificate has been granted, a person or child subject to it may be recalled if the managers are on the opinion that it is necessary for such person's protection. A person upon being recalled may be detained in the school for no longer than three months and may at any time again be placed out on a supervision certificate.[96] If the Minister discharges a child under (1) above the managers have no further responsibility for him.

CRITICISMS AND SUGGESTED REFORMS[97]

In 1970, the Kennedy Report stated that "The Child Care system has evolved in a haphazard and amateurish way and has not altered radically down the years. It may have been admirable at one time but it is now no longer suited to the requirements of our modern and more scientific age and our greater realisation of our duty to the less fortunate members of society". The need for a new Children's Act and a complete overhaul of the law as to children has been

---

92. Children Act, 1908, Sect. 68 (1).
93. *Ibid.*, as amended by Children Act, 1941, Sect. 14 (a).
94. *Ibid.*, Sect. 68 (2) as amended by the Children Act, 1941, Sect. 14 (b).
95. *Ibid.*, Sect. 68 (2).
96. *Ibid.*, Sect. 68 (3).
97. See generally *Some of our Children: A Report on the Residential Care of the Deprived Child in Ireland*, Tuairim (London 1966); *Reformatory and Industrial Schools Systems Report* 1970 (The Kennedy Report), (Stationery Office, Dublin 1970); *Children Deprived–The CARE Memorandum on Deprived Children and Children's Services in Ireland*, (CARE Dublin, 1970); A.R. Byrne, *Report on Children's Hearing in Scotland*, (N.Y.C. of Ireland, Jan. 1974); J.P. Grant, "The Children's Hearing System in Scotland: Its Strength and Weaknesses" (1975) 10 I.J. (n.s.) 24; First and Second Interim Reports of the Interdepartmental Committee on Mentally and Maladjusted Persons (Stationery Office, Dublin 1974); North Dublin Social Workers, Suffer Little Children (Dublin 1976); Task Force on Child Care Services–*Interim Report*, (Stationery Office, Dublin 1975); *Report of Joint Committee on Non-Accidental Injury to Children*, (I.S.P.C.C. and North Dublin Social Workers, Dublin, Nov. 1975); *Report of the Committee on Non-Accidental Injury to Children*, (Stationery Office, Dublin 1976); "Second Submission to the Task Force on Child Care Services", *Children First*, (Dublin 1976); C. Delaney, "Child Battering in Ireland", Children First Newsletter No. 3, Spring 1976; P. Brennan, "The Role of Residential Care Services of Ireland", Children First Newsletter No. 6, Winter 1976; "Proceedings of The Children First Conference on Substitute Parenting", Children First Newsletter No. 7, Spring 1977; "Containment of Young Offenders", Children First Newsletter Nos. 12 and 13, Summer and Autumn 1978; *Care Newsletter* (Vol. 1 No. 2, Nov. 1974); *Care Newsletter*, (Vol. 1 No. 3, July 1975); M.V. O'Mahony, "Legal Aspects of Residential Child Care, 1971), 6 I.J. (n.s.) 219; F.J. Elliott, "Residential Child Care Health Act Admissions (1972)", 7 I.J. (n.s.) 358; Dr. P.E. McQuaid, "Reform in the Law Relating to Children", S.Y.S. Lecture No. 67 (1972); Dr. P.E. McQuaid, "Problem Children and their Families", *Studies*, Vol. 60 (Summer 1971); I. Hart, "The Social and Psychological Characteristics of Institutionalised Young Offenders in Ireland", 16 *Administration*, (Summer 1968); E. Stewart, "Young Offenders and the Criminal Law", *supra*, I.C.C.L. Report No. 2 (Dublin, 1977); C. Mollan, *Children First*, (Arlen House, Dublin 1979); D. Green, "The Child and the Law– The Practising Lawyer's Viewpoint" (1979) Vol. 73 *Gazette of the Incorporated Law Society of Ireland* 143 and "Legal Aspects of Non-Accidental Injury to Children" (1980) Vol. 74

apparent for some time. It is intended here to briefly mention only some of the reforms required in children's legislation. Footnote 97 below lists some of the recent Irish literature in which the deficiencies of the present child care system and legislation are discussed.

(1) An entirely new court structure should be set up to deal with children in need of care or children who have committed an offence. Upon the establishment of a family court or family tribunal, such a court should be taken into the family court structure. Apart from legal training, the personnel of such a court should have specialised training in child care.[98]

(2) There is a need to centralise administrative and legislative responsibility for all aspects of child care within one government department. At present it is divided between the Departments of Education, Justice and Health.

(3) Proper training should be provided for all those persons engaged in or wishing to engage in work in the child care services.

(4) All laws relating to children and child care should be brought up to date and incorporated into one Children's Act. Such an Act should

(a) raise the age of criminal responsibility, (suggestions in different reports produced in recent years as to what the age of responsibility should be have varied between 12 and 16 years),

(b) provide for the automatic assessment by professionally qualified persons of all children who come before a court as in need of care and attention or for the commission of an offence. Upon a dispute arising between parents, or parents and a stranger, as to the custody of a child, the court should be empowered to obtain independent reports as to what course of action is in the interests of a child's welfare from professionally qualified personnel attached to the court.

(c) provide for a wide range of services to meet the needs of deprived children. These should include (i) the provision of preventative and day care services in local areas to meet the needs of children whose parents are unable to do so, (ii) extension of the Juvenile Liaison Officer scheme, (iii) the provision of a wide range of residential facilities, placed as near as possible to the population centres from which the children placed in them come. The placing of children in places far away from their family home frequently contributes further to the breakdown of an already disintegrating family unit. The type of care provided and the activities available in residential homes should vary in accordance with the needs of the group of children the particular home caters for, (iv) provision for proper after care services and supervision of children. At present, children released from reformatory or industrial schools may in theory be still under the supervision of the manager of the school, but in reality lose all connection with the school. Upon release they may find themselves face to face with the same problems that caused their

Gazette of the Incorporated Law Society of Ireland 152; "The Child and the Law—The Child Psychiatrist's Viewpoint, (1979) Vol. 73 *Gazette of the Incorporated Law Society of Ireland* 189.
98. See Chapter 2.

institutionalisation in the first place, with no one to turn to for support and help, (v) empower the court to make a supervision order in respect of any child who comes before it, whether as being in need of care or for the committal of an offence. Such orders should give professional workers the statutory authority to supervise a child in his own home.

(d) redefine the circumstances in which a child or young person may be taken into care. The provisions of the 1908 Act in this area are in need of a total revision. At present there are a variety of circumstances in which a child's welfare may be at risk but in respect of which the courts possess no specific jurisdiction under the 1908 Act to place the child in care.[99] However, the power of a parent to bring his child before the court on the grounds that he is beyond control should be revoked. Such proceedings, the Kennedy Report noted, "are harmful to family relationships and for the child often a final repudiation by the parent. Essentially the parents are seeking help for themselves and the child". Such help should be provided by social and welfare services near to where the parties live.

(e) amend section 11 of the Guardianship of Infants Act, 1964, to permit any person apply to the court for a direction in respect of any matter concerning the welfare of a child, such applications to include applications for custody of a child by a person who is neither the parent or a guardian of the child.

(f) recognise adoption as an important part of the child care system and integrate adoption law within child's law generally. The role that adoption may play in relation to the unwanted or institutionalised legitimate child should be recognised and the adoption of such children permitted in circumstances where it would be in the best interests of the child to be adopted.

(g) permit the court to make a care order or supervision order in respect of a child, when adjudicating in a dispute as to custody between parents, or parents and strangers. The court should have jurisdiction to make a care order if of the opinion that the child is in need of care and that having regard to the particular circumstances, it is undesirable for the child to be placed in the custody of either of the parties before the court. At present, even if both parties are totally inadequate or if it could be positively harmful to a child to place him in either of their custody, the court in hearing proceedings brought under the Guardianship of Infants Act, 1964, must award custody to one of the parties before the court and has no specific power to make any order to ensure the child is properly protected against parental abuse.

(5) In all proceedings relating to children, e.g. care, custody, guardianship, adoption proceedings etc., the court should be empowered to appoint a separate legal representative to ensure that the child's interests are properly presented to the court.[100]

---

99. In all circumstances in which a child is at risk the wards of court jurisdiction of the High Court can be invoked but in practice it has generally not been used by Health Boards or other voluntary children's agencies to afford protection to children at risk.

100. See Goldstein, Solnit, Freud, *Beyond the Best Interests of the Child* (The Free Press, MacMillan Publishing Co. Inc., U.S.A. 1973) Chap. 5.

(6) Provision should be made for the establishment within each Health Board area of a central registry of non-accidental injuries to children. Such a registry was described as a "vital element" in attempting to deal with the problem of battered children in a recent report made to the Department of Health.[101]

In England in 1927 the Committee on the Treatment of Young Offenders[102] which reported on the deficiencies of the 1908 Act noted that there was "little or no difference in character and needs between the neglected and delinquent child". All children who come before the courts, whether in need of care, or for the commission of an offence, are deprived in some important aspect of their lives. At the time of writing, a government committee set up to prepare a new Children's Bill and to make recommendations for the improvement of services for deprived children is in its seventh year of sittings. It is to be hoped that it will soon conclude its deliberations and that its report, when finally published, will result in the rapid introduction of the many reforming measures discussed in these pages.

101. *Report of the Committee on Non-Accidental Injury to Children, supra*, p. 16.
102. (1927) Cmnd. 2831, see pp. 17–20. In England the law as to children has been radically changed since 1908.

CHAPTER 14

FAMILY RIGHTS TO MAINTENANCE

MAINTENANCE FOR SPOUSES

Introduction

A husband at common law has always been under a legal duty to maintain his wife. The duty, however, only extends to the provision of the bare necessities of life. The wife on the other hand has never been under a corresponding common law duty to maintain her husband.

Prior to 1922, if a husband sought a Private Divorce Bill, an official of the House of Commons, who became known as "the lady's friend", was empowered to ensure that the husband made provision for his wife so as not to leave her destitute upon being divorced. While supervision of all other matrimonial matters was vested in the Ecclesiastical Courts, the common law courts provided no remedy whereby a wife could compel her husband to give her a sum of money specifically for her support. The Ecclesiastical Courts themselves would only order a husband to support his wife pending the hearing of a suit or upon making a decree of divorce *a mensa et thoro*.

The transfer of the Ecclesiastical Jurisdiction over marriage to the Court for Matrimonial Causes in 1870 effected no direct change in the substantive law relating to the maintenance of wives. It retained the principle that maintenance of the wife was only an ancillary matter to the main matrimonial reliefs of annulment, restitution of conjugal rights, or divorce *a mensa et thoro*, and this power to award alimony (as maintenance in such proceedings is called) was in any case available only to a small fraction of the population who could afford litigation in this court.

It was not until the passing of the Matrimonial Causes Act, 1878, that magistrates were given the power to order a husband to pay maintenance directly to support his wife. This Act provided that a husband convicted of an aggravated assault[1] upon his wife, could be ordered to pay her a weekly sum by way of maintenance. If the court in which the husband was convicted was satisfied that the future safety of the wife was in peril, it could order that she was no longer bound to cohabit with her husband. The order was to have the same force and effect as a decree for judicial separation on the ground of cruelty. No limit was placed on the amount of maintenance the court could order, and it was empowered to grant to the wife legal custody of any children of their marriage under ten. This Act was repealed in 1895 by the Summary Jurisdiction (Married Women) Act which extended the powers of magistrates in England and Wales

---

1. See Sect. 43 of Offences Against the Person Act, 1861.

but did not apply in Ireland. Thus, if the Act of 1878 applied to Ireland it continued to operate here after 1895. There is, however, some doubt as to whether it ever applied in this country.[2] Even if it did, it seems that it no longer has any effect, the offence of aggravated assault being abolished by the Criminal Justice Act, 1951.

The Married Women (Maintenance in Case of Desertion) Act, 1886, repealed in England by the Act of 1895, was until recently the principal provision under which the courts could make a maintenance order. It conferred on magistrates (now District Justices) jurisdiction to make a maintenance order in favour of a deserted wife if her husband was able, wholly or in part, to maintain her and wilfully refused or neglected to do so. This jurisdiction was extended to the High Court by the Courts Act, 1971. The present law is set down in the Family Law (Maintenance of Spouses and Children) Act, 1976. By it, the court may make a maintenance order if it appears, upon an application by either spouse that the other spouse has failed to provide such maintenance as is proper in the circumstances.[3]

The Poor Relief (Ireland) Act, 1838, imposed upon a husband a statutory obligation to reimburse a Poor Law Union for relief paid by it to support his wife.[4] By section 59 of that Act and later section 2 of the Vagrancy (Ireland) Act, 1847, a husband was rendered liable to prosecution and imprisonment for wilfully neglecting to maintain her.[5] These provisions were repealed and replaced by the Public Assistance Act, 1939, by which spouses were under a mutual obligation of support,[6] each being liable to reimburse a local authority in respect of any money paid by it for the other's maintenance.[7] Section 83(1) of that Act provided that it was a criminal offence punishable by three months imprisonment for a husband to desert, or wilfully neglect to maintain his wife so as to render her eligible for assistance. The Act of 1939 was repealed by the Social Welfare (Supplementary Welfare Allowances) Act, 1975, which has now been superseded by the Social Welfare (Consolidation) Act, 1981. Under this Act spouses are still under a mutual obligation of support, each being liable to contribute towards repayment of any allowance granted to the other spouse. However, neither spouse is liable to criminal prosecution for failing to provide the required maintenance.

In 1970 the financial protection afforded a wife was extended when the State partially recognised that it had a specific responsibility to provide support for spouses of broken marriages. Section 22 of the Social Welfare Act, 1970, created Deserted Wife's Allowance, by which a wife, deserted by her husband and unable to obtain maintenance from him, is guaranteed a specific income each week for herself and her children until the desertion terminates or until the husband meets his financial obligations to his family.[7a]

2. Sect. 2 of the Act which refers to divorce proceedings did not apply in this country. See also (1896), 30 I.L.T. & S.J. 471; and W. Duncan, "Desertion and Cruelty in Irish Matrimonial Law", (1972), 7 I.J. (n.s.) 213 at 217.
3. See below.
4. See *M'Evoy v. The Guardians of Kilkenny Union*, (1896), 30 I.L.T.R. 156, (Q.B.D.) under the Married Women's Property Act, 1870, a wife with separate property became liable to the Poor Law Authorities for the maintenance of her husband.
5. *Phillips v. The Guardians of South Dublin Union*, [1902], 2 I.R. 112 (1900), 34 I.L.T.R. 171; 1 N.I.J.R. 3, (Q.B.D.); *The Guardians of the Poor of the Drogheda Union v. M'Cann* (1905), 39 I.L.T.R. 210, 5 N.I.J.R. 216, (K.B.D.).
6. See Sect. 27.
7. This duty was not absolute. Thus if a wife left her husband without reasonable cause his duty was suspended until her desertion ended and the local authority could not recover money paid by it for her maintenance—*South Cork Board of Public Assistance v. O'Regan* [1949], I.R. 415, (S.C.). The duty of reimbursement was absolute under the 1838 Act—see *M'Evoy v. The Guardians of Kilkenny Union, supra.*
7a. See p. 292 *infra*.

It is now intended to engage in a more detailed discussion of the above law and the problems connected with it.

Necessaries

Necessaries can be defined as matters suitable to a person's station or condition in life and in accordance with his needs. They include food, clothes, lodgings and medical attention. One of the essential obligations imposed upon a husband at common law is to maintain his wife by providing her with necessaries. The rules as to the enforcement of this obligation were developed in a context where a wife had no legal power to contract on her own behalf, and lacking the capacity to hold property, usually had no resources of her own to meet any liabilities. The common law rule that neither spouse could sue the other, prevented a wife from enforcing her right to maintenance by a direct action against her husband. Thus, the presumption arose that a wife had power to pledge her husband's credit for the purchase of necessaries if he did not supply them to her himself. The husband's duty to pay the debts incurred by his wife stemmed from his express or implied authority to her to act as his agent. Her presumed authority to so act in the purchase of necessaries lasts while the spouses are living together.[8]

This presumption of agency can be rebutted. Proof that the husband has revoked his implied authority by express prohibition is sufficient. It is not necessary that such prohibition be communicated to a trader.[9] Thus a trader can be in a very weak position if he grants credit to a married woman. However, if a husband holds his wife out to a trader as having authority to pledge his credit, he is bound to give notice of the revocation of his authority to the particular trader in order to escape liability.[10]

The husband alone is the judge of the sufficiency of the allowance he gives to his wife and no finding of the court that the allowance is insufficient can render him liable for goods once the wife's authority is properly revoked.[11] Where a wife is in receipt of her husband's whole income which is ample to support both herself and her family, it has been held that she cannot pledge his credit.[12] Moreover, proof that the trader regarded the credit as being given to the wife alone, and not to the husband, frees the husband from any liability.[13]

If a wife is forced out of the matrimonial home or is deserted, her husband cannot forbid her to pledge his credit in order to support herself and her children.[14] Thus where a wife was driven out of her home by the behaviour of her sister-in-law who also lived in the house, the wife's brother was held entitled to recover from her husband the rent due for her lodgings.[15] A husband who does not

---

8. A mistress can also pledge the credit of the man she is living with. See *Munro v. De Chemant* (1815), 4 Camp. 215; 171 E.R.69, (*Nisi Prius*) and *Ryan v. Sams* (1848), 12 Q.B. 460; 116 E.R. 940, (Ct. of Q.B.).

9. *Ryan v. Nolan* (1869), I.R. 3 C.L. 319, (Ct. of C.P.).

10. *Moylan v. Nolan* (1865), 16 I.C.L.R. 427, (Ct. of Q.B.).

11. *Ryan v. Nolan, supra; Jolly v. Rees* (1864), 15 C.B. (n.s.) 628, 143 E.R. 931, (Ct. of Q.B.); *Debenham v. Mellon* (1880), 6 App. Cas. 24, (H.L.), affirming (1880), 5 Q.B.D. 394.

12. *Chappell v. Nunn* (1879), 4 L.R. Ir. 316, (Q.B.D.); *Russell v. Mulcahy* (1897), 31 I.L.T. 215, (Cir. Cas.).

13. *Switzer and Co. Ltd. v. Kennan* (1930), 64 I.L.T.R. 222, (Cir. Ct.). See also *M'Grath v. Burke* (1897), 31 I.L.T. & S.J. 429, (Cir. Cas.), where it was held that a shopkeeper cannot recover from a husband the price of goods supplied to his drunken wife, whose habit of drink was so notorious that the trader must have been aware of it.

14. *Bazeley v. Forder* (1868), L.R. 3, Q.B. 559, (Ct. of Q.B.); *Mecredy v. Taylor* (1873), I.R. 7 C.L. 256, (Ct. of Exch. Cham.).

15. *Devine v. Monahan* (1932), 67 I.L.T.R. 44, (H.C.).

comply with a court order for the payment of alimony is also liable for debts incurred by his wife in the purchase of necessaries.[16]

As has already been seen, if legal proceedings are necessary for a wife's protection from her husband, she may pledge his credit for any costs she incurs in such proceedings.[17] Finally at common law a husband is not liable to maintain an adulterous wife unless he has connived at[18] or condoned the adultery[19]. Thus in such circumstances a wife has no presumed authority to act as his agent. Similarly if a wife is in desertion he is not bound to maintain her. In such circumstances her right to maintenance is only suspended and upon the desertion coming to an end her agency may again arise.

Whilst the doctrine of the agency of necessity may have proved useful in the past its use today is very limited. The Married Women's Property Acts, now replaced by the Married Women's Status Act, 1957, removed a married woman's disabilities relating to contracts and the ownership of property. Under the Family Law . . . Act, 1976, she may obtain a maintenance order if inadequately supported and if unable to do so, may be entitled to Deserted Wife's Allowance or Benefit or Supplementary Welfare Allowance. Its usefulness in obtaining solicitor's costs so as to enable her to bring court proceedings against her husband is not great. As for traders, few, understandably, will grant credit to a deserted wife on the basis that at some future time they may be able to secure payment from her husband, if and when he turns up.

Family Law (Maintenance of Spouses and Children) Act, 1976[20]

Grounds for Application: The Act seeks to make financial need rather than matrimonial misdeed the central issue in an application by a spouse for a maintenance order. Under it, the court may make an order if it appears "on application to it by a spouse, that the other spouse has failed to provide such maintenance for the applicant spouse as is proper in the circumstances".[21] Under the Act of 1886, to obtain an order it was not sufficient to prove a refusal on the part of one's husband to provide proper maintenance. The extra element of desertion had to be present. Further, the court was restricted to ordering maintenance in favour of a wife. It now has equal powers to order either spouse to maintain the other and a maintenance order can be made even if the spouses are still residing together.

Whether a spouse is providing "proper maintenance" for the other is a question of fact to be determined by the court, having regard to the circumstances of the particular case. Moreover, the Supreme Court in *H.D.* v. *P.D.*[22] held that it is not possible for spouses to contract out of the maintenance provisions of the Act. Thus, spouses cannot by agreement prevent each other from applying for maintenance or oust the jurisdiction of the court so as to prevent it from making a maintenance order if it appears to the court, upon hearing a maintenance appli-

---

16. Married Women's Status Act, 1957, Sect. 11 (2).
17. See p. 22 *ante*.
18. *Wilson v. Glossop* (1888), 20 Q.B.D. 354, (C.A.).
19. *Harris v. Morris* (1801), 4 Esp. 41; 170 E.R. 635, *(Nisi Prius)*; see also Article entitled "Husband's liability for necessaries supplied to adulterous wife"; (1887), 21 I.L.T. & S.J. 427.
20. See generally P. Horgan, "The Irish Republic's New Maintenance Provisions", (1977) 127 N.L.J. 743; W. Binchy, "Family Law Reform in Ireland" (1976) 25 I.C.L.Q. 901.
21. Sect. 5 (1) (a). The application for maintenance must be made by a spouse. Thus, if the parties have obtained a foreign decree of divorce recognised by Irish law no maintenance order can be made. See *L.B.* v. *H.B.* (July 1980) unreported (H.C.) where the court refused to recognise a French divorce and made a maintenance order against the husband.
22. (May 1978) unreported (S.C.).

cation, that there is a failure to provide proper maintenance.[23] If there is no evidence adduced of such failure, however, no maintenance order can be made under the Act.[24]

A person on whose application a maintenance order is made is called a maintenance creditor, whilst the spouse ordered to pay maintenance is the maintenance debtor. Despite the court's power to make a maintenance order in favour of husbands, undoubtedly the great majority of orders under the Act are made in favour of wives. Thus, normally the husband will be the maintenance debtor and the wife will be the maintenance creditor.

Criteria for making an order: The court in deciding whether to make a maintenance order and the amount to be awarded must have regard to all the circumstances of the case, and in particular:

(a) the income, earning capacity (if any), property and other financial resources of the spouses and of any dependent children of the family, including income or benefits to which either spouse or any such children are entitled by or under statute, and

(b) the financial and other responsibilities of the spouses towards each other and towards any dependent children of the family and the needs of any such dependent children, including the need for care and attention.[25]

The Act does not distinguish between those matters relevant in determining whether an order should be made in favour of a spouse, or a spouse and child, or a child alone. It is intended that all the financial circumstances of the parties be taken into account. However the financial resources and needs of dependent children are essentially relevant to an application for maintenance for the support of such children. Children's maintenance is discussed in a separate section further on in this chapter.[26]

In practice, judicial application of the above criteria has produced varied and inconsistent results, different members of the judiciary possessing different views of what is a "proper" sum of maintenance to order in particular financial circumstances. As yet, no detailed judicial guidelines have emerged from decided cases describing the manner in which awards of maintenance are to be calculated.

In the majority of maintenance cases, the courts are solely concerned with "need". In such cases, it is clear that the family finances are such that if spouses separate there will be an inevitable reduction in the living standards of both spouses. The court making a maintenance order in such circumstances seeks to provide for the support of a dependant spouse whilst also ensuring that the other spouse will have sufficient money available for his own support. In some cases, however, the financial circumstances are such that the additional expense caused by separation need not affect both parties. Thus in *E.D.* v. *F.D.*[26a] Costello J.

---

23. See further p. 123 *ante*. See also section 27 of the 1976 Act.
24. See *St.J.* v. *St.J.* (June 1980) unreported (H.C.).
25. Sect. 5 (4). Earnings are defined as "any sums payable to a person—
    (a) by way of wages or salary (including any fees, bonus, commission, overtime pay or other emoluments payable in addition to wages or salary or payable under a contract of service);
    (b) by way of pension or other like benefit in respect of employment (including an annuity in respect of past services, whether or not rendered to the person paying the annuity, and including periodical payments by way of compensation for the loss, abolition or relinquishment, or diminution in the emoluments, of any office or employment);".
26. See p. 282 *infra*.
26a. (October, 1980) unreported (H.C.).

stated:

> "In fixing maintenance I do not accept the view which was urged on the Defendant's behalf that because the overall family expenses rise when a husband deserts the family home the extra burden should be borne equally by the husband and the wife and children who are living with her, and that she must be prepared to accept a reduction in their living standards. When a husband deserts his wife and children the Court should be concerned to ensure that their financial position is protected, even if this means causing a drop in the husband's living standards."

On the evidence given in that case the husband's earnings were considerable. It is clear, however, that if the husband's earnings had been at a lower level a reduction in the living standards of the wife would have been inevitable.

There is a suggestion arising from some judicial comments that "financial need" must be proved by an applicant spouse before a maintenance order can be made.[26b] It is clear, however, that the criteria set down in the Act are concerned with the totality of the parties' financial circumstances. Thus, a spouse may fail to provide an applicant spouse with "such maintenance as is proper in the circumstances" if the former is very wealthy, even though the maintenance provided meets all of that spouse's basic needs. In the case of the very affluent, the maintenance ordered to be paid may bear no relation to basic needs. In *L.B.* v. *H.B.*[26c] on the wife's application for a maintenance order, Barrington J. concluded that "Mr. B. is a man of enormous wealth" and stated:

> "I am also satisfied that he has not maintained his wife in the style to which the wife of so wealthy a man may reasonably aspire and which she formerly enjoyed . . . I am satisfied therefore that the defendant has not maintained the plaintiff in the manner which is proper in the circumstances. I accept the evidence of the plaintiff that she cannot live, with any measure of comfort, in a house the size of the family home without, at least, the services of a housekeeper and a gardener. On the assumption that she pays the housekeeper and the gardener I will fix maintenance in the sum of £300.00 per week."

Whilst in the case of those of ordinary means the courts are concerned to provide maintenance to meet "need", in the case of the wealthy, the courts, in practise, are also concerned with determining what should be the style of life and relevant standard of living of an applicant spouse.

Orders that can be made: The court only has power to order periodical payments. The District Court, and the Circuit Court on appeal from the District Court, may not order payment of a periodical sum greater than £50 per week.[27] The High Court may order payments unlimited in amount. It is not necessary that the court order weekly payments. It is possible for example for it to order monthly or quarterly payments. Such payments are to be made without deduction of income tax.[28]

26b. See *H.D.* v. *P.D.*, *supra*, at p. 9 of judgement where Walsh J. said: "It appears to me that in a case such as the present one the function of the court under the Act of 1976 is to determine whether or not there is a financial need justifying the making of the order sought under the act." See also *St. J.* v. *St. J.*, *supra*.

26c. *Supra.*

27. Sect. 23 (2) (a).

28. Sect. 24.

As initiated before the Dáil, the Courts Bill, 1980, section 12 proposes to extend the jurisdiction of the District Court to permit it to make maintenance orders of an amount up to a sum of £100.00 per week and also proposes to confer on the Circuit Court jurisdiction to make maintenance orders unlimited in amount. The Circuit Court jurisdiction will be limited to ordering maintenance at a rate no greater than £100.00 per week when that court is hearing District Court appeals.

There is no express power conferred on the court by the 1976 Act to order the making of a lump sum payment to an applicant. The Minister for Justice, however, stated in the Special Dáil Committee set up to examine the provisions of the Act, as presented to the Dáil, that the court was empowered by it to order a payment of a large sum for the first period and a lesser sum thereafter if it so wished.[30]

The court under the Act may order "periodical payments . . . for such period . . . of such amount and at such times as the court may consider proper". The more usual interpretation of the power conferred by this section would be that it enables the court to order periodical payment of a set sum until the variation or termination of the order. It is doubtful whether an order may lay down that different amounts are payable at different periods, the Act merely empowers the court to order payment of "such amount" and not "such amounts" as it considers proper.

Bars to Relief: Under the Act there are two bars to the making of an order. Desertion is an absolute bar and adultery is a discretionary bar.

DESERTION

The court may not make a maintenance order for the support of a spouse where the spouse has deserted and continues to desert the other spouse.[31] Further, the court having made a maintenance order in support of a spouse must discharge that order "where it appears to it that the spouse has deserted and continues to desert the spouse liable under the order to pay maintenance".[32]

The role played by desertion in maintenance legislation has thus been completely reversed. Under the Act of 1886 the onus was placed on the applicant to prove desertion by the defendant, such desertion being an essential prerequisite to the granting of an order by the court. Today, it may be used by the defendant as a bar to the granting of a maintenance order, or to discharge an order already made, and the onus is placed on the defendant to prove that the applicant or supported spouse is in desertion. As in most cases it is the husband that deserts, and not the wife, the former possessing greater financial independence, desertion is likely to play a far lesser role under the present Act than it played under the Act of 1886.

Desertion consists of the following four elements:

(a) A factual separation of the spouses;

(b) Absence of consent to live apart;

(c) Intention to desert;

---

29. See *St. J. v. St. J., supra*.
30. See Family Law . . . Bill, 1975–Special Committee Dáil Éireann (Official Report Unrevised), p. 15–18.
31. Sect. 5 (2).
32. Sect. 6 (2).

(d) Absence of just cause for leaving.

(a) *Separation*:[33] Unless the parties have separated and no longer live together there can be no desertion. The more usual case of separation involves spouses living in separate abodes. However it is possible for spouses to be regarded as living separate and apart although still residing under the same roof.[34] Desertion it has been said is "not the withdrawal from a place, but from a state of things".[35] Thus, if parties still reside under the same roof but "cease to be one household and become two households"[36] the factum of separation is present. Whether this has happened depends on the circumstances of the particular case. As a general rule it can be said to be a question of whether all the usual interaction of matrimonial cohabitation has come to an end. Thus, if spouses sleep in separate rooms, cease to communicate, refuse to carry out their marital duties and no longer engage in the normal interaction of man and wife, the court will hold the fact of separation to be present.[37]

Although normally, parties will live together before one deserts the other, the court may find that there is sufficient separation to constitute desertion without any previous cohabitation.[38]

(b) *Consent*: If parties agree to separate neither is in desertion. Undoubtedly there must be many a battered wife who has been more than relieved to see the departure of her husband. The test used to determine whether the latter is in desertion is whether the separation is due primarily to the conduct of the deserting spouse or to the other's voluntary consent to live apart.[39]

Consent may be by oral or written agreement, or inferred from the conduct of the parties.[40] If the parties have signed a separation agreement which is still in force neither can rely on separation subsequent to the agreement as being desertion. Similarly, if a separation agreement is signed following desertion by

---

33. See F. Bates, "Cohabitation and Separation in the Law of Desertion", (1970), 21 N.I.L.Q. 111.

34. *Powell v. Powell* [1922], P. 278, (P.D.A.); *Naylor v. Naylor* [1962], P. 253; [1961], 2 All E.R. 129, (P.D.A.); *Hopes v. Hopes* [1949], P. 227; [1948], 2 All E.R. 920, (C.A.).

35. Per Lord Merrivale, *Pulford v. Pulford* [1923], P. 18; at p. 21 (P.D.A.).

36. Per Denning L.J., *Hopes v. Hopes, supra* at p. 326. See also *Bull v. Bull* [1953], P. 224; [1953], 2 All E.R. 601, (C.A.).

37. *Naylor v. Naylor, supra*; *Walker v. Walker* [1952], 2 All E.R. 138, (C.A.); *Bartram v. Bartram* [1950], P. 1; [1949], 2 All E.R. 270, (C.A.). These were all cases where spouses were living under the same roof but as "two households" the wife being in desertion of the husband. See also *Hopes v. Hopes, supra* where the husband unsuccessfully alleged that the wife was in desertion, the parties still living under the same roof. Mere refusal to carry out some of the obligations of matrimony does not constitute desertion. See *Weatherley v. Weatherley* [1947], A.C. 628, (H.L.) where refusal by a wife to have sexual intercourse was held not to be desertion. Sect. 2 (6) of the English Matrimonial Causes Act, 1973, provides that for the purposes of the Act a "husband and wife should be treated as living apart unless they are living with each other in the same household". For the manner in which the courts have interpreted this see *Mouncer v. Mouncer* [1972], 1 All E.R. 289; *Santos v. Santos* [1972], Fam. 247; [1972], 2 All E.R. 246, (C.A.); *Fuller v. Fuller* [1973], 2 All E.R. 650, (C.A.); *Bradley v. Bradley* [1973], 3 All E.R. 750, (C.A.). See also R.L. Denyer, "Living Apart" (1974), 124 N.L.J. 735.

38. *De Laubenque v. De Laubenque* [1899], P. 42, (P.D.A.); *Timoney v. Timoney* [1926], N.I. 75, (K.B.D.); *Wells v. Wells* [1940], N.I. 88, (K.B.D.).

39. *Harriman v. Harriman* [1909], P. 123, (C.A.); *Pizey v. Pizey* [1961], P. 101, (C.A.); *Bacon v. Bacon* [1946], N.I. 110, (K.B.D.).

40. See *Joseph v. Joseph* [1953], 2 All E.R. 710; [1953], 1 W.L.R. 1182, (C.A.); the court inferred that a wife consented to live apart by her obtaining a "ghet" which by Jewish Law effects a divorce. In *Counihan v. Counihan* (July 1974), unreported, (H.C.), the wife alleged that the husband was in desertion but the court held the original separation of the parties to be by consent. The wife had subsequent to the separation obtained an English divorce which was not recognised in this country. Kenny J. did not hold that her obtaining the divorce decree also inferred consent by her to separation.

one spouse, the agreement terminates the desertion.⁴¹ Thus, if a husband concludes a separation agreement with his wife after she has deserted him, he will no longer be able to rely on her desertion as a defence against a claim by her for maintenance. Alternatively, if they sign an agreement which does not contain a clause by which they consent to live apart, any preceding desertion will continue to subsist.

It is a question of fact whether a consent to separate is real or not. Thus, if a spouse is forced into signing a separation agreement by threats of the other spouse and without legal advice, the consent to live apart may be ineffective.⁴² Where there is genuine consent it is still possible for one spouse subsequently to be held in desertion of the other. Agreement to live apart may be purely temporary e.g. for a given period of time, or until the fulfilment of a condition or until the happening of a particular event. If the period comes to an end and one of the parties then refuses to cohabit he or she will be in desertion.⁴³ On the other hand, if an agreement is intended to run forever, it will only terminate with the consent of both parties or upon a breach of a fundamental term by one party treated by the other as terminating the agreement.⁴⁴

(c) *Intention*: Intention to remain permanently separated from the other spouse is an essential ingredient of desertion. Normally, desertion will commence as soon as spouses separate. But if when the original separation took place the parties intended to return to each other, desertion begins only when the intention (*animus deserendi*) is formed.⁴⁵ Thus, if a spouse goes to Cork to mind a sick parent and subsequently decides not to return to the matrimonial home in Dublin, it is only when the latter decision is made that he or she is in desertion. Whether an insane spouse is capable of forming the requisite intention is a question of fact in each case. Thus, it has been held that a spouse who leaves under the influence of an insane delusion that the other spouse is going to kill her is not in desertion.⁴⁶ Similarly, supervening insanity may terminate desertion.⁴⁷

(d) *Just Cause*: "Grave and weighty"⁴⁸ conduct by one spouse will justify the other spouse separating so as to afford the latter a defence against desertion. Thus, if a husband assaults his wife and as a result she leaves the matrimonial home, upon her suing for maintenance, if the husband alleges that she is in desertion, she can justify her departure on the grounds of his conduct. Indeed as we shall see in the next section, it is the husband rather than the wife that may be held in desertion in such circumstances. It is, of course, not sufficient for

41. *Piper v. Piper* [1902], P. 198, (P.D.A.).
42. *Holroyd v. Holroyd* (1920), 36 T.L.R. 479, (P.D.A.).
43. *Timoney v. Timoney, supra; Shaw v. Shaw* [1939], P. 269; 2 All E.R. 381, (P.D.A.); *Bosley v. Bosley* [1958], 2 All E.R. 167, (C.A.); *Hall v. Hall* [1960], 1 All E.R. 91, (Assize); If a spouse decides before the end of the agreed period not to return, desertion begins to run as soon as the other spouse becomes aware of the decision—*Huxtable v. Huxtable* (1899), 68 L.J., P. 83, (P.D.A.); *Nutley v. Nutley* [1970] 1 All E.R. 410 (C.A.).
44. *Pardy v. Pardy* [1939], P. 288; [1939], 3 All E.R. 779, (C.A.).
45. *Henty v. Henty* (1875), 33 L.T. 263, (Ct. for Div. and Matr. Causes); *Strickland v. Strickland* (1876), 35 L.T. 767, (P.D.A.); *Chudley v. Chudley* (1893), 9 T.L.R. 491; (1893), 10 T.L.R. 63, (Q.B.D.), (C.A.); *Pulford v. Pulford, supra; Pardy v. Pardy, supra;* see also (1897), 31 I.L.T. & S.J. 15, 29—"Husband and Wife—Desertion".
46. *Perry v. Perry* [1963] 3 All E.R. 766, (P.D.A.); *Brannan v. Brannan* [1973], Fam. 20; [1973] 1 All E.R. 38, (Fam. Div.).
47. *Crowther v. Crowther* [1951] A.C. 723, (H.L.).
48. *Yeatman v. Yeatman* (1868) L.R. 1 P. & D. 489; see also *Oldroyd v. Oldroyd* [1896], P. 175, (P.D.A.), conduct that renders it "practically impossible for the spouses to live properly together"; *Buchler v. Buchler* [1947] P. 25; [1947] 1 All E.R. 319, (C.A.).

a wife alleged to be in desertion to merely make allegations of misbehaviour against her husband. She must prove her case by satisfying the court that she had "just cause" for leaving the family home.

In *P.* v. *P.*[48a] the wife was held to be in desertion for leaving the family home as she failed to prove that her departure, as she alleged, had been forced by her husband's violence and cruelty. As a consequence, the court ruled that it was debarred from making a maintenance order for her separate support. Delivering judgement in this case, Barrington J. stated:

> "When parties marry they marry for better or for worse. This, as I understand it, includes accepting quirks and difficulties in the character of the other marriage partner.
> To establish 'just cause' for leaving the matrimonial home the partner who has left must establish some form of serious misconduct on the part of the other partner. Such conduct must, as Lord Asquith said: . . . exceed in gravity such behaviour, vexatious and trying though it may be, as every spouse bargains to endure when accepting the other 'for better or worse'. The ordinary wear and tear of conjugal life does not in itself suffice."[48b]

In *M.B.* v. *E.B.*[48c] the court held that the wife had just cause for leaving the family home. The parties married in June, 1977 and separated in July, 1979. The wife established in evidence that her husband drank to excess and that since their child had been born he had gone out to a public house on his own almost every night of the week. He frequently returned home drunk and she was worried that he might, when drunk, knock over the baby. The night prior to the wife's departure the husband returned home drunk. An argument took place between them and the wife went to bed locking the bedroom door. The husband remained in the sitting-room drinking whiskey and playing a tape recorder "at full blast". The following morning, the wife found him asleep in the sitting-room with an empty bottle of whiskey beside him. She left the family home taking the baby with her. Delivering his judgement Barrington J. stated:

> "I have no doubt that she (the wife) felt that she had just cause for doing what she did. A marriage counsellor might well have advised the wife not to take so extreme a step and might have assisted the husband to a fuller awareness of the ways in which he was distressing his wife. But objectively, I have reached the conclusion that the wife had just cause for leaving the matrimonial home in the light of the picture she has given of the marriage and which I accept to be a true one."

Whether a spouse's conduct is such as to justify the departure of the other is a question of fact dependent on the circumstances of the case. Misconduct towards the parties' children may also justify a spouse's departure. Thus, in an English case it was held that where a husband developed a mental illness that led him to frighten his children, the wife was entitled to remain apart from him for as long as it was necessary for the children's sake.[49] A party may also not be in desertion if separation from his spouse is beyond his control, e.g. a spouse serving a prison term. Moreover, if a spouse has a reasonable belief that he has a good cause for leaving, such belief arising out of the other's conduct, then he will not be in desertion, even if the belief is mistaken.[50] If a spouse ceases to have a good

48a. (March 1980) unreported (H.C.).
48b. *Buchler v. Buchler* [1947] P. at p. 45; [1947] 1 All E.R. at p. 326.
48c. (February 1980) unreported (H.C.).
49. *G. v. G.* [1964] 1 All E.R. 129; [1964], P. 133, (P.D.A.).
50. *Ousey v. Ousey and Atkinson (No. 2.)* (1874) L.R. 3 P. & D. 223; [1874-80], All

cause or ceases to have a reasonable belief of a good cause for remaining apart, he will be in desertion if he fails to resume cohabitation.[51]

Constructive Desertion: It is not only the person who leaves the matrimonial home who may be in desertion. It has for long been accepted that if a spouse behaves in such a way as to force the other to leave, the former spouse is in constructive desertion.[52] Thus, desertion under the Act is said to include "conduct on the part of one spouse that results in the other spouse, with just cause, leaving and living separately and apart from him.[53] As in the case of ordinary desertion, the parties must separate and the deserted spouse (this time the one that departs) must have a just cause for doing so. Habitual drunkenness, violence, adultery and mental cruelty have, in practice, all been regarded as sufficient grounds for a spouse's departure.[54] When a husband physically throws his wife out of the matrimonial home or a spouse refuses without good cause to permit the other spouse to enter, there is an obvious case of constructive desertion. On the other hand, financial irresponsibility or inability to give a wife the amount of money which she requires to run the house according to her standards, or absence from the home during the week on account of work, have been held not to justify a wife leaving.[55]

Prior to the coming into force of the present Act, for a party to be held in constructive desertion, it was necessary to prove that he intended to end cohabitation. The Act makes no reference to intention but it is submitted that it is still required. The necessity to prove intention does not mean that a person can treat his spouse intolerably and then defend himself by saying that he never intended to make the other leave.

In *Counihan* v. *Counihan*[56] the High Court for the first time in a written judgement, discussed the meaning of constructive desertion. Kenny J. approved of the judgements of the Judicial Committee of the Privy Council in *Lang* v. *Lang*[57] and of Lord MacDermott in the Northern Ireland case of *McLaughlin* v. *McLaughlin.*[58] As a consequence of these cases, for the behaviour of a spouse to constitute constructive desertion, an intention to disrupt the marriage or to bring the cohabitation to an end must be proved against the spouse alleged to have deserted. The conduct of a spouse and its natural and probable consequences can give rise to a presumption in favour of the existence of such intention. This presumption though rebuttable, will not necessarily be rebutted by showing that

E.R. Rep. 635; (P.D.A.); *Glenister v. Glenister* [1945], 1 All E.R. 513; [1945], P. 30; But if the belief does not arise from the other's conduct or if the conduct was procured by the departing spouse, the latter has no "just cause"—*Elliott v. Elliott* [1956], 1 All E.R. 122; [1956], P. 160, (C.A.); *Hartley v. Hartley* [1955], 1 All E,R. 626; (P.D.A.).

51. *Forbes v. Forbes* [1954] 3 All E.R. 461, (P.D.A.); *Allen v. Allen* [1951], 1 All E.R. 724, (C.A.); *West v. West* [1954] 2 All E.R. 505; [1954] P. 444, (C.A.).

52. *Graves v. Graves* [1864] 3 Sw. & Tr. 350; 164 E.R. 1310, (Matr. Ct.).

53. Sect. 3 of the 1976 Act.

54. See, for example, *R.K. v. M.K.* (October 1978) unreported (H.C.) in which the plaintiff wife suffered from a motor neurone disease and consequent depression and anxiety. Finlay P. stated that: "the obligations of a husband or a wife are not obviated but may be heightened by the sickness of the spouse. From the diagnosis of the plaintiff's illness and her progressive incapacity caused by it, the defendant showed a gross lack of attention and sympathy with her real needs which amounted to cruelty justifying her departure from the home." See also, *M.B. v. E.B., supra.*

55. In *Counihan v. Counihan, supra,* Kenny J. remarked that "The Standards to be applied in judging the conduct of husband and wife are those of men and women not angels".

56. *Supra.*

57. [1954] 3 All E.R. 571; [1955], A.C. 402, (P.C.).

58. [1956] N.I. 73, (Q.B.D.).

the offending spouse did not want the other to depart, it being possible for a person to wish one thing and intend another. The more serious the conduct of the spouse the more difficult it becomes to rebut the presumption.

The facts of *Counihan* were the following:—After ten years of marriage the wife told the husband to leave the matrimonial home in Dublin. She did this because of what she said was his irresponsibility in financial matters, his recklessness in contracting large debts and his taking a job which meant he could be at home only at weekends. Kenny J. held that the matters relied on did not constitute cruelty or conduct which "a reasonable man would know would have the consequences that marriage would be disrupted". He stated that the wives of many circuit going barristers and commercial travellers very often only see their husbands at weekends, and whilst the husband was financially irresponsible it would not have justified her leaving him. Consequently, it was held that the husband was not guilty of constructive desertion upon leaving the matrimonial home, the wife not having sufficient cause to require him to go. As a result, their separation was held to be by consent.[59]

Termination of desertion: For desertion to bar an application for maintenance it is not enough that the party seeking an order deserted the defendant some time in the past, he or she must still be in desertion when the matter comes to court. Desertion is a continuing offence and may come to an end. It terminates if the parties resume cohabitation[60] or if the deserting spouse makes a genuine offer to resume cohabitation. Such an offer must be genuine and not just a ploy to obtain a maintenance order. If a spouse refuses a genuine offer of reconciliation the court may hold that desertion has ended. However, the conduct of the deserter may be such that the other spouse could not be expected to accept him back.[61] In such a case the party will remain in desertion. Finally, desertion terminates following an agreement to live apart,[62] or the obtaining by a spouse of a divorce *a mensa et thoro*.

ADULTERY

The court has a discretion to refuse to make a maintenance order for the support of an applicant spouse if that spouse has committed adultery.[63] However, if the other spouse has condoned or connived at, or by wilful neglect or misconduct, conduced to the adultery, the court has no discretion and the act of adultery is not a ground upon which the court can refuse to make an order. Further, even if the defendant spouse has not behaved in this way, the court may make an order notwithstanding the applicant's adultery, if having regard to all the circumstances (including the conduct of the other spouse) it considers it proper to do so.[64]

In *L. v. L.*[64a] the husband (D) had left his wife and continued to engage in an

59. Kenny J. did not consider the point that as the wife was unjustified in not permitting the husband to enter the house she may have been the party in desertion.
60. *Abercombe v. Abercombe* [1943] 2 All E.R. 465, (P.D.A.). "Just as you can have an act of desertion where the parties are not living under the roof of a matrimonial home, so equally you can have a resumption of cohabitation without necessarily going under the same roof". Thus, where parties go away on holiday together and resume sexual intercourse the court may adopt an inference of resumed cohabitation. Alternatively, see *Perry v. Perry* [1952] 1 All E.R. 1076; [1952] P. 203, (C.A.); *Lynch v. Lynch* [1966] N.I. 41, (Q.B.D.).
61. *Edwards v. Edwards* [1948] 1 All E.R. 157; [1948] P. 268, (P.D.A.).
62. *Supra*.
63. For the meaning of adultery see p. 132 *ante*.
64. Sect. 5 (3) of the 1976 Act.
64a. (December 1979) unreported (H.C.).

adulterous relationship with another woman. At the date of the court hearing, the wife had formed a relationship with another man. Although she lived alone, this man did from time to time stay over night in the wife's home. The court accepted, on the evidence, that he did not regularly maintain her in any way.

D. contended that the wife's adultery terminated his liability to provide her with maintenance. The court rejected this contention. It was clear that the wife's liaison was subsequent to that of D. and there was no suggestion of the wife having committed adultery prior to D's departure from the family home.

Delivering the judgement of the court, Finlay P. stated:

> "If the court is satisfied that the spouse against whom maintenance is claimed has condoned or connived at or by wilful neglect or misconduct conduced to the adultery then it has no discretion and must order maintenance provided that the other conditions contained in the Act of 1976 with regard to maintenance are fulfilled, that is to say that the other spouse has failed to provide such maintenance for the applicant spouse as is proper in the circumstances . . .
>
> If on the other hand, the Court is not satisfied that the respondent spouse has condoned or connived at or by wilful neglect or misconduct conduced to the adultery then it has a discretion and may exercise that discretion having regard to all the circumstances. All the circumstances must in my view include the financial circumstances of the applicant spouse. It seems to me that if an applicant spouse who has been guilty of adultery not condoned, connived at or conduced to by the other spouse were notwithstanding that in a position of extreme want or considerable penury that the court might have regard to that as a circumstance which would entitle it to exercise its discretion in favour of making an order for maintenance. Furthermore it seems to me that if an applicant spouse had committed adultery but has ceased at the time of application that adulterous relationship that may well be a consideration which the court should take into account. Furthermore . . . a spouse against whom maintenance was claimed who had not condoned, connived at or conduced to the adultery of the applicant spouse might by his own conduct including presumably a subsequent adultery on his part make himself liable where he otherwise would not be to the payment of maintenance. I do not intend that these should be considered an exhaustive list of the circumstances which the court may take into consideration which must, of necessity, vary with every case but they are the sort of circumstances which it appears to me may be material to this situation."

Rejecting D's denial of liability for his wife's maintenance, the learned President held that on the facts of the case D's wilful misconduct "as a matter of probability" had conduced to his wife's adultery. Her adultery was thus not a relevant factor in the court's determination of the wife's maintenance application. The court was merely concerned with the financial circumstances and needs of both spouses.[64b]

64b. On the facts of the case the court held that D. had not condoned or connived at his wife's adultery. Referring to the concept of condonation, Finlay P. stated: "I am . . . satisfied that it must be interpreted in so far as it refers to a condoning of the adultery as intended to carry the ordinary legal meaning of condonation namely a co-habiting subsequent to the discovery of the adultery."

As for the word connived, he continued "I must interpret this as indicating conduct on the part of the other spouse consisting of a knowledge of the adultery and a failure to make any remonstrance concerning it or to take any steps to try and persuade his partner from continuing with it." See further p. 136 *et seq.*

Where subsequent to the making of a maintenance order, an applicant spouse commits adultery, the court cannot discharge or vary the order if the other spouse behaved in a manner that would prevent adultery being relied on to bar the making of an order. Similarly, even if the other spouse has not behaved in such a manner the court may, notwithstanding the adultery, refuse to discharge or vary the order, where having regard to all the circumstances (including the conduct of the other spouse) it considers it proper to refuse to do so.[65]

Discharge and variation: A maintenance order may be discharged or varied at any time on the application of either party, if new circumstances exist or upon the production of evidence not available to the party applying when the order was made or last varied.[66] An increase in a party's earnings or a decrease in the value of the original order as a result of inflation could be a sufficient change in circumstances to justify the variation of a previous order.

If an application for maintenance fails and the parties' circumstances subsequently change, the applicant may be justified in applying a second time for an order. However, where a summons for maintenance has been dismissed the matter is *res judicata* and the court has no jurisdiction to hear a second summons on exactly the same cause of complaint.[67]

An order may also be discharged on the application of the maintenance debtor one year after being made, if it appears to the court that having regard to the former's record of payments and to other circumstances, the persons for whose support it provides will not be prejudiced by its being discharged.[68] As we have already seen, the court must revoke an order if the maintenance creditor subsequently deserts,[69] and has a discretion to discharge or vary an order upon his committing adultery.[70]

Section 5 provides that an order is to remain in force "for such period during the lifetime of the applicant . . . as the court may consider proper". Thus, it is also possible that the court when making the original order may limit the period for which it is to remain in force.

Finally, the Courts Bill, 1980, as initiated, also proposes to permit the District Court or Circuit Court to vary or discharge a maintenance order made by the High Court before the commencement of Section 12 of the Bill, where the spouses' circumstances have changed, provided that, in the case of the District Court, the order made was one which would have been within the jurisdiction of that court if Section 12 of the Bill had been in operation at the time when the order was made.

Interim orders: Under the Act of 1886, it was the practice of a number of District Justices upon an application for maintenance, to adjourn the proceedings before making an order, and ask the court's welfare officer to interview the parties. In doing so, a justice would sometimes "suggest" to a husband that in the meantime, until the matter came back into court, he should pay his wife a certain amount of maintenance. The court had, however, no means of enforcing such payment and no statutory basis for making the "suggestion". Now, under section 7 of the new Act both the High Court and the District Court, before

---

65. *Ibid.*, Sect. 6 (4).
66. *Ibid.*, Sect. 6 (1) (b).
67. *Downey v. Downey* [1943], Ir. Jur. Rep. 72, (Cir. Ct.).
68. Sect. 6 (1) (a) of the 1976 Act.
69. *Ibid.*, Sect. 6 (2).
70. *Ibid.*, Sect. 6 (4).

deciding whether to make or refuse to make an order, have statutory authority "if it appears proper to do so having regard to the needs of the persons for whose support the maintenance order is sought and the other circumstances of the case" to make an interim maintenance order for such periodical sum as the court thinks proper. Such an order may be in force for a specified period or until the application is adjudicated upon.

Under the provisions of the Courts Bill, 1980, the Circuit Court will also acquire jurisdiction to make interim maintenance orders.

Deemed maintenance orders: Section 8 of the Act provides that if parties enter into a written agreement (including a separation agreement) that includes either or both of the following provisions:

(a) a provision whereby one spouse undertakes to make periodical maintenance payments for the benefit of the other spouse and/or any dependent children of the family;

(b) a provision governing the rights and liabilities of the spouses towards one another in respect of the making or securing of payments (other than payments specified in 'a'), or the disposition or use of any property;

upon application by one or both spouses, the High Court or Circuit Court may by order make the agreement a rule of court, if satisfied that it is fair and reasonable and that it adequately protects the interests of both spouses and the dependent children. As a consequence of such an order, the procedure provided for payment and enforcement of maintenance orders made under the Act, may be used for the payment and enforcement of any maintenance clause in the agreement by which a spouse is obliged to make periodical payments for the benefit of the other spouse or dependent children.[70a] It is important to note that any such maintenance clause does not become a maintenance order proper, it merely is regarded as such for the purposes of payment and enforcement. For example, if a spouse wishes to obtain a greater sum than that being received under the agreement, maintenance proceedings must be issued. It is not sufficient to simply apply for a Variation Order. Moreover, there is nothing to prevent a party to any agreement ruled under section 8 from applying for a maintenance order at a future date if circumstances change, even if the agreement contains a clause prohibiting such an application, as it is not possible to contract out of the provisions of the Act.[71]

In conclusion, any maintenance order made under the Act of 1886 is deemed to be a maintenance order made under the Act of 1976 and continues in force and is payable and enforceable in the same manner as an order made under the latter act.[72]

Procedure for Payment: The court when making a maintenance order under the Act must direct that payments under the order be made to the District Court clerk rather than the maintenance creditor. The court is bound to make such a direction unless at the request of the maintenance creditor the court considers that it would be proper not to do so. If a direction of payment to the clerk is not made, the court may at any time in the future make such a direction on the *ex parte* application of the maintenance creditor.[73]

70a. See *J.H. v. C.H.* (July 1979) unreported (H.C.).
71. See *H.D. v. P.D.* (May 1978) unreported (S.C.). See further p. 123 *ante*.
72. *Ibid.*, Sect. 30 (2).
73. *Ibid.*, Sect. 9 (1).

The clerk is under a duty to transmit payments made to him to the maintenance creditor.[74] Where payments to the clerk are in arrears, upon a request in writing by the maintenance creditor, the clerk may proceed in his own name for enforcement of the arrears.[75] This does not prevent a person from taking proceedings in his or her own name for the recovery of arrears if he or she so wishes.[76] Where the court has directed payment to the court clerk it may discharge the direction on the application of the maintenance debtor if satisfied that having regard to his record of payment and other circumstances it would be proper to do so. The court must give the maintenance creditor an opportunity to oppose such an application.[77]

Alimony[76]

The High Court by virtue of the 1870 Act now exercises the powers formerly vested in the Ecclesiastical Courts to order a husband to pay his wife alimony pending suit (*pendente lite*) and to pay her permanent alimony after the granting of a divorce *a mensa et thoro*.[79] The court has no jurisdiction to order a wife pay her husband such alimony.

Alimony Pendente Lite: Provided the "*factum*" of marriage between the parties is established, alimony pending suit will be allotted to a wife, regardless of whether the suit is commenced by or against the husband,[80] in nullity petitions,[81] in suits for restitution of conjugal rights and in suits for a divorce *a mensa et thoro*.

A statement as to the husband's income must be set down in the wife's affidavit and the veracity of such statement can be contested by the husband. The amount of alimony that will be awarded depends on the discretion of the court which is formed from an equitable view of all the circumstances of the case, e.g. husband's income, wife's independent income, property interests of the parties, etc.

Permanent Alimony: A wife who has obtained a final decree of divorce *a mensa et thoro* may apply to the court for allotment of permanent alimony. A larger allowance will be made by way of permanent alimony than for alimony pending suit. If a decree has been granted by reason of a wife's adultery the court has no power to order the husband to make any financial provision for her. If a decree of nullity is made, the marriage is regarded as invalid *ab initio* and the 'husband' cannot be compelled to support his former 'wife'.

Alimony is allotted for the maintenance of the wife from year to year (the payment can of course be weekly,[82] monthly or yearly). The court has no power to order a husband to pay his wife a lump sum either instead of or as well as periodic payments. Neither has the court power to award her a separate sum for

74. *Ibid.*, Sect. 9 (4).
75. *Ibid.*, Sect. 9 (2).
76. *Ibid.*, Sect. 9 (5).
77. *Ibid.*, Sect. 9 (3).
78. See R.S.C. (S.I. No. 72 of 1962), Order 70, Rules 47-57.
79. *Keyes v. Keyes* [1919] 2 I.R. 160; (1918) 53 I.L.T.R. 190, (K.B.D.).
80. *Bain v. Bain* (1824), 2 Add. 253; 162 E.R. 286, (Consistory Ct.); *Smyth v. Smyth* (1824) 2 Add. 254; 162 E.R. 287, (Consistory Ct.); *Wilson v. Wilson* (1797), 2 Hag. Con. 203; 161 E.R. 716, (Consistory Ct.).
81. *Bird, alias Bell v. Bird* (1753), 1 Lee 209; 161 E.R. 78, (Arches Ct.).
82. See *Brolly v. Brolly* [1939], I.R. 562, (H.C.) where it was held that the husband was not entitled to deduct income tax from payments ordered to be made weekly; see also *Nolan v. Nolan* [1941], I.R. 419, (H.C.).

the support of any children in her custody.

Variation: A wife can apply to the court any time after an order for payment of alimony has been made, whether it be alimony pending suit[83] or permanent alimony, for an increase of the sum allotted by reason of the increased income of her husband or by the reduction of her own income. Similarly, a husband may apply for a diminution of the sum allotted by reason of his reduced, or the wife's increased, income.[84]

FINANCIAL PROVISION FOR CHILDREN OF SPOUSES

Introduction

Common Law: At common law a father was under a duty to maintain his legitimate children and to provide them with food, clothes, lodgings and other necessaries. This duty was, however, only a moral one and was never enforceable. Children never had an agency of necessity and thus a trader could never force the father of a child supplied with necessaries to pay for them.[85] The wife's agency of necessity did extend to the purchase of necessaries for the children of the marriage however, so a father could be compelled, through her, to pay for such goods.[86]

The Poor Law: Poor Law legislation expressly imposed upon a father an obligation to maintain his children and made him criminally liable for failing to do so.[87] Under the Public Assistance Act, 1939[88] both parents were obliged to maintain their children under 16 years, and were liable to criminal prosecution for deserting or wilfully neglecting to do so, so as to render such child eligible for assistance under the Act.[89] Under the Social Welfare (Supplementary Welfare Allowances) Act, 1975, which replaced the Act of 1939, both parents were still obliged to maintain their children under the age of 16, but it was no longer a criminal offence to fail to do so.[90] This remains the position under the provisions of the Social Welfare (Consolidation) Act, 1981.

Alimony: The law was extremely slow in making provision for the direct payment by one parent to another of sums of maintenance for the support of a child. Whilst a wife could be awarded alimony by the Ecclesiastical Courts no provision could be made for her children, and this is still the position in respect of awards of alimony made in those proceedings heard in the High Court, that were formerly within the jurisdiction of the Ecclesiastical Court.

Guardianship of Infants Act, 1964: Finally, with the coming into force of

---

83. *McArdle v. McArdle* (1940), 74 I.L.T.R. 59, (H.C.) held the court had jurisdiction to hear an application to vary an order of alimony pendente lite upon the application of the respondent who failed to appear at the original hearing.
84. See R.S.C. Order 70, Rule 55; see also *McGowan v. McGowan* [1921], 2 I.R. 314, (K.B.D.) where the amount being paid having been fixed by the consent of the parties, the consent having been made a rule of court, the court held that it had jurisdiction to vary the amount. See further p. 110 *ante*.
85. The father could of course expressly make his child his agent and so render himself liable for the child's purchases.
86. *Bazely v. Forder* (1868), L.R. 3 Q.B. 559, (Ct. of Q.B.).
87. See Sects. 53 and 59 of the Poor Relief (Ireland) Act, 1838 and Sect. 2 of Vagrancy Act, 1847.
88. See Sect. 27.
89. Sect. 83.
90. A parent who fails to maintain his children may be liable to prosecution under the Children's Acts, 1908-1957, however.

the 1964 Act, a parent was able to apply to the Circuit Court or High Court for a maintenance order to be made in his favour requiring the other parent to provide support for a child in the applicant's custody.

Family Law (Maintenance of Spouses and Children) Act, 1976

It was not until the coming into force of the Courts Act, 1971,[91] that a spouse upon applying for maintenance for her own support could simultaneously seek an extra sum for the support of her dependent children. Now a spouse may seek maintenance for dependent children under the Family Law (Maintenance of Spouses and Children) Act, 1976. Except in so far as it is differentiated below, the law under this Act in relation to the maintenance of children, is the same as the law in respect of the maintenance of spouses.

Grounds: When it appears to the court that a spouse has failed to provide such maintenance for his dependent children as is proper in the circumstances, the court may order that spouse to make periodical maintenance payments for their support.[92] The District Court, and Circuit Court on appeal, cannot award more than £15 per week for the support of a child, whilst the High Court has an unlimited jurisdiction.[93] The Courts Bill, 1980, as initiated, proposes to permit the District Court award up to £30 per week for each child and also proposes to confer an unlimited original jurisdiction on the Circuit Court.

Dependent child: A dependent child of a spouse or spouses means any child under 16 years of age—

    (a) of both spouses, or adopted by both spouses under the Adoption Acts, 1952 to 1974, or in relation to whom both spouses are in *loco parentis*, or

    (b) of either spouse, or adopted by either spouse under the Adoption Acts, 1952 to 1974, or in relation to whom either spouse is in *loco parentis*, where the other spouse being aware that he is not the parent of the child, has treated the child as a member of the family.

A person over 16 may still be a dependent child if he—

    (i) is or will be or, if an order were made under this Act providing for periodical payments for his support, would be receiving full-time education or instruction at any university, college, school or other educational establishment and is under the age of 21 years, or

    (ii) is suffering from mental or physical disability to such extent that it is not reasonably possible for him to maintain himself fully.[94]

Who may apply: The great majority of applications for maintenance for the support of dependent children are made by a spouse when seeking maintenance for her own support. However, the Act also permits a third party to seek a maintenance order for the benefit of dependent children in certain circumstances. Where a spouse

    (a) is dead;

91. See Sect. 18 of the 1971 Act.
92. Sect. 5 (1) (a) and (b) of the 1976 Act.
93. *Ibid.*, Sect. 23 (2) (a).
94. *Ibid.*, Sect. 3.

(b) has deserted, or has been deserted by the other spouse; or

(c) is living separately and apart from the other spouse

and there are dependent children of the family who are not being fully maintained by either spouse, the court may order a spouse to make periodical payments of maintenance for the support of each dependent child to the person applying for the order.[95]

This provision could be used, for example, by a grandmother or an aunt to force a grandson or nephew to support a child of his in either of their care. A social worker could also bring proceedings under this section to force a parent to maintain his or her child. An interesting question that arises is whether a child himself could bring proceedings against a parent to obtain support, in the absence of a third party or other parent seeking maintenance on his behalf. It is arguable that he could do so, as the section empowers "any person" to bring such proceedings. No such proceedings, however, could be brought against parents still living together.

Effect of parent's desertion or adultery: Desertion or adultery by a spouse does not affect the other spouse's liability to contribute towards the maintenance of any of his dependent children in the former's custody. Indeed, in *P. v. P.*[96a] where the court held the wife to be in desertion and consequently, barred from receiving maintenance for her own separate support, it went on to hold that as the parties were agreed that the wife retain custody of their child and it was also "agreed that this means she cannot work for some years to come . . . the maintenance for the child must include a sum sufficient to enable the mother to look after the child." Thus, a spouse barred from receiving maintenance for her own separate support may, if she retains custody of the children of her marriage, obtain a sum of maintenance for her support indirectly through the maintenance paid to her for the support of the children.

Other matters: A maintenance order must specify each part of the payment that is for the support of a child and may specify the period, during the lifetime of the person applying for the order, for which payment for a child's support is to be made.[97] An order for the support of a child is discharged upon the child ceasing to be a dependent child within the meaning of the Act.[98]

Guardianship of Infants Act, 1964

Since the coming into force of the Guardianship of Infants Act, 1964,[99] either parent may apply to the High Court or Circuit Court for a direction on any question affecting the welfare of an infant[100] and the court may make such order as it thinks proper. By section 11(2)(b) the court may order the father[101] or mother to pay towards the maintenance of the infant such weekly or other periodical sum as having regard to the means of the father or mother the court considers reasonable. For liability to arise under such an order the spouses must

95. *Ibid.*, Sect. 5 (1) (b).
96. *Ibid.*, Sect. 6 (5).
96a. (March 1980) unreported (H.C.).
97. *Ibid.*, Sect. 5 (1) (c).
98. *Ibid.*, Sect. 6 (3).
99. In 1966.
100. Infant means a person under 21.
101. Father includes a male adopter but does not include the natural father of an illegitimate child—see Sect. 2 of Guardianship of Infants Act, 1964.

have ceased to cohabit and if they continue to cohabit for three months after the making of such an order, it ceases to have any effect.[102]

An order for maintenance of a child may be applied for and may continue in force until a child's 21st birthday. The court has no power under the 1964 Act to award any sum for the maintenance of a spouse, and the question as to whether either spouse is guilty of a matrimonial offence is irrelevant in reaching a determination as to whether an order for the maintenance of a child should be made. It may however, be relevant if there is a dispute first of all as to custody.[103] Finally, under section 7 of the Act, if the court makes an order that a testamentary guardian is to act as a guardian of an infant to the exclusion of a surviving parent, the court may order the latter to contribute towards the infant's maintenance.

The Courts Bill, 1980, proposes to permit the District Court award up to £30 per week towards the maintenance of an infant under section 11(2)(b) of the 1964 Act.

ENFORCEMENT MACHINERY

The following is the machinery available for enforcing financial orders of support made by the High Court, Circuit Court, and District Court. Unless it is necessary to distinguish between them, all such orders are referred to below as maintenance orders. Thus, the procedure for attachment of earnings not only applies to financial orders made under the Act of 1976 but is also available to enforce orders deemed to be maintenance orders under the Act,[104] affiliation orders, orders for maintenance under the Guardianship of Infants Act, 1964, enforceable maintenance orders under the Maintenance Orders Act, 1974[105], and orders for payment of alimony pending suit or permanent alimony.

Attachment of Earnings

The Act of 1976 introduced a new method of enforcing a maintenance order—attachment of the earnings of a maintenance debtor.[106] An attachment of earnings order may be applied for by the person for whose benefit maintenance is paid or by a District Court clerk to whom payment is made. It can only be made without the consent of the maintenance debtor if the court is satisfied that he has, without reasonable excuse, defaulted in the making of any payment.[107]

An order must specify two rates:

(a) The normal deduction rate—the amount of earnings which the court considers reasonable to apply towards meeting payments falling due under an order in the future, together with arrears already due and unpaid and costs owing.

(b) The protected earnings rate—the amount below which the court considers it proper that the earnings should not be reduced by payment made in pursuance of an order of attachment, having regard to the resources and needs of the maintenance debtor.[108]

An attachment order is directed to the maintenance debtor's employer who

102. Sect. 11 (3) of the 1964 Act.
103. See p. 217 *et seq., ante.*
104. See p. 280, *ante.*
105. See p. 289 *infra.*
106. Sect. 10 of the 1976 Act.
107. *Ibid.,* Sect. 10 (3).
108. *Ibid.,* Sect. 10 (4).

is bound to make such periodical deductions from the debtor's earnings as specified by the order and to pay them over to the District Court clerk.[109] Thus, on each pay-day an employer will normally deduct the "normal deduction rate" and hand over the rest of the pay to his employee. However, if deduction of the normal deduction rate would bring the amount handed to the employee below the protected earnings rate, the employer may only withhold the amount by which the earnings exceed the protected earnings rate. When a deduction is made the employer must give the maintenance debtor a written statement of the total amount deducted.[110] The District Court clerk may post any payment received by him under an attachment order, to the person entitled to the payment.[111]

Upon the making of an attachment of earnings order, any proceedings previously commenced under section 8(1) of the Enforcement of Court Orders Act, 1940, lapse.[112] Similarly, an order made or a warrant issued under that section ceases to have effect.[113] An attachment of earnings order ceases to have effect upon the subsequent making of an order under the above provision for the enforcement of an obligation to pay maintenance.[114]

Statement of Earnings: In relation to an order of attachment or an application for such an order, the court may require the maintenance debtor to give to it a statement in writing of the name and address of any person by whom earnings are paid to him and particulars of his earnings and expected earnings, resources and needs. Notice to the debtor of an application for an attachment of earnings order may include a requirement that such particulars be given to the court within a specified time. Further, the court may order an employer of a maintenance debtor to furnish particulars of the latter's earnings and expected earnings.[115] When an attachment order is in force an employer, maintenance creditor or maintenance debtor may apply to the court for a determination as to whether payments to the debtor are earnings for the purpose of the order.[116]

Variation and Discharge: If an attachment order is served on a person and the mantenance debtor is not or subsequently ceases to be in his employment, the person served must inform the court within ten days of either being served with the order, or from the date of the maintenance debtor's departure.[117] An order in respect of an employer lapses upon his ceasing to employ the maintenance debtor. However, it still applies in respect of deductions from earnings paid by the employer after termination of employment, so as to enable payment to the person in whose favour the order was made of any deductions made by that employer.[118]

The maintenance debtor is himself under an obligation to notify the court in writing within ten days of his leaving or changing employment and must also give particulars of earnings under the new employment.[119] Upon a person

---

109. *Ibid.*, Sect. 10 (2).
110. *Ibid.*, Sect. 11 (3).
111. District Court, Family Law (Maintenance of Spouses and Children) Act, 1976, Rules 1976; (S.I. No. 96 of 1976), Rule 22.
112. See p.
113. Sect. 19 (1) of the 1976 Act.
114. *Ibid.*, Sect. 19 (2).
115. *Ibid.*, Sect. 13.
116. *Ibid.*, Sect. 14.
117. *Ibid.*, Sect. 11 (2).
118. *Ibid.*, Sect. 17 (3).
119. *Ibid.*, Sect. 14 (a) and (b).

employing a maintenance debtor and discovering that an order of attachment of earnings is in force and the court by which it was made, he must notify the court in writing that he is the debtor's employer and include a statement of the debtor's earnings.[120] The court clerk, upon learning of any employer other than the one to whom the order is directed, may serve such employer with a copy of the order.[121]

A weakness in the above provisions is the inability of the court to impose an effective sanction on the maintenance defaulter who takes up new employment without informing the court, and without telling his new employer that an order of attachment of earnings is in force against him. The Act merely provides that if a person without reasonable excuse fails to give the above required notices and a maintenance creditor, as a result, fails to obtain a sum of money due under an attachment order, the person in default may be sued for that sum as a simple contract debt. Whereas this provision may compel an employer to comply with his obligations, it will have little effect on the maintenance debtor himself, as he is already liable for the sum due. Further, whereas a maintenance debtor is guilty of an offence if he gives "false or misleading" information to the Court on any of the above matters and is rendered liable to a fine not exceeding £200 and/or a term of imprisonment up to six months, he is liable to no such penalty if he fails to inform the court at all.[122]

The court has a general power to discharge or vary an attachment of earnings order.[123] Finally, an attachment order ceases to have effect upon the discharge of the maintenance order it sought to enforce, except in relation to money payable prior to the date of discharge.[124]

Enforcement of Court Orders Act, 1940, Sect. 8[125]

This provision applies to financial orders made in the District Court under the Act of 1976, orders deemed to be maintenance orders under that Act[126] and District Court affiliation orders.[127] The section renders a person who defaults in his payments liable to distraint or imprisonment and an application under the section may be made by either the maintenance creditor or a District Court clerk where maintenance payments are being made through the District Court. Only arrears payable in respect of the six months immediately preceding the institution of enforcement proceedings can be recovered under section 8.

An application under section 8 is made by the swearing of an information before a justice of the District Court setting out the arrears payable. A justice to whom such application is made may either issue a warrant for the arrest of the maintenance debtor or if he thinks fit, issue a summons requiring the maintenance debtor to appear before the court. A justice when issuing a warrant may certify in the warrant his consent to the maintenance debtor being released on his entering into recognisance, with or without a surety or sureties, for his

---

120. *Ibid.*, Sect. 14 (c).
121. *Ibid.*, Sect. 11 (4).
122. Sect. 20 of the 1976 Act.
123. *Ibid.*, Sect. 17 (1).
124. *Ibid.*, Sect. 18 (1).
125. See District Court Rules (No. 2) 1962 (S.I. No. 8 of 1962) Part iv; District Court, Family Law (Maintenance of Spouses and Children) Act, 1976, Rules 1976 (S.I. No. 96 of 1976) Rule 30; See further J.V. Woods, *District Court Guide* Vol. II (1977), pp. 241-244.
126. Sect. 29 of the Act of 1976.
127. In this section the term "maintenance creditor" is used to include a person to whom money is payable under an affiliation order and the term "Maintenance debtor" includes the person against whom an affiliation order has been made.

appearance before the court on a date specified in the warrant and he must specify the amount in respect of which the maintenance debtor and his surety or sureties (if any) are to be bound.

Distraint: A district justice may if he thinks proper upon an application being made, direct that the arrears owed by a maintenance debtor be levied by the distress and sale of the debtor's goods. In practice this provision is rarely used.

Imprisonment: A maintenance debtor may be imprisoned for up to three months unelss he shows that his failure to pay was due neither to his wilful neglect nor culpable negligence. The release of a person imprisoned can be obtained upon payment by him, or by another person, of the sum owing. Serving a prison sentence does not operate so as to extinguish the debt.

Defence Act, 1954, Sect. 98[128]

This section applies to maintenance orders made under the Family Law ... Act, 1976, and deemed maintenance orders made under that Act, financial orders made under the Illegitimate Children (Affiliation Orders) Act, 1930, orders for alimony or for payment of any moneys due as alimony under a deed of separation and any arrears accrued and any costs and expenses payable under any of the aforesaid orders.

Under the section if any of the above orders are made against a person who is or subsequently becomes a "man of the Permanent Defence Force" and a copy of such order is sent to the Minister for Defence the prescribed authority "shall order to be deducted from the pay of such person as a man of the Permanent Defence Force and to be appropriated in satisfaction or part satisfaction of the amount ... payable under the order such portion (not exceeding, in case he holds the rank of sergeant or a higher non-commissioned army rank or the rank of petty officer or a higher non-commissioned naval rank, two thirds or, in any other case, three fourths) of his daily pay as the prescribed authority thinks fit. This section also applies to a reservist called out on permanent service.

In effect this provision permits earnings to be attached even if the payer has not defaulted in payments. It is to be noted, however, that the section does not apply to a maintenance order made under the Guardianship of Infants Act, 1964.[129] Furthermore, section 107 of the 1954 Act prohibits the making of an order of imprisonment under the Enforcement of Court Orders Act, 1940, sect. 8 against a man of the Permanent Defence Force or a reservist who has been called out on permanent service.

Other Methods of Enforcement

In practice these are not relevant to the enforcement of District Court main-

---

128. As amended by Sect. 30 of the 1976 Act.
129. See however section 99 of the 1954 Act. Sub-section one states:
"Where it appears to the Minister that a person who is or subsequently becomes a man of the Permanent Defence Force has deserted or left in destitute circumstances, without reasonable cause, his wife or any of his legitimate children under the age of sixteen years, the Minister may order to be deducted from the daily pay of such person as a man of the Permanent Defence Force and applied in such manner as the Minister thinks fit towards the maintenance of the wife or such legitimate children such portion (not exceeding, in case he holds the rank of sergeant or a higher non-commissioned army rank or the rank of petty officer or a higher non-commissioned naval rank, two-thirds or, in any other case, three-fourths) of his daily pay as the Minister thinks fit."

tenance orders. A maintenance order is not a final judgement. Thus, the successful applicant for maintenance does not have the same rights of enforcement as the successful plaintiff in a tort or contract action. The court may exercise its discretion in determining how much arrears need actually be paid and may remit them in whole or in part. It will not enforce payment of arrears that go back many years. There is no inflexible rule however and much depends on the circumstances of the case.[130] Due to the court's discretionary power maintenance payable under an order of the High Court cannot be recovered by action,[131] though it may be enforced by any of the appropriate forms of execution.

The usual means of enforcement in the High Court prior to 1976 was by use of the Debtors (Ir.) Act, 1872, Sect. 6. By this section, the court may order the payment of arrears of maintenance by instalments or may commit a defaulter to prison upon being satisfied that he had had, since the date of the order, the means to pay the sum in respect of which he is in default and has refused or neglected to pay it.[132] The court upon ordering imprisonment normally stays the order for a short time to enable the defaulter to pay his debt.[133] Imprisonment may be for a term of six weeks or until payment is made.[134] It does not operate so as to extinguish the arrears due.

RECIPROCAL ENFORCEMENT OF MAINTENANCE ORDERS

At common law a valid foreign judgement in personam is enforceable if it is for a debt or definite sum of money and is final and conclusive.[135] This is subject to the proviso that no action can be maintained on such a judgement if it is in respect of a cause of action contrary to the public policy of the country in which it is sought to be enforced. A foreign maintenance order requiring a spouse to make periodical payments to the other spouse is in foreign judgement in personam. If, as is usually the case, the foreign court has power to vary the amount of the payments, the foreign order cannot at common law be enforced in this country as it is not "final and conclusive".[136] However, if the foreign court has power to vary the amount of future payments, but may not vary arrears, then the arrears may be recovered by an action on the foreign judgement.[137] Application of the above rules meant that, at common law, an Irish maintenance order could not be enforced in any of the courts in the United Kingdom and any of the latter's maintenance orders providing for periodical payments, could not be enforced in the Irish courts. Due to the high instance of husbands deserting their wives and going to England, there was a definite need to set up some procedure whereby maintenance orders made here could be enforced in England.

The Maintenance Orders Act, 1974,[138] which came into force on the 1st April,

130. *Keys v. Keys, supra* (concerned enforcement of Alimony order).
131. *Keys v. Keys, supra.*
132. Sect. 6 (2) of the 1872 Act; see *Tees v. Tees* [1930], N.I. 156, (K.B.D.), (order of committal made in respect of non payment of permanent alimony); *Daly v. Daly* (1886), 17 L.R. Ir. 372, (Matr. Ct.).
133. See *Brolly v. Brolly, supra*; *Tees v. Tees, supra.*
134. See however the Defence Act, 1954, Sect. 107 which prohibits the imprisonment of a member of the Defence Forces under Sect. 6 of the Act of 1872.
135. *Rainford and Others v. Newell-Roberts* [1962], I.R. 95, (S.C.); *Mayo-Perrott v. Mayo-Perrott* [1958], I.R. 336, (S.C.).
136. *Leake v. Douglas* (1954), I.L.T.R. 4, (Cir. Ct.); See Dicey & Morris, *The Conflict of Laws*, 9th edition, p. 391.
137. *Beatty v. Beatty* [1924], 1 K.B. 807; [1924], All E.R. Rep. 314, (C.A.).
138. See also Family Law (Maintenance of Spouses and Children) Act, 1976, Sect. 9 (7) and (8); S.I. No. 58 of 1975—District Court (Maintenance Orders Act, 1974), Rules, 1975. See further J.V. Woods, *District Court Guide* (1977), pp. 245 *et seq.*

1975, now provides for the reciprocal enforcement of maintenance orders between Ireland and a "reciprocating jurisdiction", i.e. England, Wales, Scotland or Northern Ireland.[139] A "maintenance order" is defined in the Act so as to include alimony and affiliation orders.[140] It also includes "an order which is incidental to a decision as to the status of a natural person".[141] Thus, if upon granting a divorce, an English court makes an order as to maintenance, the maintenance order is enforceable in this country. The Act applies to maintenance orders made before and after its commencement, but does not apply to arrears which accrued prior to its commencement.[142]

Thè Act confers jurisdiction on the Master of the High Court at first instance to make an enforcement order.[143] A maintenance debtor may appeal to the High Court against the making of an enforcement order whilst a maintenance creditor may appeal against a refusal by the Master to make such an order.[144]

Upon the making of an enforcement order the maintenance order becomes an "enforceable maintenance order" for the purposes of the Act and the District Court acquires jurisdiction to hear enforcement proceedings against a maintenance debtor for arrears of maintenance. The District Court's jurisdiction in such proceedings is identical to the jurisdiction it possesses to enforce maintenance orders made in the State.[145] Thus, if enforcement proceedings are brought under the Enforcement of Court Orders Act, 1940, an order can be made only in respect of six months arrears of maintenance. Curiously, the Act does not confer jurisdiction on the High Court to enforce "enforceable maintenance orders".

The Act lays down three circumstances in which a maintenance order made in a reciprocating jurisdiction will not be recognised or enforceable here.[146] They are—

(a) if recognition or enforcement would be contrary to public policy, *or*

(b) where it was made in default of appearance, the person in default not being served with notice of the institution of the proceedings in sufficient time to enable him to arrange for his defence, *or*

(c) if it is irreconcilable with a judgement given in a dispute between the same parties in this State.

Prior to the enactment of the Act of 1974, it was suggested that Irish public policy as enunciated in *Mayo-Perrot* v. *Mayo-Perrot*[147] presented an obstacle to the enforcement in this country of maintenance orders made consequent to a foreign decree of divorce *a vinculo*.[148] In that case, the Supreme Court refused

139. The corresponding legislation in the United Kingdom is Part I of the Maintenance Orders (Reciprocal Enforcement) Act, 1972 as applied to the Republic of Ireland by "The Reciprocal Enforcement of Maintenance Orders (Republic of Ireland) order, 1974, (S.I. 1974/2140). For forms required for use in proceedings for the enforcement of orders under the Provisions of Part I of 1972 Act see Magistrates Courts (Reciprocal Enforcement of Maintenance Orders (Republic of Ireland) Rules, 1975 (S.I. 1975/286). See also (1975), 125 N.L.J. 435; and (1977) 127 N.L.J. 612; C. Latham, "Reciprocal Enforcement of Maintenance Orders in the E.E.C.", (1975), 5 Fam. Law 145.
140. Sect. 3 (1) of the 1974 Act.
141. *Ibid.*, Sect. 3 (2).
142. *Ibid.*, Sect. 4.
143. *Ibid.*, Sect. 6.
144. *Ibid.*, Sects. 7 and 8.
145. *Ibid.*, Sect. 14.
146. *Ibid.*, Sect. 9.
147. [1958] I.R. 336 (S.C.). See p.
148. See article entitled "Recognition of Foreign Divorce Decrees", by J. O'Reilly (1971) 6 I.J. (n.s.) 293; and by the same author "Enforcement Abroad of Irish Maintenance Decrees" (1972), 7 I.J. (n.s.) 106; it is submitted that the author confuses the concepts of

to enforce an order for costs made in English divorce proceedings on the grounds that it was contrary to Irish public policy "to give active assistance to facilitate" or to "aid" the effecting of a dissolution of marriage. In *N.M.* v. *E.F.M.* [149] the Master of the High Court ruled that an English maintenance order made consequent to the granting of an English divorce was an enforceable maintenance order for the purposes of the Act. The maintenance debtor appealed to the High Court and submitted that enforcement of the maintenance order was contrary to public policy. Hamilton J., finding in favour of the maintenance creditor and dismissing the appeal, stated:

> "I accept unreservedly that if recognition or enforcement of a maintenance order would have the effect of giving active assistance to facilitate in any way the effecting of a dissolution of marriage or give assistance to the process of divorce that such recognition or enforcement would be contrary to public policy . . . in enforcing and recognising this Maintenance Order . . . it cannot be said that such enforcement or recognition is giving active or any assistance to facilitate in any way the effecting of a dissolution of marriage or is giving assistance to the process of divorce. It is merely providing for the maintenance of spouses and as such cannot be regarded as contrary to public policy."[150]

As well as providing for the reciprocal enforcement of maintenance orders, the Act also sets down a procedure whereby maintenance proceedings can be brought in this jurisdiction against a person residing in a reciprocating jurisdiction.[151] An essential pre-requisite to the institution of proceedings in this country to obtain a maintenance order, or to seek enforcement of an order already made, against a person residing in the United Kingdom, is knowledge of the whereabouts of such person. In the absence of such knowledge no such proceedings can be successful.

In conclusion, the convention of the European Economic Community on Jurisdiction and the Enforcement of Civil and Commercial Judgements provides for the reciprocal recognition and enforcement throughout the European Community of maintenance orders. Ireland acceded to the Convention on the 9th October, 1978, but the appropriate legislation has to be enacted by the Oireachtas before the Convention can become part of Irish law.[152]

"enforcement" and "recognition" of a divorce decree, (see Dicey & Morris, *Conflicts of Law, supra*, p. 985-987). See also W. Duncan, "Desertion and Cruelty in Irish Matrimonial Law", (1972) 7 I.J. (n.s.) 213, esp. 231-235. See also *Leake v. Douglas, supra*; *M'Donnell v. M'Donnell* [1921], 2 I.R. 148; (1920), 54 I.L.T.R. 104, (K.B.D.).

149. (July 1978) unreported (H.C.). See also *Leake v. Douglas, supra* where it was held by the Circuit Court that an order for maintenance made consequent to divorce proceedings affected status only and that the obstacle to its enforcement was that it was not final and conclusive. This obstacle has now been removed in the case of orders made in the United Kingdom.

150. The parties in this case appear to have accepted that the divorce decree was recognised by Irish law. The evidence was that the parties had emigrated from Ireland to England in 1946 and were both still living in England in August 1967 when the decree of divorce *a vinculo* was made absolute. The maintenance debtor, the husband, had remarried and returned to Ireland to reside in 1974.

151. Sects. 17 and 18.

152. See Vol. 21 of the *Official Journal of the European Communities* No. L 304 (30th October, 1978) and Vol. 22 of the *Official Journal of the European Community* No. C 59, (5th March, 1979). See further Dáil Debates (21 October 1980) Vol. 323 col. 251 where the Minister for Justice stated that the necessary legislation to ratify the Convention would be enacted "when other urgent domestic legislation has been disposed of."

SOCIAL WELFARE LEGISLATION

Social welfare legislation is essentially part of family maintenance law. It is outside the scope of this book, however, to examine the great variety of social welfare benefits and allowances that are available. It is intended in this chapter merely to examine the two schemes of social welfare most relevant to the marital breakdown situation—Supplementary Welfare Allowance and Deserted Wife's Allowance and Benefit—and one social welfare allowance that is paid to the great majority of families residing in the State, who have children—Children's Allowance.[152a]

Supplementary Welfare Allowance

The Social Welfare (Supplementary Welfare Allowances) Act, 1975, which made provision for the payment of supplementary welfare allowance, came into force on the 1st of July, 1977.[153] This is now repealed and replaced by the Social Welfare (Consolidation) Act, 1981. By section 200 of the 1981 Act every person in the State whose means are insufficient to meet his needs and the needs of any dependants is entitled to claim the allowance.[154] Under the Act a wife is regarded as a dependant of her husband if living with him or wholly or mainly maintained by him; whilst a husband is regarded as a dependant of his wife if he is incapable of self-support by reason of some physical or mental infirmity and is wholly or mainly maintained by her.[155]

The Supplementary Welfare Allowance Scheme is administered by the Health Boards who are responsible for its day to day operation under the general direction and control of the Minister for Social Welfare.[156] A claim for the allowance is made to an officer of the health board in the area where the claimant lives and an appeal lies from his decision.[157]

The amount of supplementary welfare allowance to which a person is entitled is the amount by which his means fall short of his needs.[158] The means and needs of a claimant are assessed on a basis laid down in the Act. Whether a person has a right to claim the allowance, is determined on the basis of this assessment. It is possible however that according to the calculations of the assessment a person's means may be regarded as adequate when in reality they are not. Thus, section 209 of the Act provides that if a person is not entitled as of right to any allowance, or where a weekly allowance is paid but his income is still not sufficient to meet his needs, such a person may receive

---

152a. On 28 Feb. 1981, the Social Welfare (Consolidation) Act, 1981 came into force (See S.I. No. 63, 1981). While replacing all previous social welfare legislation it continued in force all relevant statutory instruments in force at the date of its commencement (See s. 112, 1981 Act). The relevant statutory provisions in the 1981 Act for Supplementary Welfare Allowance are in Part III, Ch. 6; for Deserted Wife's Allowance in Part III, Ch. 5; for Deserted Wife's Benefit in Part II, Ch. 13 and for Childrens Allowance in Part IV.

153. See S.I. No. 156 of 1977; see also Social Welfare (Supplementary Welfare Allowances) Regulations 1977 (S.I. No. 168 of 1977).

Supplementary Welfare Allowance replaced Home Assistance provided under the Public Assistance Act, 1939. The latter was a discretionary scheme whilst the former confers an entitlement to receive payments as of right in certain instances. For further information on Home Assistance see S. Ó Cinnéide, *A Law for the Poor* (I.P.A., Dublin, 1970); The National Economic and Social Council, *Universality and Selectivity: Social Services in Ireland* (N.E.S.C. No. 38) (Stationery Office, Dublin, 1978) p. 150 *et seq.*

154. With certain exceptions, see 1981 Act, sections 201, 202, 203 which relate to persons receiving full time education, persons in full time employment and persons affected by trade disputes.

155. S.W. (C.) Act, 1981, s. 208.

156. S.W. (C.) Act, 1981, s. 204.

157. S.W. (C.) Act, 1981, s. 205.

158. S.W. (C.) Act, 1981, s. 207.

(a) payment of an allowance, where he is receiving no allowance as of right, *or*

(b) an additional allowance where already in receipt of allowance.[159]

Such payments are "discretionary" and not as "of right". The Act does, however, provide that the Minister may make regulations prescribing (i) the circumstances in which such a payment may be made and (ii) the amount to be paid either generally or in relation to a particular class of person.

The present regulations provide that an additional allowance may be paid if

(a) the rent or mortgage interest payable by a person in respect of his place of residence exceeds £1.50 per week,

(b) a person is living alone or only with persons who are dependent on him and such person or his dependants due to ill health or infirmity have to maintain a high standard of heating in their place of residence,

(c) a person or any dependant has special dietary needs,

(d) where in circumstances other than those specified in (a) to (c) the Health Board, by reason of the exceptional needs of such person, determines that the weekly payment is not sufficient to meet the person's needs.[160]

The amount of additional payment is left totally to the discretion of the Health Board save that an additional payment under (a) above is only payable in respect of the amount payable by the person in excess of £1.50 per week and the person is not entitled as of right to the total sum above £1.50. The Health Board is only bound to give such part of that amount as it considers reasonable in the circumstances.[161] Moreover, no additional payment in excess of £5 can be made without the Minister's consent.[162]

The regulations in making provision for a person not in receipt of an allowance "as of right" merely state that "a weekly allowance may be paid to such person of such amount when taken with his other income is determined as appropriate to meet his needs."[163] However, as in the case of an additional payment the amount cannot exceed £5 per week without the consent of the Minister.[164]

Regulations under section 209 may also provide for the granting of an allowance in kind to meet a person's specific needs. Thus, under the regulations, upon a determination under the section that an allowance is payable to a person in respect of heating needs the allowance may be granted "in the form of an allowance in kind" (i.e. free coal or turf) if the Health Board deems it appropriate.[165] Health Boards may also arrange for the provision of footwear for a child dependant of a person who because of insufficient means is unable to provide such footwear.[166]

In determining entitlement the needs and means of a husband and wife living together are aggregated,[167] and the needs of a child under 18 are included in the needs of a person on whom he is dependent for support.[168] Thus, if an un-

---

159. S.W. (C.) Act, 1981, s. 209 (Formerly section 11 of the 1975 Act).
160. Social Welfare (Supplementary Welfare Allowances) Regulations 1977, *supra*, para. 6 (1) and para. 6 (4).
161. *Ibid.*, para. 6 (2).
162. *Ibid.*, para. 6 (6).
163. *Ibid.*, para. 6 (3).
164. *Ibid.*, para. 6 (6).
165. *Ibid.*, para. 6 (5).
166. *Ibid.*, para. 7.
167. S.W. (C.) Act, 1981, s. 207(2)(a).
168. S.W. (C.) Act, 1981, s. 207(2)(b).

supported wife is living apart from her husband with dependant children, her means and needs will be calculated on the basis of the income of herself and the children. However, if she is living with a husband who does not support her, as their means are aggregated, it is possible that on the basis of the Act's assessment her means will be regarded as sufficient, although she may be in receipt of no money. In such cases she may claim Supplementary Welfare Allowance under section 11 of the Act. In the former case, her allowance is paid as of right. In the latter, at the discretion of the officer of the health board.

Instead of making a payment, the Health Board may determine in exceptional circumstances that the needs of a person can best be met by the provision of goods or services.[169] Further, the latter may also be supplied when it is necessary to meet a sudden and urgent need. If a person has an exceptional need the Board may dispense with an inquiry into means and determine that a single payment be made to such person to meet that need.[170] Similarly, the Board has a wide discretion to make a payment of supplementary welfare allowance in an urgent case without being bound by Ministerial regulations, or the provisions of the Act as to the assessment of means and needs.[171]

For the purpose of the Act, a man is liable to maintain his wife, his legitimate children under 16 and his wife's children born before her marriage to him. A woman is liable to maintain her husband and both any legitimate or illegitimate children of hers under 16. A child is not under the Act liable to maintain his parents.[172] Where a spouse or child who is liable to be maintained by another is granted an allowance, the person liable for maintenance is liable to contribute according to his ability to such allowance. The Health Board is empowered to apply for a District Court order where necessary for this purpose.[173]

Under the supplementary welfare allowance scheme in specified circumstances a person is entitled to receive payments as of right. However, as has been seen, an officer of the Health Board has considerable discretion in certain circumstances in determining a person's entitlement to an allowance and the amount of allowance to be paid. A major difficulty in practice has been the considerable divergence in approach between different supplementary welfare allowance officers when dealing with applicants seeking a discretionary allowance. A further difficulty arises due to the fact that applicants for supplementary welfare allowance are generally unaware of their right to appeal against a decision made by the supplementary welfare allowance officer. Whereas the Act empowered the Minister to provide regulations for the making and determination of appeals no detailed regulations in respect of appeals have yet been made and no formal appeals procedure has been provided. The Minister has, however, appointed a person in each Health Board area to determine appeals.[174]

The role of supplementary welfare allowance in the area of marital breakdown is to provide interim relief for a spouse without means until a maintenance order is obtained against the other spouse or until, in the case of a wife, she becomes entitled to Deserted Wife's Allowance or Benefit. It also provides relief where a spouse fails to comply with a maintenance order or where a spouse requires the sum paid to her, on foot of such an order, to be supplemented.

169. S.W. (C.) Act, 1981, s. 211.
170. S.W. (C.) Act, 1981, s. 212.
171. S.W. (C.) Act, 1981, s. 213.
172. S.W. (C.) Act, 1981, s. 214.
173. S.W. (C.) Act, 1981, s. 215.
174. S.W. (C.) Act, 1981, s. 205. For further discussion on the workings of the S.W.A. scheme see Relate: The Information Bulletin of the National Social Service Council Vol. 4 No. 10 (July 1977); Vol. 5 No. 1 (October 1977). See also N.E.S.C. No. 38, supra, pp.154-155.

Deserted Wife's Allowance and Benefit

The Social Welfare Act of 1970 made provision for payment by the Dept. of Social Welfare of an allowance to a wife deserted by her husband. This Act was repealed and replaced by the Social Welfare (Consolidation) Act, 1981. Stringent conditions are laid down for eligibility for deserted wife's allowance. As well as being deserted, the wife must satisfy a means test, and if she is less than 40 years of age[175] in order to get an allowance she must have at least one qualified[176] child residing with her. Formerly, a wife had to be resident in the State at any time for a period of two years to qualify for the allowance but in 1978 this requirement was abolished.[177]

A qualified child is one who

(a) is under 18 years of age or, if over that age, is under 21 years and is receiving full time instruction by day at any university, college, school or other educational establishment,

(b) is ordinarily resident in the State, and

(c) is not detained in a reformatory or an industrial school.

A woman is regarded as deserted for the purpose of the Act if:

(a) her husband has of his own volition left her and has not at any time during the three months immediately preceding the date of her claim for an allowance lived or cohabited with her; and

(b) her husband wilfully refuses or neglects to contribute to the support and maintenance of her and her children; and

(c) she has made and continues to make reasonable efforts within the means available to her to trace her husband's whereabouts and to prevail on him to contribute to the support and maintenance of her and her children; and

(d) her husband has not resumed living or cohabiting with her.[178]

In determining whether or not a husband contributes to the support and maintenance of his wife, monetary payments and other contributions which are inconsiderable may be disregarded.[179] Thus, if a husband in desertion, regularly or irregularly pays his wife small sums of maintenance, such payments may not disqualify her from entitlement to the allowance.

If a husband is still in the country and his wife knows of his whereabouts she is expected to bring maintenance proceedings against him to force him to contribute towards her support. If she does not do so, her application for the allowance may be refused due to her failure to make "reasonable efforts" to prevail on him to provide maintenance.[180] The underlying assumption of the Act is that the State's responsibility is secondary to that of the deserting husband. Originally Deserted Wife's Allowance payments ceased upon the husband obtain-

175. S.W. (C.) Act, 1981, s. 195(1)(b).
176. S.W. (C.) Act, 1981, s. 195(3).
177. Social Welfare (Deserted Wife's Allowance) Regulations, 1970 (S.I. No. 227 of 1970) Article 6, revoked by the Social Welfare (Deserted Wife's Allowance) (Amendment) Regulations 1978 (S.I. No. 92 of 1978) Article 3.
178. *Ibid.,* Article 4 (1) as amended by the Social Welfare (Deserted Wife's Allowance) (Amendment) Regulations, 1974, (S.I. No. 178 of 1974) Article 3.
179. Social Welfare (Deserted Wife's Allowance) Regulation 1970, *supra*, Article 4 (2) as amended by the Social Welfare (Deserted Wife's Allowance) (Amendment) Regulations 1972 (S.I. No. 74 of 1972) Article 2.
180. See, N.E.S.C. No. 38, *supra*, at pp. 120-122.

ing a divorce abroad, the "wife" in such circumstances being regarded as no longer married.[181] This is no longer the position and now if a wife having been deserted is divorced abroad, the decree is ignored by the Department of Social Welfare and the allowance is paid. Finally, a woman is disqualified from receiving an allowance if and so long as she is cohabiting with any other man as husband and wife.[182] Upon the termination of such cohabitation she can again be eligible for an allowance.

Section 17 of the Social Welfare Act, 1973, made provision for Deserted Wife's Benefit,[182a] obtainable under conditions similar to those required for a Deserted Wife's Allowances except the Benefit has no means test. Thus, if a deserted wife works or has some other income, it will not affect her entitlement to benefit or the amount she receives. The Benefit is payable if either the wife or husband have satisfied the relevant contribution conditions under the Social Welfare Acts.[183] The amounts receivable under benefit are slightly more than those under the allowance.

Children's Allowance

Children's allowance becomes payable from the first day of the month following that in which a child is born to the person with whom the child normally resides. Usually the mother is the person with whom the child is regarded as residing and it is she who is entitled to claim the allowance. The allowance is given for each "qualified child" and is not dependent on any means test or social insurance contributions.

A child is a "qualified child" for the purpose of obtaining the allowance if

(a) he is under 16 years or

(b) having attained the age of 16, he is under 18 years and—

   (i) is receiving full-time instruction by day at any university, college, school, or other educational establishment *or*

   (ii) is an apprentice *or*

   (iii) is, by reason of physical or mental infirmity, incapable of self-support and likely to remain so incapable for a prolonged period,

   and

(c) he is ordinarily resident in the State

(d) he is not detained in a reformatory or an industrial school and is not undergoing imprisonment or detention in legal custody.

The allowance is paid in respect of each qualified child and the sum payable increases as the number of qualified children increase.[184]

---

181. See Report of the Commission on the Status of Women, December 1972, paragraphs 464 and 465.
182. See 1970 Regulations, *supra*, Article 7.
182a. Now see S.W. (C.) Act, 1981, Part II Ch. 13.
183. See S.W. (C.) Act, 1981, s. 101. See further Social Welfare (Deserted Wife's Benefit) Regulations, 1973 (S.I. No. 202 of 1973). See also S.I. No. 202 of 1974, S.I. No. 232 of 1975 and S.I. No. 84 of 1978.
184. See generally the Social Welfare (Consolidation) Act, 1981, Part IV. See also Social Welfare (Children's Allowances) (General) Regulations, 1952 (S.I. No. 222 of 1952); Social Welfare (Children's Allowances) (General) (Amendment) Regulations 1974 (S.I. No. 197 of 1974); Social Welfare (Children's Allowances) (Normal Residence) Rules 1974 (S.I. No. 198 of 1974).

CRITICISMS AND SUGGESTED REFORMS

Although undoubtedly the Act of 1976 has afforded far greater protection to unsupported spouses and their children than any preceding legislation, the law in relation to maintenance is still defective in a number of respects. In criticising the law and suggesting various reforms the term "maintenance" is taken in the following pages as including alimony, unless otherwise stated.

1. The most fundamental defect is the absence of a consistent philosophy as to the purpose of maintenance legislation. The Act of 1976 whilst making financial need rather than matrimonial misdeed the central issue in maintenance proceedings, still retains the concept of the matrimonial offence. Adultery is a discretionary bar and desertion an absolute bar to a maintenance order under the Act, whilst adultery is still an absolute bar to an award of alimony subsequent to the granting of a *mensa et thoro* decree.

In an earlier chapter the role of the matrimonial offence in separation proceedings was discussed and it was suggested that it be replaced by the concept of marital breakdown. If this is deemed desirable, the role of the matrimonial offence in maintenance proceedings will also have to be reviewed.

In England, following divorce proceedings, the court when assessing the amount of maintenance payable by a spouse now takes misconduct into account only if "obvious and gross". To take it into account in other circumstances according to Lord Denning "would be to impose a fine for supposed misbehaviour in the course of an unhappy married life".[185]

In Australia, under the Family Law Act, 1975,[186] liability of a spouse to maintain the other spouse is made conditional upon the extent to which he or she is able to do so and limited to when the other party is unable to support herself or himself adequately. In exercising this jurisdiction the court is to take into account such matters as the age and state of health of the parties, their income, property and financial resources, their capacity for work, whether either has the care of children, their financial needs, the responsibility of either to support another person, the eligibility of either for a pension, the extent to which maintenance would increase the earning capacity of the applicant by enabling her or him to undertake education or training, the duration of the marriage, and the extent to which it has affected the earning capacity of the applicant and the terms of any property settlement made. Conduct of either party is not listed as such, although if of a "gross nature" it may be regarded as relevant under a provision which permits the court to take into account "any fact or circumstance which, in the opinion of the court, the justice of the case requires to be taken into account".[187]

Curiously, the Committee on Court Practice and Procedure, in their Report on Desertion and Maintenance which preceded the enactment of the 1976 Act, completely omitted to discuss what role misconduct should play in maintenance applications.[188]

2. Whereas misconduct may bar a spouse from obtaining maintenance under

185. *Wachtel v. Wachtel* [1973], Fam. 72 at p. 81; [1971], 1 All E.R. 829, (C.A.).
186. Sect. 72.
187. Australian Family Law Act, 1975, Sect. 75 (2). See also K. Enderby, "The Family Law Act 1975", (1975), 49 A.L.J. 477; P.E. Nygh, *Guide to the Family Law Act*, 1975, p. 98 *et seq.*
188. See the Nineteenth Interim Report of the Committee on Court Practice and Procedure, (Dublin Stationery Office 1974). The Report of this Committee laid the foundations for the enactment of the Act of 1976.

the Act of 1976, it is not to affect the amount of maintenance ordered for the support of a child. It is intended that the former's misconduct should not affect the money payable to provide for the latter's needs. It is submitted that this intention cannot be complied with. Whereas the court may assess separate sums payable for the support of a spouse and each child, it is inevitable that whatever money is obtained will be used to meet the needs of the household. If no sum is to be paid to support a spouse, undoubtedly the standard of living of all, not just the spouse punished for misconduct but also any children in her custody, will fall.[188a]

3. If misconduct is to remain as a barrier to the obtaining of a financial order of support, it is submitted that it should in all cases be a discretionary bar. It is illogical that adultery should be an absolute bar in the case of alimony applications and a discretionary bar in the case of maintenance. Further, it seems that under the Act of 1976, desertion is regarded as a more reliable indicator of "guilt" than adultery, in that the former is an absolute bar. Yet desertion by one party may no more indicate sole responsibility for the destruction of the marital bond than any other behaviour.[189] For example, spouses may continuously bicker and argue; each being equally responsible for the unhappiness that is created. The wife may decide that she no longer wishes to lead such an unhappy life and may leave the matrimonial home with her children. The behaviour of the husband may not however be such as to justify her departing and she may be held to be in desertion, and thus disentitled to maintenance. It is submitted that such a decision would be unjust and that if the bars are to remain, desertion should merely be a discretionary bar.

4. The court when ordering periodical payments should be empowered to require the paying spouse to secure the order where it thinks appropriate. This would have the advantage of providing a tangible fund for enforcement if a spouse defaults in his payments. The ability of the court to require security would be particularly advantageous to ensure payment by a self-employed maintenance debtor against whom no order for the attachment of earnings can be made.[190]

5. The court should be empowered to order the payment of a lump sum in addition to any periodical payments ordered. There are a number of circumstances in which such a power might be useful. If a husband has left home and is not maintaining his wife and children he may have left behind him an outstanding hire purchase debt or gas or electricity bill, or a wife forced to leave the matrimonial home may have various expenses to meet in establishing a new home. Similarly, a wife already in receipt of periodical payments may suddenly be faced with a large medical bill in respect of herself or her children. Power to make a lump sum order would also confer on the courts the means of providing some financial security for a dependent wife and children in the event of a husband leaving the jurisdiction.

6. As already stated in the chapter on nullity, the court upon declaring a marriage void or upon granting a decree of annulment should be empowered to

188a. This appears to have been recognised by the High Court in *P. v. P.* (March 1980) unreported. See p. 284 *ante*.
189. See K. O'Higgins, *Marital Desertion in Dublin*, (1974), p. 134 where the author points out that in the majority of cases studied by her "desertion and separation are . . . the result of an already disrupted family life".
190. See for example the English Matrimonial Causes Act, 1973, Sect. 23.

make financial orders for the support both of a 'spouse' and any children of the parties. As we have already seen, the discussion paper on the Law of Nullity in Ireland makes such a recommendation.[191]

7. The Act of 1976 contains elaborate provisions to ensure that the court obtains accurate information in relation to a maintenance debtor's earnings prior to the making of an order of attachment. It is submitted that similar provisions should apply when a maintenance order is first sought. Prior to the hearing of maintenance proceedings both spouses and their employers should be obliged to furnish the court with information as to their earnings and resources.

8. The jurisdiction conferred on the courts by the Act of 1976 to make attachment of earnings orders has undoubtedly rendered maintenance orders more easily enforceable and made it more difficult for a maintenance debtor in regular employment to evade his maintenance obligations. However, a spouse determined not to comply with a maintenance order may, by moving from job to job, lessen the effectiveness of the attachment of earnings procedure. Although the act imposes a duty on a maintenance debtor to inform the court of any change in his employment, as we have already seen, there is no effective penalty that the court can impose if it is not so informed. It is submitted that the sanction that may be imposed on a maintenance debtor who gives "false and misleading" information to the court in relation to a change in his employment, should be extended to apply to the maintenance debtor who fails to inform the court that any change at all has taken place.

Liability to a fine or imprisonment may not, however, be an effective deterrent to spouses changing jobs to avoid their maintenance obligations. In *Separated Spouses*,[192] the authors point out that "a system of attachment may work very efficiently in countries which have a complete system of national registration and of reporting changes of address and occupation to the police",[193] but in countries that lacked such a system they doubted the efficiency of attachment procedures, and were sceptical that they could produce any significant improvements.

It is the author's experience that attachment of earnings has proved effective in a number of cases in forcing maintenance defaulters to comply with maintenance orders made against them. No detailed research has, however, been carried out in Ireland to assess the impact of attachment of earnings on the general rate of recovery on maintenance orders. It is submitted that the efficiency of attachment orders would be considerably increased if there was a statutory obligation on employers to state on an employee's P.45 form, upon that employee leaving employment, that an attachment order has been made and to insert all relevant information concerning the order, so that upon a change of employment, the new employer would automatically discover the existence of such an order and become bound by its terms.

9. The District Court is limited to ordering weekly payments of £50 for the support of a spouse and £15 for the support of each dependent child. It is

191. In relation to suggestions 4 to 6 see Sect. 10 of the proposed Nullity of Marriages Bill printed in the Appendix.
192. By McGregor, Blom-Cooper and Gibson, (London 1970), p. 200.
193. A.I.M. suggested the introduction of such a system in Ireland. *The A.I.M. Group Report*, (Dublin 1972), p. 13. In "*Separated Spouses*" the authors stated that "this degree of control over the citizen is not compatible with British notions of liberty". It is submitted that this equally applies to Ireland.

almost 5 years since the Act of 1976 came into force. Within that period inflation has reduced the value of money by over 80%. The need to increase the amount of weekly maintenance that the District Court can order has been recognised in the Courts Bill, 1980. However, the increase as proposed will in real monetary terms still leave the District Court with a lesser jurisdiction than that conferred on it originally in May, 1976. The monetary limits of the District Court should be regularly revised after the 1980 Bill comes into force, so as to ensure that the court will continue to be able to make realistic orders that provide for the proper support of those who bring maintenance proceedings before it.

10. The Committee on Court Practice and Procedure noted that in evidence submitted to it, "the sanction of imprisonment where a husband defaults in payment of maintenance was criticised for being one that did not really help the situation but rather aggravated it".[194] Despite this, no further mention of the problems associated with imprisoning maintenance defaulters was made by it, and its report contained no recommendations as to the future role of imprisonment in the maintenance process.

Whilst imprisonment as a threat can in certain cases be useful in persuading a recalcitrant spouse to meet his obligations, it is submitted that the carrying out of the threat is totally undesirable. The imprisonment of a husband in no way alleviates the financial distress of an unsupported wife, and can only serve to further exacerbate their matrimonial difficulties. In England, in 1974, the Finer Committee's Report on One Parent Families recommended the abolition of imprisonment for maintenance defaulters.[195] The question of its abolition in this country needs to be examined.

11. As we have seen the age up to which a child is regarded as dependent varies between 16 and 21. There is a need for a uniform provision to be enacted to determine dependency under both Family and Social Welfare legislation.[196]

12. The existing social welfare scheme for deserted wives can be criticised on the following grounds:

(a) Desertion as a criteria for eligibility for payments under the scheme is arbitrary and illogical. For example, a wife whose husband leaves home to live with another woman may be eligible for deserted wife's allowance or benefit but a wife who enters into a deed of separation with a husband who has previously violently assaulted her is not eligible as she is not deserted, having separated by agreement. Rather than determining eligibility on the basis of financial need, the scheme places undue emphasis on the final events immediately preceding the separation of spouses.[197]

(b) In many cases establishing the fact of desertion is particularly difficult. In practice, an official of the Department of Social Welfare normally interviews both the applicant and her husband, if the latter's whereabouts are known. Few husbands admit to deserting their wives and there is no prescribed procedure

194. *Supra*, p. 12.
195. Report of the Committee on One Parent Families, (Cmnd. 5629, H.M.S.O. 1974), p. 128-132. See also *"Separated Spouses"*, *supra*, p. 200-207; P. Morris, *"Prisoners and their Families"*, (1965).
196. See, The Law Reform Commission: Working Paper No. 2 (Dublin 1977), pp. 54-70.
197. See the National Economic and Social Council, *Universality and Selectivity, Social Services in Ireland* (N.E.S.C. Report No. 38) (Stationery Office, Dublin, 1978) at p. 120, para. 8.81.

laying down the manner in which the competing claims of the spouses are to be determined. The matter is essentially left to the judgement of the departmental official who carries out the interviews and there is no information available as to the criteria used by the officials in making the necessary determination.

(c) As desertion is no longer a pre-requisite for the bringing of maintenance proceedings, it should similarly not be a pre-requisite to obtaining a special welfare payment upon the principal family breadwinner ceasing to provide maintenance. Matrimonial misconduct should be irrelevant in determining a spouse's entitlement to such payments. Whereas it may be unjust in certain circumstances to require a spouse to maintain the other spouse, if that other has committed a matrimonial offence, such considerations are not relevant to the State's duty to provide support. Even if a spouse can be held solely responsible for the breakdown of a marriage, which is very rarely the case, the needs of that spouse and his or her children still need to be met. Retributive measures on the part of the State can only lead to further bitterness and exacerbate the matrimonial dispute between the spouses.

(d) To obtain the allowance or benefit a wife must be deserted for three months. The Commission on the Status of Women in 1972 recommended that the Department of Social Welfare be enabled to grant the allowance during the qualifying period if undue hardship would be caused by withholding payments until the end of the period.[198] It is submitted that the qualifying period serves no useful purpose and should be abolished.

(e) In determining eligibility, maintenance payments of an "inconsiderable sum" made by a husband may be disregarded but this is a discretionary provision and there is no information available as to what is regarded as an "inconsiderable sum".[199] In practice, if payments of any nature are being made by a husband to his wife, it is extremely unusual for the latter to be successful upon her claiming assistance under the scheme.

(f) The permanent absence of a spouse from the family home can in many instances give rise to additional family expenditure. The provision of Deserted Wife's Benefit recognises the extra financial burden imposed on deserted wives by providing a weekly social welfare payment to wives who qualify for benefit on their own or their husband's insurance record without a means test. The benefit is paid to an eligible wife whether or not she is in employment and the amount paid to her is not affected by any other income that she receives. The provisions as to Deserted Wife's Allowance do not afford similar recognition to the burden imposed on wives who are in receipt of the allowance. The means test renders it impossible for a wife to make any significant financial gain by combining part-time work with the allowance as most of the earnings received in such work are offset against the allowance. It also acts as a disincentive to a deserted wife obtaining full-time employment, in that a wife will normally lose her total allowance upon obtaining such employment even though she has to meet the additional expenses that arise from her work, such as the employment of a child minder. As a consequence, there will often be little net improvement

---

198. Report of the Commission on the Status of Women (Dublin 1972 Stationery Office) paras. 384 and 385. When the Commission made this recommendation there was a six months qualifying period.
199. See N.E.S.C. Report No. 38, *supra* at p. 119, para. 8.80.

in her financial circumstances if she obtains such employment. Moreover, a wife in receipt of the allowance receives less money than a wife in receipt of the benefit, despite the fact that the latter is often in employment and in receipt of a salary, whilst the former is usually solely dependent on the allowance to support herself and her children. In essence, the deserted wife dependent on Deserted Wife's Allowance is liable to be caught in a poverty trap.[200]

(g) To a great extent the problems of a separated husband bringing up children and those of a separated wife bringing up children are identical. Each has to provide a home for the family and has to fill both parental roles. In financial terms, the expense of running a house does not vary greatly if one parent or spouse is absent. The costs of items such as heating, lighting, cooking, mortgage or rent and family transport remain largely the same. Additional expense is usually incurred in the necessity to employ others to do work usually done by the departed spouse. This can include items such as cooking, washing, shopping, house maintenance and decoration and household repairs. Child minding is a further expense for either fatherless or motherless families. This expense not only applies solely to those parents who go out to work but to all parents, if they are to continue to lead a normal social life. The absence of an allowance or benefit payable to deserted or separated fathers is a further anomaly in the existing scheme and indicative of its failure to come to terms with the financial needs of the single parent family.[201]

It is submitted that the present scheme of social welfare assistance for deserted wives should be replaced by a scheme for single parent families. Within this scheme provision should also be made for dependent unsupported spouses who have no children or whose children have attained the age of majority.

Any such scheme should fully take into account the interaction between Family Law and Social Welfare Law in the provision of income maintenance. At present, the State plays a secondary role in providing support for the broken family, only intervening when the spouse obliged to provide it fails to do so. Despite the fact that maintenance payable under a court order normally is in excess of that payable to a deserted wife under the Social Welfare Acts, many wives after experiencing the difficulties involved in securing regular payments under the former, express a preference for the latter. The granting of a maintenance order very often marks not the end but merely the beginning of a wife's problems. Many wives never know from one week to the next whether they will receive the sum ordered to be paid by the court or whether they will have to rely on Supplementary Welfare Allowance. Moreover, every few weeks they may find themselves returning to court to seek payment of arrears. Alternatively, a wife in receipt of Deserted Wife's Allowance or Benefit avoids much of the stress and anxiety associated with maintenance proceedings and she has a guaranteed regular weekly income.[202]

In England, the Finer Committee has suggested that the primary responsibility for providing support for single parent families should be borne by the State in the form of a Guaranteed Maintenance Allowance.[203] In the hands of the

---

200. See the National Economic and Social Council, *Alternative Strategies for Family Income Support* (N.E.S.C. Report No. 47) (Stationery Office, Dublin, 1980) at pp. 114-115.
201. See further, N.E.S.C. Report No. 47 at p. 120.
202. See K. O'Higgins, *supra*, p. 98-102.
203. *Supra*, p. 276-334; See also O'Higgins, *supra*, p. 125-126; D. Marsden, *Mothers Alone*, (Pelican Books, 1973) in particular chapter 15.

recipient such an allowance would be a substitute for maintenance payments under a court order. Maintenance payments would be assessed and collected by the Welfare Authority administering the allowance and they would be offset against the allowance paid and any excess paid to the recipient of the allowance. A spouse could still, under such a scheme, bring maintenance proceedings against the other spouse, if he or she so wished, but the primary responsibility to do so would rest with the State.

The provision of such a State allowance would relieve the unsupported spouse, to the maximum extent possible, of the pressures and anxieties attendant upon court proceedings for the assessment and enforcement of maintenance orders and would ensure the receipt of a regular and stable income, regardless of the extent to which the absent spouse or parent fulfills his or her obligation to provide support. As all single parents and dependent unsupported spouses would be entitled to receive such an allowance as of right the anomalies and inequities in the existing scheme for deserted wives would be avoided.

In New Zealand, the Social Security Amendment Act, 1973, introduced a social welfare scheme very similar to the form of single parent allowance suggested here.[204] Our present social welfare law in so far as it provides social assistance for deserted wives, unmarried mothers, prisoners' wives and widows already contains the foundations for such a scheme. Its introduction would bring to an end the present fragmented and unco-ordinated approach to income maintenance. It would not only provide a regular income for those entitled to it but would also enable the State to recover payments made from spouses who fail to meet their obligations, while eliminating the necessity for a direct confrontation between spouses before the courts.[205]

204. See 1975 N.Z.L.J. 6. See also J. Eekelaar, *Family Law and Social Policy* (Weidenfeld and Nicolson, London 1978) p. 203-204. See further R. Sackville, *Social Security and Family Law in Australia* (1978) 27, I.C.L.Q.127.

205. The Committee on Court Practice and Procedure in its 19th interim report recommended that as a long term reform "all maintenance orders should be met in the first instance by the local authority or Department of Social Welfare". However, the Committee failed to work out the manner in which such a system could operate. For example, under the Committee's recommendation, following the making of a maintenance order, the welfare authority would be required to pay such amount of maintenance as the court considered it reasonable for the defaulting spouse to pay, rather than such amount as is necessary to meet the needs of the recipients. Under such a system people with identical needs would receive different social welfare payments. Further, the Committee's recommendation assumes that responsibility for proceedings against the defaulting spouse will rest with the other spouse. For a brief discussion of the Committee's recommendations see W.R. Duncan, "Desertion and Maintenance" (1974), 9 I.J. (n.s.) 321. See also N.E.S.C. Report No. 47, *supra*, at p. 19 where the Council recommends "that a deserted wife who has children should be entitled to the Deserted Wife's Benefit or Allowance and that the State should collect any maintenance due from the deserting husband." Chapter 5 of the same report examines the Social Welfare Benefits payable to one parent families. It does not, however, elaborate further on the manner in which the Council's recommendation should be implemented.

CHAPTER 15

MATRIMONIAL PROPERTY

INTRODUCTION

At common law a married woman had no contractual capacity and any contract entered into by her prior to her marriage automatically vested in her husband. Similarly any property, whether real or personal, owned by her at the time of the marriage or acquired thereafter became his.

A husband's interest in his wife's freehold property only lasted during his lifetime. Upon his death, it reverted to his wife, if she survived him or to her heir, if she did not. An absolute disposition of a wife's freehold property could be made however if both spouses joined in the disposition.

A husband had greater power over his wife's leasehold property and could make an absolute disposition of it, during his lifetime without her consent but if he did not do so, she could claim it upon his death.[1] A wife's personal property was absolutely owned by her husband. An exception to this rule related to a wife's "paraphernalia" i.e. those articles of apparel and personal ornament as were suitable to her rank and degree, e.g. brooches or a coat. While these were the property of the husband during his lifetime, they reverted to the wife upon his death.

Equity mitigated the harshness of the common law rules by the development of the concept of property for a wife's 'separate use'. If property was transferred to trustees or to a wife's husband to apply it for the wife's 'separate use', it remained her separate property and she could deal with it as if she were unmarried. This doctrine conferred on a married woman a limited contractual capacity, as any property so held by her could become bound by a contract, although she herself was not personally bound on any agreement.[2]

The Married Women's Property Acts[3] extended a wife's contractual capacity but her liability still remained proprietary and not personal. The Act of 1882 provided that any property acquired by a wife after 1882 and all property belonging to a woman who married after that date, should remain her separate property and conferred capacity on a wife to avail of the same civil remedies for the protection and security of her own property as a *femme sole*. By the Act of 1893 every contract entered into by her, otherwise than as agent of her husband, was held to bind her.

The above Acts did not abolish the equitable concept of restraint upon anticipation. This doctrine arose in order to protect a wife from making an

---

1. See J.C.W. Wylie, *Irish Land Law* (Professional Books Ltd., London 1975) p. 876.
2. See G.W. Keeton and L.A. Sheridan, *Equity* (N.I.L.Q. Inc., 1969) Chap. XV.
3. 1865, 1870, 1874, 1882, 1884, 1893, 1907.

improvident disposition of her separate property. Upon equity vesting in the wife the beneficial interest in property given to her separate use, there was nothing to prevent her from conveying her interest to a money-grabbing husband. Thus, equity held that if a clause restraining alienation or anticipation was inserted in a grant of property, any disposition by which she purported to alienate such property or deal with its income was rendered void. Whilst this rule protected a wife against her husband's influence, it simultaneously prevented a wife from selling property subject to such restraint when it was in her interests to do so.[4] The Conveyancing Act, 1881, conferred power on the courts to remove a restraint and authorise a disposition of property, if a wife consented and it was for her benefit.[5] A restraint ceased to have effect upon the death of a husband.

The present law is governed by the Married Women's Status Act, 1957, under which a husband and wife are treated as two separate persons for all purposes of acquisition of property.[6] The doctrine of restraint upon anticipation is abolished.[7] A married woman can now acquire, hold and dispose of any property and is capable of contracting and being rendered personally liable in respect of her contracts and debts.[8] Any property she owns no longer automatically vests in her husband upon marriage and her husband is no longer liable for any contract entered into, or debt incurred, by her. As has been seen, however, he may be liable for necessaries supplied to his wife in certain circumstances[9] and in accordance with the general law of contract, he may be bound by any contract entered into or debt incurred by her acting as his agent.

PROPERTY RIGHTS DURING MARRIAGE

The general principle of separate property is that each spouse has independent and equal power to acquire and deal with his or her own property. Marriage as such no longer affects rights of ownership during the parties' lifetime. Whatever a party owns prior to marriage continues to belong to him after the ceremony. Each spouse owns his own income and any property that is acquired with it. There are nevertheless certain rules which curb spouses' proprietary freedom and statutes which provide special procedures for determining their property disputes. It is these that form the principal subject matter of the rest of this chapter.

The Resolution of Proprietary Disputes: The doctrine of separate property does not in practice provide easy solutions to disputes between a husband and wife over the ownership of property. Spouses tend to regard their earnings and property as part of the family assets rather than as belonging to either of them to the exclusion of the other. Arrangements as to domestic expenditure and ownership of property tend to be informal and undocumented. This is, of course, as it should be and will rarely give rise to any problems while spouses are living happily together. It is when a marriage breaks down and a dispute occurs that the domestic arrangements have to be unravelled and a determination

---

4. See Keeton and Sheridan, *supra*; Wylie, *supra* p. 877.
5. Sect. 39, subsequently replaced by the Conveyancing Act, 1911, Sect. 7.
6. Sect. 5.
7. Sect. 6.
8. *Ibid.*, Sect. 2 and Sect. 11. Although the Married Woman's Property Acts rendered a wife suable on her contracts and debts, she could only be sued to the extent of her separate estate. See *The State (Kingston) v. Circuit Court Judge of Cork* [1943] I.R. 611, (S.C.).
9. See p. 241 *ante*.

as to the rights of the parties over the 'family property' has to be made. The great majority of disputes relate to rights of ownership and possession of the matrimonial home and its contents. The respective rights of a husband and wife to such property and the means for ascertaining these rights are examined in the following pages.

THE MARRIED WOMEN'S STATUS ACT, 1957, SECT. 12

The Married Women's Status Act 1957, Section 12, provides a procedure for determining disputes "between husband and wife as to the title to or possession of any property". Either party may make a summary application to the Circuit Court or High Court for such determination and the court "may make such order, with respect to the property in dispute . . . as the Court thinks proper".[10] Section 12 of the Act of 1957 replaced section 17 of the Act of 1882 which permitted the Court upon such an application to make such order as it thought "fit".

If an application is made to the Circuit Court and the dispute concerns personal property (other than chattels real), the value of which exceeds £2,000 or land, the rateable valuation of which exceeds £60, upon a request by the defendant, the proceedings must be transferred to the High Court. Any order made or act done in the course of such proceedings before such transfer remains valid unless discharged or varied by order of the High Court.

The Courts Bill, 1980, as initiated, proposes to increase from £60 to £200 the limit of rateable value of land beyond which proceedings may be transferred from the Circuit Court to the High Court and to remove the limitation placed on the jurisdiction of the Circuit Court when dealing with personalty.

Section 12 procedure may be used for the determination of all proprietary disputes between spouses, whether the subject matter of the dispute is real or personal property and if the former, whether the dispute concerns the matrimonial home or any other real property. It is, however, the resolution of disputes as to title in and possession of the family home that is the particular concern of this section.

Disputes as to Title in the Matrimonial Home

The Married Women's Property Act, 1882, section 17 is still in force in England and Northern Ireland. The case law developed in these jurisdictions under section 17 is at the foundation of the decisions delivered by the Irish High Court under section 12 of the 1957 Act. Thus, it is intended first to examine the manner in which the courts in England and Northern Ireland have exercised their jurisdiction under section 17 of the 1882 Act. We shall then discuss the relevant Irish case law.

Section 17 of the 1882 Act[11]

There has been in recent years much judicial controversy as to the scope of

10. Sect. 12 (3); The provisions of Sect. 12 are said to be without prejudice to the rights conferred by Sect. 2. Thus, a spouse may, if he or she so wishes protect an interest in property by suing the other in tort rather than by bringing Sect. 12 proceedings.
11. For a more extensive coverage of the English decisions under Sect. 17 see generally J.G. Miller, *Family Property and Financial Provision* (Sweet & Maxwell, 1974); P.M. Bromley, *Family Law*, 6th edition (Butterworths, 1976) chapter 14; S.M. Cretney, *Principles of Family Law*, 3rd edition (Sweet & Maxwell, 1979), chapter 8; B. Passingham—*Law and Practice in Matrimonial Causes*, 2nd Ed. (1974 Butterworths, London) Ch. 15; J. Jackson and D.T.A. Davies, *Matrimonial Finance and Taxation* 2nd Ed. (1975 Butterworths, London),

the court's power under section 17. At one time it was said that the jurisdiction conferred by this section was purely discretionary, enabling the court to make such orders as appear to be fair and just in all the circumstances of the case. Building on the court's discretion, a doctrine of "family assets" was enunciated.[12] By this doctrine it was stated that

"Where a couple by their joint efforts, get a house and furniture, intending it to be a continuing provision for them for their joint lives, it is the *prima facie* inference from their conduct that the house and furniture is a 'family asset' in which each is entitled to an equal share. It matters not in whose name it stands; or who pays for what; or who goes out to work and who stays at home. If they both contribute to it by their joint efforts, the *prima facie* inference is that it belongs to them both equally: at any rate, when each makes a financial contribution which is substantial".[13]

The House of Lords in *Pettitt* v. *Pettitt*[14] and *Gissing* v. *Gissing*[15] denied the existence in English law of a doctrine of family assets. Section 17 of the Act of 1882 was held to confer on the court no wider powers than it had in relation to the determination of proprietary disputes in other types of proceedings.[16] The section was held to be purely procedural, giving the court no power to confer or vary property rights.[17] Lord Morris stated that in a question as to title or ownership of property the job of the court is to ask "whose is this" and not "to whom shall this be given".[18] The fact that the contesting parties' marriage has broken down does not affect the answer to that question. Their proprietary rights are in no way altered by their changed matrimonial circumstances.

While these cases determined the question of whether the court possessed any discretionary power, the difficulty of ascertaining the interest of the parties still exists. The following principles can be gleaned from the relevant English authorities:

I. In the first place, the beneficial ownership of the property in question depends on the agreement of the parties at the time of acquisition. Where the conveyance or lease declares not merely in whom the legal title is to vest but in whom the beneficial title is to vest, that concludes the question of title as between the spouses for all time and in the absence of fraud or mistake at the time of the transaction, the parties cannot go behind it at any future time.[19]

Ch. 16. See also A.A.S. Zuckeman, "Ownership of the Matrimonial Home; Common Sense and Reformist Nonsense" (1978) 94 L.Q.R. 26.

12. See *Hine* v. *Hine* [1962] 3 All E.R. 345 (C.A.); *Appleton* v. *Appleton* [1965] 1 W.L.R. 25 (C.A.); *Fribrance* v. *Fribrance* (No. 2) [1957] 1 All E.R. 357 (C.A.); *Ulrich* v. *Ulrich* [1968] 1 All E.R. 67 (C.A.); *Gissing* v. *Gissing* [1969] 2 Ch. 85 (C.A.).

13. Per Lord Denning, *Gissing* v. *Gissing, supra*, at p. 93 (C.A.).

14. [1970] A.C. 777 (H.L.).

15. [1971] A.C. 886 (H.L.).

16. ". . . in my opinion the decision in *Pettitt* v. *Pettitt* has established that there is not one law of property applicable where a dispute as to property is between spouses and another law of property where the dispute is between others" (per Viscount Dilhorne in *Gissing* v. *Gissing* at p. 899).

17. See also *Cobb* v. *Cobb* [1955] 2 All E.R. 696 (C.A.); *National Provincial Bank* v. *Ainsworth* [1965] A.C. 1175 (H.L.); *Cowcher* v. *Cowcher* [1972] 1 All E.R. 943 (Fam. D.); *McFarlane* v. *McFarlane* [1972] N.I. 59 (C.A.).

18. *Pettitt* v. *Pettitt, supra* at p. 798; See also *Bothe* v. *Amos* [1976] Fam. 46 at p. 54 (C.A.). The question to be determined is "What the title is: not what the title ought to be" per Megaw L.J.

·19. Per Lord Upjohn in *Pettitt* v. *Pettitt* at p. 813. See also *Leake* v. *Bruzzi* [1974] 2 All E.R. 1196 (C.A.); *Re Johns Assignment Trusts, Niven* v. *Niven* [1970] 2 All E.R. 210 (Ch. D.); *Bedson* v. *Bedson* [1965] 2 Q.B. 666 (C.A.); *Wilson* v. *Wilson* [1963] 2 All E.R. 447 (C.A.). (As for fraud see footnote 25.).

II. If the title documents are silent as to beneficial interest, in the absence of all other evidence, property conveyed into the name of one spouse *prima facie* confers on that spouse the whole beneficial interest, whilst property conveyed to the spouses jointly *prima facie* results in a joint acquisition of the beneficial interest.[20]

III. However, evidence is admissible that the spouse in whom legal title is vested holds all or part of that title on trust for the other spouse. Evidence is admissible as to the intention of the parties at the time of acquisition of the property.[21] In the absence of an agreement between the parties in order to discover their intentions, the court may draw an inference from their conduct[22] and the facts may result in the court holding all or part of the property to be held on an implied, constructive or resulting trust.[23]

IV. Two equitable presumptions may assist the court. By the presumption of resulting trust, if property is conveyed into the name of a person other than the one that provides the purchase price, the former is presumed to hold the property on trust for the purchaser. Thus, if a wife provides all or part of the purchase money for a house that is bought in her husband's name, he is regarded as holding all or part of the property on trust for her, i.e. she owns a beneficial interest in the property, proportionate to her contribution to its purchase, although the whole legal estate is vested in him. The presumption of advancement, however, comes into play where a husband puts property into his wife's name. By this, it is presumed that he intends to make a gift to her.[24] Both these presumptions are rebuttable by evidence that the wife intended a gift or that a husband intended to retain the beneficial interest. In recent English cases these presumptions have been said to have little relevance today and to be easily rebuttable.[25]

V. In determining the parties' proprietary interests, the court will look to both direct and indirect contributions made by the parties to the purchase of the property.[26] Thus, if the property is held in the name of one spouse (for example, the husband) but the other spouse has made a direct payment out of her own money towards the purchase price, the deposit, legal charges or mortgage instalments, the former will hold the property subject to a beneficial interest vested in the latter.[27] More complex is the position where a spouse contributes indirectly to the purchase. The relevant authorities concur in holding that for an indirect contribution to give rise to a share in the house, it must be of a substantial nature.[28] That, however, is the extent of their agreement.

---

20. Per Lord Upjohn, *Pettitt v. Pettitt, supra,* at p. 814.
21. *Re Rogers Question* [1948], 1 All E.R. 328, (C.A.).
22. Per Lord Upjohn, *Pettitt v. Pettitt, supra,* at p. 813. See also Lord Diplock and Lord Dilhorne in *Gissing v. Gissing, supra,* at p. 906.
23. Per Lord Reid and Lord Diplock, in *Gissing v. Gissing, supra,* pp. 897, 905.
24. See J.C. Wylie, *Irish Land Law, supra,* p. 450. See further *Watters v. Watters* (April 1979) Northern Ireland Law Reports Bulletin of Judgements (No. 3 of 1979) (H.C., N.I.).
25. See particularly the comments made in *Pettitt v. Pettitt, supra.* Evidence rebutting the presumptions is not admissable however if it discloses an improper or fraudulent motive, *Gascoigne v. Gascoigne* [1918], 1 K.B. 223; (K.B.D.); *Re Emery's Investment Trust* [1959], Ch. 410, (Ch. D.); *Tinker v. Tinker* [1970], P. 136; (C.A.); *Heseltine v. Heseltine* [1971], 1 All E.R. 952, (C.A.).
26. *Gissing v. Gissing, supra,* Lord Reid at p. 896, Lord Pearson at p. 903. Lord Diplock at p. 907.
27. See *Muetzel v. Muetzel* [1970], 1 All E.R. 443, (C.A.); *Cowcher v. Cowcher, supra;* *Falconer v. Falconer* [1970], 3 All E.R. 349, (C.A.); *Watters v. Watters, supra.*
28. The contribution may be by labour rather than cash—see *Smith v. Baker* [1970], 2 All E.R. 826, (C.A.). H and W built home themselves. W gave up job in order to participate

In *Gissing* and *Pettitt*, the Law Lords expressed conflicting views and as a result two streams of opinion have emerged.

(a). The English Court of Appeal has in a number of cases followed the *dicta* of Lord Reid in *Gissing* v. *Gissing* that if a wife assists a husband to purchase the matrimonial home by relieving him of other expenses which he would otherwise have had to bear, she makes an indirect contribution which entitles her to a share. Thus, in *Falconer* v. *Falconer* Lord Denning stated that the contribution

"may be indirect as where both go out to work and one pays the housekeeping and the other the mortgage instalments. It does not matter which way round it is. It does not matter who pays what. So long as there is a substantial financial contribution to the family expenses, it raises an inference of trust."[29]

In *Hazell* v. *Hazell* he stated

"it is sufficient if the contributions made by the wife are such as to relieve the husband from expenditure, which he would otherwise have had to bear. By so doing the wife helps him indirectly with the mortgage instalments because he has more money in his pocket with which to pay them. It may be that he does not strictly need her help—he may have enough money of his own without it—but if he accepts it (and thus is enabled to save more of his own money) she becomes entitled to a share."[30]

In *Hargrave* v. *Newton*[31] the Court of Appeal held that a wife had a beneficial interest in the matrimonial home which was solely in the husband's name. The money for the house was raised by the husband. So as to help meet all the family expenses, the wife went out to work. Some time later she was fortunate enough to obtain a reward upon finding stolen money. The wife's earnings and the reward money were used to meet household expenses such as clothes, food, telephone bills, etc. The court held that the substantial indirect contributions by the wife were such as to permit the court impute that the husband held the matrimonial home on trust for them both jointly, beneficially in equal shares. A comparison between the decision in this case and that of the House of Lords in *Gissing* v. *Gissing*[32] is instructive.

In the latter, the house was purchased by the husband and was also held solely in his name. The wife made no direct contribution to the purchase price but paid for some household items and the cost of laying the lawn. She went out to work and paid for her own clothes and those of her son.

The House of Lords unanimously held that she possessed no interest in the house. It is submitted that the decisions in these two cases cannot be reconciled. In both, the wife "relieved the husband from expenditure which he would otherwise have had to bear", yet in the former, she was held to have an interest in the house, whilst in the latter, she was held to have none.

(b). Lord McDermott in the Northern Ireland Court of Appeal in *McFarlane*

---

in building. See also *Cooke* v. *Head* [1972], 2 All E.R. 38, (C.A.).
   29. [1970], 3 All E.R. 449 at p. 452, (C.A.).
   30. [1972], 1 All E.R. 923 at p. 926, (C.A.). See also *Cooke* v. *Head, supra*; *Kowalczuk* v. *Kowalczuk* [1973], 2 All E.R. 1042, (C.A.)—held that a wife's indirect contributions gave her no interest in the matrimonial home which was purchased by husband before the parties met each other.
   31. [1971], 3 All E.R. 866, (C.A.).
   32. *Supra*.

v. *McFarlane*, relying on statements made by the majority in *Gissing*, stated that

"the indirect contributions of a spouse must, if they are to earn or generate a beneficial interest . . . in the property acquired, be the subject of some *agreement* or *arrangement* between the spouses sufficient to show a mutual intention that the indirect contributions will benefit the contributor in this way . . . I do not refer to a contractual relationship solely, but would include any understanding between the spouses, which shows a mutual intention that the indirect contributions of one or the other will go to create a beneficial proprietary interest in the contributor."[33]

An initial direct payment to the purchase price may constitute sufficient evidence of such mutual intention.[34]

In *McFarlane* it was held that the wife had no beneficial interest in the matrimonial home, which was held in the husband's name, despite the considerable indirect contribution made by her towards its acquisition. The wife had done part-time clerical work in her husband's business for no pay. The salary she earned from other work was used to meet ordinary household expenses including food for all the family and clothes for herself and her children. The husband paid rates, gas, electricity etc. Later on, she gave up her other job and entered her husband's business full-time and was paid a salary. This she also used for the household expenses. Subsequently the husband purchased a house, the title of which was in his sole name.

The court agreed that the wife's efforts made a substantial if indirect contribution to the funds out of which the house was purchased. As, however, there was no agreement or arrangement between the spouses as to ownership, the court held she had no beneficial interest in the property. On the principles used and applied by the English Court of Appeal in *Hargrave* v. *Newton* she would undoubtedly have been held to have a share in the home.[35]

Circumstances in which an indirect contribution *may* result in the acquisition of a beneficial interest in the matrimonial home

(a) If a spouse contributes to the finance available to purchase the home, by working for the other spouse in his business for no pay.[36]

(b) Where a spouse makes substantial improvements to property held by the other spouse.[37] Where however, "do-it-yourself" jobs are done by one spouse

---

33. [1972], N.I. 59, at p. 71. In *Gissing v. Gissing* Lord Dilhorne stated that "Proof of expenditure for the benefit of the family by one spouse will not of itself suffice to show any such common intention as to the ownership of the matrimonial home" (at p. 901). Lord Pearson stated "Contributions are not limited to those made directly in part payment of the price of the property or to those made at the time when the property is conveyed into the name of one of the spouses. For instance there can be a contribution if by arrangement between the spouses one of them by payment of the household expenses enables the other to pay the mortgage instalments", (at p. 903). See also *Cowcher v. Cowcher, supra*; *In re Barnes, a Bankrupt* (May 1979) Northern Ireland Law Reports, Bulletin of Judgements (No. 4 of 1979) (H.C., N.I.).

34. Per Lord Diplock, *Gissing v. Gissing, supra*, at p. 907. See also *Watters v. Watters, supra*.

35. See further L.J. Gibson, A Wife's Rights in the Matrimonial Home (1976) 27, N.I.L.Q. 333.

36. *Nixon v. Nixon* [1969], 3 All E.R. 1133, (C.A.). (Disapproved of by Lord McDermott in *McFarlane v. McFarlane*, the judgement in this case was delivered after the decision of the House of Lords in *Pettitt v. Pettitt* but before their decision in *Gissing v. Gissing*); see also *Muetzel v. Muetzel, supra*; *Re Cummins* [1972] Ch. 62; [1971] 3 All E.R. 782 ( )

37. *Jansen v. Jansen* [1965], P. 478, (C.A.) approved by Lord Reid and Lord Diplock in *Pettitt v. Pettitt*, disapproved of by Lords Hodson and Upjohn. See English Law Commission *Report on Financial Provision in Matrimonial Proceedings*, paras. 56–58. Law

on the property of the other, the former acquires no beneficial interest in the property.[38]

(c) Where a spouse assists in the building of the matrimonial home.[39]

(d) Where the wife's own finance is used to pay for food and other general family expenses, thus enabling the husband to make mortgage payments.[40]

(e) Where all or part of the purchase money comes from "joint savings" or a "common pool".[41]

Section 12 of the 1957 Act

The first High Court case in which a written judgement was delivered in the determination of a dispute under Section 12 of the 1957 Act is that of *Conway* v. *Conway*,[42] in which Kenny J. cited with approval a number of cases decided under Section 17 of the 1882 Act. *Conway* v. *Conway* has been expressly followed in a number of subsequent decisions and it is this case which shall be discussed first.

In *Conway* v. *Conway* the parties married in 1961. In 1963 a house was purchased by the husband, (the defendant in these proceedings) in his name only. The wife (the plaintiff) had inherited a sum of £242 and she gave it to the husband so that he could pay the deposit and the expenses of the purchase of the house. The rest of the money was obtained by the husband by way of a mortgage of £2,005. At various times the husband was unable to make the mortgage repayments and as a consequence the wife gave him money of her own so that he could pay the instalments due. The total amount contributed by her to the purchase price of the house and the mortgage repayments was £1,027. Upon the parties' marriage breaking down, the wife brought proceedings and succeeded in claiming a right to half of the beneficial interest in the house. Giving judgement Kenny J. stated:

> "When the matrimonial home is purchased in the name of the husband either before or after marriage, the wife does not as wife become entitled to any share in its ownership either because she occupies the status of wife or because she carries out household duties.[43] In many cases however, the wife contributes to the purchase price or mortgage instalments. Her contributions may be either by payment to the husband of moneys which she has inherited or earned or by paying the expenses of the household so that he has the money which makes it possible for him to pay mortgage

Commission No. 25 and The Matrimonial Proceedings and Property Act, 1970, Sect. 37. See also *Davis v. Vale* [1971], 2 All E.R. 1021, (C.A.); *Harnett v. Harnett* [1974], 1 All E.R. 764 (C.A.); *Re Nicholson, Nicholson v. Perks* [1974], 2 All E.R. 386, (Ch. D.).

38. *Button v. Button* [1968], 1 All E.R. 1064, (C.A.); *Pettitt v. Pettitt, supra*; *Gissing v. Gissing, supra*.

39. *Smith v. Baker, supra*; *Cooke v. Head, supra*—Here an unmarried couple together built a bungalow, in which they intended to live when finished. L did a great deal of heavy building work and was held to have a beneficial interest in the property.

40. See e.g. *Falconer v. Falconer, supra*; *Hazell v. Hazell, supra*; *Hargrave v. Newton, supra*; alternatively see *Gissing v. Gissing, supra*; *Cowcher v. Cowcher, supra*; *McFarlane v. McFarlane, supra*.

41. See *Re Densham*, [1975], 3 All E.R. 726, (Ch. D.); *Davis v. Vale, supra*; *Jones v. Maynard* [1951], Ch. 572, (C.A.); *Heseltine v. Heseltine* [1971], 1 All E.R. 952 (C.A.). *Re Bishop* [1965], 1 All E.R. 249; [1965], Ch. 450 (Ch. D.); *Watters v. Watters, supra*.

42. [1976] I.R. 254 (H.C.); (1975) 111 I.L.T.R. 133 (H.C.).

43. See also *R.K. v. M.K.* (October 1978) unreported, (H.C.) in which Finlay P. stated "The extent of her (the wife's) work in the household and in the care of her children was very considerable but our law does not recognise so far at least a right arising from that type of work to a part ownership of any family or marriage property".

instalments".[44]

He then noted that domestic arrangements between spouses are usually informal and continued:

"When there is an agreement between them as to the ownership of the house which is in the husband's name only, the Court will enforce it but the number of cases in which this happens is small".[45]

Where there is no agreement, however, he stated

"Trying to infer what was the implied agreement which arose when payments were made or expenses paid by a wife is a futile task because when the spouses are living happily together, they do not think of stipulating that payments by one of them are made to acquire a share in the matrimonial home or furniture. I think that the correct and most useful approach to these difficult cases is to apply the concept of a trust to the legal relationship which arises when a wife makes payments towards the purchase of a house or the repayment of the mortgage instalments when the house is in the sole name of the husband. When this is done, he becomes a trustee for her of a share in the house and the size of it depends upon the amount of the contributions which she has made towards the purchase or the repayment of the mortgage".[46]

He concluded this part of his judgement by stating that the decisions in *Pettitt*, *Gissing*, *McFarlane*, *Hazell*, *Kowalczuk* and his earlier judgement in *Heavey* v. *Heavey*[47] supported the above stated principles. As we have seen, however, the above cited cases are by no means consistent, in certain respects conflicting principles being stated by different judges. Whereas the actual decision in *Conway* cannot be faulted it left undecided the question of whether a wife may obtain a beneficial interest in the matrimonial home if by paying the household expenses she relieves the husband from expenditure which he would otherwise have to bear, or whether before such expenditure can give rise to an interest, there must be an agreement or arrangement between the spouses as to ownership.

In *M.* v. *M.*[48] a property was purchased by the defendant wife in her sole name in 1972 to provide a source of income. The purchase price was £8,500 and renovations were carried out at a cost of a further £4,000 to convert it into a number of bedsittingrooms. A loan for the deposit was obtained by the wife from her sister in the sum of £2,225. The balance of the purchase price, a sum just in excess of £6,000, was obtained on loan from a bank. The sum of £4,000 was provided out of the proceeds of sale of a public house in which the court held the plaintiff's husband had a 19% share, the wife owning the remainder, 81%. For a considerable time after the purchase of the premises, the rents were used solely to pay off the two loans and at the date of the court hearing they had both been discharged. From the date of the purchase, the husband who was working in the United States, sent a large portion of his earnings home for the maintenance of his wife and children. It was admitted by the wife in evidence that if she had not received these moneys she could not have fully discharged both loans. Throughout the period when the loans were being paid off, the wife and her children lived rent free with the wife's sister. The court held that 60% of

44. *Supra* at pp. 257 and 134.
45. *Ibid.*
46. [1976] I.R. at p. 258; (1975) 111 I.L.T.R. at pp. 134–135.
47. (1974) 111 I.L.T.R. 1 (H.C.). See p. 314 *infra*.
48. (1978), 114 I.L.T.R. 46 (H.C.).

the beneficial interest in the property was vested in the wife and 40% in the husband. Apart from the sum of £4,000 which was held by the parties in the above stated shares, Finlay P. stated that he must on the evidence

"take the view that(the)loans were ultimately equally discharged by the contributions of the plaintiff and the defendant. It is quite clear to me . . . that the plaintiff's contributions from his salary and working in New York to the family made a clear indirect contribution towards the clearing of these loans. At the same time the arrangement made by the defendant (wife) with her own family...in particular with her sister, which provided free board and lodging for herself and her children together with what I am satisfied, on the evidence, was an active participation by her in the running and letting of the premises constituted a contribution on her part towards the reduction of the loans. It is not possible for me to make any precise calculation as to the shares in which these contributions were made but I take the view that, having regard to the relationships of the parties and the financial arrangements between them, the equitable conclusion is that they contributed equally to the clearing of these amounts of loans off the property and to the consequential enlargement of the equity in it."[48a]

In *K.* v. *K.*[49] Finlay P. held that the plaintiff wife had a 28% share of the beneficial interest in the family home and a 50% share of the beneficial interest in the leases of two shops, the legal title in all three being held by the husband in his sole name. The former share arose as a result of contributions made by the wife towards the maintenance of the family including the mortgage repayments and other household expenses. The latter share arose due to the fact that the rents payable for both shops came out of profits made in a limited liability company in which the wife held a 50% share and in which she was an active participant. No moneys were paid for the leases and the court held that the real cost of their acquisition consisted of the payment of rent and observance of the other covenants in the leases.

In *M.* v. *M.* and *K.* v. *K.* both direct and indirect contributions had been made to the purchase of the properties in dispute by the spouses who successfully claimed a beneficial interest in them.[50]

In *R.* v. *R.*[51] a claim to a beneficial interest in a family home succeeded solely on the basis of a spouse's indirect contributions. The parties, in this case, had married in 1968. A year later the family home was purchased in the husband's sole name and the deposit and mortgage repayments were all paid by the husband. Between 1968 and 1973, when the parties separated, the wife worked on average thirty-three weeks per year.

The court held that had the wife not been working, the husband would not have been able to keep up the mortgage repayments, maintain their standard of living and run a car, which he required for his job. The wife spent some of her earnings on providing food and other household requisites and she spent some on clothes for herself and visits to the hairdressers.

McMahon J., holding that the wife had an 18% beneficial interest in the home, stated that there was no distinction between moneys used by the wife for

48a. *Ibid.*, at p. 49.
49. (1978) 114 I.L.T.R. 50 (H.C.). See also the unreported High Court judgement delivered by Barrington J. in the same case in October 1980. See Ftn. 89 *infra*.
50. In *M.* v. *M.*, *supra*, Finlay P. held the total cost of acquisition and renovation of the property to be the purchase price i.e. the sum of £12,500. Thus, the plaintiff husband contributed directly with his 19% share in the sum of £4,000 spent on renovations and indirectly with the moneys sent home from New York.
51. (January 1979), unreported, (H.C.). See also *W.* v. *W.* (March 1981) unreported (H.C.) in Appendix E.

necessaries for herself or for household purposes. He stated "so far as the money was spent on the wife's needs it seems to me that these were expenses which the husband would have been forced to meet if she were not able to pay for them herself". He continued

> "both kinds of expenditure come within the principles enunciated by Kenny J. in *Conway* v. *Conway* . . . namely that the wife's contribution which will give her a claim to a beneficial interest in the matrimonial home may take the form of paying the expenses of the household so that her husband has the money which makes it possible for him to pay the mortgage instalments. In either case there is a saving to the husband and if that enables him pro tanto to meet the mortgage repayments the wife should be regarded as contributing towards these repayments".

In the subsequent case of *M.B.* v. *E.B.*[51a] a wife's financial contributions to the purchase of furniture and other household goods and towards the general household expenses were held to confer on the wife a beneficial interest in the family home. The legal title in the home was held by the husband in his sole name and no direct payments had been made by the wife towards its acquisition. The wife in evidence had stated that there was "a kind of an agreement" between them under which the husband paid the mortgage and the electricity bills and she bought virtually everything else that was required for the house.

Barrington J. stated that:

> "Marriage partners seldom enter into formal agreements when the marriage is going well. But, the understanding between them may, at times, be seen in their actions or course of conduct. If they appear to be acting on the principle that all things are common between friends, then . . . a court can readily infer that that principle gives the basic understanding between them."

The wife merely claimed an interest in a two fifths share of the house, as three fifths of the purchase price had been paid in cash by the husband at the time of the purchase and the wife had made no contribution to this sum. The wife also claimed, in the alternative, an interest in the household goods and furniture.

Barrington J. found that on the facts of the case, there clearly was an understanding between the parties that they were, by their joint efforts, to buy and furnish a home and held that the wife was entitled to a one fifth share in the beneficial interest in the home and to a one half share in the household goods and furniture. The learned judge cited with approval both the judgements of McMahon J. in *R.* v. *R.* and of Lord Denning in *Hazell* v. *Hazell* and it appears from the judgement delivered, that even in the absence of such a finding, the court would have held that the indirect contributions made by the wife gave rise to the acquisition by her of a beneficial interest in both the home and household chattels.[51b]

It is clear from the decided cases that if the legal title in the family home is vested in the sole name of one spouse, in the absence of proof of an agreement or arrangement to the contrary, the size of the beneficial interest the other spouse may successfully claim is dependent upon the proportionate value of that spouse's contribution towards the acquisition of the home when compared with the contribution made by the spouse in whose name the legal title is vested.[52] More-

---

51a. (February 1980) unreported (H.C.).
51b. See further *W.* v. *W.* (March 1981) unreported (H.C.) summarised in Appendix E.
52. See also *L.* v. *L.* (December 1979), unreported, (H.C.) where the court held a wife

over, it appears from the decision in *R.* v. *R.* that if a spouse contributes to the household expenses and in so doing relieves the other spouse from expenditure he would otherwise be bound to meet, leaving him free to make the mortgage repayments, the former may acquire a beneficial interest in the family home without making any direct contributions towards its purchase or without any agreement or arrangement existing between the spouses. Thus, Irish case law at this stage appears to be following the line of English authorities that have resulted from the judgement of Lord Reid in *Gissing* v. *Gissing* and to be rejecting the narrower approach illustrated by the judgement of Lord McDermott in *McFarlane* v. *McFarlane.*[53] However, until the Supreme Court has clearly set down the circumstances in which an indirect contribution towards the purchase of property by itself gives rise to a beneficial interest in it, the law will remain uncertain.

The judgement in *Heavey* v. *Heavey*[54] sheds no further light on the above issue but is of interest in so far as it indicates the approach of the courts when dealing with a claim by a husband to property purchased by him with funds contributed by both spouses but which is purchased by the husband in his wife's sole name.[55]

In 1967 the husband purchased a house with money from a joint bank account in the name of his wife and himself. The house was conveyed at the time of purchase into the wife's name. The husband gave two reasons for vesting title in his wife (a) to help avoid death duties after his death and (b) to invest money given to him by his wife over the previous years.

The total cost of purchase was £16,904. The property was converted into luxury flats at a further cost of £16,560 which was financed by an overdraft given by the Bank of Ireland to the husband. From the date of conversion until May 1973 the husband received most of the rents from the house. After the latter date they were collected by the wife. In proceedings brought under section 12, the court held the wife to be beneficially entitled to the entire interest in the property. No reasons are given for this decision in the only available written judgement relating to the dispute between the parties. Subsequent to that decision the wife applied for an account of the rents and profits arising out of the house, received by her husband, from the date of purchase until May 1973. The wife then claimed payment of £23,000 from her husband, which was that part of the rent received by him that had not been made over to her. The court held the husband to be entitled to credit against the rents which he collected for the amount which he owed to the bank in connection with the purchase and conversion of the premises by him, together with the probable amount of interest which he had to pay.

Kenny J. giving judgement stated that

"It is a presumption of law that when a husband makes a purchase of property or transfers money or securities into the name of his wife solely, it is intended as a gift to her absolutely at once and there is no resulting trust in his favour . . . The same principle applies when a husband expends his own money on the property of his wife even if that property has been

had a 35% beneficial interest in the family home. This interest resulted from the wife contributing to a family fund out of which mortgage repayments were made and using a large portion of her own earnings to meet other family and household expenditure. See further *O'R.* v. *O'R.* (October 1978), unreported, (H.C.).

53. See also *W.* v. *W.* (March 1981) unreported (H.C.) in Appendix E. See, however, *McGill* v. *S.* [1979] I.R. 283 (H.C.) discussed on p. 376 *et seq.*

54. *Supra.*

55. See further *M.* v. *M., supra.* Here the spouse who made the arrangements for purchase appears to have been the wife.

transferred by him to her. It is, however, not an absolute rule of law that the wife gets the benefit of the expenditure, it is a presumption only which may be rebutted by evidence so that if the wife leads the husband to believe that money which he spends on improving her property will be repaid to him out of the rents of the property when improved, he has a valid claim to be reimbursed out of the rents".[56]

In the absence of a husband being so led he had no claim to reimbursement. Kenny J. continued

"This principle however, does not apply when the husband has borrowed the money to purchase the property or to carry out the improvements. If the wife is aware that the husband is borrowing the money for either of these purposes, it would, in my view, be inequitable for her, when a dispute arises between them, to retain the rents for herself and to refuse to have the outstanding debt incurred by the husband paid out of them. In this case the wife was keeping the husband's books and knew that part of the cost of purchasing the property and the entire cost of converting them was being financed by a bank loan given to the husband".[57]

The Supreme Court dismissed an appeal, made by the husband, against the above decision in July 1976. There was, however, no written judgement delivered by the court.[58]

Disputes as to Possession of the Matrimonial Home

Although the House of Lords in *Pettitt* v. *Pettitt* held that section 17 of the 1882 Act conferred on the court no jurisdiction to transfer or vary rights in property, it was stated that the section confers

"A wide discretion as to the enforcement of the proprietary or possessory rights of one spouse in any property against the other".[59]

In England this discretionary power has been exercised so as to restrain a husband from disposing of any interest in a home vested solely in his name until he has provided his wife with suitable alternative accommodation.[60]

In the Irish case of *Heavey* v. *Heavey*, whilst the wife succeeded in her claim

---

56. *Supra* at p. 3.
57. *Ibid.*, at p. 4.
58. The perfected order of the Supreme Court did not become available until January 1977. For further judgements under section 12 see *B.* v. *B.* (July 1978), unreported, (H.C.) in which Finlay P. held the spouses to have a joint beneficial interest in a farm, the legal title of which was held by the spouses jointly. The moneys used for the purchase of the farm had derived from moneys given by the wife's mother to the parties for the purchase of a house. Also *P.* v. *P.* (3, 1980) & *E.R.* v. *M.R.* (1, 1981): unreported. H.C. See Circuit Ct. judgement of Judge McWilliam in *Galligan* v. *Galligan* (1976), vol. 70 No. 7 of the *Gazette of the Incorporated Law Society of Ireland*, "Recent Irish Cases", p. 25. Here a farm purchased from a joint bank account was held to belong to the spouses jointly although purchased in the husband's sole name. Both spouses worked putting their money into a joint "pool". Cases referred to in the judgement but not mentioned in the Gazette Report included *Jones* v. *Maynard, supra*, and *Gissing* v. *Gissing, supra*.
59. Per Lord Diplock at p. 820. See also *National Provincial Bank Ltd.* v. *Ainsworth*, 1965, A.C. 1175, (H.L.) at p. 1220. "The court has a discretion (under Sect. 17) to be exercised in the interest of the parties to restrain or postpone the enforcement of legal rights but not to vary agreed or established rights in property in an endeavour to achieve a kind of palm tree justice". Per Lord Hodson. See also judgement of Lord Wilberforce at p. 1246.
60. *Lee* v. *Lee* [1952], 2 Q.B. 489, (C.A.) approved by House of Lords in *National Provincial Bank* v. *Ainsworth*, by Lord Hodson at p. 1220, Lord Cohen at p. 1228, Lord Upjohn at p. 1233, Lord Wilberforce at p. 1258. See also *Halden* v. *Halden* [1966], 3 All E.R. 412, (C.A.).

to ownership of a house converted into flats, it was held that she had no beneficial interest in the matrimonial home, the title of which was held solely by the husband. Kenny J. nevertheless made an order restraining the husband from selling the home "until he provided such alternative suitable accommodation for the wife as might be sanctioned by the court". In *Conway* v. *Conway* after declaring the parties to have a joint beneficial interest in the matrimonial home, Kenny J. granted an injunction restraining the husband from entering it because his behaviour had been so "outrageous". Thus, it seems that the court, in exercise of the jurisdiction conferred upon it by section 12, has a far-reaching discretionary power to control the manner in which a spouse exercises his proprietary rights and in so doing may protect the right of the other spouse to reside in the matrimonial home.[61]

The common law right of a wife to reside in the matrimonial home[62] has been held to be a purely personal right enforceable against her husband but unenforceable against third parties.[63] Thus, whilst it can be invoked to restrain a husband from selling the matrimonial home until he provides his wife with alternative accommodation, it cannot be invoked to prevent a purchaser obtaining possession of the home, upon it being sold by her husband without her knowledge.[64] Two recent legislative enactments have sought to give added protection to the right of a wife to occupy the matrimonial home, free from molestation or attack, without the fear of her husband selling it behind her back. The provisions of these will now be examined.

THE FAMILY HOME PROTECTION ACT, 1976[65]

The Family Home Protection Act came into force on the 12th July, 1976. Its primary object is to ensure that a spouse will not sell or otherwise dispose of the family home behind the back of his family and without the prior consent of the other spouse.[66]

Whilst the Act applies equally to a husband and to a wife, for the sake of convenience in the discussion that follows, it will be presumed that title in the property is vested in the husband alone and that the consent required is that of the wife. This is the situation that arises in practice in the majority of cases.

---

61. See also the old case of *Gaynor v. Gaynor* [1901], 1 I.R. 217, (M.R.) where the Master of the Rolls refused to grant an injunction preventing the husband from entering the matrimonial home, the title of which was in his wife's name, on the ground that he did not wish to do "indirectly that which could be done directly by proper proceedings, viz. to grant a judicial separation". It is submitted that this decision is of no importance to-day.

62. The common law right of a wife to reside in the matrimonial home by virtue of her status as wife was accepted by the House of Lords in *National Provincial Bank Ltd. v. Ainsworth, supra*. See extra-judicial comments of Kenny J. in "Some Aspects of Family Law", S.Y.S. Lecture No. 46 (1970).

63. *Ibid.*

64. If the transaction is purely a sham to enable a husband to obtain possession however, the wife's rights are protected—see *Ferris v. Weaven* [1952], 2 All E.R. 233, (Q.B.D.) Jones J. approved in *National Provincial Bank v. Ainsworth, supra.*

65. See generally J.C.W. Wylie, *Irish Conveyancing Law* (Professional Books Ltd., 1978) p. 198 *et seq.*; P. Ussher, "The Position of a Purchaser Under the Family Home Protection Act, 1976" (January 1977) Vol. 71 *The Gazette of the Incorporated Law Society of Ireland* 3; J. Macken, "The Family Home Protection Act, 1976" (March 1977) 111 I.L.T. & S.J. pp. 52, 59, 65, 71; F. Daly, "The Effect on Conveyancing Practice of the New Law Society Contract for Sale and the Family Home Protection Act, 1976" (S.Y.S. Lecture No. 79, November 1976); M. Carroll, "The Family Home Protection Act, 1976" (S.Y.S. Lecture No. 124, April 1980).

66. *Somers v. Weir* [1979] I.R. 94; (1979) 113 I.L.T.R. 81 (S.C.). See also Dáil Debates vol. 291, Cols. 54 *et seq.*

Family home: The term "family home" means primarily a dwelling in which a married couple ordinarily reside. The expression is said also to comprise a dwelling in which a spouse whose protection is in issue ordinarily resides, or if that spouse has left the other spouse, ordinarily resided before so leaving.[67] Thus, two separate houses could under this definition be regarded at the same time as a "family home". For example, B. owns house X and house Y; B. and Mrs. B. live together in house X for a number of years after their marriage, then B. forces Mrs. B. to leave and go and live in house Y with their children. House Y is the family home in which Mrs. B. is now ordinarily residing, whilst house X is the home in which she ordinarily resided before leaving.

The term dwelling includes any building, or any structure vehicle or vessel (whether mobile or not), or part thereof, occupied as a separate dwelling and includes any garden or portion of ground attached to and usually occupied with the dwelling, or otherwise required for the amenity or convenience of the dwelling. The Act does not apply to any dwelling in which the wife has never resided. Thus, if a husband leaves his wife and goes to live elsewhere, if the wife never resides in his new home, it is outside the scope of the Act.

Whilst in general the Act does not apply to the sale of business premises, in certain circumstances a wife's consent will be required for such a sale. For example, where a portion of the premises are used for residential purposes by the family and another portion for business purposes, it may not be possible or practical to dispose of the latter part of the premises without the former.

The requirement of consent: By section 3(1) of the Act, if a spouse without the prior consent in writing of the other spouse, purports to convey any interest[68] in the family home to any person except the other spouse . . . the purported conveyance is void, subject to certain specified exceptions.

1. By section 3(2), sub-s. (1) does not apply to a conveyance made by a spouse in pursuance of an enforceable agreement made before the marriage of the parties. For example, A. contracts to sell his house to B. Subsequently, A. marries C. and they reside in the house for some time before the conveyance is completed. C.'s consent to the conveyance is not required under this provision.

2. Section 3(3) provides that no conveyance is void by reason only of sub-s.(1).

   (a) If it is made to a *bona fide* purchaser for full value.[69]

   (b) If it is made by a person other than the spouse referred to in section

67. Sect. 2. A dwelling may be a family home for the purposes of the Act if a husband and wife ordinarily resided in it, either before or after the coming into force of the Act. See *Somers v. Weir* (1979) 113 I.L.T.R. 81 (S.C.) and *H. and L. v. S.* (July 1979), unreported, (H.C.). In both of these cases the spouses resided together in the home until 1973 when the wife in each case left the home taking the children with her. See also *Hegarty v. Morgan* (1979) 113 I.L.T. & S.J. 173 (H.C.).

68. "Interest" means any estate, right, title or other interest legal or equitable—Sect. 1 (1).

69. See Sect. 3 (6) which states that: "Purchaser means a grantee, lessee, assignee, mortgagee, chargeant or other person who in *good faith* acquires an estate or interest in the property". Thus, a person who does not acquire an estate or interest in good faith, is not a purchaser within the meaning of the Act.

"Full value" is said to mean "such value as amounts or approximates to the value of that for which it is given".—Sect. 3 (5).

In the text 2 (a) and (b) above should merely refer to a purchaser for full value (a) or for value (b) and the word purchaser implies that the person acquired the interest in good faith. However, for clarity the more usual term of *bona fide* purchaser is used in the text, as it is easy otherwise to lose sight of the fact that, for example in (a), to be exempt from the requirement of consent, a person must not only give full value but must also be *bona fide*.

3(1) to a *bona fide* purchaser for value.[70]

(c) If its validity depends on the validity of a conveyance in respect of which any of the conditions mentioned in sub-s. (2) or para. (a) or (b) are satisfied.

The Act attempts to strike a balance between protecting the interests of a wife and those of a *bona fide* purchaser. For example, having regard to para. (a) above, if a vendor conceals the fact of his marriage and does not obtain his wife's consent to a conveyance of what, unknown to the purchaser, is the family home, the appearance of the vendor's wife subsequent to the closing of the sale will not affect the interest in the property conveyed to the purchaser, if the latter has no notice of the marriage or the wife's existence, is *bone fide* and has given "full value".

To be *bona fide*, the purchaser must not have notice that at the time of the conveyance the property purchased was a family home. Absence of notice does not mean however that the validity of a conveyance cannot be impugned if a purchaser remains quiet and asks no questions. By virtue of the Conveyancing Act, 1882, Sect. 3, a purchaser will be held to have notice, if the fact that the property conveyed was a family home was within his own knowledge or

"would have come to his knowledge if such inquiries and inspections had been made as ought reasonably to have been made by him".

Moreover notice may be imputed to him if in the same transaction, such a fact

"has come to the knowledge of his counsel or of his solicitor or other agent or would have come to the knowledge of his solicitor or agent if such inquiries and inspections had been made as ought reasonably to have been made by the solicitor or agent".[71]

In *Somers* v. *Weir*[72] the purchaser's solicitor failed to make the enquiries he reasonably ought to have made to properly ascertain whether a wife's consent was required for the valid conveyance of a house. Her consent was not obtained and as a result the conveyance was held to be null and void.

The husband and wife resided together in the house from 1961 until 1973, when their marriage broke down and the wife left the house taking her children with her. In 1974 the parties entered into a separation agreement. The husband continued to reside in the house and on the 2nd August, 1976 entered into a written agreement to sell it. The sale was completed on the 17th August, 1976.

The Supreme Court held that the property in question was a family home and could not have been properly conveyed by the husband without the prior consent

---

70. See footnote 69, *supra*.
71. Conveyancing Act, 1882, Sect. 3 (1) para. (ii) as amended by Sect. 3 (7) of the Family Home Protection Act, 1976. See *Somers v. Weir, supra*; *M.D. v. L.D. and Ors.* (December 1978), unreported, (H.C.). See also *Hegarty v. Morgan, supra*.
72. *Supra*. See also *H. and L. v. S.* (July 1979), unreported, (H.C.) in which a conveyance was declared null and void in similar circumstances. See further *Hegarty v. Morgan, supra*, in which a contract for sale was rescinded due to the inadequacy of the vendor's Family Home Protection Act Statutory Declaration and the vendor's refusal to take further steps to establish that the property was not a "family home" within the meaning of the Act. On the other hand, see *Guckian and Anor. v. Brennan and Anor.* (March 1980), unreported, (H.C.) in which it was held that the vendors of registered land are not required for the purposes of The Family Home Protection Act to furnish a purchaser with evidence that the provisions of the Act were complied with when the property was originally assigned to them (the vendors). The court held that the duty of ensuring that the original transfer to the vendors was valid and effective fell upon the registrar at the time of registration and that the "register thereafter, in the absence of fraud, affords conclusive evidence of the validity of the title". See further p.

of his wife. If the necessary enquiries had been made by the purchaser's solicitor he would have been aware of this and, thus, the purchaser was held, by imputation, to have notice of the position at the time of the conveyance. The purchaser's solicitor had without further enquiry, wrongly accepted as sufficient for the purposes of the Act, the husband's statutory declaration stating that since he had executed a separation agreement with his wife, she had not relied on the property in question as her family home and that "by virtue of said separation agreement she has now no interest therein". The solicitor had never seen the separation agreement which in fact made no reference at all to the family home.

The guiding principle in a conveyancing transaction is *caveat emptor*—let the buyer beware.[73] It is the responsibility of the purchaser to investigate the vendor's title, and if he does not observe the appropriate conveyancing procedures, he will be held to have notice of matters which would have been discovered if the proper procedure had been observed by him. In order to comply with the above requirement and properly protect a purchaser's interests, it is now essential when purchasing property which could have been used as a family home to raise the appropriate requisitions on title, enquiring as to whether the property comes within the provisions of the Act.[74] In the event of such requisitions not being made, the appearance of a spouse after the purchase of what turns out to have been the family home may render the transaction void.[75]

73. See generally J.C.W. Wylie, *Irish Conveyancing Law, supra*, Chap. 5.

74. In a letter from the President to its members on 23rd July, 1976 the Council of the Incorporated Law Society suggested the following requisitions: (1) Is the property sold a family home within the meaning of The Family Home Protection Act, 1976? (2) If so, please furnish the consent of the other spouse to the sale by endorsement on the purchase deed. (3) If the property is stated not to be a family home by reason of the vendor being unmarried, please furnish a statutory declaration verifying the fact.*

Although it is not necessary in order to fulfil the requirement of the Act that a consent be endorsed on the deed (see p. 286) a consent so endorsed will assist the purchaser establishing proper title after the conveyance is completed if required to do so in order, for example, to raise a mortgage or simply resell the property.

*A property may, of course, not be a family home within the meaning of the Act even if the vendor is married, for example, the vendor's wife may never have resided in the property and it is suggested that the words "by reason of the vendor being unmarried" should be excluded from this requisition. As for the content of the required declaration see *Hegarty v. Morgan, supra*, in which McWilliam J. stated "in my opinion a statutory declaration should set out the facts establishing that the premises are not a family home". A bald statement that premises are not a family home within the meaning of the Act will in many cases be insufficient to satisfy the requirements of the Act.

75. For a general discussion of the Doctrine of Notice see J.C.W. Wylie, *Irish Land Law*, (Professional Books Ltd., London 1975), p. 102 *et seq*. See also *Northern Bank Ltd. v. Henry and Ors*. (June 1978) unreported, (H.C.); (April 1980), unreported, (S.C.) See, in particular, the judgements of the Supreme Court in which section 3 of the Conveyancing Act, 1882 and the Doctrine of Constructive Notice are given detailed consideration. In his judgement Kenny J. referring to decided cases stated that "a purchaser or mortgagee who omits to make such enquiries and inspections as a prudent and reasonable purchaser or mortgagee acting on skilled advice would have made will be fixed with notice of what he would have discovered if he had made the enquiries and inspections which ought reasonably to have been made by him." Further on he continued "the test then is the prudent purchaser acting on skilled advice. Such a purchaser would certainly not abstain from enquiry in an attempt to avoid having notice."

The court held that the test to determine whether a conveyancer has fully complied with the duty imposed on him is an objective one. Henchy J. stated "the test of what enquiries and inspections ought reasonably to have been made is an objective test, depending not on what the particular purchaser thought proper to do in the particular circumstances, but on what a purchaser of the particular property ought reasonably to have done in order to acquire title to it . . . (a purchaser) must expect to be judged by what an ordinary purchaser, advised by a competent lawyer, would reasonably enquire about or inspect for the purpose of getting a good title . . . and a reasonable purchaser is one who not only consults his own needs or preferences but also has regard to whether the purchase may prejudicially and unfairly affect the rights of third parties in the property."

Paragraphs (b) and (c) are not easy to construe. One of their purposes is to prevent a series of invalid transactions. For example, although a conveyance from X to Y may be void by reason of section 3(1), a subsequent conveyance by Y to Z may vest a valid title in the latter if he is a *bona fide* purchaser for value, as the conveyance is by a person (Y) other than the spouse making the purported conveyance (X) referred to in section 3(1).[76] In the event of a sale by Z, paragraph (c) guarantees the validity of Z's title.

Paragraph (b) also permits a mortgagee,[77] or if the house-owning spouse goes bankrupt, the Official Assignee in bankruptcy, to convey a family home free from the requirement of obtaining a consent. Under this paragraph, it also appears open to a spouse wishing to acquire a house for use as a "family home", to evade being bound in the future to obtain a consent if he wishes to sell it, by purchasing the house through a company in which such spouse holds the controlling interest. If the property is vested beneficially in the company, a future conveyance of it would be by "a person other than the spouse referred to in section 3(1)" and no consent would be required. Finally, if a dispute arises as to the validity of a conveyance under the Act, the burden of proving that validity is placed on the person alleging it.[78]

The language of section 3 is obscure and unnecessarily complicated. An amending section clearly spelling out the circumstances in which section 3(1) will not affect the validity of a conveyance is urgently required, if much unnecessary and difficult litigation is to be avoided.

Spouse's Prior Written Consent: The spouse whose prior consent is necessary to fulfil the requirements of the Act is the legally recognised spouse of the person conveying the family home. The Act places no age limitation on a spouse's capacity to grant a consent but it has been suggested[79] that as a consequence of a minor's common law contractual incapacity and the provisions of the Infants Relief Act, 1874, a minor spouse lacks the capacity to give a consent under the Act or, in the alternative, that a minor's consent is voidable and can be repudiated by the minor upon attaining the age of 21 years. Thus, in conveyances for which the consent of a minor spouse is required the practise has grown of an application being made to the High Court by the minor spouse's guardian under sect. 11 (1) of the Guardianship of Infants Act, 1964, for a court order approving of the minor spouse giving the required consent so as to ensure the minor will not seek to set aside the consent after attaining majority. Prior to the court making such order it is bound by sect. 3, 1964 Act, to ensure the proposed conveyance is in the interests of the welfare of the minor spouse. In *Lloyd v. Sullivan*,[79a] the vendor of a family home refused the purchaser's request that an application be made to the High Court on behalf of the vendor's wife, a minor, to obtain the court's approval to her consent to the sale. McWilliam J. stated "if the transaction were not shown to be to her advantage, she would be entitled to repudiate her consent on attaining her majority". He held the vendor had failed to show good title by his refusal to permit the requested application to be made to the court.[79b]

The Family Law Bill, 1981, as initiated before the Dáil on 20 February 1981,

---

76. The problem with this interpretation is that Y's conveyance vests an interest in Z which Y never had, the conveyance to Y being void; i.e. by Y conveying what to him is a 'nothing' he turns it into a 'something'.

77. See further p. 292 below.

78. Sect. 3 (4).

79. See J.C.W. Wylie, *Irish Conveyancing Law, supra*, pp. 208–210; M. Carroll, *The Family Home Protection Act, 1976, supra*.

79a. (March 1981) unreported (H.C.).

79b. As a consenting spouse does not enter a contractual relationship, the need for such application remains doubtful until the Supreme Court so determines.

provides that for the avoidance of doubt no consent to a conveyance given by a spouse before or after the Bill's enactment for the purposes of section 3(1) of the 1976 Act "is or was invalid by reason only that it is or was given by a spouse who has not or had not attained the age of majority". This provision when enacted should remove all doubts as to the validity of consents given by minor spouses under the Act. The 1981 Bill, as initiated, is reproduced in Appendix D.

The requirement of a spouse's "prior consent" to render a conveyance valid, raises the question of what is meant by "prior consent". Speaking on the Bill in the Seanad the then Minister for Justice, Mr. Cooney, expressed the opinion that for a wife's written consent to fulfil the requirement of the section it must be endorsed on the conveyance.[80] In the absence of such an endorsement, he stated, the title would be faulty. This interpretation of section 3(1) is questionable in that what the section requires is a written consent prior to the conveying of the family home. Use of the word "prior" indicates that it must be given in writing before the conveyance is executed. It does not require a wife to be a party to the execution of the conveyance itself. Moreover, in *Kyne* v. *Tiernan & Anor.*[80a] the High Court held that a letter signed by a wife unequivocally consenting to the sale of a family home was sufficient to comply with the requirements of the section and that a further consent endorsed on the conveyance itself was unnecessary.

A question arises as to "how prior" can a consent be? Further must a consent be given for a sale to a particular purchaser, or is a general consent to the sale of the family home to any purchaser sufficent? For example, can a wife in a deed of separation give a general consent to the selling of the family home, so as to enable her husband validly convey it to a third party at any time in the future, if he so wishes? Having regard to the wording of the section it is arguable that a sale of the family home subsequent to the giving of such a consent would be valid. The validity of such a sale could, however, be called in question if, prior to the completion of the conveyance, a wife notified the parties that she was withdrawing a consent so given. Whether the court would hold her bound by her agreement and her change of mind to be of no effect or whether it would only recognise the sale as valid in such circumstances, if a successful application to dispense with consent was made by her husband, remains to be seen.

Conveyance: A conveyance under the Act is said to include

> "a mortgage, lease, assent, transfer, disclaimer, release and any other disposition of property otherwise than by a will or a *donatio mortis causa* and also includes an enforceable agreement (whether conditional or unconditional) to make any such conveyance". "Convey" is to be construed accordingly.[81]

The Act has been held to apply to conveyances, the contracts in respect of which were entered into prior to the 12th July, 1976, but which were not completed until after that date. In *M.D.* v. *L.D. & Ors.*[82] contracts were entered into on the 5th March, 1976 between the husband L.D. and N. for the sale of the D.'s family home to N. The transfer was executed by the purchaser and the

80. Seanad Debates, Vol. 84, Cols. 1060–1062.
80a. (July 1980) unreported (H.C.).
81. Sect. 1 (1). "An enforceable agreement . . . to make any such conveyance" must be taken to mean an agreement enforceable but for the provisions of the Act. For example, if prior consent is not obtained to a contract for sale of the family home, the contract is one that would be enforceable if the Act did not render it void because of the absence of consent.
82. *Supra*. See also *H.* v. *H. and D.* (February 1980), unreported, (H.C.).

vendor and the purchase money handed over on the 5th May, 1976. Subsequently, N. decided he wished the house to be held jointly in the names of his wife and himself and a fresh transfer was executed. The house was on registered land and neither transfer was registered prior to the 12th July, 1976. N. was aware throughout the transaction that the property he was purchasing was a family home and that D. was married. At no stage was the wife asked to consent to the sale of the home. In proceedings brought by the wife, M.D., the High Court held that the transaction had been caught by the Act and that the wife's consent was required, as a transfer of registered land does not operate as a conveyance until it is registered.[83]

A wife's "prior consent" is required not only to close a sale but also to render valid and enforceable the contract for sale.[84] Thus, in order to protect the interests of the purchaser, it is not sufficient to wait until the requisition stage to enquire whether the property being sold is a "family home" within the terms of the Act. If no such inquiry is made and a wife's consent is not obtained prior to the signing of a contract for sale, if the contract is for the sale of a family home and the vendor subsequently reneges on his commitment, the contract will be of little value to the purchaser.[85] If, however, a wife has given her written consent to the sale of a family home prior to the execution of contracts for sale, it has been held that no further consent is required for the valid completion of the conveyance.[85a]

In *Kyne* v. *Tiernan & Anor*.[85b] the husband and the wife decided to sell their family home, the legal title of which was held by the husband in his sole name, and both co-operated with an auctioneer in arranging a sale. The wife was reluctant to attend at the offices of the husband's Solicitor to sign a written consent to the sale endorsed on the contract for sale but signed a letter drafted by the husband unequivocally consenting to the sale. Subsequently, the contract for sale was signed by the purchaser. Matrimonial difficulties arose between the husband and the wife and the wife refused to endorse her consent to the sale on the deed of transfer to the purchaser. In proceedings brought by the purchaser, seeking an order for specific performance of the contract for sale, the court held on the evidence that both the husband and the wife had agreed to sell the home and that the wife had given an unconditional consent to the sale in the letter signed by her. The court concluded that the consent contained in the letter was sufficient to comply with the provisions of section 3 of the Act. As for whether the section required a further written consent by the wife for the valid completion of the conveyance, McWilliam J. stated:

"I suppose it could be said on a strict interpretation of section 3 of the Act, that there must be a consent in writing to each conveyance, that is to say, both to the contract and to the final conveyance to the purchaser, but I cannot imagine that it could have been the intention of the legislature to require two consents for the completion of one transaction, namely, the sale of one house, and thus leave a purchaser in the position of conducting all the work and incurring all the expense necessary for the completion of a purchase only to find that a spouse had changed his or her mind about giving consent and require the whole transaction to be abandoned. Accord-

---

83. See the Registration of Title Act, 1964, Sect. 51.
84. See J.C.W. Wylie, *Irish Conveyancing Law, supra*, pp. 212–215.
85. See judgement of Griffin J. in *Somers v. Weir, supra*, at p. 90.
85a. See *Kyne v. Tiernan and Anor* (July 1980) unreported (H.C.).
85b. *Supra*.

ingly, I am of opinion that the consent given by the wife . . . is sufficient for the completion of the entire transaction."

A conveyance of a home which is jointly owned by a married couple and to which both spouses are parties was held by the Supreme Ct. in *Nestor v. Murphy*[86] to be outside the scope of section 3(1). The two defendants, a married couple, each signed a contract to sell their family home in which they were joint tenants to the plaintiff. Subsequently, they refused to complete the sale, contending that the contract was void because the wife did not consent to the sale in writing before the contract was signed. Delivering the judgement of the court Henchy J. stated:

> "The basic purpose of the subsection is to protect the family home by giving a right of avoidance to the spouse who was not a party to the transaction. It ensures that protection by requiring, for the validity of the contract to dispose and of the actual disposition, that the non-disposing spouse should have given a prior consent in writing. The point and purpose of imposing the sanction of voidness is to enforce the right of the non-disposing spouse to veto the disposition by the other spouse of an interest in the family home . . . an extension of that right of avoidance to spouses who have entered into a joint 'conveyance' would not only be unnecessary for the attainment of that aim but also enable contracts to be unfairly or dishonestly repudiated by parties who entered into them freely, willingly and with full knowledge . . . the spouse whose 'conveyance' is avoided(under) s. 3(1) is a spouse who has unilaterally (i.e. without the other spouse joining) purported to 'convey' an interest in the family home without having obtained the prior consent in writing of the other spouse."[86a]

The defendants' appeal was dismissed and the order for specific performance made in the High Court was affirmed.

Two months later in *M. and Anor. v. H. and Anor.*[87] the High Court held that if a family home is in the joint names of a husband and wife and they both authorise an estate agent to enter into a contract for the sale of their home, the validity of the contract is not affected by the failure of the wife to give her prior consent in writing to it. Following the Supreme Court decision in *N. v. M.* and holding that section 3(1) had no application, Keane J. stated:

> "I do not regard it as in any sense material that . . . the wife in the present case did not actually sign the contract, although she was a party to it. The judgement of the Supreme Court is plainly based on the principle that a transaction to which both spouses are parties is not captured at all by the Act; and in this context it is manifestly immaterial whether the spouse on whose behalf protection is claimed signs the contract herself or authorises someone to do it on her behalf. If, for example, the evidence in *N. v. M.* had established that the wife's solicitor had signed the contract as agent on her behalf with her full authority because she was away at the time, I do not believe that the decision would have been any different."

The Act's application to mortgages is of particular importance. The term "mortgage" is said to include "an equitable mortgage, a charge on registered land and a chattel mortgage".[88] Thus, if a husband wishes to raise a mortgage on the

86. [1979] I.R. 326 (S.C.).
86a. *Ibid*. at pp. 328, 329.
87. (December 1979), unreported, (H.C.).
88. Sect. 1 (1).

family home, he has to obtain the consent of his wife. This requirement is particularly important for the wife living in the family home. If such a wife's husband attempted to sell the home, it is unlikely that she would be unaware of his actions, as undoubtedly people would come to view it. If, however, he sought by means of a mortgage to raise money to put into a failing business, to secure his overdraft or for gambling or drinking purposes, a wife could know nothing about it until a bank or building society sought to enforce its security. Under the provisions of the Act for such a mortgage to be valid and the rights of the mortgagee to be enforceable the prior consent of the wife to the mortgage must be obtained.

The Act does not require the consent of a non-owning spouse if property that is mortgaged is not a family home at the time the mortgage is taken out. Thus, where a mortgage is raised when a house is bought, the consent of the spouse without title is not required to validate the mortgage, if the parties will not acquire possession of the house until the transaction has been completed. Only after the house has been bought and the parties have taken up residence will it become a family home as defined by the Act. In practice, however, since the coming into force of the Act, mortgagees have required the consent of the non-owning spouse to the creation of a mortgage on a newly purchased house.

Section 3(1) of the Act does not apply retrospectively to conveyances completed prior to its coming into force. Thus, a mortgage of a family home entered into by a husband without the consent of his wife prior to the 12th July, 1976, is unaffected by the section. Nevertheless, such a mortgage may be defeated in whole or in part if the wife's consent was not obtained or if she was not a party to it, if at the time of its execution she had a beneficial interest in the home. Thus, in *Northern Bank Ltd.* v. *Henry & Ors.* [89] a second mortgage on the family home granted to the bank by the husband in 1974 was held not to have priority over the wife's beneficial interest in the home which arose in 1964 and which was proved in subsequent High Court proceedings between the spouses. Prior to completing the mortgage the bank had not made any enquiries or furnished any requisitions to ascertain whether any litigation was pending or threatened in relation to the home or as to whether the wife had any beneficial interest in it. The bank was held not to have "made such enquiries . . . as ought reasonably to have been made"[90] and was held to have constructive notice of the wife's interest. Delivering judgement in the Supreme Court, Henchy J. stated:

"Notwithstanding that this purchase took place before the passing of the Family Home Protection Act, 1976, (which makes a transaction of this kind void for want of the prior written consent of the wife), the bank as purchaser ought reasonably to have adverted to the fact that there were decisions showing that a wife who had made payments towards the acquisition of the home or towards the payment of the mortgage instalments on it acquired a corresponding share in the beneficial ownership. As a matter of ordinary care, therefore, an inquiry as to threatened or pending claims was called

---

89. *Supra.* This case was concerned with unregistered land. See also the English case of *Williams & Glyn's Bank Ltd.* v. *Boland and Anor.*; *Same* v. *Brown* [1980] 2 All E.R. 408 (H.L.) in which it was held that a legal mortgagee of registered land granted to the plaintiffs by a husband alone and registered in the Land Registry was overriden by the beneficial interest in the matrimonial home of the wife "in actual occupation of the land" (home) within Sect. 70 (1) (g) of the Land Registration Act, 1925. The equivalent provision in Irish legislation is to be found in the Registration of Title Act, 1964, Sect. 72 (1) (j). See further *K.* v. *K.* (October 1980), unreported, (H.C.) in which both the judgements of the Supreme Court and of the House of Lords in the above cases are discussed and distinguished.
90. See the Conveyancing Act, 1881, Sect. 3 (1).

for."[91]

Parke J. in the course of his judgement stated:

"I have no doubt that by the beginning of the year 1974 any person who was offered a title to a matrimonial home by one spouse should have been alerted to the possibility that the other spouse might have a claim which would be upheld by the Courts to at least a share in the beneficial interest in the property. In the present case a proper investigation would have revealed that Mrs. Henry was not merely entitled to an unquantified share in the house, but to the entire beneficial ownership to the exclusion of the proposed mortgagee."[92]

Registration: Section 12 of the Act empowers a spouse to register a notice in the Registry of Deeds pursuant to the Registration of Deeds Act, 1707, (in the case of unregistered land) or under the Registration of Title Act, 1964, (in the case of registered land) stating she is married to a person having an interest in particular property or land. By registering the fact of her marriage, a wife can ensure that the defence of *bona fide* purchaser cannot be successfully used so as to uphold the validity of a conveyance of the family home made by her husband without her prior consent. It is a necessary part of the investigation of title carried out by a purchaser's solicitor prior to the completion of a conveyance to conduct a registry of deeds search, in the case of unregistered land, and a land registry search, in the case of registered land and either search would reveal the existence of a notice registered by a wife in the appropriate registry. However, even if a wife fails to register a notice she will not be prejudiced as the section provides that the fact that a notice of marriage has not been registered "shall not give rise to any inference as to the non-existence of a marriage."[93]

Section 13 of the Act states that Section 59(2) of the Registration of Title Act, 1964, (which refers to noting upon the register provisions of any enactment restricting dealings in land) shall not apply to the provisions of the 1976 Act. Section 59 imposes a duty on the Registrar to note upon the Register the "prohibitive or restrictive provisions . . . of an enactment by which the alienation, assignment, subdivision or subletting of any land is prohibited or in any way restricted". Moreover, under the section such provisions even if not registered are held to be burdens on the land concerned under section 72 of the 1964 Act.

In *Guckian & Anor.* v. *Brennan & Anor.*[94] Gannon J. stated:

"The 1976 Act does not create, nor invest a married person with any right affecting land or property of the nature of an interest in land which could fall within any of the classifications of burdens within Section 72(1) of the 1964 Act. Such right as is conferred is a right affecting the instrument of transfer and its validity. If it be invalid the transfer is ineffective, but the spouse for whose benefit it is rendered ineffective obtains no estate or interest in the land or property the subject of the transfer which can affect the ownership or title to the property."

In the view of the learned judge Section 13 took the provisions of the 1976 Act "out of the scope" of Sections 59 and 72 of the 1964 Act. He held that the

---

91. See pp. 8–9 of judgement.
92. See p. 5 of judgement.
93. Sect. 12 (2). Sect. 12 (3) provides that "no stamp duty, Registry of Deeds fee or land registration fee shall be payable in respect of any such notice".
94. (March 1980), unreported, (H.C.).

effect of section 13, taken together with section 31(1) of the 1964 Act, is that a purchaser of registered land when investigating title need only enquire into matters arising under the Family Home Protection Act in relation to "the particular intended contract of sale and the intended instrument of transfer" to that purchaser. There is no obligation on the purchaser of such land to make enquiries as to the validity under the 1976 Act of prior transactions as the Register, in the absence of fraud or mistake, is conclusive as to the validity of any such transaction.[95]

Offences: Section 15 provides

"Where any person having an interest in any premises, on being required in writing by or on behalf of any other person proposing to acquire that interest to give any information necessary to establish if the conveyance of that interest requires a consent under section 3(1), knowingly gives information which is false or misleading in any material particular, he shall be guilty of an offence and shall be liable—

(a) on summary conviction, to a fine not exceeding £200 or imprisonment for a term not exceeding twelve months or to both, or

(b) on conviction on indictment, to imprisonment for a term not exceeding five years,

without prejudice to any other liability, civil or criminal."

Thus, if a husband in answer to a purchaser's written inquiry falsely states that he is single and that the house he intends to sell is not a family home within the meaning of the Act, he is liable to a conviction under the above section. The section does not, however, make it an offence for another to masquerade as a party's spouse. For example, A has forced his wife to leave the family home and is living with B. A wishes to sell the family home and B signs the consent pretending to be his wife. Whilst A may be liable to prosecution under this section, B is not.[96]

Dispensing with Consent: Section 4 provides that if a wife "omits or refuses to consent", her consent may be dispensed with by the court subject to the following provisions.[97]

(i) The court cannot dispense with the consent of a spouse, unless it considers it is

"unreasonable for the spouse to withhold consent, taking into account all the circumstances including—

(a) the respective needs and resources of the spouses and of the dependent children (if any) of the family, and

95. Section 31 (1) of the Registration of Title Act, 1964, provides that "The register shall be conclusive evidence of the title of the owner to the land as appearing on the register and of any right, privilege, appurtenance or burden as appearing thereon; and such title shall not, in the absence of actual fraud, be in any way affected in consequence of such owner having notice of any deed, document, or matter relating to the land; but nothing in this Act shall interfere with the jurisdiction of any court of competent jurisdiction based on the ground of actual fraud or mistake, and the court may upon such ground make an order directing the register to be rectified in such manner and on such terms as it thinks just".
96. If B has made a statutory declaration she may be guilty of an offence under the Statutory Declarations Act, 1938, Sect. 6.
97. Sect. 4 (1).

(b) in a case where the spouse whose consent is required is offered alternative accommodation, the suitability of that accommodation having regard to the respective degrees of security of tenure in the family home and in the alternative accommodation".[98]

As is indicated by the use of the word "including", (a) and (b) are not all embracing, the court being able to take into account other relevant circumstances.

In *Somers* v. *Weir* it was stated that the onus of proving that the withholding of consent is unreasonable rests "fairly and squarely" on the spouse seeking an order dispensing with consent.[99]

In *H.* v. *H. and D.*[100] the prospective purchaser of a property (D) and not a spouse sought an order dispensing with a spouse's consent. In this case the husband had contracted to sell a property comprising 215 acres including the family home to D. in 1973 for £150,000. The wife, who had no proprietary interest in the property, opposed the sale as she did not want to leave the home and take up residence elsewhere. Due to his wife's opposition to the sale the husband delayed its completion and after considerable litigation D. ultimately obtained an order for specific performance by which the sale was to be completed and possession of the property delivered to D. no later than September, 1979. At no stage had the wife given her written consent to the sale in accordance with the provisions of the 1976 Act.

In July, 1979 the wife instituted proceedings under the 1976 Act seeking a declaration that a transfer of the property by her husband without her consent would be void under section 3 of the Act. D. sought an order under section 4 dispensing with the wife's consent. The court held that the Act applied to the intended conveyance, refused to dispense with the wife's consent and granted the declaration sought by the wife. Gannon J. in determining whether the wife's withholding of consent was unreasonable held that the matters referred to in (a) and (b) had no relevance as the spouses in this case were still lawfully married and that these matters referred to "a situation in which a family, so far as the two spouses are concerned, has ceased to be a family."

Further on in his judgement the learned judge stated:

"The purchaser . . . asks the Court to declare that it is unreasonable for the plaintiff to withhold her consent solely on the grounds that she does so because of sentimental attachment . . . I believe it to be the law that the determination of whether the withholding of consent is unreasonable or not is not resolved by considering whether the reasons are commendable or acceptable . . . I must take account of the circumstances of the family as a unit and consider the interests of the family to the extent that it remains a unit. There is no evidence of division in this family or between the spouses who have, at all times, supported each other and complimented each other each in his and her proper functional area of ability. To me it is natural, proper and reasonable that the wife and mother in a family would be motivated by emotional and sentimental responses and for her these would have much higher priority than financial and commercial considerations. In a united family the spouses will disclose and balance their differing priorities in the ordinary course of family life and daily decisions. For many family and domestic decisions the wife's priorities will prevail and in many others

---

98. Sect. 4 (2).
99. See judgement of Griffin J.
100. (February 1980), unreported (H.C.). At the time of writing a Supreme Court appeal is pending.

the husband's will prevail, particularly in matters pertaining to the security and maintenance and advancement of the family. It may be unusual for the wife to persist in pressing her priorities in an area of decision in which the husband's judgement would normally prevail, but I could not say that it would be unreasonable."

As for D.'s reliance on the circumstances as they existed at the time when the contract for sale was entered into, the learned judge stated that in determining whether to dispense with a consent he must consider the circumstances as they are at the time of the court proceedings. He continued:

"The evidence is that the plaintiff and her husband are both of the one mind, namely that they do not want to move . . . nor to live separately, nor to leave the family home. The value of the property is now estimated at over £640,000 and it would be impossible for the plaintiff and the first defendant (the husband) to acquire an alternative farm of land of reasonably equivalent quality of any more than 50 acres if they were to complete this sale. Without determining whether her attitude is commendable or acceptable I take the view that it is not unreasonable for the plaintiff to withhold her consent in all the circumstances to the proposed 'conveyance' and accordingly I may not dispense with her consent."[101]

The question arises here as to what attitude the court will take to a statement in a deed of separation whereby a wife renounces all proprietary and possessory interest in the matrimonial home, but subsequently refuses to consent to its sale. Whereas such a provision in a deed would undoubtedly be a circumstance to take into account in determining whether to dispense with consent, it is submitted that such a provision would not lead to an automatic dispensing with consent. The court is still bound to have regard to other circumstances, including those listed in (a) and (b).

Another question arises as to the manner in which the court would deal with a case in which a separation agreement contains a clause by which a wife promises to give her consent to the sale of the family home if required to do so at some future time, but subsequently refuses such consent. Would an order of specific performance to enforce such a clause be made? It is submitted that such a clause would again simply be one of the circumstances to be taken into account by the court upon an application being made to it, to dispense with consent.

(ii) If the spouse whose consent is required is in desertion of the other spouse, the court must dispense with the former's consent. Desertion is said to include

"conduct on the part of the former spouse that results in the other spouse, with just cause, leaving and living separately and apart from him".[102]

Thus, under the latter provision, if with just cause a wife leaves her husband, and the husband who owns the matrimonial home wishes to sell it, the husband and not the wife will be held to be in desertion, and the wife's consent to the sale will still be required.

---

101. See also *R. v. R.* (December 1978), unreported, (H.C.) in which McMahon J. refused to dispense with a wife's consent, holding that her refusal to a mortgage being raised on the family home was not unreasonable. He formed the view that on the evidence, if the husband was permitted to obtain the proposed mortgage, he would not have had sufficient income to maintain his family, support himself and be able to keep up the mortgage repayments.
102. Sect. 4 (3).

(iii) If a spouse is incapable of consenting by

"reason of unsoundness of mind or other mental disability or has not after reasonable inquiries been found, the court may give the consent on behalf of that spouse if it appears to be reasonable to do so".[103]

The President of the High Court has stated in a practice direction that where there is an application to dispense with a consent in circumstances (ii) and (iii) and the spouse whose consent is required cannot be served as a party, the fact of desertion or of unsoundness of mind or other mental disability or of inability to trace should be corroborated by an affidavit of some responsible disinterested person confirming the material facts contained in the affidavit of the applicant spouse.[104] An order to dispense with consent may in such circumstances be granted upon an *ex parte* application being made.

In *Somers* v. *Weir*,[105] the Supreme Court emphasised that an application under section 4 must be made before a conveyance takes place. The court has no jurisdiction to dispense with consent under the section after a conveyance has been completed. At that stage the court may determine, upon an application being made to it under section 3 of the Act, whether a conveyance is valid without consent or void *ab initio*, but it cannot make an order under section 4 dispensing with a consent.

Section 5 Proceedings: Section 5 of the Act confers on the court a general discretion to protect the right of a spouse to reside in the family home. Sub-s. (1) provides,

"Where it appears to the court, on the application of a spouse, that the other spouse is engaging in such conduct as may lead to the loss of any interest in the family home *or* may render it unsuitable for habitation as a family home with the intention of depriving the applicant spouse or a dependent child of the family of his residence in the family home, the court may make such order as it considers proper, directed to the other spouse or to any other person, for the protection of the family home in the interest of the applicant spouse or such child".

Judicial intervention can take place under the section in a wide variety of circumstances. The jurisdiction conferred by this section on the court may be invoked by a wife, for example, if a husband

(i) attempts to demolish part of the family home or remove slates from the roof, *or*

(ii) cuts off or has cut off the electricity, gas, water or any other essential supplies, *or*

(iii) suffers a judgement in collusive proceedings brought by a friend with the intention of ultimately being "forced" to sell the home to meet the award made in the judgement, *or*

(iv) refuses to pay any further mortgage instalments due or rent payable in respect of the home, *or*

103. Sect. 4 (4).
104. See (1977) 111 I.L.T. & S.J. 176.
105. See judgements of Griffin J. at p. 6 and Henchy J. at p. 18. See also *H. and L.* v. *S., supra*.

(v) breaches covenants in the lease of the home which could result in forfeiture, *or*

(vi) simply advertises that the family home is for sale, or puts it onto an estate agent's books.

Behaviour such as that outlined in (i) and (ii) could be such as to render a house "unsuitable for habitation as a family home", whilst (iii)–(vi) could be regarded as conduct likely to lead to the loss of an interest in the family home. Such conduct by itself will however be insufficient for a successful invocation of the court's jurisdiction. For the court to intervene in such circumstances, the section requires proof that a husband acted in such a fashion "with the *intention* of depriving" his wife or a dependent child of the family of his or her residence in the family home.

The section grants to the court a wide discretion in determining the type of order it should make. In *E.D.* v. *F.D.* [105a] it was held that in exercising this discretion the court may make an order to require a husband to transfer a family home into the sole name of his wife if the circumstances are such as to require the making of such an order for the protection of the family home.

Whilst sub-s. (1) seeks to protect a wife's right of residence, sub-s. (2) provides for the awarding of compensation to a wife deprived of her right to reside in the family home. It provides,

"Where it appears to the court, on the application of a spouse that the other spouse has deprived the applicant spouse or a dependent child of the family of his residence in the family home by conduct that resulted in the loss of any interest therein or rendered it unsuitable for habitation as a family home, the court may order the other spouse or any other person to pay to the applicant spouse such amount as the court considers proper to compensate the applicant spouse and any such child for their loss or make such other order directed to the other spouse or to any other person as may appear to the court to be just and equitable."

Not only the offending husband but also a third party can be ordered to compensate a wife under this section. Thus a party to a collusive action such as that suggested in (iii) above or a person employed by a husband to remove slates from the roof of his house in order to force a wife to leave, could be ordered to pay compensation under this section. The court under the above subsection also has wide discretionary power as to the type of order it can make. Thus, rather than ordering compensation, the court might order the husband to put the home rendered uninhabitable back into proper condition, or to provide his wife and children with an alternative place of residence. Whether the court may order a spouse to vest the beneficial interest in an alternative home, in the other spouse, under this jurisdiction, has not yet been decided.

A curious anomaly is that the conduct of the husband under sub-s. (2) need only have "deprived" his wife of her right of residence to permit the court to make an order, whilst under sub-s. (1) the court can only intervene if the husband's conduct is done with the "intention of depriving". Thus, it seems that although the court may, in certain circumstances, be unable to act to prevent either the loss of an interest in the family home or a husband from rendering it uninhabitable, it may, upon the husband's conduct causing either of the above results, order

105a. (October 1980), unreported, (H.C.).

him to compensate his wife.

Payment in arrears: Section 6(1) of the Act provides that

"Any payment or tender made or any other thing done by one spouse in
or towards satisfaction of any liability of the other spouse in respect of
rent, rates, mortgage payments or other outgoings affecting the family home
shall be as good as if made or done by the other spouse, and shall be treated
by the person to whom such payment is made or such thing is done as though
it were made or done by the other spouse."

Thus, in the event of a husband defaulting on mortgage repayments the
mortgagee is bound by this section to accept payments made by his wife and to
treat them as if they were made by the husband. Similarly, so long as a wife pays
the rent, a landlord will be unable to evict her for her husband's default. Moreover,
payment by her of rent in such circumstances will protect any rights accruing to
either spouse by virtue of their tenancy under the Rent Restrictions Acts, the
Landlord and Tenant Acts, etc. Such treatment however does not affect any
claim the wife making the payment may have to an interest in the family home.[106]

The Act further provides that in proceedings for the sale or possession of the
family home by the mortgagee or landlord, if a wife is able to pay off the arrears
or repayments within a reasonable time and is able to make future periodical
payments falling due, the court may adjourn the proceedings "for such period
and on such terms as appear . . . to be just and equitable."[107] If the wife succeeds
in making the required payments and it appears to the court that payments
subsequently falling due will continue to be paid, it may make an appropriate
declaration to that effect.[108] Upon such a declaration being made, any term
in a mortgage or lease whereby the default in payment, that gave rise to the
initial proceedings, has at any time before, or after the initial hearing of such
proceedings, resulted or would have resulted, in the capital sum advanced there-
under, or any sum other than the periodical payments, becoming due, is of no
effect for the purpose of such proceedings or any subsequent proceedings in
respect of the sum so becoming due.[109]

A defect in the above provisions is that a mortgagee or lessor is not bound to
give a wife any notice of her husband's default. Thus, if proceedings are brought
and she only discovers the amount due shortly before, or at the date of the
hearing, so much arrears may have accrued that it is impossible for her to pay it
all within "a reasonable time". However, in determining for what length of time
proceedings should be adjourned to enable arrears to be paid off, the court must

"have regard in particular to whether the spouse of the mortgagor or lessee
has been informed (by or on behalf of the mortgagee or lessor or otherwise)
of the non-payment of the sums in question or of any of them".

A further defect in the above protection, is that in order to enforce his
security a mortgagee need not always obtain a court order. The Conveyancing
Act, 1881, Sect. 19(1), confers a power of sale on all mortgagees, provided the
mortgage was made by deed. Thus, if a husband defaults on a legal mortgage, a
sale may take place without the wife's knowledge and without her being given an
opportunity to make good her husband's default. In practice however, if the

---

106. Sect. 6 (2).
107. Sect. 7 (1).
108. Sect. 8 (1).
109. Sect. 8 (2).

husband and wife are still living in the home the mortgagee will have great difficulty in finding a purchaser willing to buy the property.

Finally, if a wife discovers that the mortgage or rent payable in respect of the family home is in arrears, it is open to her to make an application under section 5 of the Act to seek a court order requiring her husband to discharge the arrears. Moreover, even if a landlord or mortgagee has obtained an order for possession of the family home, a wife may ask the court under section 5 to restrain the former from enforcing the order for possession and seek an order against her husband requiring him to discharge the arrears within a stipulated time. In practice, a number of orders of this nature have been made by the High Court in recent years.

Joint Tenancies: The Act seeks to encourage spouses where the family home is owned by one of them to place the home in joint ownership. Section 14 provides that

"No stamp duty, land registration fee, Registry of Deeds fee or court fee shall be payable on any transaction creating a joint tenancy between spouses in respect of a family home where the home was immediately prior to such transaction owned by either spouse or by both spouses otherwise than as joint tenants."

Household goods: Section 9 of the Act prevents a spouse from disposing of "household chattels" in certain circumstances. Household chattels for the purpose of this section are said to mean

"furniture, bedding, linen, china, earthenware, glass, books and other chattels of ordinary household use or ornament and also consumable stores, garden effects and domestic animals, but does not include any chattels used by either spouse for business or professional purposes or money or security for money".[110]

(1) If matrimonial proceedings[111] have been instituted by either spouse, neither spouse "can sell, lease, pledge, charge or otherwise dispose or remove any of the household chattels" in the family home until the proceedings have been finally determined. A spouse however may so act

(a) with the consent of the other spouse, *or*

(b) with the permission of the court before which the proceedings have been instituted.[112]

A spouse who contravenes this provision is guilty of an offence and liable on summary conviction to a fine not exceeding £100 or to imprisonment for up to six months.[113]

(2) Section 9(1) provides that

"Where it appears to the court, on the application of a spouse, that there are reasonable grounds for believing that the other spouse intends to sell, lease,

---

110. Sect. 9 (7).
111. Sect. 9 (3) defines matrimonial proceedings as including "proceedings under Sect. 12 of the Married Women's Status Act, 1957, under the Guardianship of Infants Act, 1964, or under Sect. 21 or 22 of the Family Law (Maintenance of Spouses and Children) Act, 1976". Curiously, Section 5 of the latter Act is not included.
112. Sect. 9 (2).
113. Sect. 9 (4).

pledge, charge or otherwise dispose of or to remove such a number or proportion of the household chattels in a family home as would be likely to make it difficult for the applicant spouse or a dependent child of the family to reside in the family home without undue hardship, the court may by order prohibit, on such terms as it may see fit, the other spouse from making such intended disposition or removal."

This section may assist a wife in various circumstances. For example, the court may make an order preventing a husband who is a compulsive gambler from selling or pledging the furniture so as to obtain money for gambling or it may prevent a husband from removing all the furniture from the family home so as to force his wife to vacate it.

If a spouse contravenes an order made under (1) or (2) above or if he

"has sold, leased, pledged, charged or otherwise disposed of or removed such a number or proportion of the household chattels in the family home as has made or is likely to make it difficult for the applicant spouse or a dependent child of the family to reside in the family home without undue hardship"

the court may order that spouse

"to provide household chattels for the applicant spouse, or a sum of money in lieu thereof, so as to place the applicant spouse or the dependent child of the family as nearly as possible in the position that prevailed before such contravention, disposition or removal".[114]

Finally, if a third person, prior to any disposition of a household chattel to him by a spouse, is informed in writing by the other spouse that he intends to

"take proceedings in respect of such disposition or intended disposition, the court in such proceedings may make such order, directed to the former spouse or the third person, in respect of such chattel as appears to it to be proper in the circumstances."[115]

Court Jurisdiction: The District Court is conferred with jurisdiction only to hear proceedings under section 9 of the Act and only if the value of the household chattels which are the subject matter of the proceedings does not exceed £1,000. The High Court and Circuit Court are conferred with concurrent jurisdiction to hear all matters arising under the Act. Where the rateable value of the land to which the proceedings relate exceeds £100 or the value of the personal property exceeds £5,000 and the proceedings are brought in the Circuit Court, that court must, at the request of a defendant transfer the proceedings to the High Court. However, any act done or order made prior to such transfer is valid until discharged or varied by order of the High Court.[116]

The Courts Bill, 1980, as initiated, proposes to increase the jurisdictional limit of the District Court under Section 9 of the Act to £2,500, to increase from £100 to £200 the limit of rateable value of land beyond which proceedings may be transferred from the Circuit Court to the High Court and to remove the limitation placed on the jurisdiction of the Circuit Court when dealing with personalty.

114. Sect. 9 (5).
115. Sect. 9 (6).
116. Sect. 10.

BARRING ORDERS

The Family Law (Maintenance of Spouses and Children) Act, 1976, section 22[117] confers jurisdiction on the District, Circuit and High Courts to make an order barring a spouse from entering the family home. Whilst the court may make an order under this section barring either a husband or a wife, the section was enacted essentially to provide protection for the battered wife. Thus, in the discussion that follows it will be presumed that the wife is the person on whose behalf such an order is sought.

Upon application being made to it by a wife, if the court is of the opinion that there are reasonable grounds for believing that the safety or welfare of the wife or of any dependent child[118] of the family so requires, it

(a) may order a husband, if he is residing at a place where his wife or a dependent child resides, to leave that place,

and

(b) may prohibit a husband from entering the place where his wife or dependent child reside.[119]

Order (b) prohibiting entry, can be made against a husband who is at the time of application to the court living apart from his wife or child, as well as against a husband who was residing in the same place as either of them, until ordered to leave by the court.

Termination of Order

(1) Either spouse may at any time apply to the court that made it, for the discharge of a barring order. The court must grant such an application if it is satisfied that it is proper to do so, and that the safety and welfare of the spouse on whose application the order was made or any dependent child will not be prejudiced by the discharge.[120]

(2) If a barring order is made by the District Court, it expires three months after the date of its making. It may however be renewed for further periods of three months upon the application of the person in whose favour the order was made.[121] If a barring order is made by the Circuit Court on appeal from the District Court, the jurisdiction of the Circuit Court to make such order is the same as that of the District Court, that is, the Circuit Court order expires three

---

117. This provision implements a recommendation made by the Committee on Court Practice and Procedure in their *Report on Desertion and Maintenance*, (Dublin, Stationery Office 1974), p. 15.
118. 'Dependent child of the family' means any child
"(a) of both spouses, or adopted by both spouses under the Adoption Acts, 1952 to 1974, or in relation to whom both spouses are in *loco parentis*, or
(b) of either spouse, or adopted by either spouse under the Adoption Acts, 1952 to 1974, or in relation to whom either spouse is in *loco parentis*, where the other spouse, being aware that he is not the parent of the child, has treated the child as a member of the family,
who is under the age of sixteen years, or, if he has attained that age—
(i) is or will be or, if an order were made under this Act providing for periodical payments for his support, would be receiving full-time education or instruction at any university, college, school or other educational establishment and is under the age of twenty-one years, or
(ii) is suffering from mental or physical disability to such extent that it is not reasonably possible for him to maintain himself fully".
119. Sect. 22 (1).
120. Sect. 22 (2).
121. Sect. 22 (4) (a).

months after the date of its making but may be renewed on further application being made to the District Court.[122]

The Courts Bill, 1980, as initiated, proposes to increase from three months to twelve months the period for which a barring order may be made in the District Court (or Circuit Court, on appeal).

(3) A barring order expires

"upon the determination of any matrimonial cause or matter in the High Court between the spouses or upon the determination of any proceedings between the spouses under the Guardianship of Infants Act, 1964, in the High Court or Circuit Court."

However, the court making such a determination may make a further barring order under section 22.[123]

The Act nowhere defines what is a matrimonial cause or matter for the purpose of this provision. Thus, it is uncertain whether it merely applies to those matters traditionally so called, that were formerly within the jurisdiction of the Ecclesiastical Courts, or whether it also applies to the determination of other matrimonial conflicts, for example, disputes as to maintenance determined under the provisions of the Family Law . , . Act, 1976, itself, disputes determined under the Married Women's Status Act, 1957, Sect. 12, or under the Family Home Protection Act, 1976.

Whilst an application to make an order must be made by a spouse, it is not necessary that the safety or welfare of the spouse be threatened before the other spouse can be barred. If the welfare of a dependent child of the family is endangered by the latter's presence, the court may make a barring order. An interesting question is whether a court, in determining whether a child's welfare or safety requires a spouse to be barred from the family home, is bound by the Guardianship of Infants Act, 1964, Sect. 3 to regard the welfare of the child as the paramount consideration in making its determination.

Effect of order: If as a consequence of a barring order, a spouse is not residing at a place for any period, he is deemed to be still residing there for the purpose of any rights he may have under the Landlord and Tenant Acts, 1967 to 1980, the Statute of Limitations 1957 or the Rent Restriction Acts, 1960-67.[124]

Breach of order: A spouse who contravenes an order made under section 22 or who "molests or puts in fear" his spouse or dependent child, whilst such an order is in force, is guilty of an offence and liable on summary conviction to a fine not exceeding £200 and/or, to a term of imprisonment not exceeding six months.[125]

Court Jurisdiction:[126] The District Court has jurisdiction to make an order irrespective of the value of the place to which the proceedings relate, but as has already been seen, unless renewed, a District Court order will lapse three months

122. Sect. 22 (4) (c).
123. Sect. 22 (5).
124. Sect. 22 (7); See also Sect. 3 (4) and the Landlord and Tenant (Amendment) Act, 1980.
125. Sect. 22 (3).
126. See Sects. 22 (4) and 23 (3).

after being made.[127] The Circuit Court (except on appeal from the District Court) may only make a barring order if the rateable valuation of the place to which the proceedings relate does not exceed £100. However, the Courts Bill, 1980, as initiated, proposes to remove this restriction on the Circuit Court's jurisdiction.

Jurisdiction to hear a section 22 application can be exercised by either a District Court or Circuit Court if one of the spouses who is a party to the proceedings "ordinarily resides or carried on any profession, business or occupation" within the jurisdiction of that court. It does not matter if the place from which a spouse is seeking to bar the other spouse is situate outside the court area.[128] Thus, if a husband and wife live in Wicklow and the husband's business is carried on within the jurisdictional area of the Dublin Metropolitan District Court, the wife may bring barring proceedings before that court, if she so wishes.

The High Court has an unlimited jurisdiction and in hearing section 22 proceedings its jurisdiction to grant a barring order is not affected by either the rateable valuation of the place from which the applicant spouse is seeking to bar the other spouse or limited by the geographical location of the place. Moreover, a barring order can be granted by the High Court upon an *ex parte* application being made in appropriate cases. However, the President of the High Court, Mr. Justice Finaly has pointed out that instances in which the court would be justified in granting an *ex parte* order are rare.[129] The more usual approach of the court upon such an application being made is to abridge time for the serving of a notice of motion by the spouse seeking a barring order on the other spouse, both to enable the matter to be dealt with speedily by the court (usually within two or three days) and to afford the other spouse an opportunity to be heard.

Appeals: Unless the court that makes the original order consents, the bringing of an appeal will not act so as to stay the effect of the order appealed against. If it consents to a stay, it may do so subject to the imposition of conditions.[130]

ALTERNATIVE TO SECTION 22 PROCEEDINGS

Prior to the coming into force of the Family Law . . . Act, 1976, there were two principal legal remedies available to a wife seeking immediate protection from the assaults of a violent husband. The first of these, discussed in an earlier chapter, is a criminal prosecution for assault.[131] The second remedy, discussed in this section, is that of the injunction.

The Injunction

An injunction may be mandatory or prohibitory. It is essentially an order of the court directing a party to do or refrain from doing a particular act. For example, if a husband has by violence forced his wife out of the family home, the court may grant a mandatory injunction ordering the husband to leave and a prohibitory injunction restraining him from re-entering the home or assaulting

---

127. For the District Court rules applicable to the bringing of Sect. 22 proceedings, see District Court [Family Law (Maintenance of Spouses and Children) Act 1976] Rules 1976 (S.I. No. 96 of 1976), para. 36 *et seq*.

128. See the order made in *The State (Mooney) v. District Justice McGrath* 1978 No. 525 S.S. (23rd October, 1978), (H.C.). There was no written judgement in this case.

129. Mr. Justice Finlay, "An Approach to Family Cases", (1977), vol. 71 *The Gazette of the Incorporated Law Society of Ireland* 175 at p. 177.

130. Sect. 22 (6).

131. See page 110 *ante*.

his wife.

An injunction may be perpetual or interlocutory. The former type of injunction is granted upon the final determination of a dispute before the court. It is made after both sides have been given an opportunity to be heard in court and to present their case in the normal way. If it appears to the court to be just and convenient to do so, it will grant an interlocutory injunction before the final determination of an action.[132] A plaintiff serves notice on the other side that on the next motion day, he will apply to the court for an injunction, thus giving the defendant an opportunity to oppose the application. If the plaintiff's affidavit makes out a sufficient case, an interlocutory injunction will be granted which is effective until the trial of the action. If, however, a person requires immediate protection against the unlawful behaviour of another, an injunction may be granted upon an *ex parte* application being made to a judge of the High Court if "the exigencies of the case require it".[133] It is this facility to obtain swift protection by way of *ex parte* applications, that makes the injunction an invaluable remedy in the family law context.

Prior to 1976 in the area of family law, injunctions were usually sought to protect a wife's right to occupy or reside in the family home and to restrain her husband from molesting or interfering with her or any of their children. Today, in the majority of cases, barring orders are sought for this purpose.

The probable success of an application for an injunction very much depends on the facts of the particular case. Neither the High Court nor the Supreme Court have yet delivered a written judgement clearly stating the legal principles applicable to the granting of family law injunctions including injunctions granted to exclude a spouse from the family home.[134] Thus, the importance that the court attaches to the proprietary interest in the home being vested in the spouse it is asked to exclude from it, or to further matrimonial proceedings pending, is uncertain. The fact of title in the home being vested in a husband's sole name has not in practice, prevented the court, by injunction, excluding a husband from the family home.

In *K.* v. *K.*[135] the husband was the sole tenant of a Dublin Corporation house. His wife was forced to leave the house following a number of serious assaults on her by the husband. Kenny J. upon an interlocutory application made by notice of motion, granted injunctions ordering the husband to vacate the matrimonial home, restraining him from entering it and from molesting or assaulting his wife or children.

In *C.* v. *C.*[136] the wife was forced to leave the matrimonial home because of her husband's violent conduct. The home was held in the husband's name. While he was away the wife returned to the home and changed the locks. Having moved

---

132. See Supreme Court of Judicature (Ireland) Act, 1877, Sect. 28 (8); R.S.C. (S.I. No. 72 of 1962) Order 50 Rule 6 (1).

133. *Ibid* Order No. 50 Rule 6 (7).

134. In England there have been a great many reported cases in this area in recent years. See, in particular, *Gurasz v. Gurasz* [1970] P. 11 (C.A.); *Bassett v. Bassett* [1975] Fam. 76 (C.A.); *Walker v. Walker* [1978] 3 All E.R. 141 (C.A.). See further the following very useful short articles—M.J. Pritchard, "The Matrimonial Castle" (1973) 32 C.L.J. 227; R.L. Denyer, 'Excluding the Husband from the Matrimonial Home' (1973) 123 *N.L.J.* 655; A. Samuels, "The Matrimonial Injunction" (1975) 125 *N.L.J.* 365; M.L. Parry, "Somewhere to Live; Excluding the Husband from Occupation of the Matrimonial Home" (1975) 5 Fam. Law 165. See also P.M. Bromley, *Family Law* 5th Edition (Butterworths', London 1976) at p. 179; S.M. Cretney, *Principles of Family Law* 3rd Edition (Sweet and Maxwell, London 1979) at p. 181–188.

135. 1975 No. 212 Sp. There was no written judgement in this case; (H.C.).

136. 1975 No. 148 Sp. There was no written judgement in this case; (H.C.).

back into the house, she successfully made an *ex parte* application to the High Court and was granted injunctions restraining her husband from entering the home and restraining him from assaulting or molesting her.

In *Conway* v. *Conway*[137] in proceedings brought under the Married Women's Status Act, 1957, Sect. 12, the court held the matrimonial home to be owned jointly by a wife and her husband, although it was purchased solely in the latter's name. At the date of the proceedings the husband was living elsewhere. Prior to that date, he had turned off the electricity supply to the house and had disconnected the phone and had on many occasions returned home late at night in a drunken state and assaulted his wife. Although he was entitled to a half share in the family home, Kenny J. granted an injunction restraining the husband from entering it because of his "outrageous" conduct.

On the other hand, the fact that title is vested only in the spouse seeking the injunction does not mean that an application to grant an injunction excluding the other spouse will be automatically granted. In *O'Malley* v. *O'Malley*[138] the court refused to grant to a wife living in the United States an interlocutory injunction requiring her husband to vacate the matrimonial home which she wished to sell. The court in refusing to grant an injunction noted that the wife was not in danger of any violence or cruelty and that there was no evidence that she would suffer irreparable damage if her application was refused.

Making the application: In practice the following injunctions may be applied for:

(1) An injunction to restrain the defendant (in the majority of cases the husband) from attending at or near or entering upon or attempting to enter upon the matrimonial home, or restraining the defendant from approaching the matrimonial home without the express invitation of the plaintiff.

(2) An injunction to restrain the defendant from molesting, assaulting or otherwise interfering with the plaintiff and the children of the plaintiff.

(3) A mandatory injunction compelling the defendant to vacate the matrimonial home.

(4) An injunction to restrain the defendant from taking a child or children out of the custody of the plaintiff, and/or

(5) Out of the jurisdiction of the court (i.e. out of the country).

Application for an injunction on grounds 4 and 5 above may of course be made when there is no dispute as to occupation of the matrimonial home or no question of a spouse being attacked.[139]

Breach of injunction: The court may commit to prison for contempt of court a person who acts in breach of an injunction.

Court jurisdiction: Proceedings claiming an injunction may be brought in

137. [1976] I.R. 254; (1973) 111 I.L.T.R. 133 (H.C.). In this case Kenny J. expressed approval of *Gurasz v. Gurasz* [1970] P. 11 (C.A.).
In *K. v. K, supra* he approved of a statement by Lord Denning in *Gurasz* that at common law it is the husband's duty to provide his wife and children with a roof over their heads.
138. (1951) I.L.T.R. 213 (S.C.).
139. See, for example, *L. v. L.* where Hamilton J., upon an *ex parte* application, granted interim custody to Mr. L. and an injunction to restrain Mrs L. from taking her children out of the custody of the father or out of the jurisdiction of the court. December 1976 (H.C.) 1976 No. 558 Sp. There was no written judgement in this case. See also p. 224. *ante.*

either the High Court or the Circuit Court. The High Court has unlimited jurisdiction but the Circuit Court can only hear a claim for an injunction, otherwise than as ancillary to other relief, where the property concerned consists of personality not exceeding £5,000 in value, or land the rateable valuation of which does not exceed £100.[140] In practice, the great majority of applications for an injunction are made in the High Court. The Courts (Supplemental Provisions) Act, 1961, Sect. 45(1) permits "applications of an urgent nature for relief by way of injunction" to be heard "otherwise than in public."[141]

PROPERTY IN HOUSEHOLD ALLOWANCE

If a husband gave his wife housekeeping money out of his own income, any money not spent by her or any property acquired by her with it, was at common law, regarded as belonging to the husband, unless it could be shown that it was his intention to make a gift to her.[142] The Commission on the Status of Women in 1972 recommended that money saved or property bought out of a wife's housekeeping allowance should be treated as belonging to the spouses in equal shares. The Family Law (Maintenance of Spouses and Children) Act, 1976, Sect. 21, implements this recommendation. It provides that

"Any allowance made by one spouse to the other spouse after the commencement of this Act for the purpose of meeting household expenses, and any property or interest in property acquired out of such allowance, shall, in the absence of any agreement, whether express or implied, between them to the contrary, belong to the spouses as joint owners."

The following points should be noted:

(a) The section applies to a household allowance provided by either spouse.

(b) It only relates to allowances made on or after 6th May 1976, the date when the Act came into force.

(c) Its application can be excluded by an express or implied agreement between the spouses, e.g. a clause in a separation agreement.

(d) If an allowance is made for household expenses, the allowance, any money saved out of it and also any property acquired with it belongs to the spouses as joint owners. Thus, if a wife purchases furniture or a television out of housekeeping money that she has saved, in the absence of a contrary agreement, it will belong to both spouses jointly.

(e) On the death of one spouse it seems that the whole beneficial interest in money and property jointly owned by virtue of this provision, will pass to the surviving spouse, unless the joint interest has been severed by either of the parties.

There are however certain ambiguities in the section. For example, what is the meaning of the phrase "an allowance . . . made for the purpose of meeting

---

140. Courts (Supplemental Provisions) Act, 1961, Sect. 22 (1) and Third Schedule, Ref. No. 27, as amended by the Courts Act, 1971, Sect. 2 (1). See further section 2 of the Courts Bill, 1980, as initiated.
141. For a comparative examination of Irish and English law in relation to injunctions and barring orders see P.T. Horgan, "Legal Protection for the Victim of Marital Violence" (1978) 13 I.J. (n.s.) 233; G. McGann, "The Domestic Violence Jurisdiction of the District Court and the Magistrates Court" (1979) vol. 73 *Gazette of the Incorporated Law Society of Ireland* 137.
142. *Blackwell v. Blackwell* [1943] 2 All E.R. 579 (C.A.); *Hoddinott v. Hoddinott* [1949] 2 K.B. 406 (C.A.).

household expenses."? If a wife is given an allowance every week by her husband, part of which she has to use to pay off mortgage instalments on the matrimonial home, does she thereby acquire an interest in the home? Or is that part of the allowance intended to meet mortgage repayments not made for the purpose of meeting a 'household expense', but rather for meeting the expense of purchasing or acquiring a house.[143] If a wife is given money every week by her husband to meet hire purchase or credit sale instalments payable for carpets or a washing machine, is that an "allowance given to meet a household expense" and will the wife by reason of making such payments acquire an interest in the property, or is she merely acting as the agent of her husband when making the weekly payments? In what circumstances will the court hold an implied agreement excluding the application of the section to exist? Will such an agreement be implied where money from the household allowance is used by the wife to purchase goods or clothes for her own use, or will a husband be held to be the joint owner of such purchases? If a wife uses part of the household allowance to buy a sweepstake ticket or to play bingo, will a husband be the joint owner of her winnings? Many of these questions will, without doubt, give rise to litigation.

CRITICISMS AND SUGGESTED REFORMS

I. There is a need for a clear exposition by the Supreme Court of the law applicable to the determination of proprietary disputes under the Married Women's Status Act, 1957, Sect. 12.

(a) In all the written judgements delivered to date it is clear that the section has been regarded as purely procedural and as conferring on the court no power to create or vary interests in property. However, it is possible that the powers conferred on the courts by this section are not identical to, or as limited as those conferred by the Married Women's Property Act, 1882, Sect. 17. Whereas section 17 enables a court to make such order as it "thinks fit", section 12 confers power to make such order as it "thinks proper". Curiously, when the Married Women's Status Act was passing through the Oireachtas, neither the Minister responsible for the Act or any T.D. or Senator commented on or gave any reason for the different phraseology used in section 12 as compared to that used in section 17 which it was replacing.[144]

(b) In *Conway* v. *Conway*, Kenny J. stated that

"when the matrimonial home is purchased in the name of the husband either before or after marriage, the wife does not as wife become entitled to any share in its ownership either because she occupies the status of wife or because she carried out household duties."[145]

---

143. The English Courts have not, as yet finally determined this question under a similar legislative provision in force there. (See the Married Women's Property Act, 1964, Sect. 1). In *Tymoszczuk* v. *Tymoszczuk* (1964) 108 Sol. Jo. 676 it was held that mortgage repayments made by a wife from an allowance given by her husband were not "expenses of the matrimonial home". In *Re Johns Assignment Trusts, Niven v. Niven, supra* this point was referred but not decided. However, Goff J. stated that he must "not be taken as accepting the view that where Sect. 1 (of 1946) does apply, moneys paid to discharge a mortgage in the marital home are not expenses of the matrimonial home . . ."
144. See *Dáil Debates* Vol. 160 Cols. 513, 831, 1552, 2278, 2381, 2383. *Seanad Debates* Vol. 47 Cols. 72, 271, 305.
145. [1976] I.R. at p. 257; (111) I.L.T.R. at p. 134. See also *R.K.* v. *M.K.* (October 1978), unreported, (H.C.) where Finlay P. stated: "The extent of her (the wife's) work in the household and in the care of her children was very considerable but our law does not recognise so far at least a right arising from that type of work to a part ownership of any family or marriage property."

In the cases determined under the Act of 1882, whilst there is disagreement as to the principles applicable to determine whether an indirect contribution by a wife, to the purchase of the matrimonial home, confers on her an interest in the home, the authorities agree in holding that no beneficial interest is acquired by the wife, who merely remains in the home and who does the housework. The law in this respect fails to recognise that the contribution a wife makes in managing the home is very often equally as important to the family fortunes as that made by the husband as breadwinner. It is arguable that in this area Irish law differs from English law.[146]

The State in Article 41.2 of the Constitution recognises the importance of the mother's role in the home and pledges itself to "endeavour to ensure that mothers shall not be obliged by economic necessity to engage in labour to the neglect of their duties in the home". In *De Burca and Anderson* v. *A.-G.*[147] it was stated that "some preferential treatment of women citizens seems to be contemplated by the Constitution"[148] and it was noted that Article 41.2 "makes special provision for the economic protection of mothers who have home duties".[149] It is thus open to the courts, by reliance on this Article and the constitutional guarantee to "protect the Family", to hold that a wife by her work in the home, acquires some beneficial or proprietary interest in it.

(c) Even if the jurisdiction conferred on the court by section 12 is identical to that conferred by section 17 of the 1882 Act, the principles to be applied in determining when an indirect contribution by a spouse will be regarded as conferring on that spouse a beneficial interest in the matrimonial home, need to be clearly enunciated. As has been seen, the law on this point is, at present, unclear.

(d) The type of order that the court may make in exercise of its jurisdiction under section 12 is uncertain. For example, can it upon determining that spouses have a joint beneficial interest in the matrimonial home, order that the home be sold and the proceeds divided between the parties? Alternatively, upon holding a spouse to have a one-third interest in the home, the value of which is assessed at £12,000, can it order the spouse who owns the other two-thirds to pay the former, £4,000 and upon such payment require the one-third share to be transferred to the latter?[150] Both these questions have not as yet been finally determined.[151]

---

146. In England, the importance of Sect. 17 of the Act of 1882 has been reduced. Under the Matrimonial Causes Act, 1973, the English court may now re-adjust interests in property in all cases of divorce, judicial separation and nullity. See *Fielding v. Fielding* [1978] 1 All E.R. 267 (C.A.). See also S.M. Cretney, *Principles of Family Law, supra*, p. 279 *et seq*.
147. [1976] I.R. 38 (S.C.).
148. *Ibid* at p. 61 per O'Higgins C.J.
149. *Ibid* at p. 70 per Walsh J.
150. If parties, held in Sect. 12 proceedings to be beneficial joint tenants (or tenants in common) of the matrimonial home, cannot agree on a sale, and if the court in such proceedings is unable to order one, it is open to either party to bring fresh proceedings under the Partition Acts, 1868 and 1876 so as to obtain the desired court order for sale and division of the proceeds. On this see Wylie, *Irish Land Law* p. 369.
151. See particularly the English cases of *Tunstall v. Tunstall* [1953] 2 All E.R. 319 (C.A.); After this case in England the Matrimonial Causes (Property and Maintenance) Act, 1958, was enacted, Sect. 7 (7) of which provides that "for the avoidance of doubt it is hereby declared that any power conferred by (Sect. 17 of 1882) to make orders with respect to any property includes power to order a sale of the property." See further *Bothe v. Amos* [1976] Fam. 46 (C.A.).
Although the court may not vary or create interests in property in proceedings under Sect. 17, in determining the sum of money a party is entitled to in respect of his proprietary interests, the Courts in England and N. Ireland have held they may have regard to a party's

II. Section 12 of the 1957 Act can only be utilised to determine property questions between 'husband and wife'. Thus, such proceedings cannot be commenced to determine a dispute between parties whose marriage has been annulled. Whether the court has jurisdiction to determine a dispute under section 12 if proceedings are commenced prior to the courts' determination of nullity is an open question. If a marriage is declared void, it is submitted that the court will at all times lack jurisdiction under this section; if however a voidable marriage is annulled, as parties are 'husband and wife' until the decree of nullity retrospectively invalidates their marriage, it could be argued that the court would have jurisdiction to determine proprietary disputes between them in proceedings commenced prior to the granting of the decree, the parties being 'husband and wife' at the date when the summons issued. The success of this argument is however doubtful. It is submitted that section 12 procedure should be extended by statute to the determination of proprietary disputes between parties to void and voidable marriages.

III. The Report on the Law of Nullity issued by the Office of the Attorney-General recommended that the High Court, subsequent to granting a nullity decree, should be conferred with jurisdiction, not only to order one party to pay maintenance to the other, but also be empowered to order the transfer of property from one party to the other or to any children of the parties and to vary any ante-nuptial or post-nuptial settlement.[152]

To help the court decide on the type of order that it should make, the Report sets down specific matters that the court should investigate. Essentially, it should be required to take into account all matters relating to the financial circumstances of the parties and their children. Of particular importance to the 'wife' is the stipulation that in deciding whether to exercise its powers, the court should have regard to "the contributions made by each of the parties to the welfare of the family, including any contribution made by looking after the home or caring for the family".[153] This provision if enacted will enable the court to give proper recognition to the contribution made to the family assets by the 'wife' who remains at home and manages the household.

By suggesting essentially the same criteria for the determination of the type of financial orders and property orders the court should consider making, the Report recognises the interdependent and complementary relationship between rights to property and rights to maintenance. For example, a wife who owns the matrimonial home or has it transferred to her, will be less dependent on the support provided by a maintenance order, than a wife who has no home at all.

It is submitted that the jurisdiction to make ancillary'orders that the Report recommends should be conferred on the court to be exercised subsequent to the granting of a decree of nullity, should also be exercisable subsequent to the granting of a decree of divorce *a mensa et thoro* or upon an application being made to the court by spouses who have agreed to separate. It would be illogical to confer on the court wide discretionary powers to re-adjust property rights so as to minimise "as far as possible . . . the hardships which may result"[154] from a

---

conduct in certain limited circumstances. See in particular *Cracknell v. Cracknell* [1971] P. 356; *McKeown v. McKeown* (June 1975) unreported (Northern Ireland H.C., Ch.D); *Bothe v. Amos, supra. Shinh v. Shinh* [1077] 1 All E.R. 97 (Ch. D.); *Suttill v. Graham* [1977] 1 W.L.R. 819 (C.A.).

152. P. 15–16.
153. See proposed Nullity of Marriages Bill, Sect. 12.
154. See p. 15 of Report.

decree that a marriage has never existed (i.e. a decree of nullity) but not confer similar powers on the court to minimise the hardships that arise upon the collapse of a marriage that has existed.

IV. A number of the difficulties that arise under the Family Home Protection Act, 1976, and that could be resolved by amending legislation have already been discussed. It is merely here intended to refer to two further matters that should be dealt with by any such legislation.

(a) Whilst a spouse may make mortgage repayments upon the default of the other spouse, which under section 6 of the Act the mortgagee must accept and which-under section 7 of the Act, after the institution of proceedings for possession or sale of the home, the mortgagee can be required by a court to accept, neither section confers any specific power on the court to transfer part of the beneficial interest in the home to a spouse making such payments.[155] Thus, if the defaulting spouse, in whose sole name the property is held, wishes subsequently to sell the home, the other spouse may have to bring proceedings under section 12 of the 1957 Act in order to ascertain whether her payments gave rise to the acquisition by her of a beneficial interest in it, and if they did, the extent of that interest.[156] Alternatively, she may have to bring proceedings claiming compensation from the defaulter for the payments made by her on his behalf.[157] Whether a claim to either a beneficial interest or compensation in such circumstances would be successful is uncertain. It is submitted that the Act should be amended so as to provide that a spouse who makes mortgage repayments in default of the other spouse, acquires a beneficial interest in the family home, proportionate to the payments made.

(b) If one spouse deserts the other, the court must dispense with the former's consent, if the latter applies to it to do so upon his wishing to sell the family home. On the other hand, if a spouse, guilty of adultery or cruelty, refuses consent, upon an application to dispense with consent, the court must consider all the circumstances including the needs and financial resources of the spouse and those of any dependent children, and the suitability of any alternative accommodation that has been offered, before it can make such an order. The Act has thus retained the concept of the matrimonial offence and as in the case of the recent legislation on maintenance, desertion is regarded as a more reliable indicator of 'guilt', than any other type of marital misbehaviour. It is submitted that desertion should merely be regarded as one of the circumstances to be taken into account by the court in determining whether the requirement of a spouse's consent should be dispensed with. Proof of desertion by itself should

---

155. An application for a transfer of the home into the sole name of the spouse paying the mortgage can in appropriate circumstances be made under section 5 of the Act. See p. 330 *ante*.

156. A beneficial interest may arise upon the payment of mortgage instalments by virtue of a resulting trust. Mortgage payments by the spouse in whom no legal title is vested are taken as evidence that it was the intention of the parties at the time of the acquisition of the property that the spouse in whom legal title was vested would hold all or part of the property on trust for the other spouse. However, if such payments are made under Sects. 6 or 7 of the 1976 Act, it is questionable whether such an intention would be inferred, and if it was it would be easily rebuttable.

157. Generally speaking money paid by one person on behalf of another does not create any obligation to repay the expenditure unless the person expending the money did so at the encouragement of the owner or upon a promise by the owner to repay—See *Heavey v. Heavey, supra*. See Megarry and Baker, *Snell's Principles of Equity*, 27th Edition (Sweet and Maxwell, London 1973) p. 448.

not conclude the matter.

V. Section 22 of the Family Law . . . Act, 1976, has significantly improved the legal protection available to the battered wife. There are, however, certain problems in the manner in which the section operates that need to be resolved.

(a) There is a need to extend the period for which a District Court barring order may remain in force. The present period of three months is unnecessarily short and does not in many cases give to the parties a sufficient "cooling off" period within which to either resolve their difficulties or to conclude a separation agreement. The Coolock Community Law Centre in a report published in 1978 suggested that the District Court's jurisdiction should be extended to enable it to grant a barring order for a continuous period of six months. Such an extended order it stated "might well be of benefit, in lessening the strain placed on the wife of making applications for renewal and in allowing greater time for reconciliation to be attempted."[158] The Courts Bill, 1980, as initiated, proposes to extend the period for which a District Court barring order may remain in force to twelve months.

(b) There is a need to change the District Court rules applicable to proceedings under section 22 to enable *ex parte* applications to be made to the court when an emergency arises. Under the existing rules, if a wife is seeking a barring order or wishes to complain to the court that such an order has been contravened, a summons must usually be served on her husband at least seven days before the court sitting in which either type of application is to be made.[159] Whereas a District Justice may abridge time for the service of a summons,[160] the District Court does not, unlike the High Court, have the power to grant immediate protection to a wife even if such protection is clearly required. For a wife seeking legal protection from a violent husband, a delay of a number of days from the time when she was assaulted or threatened with violence until the court is in a position to intervene can be both terrifying and dangerous. It is submitted that the District Court rules should provide for *ex parte* applications by a spouse in need of immediate protection and empower the court to grant an interim barring order or, if the application relates to a breach of a barring order, empower the court to issue a warrant for the arrest of the offending spouse.

(c) Although a husband who contravenes a barring order is guilty of an offence and liable to six months imprisonment, he cannot be arrested without a warrant. In practice the gardai are reluctant to involve themselves in matrimonial proceedings and in the great majority of cases where a barring order is breached, the wife must herself again bring the matter before the court. It is submitted that in order to make barring orders effective in fully protecting a wife from a violent husband, statutory powers should be conferred on the gardai to arrest without a warrant a husband acting in contravention of a barring order or a husband who a guard has reasonable cause to believe is going to contravene

---

158. See generally Coolock Community Law Centre Special Report, "Barred", (Dublin 1978); P.T. Horgan, "Legal Protection for the Victim of Marital Violence" (1978) 13 I.J. (n.s.) 233; G. McGann, "The Domestic Violence Jurisdiction of the District Court and the Magistrates Court" (1979) vol. 73 *The Gazette of the Incorporated Law Society of Ireland* 137.

159. District Court (Family Law Act 1976) Rules 1976. (S.I. No. 96 of 1976) Rule 41.

160. See the District Court Rules, 1948 (Statutory Rules and Orders 1947 No. 431) Or. 51 (1).

a barring order.[161]

(d) A District Court barring order, by excluding a spouse from the matrimonial home, in many instances also effectively deprives a barred spouse of the custody of his children. If such a spouse wishes to obtain custody of, or access to his children, in the absence of the agreement of the other spouse, he must at present bring proceedings in either the Circuit Court or the High Court. Since the coming into force of the Family Law ... Act, 1976, it has been clear that there is a need to vest jurisdiction in the District Court to at least make access orders in relation to children so as to permit a barred spouse to have some contact with his children and maintain a relationship with them after the making of a barring order. The Courts Bill, 1980, as initiated, by granting to the District Court jurisdiction to determine proceedings under the Guardianship of Infants Act, 1964 will empower the court to make both custody and access orders when barring a spouse from the family home.

161. See further Mr. Justice T.A. Finlay, the President of the High Court, "An Approach to Family Law Cases" (1977) Vol. 71 *The Gazette of the Incorporated Law Society of Ireland* 175 at p. 177 where the learned judge states "I would like to see a situation, if this Act is being amended or reformed, whereby some sort of register of these (barring) orders would be kept by the Garda Siochana on a regional basis and whereby the court could officially inform the gardai who themselves could carry down the information to the local station concerned of the making of an order and of its terms."

SUCCESSION ON DEATH

Succession by will

By the Succession Act, 1965, Sect. 77 any person of sound disposing mind,[1] who has attained the age of eighteen years, or is, or has been married, may dispose of all his property by will.[2] Further, a person under eighteen and unmarried may appoint a guardian of an infant by will if entitled to make such appointment.

Prior to the coming into force of the above Act, a testator had complete freedom of disposition, and thus could disinherit both his wife and children and leave them penniless if he so desired.[3] This freedom of testamentary disposition has now been curtailed by Part IX of the Act.

The Legal Right of a spouse

Moving the Second reading of the Succession Bill, 1965, Mr. B. Lenihan, the then Minister for Justice, stated that the family provisions of Article 41 of the Constitution "cannot be reconciled with a system of law which allows a man to ignore the mother of his family and to leave his property to strangers".[4] The Act, which came into force on the 1st January, 1967, provides that if a testator leaves a spouse[5] and no children, the spouse has a legal right to one-half of the estate;[6] if a testator leaves a spouse and children, the spouse has a legal right to one-third of the estate.[7] This legal right of a spouse is given priority over devises,

---

1. *In the Goods of Farrell, Deceased* (1954) 88 I.L.T.R. 57, (H.C.); *In the Goods of Mitten, Deceased* (1934) 68 I.L.T.R. 38 (H.C.); *In Bonis Corboy, Leahy v. Corboy* [1969] I.R. 148 (S.C.).

2. For a comprehensive account of the law as to Succession, see J.C. Wylie, *Irish Land Law*, Part VI.

3. Since the coming into force of the (Irish) Statute of Distribution, 1695, a testator could deal with his property as he thought fit. Prior to that date there was not complete freedom, the law being governed by the 'custom of Ireland' described in, and abolished by Sect. 10 of the above Statute. The present law of succession in relation to spouses and children is very similar to the 'custom of Ireland' set out in that section. See *In Re Urquhart* [1974] I.R. 197 (S.C.) judgement of Walsh J. at p. 208–209.

4. Dáil Debates Vol. 215 Col. 2018.

5. The question as to who is a deceased's spouse has given rise to some litigation in circumstances in which a deceased and his first spouse have been divorced in another jurisdiction and the former has married another. See *Bank of Ireland v. Caffin* [1971] I.R. 123 (H.C.)–See footnote 13 below; *Gaffney v. Gaffney* [1975] I.R. 133 (S.C.); See also *In the Matter of N.S.M., deceased* (1973) 107 I.L.T.R. 1 (H.C.). Here the deceased and his first wife were divorced, although at all times domiciled in Ireland. The deceased married a second time and in his will, left nothing to his first wife. She commenced proceedings to obtain her share as a legal right, but the proceedings were compromised. The case in which these matters are recounted, concerned a claim by children of the first wife and the deceased to a share in his estate.

6. Sect. 111 (1); See also Sect. 109 (2) which states that references to the estate of the testator under Part IX of the Act "Are to all estate to which he was beneficially entitled for an estate or interest not ceasing on his death and remaining after payment of all expenses, debts and liabilities (other than estate duty*) properly payable thereout."
*(See now the Capital Acquisitions Act, 1975).

7. Sect. 111 (2).

bequests and shares on intestacy.[8]

If a devise[9] or bequest[10] to a spouse is said in a will to be in addition to the legal right, the testator is deemed to have made a gift consisting of both the property devised or bequeathed and a sum equal to the value of the share the spouse is entitled to as a legal right.[11] In any other case, a devise or bequest to a spouse is deemed to have been intended by the testator to be in satisfaction of the legal right of the spouse.[12]

If there is a devise or bequest to a spouse in the will of a testator, the spouse may elect to take either that which is left to him by the will or the share to which he is entitled as a legal right.[13] If the spouse fails to elect, he must take under the will and cannot claim any share as a legal right.[14] Where a person dies partly testate and partly intestate, a spouse may elect to take either a share as a legal right or a share under the intestacy, together with any devise or bequest made in the will.[15] In default of election, a spouse is only entitled to take the latter.[16]

The personal representatives of the deceased's estate must notify a spouse in writing of his right of election. The right is not exercisable either after the expiration of six months from the receipt by the spouse of such notification, or one year from the taking out of representation of the deceased's estate, whichever is the later.[17] If a spouse elects to take his share as a legal right, he may further elect to take any devise or bequest made to him less in value than the share in partial satisfaction thereof.[18]

The legal right of a spouse may be renounced in an ante-nuptial contract made in writing between the parties to an intended marriage or may be renounced in writing by a spouse after marriage and during the lifetime of the testator e.g. in a separation agreement.[19] Further, where a testator during his lifetime and

---

8. Sect. 112.
9. A devise is a gift of real property.
10. A bequest is a gift of personal property e.g. money, furniture or jewellery. A gift of a leasehold interest in property is usually also referred to as a bequest.
11. Sect. 114 (1).
12. Sect. 114 (2).
13. Sect. 115 (1) (a). See *In re Caffin, Bank of Ireland v Caffin* [1971] I.R. 123 (H.C.).
     Y was the first wife of the deceased. His marriage to her was dissolved by an English court when both the deceased and Y had an English domicile. Subsequently the deceased married K. The deceased's will contained a bequest of a pecuniary legacy to his second wife, but she, claiming to be the spouse of the deceased, elected to take her legal right to one half of his estate, instead of the legacy. The executors and trustees of the will applied to the court to determine whether Y or K was the spouse of the deceased for the purpose of Part IX of the Act of 1965. The court held that K, the second wife, was the deceased's spouse for the purpose of the Act. See further Chapter 10.
14. Sect. 115 (1) (b); See *In Re Urquhart, supra*, in which the Supreme Court decided that the share by way of legal right may not vest in a spouse until he elects to take it. Walsh J. in his judgement at p. 211 stated
     "The right to take the legal share requires a 'taking' to vest the share in the spouse. It may be an actual taking, as by an express election to take it instead of the legacy, or it may be a constructive taking by dealing with the legal share in a manner which is inconsistent with any explanation other than that the spouse, in so dealing with it, has not elected to take the legacy.
15. Sect. 115 (2) (a).
16. Sect. 115 (2) (b).
17. Sect. 115 (4). A spouse may exercise the right of election before receiving a notice from the personal representatives—see *J.H. v. W. J.H.* (December 1979) unreported (H.C.).
18. Sect. 115 (3); Sect. 115 (5) provides that in the case of a spouse being
     "a person of unsound mind, the right of election conferred by this section may, if there is a committee of the spouse's estate, be exercised on behalf of the spouse by the committee by leave of the court which has appointed the committee or, if there is no committee, be exercised by the High Court or, in a case within the jurisdiction of the Circuit Court, by that Court."
19. Sect. 113.

prior to the 1st January 1967, has made permanent provision for his spouse, whether under contract or otherwise, all property which is the subject of such provision (other than periodical payments made for her maintenance during his lifetime) must be taken as being given in or towards satisfaction of the share as a legal right of that spouse.[20] The value of property is reckoned as at the date of the making of the provision[21] and if the value is equal to or greater than the legal right, the spouse is not entitled to take any share as a legal right.[22] If the value of the property is less than the legal right, the spouse is only entitled to receive so much of the estate, as when added to the value of the property, is sufficient to make up the full amount of the legal right, as nearly as can be estimated.[23]

Provision for Children

Section 117 of the Act empowers the court, upon an application by or on behalf of a child of a testator, to order such provision to be made for the child out of the estate as the court thinks just, if it is of the opinion that "the testator has failed in his moral duty to make proper provision for the child in accordance with his means whether by will or otherwise."[24] The court must "consider the application from the point of view of a prudent and just parent." It has to take into account the position of each of the children of the testator and any other circumstances which it considers of assistance in arriving at a decision, that is "as fair as possible to the child to whom the application relates and to the other children".[25] An order under this section may not, however, affect the legal right of a surviving spouse or, if the surviving spouse is the mother or father of the child, any devise or bequest to the spouse or any share to which the spouse is entitled on intestacy.[26] Thus, if a surviving spouse is a step-parent, an order may not affect his legal right, but may affect any devise or bequest to him or his share on intestacy.

The court under section 117 must decide (i) whether a testator had a moral obligation to make provision for one or more of his children under his will; (ii) if the testator had such an obligation, whether he failed to make proper provision for such child or children in accordance with his means;[27] and (iii) if he so failed, what provision should be made out of the estate.[28]

20. Sect. 116 (1).
21. Sect. 116 (2).
22. Sect. 116 (3).
23. Sect. 116 (4).
24. Sect. 117 (1). See also *F.M. v. T.A.M. and others*, (1972) 106 I.L.T.R. 82 in which Kenny J. stated that the 'estate' for the purposes of Part IX of the Act of 1965 does not include immoveable property of which a testator was seized or to which he was entitled outside the State–(at p. 86). However he stated further on (at p. 87) that in deciding whether a testator has made proper provision in accordance with his means, "the court may have regard to immoveable property outside the Republic of Ireland owned by the testator". The court, therefore, when deciding whether the moral duty has been fulfilled, must take all the testator's property (including immoveable property outside the Republic of Ireland) into account, but if it decides that the duty has not been discharged, the provision for the child is to be made out of the estate excluding that 'immoveable property'.
25. Sect. 117 (2); See also Sect. 63 which provides that advancements made by a deceased to his children may be brought into account in determining a child's share in the estate.
26. Sect. 117 (3).
27. For a case in which it was held a testator had not so failed, see *In the Matter of the Estate of Bessie Elkinson, Deceased, Elkinson v. Jacob and Ors.* (January 1980) unreported (H.C.).
28. See *In the matter of the Estate of Henry Dowse, Deceased, Walsh v. A.I.B. and Ors.* (March 1977) unreported (H.C.); See also *Woods and Ors. v. Dowd and Ors.* (May 1975) unreported (H.C.); *L. v. L.* [1978] I.R. 288 (H.C.); *M.P.D. and Ors. v. M.D.* (February 1981) unreported (H.C.).

In *F.M.* v. *T.A.M.*[29] *and others*, Kenny J. stated that

"the obligation to make proper provision may be fulfilled by will or otherwise and so gifts or settlements made during the lifetime of the testator in favour of a child or the provision of an expensive education for one child when the others have not received this may discharge the moral duty ... It follows that the relationship of parent and child does not of itself and without regard to other circumstances create a moral duty to leave anything by will to the child".

He held that the question as to whether a parent has a moral duty to make proper provision for a child must be judged by the facts existing at the date of death and must depend upon

"(a) the amount left to the surviving spouse or the value of the legal right, if the survivor elects to take this, (b) the number of the testator's children, their ages and their positions in life at the date of the testator's death, (c) the means of the testator, (d) the age of the child whose case is being considered and his or her financial position and prospects in life and (e) whether the testator has already in his lifetime made proper provision for the child."

The fact that a child contributed financially to a parent, looked after her interests for many years and helped in the upkeep of the parents' home has also been held to give rise to a moral duty.[30] It has been emphasised that the duty is not to make "adequate provision" but to make "proper provision in accordance with the testator's means."[31] Further, its existence must be decided by objective considerations. The court must decide whether the duty exists, and the opinion of the testator, that he was not under any duty is not decisive.[32]

The fact that a court finds a parent in breach of his duty does not of necessity mean that a parent is blameworthy. It is possible, for a will made by a testator, to be completely overtaken by events, for example, by a sudden and dramatic increase in the testator's wealth prior to his death.[33]

If a court decides that a testator had a moral duty and has failed to fulfil it, it must decide what provision to make for the applicant child out of the estate from the point of view of a prudent and just parent. It has been held that a prudent and just parent when making his will would take into account all his moral obligations and not just those that arise under the Succession Act.[33a] Such obligations may require the provision of support for a testator's dependent parents. They may also extend to making provision for a testator's illegitimate children or for a second spouse, in the latter instance, even if the testator's second marriage is invalid. Thus, the court must have regard to such obligations when deciding whether the provision that has been made is proper and upon holding that it is not, when determining what provision should be made.[34]

---

29. *Supra*; See also *In the matter of N.S.M. Deceased* (1973) 107 I.L.T.R. 1 (H.C.); *McNally, decd., Jennings v. Clancy* (1974) 108 I.L.T. & S.J. 227 (H.C.); *Bray v. Bray* (February 1977) unreported (H.C.). *In the matter of the estate of Henry Dowse, Walsh v. A.I.B. and Ors.* (March 1977) unreported (H.C.).
30. *In the estate of Matilda McGarry, decsd, McGarry v. Byrne* (November 1978) unreported (H.C.).
31. See *In the matter of the estate of Henry Dowse, Walsh v. A.I.B. and Ors, supra,* where Hamilton J. held that the provision made by the deceased for his daughter was "adequate" but not "proper provision according to his means".
32. *F.M.* v. *T.A.M., supra; In matter of N.S.M. Deceased, supra.* See also *In the matter of J.R.; J.R. v. J.R.* (November 1979) unreported (H.C.).
33. *Woods and ors. v. Dowd and ors., supra.*
33a. *L. v. L., supra; M.P.D. and Ors v. M.D., supra.*
34. See *L. v. L., supra.* See also *J.H. & C.D.H. v. A.I.B. & Ors.* (November 1978) unreported (H.C.), *M.P.D. and Ors. v. M.D., supra.*

The section confers on the court a wide discretionary power to reconstruct a testator's will in order to make proper provision for his children.[35] The section does not require that equal provision be made for each of the testator's children. The court may order that one child receive a greater share of a parent's estate than the other due to the former's particular or special circumstances.[36] Moreover, the court is not required when dividing an estate to confer on a child an absolute interest in part of it. It may, if it deems it prudent and just, place property in trust for the benefit of one or more children, even if such children are over 21 years of age.[37]

An application for provision out of a parent's estate may be made by or on behalf of a child.[38] By virtue of section 110 of the Act, an application may be made for the benefit of children adopted under the Adoption Acts 1952-76[39] and children legitimated under the Legitimacy Act, 1931, as well as for the benefit of legitimate children. The Act makes no express reference to the illegitimate child and whether an application can be made for the benefit of such child under the section has yet to be determined.[40]

The right to make an application is not limited to dependent children but extends to all children of the testator, even those over twenty-one years of age and married. An application may also be made on behalf of a child of the testator, conceived prior to his death, but born thereafter.[41]

In *F.M.* v. *T.A.M. and others*,[42] a testator left all his property upon trust for his wife for life and after her death for two nephews. He had one child, an adopted son (the plaintiff) who was at the time of the testator's death thirty-two years of age and married with two children. The testator had made no provision for the plaintiff prior to his death and left him nothing in his will. The High Court held that the testator had failed in his moral duty to make proper provision by his will for the plaintiff and ordered that he be given one half of the testator's estate.[43]

In *In the matter of N.S.M. deceased*,[44] the court held that a testator, who had left a substantial estate, had failed in his moral duty to make proper provision for two married daughters (thirty and twenty-five years of age respectively) and for one son (twenty-nine years of age) and went on to make appropriate provision for them.

An application for an order under section 117 must be made within twelve months from the first taking out of representation of the deceased's estate. The

---

35. See however *Woods and Ors. v. Dowd and Ors., supra*, where Parke J. stated "(Counsel for the defendant) argued . . . that the court should disturb or interfere with the provisions of a will to the minimum extent necessary to make provision for a child or children claiming under the section. I accept at once that this is a sound principle, and one which can and ought to be applied to the majority of cases which have arisen and will arise under the section." Nevertheless, it has proved necessary for the court in many cases (including this one) to change the provisions of a will to such an extent as to render it unrecognisable to the original.

36. See, for example, *In the matter of F.F. Decsd., H.L. v. The Govenor and Company of the Bank of Ireland* (July 1978) unreported (H.C.); *In the estate of Matilda McGarry, Decsd., McGarry v. Byrne, supra; J.H. & C.D.H. v. A.I.B. Ors., supra*.

37. *Ibid*.

38. See *In the Matter of Michael Looney Deceased; O'Connor v. O'Keefe*, (November 1970) unreported (H.C.).

39. See *F.M. v. T.A.M., supra*; See also the Adoption Act 1952, Sect. 26.

40. On this question see further p. 336.

41. Sect. 3 (2).

42. *Supra*.

43. Excluding immoveable property in England which was included in the estate. See footnote 24 *supra*.

44. *Supra*.

personal representatives of the deceased are placed under no obligation to inform children of the deceased of their right to make such an application, or of the time within which such an application must be made.[45]

Restrictive Clauses in Legacies and Trusts

A testator when making a disposition in a will cannot interfere with the parental right to determine a child's religious education. In *Burke and O'Reilly* v. *Burke and Quail*[46] a testator by her will left the residue of her property upon trust for the purpose of maintaining and educating G[47] in Ireland and bringing him up as a Roman Catholic. A direction in her will that the selection of a Catholic school for G was to be at the absolute discretion of the trustees was held to be inoperative as it "would override the sacred parental authority and defy the parental right and duty of education under Article 42 of the Constitution".[48]

In *Re Blake, deceased*,[49] a trust was set up, the income of which was to be applied for the benefit of the testator's grandchildren, subject to the condition that they be brought up in the Roman Catholic faith. If they were not so brought up, the trust was to fall into residue. The condition was held to be void as an unlawful infringement of the parental right to determine a child's education. Dixon J. stated that

> "any attempt to restrict or fetter that right would be contary to the solemnly declared policy and conceptions of the community as a whole".

In conclusion, a condition in a legacy that totally restricts a party's right to marry will also be declared void, whilst a partial restraint on marriage may be permitted.[50]

Revocation of Wills and Subsequent Marriage

Under section 85(1) of the Act a will is revoked by the subsequent marriage of the testator, "except a will made in contemplation of that marriage, whether so expressed in the will or not".[51]

Intestate Succession[52]

If a person dies intestate after 1st Jan. 1967, leaving a spouse and no issue, the spouse is entitled to the entire estate.[53] If the intestate leaves both a spouse and issue, the spouse takes two-thirds of the estate and the remainder is distributed among the issue.[54] If the intestate leaves issue only, the estate is distributed

---

45. For a general discussion of children's succession rights see H.M. Fitzpatrick, "The Succession Act, 1965 Sect. 117" (1976) 110 I.L.T. & S.J. pp. 84, 89, 95, 101.

46. [1951] I.R. 216 (H.C.).

47. G. was the son of a Protestant father and Catholic mother.

48. As this was a condition subsequent its invalidity did not prevent G. from benefiting under the will.

49. [1955] I.R. 89 (H.C.).

50. There is extensive case law on this—See Wylie, *supra* p. 168—169. See also *Ryan v. A.-G.* [1965] I.R. 294 (S.C.) in which "the right to marry" was said to be one of the personal rights arising out of Art. 40.3.

51. For a general account of the Law of Revocation see Wylie, *supra*, p. 666—669.

52. For the history of intestate succession in Ireland see *ibid*, chap. 15.

53. Sect. 67 (1). See *Gaffney v. Gaffney, supra*, where the intestator's first wife was declared the lawful spouse of her husband at the date of his death, the parties' divorce not being recognised in this country. As a consequence the 'wife' of his second marriage had no rights of succession to the Estate of the intestate. See further Chapter 10.

54. Sect. 67 (2). By the Adoption Act 1952, Sect. 26 (1) if an adopter or an adopted

among the issue.[55]

If distribution is to take place among the issue, if the issue are in equal degree of relationship to the deceased, the distribution is in equal shares among them, if they are not it is 'per stirpes'.[56] If an intestate leaves neither spouse nor issue, his estate is distributed between his parents in equal shares, but if one parent only survives the intestate, that parent takes the whole estate.[57] Next in line, if none of the above survive an intestate, are his brothers and sisters, among whom the estate must be distributed in equal shares. If a brother or sister does not survive the intestate, the surviving children of the former, where any other brother or sister survives, take in equal share that part of the estate that their parent would have taken.[58] If no brother or sister survives, the estate is distributed in equal shares among the children of the intestate's brothers and sisters.[59] In the event of the deceased being survived by none of the above, the estate is distributed between his next of kin,[60] and in default of next-of-kin, the state may take it "as ultimate intestate successor".[61] Finally, the Act provides that descendants and relatives conceived before an intestate's death but born alive thereafter, are to be regarded as having been born in the lifetime of the deceased and as having survived him.[62]

Right to Home and Household Goods

If the estate of a deceased person includes a dwelling[63] in which at the time of a deceased's death the surviving spouse was ordinarily resident, the latter may require the personal representatives in writing, to appropriate the dwelling, in or towards satisfaction of his or her share in the deceased's estate.[64] A surviving

person or any other person dies intestate in respect of any property after the making of an adoption order, the property devolves as if the adopted person were the child of the adopter born in lawful wedlock. This does not apply to property subject to an entailed interest under a disposition made before the order. See further the remaining sub-section of Sect. 26. Sect. 63 of the Act of 1965 provides that advancements made by a deceased to his children may be brought into account in determining a child's share in the estate.

See also *Application of Meade* [1971] I.R. 327 (H.C.). In this case the wife of an intestate was authorised to use part of her children's share in the estate for the provision of maintenance for the children.

55. Sect. 67 (3).

56. Sect. 67 (4); Sect. 3 (3) provides that "Where a deceased person's estate or any share therein is to be distributed per stirpes among his issue, any issue more remote than a child of the deceased shall take through all degrees, according to their stocks, in equal shares if more than one, the share which the parent of such issue would have taken if living at the death of the deceased, and no issue of the deceased shall take if the parent of such issue is living at the death of the deceased and so capable of taking."

57. Sect. 68.

58. Sect. 69 (1).

59. Sect. 69 (2).

60. See Sects. 70–72. See *In the Matter of the Estate of Norman Robert Wilson, Deceased, Eric John Wilson v. The Attorney-General and John Coughlan* (May 1979) unreported (H.C.). Sect. 71 (1) provides that "the person or persons, who at the date of the death of the intestate, stand nearest in blood relationship to him shall be taken to be his next of kin". In this case it was stated that "the legislature intended to include only legitimate blood relations in the ascertainment of next of kin". As a consequence it was held that the maternal cousins of the deceased, who were the nearest surviving "blood" relations of the deceased who died intestate were not entitled to succeed to his estate. At the time of writing there is a Supreme Court appeal pending.

61. Sect. 73 (1); but the Minister for Finance may waive this right if he thinks it proper to do so – Sect. 73 (2).

62. Sect. 3 (2).

63. Dwelling means "an estate or interest in a building occupied as a separate dwelling or a part, so occupied, of any building and includes any garden or portion of ground attached to and usually occupied with the dwelling or otherwise required for the amenity or convenience of the dwelling". – Sect. 56 (14).

64. Sect. 56 (1); See also 56 (5) (b) and (6) which provides that this right is not exer-

spouse may also require the appropriation of any household chattels in or towards satisfaction of such a share.[65] If a spouse's share is insufficient to enable either or both appropriations to be made, the right may also be exercised in relation to the share of an infant for whom that spouse is a trustee.[66] Further a spouse may require appropriation partly in satisfaction of a share in the deceased's estate and partly in return for a payment of money by the spouse on the spouse's own behalf and that of any infant for whom the spouse is trustee.[67]

While a surviving spouse's right of appropriation still subsists, that spouse may apply to the court, and if the court "is of opinion that in the special circumstances of the case, hardship would otherwise be caused" to the spouse, or the spouse and any children, it may "order that appropriation to the spouse shall be made without the payment of money . . . or subject to the payment of such amount as the court considers reasonable".[68] The court may also make such "further order in relation to the administration of the deceased's estate as may appear to be just and equitable having regard to the provisions of the Act and to all the circumstances."[69]

The personal representatives must notify a spouse of his or her rights of appropriation and, as in the case of the legal right, they are not exercisable later than six months from receipt by a spouse of such notification or one year from the first taking out of representation of a deceased's estate.[70] The above rights arise whether a deceased dies testate or intestate.

---

cisable
- (a) where the dwelling forms part of a building, and an estate or interest in the whole building forms part of the estate;
- (b) where the dwelling is held with agricultural land an estate or interest in which forms part of the estate;
- (c) where the whole or a part of the dwelling was, at the time of the death, used as an hotel, guest house or boarding house;
- (d) where a part of the dwelling was, at the time of the death, used for purposes other than domestic purposes . . .

unless the court, on application made by the personal representatives or the surviving spouse, is satisfied that the exercise of that right is unlikely to diminish the value of the assets of the deceased, other than the dwelling, or to make it more difficult to dispose of them in due course of administration and authorises its exercise."

In *In the Matter of J.H. Decsd., H. v. H.* [1978] I.R. 138 sub nom (1977) 114 I.L.T.R. 1 (S.C.), it was held that the onus lies upon an applicant to so satisfy the court, that the words "assets of the deceased" refer to *all* the assets of the deceased other than the dwelling house and that the court must be satisfied that *neither* of the specified eventualities is likely to happen (i.e. the word 'or' in the subsection is not disjunctive). For the sequel to this case see footnote 70 *infra*.

65. Sect. 56 (2). Household chattels means "furniture, linen, china, glass, books and other chattels of ordinary household use or ornament and also consumable stores, garden effects and domestic animals, but does not include any chattels used at the death of the deceased for business or professional purposes or money or security for money, Sect. 56 (14)."

66. Sect. 56 (3).

67. Sect. 56 (9).

68. Sect. 56 (10) (a) and (b).

69. Sect. 56 (10) (c). See further Sect. 56 (10) (d).

70. Sect. 56 (5). See also section 55 which enables a personal representative to appropriate "any part of the estate of a deceased person . . . in or towards satisfaction of any share in the estate". See further *H. v. O.* [1978] I.R. 194 sub nom *C.H. v. D.G. O'D. and Ors.* (1978) 114 I.L.T.R. 9 (S.C.). Whereas the deceased's wife did not succeed under section 56 in having her family home appropriated towards satisfaction of her share in her husband's estate (See H. v. H. sub nom *In the Matter of J.H. Decsd., supra*) it was so appropriated as a result of her bringing proceedings to compel the personal representatives to make an appropriation under section 55. The Supreme Court however emphasised that a spouse or other beneficiary does not possess any right to compel a personal representative to exercise a power of appropriation under section 55 and stated that the proceedings were misconceived. Nevertheless, it dealt with the application on the basis of the personal representative having chosen to operate the section so as to avoid further litigation between the parties.

Part X of the Act of 1965: Unworthiness to Succeed and Disinheritance

Section 120 of the Act of 1965 sets down various types of persons who are excluded from benefiting from a deceased's estate. A sane person guilty of the murder, attempted murder or manslaughter of the deceased cannot take a share in the deceased's estate, unless a share is left to him by the latter in a will made after the act constituting the offence, and is not entitled to make an application under section 117.[71] A spouse against whom a deceased has obtained a decree of divorce *a mensa et thoro*, a spouse who has failed to comply with a decree of restitution of conjugal rights obtained by the deceased, and a spouse guilty of desertion (or constructive desertion)[72] which has continued up to the death, for two years or more, is precluded from taking any share in the estate of the deceased as a legal right or on intestacy.[73] Such a spouse is not prevented from taking a share left to him or her in the will of the deceased. A person who has been found guilty of an offence, against the deceased, or his spouse or child, punishable by imprisonment for a maximum period of at least two years, or by a more severe penalty, is precluded from taking any share as a legal right or from making an application under section 117.[74] If a person is precluded from taking a share in a deceased's estate on one of the above grounds the share is distributed as if that person had died before the deceased.[75]

Section 121 seeks to prevent a spouse, or parent disposing of his property so as to evade the obligations to his spouse and children, imposed upon him by the Act. The section applies to a disposition of property (other than a testamentary disposition or a disposition to a purchaser) under which the beneficial ownership of the property vests in possession in the donee within three years before the death of the person who made it, or on his death or later.[76] If the court is satisfied that such a disposition was made for the purpose of defeating or substantially diminishing the share of the disponer's spouse, whether as a legal right or on intestacy, or the intestate share of any of his children or of leaving them insufficiently provided for, the court may order that all or part of the disposition be deemed a devise or bequest made by will and forming part of the deceased's estate.[77] Such an order may be made regardless of whether the disponer died testate or intestate. To the extent that the court orders, the disposition is deemed never to have had effect and the donee[78] becomes a debtor to the estate for such amount as the court directs.[79] The court may also make any further order as may appear just and equitable, having regard to the provisions and the spirit of the Act and all other circumstances.[80]

An order may be made under this section for the benefit of a spouse, upon application by the spouse or the personal representatives, or for the benefit of a child, upon an application being made under section 117.[81] If, however, an

71. Sect. 120 (1).
72. Sect. 120 (3) states that "a spouse who was guilty of conduct which justified the deceased is separating and living apart from him shall be deemed to be guilty of desertion." For a discussion of the meaning of desertion see p. 244 *ante*.
73. Sect. 120 (2); This is a further example of the matrimonial offence approach to the problem of marital breakdown.
74. Sect. 120 (4).
75. Sect. 120 (5).
76. Sect. 121 (1); disposition includes a *donatio mortis causa*—Sect. 121 (10); See also Sect. 121 (8)—if a donee disposes of the property to a purchaser the section then applies to the consideration given by the purchaser.
77. Sect. 121 (2). See *M.P.D. and Ors. v. M.D.* and *M.S.D. v. M.D.* (February 1981) unreported (H.C.).
78. Or any person representing or deriving title under him.
79. Sect. 121 (3).
80. Sect. 121 (4).
81. Sect. 121 (5).

application is made by or on behalf of a child of the disponer, who is also a child of the surviving spouse, no order can be made in respect of a disposition made to the spouse.[82] Further, no order can be made affecting a disposition made in favour of any children of the disponer, if

(a) the spouse of the disponer was dead when the disposition was made, or

(b) the spouse was alive when the disposition was made but was a person who, if the disponer had then died, would have been precluded under any of the provisions of section 120 from taking a share in the estate, or

(c) the spouse was alive when the disposition was made and consented in writing to it.[83]

An application under section 121 must be made within one year from the taking out of representation of a deceased's estate.[83a]

THE LAW OF MATRIMONIAL PROPERTY IN PERSPECTIVE

There is, at present, a notable distinction between the approach of the law and the powers of the court when questions arise as to the ownership of property during the lifetime of the parties to a marriage and when they arise upon death. During the lifetime of the parties, subject to certain limited exceptions, the law as to ownership of property applies in the same manner to a married couple as to single people. Ownership is in the main determined by reference to the spouse who contributed the finance used to acquire property.

This emphasis on the origin of the financial contribution has meant that whilst a wife is legally as free as her husband to acquire property, in social reality, the great majority of wives have no real economic independence. Their dependence arises out of the attitude the law takes to the traditional roles that the respective spouses play in the marital relationship. In determining questions as to the ownership of property, the contribution which the majority of wives make towards the acquisition of family assets by their work in the home is wholly ignored. The law fails to recognise that, as pointed out in 1972 by the Commission on the Status of Women, "property rights of the husband would be less if his wife's services in the home were not available to him"[84] and fails to regard her services as conferring on her any beneficial interest in property acquired by him. Put simply, the present law fails to take into account that marriage is a form of partnership in which the parties play interdependent roles and to which the different contributions of each are of equal importance to the family welfare.

Upon the death of a spouse the law adopts a totally different attitude. The partnership element is then properly recognised and the right of a spouse to obtain a fixed share in the other's estate is fully protected.

A law such as that suggested earlier[85] by which the court would have discretionary power to adjust property rights between spouses upon marital breakdown and would, in exercise of that power, be required to have regard to the contribution made to the family welfare by the spouse who looked after the home and cared for the family, would remove some of the injustice perpetrated by the law as it presently operates. It is arguable, however, that if it is thought just that a spouse should be entitled to a fixed share in the assets of the other upon the

82. Sect. 121 (6).
83. Sect. 121 (7).
83a. See *M.P.D. and Ors. v. M.D.*, and *M.S.D. v. M.D., supra*.
84. Report at p. 177.
85. See p. 343 *ante*.

latter's death, spouses should be similarly entitled to a share in each other's assets during the subsistence or upon the breakdown of their marriage. Such legal provision, commonly referred to as a system of Community of Property, is in force in a variety of forms in a number of countries.

There has been no consistent philosophy applied to or systematic development of family property law. Although recent legislation has sought to give better protection to the right of a wife to reside in the matrimonial home, a great deal remains to be done before the great majority of wives will find themselves in a position of real equality as compared to that of their husbands. In 1972, the Commission on the Status of Women recommended that the desirability of legislation providing for a system of community of property or for a system of co-ownership of the matrimonial home be investigated.[86] Successive governments have failed to take any steps to institute any such investigation.[87]

86. See also the Council for Social Welfare, (A Committee of the Catholic Bishops Conference), Statement on Family Law p. 6 where it is also suggested that consideration be given to the introduction of a system of community of property.

87. For some comparative material on family property law see A. Kiralfy—*Comparative Law of Matrimonial Property* (A.W. Sijthoff International Publishing Co. Netherlands 1972); I.M. Pederson—Matrimonial Property Law in Denmark (1965) 28 M.L.R. 137 (This article has particular interest from an Irish perspective as the Danes have a system of community of property together with fixed succession rights). For discussion as to how family property law should be reformed see English Law Commission, *Working Paper on Family Property Law* (P.W.P. No. 42); English Law Commission No. 52; *First Report on Family Property: A New Approach*, and No. 86, *Third Report on Family Property:The Matrimonial Home and Household Goods*; K.J. Gray, *Reallocation of Property on Divorce* (Professional Books, 1977); S.M. Cretney, *supra*, ch. 16; O Kahn Freud, Matrimonial Property: where do we go from here? (Joseph Unger Memorial Lecture 1971); M.P.A. Freeman, Towards a Rational Reconstruction of Family Property Law, [1972] Current Legal Problems, 84; A.A.S. Zuckerman, "Ownership of the Matrimonial Home—Common Sense and Reformist Nonsense" (1978) 94 L.Q.R. 26.

CHAPTER 16

THE FAMILY OUTSIDE MARRIAGE

The natural family or the family outside wedlock does not in Irish law possess the same legal rights and obligations as the family based on marriage. In this chapter it is intended to examine the present legal position of natural parents *vis-à-vis* each other and their children.

THE CONSTITUTION

We have already seen in chapter one that the courts have held that the mother and father of an illegitimate child and the child are not a family for the purposes of Articles 41 and 42 of the Constitution.[1]

In the leading case of *The State (Nicolaou)* v. *An Bord Uchtála*,[2] the Supreme Court stated that the words "family" and "parents" in Articles 41 and 42 referred only to a family and parenthood based on marriage and that the guarantees in these articles do not extend to a natural mother or a natural father. A mother's natural right to the custody and care of her illegitimate child was said to be protected by Article 40.3. Twelve years later in *G.* v. *An Bord Uchtála*,[3] a majority of the Supreme Court endorsed the approach in *Nicolaou* and confirmed that the rights of the mother of an illegitimate child were protected not by the family provisions of the Constitution but by the latter Article. O'Higgins C.J. stated that the plaintiff, who was the mother of an illegitimate child

> "as such . . . has rights which derive from the fact of motherhood and from nature itself. These rights are among her personal rights as a human being which the State is bound under Article 40.3.1. of the Constitution to respect and to defend and vindicate. As a mother she has the right to protect and care for and to have the custody of her infant child . . . This right is clearly based on the natural relationship which exists between a mother and child."[4]

The courts have held that the position of the illegitimate child is not constitutionally inferior to that of the legitimate child. Thus, in *G.* v. *An Bord Uchtála*, Henchy J. stated,

---

1. See *State (Nicolaou)* v. *An Bord Uchtála* [1966] I.R. 567, (S.C.); *G.* v. *An Bord Uchtála* (1978) 113 I.L.T.R. 25 (S.C.); *In re M., an Infant* [1946] I.R. 334; (1946), 80 I.L.T.R. 130 (H.C.); *McNally* v. *Lee* (Jan. 1970) unreported (H.C.); *State (K.M. and R.D.)* v. *The Minister for Foreign Affairs and Ors.* [1979] I.R. 73 (H.C.).
2. *Supra.*
3. *Supra.*
4. *Supra* at p. 35. See also judgements of Parke J. and Walsh J; Kenny J. and Henchy J. both held that the mother of an illegitimate child merely has a statutory or legal right and not a constitutional right to its custody. Henchy J. did however later in his judgement state "the mother's rights in regard to the child, although deriving from the ties of nature, are given a constitutional footing only to the extent that they are found on the constitutionally guaranteed rights of the child." (*Supra* at p. 52).

"All children, whether legitimate or illegitimate, share the common characteristic that they enter life without any responsibility for their status and with an equal claim to what the Constitution expressly or impliedly postulates as the fundamental rights of children."[5]

The courts have emphasised that the "innocent" child of an extra marital union possesses the same "natural and imprescriptible rights" (under Art. 42) as a child born in wedlock to religious and moral, intellectual, physical and social education."[6]

It has been stated, however, that this constitutional equality does not mean that in all instances legitimate and illegitimate children must be treated identically. Whereas, Article 40.1 of the Constitution states that "All citizens shall as human persons be held equal before the law", it permits the State in its enactments to "have due regard to differences of capacity physical and moral and of social function". A difference in "moral capacity and social function" between legitimate and illegitimate children was held in the *State (K.M. and R.D.) v. The Minister for Foreign Affairs and Ors.*[7] to justify a difference in treatment between such children in a legislative provision concerning the removal of children under 7 years from the State. The difference in treatment was, in that case, regarded as a desirable protection of the welfare of illegitimate children. It has also been judicially suggested that the same constitutional justification may be adduced to support a difference in treatment between legitimate and illegitimate children in the law as to succession.[8]

It is submitted that in so far as the law as to succession discriminates between legitimate and illegitimate children, it cannot be upheld as justifiable discrimination. Whereas legislative discrimination may be constitutionally inviolate, if it results "from some special abilities or some deficiency or from some special need"[9] or from "differences in relevant circumstances"[10] it cannot be "invidious or arbitrary."[11]

---

5. *Supra* at p. 51.
6. Per Gavan Duffy P. in *In re M., an Infant, supra* at p. 344. See also *State (Nicolaou) v. An Bord Uchtála, supra* at p. 642—"These 'natural and imprescriptible rights' cannot be said to be acknowledged by the Constitution as residing only in legitimate children" per Walsh J; *G. v. An Bord Uchtála, supra*, in particular judgements of Walsh J at p. 41 and Henchy J. at pp. 51—52. See further p. 3, footnote 7 *ante*.
7. *Supra*. The constitutional challenge in this case was however successful on another ground. See p. 114 *ante*.
8. See *G. v. An Bord Uchtála, supra*, judgement of Henchy J. at p. 51. See also *State (Nicolaou) v. An Bord Uchtála, supra*, at p. 642—"An illegitimate child has the same natural rights as a legitimate child though not necessarily the same legal rights—per Walsh J. For the succession rights of illegitimate children see p.
9. *State (Nicolaou) v. An Bord Uchtála, supra* at p. 639 per Walsh J.
10. *O'Brien, an infant, v. Keogh* [1972] I.R. 144 (S.C.) per O'Dalaigh C.J. at p. 156.
11. *De Burca and Anderson v. The Attorney-General* [1976] I.R. 38 (S.C.) per Walsh J. at p. 68. See also O'Higgins C.J. at p. 59. See further *In The Matter of the Estate of Norman Robert Wilson, Deceased, Eric John Wilson v. The Attorney-General and John Coughlan* (May 1979) unreported (H.C.). In this case the claim of maternal cousins to be entitled to succeed to the estate of the deceased, who died intestate and was illegitimate was unsuccessful in the High Court. However, McWilliam J. in his judgement stated "There is a great deal to be said for the point of view that it is invidious to make a distinction for the purpose of inheritance between legitimate and illegitimate persons although it does not necessarily follow the depriving an illegitimate person of a right to inherit as next of kin offends against the provisions of the Constitution. In this case, however, it cannot be suggested that there is or was any discrimination against the illegitimate person. He is not deprived of any benefit or of any rights. He had full power of disposal over his property but did not choose to exercise it. The claim that must be made is that, because he was illegitimate, there was discrimination against his first cousins. Whatever claim might be made by him if he were deprived of rights to succeed to property of next of kin of his natural relations, I do not see how the converse can possibly give rise to the claim which can succeed on a constitutional

It is submitted that a legislative discrimination based solely upon the circumstances of a person's birth, a matter over which a person has no control, comes within the area of an invidious and arbitrary discrimination that is contrary to Article 40.1.[12]

As for the father of an illegitimate child, Walsh J., giving judgement for the Supreme Court in *Nicolaou*, stated,

> "It has not been shown to the satisfaction of this Court that the father of an illegitimate child has any natural right as distinct from legal rights, to either the custody or society of that child and the court has not been satisfied that any such right has ever been recognised as part of natural law."[13]

The court thus withheld constitutional recognition from the natural father not only under Articles 41 and 42 but also under Article 40.3.

Professor John Kelly has criticised the failure of the Supreme Court in its judgement in *Nicolaou* to extend constitutional recognition to the position of the natural father. "Suppose a case in which the custody of a child is disputed between its natural father (its mother having died or gone away) and an outsider, in circumstances where the child's welfare would be equally assured with either, and no complications of religion or of disturbing a settled habitat exist. What judge would not prefer the father's claim?" he asks. "And if he were asked why he preferred it, would he not refer his judgement to "nature" in one guise or another".[14]

It is submitted that there is no reason why the constitutional guarantees to the family should not be taken to apply to the family outside wedlock. Whereas the State pledges itself "to guard with special care the institution of Marriage, on which the Family is founded and to protect it against attack" there is nothing

---

ground." At the time of writing a Supreme Court appeal is pending.

In *Murphy v. A.G.* (January 1980) unreported (S.C.) the Supreme Court cast doubts on the use of the phrase "invidious discrimination" in the context of Article 40.1.

12. See the decisions of the United States Supreme Court in *Levy v. Louisiana*, 391 U.S. 68; *Weber v. Aetna Casualty and Surety Co.*, 406 U.S. 164; *Jimenez v. Weinberger* 417 U.S. 628; *Gomez v. Perez*, 409 U.S. 535 (U.S.A.); *Trimble v. Gordon* 3 F.L.R. 3081.

See however *Labine v. Vincent*, 401 U.S. 532, in which the U.S. Supreme Court held a statutory scheme that barred an illegitimate child from sharing equally with legitimate heirs in his father's estate not to constitute an invidious discrimination against illegitimate children in violation of the due process and equal protection clauses of the U.S. Constitution. See also *Mathews v. Lucas* 2 F.L.R. 3074. See further W. Binchy, "The American Revolution in Family Law" (1976) 27 N.I.L.Q. 371; M. Staines, "The Concept of 'The Family' Under the Irish Constitution" (1976) 11 I.J. (n.s.) 223; T. O'Connor, "Illegitimate Children and Succession" (1979) vol. 73 *The Gazette of the Incorporated Law Society of Ireland* 53 and "Illegitimacy and the European Convention on Human Rights" (1978) 112 I.L.T. & S.J. at p. 167 *et seq*; S. Maidment, "The Marckx Case" (1979) 9 Fam. Law 228. In Marckx, The European Court of Human Rights held that provisions of the Belgian Civil Code, relating to illegitimate children violated Articles 8 and 14 of The European Convention for the Protection of Human Rights and Fundamental Freedoms. The court in its judgement found certain limitations and discriminations in the area of succession to be in breach of the Convention. It is submitted that in the event of such proceedings being brought against this country, Irish succession laws would similarly be held to be contrary to the Convention.

13. [1966] I.R. at p. 643. See also *State (K.M. and R.D.) v. The Minister for Foreign Affairs and Ors., supra.*

14. *Fundamental Rights in Irish Law*, p. 244. In *R. v. Nash* (1883), 10 Q.B.D. 454, (C.A.). The Master of the Rolls, Sir G. Jewel M.R., stated at p. 456 "The court is now governed by equitable rules, and in equity regard was always had to the mother, the putative father, and the relations on the mother's side. Natural relationship was thus looked to with a view to the benefit of the child. There is in such a case a sort of blood relationship, which, though not legal, gives the natural relation a right to the custody of the child". See also *Re Hyndman, Infants* (1905) 39 I.L.T.R. 191 (K.B.D.), judgement of Lord O'Brien, L.C.J. at p. 192.

in the wording of the Constitution which of necessity withholds constitutional recognition from the family not based on marriage. If a widow and her child are a family for the purposes of Articles 41 and 42 why not an unmarried mother (and/or an unmarried father) and her/his child? Recognition of the latter as such could not in any way be construed as an attack on marriage as an institution, but just a recognition of the factual existence of a family.

Following the limitation of the application of Articles 41 and 42 to married couples, it has been held that a natural father has no right to appear before the Adoption Board upon an application by a third party for the adoption of his child.[15] It also seems that whereas married persons have a constitutional right to have access to contraceptives, a denial of such access being an invasion of marital privacy, a single person has no such right.[16] Further as these articles do not apply to the relationship between natural parents and their illegitimate child, there can be no constitutional objection to the welfare of such child being given paramount consideration in determining disputes between a parent and a stranger as to its custody.[17] Finally, as we have seen in the chapter on adoption, the unmarried mother of an illegitimate child, by adopting her child may place it in the same legal position as a child born to her in marriage. Whether such an adoption renders the mother and child "a family" within the meaning of Articles 41 and 42 has never been judicially decided.

GUARDIANSHIP AND CUSTODY

At common law a child born outside wedlock was said to be illegitimate or a bastard. He was a *filius nullius* (the child of no one) with no parents and no relations. None of the legal rights and duties which flowed from the relationship of parent and legitimate child were accorded to him or his parents. Natural parents were neither the guardians of their child nor did they have any rights to its custody.[18]

In the 19th century the notion that the mother had some rights to her child slowly emerged. Initially her rights arose as a corollary to the duty imposed on her by the Poor Law legislation to provide maintenance. Although she was not regarded as the guardian of her child,[19] and her rights in relation to it were said not to be the same as the rights of the father of a legitimate child,[20] it became established that the "natural" relationship gave the mother a right to her child's custody.[21] Her wishes were to be primarily considered and observed unless contrary to its welfare.[22] However, the mother's wishes in relation to such a

---

15. *The State (Nicolaou) v. An Bord Uchtála, supra.* In contrast to the decision in *Nicolaou*, see *Stanley v. Illinois*, 405 U.S. 645 in which the United States Supreme Court held contrary to the equal protection clause of the U.S. Constitution a statutory provision which enabled the State of Illinois deprive a father of the custody of his illegitimate child without affording him a hearing. See further W. Binchy, *supra*; M. Staines, *supra*.

16. See *McGee v. A.-G.* [1974], I.R. 284; (1973), 109 I.L.T.R. 29, (S.C.). See, however, the decision of the American Supreme Court in *Eisenstadt v. Baird*, 405 U.S. 438. See further p. 103 *ante*.

17. See p. 235 *et seq. ante*.

18. See article entitled "The right to the Custody of Children" (1883), 17 I.L.T. & S.J. 417–8, 431–2, 445–6, 459–60, 473–4, 483–4. See also *Children in English Society*, by I. Pinchbeck and M. Hewitt ch. XIX.

19. See *R. v. Nash* (1883), 10 Q.B.D. 454, (C.A.); *In re Ullee, Infants* (1885), 1 T.L.R. 667, (Ch. Div.); contra the dicta in *In re Darcys* (1860), 11 I.C.L.R. 298, (Ct. of C.P.).

20. *Barnado v. McHugh* [1891], A.C. 388, (H.L.); *In re Connor*, [1919], 1 I.R. 361, 367 (M.R., C.A.).

21. *R. v. Nash, supra*.

22. *Barnado v. McHugh, supra. In re Connor, supra; In re Tamburrini* [1944], I.R. 508, (H.C.); *In re Cullinane, an Infant* [1954], I.R. 270, (H.C.).

child could only prevail during her lifetime and if she was survived by the putative or natural father, he was entitled to the custody of the child as against any guardian appointed by the mother.[23]

Section 6(4) of the Guardianship of Infants Act, 1964, clarified the legal position of a mother *vis-à-vis* her illegitimate child by providing that the mother of such child shall be its guardian. As such, she can apply to the High Court or Circuit Court under section 11 of the Act for a direction on any question affecting the welfare of her child and can appoint a testamentary guardian to act after her death. Section 11(4) of the Act affords recognition to the natural father by providing that he can make an application to the court for an order regarding the custody of his child and a right of access to it.

This Act was passed while the *Nicolaou* case was under litigation. Today, if the natural father of a child was refused a hearing by the Adoption Board, or the Board were going to make an order contrary to his wishes, he could at least delay the adoption process by applying for a custody order under the 1964 Act. The 1964 Act does not confer jurisdiction on the court to order a natural father to maintain his child. The mother is left to her rights under the Illegitimate Children (Affiliation Orders) Act, 1930.

Upon legal proceedings arising out of any dispute concerning the upbringing or custody of an illegitimate child, the court must, as in the case of legitimate children, regard the welfare of the child as the paramount consideration. Moreover, as Articles 41 and 42 of the Constitution do not apply to the legal relationship between natural parents and their illegitimate child, there can be no constitutional objection to the welfare of such child being given paramount consideration in determining disputes between a parent and a stranger.[24] In *McNally* v. *Lee*[25] the High Court refused to make an order of custody in favour of the mother of an illegitimate child. In this case the mother M. having given birth to her child in 1959 "freely and fully" consented to its being adopted in 1960. The child was given to the L's but as Mrs. L. was under 30 an adoption order could not be made until she reached that age.[26] In 1964 the statutory form of consent was sent to the mother and she refused to sign it. That same year the mother married a man who was not the father of the child. In 1969 an application by the mother for custody of the child was made to the High Court. Evidence was given that if the child was taken away from Mr. L.[27] the child would become emotionally disturbed. Kenny J. held that

> "the welfare of the child requires that he should remain with Mr. L. and that giving him to the custody of M. would be foolish and would probably destroy any prospect he has of a stable, settled life".

He also held that M. had abandoned the child and that under section 14 of the 1964 Act he would refuse to grant her custody.

In *J.L. (A Minor)*[28] an 8½ year old girl was placed in the custody of a third

---

23. *In re Kerr, an Infant* (1889), 24 L.R. Ir. 59, (Appeal); *In re Connor, supra*; *In re Crowe* (1883), 17 I.L.T.R. 72, (Q.B.D.). If the mother of an illegitimate child married there arose out of the husband's statutory duty to support her child, a right to the custody of the child—see *In re Gavagan, an Infant* [1922], 1 I.R. 148; (1922), 57 I.L.T.R. 33, (Ch. Div.).

23a. Under the provisions of the Courts Bill, 1980, as initiated it will be possible for applications under the 1964 Act to be determined by the District Court.

24. See p. 235 *ante*.

25. *Supra*.

26. Sect. 11 (3) of the Adoption Act, 1952 which was amended by the Act of 1964.

27. Mrs. L. had by this time died.

28. (March 1978), unreported (H.C., Finlay P.).

party (M) who was regarded by the girl as her mother and the court refused to make a custody order in favour of the girl's real mother, (K). J.L. was born in August, 1969. Her mother, who had married a man who was not J.L.'s father in July, 1969, was deserted within a few weeks of the child's birth. In November, 1970, J.L. came with her mother to reside in F.'s household. F. was a widower with four children. For a period, K. did the housework in F.'s home and reared her child there. In August, 1972, M., a spinster, moved into the house and assisted F. in both running the household and in his business. Shortly after M.'s arrival J.L. went to sleep in M.'s bedroom and started to refer to her as "mammy".

In September, 1974, K. left F.'s household, leaving J.L. behind her, returning only for short visits between then and January 1975. She stayed again for about 5 weeks in February, 1975, but never again returned to stay. J.L. remained part of F.'s household being brought up by F. and M.

In March, 1978, Finlay P., holding that this was a case that came within sections 14 and 16 of the 1964 Act, ruled that it was in the interests of J.L.'s welfare that she remain in F.'s household. He concluded that on the evidence the child "had no overt awareness" of her relationship with K. Whilst making a custody order in favour of M., he also made elaborate access arrangements to enable a "gradual re-familiarisation" between K. and J.L. to take place.

Finally, as we have already seen, in *G.* v. *An Bord Uchtála*,[29] the mother of a ·one year old illegitimate child succeeded in obtaining an order returning her child to her custody and the prospective adopters with whom the child had been placed, failed to obtain an order dispensing with the consent of the mother to the making of an adoption order. In *S.* v. *E.H.B. and Ors.*[30] a mother failed in her application for custody of her one and a half year old child and the adopters with whom the child had been placed were granted an order dispensing with her consent.

FINANCIAL SUPPORT

Introduction

Under Poor Law legislation a mother was under a duty to maintain her illegitimate child until it reached the age of 15 and any relief given to her child by a Poor Law Union was recoverable from her.[31] Upon her marrying, her husband came under the same duty.[32] The Public Assistance Act, 1939[33] re-enacted these provisions, liability to maintain continuing until the child became 16 years of age. The Social Welfare (Supplementary Welfare Allowances) Act, 1975 retains this liability,[34] and a health board may recover from a mother or her husband, if the child was born prior to their marriage, a contribution towards any allowance granted by it for the child's support.[35]

The Courts Act, 1971,[36] enabled a deserted wife to seek maintenance from

---

29. *Supra.*
30. (February 1979), unreported, (H.C.).
31. See the Poor Relief (Ireland) Act, 1838, Sects. 53–55.
32. See *In re Gavagan, an Infant* [1922], 1 I.R. 148, (1922), 57 I.L.T.R. 33, (Ch. Div.), where it was held that by virtue of his observance of his obligation to maintain his wife's illegitimate child under the 1838 Act the husband acquired a right to the custody of such child. The husband in this case was the father of the child but the same right of custody would have arisen even if he was not.
33. Sect. 27. See also Sect. 28 which enabled a public assistance authority to recover from those under an obligation to support an illegitimate child, the sum paid out by it to maintain such child.
34. See Sect. 16 of the 1975 Act.
35. *Ibid.*, Sect. 17.
36. Sect. 18 (6).

her husband for any illegitimate child under 16 who immediately prior to the husband's desertion was wholly or partly supported or maintained by the spouses. Under The Family Law . . . Act, 1976, either spouse may seek maintenance from the other for a dependent child of the family. Amongst the children within this category is a child of one spouse which the other spouse has treated as a member of the family, although aware that he is not the parent of the child.[37] A third party may also obtain an order requiring either spouse to maintain such a child in certain circumstances under this Act.[38] The Bastardy Law (Ireland) Act, 1863[39] enabled the Guardians of a Poor Law Union to recover the cost of relief given to an illegitimate child from the putative father of the child. In order to recover such costs it was necessary for the mother to identify the father upon oath and for her allegation of paternity to be supported by corroborative evidence.[40] It was not until the passing of the Illegitimate Children (Affiliation Orders) Act, 1930, that the mother of an illegitimate child was given power to directly force the father of her child to make a financial contribution towards its maintenance. The Act of 1930 repealed the one of 1863 in toto. Since the coming into force of the Family Law . . . Act, 1976, a third party may also seek a court order to require natural parents to maintain their child. Finally, whilst the mother of an illegitimate child is unable to claim maintenance for her own benefit from the father of her child, she has since 1973 been entitled to receive Unmarried Mother's Allowance.

It is now intended to engage in a detailed examination of the present law.

Affiliation Orders

The Illegitimate Children (Affiliation Orders) Act, 1930,[41] makes provision for the mother of an illegitimate child to bring proceedings against the person she alleges to be the father of her child, to oblige him to contribute towards the mainteance of such child.[42]. Formerly such proceedings could only be commenced in the District Court bu the Courts Act, 1971,[43] confers on the High Court jurisdiction concurrent to that of the District Court. The Courts Bill, 1980, as initiated, proposes to also confer jurisdiction on the Circuit Court to hear such proceedings.

An order adjudging that a person alleged to be is the father of an illegitimate child is called an affiliation order.[44]

Who may apply for an order: The mother of a child[45] or a local body ad-

---

37. Sect. 3 of the 1976 Act. An order may be made to maintain such a child until he reaches the age of sixteen "or if he has attained that age—
    (i) Is or will be or, if an order were made under this Act providing for periodical payments for his support, would be receiving full-time education or instruction at any university, college, school or other educational establishment and is under the age of twenty-one years, or
    (ii) is suffering from mental or physical disability to such extent that it is not reasonably possible for him to maintain himself fully."
38. Sect. 5 (1) (b), see p. 254 *ante*.
39. Replacing Sect. 18 of the Poor Relief (Ireland) Act, 1862.
40. See Sect. 2 and Sect. 3 of the Act of 1863.
41. See also the District Court Rules (No. 2) 1962, (S.I. No. 8 of 1962).
42. Illegitimate Children (Affiliation Orders) Act, 1930, sect. 2.
43. Sect. 19 (2) (a). See further *O. v. M.* [1977] I.R. 33 (S.C.).
44. Sect. 3 of the 1930 Act.
45. A " 'child' means any child who is under the age of sixteen years, or, if he has attained that age—
    (i) is or will be or, if an order were made under this Act providing for periodical pay-

ministering relief to the poor[46] and actually giving relief to the mother or to her illegitimate child. In practice no body that comes within the latter definition has ever applied under the Act. An application for an affiliation order is always made by the mother. The mother may only apply if a single woman, a widow, a married woman living separate from her husband[47] or a married woman living with her husband who gave birth to an illegitimate child before her marriage.[48] Thus, if a woman becomes pregnant by a man other than the one that she subsequently marries, and her child is not born until after the marriage, she may only bring affiliation proceedings if she separates from her husband, or if he dies, or if their marriage is otherwise validly terminated.

There seems little valid reason for limiting in the above manner the circumstances in which an application may be made. It is illogical to deprive a family of extra support where a husband marries knowing his wife to be pregnant by another, and yet permit it to seek such support if the parties marry a week after the birth.

The issuing of Summons: In order for a summons to be issued the mother must first upon oath in writing identify the father of the child.[49] There are specific time limits laid down in the Act, within which a mother can apply for a summons to be issued. By section 2(2) as amended by the Family Law . . . Act, 1976,[50] an application can be made only:

(a) Before the birth of the child,[51]

(b) Within three years after the child's birth;

(c) At any time, if the alleged father has contributed towards the main-

ments for his support, would be receiving full-time education or instruction at any university, college, school or other educational establishment and is under the age of twenty-one years,
(ii) is suffering from mental or physical disability to such extent that it is not reasonably possible for him to maintain himself fully".—Sect. 1 of the 1930 Act, as amended by the Family Law . . . Act, 1976, Sect. 28 (1) (a).
46. Whilst in theory such a body could bring affiliation proceedings there is no reported case of a body doing so since the Act's inception. The Illegitimate Children (Maintenance and Succession) Bill, 1974 proposed in Sect. 3 (a) the deletion in Sect. 2 subs. (1) of "On the application within the time hereinafter limited, of a local body administering the relief of the poor then giving relief to the mother of an illegitimate child or to an illegitimate child" and the substitution of "other person having lawful custody of an illegitimate child other than by virtue of an adoption order made under the Adoption Acts, 1952, and 1964". The latter may now seek a "maintenance order" from the natural parents—see Third Party Maintenance Orders, p. 334 below.
47. A married woman seeking an affiliation order in respect of a child born to her during marriage will usually have the difficulty of having to rebut the presumption of legitimacy and establish paternity without being able to give direct evidence herself of not engaging in intercourse with her husband at any time during which conception could have taken place. See p. 170 *et seq*. See, however, *O'Connell v. Broderick* (February 1977) unreported (H.C.) where this difficulty does not appear to have been considered. See further J. O'Reilly, "Affiliation Proceedings in the High Court: An Appreciation by a Married Woman", (1976) II I.J. (n.s.) 340.
48. See Sects. 1 and 2 of the 1930 Act.
49. *Ibid*., Sect. 2 (1); see *The State (O'Neill) v. Shannon* [1931] I.R. 691. A District Court affiliation summons is issued by a District Justice. A special summons to commence High Court affiliation proceedings may only be issued with the "prior leave" of a judge of that Court. The issuing of either is dependent on the making of a sworn information (District Ct.) or sworn affidavit (High Court) by the mother identifying the father of her child. An *ex parte* application is made to a judge of the relevant court grounded on the information or affidavit for leave to issue a summons. See *O. v. M. supra*.
50. Sect. 28 (1) (b).
51. By Sect. 2 (3) where a summons is issued before the birth of a child the date for which the father is summoned to the court "shall not be earlier than 14 days after the day on which such child is expected to be born".

tenance of the child within three years of its birth;[52]

(d) Within three years after the alleged father first takes up residence in the State,[53] if he was not resident in the State at the date of the child's birth, or if he ceased to be so resident within three years of its birth.

For time to run against the mother it is not necessary for her to know the place of residence of the father. Thus, if the father disappears before proceedings are commenced, without contributing to the child's maintenance and unknown to the mother takes up residence in Cork, if the mother living in Dublin does not discover his whereabouts until three years after the child's birth she will be unable to succeed in an application for an affiliation order. Similarly knowledge by the mother, of the father having taken up residence in the State is not required for time to run under (d) above.

The reason for limiting the time by which proceedings must be brought is to prevent a mother bringing proceedings a long time after the birth of a child, when it might prove impossible for the defendant to adduce rebutting evidence. The present law, however, is weighted to an unnecessary degree against the mother and child and in favour of the father.

The Illegitimate Children (Maintenance and Succession) Bill, 1974, introduced in the Seanad by Senator Mary Robinson on the 10th May, 1974 but subsequently withdrawn,[54] proposed to permit an application for an affiliation summons "either before or after the birth of the illegitimate child in respect of whom the application is made provided that the application is made within the period during which a weekly sum for the maintenance and education of such child may be made payable". The enactment of this provision would not only have simplified an unnecessarily complicated area of the law, it would also have more effectively sought to prevent unmarried fathers from evading their responsibilities.

The Act places the onus on the mother to prove to the satisfaction of the court that the person she alleges to be, is, the father of her child, and she cannot do this without corroborative evidence. It is submitted that there is no valid reason for restricting the period within which a mother can bring affiliation proceedings. Whereas it may be difficult for the person alleged to be the father to rebut a mother's allegation a number of years after the child's birth, it will be equally difficult for her in such circumstances to adduce adequate evidence to substantiate her own case. Moreover, the mother has to establish a *prima facie* case before the alleged father is required to rebut it.

Effect of criminal charge: In relation to the bringing of affiliation proceedings, it has been held by the High Court in *O'Donnell* v. *Hegarty*[55] that an acquittal of a person on a charge of unlawful carnal knowledge of a girl aged between 15 and 17 is no bar to a subsequent application for an affiliation order by the same girl against that person in respect of an illegitimate child born to her as a result of the intercourse which grounded the criminal charge. The affiliation proceedings are not as a result of the acquittal *res judicata*; the acquittal does not work any

---

52. See *O'Connell v. Broderick, supra*. A contribution is not limited to a financial contribution, it can be a contribution in kind.
53. Prior to the coming into force of the Act of 1976 all the time limits were of six months. Further time under (d) started to run six months after the alleged father first "entered the State". On this see *The State (O'Callaghan) v. Buckley* [1960] I.R. 429, (H.C.).
54. On the 13th Feb. 1975 upon the Minister for Justice giving a specific undertaking that a Family Law Reform Bill on the subject would soon be introduced. This was the Bill that was finally passed in 1976.
55. [1941] I.R. 538; (1941), 76 I.L.T.R. 12, (H.C.).

estoppel in favour of the father and the plea of *autrefois acquit* by him in answer to the affiliation proceedings is bad. The reason for this is that different matters are in issue in the two types of proceedings. Similarly, if a person is acquitted on a charge of rape, the girl who it was alleged he raped is not estopped from bringing affiliation proceedings alleging that the person acquitted of the charge is the father of her child.

Procedure: The hearing takes place in the District Court or High Court and if the District Justice or the High Court is satisfied that the alleged father is the father of the child an order can be made adjudging him to be the "putative" father.

By section 3(2) of the Act—

"No justice of the District Court[56] shall be satisfied that a person is the putative father of an illegitimate child without hearing the evidence of the mother of such child and also evidence corroborative in some material particular or particulars of the evidence of such mother."

This involves two factors: (1) The giving of evidence by the mother; (2) The requirement of evidence corroborative of the mother's in some material particular.

1. As was seen earlier, no summons can be issued unless the mother upon oath in writing identifies the father of the child, and by section 3(2) she must give evidence in court. Thus, if she dies at the birth of the child or afterwards, but before the application is finally heard, or cannot give evidence for any other reason, no order can be made and the father cannot be legally obliged to support the child.[57] This can result in considerable injustice in that if the mother dies, a relation may wish to bring up the child. Such a third person should in such circumstances be able to get an order to force the father to meet his obligation to provide maintenance for the child. Obviously it would be more difficult for such a person to provide the necessary proofs for the court to make an order, but he or she should be given an opportunity to do so. There seems little point in not permitting the bringing of such proceedings. If they were successful it can be only for the benefit of the child.

2 A difficult factor and one that has been discussed in a large number of cases is that of finding evidence corroborative of the mother's evidence in some material particular. The burden of proving paternity is upon the applicant, and her evidence by itself is not sufficient for an order to be made. There must be corroborative evidence of some fact that implicates the alleged father.[58] The best evidence is a corroborated admission of paternity by the father but evidence of such will rarely be forthcoming.[59] Mere evidence of opportunity for intercourse is not sufficient,[60] nor is evidence that the defendant sought and obtained an interview with the applicant on hearing that she accused him of being the father.[61]

56. Similarly by virtue of the Courts Act, 1971, Sect. 19 "No judge of the High Court". See *O. v. M., supra.*
57. See further on section entitled "Third Party Maintenance Orders". Where a person has been adjudged the putative father or is the admitted father, a third person in charge of the child may bring maintenance proceedings against him.
58. *The State (Reilly) v. District Justice for Clones* [1935] I.R. 908, (H.C.).
59. *O'Neill v. Kelly* [1957], Ir. Jr. Rep. 81, (Cir. Ct.).
60. See *Seaver v. O'Toole* [1937], Ir. Jur. Rep. 8, (Cir. Ct.); *The State (Smyth) v. Fawsitt* [1950] Ir. Jur. Rep. 25, (H.C.).
61. *McCarthy v. Hourihane* [1935], Ir. Jur. Rep. 37, (H.C.).

The leading case is *Morrissey* v. *Boyle*.[62] The applicant, Morrisey, brought affiliation proceedings against the defendant, Boyle. She stated in evidence that on two occasions B. who was introduced to her as Mr. Manning, took her with another girl and a civic guard for a motor drive; that they stopped at a public house and that they then went off walking in pairs through the fields near Stepaside; that B. had intercourse with her on one of these occasions, and on subsequent occasions, and that as a result of this intercourse a child was born. Some weeks after the birth of the child she met B. and told him that she had been in trouble and that "the baby is in a nursing home"; that he had asked her in what home and she told him; she also told him that she had been in trouble with her parents and that her father wanted to see him, and that B. then said he would arrange to meet her father but that it was too late that night; that her father then came up and B. arranged to meet him on the following night.

Her father gave evidence that he met B. on the same occasion and asked him was he Mr. B. and when he said "Yes" he brought B. to the applicant and said "Now Mr. Manning this is my daughter and she will tell you her tale". The father then left them for 10 or 12 minutes and on his return the applicant said to her father "Mr. Boyle wants to make an appointment to see you" and they arranged to meet on the following night. Boyle did not keep the appointment.

On the following evening the applicant's father wrote to B. saying that he was surprised that he did not keep the appointment; that he was willing to meet him any evening and that he did not intend to allow the matter to remain any longer in abeyance, and should he wish to come to an amicable agreement he would expect an early reply to his letter. B.'s solicitor replied to the father's letter stating that if he wished to discuss any matter he should first communicate with him and not directly to B.

The guard also gave evidence which was at variance with that of the applicant as to the material dates and as to the parties separating when they left the motor car.

The District Justice dismissed the summons. On Appeal to the Circuit Court at the conclusion of the applicant's case, B. applied for a direction on the ground that there was no evidence "corroborative in some material particular" of the evidence of the applicant but the Circuit Court judge refused the application holding that there was such evidence. He, however, stated a case for the opinion of the Supreme Court.

There it was held that the Circuit Court was correct in holding that there was evidence corroborative in some material particular of the evidence of the applicant and that the application for a direction was rightly refused.

Because of its importance Sullivan C.J.'s judgement is quoted in *extenso*. Sullivan C.J., referring to section 3(2) stated[63]

"A similar provision in Sect. 4 of the Bastardy Laws (Amendment) Act, 1872, was considered by the Court of Appeal in England in *Thomas* v. *Jones*.[64] In his judgement in that case Scrutton L.J. there said:—"What is meant by 'Corroboration in some material particular'—that is in a material fact? The vital fact to be proved in a bastardy case is that a child has been born to the applicant as a result of sexual connection with the man. From the nature of the case it is almost inevitable that there never will be any direct corroboration of sexual connection. The evidence in corroboration

62. [1942] I.R. 514; (1941), 75 I.L.T.R. 228, (S.C.).
63. *Supra* at p. 520, 521.
64. *Thomas v. Jones* [1921], K.B. 22, (C.A.).

must always be circumstantial evidence of the main fact, that is to say, evidence from which it may be inferred that the main fact happened. For instance, the fact that the man has had connection with the woman and a child has resulted is sometimes inferred from evidence of previous affection, that they had been seen together showing affection to each other. Sometimes it is inferred from the fact of subsequent affection—that the man and woman are seen together showing signs of affection. Sometimes it is inferred from the fact that the man has done acts which may be treated as recognising responsibility for the child as his child, statements that he will provide for the child, payments for the child, all facts from which as a matter of inference and probability it is more probable that the intercourse did take place than not . . . If the fact is such that the probabilities are equal one way or the other, an inference cannot legitimately be drawn from it one way or the other. It must show, even only slightly, more probability that intercourse took place than not, and if there is that balance of probability it is not for the Court to say that it is so slight that it would not have acted upon it."

Sullivan C.J. continued[65]

"In my opinion the only reasonable interpretation of the appellant's evidence is that in the interview in question she charged the respondent with the paternity of her child. That such a charge was made is, I think, the reasonable inference from the fact that the respondent without asking for any explanation of the letter . . . instructed his solicitors to reply to it in the terms 'stated'. If such a charge was made, then the fact that the respondent did not repudiate it in the presence of the appellant's father, but made an appointment to meet him on the following night obviously with the object of discussing the matter is to my mind a most material circumstance from which the more probable inference is that the charge was well founded.

The appellant's evidence as to that material circumstance was corroborated by the evidence of her father."

In the same case Meredith J. stated

"corroboration has not to go the length of being an unambiguous admission, for that would be conclusive: it is enough if there be something which tends to make you believe the story of the applicant to be the truth".[66]

Following Morrissey's case, in *Kiely* v. *Mulvihill*,[67] evidence was given that the appellant had shown affection towards the applicant over a long period of time and that, on one occasion the appellant entered a field with the applicant at about 3 a.m. and remained there for about two hours.

The court held that the entering of the field at that time of night was more than evidence of mere opportunity and that "[it] must show even only slightly more probably that intercourse took place than not".[68] Taking this fact together with evidence of affection it was held that there was sufficient corroboration of the applicant's evidence to satisfy the statute.

Alternatively, in *Cahill* v. *Reilly*,[69] evidence was given that the applicant and the defendant who were engaged to be married were sitting in the kitchen of the

65. *Supra* at p. 523.
66. *Supra* at p. 526.
67. (1947) 82 I.L.T.R. 1, (Cir. Ct.).
68. *Supra* at p. 2 per Judge B. O'Briain.
69. [1957] Ir. Jur. Rep. 77, (Cir. Ct.).

applicant's home at 2.30 a.m. in the morning. The applicant's sister corroborated the fact that they were in the kitchen at that time as she had shortly before, left the room.

Judge Deale reached the conclusion that it was unlikely that the couple would have engaged in intercourse so soon after the interruption of their privacy. At best "the probabilities of intercourse and no intercourse are equal". Thus the fact that the sister corroborated the presence of the parties in the kitchen did "not corroborate the material fact that they had sexual intercourse in her absence".

There seems on the face of it to be little difference between the facts of the two above cases. In both cases they were young people who had previously exhibited affection towards each other, in the latter instance, the parties being engaged. The difference between the cases was that it was regarded as more likely that parties would engage in sexual intercourse in a field at 3 a.m. in the morning than they would do so in a kitchen at 2.30 a.m. in the morning.

These two cases illustrate the difficulty in predicting the outcome of affiliation proceedings, an unknown factor in each case and one that may be crucial, being what sexual behaviour the court will regard as more probable than not in particular circumstances.[70] Finally, an order that is obtained as a result of perjured evidence by the corroborating witness will be quashed whether or not the party obtaining the order was privy to the perjury.[71]

Blood and Tissue Testing

As has already been seen, blood testing and tissue testing of both a mother, child and the alleged father can provide considerable assistance to a court in determining the question of paternity.[72] Tissue testing in particular can now establish to a high degree of certainty whether a person alleged to be, in fact is the father of a child. However, the 1931 Act does not empower the courts to require the parties to an affiliation action to undergo blood or tissue testing. In practice it is now usual for parties to such proceedings to voluntarily undergo such testing and if the tissue tests establish paternity the issue of paternity is not usually contested. Similarly, if the tests establish that an alleged father could not be the father of a particular child, it is usual that the plaintiff discontinues her proceedings against him.

A question that has yet to be determined by the Irish courts is whether an alleged father's refusal, without a reasonable excuse, to undergo tissue and blood testing at the request of the mother of an illegitimate child constitutes "evidence corroborative in some material particular" within the meaning of Sect. 3(2) of the 1931 Act so as to enable the mother in affiliation proceedings to obtain an affiliation order. If an alleged father contests paternity in affiliation proceedings after the results of such testing have proved consistent with the allegation of paternity, there is little doubt that the results of the tests carried out would constitute the necessary corroborative evidence.[73]

Orders that may be made:[74] If the court adjudges the defendant to be the

---

70. See also *Norwood v. Scott* (1939), 73 I.L.T.R. 200, (N.I. Recorders Ct.); *Edgar v. Wallace* [1957], N.I. 64, (C.A.).
71. *R. (Burns) v. Tyrone County Court Judge* [1961], N.I. 167, (Q.B.D.).
72. See p. 172 *ante*.
73. See (1932) 66 I.L.T. & S.J. 64 "Bernstein Blood Test as Evidence" in which is recounted the first occasion in which the results of blood testing was successfully used in affiliation proceedings in this country.
74. See Sect. 3 of 1930 as amended by the Family Law . . . Act, 1976, Sect. 28.

putative father of the child, it may order him to make various payments. He may be ordered to pay the expenses incidental to its birth,[75] and if the child has died before the making of the order, also the funeral expenses to a sum not exceeding £200. In addition he may be ordered to pay a weekly sum for the maintenance and education of the child and the court may attach such conditions as it thinks proper to the payment or receipt of the money. The weekly sum that can be ordered in the High Court is unlimited and left to the judge's discretion, but no more than £15 can be ordered in the District Court.[76] A weekly sum may not commence earlier than the date on which the order is made.[77] As an alternative to a weekly sum, where the court deems it appropriate and the putative father consents, the latter can pay a lump sum fixed by the court in commutation of a weekly sum.[78]

The court may also order the putative father to pay a sum not exceeding £200 for the purpose of apprenticing a child to a trade. An application for such an order cannot be made until the child is 14, and must be made not later than six months after such child has attained the age of 16.[79] If a child in respect of whom a weekly sum is payable dies, upon an application being made within two months of the death of such child, the court can order the putative father to pay the funeral expenses to an amount not exceeding £200.[80]

The Courts Bill, 1980, as initiated, proposes to grant an unlimited jurisdiction to the Circuit Court in affiliation matters and to extend the jurisdiction of the District Court to permit the court award payments of an amount up to £30 per week for the maintenance of a child.

Normally money due under an affiliation order is payable to the mother. If the mother dies or for any reason the child is not in her custody the order is made payable to the person in whose custody the child is. It can also be made payable to a local body if the child or mother is in receipt of poor relief from them.[81]

If a putative father, liable to pay a weekly sum dies, liability for such sum attaches to his estate as a civil debt and is recoverable by the person to whom the weekly sum is payable.[82] Similarly, in such circumstances his personal representative can be ordered to pay the funeral expenses of such child or the sum fixed to enable the child to become apprenticed.[83]

Appeals: Either party may appeal from a court's decision. Formerly, any party who wished to do so, had to enter into a recognizance. This however is no longer necessary.[84] An appeal to the Circuit Court is virtually a rehearing of the case and the mother again has to give evidence which must be corroborated. Consequently if she were to die before the appeal was heard the court would be

---

75. By the Social Welfare (Consolidation) Act, 1981, sect. 28(2) in deciding whether or not to make an order for payment of expenses incidental to the birth of a child the court cannot take into consideration the fact that the mother of the child is entitled to maternity allowance.
76. Courts Act, 1971, Sect. 19 (3) (a) as amended by the Family Law . . . Act, 1976, Sect. 28 (3). See also *M.R. v. R. O'F.* (1974), 109 I.L.T. & S.J., 25 (H.C.).
77. Sect. 4 (1) of 1930 as amended by the Family Law . . . Act, 1976, Sect. 28 (1) (h).
78. Sect. 3 (1) (c) of the 1930 Act.
79. *Ibid.*, Sect. 6 as amended by the Family Law . . . Act, 1976, Sect. 28 (1) (j).
80. *Ibid.*, Sect. 7 as amended by the Family Law . . . Act, 1976, Sect. 28 (1) (j).
81. *Ibid.*, Sect. 9 (3).
82. *Ibid.*, Sect. 4 (5) as amended by the Family Law . . . Act, 1976, Sect. 28 (1) (h).
83. *Ibid.*, Sect. 6 (1) and 7.
84. See Illegitimate Children (Affiliation Orders) Act, 1930, Rules 1931, para. 7. See also *Lonergan v. Morrisey* [1947], 81 I.L.T.R. 130, (Cir. Ct.). The 1931 Rules were repealed by the District Court Rules (No. 2.), 1962, *supra*.

bound to find for the defendant.

Variation Orders: Upon the application of either the person by whom or to whom a weekly sum is payable, the court has full powers to vary the amount payable, change the person to whom it is payable, or vary all or any of the conditions relating to the payment or receipt of the money.[85] Upon the application by a person liable to pay a weekly sum, or upon the death of such person, upon the application of the person to whom such weekly sum is payable, the court can authorise the commutation of the weekly sum by payment of a lump sum.[86] Every lump sum fixed as a result of such an application has to be fixed with a view to securing for the illegitimate child benefits at least equal to those he would derive from a continuation of the weekly sum.

Concurrent jurisdiction: Under section 19(2)(a) of the Courts Act, 1971, the High Court has concurrently with the District Court, jurisdiction to hear and determine affiliation proceedings. Section 19(3)(b) states that nothing in the section shall be construed as conferring on the District Court jurisdiction to make an order in any matter in relation to which the High Court has made an order. However, the section says nothing about the power of the High Court to make an order in relation to a matter previously dealt with before the District Court. In *M.R.* v. *R.O'F.*[87] it was held that the High Court has power to modify or vary affiliation orders made in the District Court. In that case, an order was made increasing the amount to be paid by the father from the then District Court maximum of £5 to £10.

Termination of Affiliation Orders:[88] An order providing for periodical payments continues to be payable for the length of time specified in the order. All such payments cease to be payable upon

(a) the death of the child

(b) their commutation by payment of a lump sum

(c) an order of the court terminating the payments

(d) the child becoming 16 years of age, unless at the time of the making of the order, or at any time thereafter, before his attaining 16, the court on account of his educational needs or a physical or mental disability orders otherwise

(e) the attainment by the child of the age of 21 where the court on account of his education needs has ordered that payment be made after he has attained 16

(f) the adoption of the child by a person other than the natural mother.[89] Where a mother adopts her own child, the affiliation order remains in force.

The court may at any time on the application of the person making weekly payments under an affiliation order terminate the payments if satisfied

(i) that liability has ceased under the Act, *or*

---

85. Sect. 5 (1) of the 1930 Act.
86. *Ibid.*, Sect. 8.
87. (1974), 109 I.L.T. & S.J. 25, (H.C.).
88. See Sect. 4 of the 1930 Act as amended by Sect. 28 (1) (h) of the 1976 Act.
89. Adoption Act, 1952, Sect. 31.

(ii) that justice requires that liability should cease.[90]

(a), (b), (d), (e) and (f) list the circumstances in which liability terminates under the Act. Despite none of these circumstances existing it is still possible for the court under (ii) above to terminate the order upon application by the party subject to it. An example of a situation in which the court may terminate an order in the interests of justice would perhaps be where the mother had become financially very well off, while the putative father was impecunious. The fact that the mother of the child marries subsequent to the making of an order does not automatically terminate liability under the order. If, however, she adopts the child together with her husband, liability ceases upon the adoption order being made.

The Family Law . . . Act, 1976,[91] empowers the court to require a putative father to make further payments although the original affiliation order is discharged or payments have ceased. The amount payable and the period of time for which it is to be paid is left to the court's discretion. The court may only require the father to make such payments while the person for whose benefit they are made is still a child within the meaning of the Act. This provision introduces considerable flexibility to the law. Thus, if a father pays a lump sum in commutation of weekly payments, it is possible that the court will at some time in the future order him to make further payments. Similarly, if payments cease upon a child reaching 16 because the child is no longer attending school, and the child subsequently, when still under 21, resumes full-time education the court may require further payments to be made.

Voluntary Agreements for the Maintenance of an Illegitimate Child:[92] A voluntary agreement can be made between the mother and the father of an illegitimate child whereby the father agrees to provide for the child. Such an agreement can be made either before or after the making of an affiliation order. It can be submitted to the court by either party and provided the benefits are substantially as beneficial as those which would be obtained under the 1930 Act, although they differ wholly or partly from such benefits, the court can record its approval. The recording of such approval acts as a complete bar to any proceedings or further proceedings (where an order has previously been made) being brought under the act for an affiliation order.[93] Before a mother of an illegitimate child in respect of whom an order has not previously been made can apply for the approval of the court for such an agreement, she must upon oath make an information in writing identifying the father of the child.[94] The

---

90. Sect. 5 (2) of the 1930 Act.
91. Sect. 4 (4) of the 1930 Act as amended by Sect. 28 (1) (h) of the 1976 Act.
92. See Sect. 10 of the 1930 Act.
93. *Ibid.*, Sect. 10 (4). There is some doubt as to the accuracy of this statement. By virtue of Sect. 10 (4) of the 1930 Act it is accurate. However, the Act of 1930, as amended by the Family Law . . . Act, 1976, Sect. 28, now states in Sect. 4 (4) (a) that "Where an affiliation order . . . has been discharged . . . or where payments under an affiliation order have ceased to be payable by virtue of this Act, the . . . court may at any time thereafter, notwithstanding anything in this Act, by order direct the making by the putative father of further payments". An order to make further payments is regarded as an affiliation order. Thus it seems from this section that if prior to concluding an agreement a father has been subject to an affiliation order, despite the obtaining of the court's approval for the agreement, it will not bar the mother from bringing proceedings for further payments. However, if such an agreement is approved, without an affiliation order ever having been made as the father is never adjudged a "putative father" it seems that future affiliation proceedings cannot be brought.
94. Sect. 10 (5) of the 1930 Act. As we shall see further on whether or not the father was previously subject to an affiliation order, as the "admitted father" under the agreement, he may be subject to maintenance proceedings brought by a third party.

father who signs such an agreement is known as the "admitted father".

In the case of an agreement made which is not submitted to the court for its approval, the question arises as to whether it is a bar to an affiliation action being brought in the future. Obviously, if such an agreement is concluded outside the statutory time limit for bringing proceedings, no problem arises as no proceedings could be brought in any case. However, if the father has contributed to the maintenance of such child within the statutory time limit, either by virtue of such an agreement or prior to its being concluded, an agreement not submitted to the court should not be a bar to the mother bringing affiliation proceedings. The Act provides that those agreements concluded and expressly approved by the court bar future proceedings. The purpose of the court seeing and approving an agreement is to protect the interests of the child by ensuring that an agreement is equally as beneficial to the child as any order that could be made by the court.

It is submitted that if an agreement was concluded containing a provision whereby the mother promised not to take affiliation proceedings, and if the circumstances were such that in the absence of such a provision the court would have jurisdiction to make an order, if such an agreement did not receive the approval of the court, such a provision would be unenforceable as contrary to the policy of the Act.[95]

Procedure for Payment: The law as to the payment of an affiliation order is the same as that applying to payment of a maintenance order under the Act of 1976.[96] The court when making an order must direct that payment be made to the District Court clerk. The court is bound to make such a direction unless, at the request of the person on whose application the order was made, the court considers that it would be proper not to do so. If a direction of payment to the clerk is not made the court may at any time in the future make such a direction. The clerk is under a duty to transmit payments made to him to the person entitled to receive them. Where payments to the clerk are in arrears, upon a request in writing by the latter, the clerk may proceed in his own name for enforcement of the arrears. This does not prevent a person from taking enforcement proceedings in her own name if she wishes. Where the court has directed payment to the court clerk, it may discharge the direction on the application of the putative father if satisfied that having regard to his record of payments and other circumstances it would be proper to do so. The court must first give the person in receipt of the payments an opportunity to oppose the application.

Normally, the mother is the person entitled to receive the payments ordered by the court. If she dies or if for any reason the child is not in her custody, the money will be paid to the person that has custody of the child. It may also be paid to a local body if the child or mother receives poor relief from it.[97]

---

95. See *Follit v. Koetzow* (1860), 2 El & El. 730, 121 E.R. 274 (Ct. of Q.B.) where it was held that a mother could apply under Sect. 3 of the Poor Law Amendment Act, 1844, for an affiliation order, despite the existence of a legally enforceable agreement between her and the father, whereby she promised in effect not to bring affiliation proceedings in return for his paying her a sum for the support of the child. The agreement was held not to bar such proceedings. Payments ordered under the Act "not being made solely for the mother's benefit, she cannot renounce the right to it". Per Blackburn J. at p. 741. For the enforcement of agreements to contribute towards the support of one's illegitimate child see *Jennings v. Brown* (1842), 9 M. & W. 496; 152 E.R. 210 (Ct. of Exch.); *Ward v. Byham* [1956] I.W.L.R. 496; [1956], 2 All E.R. 318, (C.A.).

96. See Sect. 28 (1) (g) of the 1976 Act.

97. See Sect. 9 (3) and (4) of the 1930 Act.

Enforcement of Orders: Every weekly or other sum ordered to be paid under the Act of 1930 may be recovered as a civil debt.[98] Other means of enforcing payment of affiliation orders are discussed in Chapter 14, commencing at page 284.

Third Party Maintenance Orders

Under section 4A of the Act of 1930, as appended by the Family Law . . . Act, 1976, Sect. 28(1)(h) it is possible for a third party to seek a maintenance order for the benefit of an illegitimate child. If it appears to the court that a parent of an illegitimate child has failed to provide such maintenance for the child as is proper in the circumstances, the court may order the parent to make periodical payments for the support of the child to the person applying for maintenance. These payments are to be made for such period during the lifetime of the applicant, as the court determines. The court also has a general discretion to determine the amount of the payments and the times at which they are to be made. A parent under this provision means the mother, putative father or an admitted father of the child.

An order may not be made in relation to a parent, if that parent is already obliged by virtue of one of the other provisions of the 1930 Act to make payments for the child's benefit unless (a) he is not complying with his obligation and (b) the court having regard to all the circumstances thinks it proper to make an order. If the court does make such an order, any sums that would fall due for payment by virtue of other provisions of the Act, cease to be payable.

Under this provision not only the father but also the mother of an illegitimate child may be ordered to pay maintenance. Thus, the father, a relative of the mother, a social worker, or an institution looking after the child, could bring maintenance proceedings against her, to require her to make some financial contribution towards its upbringing. In so far as is appropriate, the provisions of the Act of 1976 relating to maintenance orders also apply to orders made under this section.

Unmarried Mother's Allowance

Family Law only provides for the maintenance of the child. Social Welfare legislation seeks to provide for unmarried mothers. Under section 197 of the Social Welfare (Consolidation) Act, 1981, an unmarried mother whose child or children are residing with her may qualify for Unmarried Mother's Allowance.[98a] For the purposes of the section a woman is regarded as being an unmarried mother "if, not being or having been a married woman she is the mother of a child who has not been adopted".[99] Thus, if an unmarried mother adopts her own child it appears that by so doing she disqualifies herself from receipt of the allowance. To obtain the allowance a mother must satisfy a means test and the means test and the amount of allowance payable is the same as that applicable to a deserted wife with one child under the deserted wife's allowance scheme. If an unmarried mother has more than one child outside wedlock, she may claim for each additional child. The allowance ceases to be payable in the same circumstances as an allowance in respect of a child ceases to be payable to a deserted wife in receipt of Deserted Wife's Allowance. There is no benefit payable to an unmarried mother equivalent to the deserted wife's benefit.

98. Sect. 11 of the 1930 Act.
98a. This provision replaced the Social Welfare Act, 1973, Sect. 8 which originally established unmarried mother's allowance.
99. See S.I. No. 190 of 1973.

Other Social Welfare Schemes

Since the coming into force of the Social Welfare (Supplementary Welfare Allowances) Act, 1975, an unmarried mother, whose means are insufficient to meet her needs and those of her dependants, qualifies for supplementary welfare allowance. Children's Allowance is also payable to an unmarried mother subject to essentially the same conditions under which payment is made to a married parent.[99a]

PROPERTY RIGHTS

The provisions of section 12 of the Married Womans Status Act, 1957, do not apply to and cannot be used for the determination of proprietary disputes between a co-habiting unmarried couple. Similarly, a cohabitee cannot invoke the provisions of section 22 of the Family Law . . . Act, 1976, to obtain a barring order if her safety or welfare or the safety or welfare of any of her children are threatened by the person with whom she is residing. In appropriate circumstances, however, an injunction may be sought or criminal proceedings for assault instituted to obtain the necessary protection or relief. The Family Home Protection Act, 1976, provides no protection for the cohabitee. Thus, if a woman is residing with a man in a home which is in the man's sole name and in which she has no proprietary or beneficial interest, her consent is not required prior to the home being validly conveyed to another. Moreover, if a cohabitee refuses to vacate a home owned solely by the person with whom she is residing, the latter may successfully bring ejectment proceedings against her. A cohabitee who claims to have a proprietary or beneficial interest in property the legal title of which is vested in the sole name of the person with whom she is residing may, of course, in ejectment proceedings or in separate proceedings instituted by her, seek a court order to declare the extent of her interest in the property.

In *McGill* v. *S.*[99b] the plaintiff and the defendant, who were not married to each other, lived together for a number of years in the defendant's flat in Germany. They spent holidays together in Ireland and on one of these, in 1967, the plaintiff purchased a house which was to be used by both of them as a holiday home. The plaintiff paid the entire purchase price of £1,775 and spent the sum of £9,750 on renovating and redecorating the house. The defendant believed the house was purchased for both of them but at no stage did any discussions take place between the parties concerning the defendant acquiring a beneficial interest in the house and the house was purchased in the plaintiff's sole name. The parties spent several holidays in Ireland working on the house and a considerable amount of work, mostly in the nature of cleaning, decoration and supervising tradesmen, was done by the defendant. She also spent £1,000 of her own money in repairing out-buildings as a present for the plaintiff. Early in 1973, following discussions with the plaintiff, the defendant came to reside permanently in the house with his permission. Towards the end of that year the plaintiff went to the United States of America on business and the parties' relationship ended. The defendant continued to reside in the house and subsequently the plaintiff, in Circuit Court ejectment proceedings, sought possession of the house from the defendant and the defendant, who contested the proceedings, counter-claimed that she was entitled to an equitable or proprietary interest in the house. The Circuit Court, rejecting the counter-claim, granted possession of the house to the

99a. See further p. 292 *ante*.
99b. [1979] I.R. 283 (H.C.).

plaintiff and this decision was affirmed by the High Court, dismissing the appeal by the defendant.

It is clear from the judgement delivered by Gannon J. in the High Court that whilst the procedure provided by the Married Womans Status Act, 1957, section 12, cannot be invoked by cohabitees, legal principles enunciated in the cases determined under that section are generally applicable in determining proprietary disputes between cohabitees. Rejecting the defendant's claim to a beneficial interest in the house, Gannon J. stated:

> "In the case of two persons who are not spouses evidence of a consensus derived from words or conduct and intended to have legal consequences would support a trust expressed or implied or constructive. But whether the party having the legal estate and the party claiming an equitable interest be spouses or not, the Court will not impute a relationship of trustee and cestui que trust from the facts of a couple living together in (or seemingly in) the married state and sharing expenses without any more cogent evidence . . ."[99b]

As the counter-claiming defendant is not a spouse but claims to be a cestui que trust by virtue of indirect contributions in circumstances of a close domestic relationship corresponding to that between spouses, I think it is necessary to point out that indirect contributions which are unrelated to the acquisition of the property cannot found an equitable interest in it . . . the evidence of the defendant in support of her claim falls far short of what is required to enable the court to hold, by the implication of a trust for her benefit, that she has acquired any beneficial interest in the property which is the subject of the claim. In spite of having the means and the opportunity, she took no part in the negotiations and contributed no amount of the purchase price for the acquisition of the property of which the plaintiff is sole owner. Such as were her indirect contributions all came after the acquisition of the property had been completed (without continuing instalment payments) and did not bear any significant relationship whatever to either the capital sum of £1,775 or to the sum of £9,750 spent by the plaintiff."[99c]

In these proceedings, the defendant also claimed that she had an irrevocable licence to continue to reside in the house. Rejecting this contention, Gannon J. stated:

> "On the facts of this case I am satisfied that the defendant was lawfully in occupation of the property which is the subject of the claim with the licence or permission of the plaintiff, but only as a licensee at will. For so long as the domestic and personal relations between the parties remained stable it was unlikely that the licence would be terminated, but the evidence does not support a licence by implied contract which could continue against the will of the plaintiff or even beyond the period of their mutual association. I am satisfied that the defendant's licence to occupy and have possession of the property was validly and effectively terminated by the institution of these proceedings at the latest."[99d]

99b. *Ibid* at p. 289.
99c. *Ibid* at p. 291–292. In his judgement Gannon J. clearly followed the judgement of Lord McDermott in *McFarlane v. McFarlane*, [1972] N.I. 59 (C.A.) and the majority judgements delivered in *Pettitt v. Pettitt*, [1970] A.C. 777 (H.L.) and *Gissing v. Gissing*, [1971] A.C. 886 (H.L.) rather than the judgement of Lord Reid in the later case and the judgements delivered in subsequent cases in which Lord Reid's approach to the question of indirect contribution has been adopted. See further p. 306 *ante et seq.*
99d. [1979] I.R. at p. 293.

The learned judge also concluded that the defendant had no grounds for a claim to compensation for the termination of her licence to reside in the house.[99e]

SUCCESSION RIGHTS

No matter how long a couple cohabit, if not married to each other, upon the death of one, in the absence of a specific disposition, the surviving party has no legal right to a share in the deceased's estate. Thus, if a person in good faith enters into a void marriage with a person now deceased and the latter makes no provision for the former in his will or dies intestate, then no claim can be made on the deceased's estate. This is particularly unjust where a person marries another, not knowing, for example, that the latter's first marriage is still subsisting. Having regard to the increased use being made by persons domiciled in this country of the divorce *a vinculo* jurisdiction exercised by the courts of the United Kingdom, there must be many persons in such a position. Moreover, if provision is made for a second spouse in a will, the latter's share of the estate may be considerably reduced if a successful claim is made by the first spouse to her legal rights under the Succession Act, 1965.[100]

An illegitimate child, being a *filius nullius* at common law, had no succession rights to either his parents or relations and if he died intestate and unmarried there was no one to whom his property could pass. The Legitimacy Act, 1931, enacted a minor reform by giving an illegitimate child and his mother limited reciprocal rights of succession on the other's intestacy. By section 9(1) of the Act if the mother of an illegitimate child "dies intestate as respects all or any of her real or personal property" and she is not survived by any legitimate children, "the illegitimate child, or if he is dead, his issue" are entitled to take any interest "to which he or such issue would have been entitled if he had been born legitimate". Thus, such child has no rights of succession to his mother under the Act if she later marries and has children, or otherwise disposes of her property by will. The Act confers on him no rights of succession whatever to the estate of his natural father.

There is of course nothing to prevent the natural parents of an illegitimate child leaving property to such child in their wills. If either parent does wish to so dispose of property in a will it is essential that the illegitimate child is clearly identified. It is an established rule of construction that in the absence of evidence clearly showing a contrary intention, words in a will or other disposition denoting family relationships are construed as referring to legitimate relations only. Thus, a disposition to "my children" would be presumed to apply to legitimate children only.[101]

By section 9(2) of the 1931 Act if an illegitimate child "dies intestate in respect of all or any of his real or personal property", his mother, if still alive, possesses the same rights of succession as a last surviving parent to his legitimate child. Sect. 9 does not apply to or affect the right of any person to take by purchase or descent an estate in tail in real property.[102]

99e. For a discussion of relevant English cases concerning proprietary disputes between cohabitees see S.M. Cretney, *Principles of Family Law*, Third edition, *Supra*, p. 244 *et seq.*
100. See p. 347 *ante.*
101. See however *O'Loughlin v. Bellew* [1906], 1 I.R. 487, (L.C.)—Whereas "children" is usually taken as referring to legitimate children, in this case, having regard to the surrounding circumstances, the court held that there was sufficient indication of intention to show that the testatrix used the word to include illegitimate children. See also *B, Deceased O. v. D.* [1916] 1 I.R. 364 (K.B.D.); *Andrews v. Andrews* (1885) 15 L.R. Ir. 199 (App.).
102. Sect. 9 (3) of Legitimacy Act, 1931. If an illegitimate child dies intestate and unmarried with no children of his own and is not survived by his mother, it appears that the State will take his property "as ultimate intestate successor." See the Succession Act, Sects.

By the Succession Act, 1965, Sect. 117 the court can order such provision as is just, to be made for a child out of the estate of a testator, where the court is of the opinion that the testator has failed in his moral duty to make proper provision for the child in accordance with his means. It is possible that this section could be held to apply to an illegitimate, as well as a legitimate child, but no claim by an illegitimate child under the section has yet been determined by the courts. The question of whether a testator has a moral duty towards his illegitimate child was however raised in a recent case.

In *L.* v. *L.*[103] a claim under section 117 was made by the two children of the deceased's first marriage. The deceased having been divorced by his first wife had remarried and a further two children had been born as a result of this marriage. Under the deceased's will, all his property had been left in trust for the benefit of his second wife.

Costelloe J. on a preliminary issue, held that in deciding a claim under section 117, the court must have regard to all a testator's moral duties. The deceased had a moral duty towards his second wife and the children of the second marriage, the nature and extent of which, he stated, could not be affected by the court failing to recognise the validity of the second marriage. It was thus not necessary to determine whether the second marriage was valid or not. Although the question of whether an illegitimate child could succeed in a claim under Section 117 was not raised, this decision is important in that for the first time it has been judicially recognised that in so far as a father owes a moral duty to provide by will for his children, that duty applies to both his legitimate and illegitimate children.[103a]

An obstacle to section 117 being construed as applicable to illegitimate children lies in the general principle of construction that where in any instrument children are referred to, in the absence of an expression of contrary intention, the instrument is taken to refer to legitimate children only.[104] It is arguable however, that if the section excludes claims by illegitimate children, it is unconstitutional.[105]

FURTHER CRITICISMS AND SUGGESTED REFORMS[106]

(1) *The Illegitimate Child*: The Episcopal Council for Social Welfare in their "Statement on Family Law Reform" stated "We regard it as unchristian that children born out of wedlock should, as a result of the actions of their parents, be victimised by legal distinctions between them and children born to married parents. Consequently we wish to urge that the legal disabilities imposed on these children should be removed".

Under the present law the child born outside wedlock is discriminated against and punished for his parents' behaviour. Such a child is looked upon as a threat to the institution of marriage. He is regarded as a living symbol of his parents'

67–73 and *In the Matter of the Estate of Norman Robert Wilson, Deceased, Eric John Wilson v. The Attorney-General and John Coughlan* (1979) unreported (H.C.).
103. [1978] I.R. 288 (H.C.).
103a. See also *M.P.D. and Ors. v. M.D.* and *M.S.D. v. M.D.* (February 1981) unreported (H.C.).
104. See P.T. Horgan, The Financial Support of Illegitimate Children (1976) 11 I.J. (n.s.) 59; H.M. Fitzpatrick, "The Succession Act, 1965, Sect. 117 Provision for Children", (1976), 110 I.L.T. & S.J. at p. 96. See also J. O'Reilly, "Legitimacy and the Law", *Irish Times*, 16th Oct. 1974 and Cherish Booklet, "Conference on the unmarried parent and child in Irish Society", (Dublin 1974), p. 11.
105. See p. 359 *ante*.
106. See Cherish Booklet, "Conference on the unmarried parent and child in Irish Society". "Statement on Family Law Reform", by The Episcopal Council for Social Welfare; a committee of the Catholic Bishops Conference, pages 16–18; Irish Council for Civil Liberties, *Children's Rights and The Constitution* (Dublin 1977).

"immorality", and as such held vicariously responsible for it. He is an object to be distinguished from all other children by the status of illegitimacy. This is despite the fact that such child has no more to do with the manner in which he is conceived and brought into the world than has the child born to married parents. Such victimisation of an innocent child is indefensible in a civilised society.

It is submitted that the legal concepts of legitimacy and illegitimacy serve no useful function and should be abolished. The biological link between parents and their children should, in so far as is legally possible, by itself determine the legal consequences of the parental relationship. Whilst the removal of the legal disabilities imposed on a child born outside wedlock would probably not have any immediate effect on social attitudes to such children, the influence of such legal change, would in the long term lead to a reformulation of public opinion and contribute towards the removal of much of the social stigma that at present attaches to them.[107]

The New Zealand Status of Children Act, 1969, provides a valuable example of the type of legislation that is required in this country to implement the above suggested reform. The Act is entitled "An Act to remove the legal disabilities of children born out of wedlock". Section 3(1) of the Act states

> "For all purposes of the law of New Zealand the relationship between every person and his father and mother shall be determined irrespective of whether the father and mother are or have been married to each other and all other relationships shall be determined accordingly".

This provision abolishes the status of illegitimacy from the law of New Zealand. Other sections of the Act deal with consequent legal problems such as interpretation of documents, presumptions as to parenthood, and succession rights. The Act goes so far as to provide that in construing any instrument the use of the words legitimate or lawful shall not by themselves exclude illegitimate relationships.[108]

The enactment of such legislation would mean that children born out of wedlock would possess the same rights of succession as children born in wedlock. To implement this, a procedure would have to be set up whereby paternity could be established. The Episcopal Council for Social Welfare recommended the passing of a law to "allow voluntary acknowledgement of a child born out of wedlock". Under the 1969 Act in New Zealand, an instrument signed by both parents, if executed as a deed, or if signed in the presence of a solicitor is *prima facie* evidence that the person named as the father, is the father of the child.[109] The registration of the father's name with his consent in the Register of Births has the same effect. The Act further enables the mother of a child, a child, a person purporting to be the father of a child and "any person having a proper interest in the result" to apply to the Supreme Court for a declaration of paternity.[110]

Whereas the Irish courts have at present power to make a declaration of legitimacy, they have no power to make paternity declarations. The making of

---

107. See the 6th Amendment of the Constitution Bill, 1978, introduced by the Labour Party which proposed to amend Articles 41 and 42 of the Constitution. It was proposed that the following section would be added to Article 41: "Equality of rights under the law shall not be denied to any child on the basis of status at birth or parentage". The Bill, however, failed to pass through the Dáil. A constitutional amendment is not required to place legitimate and illegitimate children in a position of legal equality.
108. Sect. 3 (3).
109. Sect. 8 (2).
110. Sect. 10.

an affiliation order could be said to be similar to a paternity declaration, but at present the effect of such an order is limited to imposing an obligation of support on the person subject to the order. Finally, as in the case of legitimacy declarations and affiliation proceedings, in proceedings to determine paternity, the court should be empowered to direct persons to undergo blood testing and tissue testing.[111]

(2) *The Unmarried Couple*: (a) It is submitted that a person who in good faith enters into a void marriage with another, now deceased should be able to apply to the court for reasonable provision out of the deceased's estate.

(b) A party to a void or annulled marriage should be able to obtain a maintenance order directed to the other party for the support of herself (or himself) and their children following a High Court determination of nullity.[112]

(c) Parties to a void or annulled marriage should be the joint guardians of any children born to them, unless a court order to the contrary is made.[113]

111. See Chapter 11.
112. See p. 87 *ante*.
113. On this see The Law of Nullity in Ireland, (Dublin, Stationery Office, Aug. 1976), p. 15.

APPENDIX A

Legal Aid Board, 47 Upper Mount Street, Dublin 2. Phone: 609120

Law Centres

45, Lower Gardiner Street, Dublin 1. Phone: (01) 787295/787753.

Aston House, Aston Quay, Dublin 2. Phone: (01) 712177/712725.

84 North Mall, Cork. Phone: (021) 500558/500365.

108 Prospect Hill, Galway. Phone: (091) 61650/65401.

84 O'Connell Street, Limerick. Phone: (061) 44599/44223.

1 Teeling Street, Sligo. Phone: (071) 61670/61658.

5 Catherine Street, Waterford. Phone: (051) 55814/55907.

APPENDIX B

NULLITY OF MARRIAGES BILL, 1976

Arrangements of Sections

Section

1. (1) This Act applies to every marriage whether celebrated before or after the passing of this Act. Application and Interpretation

    (2) Where the parties to a marriage have adopted a child pursuant to the Adoption Acts 1952 to 1976, then for the purposes of *sections* 10, 11 and 12 of this Act the child shall be regarded as being a child of the marriage. 1952, No. 25.

2. (1) This section applies to— Presumption of validity of certain marriages.
    (*a*) any marriage celebrated in the State and purporting to have been solemnised in accordance with law, and

(*b*) any marriage celebrated outside the State and which is recognised in the State.

(2) Every marriage to which this section applies shall for all purposes be treated as being valid until—

(*a*) an order decreeing its nullity has been made pursuant to this Act, or

(*b*) a judgment (whether by way of an order, decree, writ or other instrument, or by whatever name the judgment is called) which is recognised in the State has been given in a court or tribunal of a country or territory outside the State whereby its nullity is declared, decreed or otherwise pronounced.

Jurisdiction in nullity proceedings.

3. The court shall have jurisdiction to grant a decree of nullity of marriage only in accordance with *section 4*, or by virtue of *section 12*, of this Act and in any proceedings the court shall grant such a decree if, and only if, the court is satisfied that the marriage to which the proceedings relate was void.

Grounds on which a marriage is void.

4. (1) A marriage is void on the following, and no other, grounds, namely:

(*a*) that it is not a valid marriage in law

(i) in a case where the marriage took place before the 1st day of January, 1975, by reason of the fact that the husband was on the date of the marriage under fourteen years of age or the wife was on the said date under twelve years of age;

1972, No. 30.

(ii) In case the marriage took place on or after the said 1st day of January, under the provisions of section 1 of the Marriages Act, 1972 (that is to say where either party was on the date of the marriage under the age of 16 and an exemption had not been obtained pursuant to subsection (2) of the said section 1 before the marriage);

(*b*) that at the time of the marriage either party was already lawfully married;

(*c*) that the parties are within the prohibited degrees of relationship;

(*d*) that the parties are not respectively male and female;

1844, c. 81.

1870, c. 110.

(*e*) that the parties have inter-married in disregard of the requirements of section 25 or 49 of the Marriages (Ireland) Act, 1844, or section 29 of the Matrimonial Causes and Marriage Law (Ireland) Amendment Act, 1870;

(*f*) that at the time of the marriage either party was suffering from impotence and that the marriage has not been consummated owing to the impotence;

(*g*) that at the time of the marriage either party was suffering (whether continuously or intermittently) from a mental disorder of a kind or to an extent that rendered him or her unfitted for marriage;

(*h*) that either party made a mistake as to the fact that the particular ceremony was a marriage ceremony;

(*i*) that the apparent consent to marry of either party was not a true consent;

(*j*) that the marriage purported to be celebrated under common law but was not solemnised in the presence of a clergyman in Holy Orders.

(2) Without prejudice to the generality of *sub-section* (*1*) (*i*) of this section, in deciding whether the apparent consent to marry was a true consent the court shall have regard to any one or more of the following that it considers relevant, namely:

(*a*) mental incapacity or deficiency of the party at the date of the marriage, including a mental incapacity to appreciate the nature of the marriage contract and the responsibilities attached to marriage;

(*b*) a threat based on any financial or social obligation or liability of the party which existed, or was alleged by the threat to exist, or would have arisen, or it was alleged would have arisen, if the party had not married and which the court considers was in the particular circumstances a material inducement to the party to marry;

(*c*) deceit practised on the party by any person as regards a feature of the marriage which in the particular circumstances of the case the court considers the party reasonably regarded as fundamental and which induced, to a material extent, the marriage;

(*d*) duress or undue influence exercised over the party whether exercised by or on behalf of the other party or not;

(*e*) a mistake of either party to the marriage as to the identity of the other party.

(3) In this section "impotence" means the incapacity to consummate the marriage in question due either to physical or psychological reasons or to partly physical or partly psychological reasons and which is not curable by ordinary means;

"mental disorder" means mental illness, arrested or incomplete development of mind or personality psychopathic disorder and any other disorder or disability of mind or personality;

"psychopathic disorder" means a persistent disorder (whether or not including subnormality of intelligence) which results in abnormally aggressive or seriously irresponsible conduct on the part of the person.

5. (1) Where, apart from this Act, any matter affecting the validity of a marriage would fall to be determined (in accordance with the rules of private international law) by reference to the law of a country other than the State, nothing in *Section 4* of this Act shall— *Marriages governed by foreign law or celebrated outside the State under the law of the State.*

(*a*) preclude the determination of that matter in the manner aforesaid, or (*b*) be construed as requiring the application to the marriage of any grounds therein mentioned except insofar as the grounds are applicable under those rules.

(2) In the case of a marriage which has taken place outside the State and purports to be marriage under common law, *section 4* of this Act shall not be construed as prejudicing any ground on which the marriage may be void by virtue of any rule governing the celebration of marriages outside the State under common law.

Bars to relief.   6. (1) Subject to *sub-section* (2) of this section, the court shall not grant a decree of nullity if the respondent satisfies the court that—

(i) the petitioner, with knowledge that it was open to him (or to her) to have the marriage avoided, so conducted himself (or herself) in relation to the respondent as to lead the respondent reasonably to believe that he (or she) would not seek to do so, and

(ii) in the circumstances of the case it would be injust, as between the parties to the marriage, to grant the decree.

(2) *Sub-section* (*1*) of this section shall not apply in relation to any ground mentioned in *paragraph* (*b*), (*c*), (*d*), (*e*) or (*j*) of *section 4* (*1*) of this Act.

(3) Any bargain or other agreement or any understanding or arrangement between the parties to a nullity suit whereby false evidence is to be given to, or relevant evidence to be withheld from, the court shall be a bar to the granting of a decree of nullity.

(4) *Sub-sections* (*1*), (*2*) and (*3*) of this section replace—

(*a*) any rule of law whereby a decree of nullity of marriage may be refused by reason of approbation, ratification or lack of sincerity on the part of the petitioner,

(*b*) any rule of law whereby collusion is a bar to the granting of such a decree.

Further provisions relating to nullity proceedings.   7. (1) Subject to *sub-section* (7) of this section, proceedings for a decree of nullity of marriage shall only be instituted either—

(*a*) during the life of either of the parties to the marriage, or

(*b*) in case the said parties are dead, within the period of six years beginning on the date of the death of the surviving spouse.

(2) Subject to *sub-section* (4) of this section, where the parties to the marriage are alive the court shall have jurisdiction to entertain and determine proceedings for nullity of marriage, if—

(*a*) the marriage was celebrated in the State,

(*b*) either party to the marriage is domiciled in the State when the proceedings are instituted,

(*c*) the said parties are ordinarily resident in the State when the proceedings are instituted.

(3) Subject to *sub-section* (*4*) of this section, the court shall have jurisdiction to entertain and determine proceedings by a wife for nullity of marriage, notwithstanding that the husband is not domiciled in the State, if the wife has been deserted by her husband and immediately before the desertion—

(*a*) the husband was domiciled in the State, or

(*b*) the parties were ordinarily resident in the State.

(4) The court shall grant a decree of nullity of a marriage on any of the grounds mentioned in *sub-section 5* of this section if, and only if, the proceedings are instituted by a party to the marriage.

(5) The grounds referred to in *sub-section* (*4*) of this section are the following, namely, that the marriage was void on the grounds mentioned in *section 4* (*1*) (*a*), 4 (*1*) (*f*), 4 (*1*) (*g*) or 4 (*1*) (*i*) of this Act.

(6) Where either of the parties to a marriage is, or both of such parties are, dead, the following provisions shall apply namely:

(*a*) the court shall have jurisdiction to entertain and determine an application for a decree of nullity if, and only if,

    (i) the marriage was celebrated in the State, or

    (ii) immediately after the death of the spouse first dying the surviving party was domiciled in the State, or

    (iii) immediately before such death the said parties were ordinarily resident in the State, and

(*b*) the court shall grant a decree of nullity of the marriage if, and only if, it is proved that,

    (i) the parties were within the prohibited degrees of relationship, or

    (ii) at the time of the marriage either party was already lawfully married, or

    (iii) the ceremony of marriage was invalid, that is to say, that the parties inter-married in disregard of the requirements of section 25 or 49 of the Marriages (Ireland) Act, 1844, or section 3 of the Matrimonial Causes and Marriage Laws (Ireland) Amendment Act, 1870, or

    (iv) the marriage purported to be celebrated under common law but was not solemnised in the presence of a clergyman in Holy Orders.

(7) Where the parties to a marriage are dead and the period mentioned in *sub-section* (*1*) (*b*) of this section has expired, subject to *sub-section* (*6*) of this section, nullity proceedings as regards the marriage may be instituted with the leave of the court, and where an application for such leave is made the court shall allow the application if, and only if, the person seeking leave to institute the proceedings satisfies the court that in the particular circumstances of the case the institution of the proceedings would be justified.

8. (1) Notwithstanding section 6 of the Guardianship of Infants Act,

Guardianship
of Infants
Act.
1964, No. 7. 1964, the court may, on granting a decree of nullity of marriage or at any subsequent time at which the parties to the marriage concerned are alive, by order declare that the parties to the marriage shall, as on and from a day specified in the order, cease jointly to be guardians of any infant of the marriage and that as and from such day the parent specified in the order shall be guardian of the infant, either alone or jointly with any guardian (not being a parent) appointed by that parent or by the court.

(2) In case an order is made by the court under this section, as on and from the day mentioned in *sub-section* (*1*) of this section, section 6 of the Guardianship of Infants Act, 1964, shall as regards the infant concerned cease to apply to—

(*a*) in case the order declares the father of the infant to be guardian of the infant either alone or jointly, the mother of the infant, and

(*b*) in case the order declares the mother of the infant to be such guardian, the father of the infant.

(3) In lieu of making an order under *sub-section* (*1*) of this section, the court may give directions on any question affecting the welfare of an infant and make such order as it thinks proper and for that purpose may exercise all or any of the powers conferred on it by section 11 of the Guardianship of Infants Act, 1964.

(4) The court may vary or discharge any order previously made by the court under this section.

Maintenance
pending suit.
  9.   In proceedings for nullity of marriage the court may make an order for maintenance pending suit, that is to say, an order requiring either party to the marriage to make to the other such periodical payment for his or her maintenance and for such term, being a term beginning not earlier than the date on which the proceedings were instituted and ending with the date of the determination of the suit, as the court thinks reasonable.

Financial
provision
orders in
connection
with nullity
proceedings,
etc.
  10. (1) On granting a decree of nullity of marriage, or at any time thereafter, the court may make any one or more of the following orders, namely:

(*a*) an order that either party to the marriage shall make to the other such periodical payments, for such term as may be specified in the order;

(*b*) an order that either party to the marriage shall secure to the other to the satisfaction of the court such periodical payments, for such term, as may be so specified;

(*c*) an order that either party to the marriage shall pay to the other such lump sum or sums as may be so specified;

(*d*) an order that a party to the marriage shall make to such person as may be specified in the order for the benefit of a child of the marriage so specified, or to such a child such periodical payments, for such term, as may be so specified;

(*e*) an order that a party to the marriage shall secure to such person as may be so specified for the benefit of such a child, or to such a child, to the satisfaction of the court, such periodical payments, for such term, as may be so specified;

(f) an order that a party to the marriage shall pay to such person as may be so specified for the benefit of such a child, or to such a child, such lump sum as may be so specified;

(g) an order that such a child of the marriage shall not be entitled to any share in the estate of any party to the marriage so specified in the event of such party dying intestate;

(h) an order providing that in respect of such a child the provisions of Part IX of the Succession Act, 1965, No. 27, shall not apply or shall apply with such limitations as are specified in the order in relation to a parent specified in the order.

(2) The court may also make any one or more of the orders mentioned in *paragraph* (*d*), (*e*) and (*f*) of *sub-section* (*1*) of this section—

(a) in any proceedings for nullity of marriage, before granting a decree; and

(b) where any such proceedings are dismissed after the beginning of the trial, either forthwith or within a reasonable period after the dismissal.

(3) Without prejudice to the generality of *paragraph* (*c*) or (*f*) of *sub-section* (*1*) of this section—

(a) an order under this section that a party to a marriage shall pay a lump sum to the other party may be made for the purpose of enabling that other party to meet any liabilities or expenses reasonably incurred by him or her in maintaining himself or herself or any child of the marriage before making an application for an order under this section in his or her favour;

(b) an order under this section for the payment of a lump sum to or for the benefit of a child of the marriage may be made for the purpose of enabling any liabilities or expenses reasonably incurred by or for the benefit of that child before the making of an application for an order under this section in his favour to be met; and

(c) an order under this section for the payment of a lump sum may provide for the payment of that sum by instalments of such amount as may be specified in the order and may require the payment of the instalments to be secured to the satisfaction of the court.

(4) The power of the court under *sub-section* (*1*) of this section or the power of the court under *sub-section* (*2*) of this section to make an order in favour of a child before granting a decree shall be exercisable from time to time; and where the court makes an order in favour of a child in a case in which proceedings were dismissed after the beginning of the trial, it may from time to time, make a further order in his favour of any of the kinds mentioned in *paragraph* (*d*) or (*f*) of the said *sub-section* (*1*).

11. (1) On granting a decree of nullity of marriage, or at any time

Property
adjustment
orders in
connection
with nullity
proceedings.

thereafter, the court may make any one or more of the following orders, namely:

(a) an order that a party to the marriage shall transfer to the other party, to any child of the marriage or to such person as may be specified in the order for the benefit of such a child, such property as may be so specified, being property to which the first-mentioned party is entitled, either in possession or reversion;

(b) an order that a settlement of such property as may be so specified, being property to which a party to the marriage is so entitled be made to the satisfaction of the court for the benefit of the other party to the marriage and of the children of the marriage or either or any of them;

(c) an order varying for the benefit of the parties to the marriage and of the children of the marriage or either or any of them any ante-nuptial or post-nuptial settlement (including such a settlement made by will or codicil) made on the parties to the marriage;

(d) an order extinguishing or reducing the interest of either of the parties to the marriage under any such settlement.

(2) The court may make an order mentioned in *paragraph* (c) of *sub-section* (1) of this section notwithstanding that there are no children of the marriage.

Matters to
which court
is to have
regard in
deciding how
to exercise its
powers under
section 10
or 11.

12. (1) In deciding whether to exercise its powers under *section 10* or *11* of this Act in relation to a party to the marriage and, if so, in what manner, the Court may have regard to all or any of the circumstances of the case including in particular the following matters, namely:

(a) the income, earning capacity, property and other financial resources which each of the parties to the marriage has or is likely to have in the foreseeable future;

(b) the financial needs, obligations and responsibilities which each of the parties to the marriage has or is likely to have in the foreseeable future;

(c) the standard of living enjoyed by the family before proceedings were instituted;

(d) the age of each party to the marriage and the duration of the marriage;

(e) any physical or mental disability of either of the parties to the marriage;

(f) the contributions made by each of the parties to the welfare of the family, including any contribution made by looking after the home or caring for the family;

(g) the value to either of the parties to the marriage of any benefit (for example, a pension) which, by reason of the annulment of the marriage, that party will lose the chance of acquiring.

(2) Without prejudice to *sub-section* (3) of this section the court may in deciding whether to make an order mentioned in *paragraph* (d),

(*e*) or (*f*) of *sub-section* (*1*) of *section 10* of this Act, or to exercise its powers under *sub-section* (*2*) or (*4*) of the said *section 10* or under *section 11* of this Act, in relation to a child of the marriage and, if so, in what manner, have regard in particular to the following matters, namely:

(*a*) the financial needs of the child;

(*b*) the income, earning capacity (if any), property and other financial resources of the child;

(*c*) any physical or mental disability of the child;

(*d*) the standard of living enjoyed by the family before the proceedings were instituted;

(*e*) the manner in which he was being and in which the parties to the marriage expected him to be educated or trained;

and the court shall exercise those powers so as to place the child, so far as it is practicable and, having regard to the considerations mentioned in relation to the parties to the marriage in *paragraph* (*a*) and (*b*) of *subsection* (*1*) of this section, just to do so, in the financial position in which the child would have been had the marriage been valid and had each of those parties properly discharged his or her financial obligations and responsibilities towards him.

(3) In deciding whether to make an order mentioned in *subsection* (*2*) of this section or to exercise a power so mentioned against a party to a marriage in favour of a child of the family who is not the child of that party and, if so, in what manner, the court may have regard (among the circumstances of the case)—

(*a*) to whether that party had assumed any responsibility for the child's maintenance and, if so, the extent to which, and the basis upon which, that party assumed such responsibility and to the length of time for which that party discharged such responsibility;

(*b*) to whether in assuming and discharging such responsibility that party did so knowing that the child was not his or her own;

(*c*) to the liability of any other person to maintain the child.

13. (1) Where in any proceedings in the High Court (not being proceedings for nullity of marriage) the court is of opinion that in order to determine a question falling to be determined by it in the proceedings the question as to whether or not a particular marriage is or was void required to be determined, then if the Court considers that in the circumstances of the case it would be just so to do, the court may in the proceedings, and on such terms and conditions (if any) as to notice, costs or otherwise as it thinks fit to impose, determine the question in accordance with and subject to the provisions of this Act apart from this section. *(Power of High Court to determine validity of marriage in proceedings other than nullity proceedings.)*

(2) Where in any proceedings the High Court, by virtue of *subsection* (*1*) of this section, determines the validity of a marriage, the court shall have as regards the proceedings the same power to grant decrees and make orders as it has in proceedings for nullity of marriage.

Procedure   14. Unless it is otherwise provided for by Rules of Court:—

(*a*) proceedings under this Act for a decree of nullity of marriage shall be instituted by special summons, and

(*b*) an application made for an order under *Section 8* of this Act, other than an application made in proceedings under this Act for such a decree, shall be made by such summons.

Repeals.   15. The Marriage of Lunatics Act, 1811, and Section 13 of the Matrimonial Causes and Marriage Law (Ireland) Amendment Act, 1870, are 1811, c. 64. hereby repealed.

Short title.   16. This Act may be cited as the Marriages (Nullity) Act, 1976.

APPENDIX C

NAMES AND ADDRESSES OF ADOPTION SOCIETIES

Cairdeas Adoption Society,
20, Harcourt Terrace, Dublin.

Catholic Protection and Rescue Society of Ireland,
30, South Anne Street, Dublin.

Limerick Catholic Adoption Society,
39, Catherine Street, Limerick.

Ossory Adoption Society,
c/o Sion House, Kilkenny.

Protestant Adoption Society,
71, Brighton Road, Rathgar, Dublin 6.

Rotunda Girls' Aid Society,
82, Marlboro Street, Dublin 1.

Sacred Heart Convent,
Bessboro, Cork.

St. Anne's Adoption Society,
Assumption Convent, Blackpool, Cork.

St. Attracta's Adoption Society,
St. Mary's Cathedral, Sligo.

St. Brigid's Orphanage,
68, Iona Road, Dublin 9.

St. Catherine's Adoption Society,
Bank Place, Ennis, Co. Clare.

St. Clare's Convent,
Stamullen, Co. Meath.

St. John's Adoption Society,
Parochial House, Butlerstown, Waterford.

St. Kevin's Adoption Society,
Arus Brugha, Dungarvan, Co. Waterford.

St. Louise Adoption Society,
1, James's Street, Dublin 8.

St. Mary's Adoption Society,
New Road, Bridge Street, Tralee, Co. Kerry.

St. Mura's Adoption Society,
Fahan, Lifford, Co. Donegal.

St. Nicholas's Adoption Society,
Hibernian House, Eyre Square, Galway.

St. Patrick's Guild,
82, Haddington Road, Dublin 4.

St. Therese Adoption Society,
Carmelite Priory, Whitefriar Street, Dublin 8.

APPENDIX D

FAMILY LAW BILL, 1981 [No. 3 of 1981]
as initiated
ARRANGEMENT OF SECTIONS

Section

ACTS REFERRED TO

Married Women's Status Act, 1957	1957, No. 5
Courts (Supplemental Provisions) Act, 1961	1961, No. 39
Family Home Protection Act, 1976	1976, No. 27

BILL ENTITLED AN ACT TO ABOLISH ACTIONS FOR CRIMINAL CON-VERSATION, ENTICEMENT AND HARBOURING OF A SPOUSE AND BREACH OF PROMISE OF MARRIAGE, TO MAKE PROVISION IN RELA-TION TO THE PROPERTY OF, AND GIFTS TO AND BETWEEN, PERSONS WHO HAVE BEEN ENGAGED TO BE MARRIED AND IN RELATION TO THE VALIDITY OF THE CONSENT OF A MINOR SPOUSE FOR THE PURPOSES OF THE FAMILY HOME PROTECTION ACT, 1976, AND TO PROVIDE FOR RELATED MATTERS.

BE IT ENACTED BY THE OIREACHTAS AS FOLLOWS:

1.—(1) After the passing of this Act, no action shall lie for criminal conversation, for inducing a spouse to leave or remain apart from the other spouse or for harbouring a spouse.

Abolition of actions for criminal conversation, enticement and harbouring of spouse.

(2) Subsection (1) shall not have effect in relation to any action that has been commenced before the passing of this Act.

2.—(1) An agreement between two persons to marry one another, whether entered into before or after the passing of this Act, shall not under the law of the State have effect as a contract and no action shall be brought in the State for breach of such an agreement, whatever the law applicable to the agreement.

Engagements to marry not enforceable at law

(2) Subsection (1) shall not have effect in relation to any action that has been commenced before the passing of this Act.

3.—Where two persons have agreed to marry one another and any property is given as a wedding gift to either or both of them by any other person, it shall be presumed, in the absence of evidence to the contrary, that the property so given was given—

Gifts to engaged couples by other persons.

(a) to both of them of joint owners, and

(b) subject to the condition that it should be returned on request if the marriage for whatever reason does not take place.

4.—Where a party to an agreement to marry makes a gift of property (including an engagement ring) to the other party, it shall be presumed, in the absence of evidence to the contrary, that the gift—

Gifts between engaged couples.

(a) was given subject to the condition that it should be returned on request if the marriage does not take place for any reason other than the death of the donor, or

(b) was given unconditionally, if the marriage does not take place on account of the death of the donor.

5.—(1) Where an agreement to marry is terminated, the rules of law relating to the rights of spouses in relation to property in which either or both of them has or have a beneficial interest shall apply in relation to any property

Property of engaged couples

in which either or both of the parties to the agreement had a beneficial interest while the agreement was in force as they apply in relation to property in which either or both spouses has or have a beneficial interest.

(2) Where an agreement to marry is terminated, section 12 of the Married Women's Status Act, 1957 (which relates to the determination of questions between husband and wife as to property) shall apply, as if the parties to the agreement were married, to any dispute between them, or claim by one of them, in relation to property in which either or both had a beneficial interest while the agreement was in force.

Application to the court in case of substantial expenditure incurred by or on behalf of a party to a broken engagement.

6.—Where an agreement to marry is terminated and it appears to the court, on application made to it in a summary manner by a person other than a party to the agreement, that a party to the agreement has received a benefit of a substantial nature (not being a gift to which section 3 applies) from the applicant in consequence of the agreement, the court may make such order (including an order for compensation) as appears to it just and equitable in the circumstances.

Recovery of substantial expenditure incurred by or on behalf of a party to a broken engagement.

7.—Where an agreement to marry is terminated and it appears to the court, on application made to it in a summary manner by a party to the agreement or another person, that, by reason of the agreement—

(a) in the case of the party to the agreement, expenditure of a substantial nature has been incurred by him, or

(b) in the case of the other person, expenditure of a substantial nature has been incurred by him on behalf of a party to the agreement.

and that the party by whom or on whose behalf the expenditure was incurred has not benefited in respect of the expenditure, the court may take such order (including an order for the recovery of the expenditure) as appears to it just and equitable in the circumstances.

Jurisdiction (sections 6 and 7).

8.—(1) The Circuit Court shall, concurrently with the High Court, have jurisdiction to hear and determine proceedings under section 6 or 7 subject, in the case of a claim exceeding £15,000, to the like consents as are required for the purposes of section 22 of the Courts (Supplemental Provisions) Act, 1961.

(2) The District Court shall have jurisdiction to hear and determine proceedings under section 6 or 7 where the

amount claimed does not exceed £2,500.

9.—Proceedings to enforce a right conferred by this Act arising out of the termination for whatever reason for an agreement to marry shall not be brought after the expiration of three years from the date of the termination of the agreement.

10.—(1) For the avoidance of doubt, it is hereby declared that no consent given by a spouse, whether before or after the passing of this Act, for the purposes of section 3 (1) of the Family Home Protection Act, 1976 (which provides that a conveyance by one spouse of an interest in the family home without the written consent of the other spouse shall be void) or of section 9 (2) of that Act (which restricts the right of a spouse to dispose of household chattels without the consent of the other spouse) is or was invalid by reason only that it is or was given by a spouse who has not or had not attained the age of majority.

(2) Subsection (1) shall apply to a consent given for the aforesaid purposes before the passing of this Act by a guardian or a court on behalf of a spouse who had not attained the age of majority as if the consent had been given by the spouse.

11.—This Act may be cited as the Family Law Act, 1981.

APPENDIX E.

W. v. W.

In *W. v. W.* (March, 1981) unreported (H.C.) the evidence established that a farm of 70 acres was transferred into the husband's sole name by the husband's brother and mother. The transfer was voluntary, in the sense that it was not in consideration of any purchase price, but the wife believed that it was transferred subject to certain encumberances. Both the husband and wife applied their savings and monies kept in a joint account on equiping and stocking the farm and improving the land. The wife worked on the farm for a number of years and also put money that she received as a result of a car accident and money received by way of gift in a bank account used by the husband for farming activities. Among the many improvements made to the farm was the provision of a modern and mechanised milking parlour for the building of which the husband obtained a loan. Both the original encumberances on the land and the loan obtained for the milking parlour were fully discharged. The court upheld the wife's claim that in so far as both her work on the farm and the financial and other contributions made by her to it had contributed towards discharging the encumberances and the loan she was entitled to an equitable interest in it proportionate to the contribution made by her but dismissed her claim that her contribution to other improvements as such entitled her to a further equitable interest. Delivering judgement, Finlay P. gave a detailed exposition of the principles applicable to determining proprietary claims made under Section 12 of the Married Woman's Status Act, 1957. He stated:

"I am satisfied that the following broad propositions of law arise which are applicable to the facts of this case.

1. Where a wife contributes by money to the purchase of a property by her husband in his sole name in the absence of evidence of some inconsistent agreement or arrangement the Court will decide that the wife is entitled to an equitable interest in that property approximately proportionate to the extent of her contribution as against the total value of the property at the time the contribution was made.

2. Where a husband makes a contribution to the purchase of property in his wife's sole name he will be presumed by a rebuttable presumption to have intended to advance his wife and will have no claim to an equitable estate in the property unless that presumption is rebutted. If it is, he would have a claim similar to that indicated in respect of the wife with which I have already dealt.

3. Where a wife contributes either directly towards the repayment of mortgage instalments or contributes to a general family fund thus releas-

ing her husband from an obligation which he otherwise would have permitting him to discharge liabilities out of that fund and . . . to repay mortgage instalments she will in the absence of proof of an inconsistent agreement or arrangement be entitled to an equitable share in the property which had been mortgaged and in respect of which the mortgage was redeemed approximately proportionate to her contribution to the mortgage repayments: to the value of the mortgage thus redeemed and to the total value of the property at the relevant time. It is not expressly stated in the decisions to which I have referred but I assume that the fundamental principle underlying this rule of law is that the redemption of any form of charge or mortgage on property in truth consists of the acquisition by the owner or mortgagor of an estate in the property with which he had parted at the time of the creating of the mortgage or charge and that there can be no distinction in principle between a contribution made to the acquisition of that interest and a contribution made to the acquisition of an interest in property by an original purchase.

4. Where a husband contributes either directly or indirectly in the manner which I have already outlined to the repayment of mortgage charges on property which is in the legal ownership of his wife subject to the presumption of advancement and in the event of a rebuttal of that presumption he would have a like claim to an equitable estate in the property.

5. Where a wife expends monies or carries out work in the improvement of a property which has been originally acquired by and the legal ownership in which is solely vested in her husband she will have no claim in respect of such contribution unless she establishes by evidence that from the circumstances surrounding the making of it she was lead to believe (or of course that it was specifically agreed) that she would be recompensed for it. Even where such a right to recompense is established either by an expressed agreement or by circumstances in which the wife making the contribution was lead to such belief it is a right to recompense in monies only and cannot and does not constitute a right to claim an equitable share in the estate of the property concerned.

6. A husband making contributions in like manner to property originally acquired by and solely owned as to the legal estate by his wife may again subject to a rebuttal of a presumption of advancement which would arise have a like claim to compensation in similar circumstances but would not have a claim to any equitable estate in the property."

The learned President prior to enunciating the above principles specifically stated that he had been referred to and had carefully considered the decisions in *Conway v. Conway, Heavey v. Heavey* and *McGill v. S.*

VOID MARRIAGE See NULLITY OF
MARRIAGE; FORMALITIES OF
MARRIAGE

VOIDABLE MARRIAGE See NULLITY
OF MARRIAGE; IMPOTENCE

WARD OF COURT
minor as, 243, 244, 245

WELFARE OF CHILDREN
adoption, in, 176, 177, 186, 187, 188,
193, 194

guardianship and custody, in, 211 et seq.
paramount, and the constitution, 6, 9,
235 et seq.

WILFUL REFUSAL TO CONSUM-
MATE
nullity, whether a ground for, 69, 70,
71, 72, 73

WILL
capacity to make, 347
See also SUCCESSION

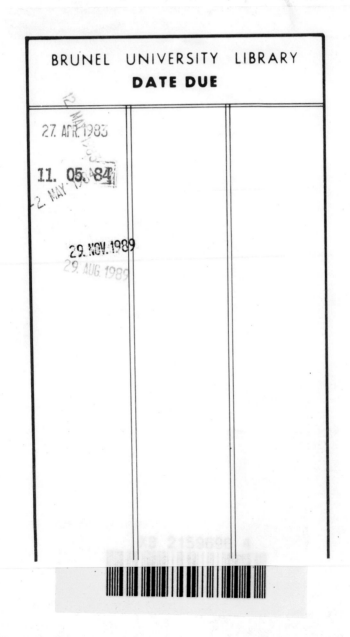